CHRISTIAN COUNSELING

OTHER BOOKS BY GARY R. COLLINS

Search for Reality
Living in Peace
Our Society in Turmoil (edited)
Man in Transition
Effective Counseling
Fractured Personalities
Man in Motion
Overcoming Anxiety
The Christian Psychology of Paul Tournier
Coping with Christmas
It's OK to be Single (edited)
Make More of Your Marriage (edited)
The Secrets of Our Sexuality (edited)
Facing the Future (edited)
Living and Growing Together (edited)
How to be a People Helper
People Helper Growthbook
*The Rebuilding of Psychology: An Integration of
    Psychology and Christianity*
You Can Profit from Stress
Family Talk
Helping People Grow (edited)

CHRISTIAN COUNSELING:

A Comprehensive Guide

By

Gary R. Collins

WORD BOOKS
PUBLISHER
4800 WEST WACO DRIVE
WACO, TEXAS
76703

ISBN 0-8499-2889-3
Libr. of Congress Catalog Card No.: 79-67361

Printed in the United States of America

First Printing, April 1980
Second Printing, May 1981
Third Printing, January 1982
Fourth Printing, September 1982
Fifth Printing, March 1983
Sixth Printing, September 1983
Seventh Printing, March 1984
Eighth Printing, September 1984

Contents

Preface

This manuscript was completed and sent to the publisher exactly ten years after the completion of my first book. It is interesting for me to look back over a decade of writing to ponder how my work has changed and hopefully improved through the production of more than two dozen books. Some of these works have been well received and sold many copies; others have had less influence, but each has forced me to face the discipline, the long, lonely hours, and the risk of expressing ideas in print, where all can see, criticize, and sometimes applaud.

I once asked Paul Tournier which of his many books was the best. "That's easy," he said with a twinkle in his eye—"the next one." I can appreciate Tournier's sentiments. I am not interested in judging whether this book will be better or worse than the next one, but I do know that this volume has been the most difficult to write and the most time-consuming. It is also the lengthiest of all my books. I hope it will also be the most helpful to date.

In the following pages I have tried to summarize much of what we know about counseling methodology and about the major problems which people face today. This book has been prepared as a resource tool for pastors and other Christian counselors, as a study guide for lay helpers, and as a textbook for use in seminaries and colleges. Besides being written for these audiences, this is the reading book for a multi-media resource entitled *The Christian Counselor's Library*. The library contains twenty-eight audio cassettes, a Counselor's Manual, and counselee worksheets (besides this book), and was produced by Educational Products Division of Word, Incorporated, 4800 W. Waco Drive, Waco, Texas 76710.

In the past decade of writing, I have never before felt the support and encouragement of so many people. Joey Paul and his colleagues at Word, Incorporated, first invited me to do this project, gave constant encouragement, and waited more or less patiently through several delays as the work was completed. My secretary Marlene Terbush and my graduate assistants Charles Romig and James Beesley helped in innumerable ways as did a team of typists which included Kathy Cropp, Marilyn Secor, Lenore Scherrer, Sharon Regan, Nancy Fister and Lora Beth Norton.

In addition each of the people who produced tapes made a significant contribution. Their names are listed elsewhere. Dr. Kenneth Meyer, President of Trinity Evangelical Divinity School, my colleagues in the psychology department, and my students all showed incredible flexibility

7

and encouragement, allowing me to juggle my schedule to complete this project in the midst of a busy school year.

My family has always stood with me as I have written books, but I have especially appreciated their support this time. My wife Julie and my daughters Marilynn and Janice have tolerated my long absences with good will and have given constant encouragement. In the weeks ahead they will be getting more of my "prime time."

The one person, however, who has made the greatest contribution to this book is my administrative assistant, Lawrence M. Tornquist. Working full time on this project for several months, he did background research, reviewed and critically evaluated each of the chapters as they were written, and discussed many of the concepts with the clarity and insight that I have come to expect. He never wrote any of the following paragraphs but in terms of input and influence he is in many respects a coauthor.

It is humbling to realize, however, that in all of this, we write, read, and counsel only because God has given us the capacities and desires to do so. This book goes forth, therefore, with thanks to God, with the prayer that it will bring honor to Jesus Christ, and with the hope that the Holy Spirit will use it to help many Christian counselors to care more effectively for their counselees.

Gary R. Collins

How to Use This Book

Christian Counseling: A Comprehensive Guide was prepared to assist Christian leaders in their day-to-day counseling ministry. The first four chapters of *Christian Counseling* are designed to give an overview of counseling and may be read consecutively. The remaining twenty-seven chapters deal with specific problems, and since each chapter stands alone, they can be read in any order. Each chapter gives several perspectives on the problem being considered: what the Bible says about the problem, its causes, its effects, counseling techniques, and ways in which the problem can be prevented. This provides background information for individual counseling.

Early in the preparation of this material, it became apparent that this could be a tool first for teaching counseling skills to students—especially those preparing for various Christian ministries—and secondly for helping individual Christians to understand themselves and to help one another. In addition to its use as a counseling resource book, therefore, this volume can be useful for students and lay people who want a greater understanding of human behavior and an awareness of people-helping skills.

When the materials are used as part of a formal training program, it is recommended that the complete resource, *The Christian Counselor's Library,* be secured. The study group should begin by reading the first four chapters of this reading book individually and then discuss them in the group. Then, each of the remaining chapters can be studied in the following way:

First, it is suggested that the appropriate chapter be read in *Christian Counseling*. Second, students should listen to the tape (or read the transcript in the *Guidebook*) and then complete the tape-worksheet. At times it will be difficult to complete these assignments. Young people, for example, may have difficulty imagining what it would be like to face retirement and the later years; single people may have difficulty completing the assignments on marriage or divorce. To complete as many assignments as possible, however, will give a "feel" for the counselee and the problem being discussed. It is assumed that these two steps will be completed by individuals prior to meeting with the group.

The third step involves group discussion, led by the leader, counselor, or pastor. The instructor may wish to give a brief lecture or comment on the subject being considered and then the group may discuss the questions which are printed below. These are designed to apply to chapters 5 through

9

31, although there may be need for slight adaptation with some of the chapters.

1. What questions do you have about the chapter?

2. Can you summarize biblical teaching on the problem discussed in this chapter?

3. Summarize the causes and effects of this problem.

4. What have you learned about counseling people with this problem?

5. Can anyone give examples of people who have had this problem? Be sure not to reveal the name of the person involved and do not give identifying details. How could this person have been counseled?

6. Outline a program for preventing the development of this problem.

7. Summarize what you have learned from this chapter and from the tape.

8. What questions do you still have which have not been answered? Where can you find answers?

This approach is designed to stimulate discussion of common *problem areas.* Suggestions for further reading are given at the end of each chapter.

For a consideration of counseling *skills,* it is recommended that this book and *The Christian Counselor's Library* be used in conjunction with the author's *How to be a People Helper* along with the accompanying *People Helper Growthbook* (both available from Vision House, 1651 E. Edinger, Santa Ana, California, 92705). Lawrence Brammer's *The Helping Relationship* (Prentice-Hall) is slightly more technical and has no Christian emphasis for study guide material, but it is a concise and excellent introduction to the skills involved in counseling. These books may be read before or after you consider the material in the book which you now hold in your hands.

Part I
Introductory
Issues

1

The Church and Counseling

NOT LONG AGO THE PASTOR OF A CHURCH IN THE EASTERN UNITED States wrote a provocative article which he titled "Counseling Is a Waste of Time." [1] Frustrated with his lack of counseling success, the writer complained of spending "hours upon hours . . . talking *ad infinitum* with scores of persons who simply do not follow through" on his "pastoral advice."

The church leader was honest enough to acknowledge that his low rate of success might have resulted from the fact that he did not have what it takes to counsel effectively. He agreed that there is a place for doctrinal and biblical discussions between a minister and parishioner, for talking about marriage with those who are approaching the altar, or for ministering personally to the sick and grieving. But he concluded that there is no place for "the traditional pastoral counseling which yields such little fruit."

A similar conclusion was expressed recently by a college president who maintained that "the only reason pastors counsel is to play psychiatrist and boost their egos in an unhealthy way." Pastors should stick to preaching and avoid counseling, this educator maintained, apparently without realizing that preaching can also be ego boosting and that unhealthy motives can cloud any activity, not just counseling. As we continued our discussion, he didn't say how a pastor or other church leader can minister to people, care for their needs, and still avoid helping them on a small-group or one-to-one basis.

In one of his earlier books Wayne Oates wrote about this issue with startling clarity:

> The pastor, regardless of his training, does not enjoy the privilege of electing whether or not he will counsel with his people. They inevitably bring their problems to him for his best guidance and wisest care. He cannot avoid this if he stays in the pastoral ministry. His choice is not between counseling or not counseling, but between counseling in a disciplined and skilled way and counseling in an undisciplined and unskilled way. [2]

Regretfully, it isn't easy to counsel in a disciplined and skilled way. Literally thousands of counseling techniques are in use; books on therapy and people-helping roll off the presses with disturbing regularity; there are almost as many theories and approaches to counseling as there are counselors; and with all of this advice and activity even the full-time counselor can become overwhelmed.

It would be good if all of this publishing, theorizing, and counselor training really helped counselors to be more effective, but some of the so-called "counselor helps" are of questionable validity. Even well-trained, experienced counselors who keep abreast of the professional literature and apply the latest techniques find nevertheless that their counselees do not always improve. Sometimes individuals even get worse as a result of counseling. It is hardly surprising, therefore, that some people give up and conclude that counseling really is a waste of time.

If everybody gave up, however, where would people go with their problems? Jesus, who is the Christian's example, spent much time talking to needy people in groups and in face-to-face contact. The Apostle Paul, who was very sensitive to the needs of hurting individuals, wrote that "we who are strong ought to bear the weaknesses of those without strength and not just please ourselves."[3] Probably Paul was writing here about those who had doubts and fears, but his compassionate concern extended to almost every problem area that might be encountered today. In the Bible helping people is not presented as an option. It is a requirement for every believer, including the church leader.[4] At times, counseling may seem like a waste of time but it nevertheless must be an important, necessary, and biblically established part of any ministry.

As a way of helping people, counseling seeks to stimulate personality growth and development; to help individuals cope more effectively with the problems of life, with inner conflict and with crippling emotions; to provide encouragement and guidance for those who are facing losses or disappointments; and to assist persons whose life patterns are self-defeating and causing unhappiness. In addition the Christian counselor seeks to bring people into a personal relationship with Jesus Christ and has the ultimate goal of helping others to become first disciples of Christ and then disciplers of others.

In reaching these aims, it is important for counselors to have an understanding of problems (how they arise and how they might be resolved), and a familiarity with counseling skills. If we can believe recent research, however, it appears that the personal characteristics of the counselors are of even greater significance. After reviewing nearly 100 studies on the effectiveness of counseling, one pair of authors concluded that therapeutic techniques can only be potent when the counselor has a personality which is "inherently helpful"—that is, characterized by warmth, sensitivity, understanding, concern, and a willingness to confront people in an attitude of love.[5] A psychologist named C. H. Patterson reached a similar conclusion after writing an in-depth book on contemporary theories of counseling:

> To be most effective the therapist must be a real, human person . . . offering a genuine human relationship. . . . Much of what therapists do is superfluous or unrelated to their effectiveness; in fact, it is likely that much of their success is unrelated to what they do or even occurs in spite of what they do, as long as they offer the relationship that it appears therapists of very differing persuasions do provide. . . . It is a relationship characterized not so much by what techniques the therapist uses as by what he is, not so much by what he does as by the way he does it.[6]

Surely Jesus Christ is the best model we have of an effective "wonderful counselor" whose personality, knowledge and skills enabled him effectively to assist those people who needed help. When one attempts to analyze the counseling of Jesus, there is always the tendency, unconscious or deliberate, to view Christ's ministry in a way which reinforces our own views about how people are helped. The directive-confrontational counselor recognizes that Jesus was confrontational at times; the nondirective "client-centered" counselor finds support for this approach in other examples of Christ's helping the needy. It is undoubtedly more accurate to state that Jesus used a variety of counseling techniques depending on the situation, the nature of the counselee and the specific problem. At times he listened to people carefully and without giving much overt direction, but on other occasions he taught decisively. He encouraged and supported but he also confronted and challenged. He accepted people who were sinful and needy, but he also demanded repentance, obedience and action.

Basic to Jesus' style of helping, however, was his personality. In his teaching, caring and counseling he demonstrated those traits, attitudes and values which made him effective as a people helper and which serve as a model for us. Jesus was absolutely honest, deeply compassionate, highly sensitive and spiritually mature. He was committed to serving his heavenly Father and his fellow human beings (in that order), prepared for his work through frequent periods of prayer and meditation, was deeply familiar with Scripture, and sought to help needy persons turn to him where they could find ultimate peace, hope and security.[7]

Jesus often helped people through sermons but he also debated skeptics, challenged individuals, healed the sick, talked with the needy, encouraged the downhearted and modeled a godly life style. In his contacts with people, he shared examples taken from real-life situations and he sought constantly to stimulate others to think and act in accordance with divine principles. Apparently he believed that some people need an understanding helper to listen, comfort and discuss before they can learn from confrontation, challenge, advice-giving or public preaching.

According to the Bible, Christians are to teach *all* that Christ commanded and taught us. This surely includes doctrines about God, authority, salvation, spiritual growth, prayer, the church, the future, angels, demons and human nature. However, Jesus also taught about marriage, parent-child interactions, obedience, race relations, and freedom for both women and men. And he taught about personal issues such as sex, anxiety, fear, loneliness, doubt, pride, sin, and discouragement.

All of these are issues which bring people for counseling today. When Jesus dealt with such people he frequently listened to the inquirers and accepted them before stimulating them to think or act differently. At times he told people what to do but he also led people to resolve their problems by skillful and divinely guided questioning. Thomas was helped with his doubts when Jesus showed the evidence; Peter apparently learned best from reflecting (with Jesus) on his mistakes; Mary of Bethany learned by listening; and Judas didn't seem to learn at all.

Teaching all that Christ taught, therefore, includes instruction in doctrine, but it also includes helping people to get along better with God, with others, and with themselves. These are issues which concern almost everyone. Some learn from lectures, sermons or books; others learn from personal Bible study or from discussion; still others learn from formal or informal counseling; and perhaps most of us have learned from some combination of the above.

At the core of all true Christian helping, private or public, is the influence of the Holy Spirit. He is described as a comforter or helper who teaches "all things," reminds us of Christ's sayings, convicts people of sin, and guides us into all truth.[8] Through prayer, meditation on the Scriptures and deliberate daily commitment to Christ, the counselor-teacher makes himself or herself available as an instrument through whom the Holy Spirit may work to comfort, help, teach, convict, or guide another human being. This should be the goal of every believer—pastor or layman, professional counselor or lay helper: to be used by the Holy Spirit to touch lives, to change them, and to bring them toward spiritual as well as psychological maturity.

The Church As a Healing Community

As we have seen, Jesus often talked with individuals about their personal needs and he met frequently with small groups. Chief among these was the little band of disciples whom he prepared to "take over" after his ascension into heaven. It was during one of these times with the disciples that Jesus first mentioned the church.[9]

In the years that followed it was this church of Jesus Christ which continued his ministry of teaching, evangelizing, ministering and counseling. These activities were not seen as the special responsibility of "superstar" church leaders; they were done by ordinary believers working, sharing and caring both for each other and for the nonbelievers outside of the body. If we read the book of Acts [10] and the Epistles it becomes apparent that the church was not only an evangelizing, teaching, discipling community, it was also a healing community.

Within recent years, mental health professionals have come to see the value of therapeutic groups in which group members help each other by providing support, challenge, guidance and encouragement that might not be possible otherwise. Of course such groups can be harmful, especially when they become uncontrolled encounters which seek to criticize and embarrass the participants rather than to build them up or to challenge them to openness or effective actions. If conducted by a sensitive leader, however, group sessions can be very effective therapeutic experiences for all the people involved.

Such therapeutic groups need not be limited to counselees meeting with each other and with a trained counselor. Families, study groups, trusted friends, professional colleagues, employee groups and other little bands of people often provide the help that is needed both in times of crisis and as individuals face the daily challenge of living. In all of society, however, the church undoubtedly has the greatest potential for being a therapeutic community. Local bodies of believers can bring support to the members, healing to troubled individuals, and guidance as people make decisions and move toward maturity.

Recent books on the church have carried some intriguing titles: *The Communion of Saints, A Living Fellowship—A Dynamic Witness, The Incendiary Fellowship, The Body of Christ, The Company of the Committed.*[11] In contrast to this optimistic tone, it may be that for many people the contemporary church is more accurately described as *A Gathering of Strangers,* with *Crowded Pews and Lonely People.*[12] The body of believers, which has potential for being a dynamic growth-producing fellowship, too often degenerates into a listless, rigid group of people who never admit to having needs or problems, attend services out of habit, and leave most of the action to an overburdened pastor. Such a picture is overstated, perhaps, but for many people the local church really isn't very helpful or meaningful. This surely was not Christ's intention when the church was first established.

Why was the church begun? Surely the answer lies in Jesus' final words to his followers before he went back into heaven:

> Go therefore and make disciples of all the nations, baptizing them in the name of the Father and the Son and the Holy Spirit, teaching them to observe all that I commanded you; and lo, I am with you always, even to the end of the age.[13]

The church was established to fulfill the great commission of making disciples (which implies evangelism) and teaching. It now is headed by Jesus Christ who showed us how to evangelize and teach, who by his life and instruction pointed us to the practical as well as the theoretical aspects

of Christianity, and who summarized his teaching in two laws, to love
God and to love others.

All of this is meant to take place within the confines of a group of
believers, each of whom has been granted the gifts and abilities needed
to build up the church. As a group, guided by a pastor, the believers direct
their attention and activities upward through worship of God, outward
through evangelism, and inward through teaching fellowship and burden
bearing.[14] When one of these is missing the group is unbalanced and the
believers are incomplete.

The remaining chapters of this book are written to assist pastors, students and other church leaders in one important aspect of the church's
work: burden bearing.[15] The twenty-six issues discussed in this book are
among the most common problem areas faced by both Christians and nonbelievers: problems which interfere with worship, evangelism, teaching
and fellowship. For each of these topics we will consider what causes the
problems, how people are affected by them, how they can be reduced or
eliminated especially through counseling, how we can prevent their reoccurrence, and where we can get further information. The chapters will
summarize biblical teaching about these issues and will draw on recent
psychological research and insights.

Can Psychology Help?

To increase counseling effectiveness, many church leaders have turned
to the insights of psychologists and other mental health professionals.
Psychology, of course, is a highly complex and currently popular field of
study dealing with both animal and human behavior. The college student
who takes an introductory course in general psychology often encounters
a mass of statistics, technical terms, and "scientific data" about a host of
seemingly unimportant topics. Seminary level courses in pastoral counseling tend to be more people-centered and relevant, but even here the student may be lost in a maze of theories and techniques which are not very
useful when one is face-to-face with a confused, hurting human being.

This has led some writers to reject psychology, including the field of
counseling, and to conclude that a Bible is all that a Christian people-
helper needs to assist others. Jay Adams, for example, argues that psychiatrists (and presumably psychologists) have usurped the work of
preachers, and are in the dangerous occupation of trying to change the
people's behavior and values in an ungodly manner. Writing to pastors,
Adams maintains that "by studying the Word of God carefully and observing how the biblical principles describe the people you counsel . . .
you can gain all the information and experience that you need to become
a competent, confident Christian counselor without a study of psychology." [16] Clearly this influential writer sees little hope that psychology or
related fields of study will be able to help the church leader to counsel
more effectively.

But was the Bible really written as a textbook on counseling? It deals with loneliness, discouragement, marriage problems, grief, parent-child relations, anger, fear and a host of other counseling situations. As the Word of God, it has great and lasting relevance to the counselor's work and the needs of his or her counselees, but it does not claim to be and neither is it meant to be God's sole revelation about people-helping. In medicine, teaching and other "people-centered" helping fields, mankind has been permitted to learn much about God's creation through science and academic study. Why, then, should psychology be singled out as the one field that has nothing to contribute to the work of the counselor?

As a field of study, scientific psychology is about 100 years old. During the past century, God has permitted psychologists to develop careful research tools for studying human behavior and professional journals for sharing their findings. Perhaps hundreds of thousands of people have come for help and professional counselors have learned what makes people tick and how they can change. Our knowledge is far from complete and neither is it error-free, but careful psychological research and data analysis have led to a vast reservoir of conclusions which are known to be of help to counselees and to any person who wants to be an effective people-helper. Even those who would dismiss the field of psychology frequently use psychological terms in their writings and psychologically derived techniques in their counseling.

In the following chapters, the writings of social scientists are frequently cited on the assumption that all truth comes from God, including truth about the people whom God created. He has revealed this truth through the Bible, God's written Word to mankind, but he also has permitted us to discover truth through experience and through the methods of scientific investigation. Discovered truth must always be consistent with, and tested against, the norm of revealed biblical truth. But we limit our counseling effectiveness when we pretend that the discoveries of psychology have nothing to contribute to the understanding and solution of problems. We compromise our integrity when we overtly reject psychology but then smuggle its concepts into our counseling—sometimes naïvely and without even realizing what we are doing.

Let us accept the fact that psychology can be of great help to the Christian counselor. How, then, do we wade through the quagmire of techniques, theories, and technical terms to find the insights which truly are helpful? The answer involves our finding a guide—some person or persons who are committed followers of Jesus Christ, familiar with the psychological and counseling literature, trained in counseling and in research methods (so that the scientific accuracy of psychologists' conclusions can be evaluated), and effective as counselors. Of crucial importance is that the guides must be committed to the inspiration and authority of the Bible, both as the standard against which all psychology must be tested and as the written Word of God with which all valid counseling must agree.

The pages which follow, and the cassette tapes which accompany this book, have been prepared by guides who can assist Christian counselors in the joyful but demanding task of helping others. This is not meant to be a cookbook volume of never-fail recipes designed for producing master counselors. Human beings are far too complicated to always be changed even through the intervention of the most skilled counselors. All counselors have failures, sometimes because of the counselor's inability or error; often because the counselee cannot or will not change. But improvement is more likely when the counselor has some understanding of the problems and some knowledge of how to intervene. The following chapters have been written to help with this understanding and we hope they will provide some of the needed knowledge.

Before we begin our analyses, however, let us pause to get an overview of effective counseling techniques. For the beginner this next chapter is meant to be a helpful introduction. For the experienced counselor it is presented as an "update" and review.

Suggestions for Further Reading

Evans, Louis H., Jr. *Creative Love*. Old Tappan, NJ: Revell, 1977.
Getz, Gene A. *Building Up One Another*. Wheaton, IL: Victor Books, 1976.
Snyder, Howard A. *The Problem of Wine Skins: Church Structure in a Technological Age*. Downers Grove, IL: Inter-Varsity, 1976.
Stedman, Ray C. *Body Life*. Glendale, CA: Regal Books, 1972.
Trueblood, Elton. *The Incendiary Fellowship*. New York: Harper & Row, 1967.

Footnotes

1. J. G. Swank, Jr., "Counseling Is a Waste of Time," *Christianity Today,* July, 1977, p. 27.
2. W. E. Oates, ed., *An Introduction to Pastoral Counseling* (Nashville: Broadman, 1959), p. vi.
3. Rom. 15:1.
4. As an example of the need for helping, note the number of times that the words "one another" appear in the Bible. We are instructed to build up, accept, admonish, be devoted to, be at peace with, serve, bear the burdens of, be kind to, teach, encourage, confess our faults to, pray for, and love one another, (Rom. 14:19; 15:7, 14; 12:10, 18; Gal. 5:13; 6:2; Eph. 4:32; Col. 3:16; 1 Thess. 5:11; James 5:16; 1 John 4:7). While this clearly extends beyond counseling, it also includes much of what is involved in the counseling process.
5. For a summary of this research see C. B. Truax and K. M. Mitchell, "Research on Certain Therapist Interpersonal Skills in Relation to Process and Outcome," in *Handbook of Psychotherapy and Behavior Change,* ed. Allen E. Bergin and Sol Garfield (New York: Wiley, 1971), pp. 299–344.
6. C. H. Patterson, *Theories of Counseling and Psychotherapy* (New York: Harper & Row, 1973), pp. 535–36.
7. John 14.
8. John 14:16, 26; 15:7–14.
9. Matt. 16:18.
10. See especially Acts 2:42–47; 4:32–35.
11. Dietrich Bonhoeffer, *The Communion of Saints* (New York: Harper & Row,

1961); Richard C. Halverson, *A Living Fellowship—A Dynamic Witness* (Grand Rapids: Zondervan, 1972); Elton Trueblood, *The Incendiary Fellowship* (New York: Harper & Row, 1967); John MacArthur, Jr., *The Church: The Body of Christ* (Grand Rapids: Zondervan, 1973); Elton Trueblood, *The Company of the Committed* (New York: Harper & Row, 1961).

12. Robert C. Morley, *A Gathering of Strangers* (Philadelphia: Westminster, 1976); Marion L. Jacobsen, *Crowded Pews and Lonely People* (Wheaton: Tyndale, 1972).

13. Matt. 28:19, 20.

14. For this three-fold concept I am grateful to Rev. Theodore Olsen, pastor of the Arlington Heights Evangelical Free Church, Arlington Heights, Illinois.

15. Gal. 6:2, 10.

16. Jay Adams, *The Big Umbrella* (Philadelphia: Presbyterian and Reformed Publishing Company, 1972), pp. 23, 24.

2

The Core of Counseling

AS ALMOST EVERYONE KNOWS, THE BIBLE CONTAINS MANY EXAMPLES of human need. Throughout its pages we read of loneliness, discouragement, doubt, grief, sadness, envy, violence, poverty, sickness, interpersonal tension, and a variety of other personal problems—sometimes exhibited in the lives of the greatest saints.

Consider Job, for example. He was a godly man, famous, wealthy and highly respected by his contemporaries. Then things suddenly fell apart. He lost all of his wealth. His family was all killed except for his wife, who under pressure showed a tendency to complain and nag. Job lost his health, his friends offered little help, and God must have seemed far away.

Then, along came Elihu. He was a young man who listened to Job and heard his struggles. Elihu was critical of those who had lectured and given advice in an attempt to help. He showed acceptance and concern, a humble willingness to be on the same level as Job (with no holier-than-thou attitude), a courage to confront, and an unswerving desire to point the counselee to God who alone is sovereign in the universe. Elihu was the one counselor who helped. He succeeded where three others had failed.

Several years ago a former president of the American Psychological Association estimated that even today, three out of every four counselors are ineffective. The ratio rose, but only slightly, in the findings of some more recent writers who studied the effectiveness of counseling. According to this research, we can be "quite certain" that two out of three practitioners are ineffective or even harmful; involved in spending energy, commitment and care in a wasteful manner.[1]

There are counselors who do succeed, however, and they counsel very effectively. These people are characterized by a personality which radiates sincerity, understanding, and an ability to confront in a constructive manner. These counselors also are skilled in the application of techniques which help counselees move toward specific therapeutic goals.[2] In this chapter we will begin with a consideration of these counseling goals, dis-

22

cuss the characteristics of a good helper, summarize some basic counseling techniques, give a brief overview of the counseling process and conclude with a look at counseling homework.

The Goals of Counseling

When he was teaching some of his followers one day, Jesus stated why he had come to earth: to give us life in abundance and in all its fullness.[3] Earlier, in what now is surely the most famous verse in Scripture, Jesus had told God's purpose in sending the Son—"that whoever believes in Him should not perish but have eternal life."[4] Jesus, therefore, had two goals for individuals: abundant life on earth and eternal life in heaven.

The counselor who is a follower of Jesus Christ has the same ultimate overarching goal of showing people how to have an abundant life and of pointing individuals to the eternal life which is promised to believers. Notice the words "ultimate" and "overarching" in the previous sentence. If we take the great commission seriously we will have a strong desire to see all of our counselees become disciples of Jesus Christ. If we take the words of Jesus seriously we are likely to reach the conclusion that a fully abundant life only comes to those who seek to live in accordance with his teachings.

Let us recognize, however, that there are many sincere Christians who will have eternal life in heaven but who are not experiencing a very abundant life on earth. These people need counseling which involves something other than evangelism or traditional Christian education. Such counseling might, for example, help counselees recognize unconscious harmful attitudes, teach interpersonal skills and new behaviors, or show how to mobilize one's inner resources to face a crisis. At times such counseling, guided by the Holy Spirit, can free a counselee from hang-ups which prevent him or her from growing to Christian maturity. For the nonbeliever, such counseling can serve as a kind of "pre-evangelism" to use Schaeffer's term,[5] which clears away some of the subtle obstacles to conversion. Evangelism and discipleship, therefore, are the Christian counselor's "ultimate overarching" goals, but they are not the only goals.[6]

What are some other goals? Any list must include at least the following.

1. *Self-understanding.* To understand oneself is often a first step in healing. Many problems are self-imposed but the one being helped may fail to recognize that he or she has biased perceptions, harmful attitudes or self-destructive behavior. Consider, for example, the person who complains, "Nobody likes me," but fails to see that the complaining is one reason for this rejection by others. One goal of counseling is for an objective, perceptually alert helper to assist those being helped to get a true picture of what is going on within themselves and within the world around them.

2. *Communication.* It is well known that many marriage difficulties relate to a breakdown in husband-wife communication. The same is true

of other problems. People are unable or unwilling to communicate. The counselee must learn how to communicate feelings, thoughts, and attitudes both accurately and effectively. Such communication involves the expression of oneself, and the ability to receive accurate messages from others.

3. *Learning and Behavior Change.* Most, if not all, of our behavior is learned. Counseling, therefore, involves helping counselees unlearn ineffective behavior and learn more efficient ways of acting. Such learning comes from instruction, imitation of a counselor or other model, and trial and error. The helper must encourage the person he or she is helping to "launch out" and practice the new learning. At times it also will be necessary to analyze what goes wrong when there is failure and the counselee must be urged to try again.

4. *Self-actualization.* Recent humanistic writers have stressed the importance of an individual's learning to achieve and maintain one's optimal potential.[7] This is termed "self-actualization" and is proposed by some counselors as the goal of all human beings whether or not they are in counseling. To the Christian, a term like "Christ-actualization" might be substituted to indicate that the goal in life is to be complete in Christ, developing our greatest potential through the power of the Holy Spirit who brings us to spiritual maturity.

5. *Support.* Often people are able to meet each of the above goals and to function effectively, except for temporary periods of unusual stress or crisis. Such persons can benefit from a period of support, encouragement, and "burden bearing" until they are able to remobilize their personal and spiritual resources to effectively meet the problems of living.

In any kind of counseling it often is helpful if the counselor and counselee establish clear goals or objectives for the counseling. Such goals should be specific rather than vague, realistic, and (if there are several) organized into some logical sequence which identifies the goals to be worked on first and, perhaps, for how long.

The Characteristics of Effective Counselors

What makes a good counselor? In a four-year study conducted with hospital patients and a variety of counselors it was found that patients improved when their therapists showed high levels of warmth, genuineness and accurate empathic understanding. When these counselor qualities were lacking, the hospital patients grew worse.[8] These early findings have been supported by subsequent research both with patients and with counselees who were not hospitalized.[9] So important are counselor characteristics that it is important to consider these in more detail.

1. *Warmth.* This word implies caring, respecting, or possessing a sincere, nonsmothering concern for the counselee—regardless of his or her actions or attitudes. Jesus showed this when he met the woman at the well. Her morals may have been low, and he certainly never condoned sinful

behavior. But Jesus nevertheless respected the woman and treated her as a person of worth. His warm, caring attitude must have been apparent wherever he went.

2. *Genuineness.* The genuine counselor is "for real"—an open, sincere person who avoids phoniness or the playing of some superior role. Genuineness implies spontaneity without impulsiveness and honesty without cruel confrontation. It means that the helper is deeply himself or herself— not thinking or feeling one thing and saying something different.

3. *Empathy.* What does a counselee think? How does he or she really feel inside? What are the counselee's values, beliefs, inner conflicts and hurts? The good counselor is continually sensitive to these issues, able to understand them, and effective in communicating this understanding (by words or gestures) to the counselee. This ability to "feel with" the counselee is what we mean by accurate empathic understanding. It is possible to help people, even when we don't completely understand, but the counselor who can empathize (especially near the beginning of counseling) is most likely to be effective as a people-helper.

While warmth, genuineness and empathy are among the most frequently cited attributes of a good counselor, there are other important helper characteristics. The good counselor, for example, is able to get along efficiently, having a relative absence of immobilizing conflicts, hang-ups, insecurities or personal problems. The effective counselor is also compassionate, interested in people, alert to his or her own feelings and motives, more self revealing than self-concealing, and knowledgeable in the field of counseling. The Christian might summarize all of this by stating that the counselor must be loving.

This was emphasized several years ago in a book by Gordon Allport, Harvard professor and former President of the American Psychological Association.[10] He called love "incomparably the greatest psychotherapeutic agent . . . something that professional psychiatry cannot of itself create, focus, nor release." [11] Allport suggested that the secular counselor often is unable to supply the love which a counselee needs and unable to receive the love the counselee wants to give. Might it be, he suggested, that Christianity offers an approach to life which is based wholly upon love and thus is able to help where secular counseling fails? This raises a thought-provoking challenge for the Christian counselor: a basic way to help is to love—asking God to love needy people through us and asking him to make us more loving.

But is love enough? For some people and with some problems love is all they need, but for others more help is required. Several years ago a famous child psychiatrist wrote a book entitled *Love Is Not Enough* and discussed the importance of discipline, structure and other therapeutic influences.[12] The effective Christian helper is loving. This is basic. But he or she also seeks to develop therapeutic characteristics and attempts to become proficient in the knowledge and use of basic counseling techniques.

The Techniques of Counseling

Counseling is primarily a relationship in which one person, the helper, seeks to assist another human being with the problems of living. Unlike casual discussions between friends, the helping relationship, at least for professionals, is characterized by a clear purpose—that of helping the counselee. The helper's needs are mostly met elsewhere and he or she does not depend on the counselee for love, affirmation or help. The counselor attempts to step out of his or her own conflicts, to become aware of the counselee's needs, and to communicate both understanding and a willingness to help. The giving of help can be a complicated process, impossible to describe adequately in a few paragraphs. We can, however, summarize some of the more basic techniques that are used in any helping situation.

1. *Attending.* The counselor must try to give undivided attention to the counselee. This is done through (a) eye contact—looking without staring as a way to convey concern and understanding; (b) posture, which should be relaxed rather than tense, and generally involves leaning toward the counselee and; (c) gestures that are natural but not excessive or distracting. The counselor should be courteous, kind, strongly motivated to understand. He or she should be alert to some of the inner distractions which prevent us from attending carefully: fatigue, impatience, preoccupation with other matters, daydreaming and restlessness. People-helping clearly is difficult and demanding work which involves sensitivity, genuine expressions of care, and alertness in attending to another both physically and psychologically.

2. *Listening.* This involves more than a passive reception of messages. According to psychiatrist Armand Nicholi, effective listening involves:

—having sufficient awareness and resolution of one's own conflicts to avoid reacting in a way that interferes with the counselee's free expression of thoughts and feelings;
—avoiding subtle verbal or nonverbal expressions of disdain or judgment toward the content of the counselee's story, even when that content offends the counselor's sensibilities;
—waiting patiently through periods of silence or tears as the counselee summons up courage to delve into painful material or pauses to collect his or her thoughts or to regain composure;
—hearing not only what the counselee says but what he or she is trying to say and what is left unsaid;
—using both ears and eyes to detect messages which come from tone of voice, posture, and other nonverbal clues;
—scanning one's own reactions to the counselee;
—avoiding looking away from the counselee as he or she speaks;
—sitting still;
—limiting the number of mental excursions into one's own fantasies;
—controlling those feelings toward the counselee that interfere with an accepting, sympathetic, nonjudgmental attitude;

—realizing that full acceptance of the counselee is possible without condoning or sanctioning attitudes and behavior destructive of the counselee or of others.[13]

It is easy to ignore all of this, and to slip quickly into advice-giving and excessive talking. This prevents the counselee from really expressing hurts, clarifying a problem through talking, sharing all of the details of an issue or experiencing the relief that comes with catharsis. Counselors who talk a lot may give good advice but it is seldom heard and even less likely to be followed. In such situations counselees feel that they have not been understood. In contrast, listening is a way of telling a counselee, "I care." When we don't listen but counsel by talking, this is often an expression of the counselor's own insecurity or of an inability to handle ambiguous, threatening or emotional situations.

3. *Responding.* It should not be assumed, however, that the counselor does nothing but listen. Jesus was a good listener (consider his time with the perplexed pair on the road to Emmaus, for example) but his helping also was characterized by action and specific verbal responses.

Leading is a skill by which the counselor slightly anticipates the counselee's direction of thought and responds in a way that redirects the conversation. "Can you elaborate on . . . ?" "What happened then?" "What did you mean by . . . ?"—all are brief questions which hopefully direct the discussion into maximally productive directions.

Reflecting is a way of letting counselees know that we are "with them" and can understand their feelings or thinking. "You must feel . . . ," "I bet that was frustrating," "That must have been fun"—all of these reflect what is going on in counseling. Be careful not to reflect after every statement (do it periodically) and try to avoid stereotype responses (e.g., frequently repeating sentences beginning with phrases such as "You must think . . ." or "I hear you saying that . . ."). A brief summary of what has been going on can also be a way of reflecting and stimulating more counselee exploration. The counselor may summarize feelings ("that must have hurt") and/or general themes of content ("from all of this it sounds like you have had a whole string of failures"), but always give the counselee time and opportunity to respond to such reflecting—summarizing.

Questioning, if done skillfully, can bring forth a great deal of useful information. The best questions are those which require at least a sentence or two from the counselee (e.g., "Tell me about your marriage") rather than those which can be answered in one word ("Are you married?" "What is your age?"). Beginning counselors ask more questions than experienced counselors,[14] and since extensive questioning can stifle communication, students are often instructed to ask few questions. Also, questions beginning with "Why" are usually avoided since these tend either to sound judgmental, or to stimulate long intellectual discussions which avoid coming to grips with the real feelings or hurts that the counselee may have.

Confronting means presenting some idea to the counselee that he or she might not see otherwise. Counselees can be confronted with sin in their lives, failures, inconsistencies, or self-defeating behavior and they should be encouraged to change their behavior or attitudes. Confrontation is best done in a loving, gentle, nonjudgmental manner. Nevertheless it often brings resistance, guilt, and sometimes anger from the counselee. It becomes important, therefore, that the counselor allow time for the counselee to respond verbally to the confrontation and to discuss alternative ways of behaving. At times such a confrontation leads to confession and a significant experience of forgiveness. Some Christians have suggested that counseling and confrontation are synonymous terms. This has neither psychological nor biblical support. Confrontation is an important and sometimes difficult part of counseling, but it is not the only skill involved in helping people.

Informing involves giving facts to people in need of information. This is different from a counselor sharing opinions or giving advice. Informing is commonplace and an accepted part of counseling; advice-giving is much more controversial. Advice-givers often lack enough knowledge of a situation to give competent advice, their advice-giving encourages the counselee to be dependent, and if the advice proves invalid it is the counselor who later is made to feel responsibility for giving bad direction. Whenever you are asked for advice or inclined to give advice, be sure that you are well-informed about the situation. Do you have enough information and expertise to validly advise another? Then ask yourself what might be the end results of this advice-giving. Is it likely to make the counselee more dependent? Can you handle the feelings that might come if your advice is rejected or proven wrong? If you then do give advice, offer it in the form of a tentative suggestion, give the counselee time to react and talk through your advice, and follow up later to see the extent to which the advice was helpful.

Interpretation involves explaining to the counselee what his or her behavior or other events mean. This is a highly technical skill with great potential for enabling counselees to see themselves and their situations more clearly. But interpretations can also be harmful, especially if they are introduced before the counselee can handle the material emotionally, or if the interpretations are wrong. If, as a counselor, you begin to see some possible explanations for another person's problems, ask yourself if the counselee is intellectually and emotionally ready to handle such an insight, keep the terms simple as you interpret, present your interpretation in a tentative way (e.g., "Could it be that . . . ?") and allow time for the counselee to respond. As you discuss the interpretation the counselee often develops even greater insights and is able to explore future courses of action with the counselor.

Supporting and encouraging are important parts of any counseling situation, especially at the beginning. When people are burdened by needs and conflicts they can benefit from the stability and care of an empathic person who shows acceptance and can give reassurance. This is more than holding up the downtrodden, however. Support includes guiding the counselee to take stock of his or her own spiritual and psychological resources, encouraging action, and helping with any problems or failures that may come as a result of this action.

4. *Teaching*. All of these techniques are really specialized forms of psychological education. The counselor is an educator, teaching by instruction, by example, and by guiding the counselee as he or she learns to cope with the problems of life. As with other less personal forms of education, counseling is most effective when the discussions are specific rather than vague, and focus on concrete situations ("How can I control my temper when I am criticized by my wife?") rather than on nebulous goals ("I want to be happier").

One of the most powerful learning tools is what psychologists call *immediacy* responses. This involves the ability of the counselor and counselee to discuss directly and openly what is happening in the here-and-now of their relationship.[15] "I feel very frustrated with you right now," someone may state, for example, or "I'm getting angry because I think you're putting me down." Such honest on-the-spot expressions of how one person feels in a situation are therapeutic in that they deal with feelings before they fester and build up. Immediacy responses also help counselees (and counselors) better understand both how their actions affect others and how they respond emotionally to interpersonal relationships. Such understanding is an important educational aspect of counseling.

The Process of Counseling

Counseling is not a step-by-step process such as baking a cake, or changing a tire, or even preparing a sermon. Each counselee is unique—with problems, attitudes, values, expectations and experiences that are unlike any other. The counselor (whose own problems, attitudes, values, expectations and experiences are also brought to the counseling situations) must approach each individual a little differently and will discover that the course of counseling will vary from person to person.

In every counseling relationship, however, it would appear that there are several steps, the first three of which may be repeated several times as problems are considered and reconsidered. These steps involve building and maintaining a relationship between counselor and counselee; exploring problems to clarify issues and determine how the problems can be handled; deciding on a course of action; stimulating the counselee to act; evaluating progress and deciding on subsequent actions; and terminating the counseling relationship by encouraging and guiding the counselee to launch out without the counselor's continuing help. On paper, all of this sounds straightforward and simple but the process of counseling can be very complicated and demanding of one's time and energy.

One reason for this is that the steps are rarely identified so clearly or easily as the previous paragraphs might imply. For example, the first step of building a relationship is especially important at the beginning when counselees (and counselors) might be nervous and apprehensive. However, once a relationship has begun it must be maintained, so the counselor must never completely lose sight of step one. In counseling there is a vacillation back and forth between these stages as problems become clearer, solutions are found, and the counseling moves to termination.

Regardless of how effective the counseling hour might be, its influence can be undermined if the counselee leaves the session and forgets or ignores what has been learned. To meet this problem, many counselors give homework assignments—projects which are designed to strengthen, expand and extend the process of counseling beyond the counselee's time with the counselor.

Homework in Counseling

In his excellent book on helping,[16] psychologist Paul Welter notes that each person has a special way of learning. Some people learn best through *hearing*—listening to the words of others. Some learn best through *seeing*—reading books, watching movies, and looking at diagrams. Then there are people who learn best through *doing*—completing projects, doing role plays, or acting out their feelings. Although there have been some recent exceptions (especially in some of the experience-oriented approaches to counseling), traditional people-helping has involved a talk-listen approach. People have come for counseling sessions which last approximately one hour and are separated by a week or so of other activities.

Homework assignments enable people to extend their learning beyond the counseling sessions and permit seeing and doing in addition to hearing. Homework, writes Adams,

> is the essence of good counseling. The counselor who perfects his ability to do homework soon will see the difference in his effectiveness in helping people. Learning how to give good homework, homework that is biblical, homework that is concrete, and homework that creatively fits the situation, takes time and effort, but is worth both.[17]

Since the term "homework" often raises thoughts of dull busywork imposed upon an unwilling recipient, it has been suggested that "task agreements"[18] might be a better and more accurate term. The counselor and counselee agree on tasks that can be done between counseling sessions. These tasks help counselees to keep aware of the counseling goals, to gain additional information (through reading or listening to tapes), to develop and practice new skills, to eliminate harmful behavior, to test what has been learned in counseling, and to try out new ways of thinking and acting.

Task agreements can be of various types and may include such specific behaviors as giving one compliment each day, refraining from criticism, reading a daily chapter in the Bible, spending time with a significant relative, keeping a record of time-use, or making a list of one's values and priorities. At the end of each counseling session the counselor and counselee might ask, "Following this counseling period, in what specific ways can the counselee practice what was learned today or get new learning which will be of further help?" The answers, and hence the potential task agreements, are almost limitless.

In spite of this potential for diversity five types of homework task agreements have been used most often:

1. *Testing.* This includes questionnaires, sentence completion forms, standardized tests, and writing assignments (such as preparing a brief biography, listing life goals, making a list of what one likes and dislikes about a job, and so on). These written responses are then taken back to the counselor where they are discussed.

2. *Discussion and Study Guides.* These sometimes appear in the appendixes of books but entire volumes have been devoted to guiding home study or small group discussion. Sometimes this study takes place independently of any counseling. Sometimes the study is a task agreement to be completed between counseling sessions and discussed subsequently in counseling.[19]

3. *Behavior Assignments.* Counselees sometimes are encouraged to change their actions in some small but important ways between counseling sessions. Saying "thank you," giving periodic compliments, not complaining about some annoying practice of one's mate, getting to work on time, reading the Bible for ten minutes daily—these are the kinds of behavior change suggestions which counselors give and then discuss with counselees.

4. *Reading.* Books and articles often contain helpful information which can supplement the counseling sessions. There is always the danger that counselees will misinterpret what has been written or that something will be pulled out of context. Few counselors have time to screen all potentially relevant books and it will be difficult to find written materials with which the counselor agrees totally. In spite of these limitations, articles and books can be a helpful adjunct to counseling, especially if the reading is discussed subsequently with the counselee.[20]

5. *Recordings.* Music therapy—the use of music to help people with their problems—is at least as old as the soothing melodies that David played to calm the troubled King Saul. Many people today relax by turning on the stereo after a busy day of work.

But the recent upsurge of interest in cassette recordings and the widespread availability of inexpensive playback equipment has given the counselor a potentially powerful but as yet unexamined resource. Literally thousands of tapes currently are available on a wide variety of subjects. The quality of the tapes and the accuracy of the information is not always good, but these can be improved and used as a helpful supplement to personal counseling.

For example, several years ago at the University of Austin, a number of cassette recordings were prepared, each of which ran for seven to ten minutes and contained practical counseling advice plus information about where to get further help. These tapes became part of a twenty-four-hour telephone service in which people could call at any time and listen to the tape of their choice. Initial research has demonstrated that the tapes are widely used, helpful, and often stimulate people to seek further counseling.[21]

Chapters 5–31 of this book include information to help counselors deal with a number of practical counseling issues. At the end of each chapter, suggestions are given for further reading—including books that could be helpful for counselees. In addition, each chapter has an accompanying cassette tape and assignment sheet prepared by a skilled Christian counselor to (a) give information to counselees that can supplement private counseling, and (b) suggest exercises to stimulate further thought and learning. When the tapes and assignment sheets are given to counselees, they can experience task agreement (homework) exercises which involve hearing, seeing and doing—all in an attempt to help in the attainment of counseling goals.

Suggestions for Further Reading

Brammer, Larry M. *The Helping Relationship.* Englewood Cliffs, NJ: Prentice-Hall, 1973.
Clinebell, Howard J. *Basic Types of Pastoral Counseling.* Nashville: Abingdon, 1966.
Collins, Gary R. *Effective Counseling.* Carol Stream, IL: Creation House, 1972.
———. *How to be a People Helper.* Santa Ana: Vision House, 1976.
Crabb, Lawrence J., Jr. *Effective Biblical Counseling.* Grand Rapids: Zondervan, 1977.
Kennedy, Eugene. *On Becoming a Counselor: A Basic Guide for Non-Professional Counselors.* New York: Seabury, 1977.
Welter, Paul. *How to Help a Friend.* Wheaton: Tyndale, 1977.

Footnotes

1. For a summary of this research see C. B. Truax and K. M. Mitchell, "Research on Certain Therapist Interpersonal Skills in Relation to Process and Outcome," in *Handbook of Psychotherapy and Behavior Change,* ed. Allen E. Bergin and Sol Garfield (New York: Wiley, 1971), pp. 299–344.
2. Ibid. In the same book see also A. E. Bergin, "The Evaluation of Therapeutic Outcomes," pp. 217–70.
3. John 10:10.
4. John 3:16.
5. F. A. Schaeffer, *The God Who Is There* (Chicago: Inter-Varsity, 1968).
6. Let us be honest in recognizing that some counselees will accept our psychological help but then conclude that they don't want our gospel. Jesus must have experienced this with the ten lepers (Luke 17:11–19). Ten lepers were healed but only one praised God and is described as having faith.

It should also be added that in some secular counseling settings the Christian

counselor is forbidden to present a Christian message. In such cases surely th...
tian's belief will come out in more indirect ways. Sometimes the counselee w...
about this and the Christian can discuss the meaning of discipleship. If ever...
is forbidden some Christians feel they can no longer work under such repres...
conditions. These are issues which pastors and other church leaders rarely have
face in the settings where they work.

7. See for example, Carl R. Rogers, *Client-Centered Therapy* (Boston: Hough-ton-Mifflin, 1951), p. 195; Rollo May, *Psychology and the Human Dilemma* (Princeton, NJ: Van Nostrand Reinhold, 1967), p. 109; and C. H. Patterson, *Relationship Counseling and Psychotherapy* (New York: Harper & Row, 1974).

8. C. R. Rogers, G. T. Gendlin, D. V. Kiesler, and C. B. Truax, *The Therapeutic Relationship and Its Impact* (Madison: University of Wisconsin Press, 1967).

9. Bergin and Garfield, eds., *Psychotherapy and Behavior Change.*

10. G. W. Allport, *The Individual and His Religion* (New York: Macmillan, 1950).

11. Ibid., p. 90.

12. B. Bettleheim, *Love Is Not Enough: The Treatment of Emotionally Disturbed Children* (Glencoe, IL: The Free Press, 1950).

13. A. M. Nicholi, Jr., "The Therapist-Patient Relationship," in *The Harvard Guide to Modern Psychiatry*, ed. A. M. Nicholi, Jr. (Cambridge, MA: The Belknap Press of Harvard University Press, 1978), p. 12.

14. From research cited in Patterson, *Relationship Psychotherapy*, p. 112. Much of this discussion is adapted from Patterson and from L. M. Brammer, *The Helping Relationship* (Englewood Cliffs, NJ: Prentice-Hall, 1973).

15. G. Egan, *The Skilled Helper.* (Monterey: Brooks/Cole, 1975), p. 173.

16. Paul Welter, *How to Help a Friend* (Wheaton: Tyndale, 1978).

17. J. E. Adams, *The Christian Counselor's Manual* (Grand Rapids: Baker, 1973), p. 343.

18. This term was suggested by Welter, *How to Help a Friend.*

19. For an excellent study guide approach see Waylon D. Ward, *The Bible in Counseling* (Chicago: Moody Press, 1977). This book contains almost fifty study guides on a variety of topics related to counseling. Somewhat different is the author's family book which includes sixty topics for family discussion supplemented by ten discussion guides for church groups. See Gary R. Collins, *Family Talk* (Santa Ana: Vision House, 1978).

20. The use of reading as an adjunct to counseling is termed "bibliotherapy." For more information see Welter, *How to Help a Friend,* chapter 34; Eleanor Francis Brown, *Bibliotherapy and Its Widening Applications* (Metuchen, NJ: Scarecrow, 1975); and J. S. Zaccaria and H. A. Moses, *Facilitating Human Development through Reading: The Use of Bibliotherapy in Teaching and Counseling* (Champaign, IL: Stipes, 1968).

21. For information on the University of Austin program write CounseLine, University of Texas Press, Box 7819, Austin, Texas, 78712. Christian tapes are available from a number of resources including One Way Tapes, 1651 E. Edinger, Santa Ana, CA, 92705, and Creative Resources, Word, Inc., 4800 W. Waco Drive, Waco, Texas, 76703. The cassette tapes made to accompany this book are also available from Word, Inc.

The Counselor and Counseling

MOST OF US HAVE MET PEOPLE WHO WOULD LIKE TO BE COUNSELORS, often because this is seen as glamorous activity of giving advice and helping people solve their problems. Counseling, of course, can be very gratifying work, but it doesn't take long for any of us to discover that counseling also is emotionally draining, hard work. It involves intensive concentration and sometimes brings feelings of pain as we see so many people hurting. When these people fail to improve, as often happens, it is easy to blame ourselves, try harder and wonder what went wrong. As more and more needy people come for counseling, there is a tendency to keep increasing our counseling load, thus pushing ourselves closer to the limits of our endurance. Sometimes the counselees' problems remind us of our own insecurities or conflicts and this can threaten our stability or feelings of self-worth. Little wonder that counseling has been seen as both a fulfilling and a hazardous occupation. In this chapter we will discuss some of these hazards and consider some ways in which the counselor's work can be more fulfilling and successful.

The Counselor's Motivation

Why do you want to counsel? Some Christian counselors, especially pastors, have been thrust into this work by people who have come unsolicited for help with their problems. Other counselors have encouraged counselees to come and may have taken special training, based on the valid assumption that counseling is one of the most effective ways to minister to others. As we have seen, the Bible commands mutual caring and this surely involves counseling.

It is always difficult to evaluate one's own motives. Perhaps this is especially true when we examine our reasons for counseling. A sincere desire to help people grow is a valid reason for becoming a counselor, but there are other reasons which motivate counselors and which interfere with their counseling effectiveness.[1]

1. *Curiosity—The Need for Information.* In describing their problems, counselees often give interesting tidbits of information which might not be shared otherwise. When a counselor is curious he or she sometimes forgets the counselee, pushes for extra information and often is unable to keep confidences. For these reasons, people prefer to avoid curious helpers.

2. *The Need for Relationships.* Everyone needs closeness and intimate contacts with at least two or three other people. For some counselees, the counselor will be their closest friend, at least temporarily. But what if counselors have no close friends apart from counselees? In such cases the counselor's need for a relationship may hinder the helping. The counselor does not really want counselees to improve and terminate counseling since this would terminate the relationship. If you look for opportunities to prolong the counseling hour, to call the counselee, or to get together socially, the relationship may be meeting your needs for companionship as much (or more) as it is helping the counselee. At this point the counselor-counselee involvement has ceased to be a professional helping relationship. This isn't always bad, but friends are not always the best counselors.

3. *The Need for Power.* The authoritarian counselor likes to "straighten out" others, give advice (even when it is not requested), and play the "problem solver" role. Some dependent counselees may want this but they are not helped if their lives are controlled by someone else. And most people eventually will resist the controller type of counselor. He or she is not really a helper.

4. *The Need to Rescue.* The rescuer takes responsibility away from the counselee by demonstrating an attitude which says "you can't handle this; let me do it for you." This has been called the "do-good," messiah approach. It may satisfy the counselee for a while but it rarely helps permanently. When the rescue technique fails (as often happens) the counselor feels guilty and inadequate—like a messiah unable to save the lost.

It is probable that every perceptive counselor will experience these tendencies at times but such tendencies must be resisted. When a person comes for counseling he or she takes the risk of sharing personal information and committing himself to the counselor's care. The counselor violates this trust and hence undermines counseling effectiveness if the helping relationship is used primarily to satisfy the helper's own needs.

The Counselor's Effectiveness

It is well known that some people are better counselors than others. This raises an important, basic question. Is it possible for every Christian to be an effective counselor or is counseling a gift which is reserved for selected members in the body of Christ? According to the Bible all believers should have compassionate concern for their fellow human beings, but from that it does not follow that all believers are or can become gifted counselors. In this respect, counseling is like teaching. Every parent has a responsibility for teaching children, but only some are especially gifted as teachers.[2]

In Romans 12:8 we read of the gift of exhortation (*paraklesis*), a word which means "coming alongside to help," and implies such activities as admonishing, supporting and encouraging others. This is listed among the spiritual gifts which some people have and others do not. Those who have and are developing this gift will see positive results in their counseling as people are helped and the church is built up. If counseling seems to be your special gift, praise God and learn to do it better. If your counseling seems ineffective, perhaps God has gifted you in some other way. This does not excuse anyone from being a people-helper but it may encourage some people to put their major efforts elsewhere and leave the counseling to those who are more gifted in that area.

To paraphrase 1 Corinthians 12:14–18:

> The Body is not one member but many . . . . If the counselor should say, "Because I am not a teacher, I am not part of the body," he is not for this reason any less a part of the body. If the whole body consisted of counselors, where would the formal teaching ministry be? If everyone were a teacher, who would do the deacon's work?
> But God has placed the members, each one of them, in the body just as he desired. . . . The teacher cannot say to the counselor, "I have no need of you," or again the evangelist to the teacher, "I have no need of you."

Clearly we need each other and counseling is a part—but only a part —of the functioning church. We help people by counseling, but we also help by evangelism, teaching, social concern, and other aspects of the ministry.

The Counselor's Role

Counseling, especially pastoral counseling, sometimes becomes ineffective because the counselor does not have a clear picture of his or her role and responsibilities. In a perceptive series of articles published several years ago, Maurice Wagner identified several potential areas of role confusion.[3]

1. *Visiting Instead of Counseling.* Visiting is a friendly, mutual sharing. Counseling is a problem-centered, goal-directed conversation which focuses primarily on the needs of one person, the counselee. All counseling will involve periodic visiting but when visiting is prolonged or primary, counseling problems are avoided and counseling effectiveness is reduced.

2. *Being Hasty Instead of Deliberate.* Busy, goal-directed people often want to hurry the counseling process to a quick and successful termination. It is true that counselors should not waste time but it is also true that counseling cannot be rushed. "Much of any counselor's success rests upon his own quiet, thoughtful attention to what the counselee is saying.

His poise is often a resource of strength for the troubled person . . . . If the counselor is hurried, or divided in his attention, his remarks of encouragement are likely to be taken with the suspicion that he is only saying something the counselee wants to hear so he can get on to something else.

"A relaxed and deliberate pace also makes the counselee feel the undivided attention and serious interest of his counselor . . . . When the counselor is hasty and hurried, he is inclined to formulate judgments based on immature impressions . . . . Deliberation cannot be accomplished if one is in a hurry to get finished with the problem." [4]

3. *Being Disrespectful Instead of Sympathetic.* Some counselors quickly categorize people (for example, as a "carnal Christian," a "divorcee," or a "phlegmatic type") and then dismiss individuals with quick confrontation or rigid advice. No one likes to be treated with such disrespect and the helper who does not listen sympathetically is unlikely to counsel effectively.

4. *Being Judgmental Instead of Unbiased.* There are times when counselees must be confronted about the sin or unusual behavior in their lives, but this is not the same as preaching and condemning in the counseling office. When counselees feel attacked they either defend themselves (often in anger) with a "what's the use?" attitude, or they go along with the counselor temporarily and grudgingly. None of these kinds of reactions contributes to counselee growth and all are in response to a counseling technique which usually reflects the counselor's own anxiety, uncertainty, or need to control. Jesus is described as one who was "touched with the feelings of our infirmities." He *never* winked at sin, but he understood sinners and always showed kindness and respect to those, like the woman at the well, who were willing to learn, repent and change their behavior.

5. *Overloading the Session Instead of Pacing the Counseling.* With his or her enthusiasm for helping, the counselor sometimes attempts to do too much in one session. This overwhelms the counselee and leads to confusion. Since it is probably true that counselees can only assimilate one or two major insights in each session, the counseling should be paced, even if this means shorter but more frequent sessions.

6. *Being Directive Instead of Interpretive.* This is a common error and, as we have seen, may reflect the counselor's unconscious need to dominate. When counselees are told what to do, they confuse the Christian counselor's opinion with the will of God, feel guilty and incompetent if they don't follow the advice, and never learn how to mature spiritually and emotionally to the point where they can make decisions without the help of a counselor. The counselor and counselee must work together as a team in which the counselor serves as a teacher-coach whose eventual goal is to withdraw from the playing field.

7. *Being Emotionally Involved Instead of Remaining Objective.* There is a fine line between caring and becoming too involved to be helpful when

a counselee is exceptionally disturbed, confused, or struggling with a problem that is similar to the counselor's own struggles. Then there is a tendency to worry and to let counselees interrupt our schedules at their convenience. Such emotional involvement can cause the counselor to lose objectivity and this in turn reduces counseling effectiveness. At times compassionate people will not be able to avoid emotional involvement, but the Christian counselor can resist this tendency by viewing the counseling as a professional helping relationship that clearly is limited in terms of issues such as length of appointments, number of conversations, resistance to touching, and so on. This is not designed to set the counselor apart. It is intended to help keep him or her objective enough to be helpful.

8. *Being Defensive Instead of Empathic.* At times most counselors feel threatened in counseling. When we are criticized, unable to help, made to feel guilty, anxious or in danger of being harmed, our ability to listen empathically is hindered. When empathy goes, so does much of our counseling effectiveness.

When such threats arise it is often good to ask ourselves why. If we don't know the answer, there is value in discussing this with a friend or other counselor. The more we know and accept about ourselves, the less we are likely to be threatened by counselees.

The counselor must maintain a vigilant attitude if he or she is to avoid these eight hazards.[5] As Christian helpers we honor God by doing the best job possible, by apologizing when we make mistakes, and by using our mistakes as learning situations and stepping stones to improvement.

If, in our desire to help, we have slipped into unhealthy counseling roles, we must restructure the relationship, at times even telling people how we intend to change (by such actions as setting more rigid counseling hours, refusing to drop everything else when the counselee calls, being less directive, and so on). This restructuring is always difficult because it often involves taking back something which has been given. The alternative is further role confusion and ineffective counseling. Mistakes and role confusions are not irreversible tragedies, however. Good rapport with counselees can cover a multitude of counseling mistakes, but we do not use this as an excuse for sloppy counseling and incompetence. "The most important concept to keep in mind is that Christ is really the Counselor; we are His agents doing His work, representing Him. His Holy Spirit is our Comforter and Guide and will lead us to deliver those He has brought to us for help."[6]

The Counselor's Vulnerability

Counseling would be easier if we could assume that every counselee wanted help, was honest, and would cooperate fully in the counseling. Regretfully this does not always happen. Some counselees have a conscious or unconscious desire to manipulate, frustrate, or not cooperate. This is a difficult discovery for the counselor who wants to succeed and whose success chiefly comes when people change. It is always difficult to work with people like this, especially when the people might not cooperate. By agreeing to help we are opening ourselves to the possibility of power struggles, exploitation and failure.

There are at least two major ways in which people frustrate the counselor and increase his or her vulnerability.

1. *Manipulation.* Some people are masters at getting their own way by controlling others. The story is told of a young counselor who felt insecure and wanted to please. Not wishing to be labeled like the "previous counselor who didn't care," the new counselor was determined to be helpful. The counseling sessions lengthened and became more frequent. Before long the counselor was making phone calls, running errands, giving small loans and even shopping for the counselee, who constantly expressed gratitude and mournfully asked for more.

Manipulated counselors are rarely helpful counselors. People who attempt to manipulate the counselor have often made manipulation a way of life. They do it subtly and well, but they are not free to live apart from deception and the art of controlling. The counselor must challenge these tactics, refuse to be moved by them, and teach more satisfying ways of relating to others.

It is wise to ask continually: "Am I being manipulated?" "Am I going beyond my responsibilities as a counselor?" "What does this counselee really want?" Sometimes people claim that they want help with a problem but they really want your attention and time, your sanctioning of sinful or otherwise harmful behavior, or your support as an ally in some family conflict. Sometimes people come because they believe that concerned mates, family members and employers will stop complaining about the counselee's behavior if it appears that counseling is taking place. When you suspect such dishonesty and manipulation it is wise to raise this with the counselee, expect denial, and then structure the counseling in a way that prevents manipulation and exploitation of the counselor in the future. Remember that truly helpful counseling is not always pleasing to the counselee or convenient for the counselor, but it does contribute to the growth and development of the person who comes for help. It doubtlessly is true that "people who are genuine in their desire for help are seldom demanding," dishonest or manipulative.[7]

2. *Resistance.* People sometimes come for help because they want immediate relief from pain but when they discover that permanent relief might require time, effort and greater pain they resist counseling. Sometimes the problems provide benefits which the counselee is unwilling to give up (personal attention from others, for example, or disability compensation, decreased responsibility, or more subtle gratifications such as punishment or the opportunity to make life difficult for others).[8] Since successful counseling would take away these benefits the counselee does not cooperate. Then there are people who get a sense of power and ac-

complishment by frustrating the efforts of others—such as professional counselors. These people often convince themselves, "I'm beyond help— but then that counselor who couldn't succeed with me isn't any good either." So the counselor continues to counsel, the counselee pretends to cooperate, but no one gets better.

Resistance is a powerful force which often requires in-depth professional counseling. When counselors begin to work, the counselee's psychological defenses are threatened and this leads to anxiety, anger and noncooperation which sometimes is not even conscious. When counselees are relatively well-adjusted this resistance can be discussed gently and openly. Let the counselee know that he or she (not the counselor) is responsible ultimately for improvement or nonimprovement. The counselor provides a structured relationship, avoids getting on the defensive, and must recognize that one's effectiveness as a counselor (and certainly as a person) is not always correlated with the improvement rate of counselees.

It has been suggested that counselors get lost not only when they do not know where they are going, but also when they do not know themselves. We can remain alert to potential problems when we frequently ask ourselves (and each other) questions such as the following: [9]

Why do I say this is the worst (or best) person I have ever counseled?

Is there a reason why I or the counselee is always late?

Is there a reason why I or the counselee wants more (or less) time than we had agreed previously?

Do I overreact to statements this counselee makes?

Do I feel bored when I am with this person? Is the problem with me, or with the counselee, or both?

Why do I always disagree (or agree) with the counselee?

Do I find myself wanting to end this relationship or to hold on to it even though it should end?

Am I beginning to feel too much sympathy for the counselee?

Do I think about the counselee frequently between sessions, daydream about him or her, or show more than average interest in the counselee or problem? Why?

The Counselor's Sexuality

Whenever two people work closely together towards a common goal, feelings of camaraderie and warmth often arise between them. When these people are of similar background, and especially when they are of the opposite sex, the feelings of warmth almost always have a sexual component.[10] This sexual attraction between counselor and counselee has been called "the problem clergymen don't talk about." [11] But it is a problem that almost *all* counselors encounter, at times, whether or not they talk about it with others.

Counseling often involves the discussion of intimate details which would never be discussed elsewhere—especially between a man and a woman who are not married to each other. This can be sexually arousing to both the counselor and counselee. The potential for immorality is even greater if the counselee is attractive and/or tends to be seductive, if the counselor is not having emotional and sexual needs met elsewhere, if the counselee indicates that he or she really needs the counselor, and/or if the counseling involves detailed discussions of sexually arousing material. Such subtle influences, wrote Freud many years ago, "bring with them the danger of making a man forget his technique and medical task for the sake of a fine experience." Perhaps almost every reader of this book knows of counselors, including pastoral counselors, who have compromised their standards "for the sake of a fine experience" and discovered that their ministries, reputations, counseling effectiveness and sometimes their marriages have been destroyed as a result—to say nothing of the adverse effects that this can have on the counselee.[12] Sexual feelings toward a counselee are common and the wise counselor would make special effort at self-control.

1. *Spiritual Protection.* Meditation on the Word of God, prayer (including the intercession of others) and reliance on the Holy Spirit to protect us are all crucially important. In addition, counselors should watch what they do with their minds. Fantasy often precedes action and the wise counselor makes a practice of not dwelling on lustful thoughts, but focusing instead on that which is true, honorable, right, pure, lovely and good.[13] There is also value in finding another believer to whom you can regularly be accountable for your actions. This can have a powerful impact on your own behavior. Finally, be careful not to fall into the dangerous trap of thinking, "It happens to others but would never happen to me." This is the kind of pride which often precedes a yielding to temptation. It ignores the scriptural command that he (or she) who thinks he stands should take heed lest he fall.[14]

And what if you do fall? We serve a God who forgives [15] even though the scars—in the form of a ruined reputation or a marriage breakdown, for example—may remain a lifetime. If we confess any sin we are forgiven, but then we have the obligation to change our subsequent behavior to make it more consistent with the Scriptures.

2. *Awareness of Danger Signals.* In an entire book dealing with counselor-counselee sexual feelings,[16] Rassieur indicated several clues that can indicate a potential shift from counseling professionalism to dangerous intimacy. This includes:

the communication of subtle messages of a more intimate quality (smiles, raising of the eyebrow, physical touches, and so on);

the desire of both counselor and counselee to maintain the relationship;

eagerness, especially by the counselee, to divulge details of sexual experiences or fantasies;

the counselor's permitting himself or herself to be manipulated by the counselee;

the counselor's recognition that he or she needs to see the counselee (this is a sign of going under);

increasing frustrations in the counselor's own marriage; and

the lengthening of time and frequency of interviews, sometimes supplemented by telephone calls.

3. *Limit Setting*. When the sexual attraction is present and recognized the counselor can stop the counseling, make a referral, or even discuss these feelings with the counselee. Before any of this, however, it is best to set some clear limits. Clearly prescribe the frequency and length of counseling sessions, then stick with these limits; refuse to engage in long telephone conversations; discourage lengthy detailed discussions of sexual topics; avoid physical contact; and meet in a place and seat yourself in a way which discourages wandering eyes or an opportunity for personal intimacies.

4. *Examining Attitudes*. There is nothing to be gained by denying your sexual feelings. They are common, often embarrassing and quite arousing, but controllable. Remember the following:

(a) Social Consequences. Yielding to sexual temptation can ruin one's reputation, marriage, and counseling effectiveness. This realization can be an important deterrent.

(b) Professional Image. Remember that you are a professional counselor and hopefully a maturing man or woman of God. Sexual intimacies with counselees never help those with problems and never advance the counselor's professional work.

(c) Theological Truth. Sexual involvements outside of marriage are sins and must be avoided. It is true that circumstances influence our present behavior and past experiences may limit our current range of choices, but these do not absolve us of responsibility. Each counselor and counselee is responsible for his or her own behavior.[17] The person, writes psychiatrist Vicktor Frankl, "is *not* fully conditioned and determined; he determines himself whether to give in to conditions or stand up to them. . . . Every human being has the freedom to change at any instant."[18] We may complain that "the devil made me do it," but the devil only tempts. He never *makes* us do anything. We choose to sin by deliberating and acting contrarily to the promptings of the Holy Spirit, who resides within the believer and is greater than Satan.[19] This is important for both counselors and counselees to realize.

5. *Support Group Protection*. Effective coping involves an honest recognition of the sexual attraction. Then there is great value in discussing this with one or two trusted confidants.

First on the list is one's spouse. A good marriage does not prevent one's being sexually attracted to a counselee, but it has a significant influence on the counselor's ability to cope.[20] Sometimes because of fear, embarrassment or a desire not to hurt, the counselor never discusses this issue with his or her mate. As a result the counselor misses a good opportunity for in-depth marital communication, support, and reassurance of one's mate. And if a counselee becomes a serious threat to the counselor's marriage, it is probable that there were underlying problems in the marriage before the counselee came along.[21]

Then there is value in discussing one's feelings with another trusted counselor or close friend. In this way the problem can be kept in perspective, the Christian friend can pray for protection, and the counselor has someone to whom he or she can be accountable.

Should the sexual attraction ever be discussed with the counselee? At times this may be appropriate in that it can help counselee understanding and growth. But the risks involved in such discussions are very high. Some counselees may interpret such discussions as an invitation to greater intimacy. Others, especially immature or flattered counselees, may talk about your discussion and this could have professionally disastrous consequences. Before discussing one's sexual feelings with a counselee, it would be wise to discuss this with another friend or professional consultant.

If you decide not to share your feelings with the counselee, try to apply the suggestions given in the previous paragraphs: avoid all flirting, and seriously consider referral to another counselor if you observe such clues as continuing anxiety during the counseling sessions, poor concentration interrupted by sexual fantasies, fear of displeasing the counselee; preoccupation with thoughts and fantasies about the counselee between sessions, and obvious anticipation of the next appointment coupled with fears that the session may be canceled or the counseling will be terminated.[22]

The Counselor's Ethics

Most professional counseling organizations (such as the American Psychological Association or the American Personnel and Guidance Association) have developed ethical codes to guide counselors in ethical decisions and to protect the public from unethical practices. In general, Christian professionals seek to comply with these ethical codes but, since we view the Bible as God's Word, the Scriptures become the ultimate standard against which we make all ethical decisions.

The Christian counselor respects each individual as a person of worth, created by God in the divine image, marred by mankind's fall into sin, but loved by God and the object of divine redemption. Each person has feelings, thoughts, a will, and the freedom to behave as he or she deems fit. As a people-helper, the counselor sincerely seeks the best for the counselee's welfare and does not attempt to manipulate or meddle in the counselee's life. As a servant of God, the counselor has a responsibility to live, act and counsel in accordance with scriptural principles. As an employee, the counselor attempts to fulfill his or her responsibilities and perform duties faithfully and competently. As a citizen and a member of society, the counselor seeks to obey governmental authorities and contribute to the good of the culture.

When there are no conflicts between these assumptions and values, the counselor's work can proceed smoothly. Ethical problems arise when values conflict and different decisions must be made. Many but not all of these decisions involve issues of confidentiality. Consider, for example, the following:

A counselee, in confidence, reveals that he has broken the law or that he intends to harm another person. Do you tell the police or the intended victim?

The daughter of the church chairman reveals that she is pregnant and plans to have an abortion. What do you do with this information?

A young man comes requesting help in gaining self-confidence around women so he can more comfortably encourage his girl friends to have sexual intercourse with him. What is your responsibility as a counselor who believes premarital sex is wrong?

A seminary graduate currently seeking pastoral placement reveals in counseling that he is a practicing homosexual. As a church member do you reveal this or say nothing when completing a recommendation form?

The counselor is committed to keeping information confidential except when the welfare of the counselee or some other person is at stake. At such times the counselee should be encouraged to share information directly with persons involved (police, employers, parents, and so on), and as a general rule, information should not be shared by the counselor without the counselee's knowledge. In addition the counselor refrains from test administration or interpretation, giving medical or legal advice, and otherwise offering services for which he or she is neither trained nor qualified. In states and countries where counselors are licensed or certified, the counselor advertises his or her services accurately and in accordance with the law.[23]

In every ethical decision the counselor seeks to act in a way which will honor God, be in conformity with biblical teaching, and respect the welfare of the counselee and others. When different decisions must be made, counselors have an obligation to discuss the situation in confidence with one or two other Christian counselors and/or with specialists such as a lawyer or physician who need not know the identity of counselees, but who can help in making ethical decisions. Such decisions are never easy, but the Christian counselor gets as much factual data as possible (including biblical data), sincerely trusts that God will lead, and then makes as wise a decision as possible based on the best evidence available.

The Counselor's Burnout

Graduate students in counseling often assume that the act of helping people will provide a lifetime of satisfaction and vocational fulfillment.

At some time after graduation, however, most counselors discover that counseling is hard work, that many counselees do not get better, and that constant involvement with the problems and miseries of others is psychologically and physically draining. In a widely reported study, researchers at the University of California in Berkeley recently conducted in-depth interviews with 200 physicians, psychiatrists, psychologists, social workers, school counselors, mental health nurses, and other helpers. It was discovered that most counselors have difficulty coping with the emotional stresses which come from continual intimate work with troubled human beings, many of whom do not get better. All of this contributes to counselor "burnout"—a feeling of futility, powerlessness, fatigue, cynicism, apathy, irritability and frustration.[24] In a subtle and sometimes unconscious effort at self-protection, counselors who believe in the importance of warmth, genuineness and empathy, instead become cold, aloof, unsympathetic, detached, worn-out helpers. The professional, concluded one report, dons such a thick armor that no one can get through.

Burnout probably is common in all helping professions, including the ministry, but can it be prevented? Apparently there are some steps we can take to avoid becoming tired, detached helpers. First, to prevent burnout we need the spiritual strength which comes through regular periods of prayer and meditation on the Scriptures. Second, we need support from a few others who accept us for who we are rather than for what we do. Each of us needs at least one loving and understanding person with whom we can cry; one person who knows our weaknesses but can be trusted not to use this knowledge against us. Third, we need to take time off—regular periods away from demanding, needy people. Jesus did this and so must we if we are to remain efficient and capable helpers. Finally, it helps if we can share the load by encouraging other believers[24] to be sensitive lay counselors and burden bearers. The church leader or other Christian counselor who seeks to do all of the helping alone is heading for inefficiency, if not eventual burnout.

And what about the helper who is burned out already? As soon as possible take your phone off the hook and get away for at least a brief period of reevaluation. Consider how you can apply the suggestions listed in the preceding paragraph. Then think about your leisure activities. How can these lighten your load and add self-fulfillment and relaxation? The counselor needs to find balance in his or her activities, a time for rest or play, and an opportunity to laugh. Otherwise life becomes boring, routine and lackluster. This isn't pleasant for the counselor and it certainly does nothing to help counselees effectively deal with the stresses of life.

The Counselor's Counselors

Many professional training programs require that students have personal counseling, supervised practice, sensitivity group training, or similar experiences in an effort to increase self-awareness, facilitate self-acceptance and remove those emotional and psychological blocks which hinder counseling effectiveness. While such counseling is often helpful and highly recommended, it frequently overlooks the greatest available source of strength and wisdom for Christian counselors—the Holy Spirit who guides and dwells in the life of each believer.[25] "I get concerned," wrote one pastoral counselor. "Christian helpers become so involved in the technicalities and theories of counseling which come to us through other helping professions, that they overlook or never become aware of the Source from which all such helpfulness comes—God himself." [26]

The Bible describes Jesus Christ as the Wonderful Counselor.[27] He is the counselor's counselor—ever available to encourage, direct and give wisdom to human people-helpers. It bears repeating that the truly effective Christian counselor is basically a skilled and available instrument through whom the Holy Spirit works to change lives. When the counselor's work brings anxieties and confusion, these can be cast on God himself, who has promised to sustain and help.[28] Daily prayer and Bible reading keep us in active communication with the One who is our own advisor and helper.

Throughout the Bible, however, we see that God also works through other human beings. He helps counselors through other people with whom the counselor can share, maintain perspective, relax—and occasionally cry. Without the support, encouragement and viewpoint of a trusted Christian friend, the counselor's work is likely to be more difficult and less effective. Often two or more counselors can meet regularly to sustain and pray for each other. If you lack such a relationship ask God to help you find a colleague with whom you can share.

Recently, two researchers asked a group of counselors to answer the following question: How would you spend the rest of your life if you had the means to do anything you wanted? Of more than 100 counselors surveyed, only three persons indicated that they would spend their lives doing counseling and of these, one person preferred to do counseling as a spare-time leisure activity.[29] Counseling can be fulfilling work but it is not easy. The sooner this is recognized and faced honestly, the more satisfying will be one's helping ministry, and the more effective will be one's counseling.

Suggestions for Further Reading

Crane, William E. *Where God Comes In: The Divine 'Plus' in Counseling.* Waco, TX: Word, 1970.

Hiltner, Seward. *The Counselor Is Counseling.* Nashville: Abingdon, 1952.

Kennedy, Eugene. *On Becoming a Counselor: A Basic Guide for Non-Professional Counselors.* New York: Seabury, 1977.

Powell, John. *Why Am I Afraid to Love?* Niles, IL: Argus Communications, 1967.
———. *Why Am I Afraid to Tell You Who I Am?* Niles, IL: Argus Communications, 1969.

Rassieur, Charles L. *The Problem Clergymen Don't Talk About.* Philadelphia: Westminster, 1976.

Footnotes

1. Paul Welter, *How to Help a Friend* (Wheaton: Tyndale, 1978), pp. 35–36.
2. Rom. 12:7; Eph. 4:11.
3. Maurice E. Wagner, "Hazards to Effective Pastoral Counseling," part one, *Journal of Psychology and Theology*, 1 (July, 1973): 35–41; part two, 1 (October, 1973): 40–47.
4. Ibid., part one, p. 37.
5. In his articles Wagner listed ten hazards. Later in the chapter we will discuss the remaining two: Being divulging instead of strictly confidential, and trying to help the emotionally ill instead of making prompt referrals.
6. At this point Wagner quotes 2 Tim. 2:24–26.
7. William E. Hulme, "The Counselee Who Exploits the Counselor," *Pastoral Psychology* (June, 1962): 31–35.
8. Armand M. Nicholi, Jr., ed., *The Harvard Guide to Modern Psychiatry* (Cambridge, MA: Howard University Press, 1978), p. 9.
9. Adopted from Eugene Kennedy, *On Becoming a Counselor* (New York: Seabury, 1977).
10. Nathaniel S. Lehrman, "The Normality of Sexual Feelings in Pastoral Counseling," *Pastoral Psychology* 105 (June, 1960): 49.
11. Charles L. Rassieur, *The Problem Clergymen Don't Talk About* (Philadelphia: Westminster, 1976).
12. The adverse effects on counselees are documented by Nicholi, *Harvard Guide*.
13. Phil. 4:8.
14. 1 Cor. 10:12.
15. 1 John 1:9.
16. Rassieur, *The Problem*.
17. Ibid., p. 58.
18. Vicktor, Frankl, *Man's Search for Meaning: An Introduction to Logotherapy* (New York: Pocket Books, Inc., 1963), pp. 206–207.
19. 1 John 4:4.
20. Rassieur found this in his survey of pastors. Reported in *The Problem*, pp. 32–34 and elsewhere.
21. Ibid., p. 131.
22. Ibid., pp. 116–17.
23. A letter to the state or provincial licensing office usually is sufficient to bring information about licensing laws. In some places, for example, a person cannot call himself or herself a psychologist unless this person has passed state licensing examinations and/or been certified by the government. Even a Ph.D. in clinical psychology cannot be called a psychologist until the state requirements are met. Such legal requirements differ widely.
24. For more detailed information on burnout see Gary R. Collins, "Burn-Out: The Hazard of the Professional People Helper." *Christianity Today*, 1 April 1977, pp. 12–14; Christina Maslach, "Burned-Out," *Human Behavior* (September, 1976): 16–22; and Charles F. Warnath and John F. Shelton, "The Ultimate Disappointment: The Burned-Out Counselor," *Personnel and Guidance Journal* 55 (December, 1976): 172–95.
25. Rom. 8:9, 10; 1 Cor. 3:16; 6:19.
26. William E. Crane, *Where God Comes In*, p. 26.
27. Isa. 9:6.
28. Ps. 55:22; 1 Pet. 5:7.
29. Sumner H. Garte and Mark L. Rosenblum, "Lighting Fires in Burned-Out Counselors," *Personnel and Guidance Journal* (November 1978): 158–60.

4

The Crises in Counseling

AS WE MOVE THROUGH LIFE, MOST OF US BEHAVE IN FAIRLY CONSISTENT ways. There are emotional and spiritual ups and downs, of course, and at times we must exert extra effort to deal with emergencies or unexpected problems, but as we approach adulthood, each person develops a repertoire of problem-solving techniques based on one's personality, training and past experience. We use these techniques repeatedly and thus are able to meet the challenges of life successfully.[1]

At times, however, situations arise which are most severe and thus threaten our psychological equilibrium. These situations, or life events, are also known as crises. They may be expected or unexpected, real or imagined, actual (as when a loved one dies) or potential (as when it appears that a loved one *might* die soon).

Several writers have pointed out that the Chinese word for "crisis" involves two characters.[2] One means danger; the other means opportunity. A crisis is a *danger* because it threatens to overwhelm the person or persons involved. Crises involve the loss of someone or something significant, a sudden shift in one's role or status, or the appearance of new and threatening people or events. Because the crisis situation is so intense and unique, we discover that our customary ways of handling stress and solving problems no longer work. This leads to a period of confusion and bewilderment, often accompanied by inefficient behavior and emotional upsets including anxiety, anger, discouragement, sorrow or guilt. Although this intellectual, behavioral and emotional turmoil often is short-lived, it may persist for several weeks or even longer.

Crises, however, present people with the *opportunity* to change, grow, and develop better ways of coping. Since people in crises often feel confused, they are more open to outside help, including the help which comes from God and that which comes from a counselor. What one does with this help and how one resolves the crisis has:

> . . . considerable significance for the future mental health of the individual. His new equilibrium may be better or worse than in the past. . . .

He may deal with the crisis problems by developing new socially acceptable, reality-based problem-solving techniques which add to his capacity
to deal in a healthy way with future difficulties. Alternatively, he may,
during the crisis, work out new coping responses which are socially unacceptable and which deal with difficulties by evasion, irrational fantasy
manipulations, or regression and alienation—all of which increase the
likelihood that he will also deal maladaptively with future difficulties.
In other words, the new pattern of coping that he works out in dealing
with the crisis becomes thenceforward an integral part of his repertoire
of problem-solving responses and increases the chance that he will deal
more or less realistically with future hazards.[3]

When doctors talk of a medical crisis they often refer to that crucial
point in time when there is a change, either toward improvement and recovery or toward decline and death. Emotional and spiritual crises likewise are unavoidable turning points in life. To live is to experience crises.
To experience crises is to face turning points which will bring either growth
and maturation, or deterioration and continuing immaturity. The Christian counselor is in a vital position to influence which direction the crises'
resolutions will take.

The Bible and Crisis Types

Much of the Bible is concerned with crises. Adam, Eve, Cain, Noah,
Abraham, Isaac, Joseph, Moses, Samson, Jepthah, Saul, David, Elijah,
Daniel, and a host of other figures faced crises which the Old Testament
describes in detail. Jesus faced crises (especially at the time of his crucifixion) and so did the disciples, Paul, and many early believers. Several
of the Epistles were written to help individuals or churches meet crises,
and Hebrews 11 summarized both crises which had happy endings and
those which resulted in torture, incredible suffering and death.

Contemporary writers have identified three types of crises, each of
which has both modern and biblical examples. *Accidental or situational
crises* occur when there is a sudden threat or unexpected loss. The death
of a loved one, the onset of a sudden illness, the discovery of a pregnancy
out of wedlock, social disruptions such as war or economic depression,
the loss of one's house or savings, a sudden loss of respect and status—
these are all situational stresses, many of which were seen in one Old
Testament man, Job. Within a short period he lost his family, wealth,
health and status. In addition, his marriage appears to have been strained
and he experienced considerable confusion, anger and inner turmoil.

Developmental crises happen in the course of normal human development. Starting school, going away to college, adjusting to marriage and
then to parenthood, handling criticism, facing retirement or declining
health, and adapting to the deaths of one's friends can all be crises which
demand new approaches to coping and problem-solving. Abraham and
Sarah, for example, coped with moving, criticism, many years of childlessness, family stress, and even the command of God that young Isaac

should be sacrificed. We might wonder how an elderly couple like Zacharias and Elizabeth handled a son as unique as John the Baptist, or how Mary and Joseph were able to raise one so unusual and brilliant as the boy Jesus. Surely there were developmental crises—turning points which demanded prolonged periods of wise decision-making but which also led to increased growth.

Existential crises, which often overlap the above, come when we are forced to face such disturbing truths as the realization that:

> I'm a failure
> I'm too old to reach my life goals
> I've been "passed over" for a promotion
> I'm now a widow—single again
> My life has no purpose
> My marriage has ended in divorce
> My illness is incurable
> I have nothing to believe in
> My house and possessions are all gone because of the fire
> I'm retired
> I've been rejected because of my skin color

These, and similar realizations, take time and effort to assimilate. They are changes in self-perception which can be denied temporarily but which in time must be faced realistically.

After a great spiritual victory, Elijah was chased by Jezebel and ran to the wilderness where he concluded that he was a failure. Jonah had similar thoughts as he debated with God and surely after his calamities Job struggled with the question, "What has become of me, and what will happen now?"

The Bible speaks to all three of these crises and gives direction both to the counselee and to the counselor who is concerned with crisis intervention. In the chapters which follow crises of all three types will be discussed in detail, but there are counseling techniques which apply to every crisis situation. These should be understood by any Christian counselor before we turn to more specific problem areas.

Crisis Intervention

Crisis counseling has several goals:

—to help the person cope effectively with the crisis situation and return to his usual level of functioning;

—to decrease the anxiety, apprehension and other insecurities that may persist after the crisis has passed;

—to teach crisis-solving techniques so the person is better prepared to anticipate and deal with future crises; and

—to consider biblical teachings about crises so the person learns from the crisis and grows as a result.

In helping people face their crises, individual differences must be recognized. People differ in their flexibility, customary ways of coping, ability to learn new coping techniques, physical and psychological strength, and level of spiritual and emotional maturity. Keeping these differences in mind, the counselor can help in several ways.[4]

1. *Make Contact.* People in crisis don't always come to a counselor for help. More often we must go to others and show our warmth, understanding and genuine interest. One should expect that crisis counseling may take time, and that the counselee's point of view needs to be understood before other suggestions for action are made.

Sometimes the person in a crisis slips into a state of daydreaming, fantasy, or deep thought, and must be pulled back to reality. Whether or not this happens, it is often helpful to make eye contact, since this can be reassuring to the counselee and helps to keep the person in touch with his or her supporters.

Touching can be another way to make contact and give reassurance. Even without words, touching and other forms of physical contact can bring great comfort, although in America we seem to have strong taboos against touch. It is acceptable to shake hands, to "slap" a friend on the back, or to hug athletes briefly after the team scores, but hand holding or putting your arms around a person in crisis is usually discouraged in counseling. This is because counselees sometimes misinterpret the physical contact and see it as having sexual overtones.

For many people there is also a fear of intimacy and this makes touching seem threatening. Realizing the value and risks involved in touching, the counselor in each counseling session should decide if physical contact really will help the counselee, and whether it is likely to be misinterpreted. Ask also, what is your own motivation for touching? Is this more likely to meet your sexual and affiliation needs, rather than the needs of the counselee? Touching can be an excellent way to make contact and give support, but perhaps it should be guided by the rule: if in doubt—don't!

2. *Reduce Anxiety.* The counselor's calm, relaxed manner can help to reduce anxiety in the counselee, especially when this calmness is accompanied by reassurance. Listen patiently and attentively as the counselee describes his or her situation, provide reassuring facts ("There *are* ways to deal with this problem"), state your approval when something is done effectively ("I think that was a good decision—it shows you're on the right track"), and when possible, offer a prediction about what will happen ("I know it's tough but I think you can handle this OK").[5] At times you may want to encourage the taking of deep breaths, the conscious tension and relaxing of muscles, or the periodic use of other techniques for reducing muscle tension.[6] The calming effect of Bible verses such as 1 Corinthians 10:3 can also be helpful. Each of these anxiety reduction methods can be overused, causing the counselee to feel trapped or smothered, but each can reduce the effects of stress and make it easier to deal constructively with the crisis issues.

3. *Focus on Issues*. In times of crises it is easy to be overwhelmed by what appears to be a mass of confusing facts and problem situations. Help the counselee decide what are the specific issues which must be faced and problems which must be solved. Try to focus on the situation as it presently exists rather than on what might happen in the future.

4. *Evaluate Resources*. The counselor's willingness to help is one important resource for the counselee in crisis, but there are others.

Spiritual resources include the indwelling presence and guidance of the Holy Spirit, along with the comforting words and promises of Scripture. These can be a source of great strength and direction during crises. Some counselors use Scripture as a hammer to push or manipulate counselees into doing what the counselor thinks should be done. This is neither helpful nor ethical. Instead, Scripture should be presented as truth with the expectation that the Holy Spirit will use it in the counselee as he desires.[7]

Personal resources include the counselee's intellectual abilities, skills, past experience or learning, and motivation. Be careful, once again, to be realistic, but remember that a simple listing of counselee strengths and a reminder of past successes in coping can be both reassuring and helpful.

Interpersonal resources refer to people—friends, family members, community and church members who could help, and often would help eagerly if they knew of the need.

Additional resources can include money and other tangible help that might be available, time that remains before decisions must be made, and the availability of legal, medical, psychological, financial, educational and other community helps.

5. *Plan Intervention*. Having evaluated the problem and considered available resources, it is helpful to decide on a course of action which asks "Specifically, what will we do now?" The counselor and counselee together can look at the available facts and list alternative courses of action. How realistic is each of these? Which should be done first, second, and subsequently?

Some counselees will have difficulty making these decisions. Our goal is not to put more pressure on the counselees by forcing them to make decisions, but neither do we want to encourage dependence and an attitude of letting someone else solve the problems. Gently, but firmly, the counselor can help the counselee to make plans and, if necessary, think of better alternatives when an earlier plan is unsuccessful. One writer has suggested that "the golden rule for the therapist in crisis intervention is to do for others that which they cannot do for themselves and no more!"[8]

6. *Encourage Action*. It is possible for people to decide on some course of action but then be afraid to move ahead with the plan. The counselor, therefore, must encourage counselees to take action, to evaluate progress, and to modify plans and actions when experience would indicate that this is wise.

Taking action always involves at least some risk. There is possibility for failure or later regret, especially if the action involves major life changes such as moving or changing jobs.

It also should be recognized that in some situations, the crisis can never be resolved completely, even by taking action. When one loses a loved one in death, discovers the existence of an incurable disease, or fails to attain an important promotion, the crisis may bring permanent change. The counselee then must be helped to face the situation honestly, acknowledge and express feelings, readjust his life style, realistically plan for the future, and rest in the knowledge that God, in his sovereignty, knows our pain and cares. In all crises, but especially in times of permanent change, it helps if people are surrounded by sincere, concerned, helpful, praying friends who are available to assist whenever and however they are needed.

7. *Instill Hope.* In all counseling, improvement is more likely if counselees can be given a sense of realistic hope for the future. Hope brings relief from suffering, based on a belief that things will be better in the future. Hope helps us avoid despair and releases energy to meet the crisis situation.

The Christian counselor instills hope in three ways (which are not necessarily listed here in the order that they would be used). First, there is the sharing of scriptural truths which can give reassurance and hope based on the unchanging Word and nature of God. This is an approach which instills hope by stimulating faith in God. Second, we can help counselees examine their self-defeating logic. Ideas like "I'll never get better" or "Nothing can be worse" often enter the counselee's thinking in times of crisis. Such ideas should be challenged gently. What is the evidence for the conclusion that "I'll never get better"? What is the evidence for a more hopeful outcome? [9] Third, counselors can get the counselee moving and doing something. Even minimal activity gives the feeling that something is being done and that the counselee is not helpless. This, in turn, can arouse hope—especially if the activity accomplishes something worthwhile.

8. *Environmental Intervention.* Sometimes there is value in changing the counselee's environment—encouraging others to pray, give money or supplies, give practical help, or otherwise assist the person in crisis.

Such community mobilization is beyond the scope of traditional counseling, but some Christian people-helpers may wish to intervene like this, nevertheless. In doing so, be sensitive to the counselee's possible feelings about such help. Some people may have difficulty in accepting outside assistance. They may feel embarrassed by the attention, threatened by the implication that they need help, and become angry at the counselor who tried to do something nice. At times, the outside help encourages dependency and a "do-nothing" attitude in the counselee. It is important to discuss all of this with the counselee who, whenever possible, should be encouraged to seek help from others without the counselor's assistance.

9. *Follow-up.* Crisis counseling often is short-lived. After one or two sessions the counselee returns to the routines of life and does not come for counseling again. But was anything learned? Will the next crisis be handled more efficiently? Is the person getting along satisfactorily now that the major point of crisis is past?

These issues should concern the counselor, who often can follow up with a phone call or visit. Even when counseling is no longer needed, such "follow-up" interest can encourage the counselee and remind him or her that someone still cares and remembers.

Referral

Sometimes we help counselees most by referring them to someone else whose training, expertise and availability can be of special assistance. Referral does not mean, necessarily, that the original counselor is incompetent or trying to get rid of the counselee. In contrast, referral can reflect the counselor's concern for the counselee, and can show the counselor's realization that no one person is skilled enough to counsel everyone.

People should be referred when they are not showing signs of improvement after several sessions, have severe financial needs, need medical attention or legal advice, are severely depressed or suicidal, show extremely aggressive behavior, appear to be severely disturbed emotionally, stir strong feelings of dislike or sexual arousal in the counselor, or have problems which are beyond the counselor's felt area of expertise.

Counselors should be familiar with community resources and persons to whom counselees can be referred. These include private practitioners such as physicians, lawyers, psychiatrists, psychologists and other counselors; pastoral counselors and other church leaders; service agencies such as the Retarded Children's Society or the Society for the Blind; government agencies such as the State Department of Welfare or the Unemployment Bureau; private and public counseling clinics or hospitals; private employment agencies, suicide prevention centers; and groups like Alcoholics Anonymous. In considering referral, do not overlook the importance of church groups which often can give support and practical help in time of need.

Before suggesting referral it can be helpful to check with the referral source to be sure that a referred person can be accepted for help. In suggesting referral to the counselee, be sure to indicate your reasons for this recommendation. Try to involve the counselee in the decision to refer, making sure that you present this as a positive way to get further help and not as your belief that the counselee is too disturbed or too much of a problem for you to help.

It is best to let counselees make their own appointments with the new counselor. Sometimes these new counselors will want information about the counselee but this should only be given if the counselee has granted his or her consent. When the referral has been made it is good to keep an interest in the counselee but remember that someone else now is responsible for the counseling.

The Future of Counseling

Traditionally, counseling has been divided into three areas: remedial, preventive, and educative.[10] Remedial counseling involves helping people to deal with the existing problems of life. Preventive counseling seeks to stop problems from getting worse or to prevent their occurrence at all. Educative counseling involves the counselor's taking the initiative to teach principles of mental health to larger groups. It is impossible to estimate the percentage of counselor involvement in each of these three areas, but it is probable that remedial counseling takes the vast majority of counselor energy and time. Graduate training programs have contributed to this lopsided emphasis and professionals have discovered that it is much easier to make a living with rehabilitative counseling than with preventive and educative work. Most people will pay to get help with a problem; few will pay to have a problem prevented.

Several years ago, a committee of the American Psychological Association recommended that the three counseling roles be reversed.[11] We should put greatest emphasis on educative counseling, the committee concluded, secondary emphasis on prevention, and least emphasis on traditional remedial, rehabilitative helping. Such a change would broaden and vastly alter the field of counseling. Instead of focusing on individuals with problems, there would be greater emphasis on groups of people within the community. Rather than waiting for counselees to come to the office, helping would take place more often where people are. In addition to the emphasis on counseling techniques, there would be a focus on the use of books, programed learning, audio cassettes, and other educative methods. None of this assumes that remedial counseling will fade from the scene. Probably it will always be present and needed. But the field of counseling is changing and Christian counselors are beginning to feel the changes.

In a very real sense, however, Christians are ahead of the trends. Since the time of Christ, the church has been concerned about prevention and education. When the pastoral counseling movement arose, the church increased its emphasis on individual helping, but the larger role of educating people and helping them find spiritual and mental health has never been abandoned. Our educative and preventive efforts have not always been effective, and neither have our goals been clear, but within the church there already exists a way of thinking which gives education a place of prominence which often surpasses the emphasis on remedial counseling.

The chapters which follow have attempted to reflect both the traditional rehabilitative approach to counseling and the educative-preventive approach. The chapters are written (1) to convey an understanding of each problem area, (2) to present guidelines for helping those who are experiencing problems, and (3) to suggest ways in which Christians can be educated so that the problems can be prevented in the future. Each of the following chapters is designed to stand alone—they need not be read in any special order. This allows the book to be a handbook with chapters which can be used for general information and used for reference when specific counseling issues arise. It also is anticipated that the book and accompanying cassette tapes will be used as a training program for counselors and as a basis for the education of lay people. This was discussed more fully at the beginning of the book.

Christian counseling is a difficult but challenging task. It involves the development of therapeutic personality traits, the learning of skills, a sensitivity to people, an understanding of the counseling process, an alertness to the dangers involved, an in-depth familiarity with the Scriptures, and a sensitivity to the guidance of the Holy Spirit. Counseling can be discussed in a book but it cannot be learned completely from a book. We become good Christian counselors through commitment to Christ, through training and through the experience of helping people with their problems. It is to these problems that we turn in the following chapters.

Suggestions for Further Reading

Aguilera, Donna C., and Messick, Janice M. *Crisis Intervention: Theory and Methodology*. (3d ed.) St. Louis: Mosby, 1978.

Switzer, David K. *The Minister As Crisis Counselor*. Nashville: Abingdon, 1974.

Whitlock, Glenn E. *Understanding and Coping with Real-Life Crises*. Monterey: Brooks/Cole, 1978.

Footnotes

1. Lee B. Macht, "Community Psychiatry," in *The Harvard Guide to Modern Psychiatry*, ed. Armand M. Nicholi, Jr. (Cambridge, MA: Belknap Press of Harvard University Press, 1978), p. 632.

2. Glenn E. Whitlock, *Understanding and Coping with Real-Life Crises* (Monterey: Brooks/Cole, 1978).

3. Gerald Caplan, *Principles of Preventive Psychiatry* (New York: Basic Books, 1964), p. 43.

4. This section is adapted from an earlier book by the author: Gary R. Collins, *How to be a People Helper* (Santa Ana: Vision House, 1976), pp. 76–80.

5. Lawrence M. Brammer, *The Helping Relationship: Process and Skills* (Englewood Cliffs, NJ: Prentice–Hall, 1973), p. 127.

6. Some of these techniques are summarized in Gary R. Collins, *You Can Profit from Stress* (Santa Ana: Vision House, 1977), chapter 13.

7. Paul Welter, *How to Help a Friend* (Wheaton: Tyndale, 1978), p. 70.

8. Thomas N. Rusk, "Opportunity and Techniques in Crisis Psychiatry," *Comprehensive Psychiatry* 12 (May, 1971): 251.

9. This approach was first suggested by Albert Ellis, *Reason and Emotion in Psychotherapy* (New York: Lyle Stewart, 1962).

10. Much of the discussion in this section is adopted from Chris Hatcher, Bonnie S. Brooks, and associates, *Innovations in Counseling Psychology* (San Francisco: Jossey-Bass, 1977).

11. A. E. Ivey, *Professional Affairs Committee Report*, Division 17—Counseling Psychology, (Washington, DC: American Psychological Association, 1976).

Part II
Personal
Issues

5

Anxiety

ANXIETY, STRESS, FEAR, TENSION—TECHNICALLY THESE WORDS HAVE
different meanings but they are often used interchangeably to describe
one of the most prevailing characteristics of twentieth-century human
beings. Psychologist Rollo May has called anxiety "one of the most urgent
problems of our day."[1] It has been termed the "official emotion of our
age," the basis of all neuroses, and "the most pervasive psychological
phenomenon of our time." Although anxiety is as old as human existence,
the complexities and pace of modern life have alerted us to its presence
and perhaps have increased its influence.

Anxiety might be defined as an inner feeling of apprehension, uneasi-
ness, concern, worry, and/or dread which is accompanied by heightened
physical arousal. It can arise in reaction to some specific identifiable
danger (many writers call this "fear" rather than anxiety), or it can come
in response to an imaginary or unknown danger. This latter kind of
anxiety has been termed "free-floating." The person senses that something terrible is going to happen but he or she does not know what it is
or why.

Various kinds of anxiety have been identified (e.g., real, phobic, ego
neurotic, basic, and separation), but for our purposes let us consider only
a few of these: acute and chronic, normal and neurotic, moderate and
high.

Acute anxiety comes quickly, is of high intensity, and has a short
duration. When people are suddenly and unexpectedly overwhelmed by
anxiety, the condition usually is acute. *Chronic* anxiety, in contrast, is
persistent and long-lasting, but of lower intensity. Chronically anxious
people seem to worry all the time and in response to a variety of situations.
Much of their anxiety is free-floating.

Normal anxiety comes when there is real threat or situational danger.
The anxiety is proportional to the danger (the greater the threat the
greater the anxiety). It can be recognized, managed, and reduced, espe-

59

cially when outward circumstances change. *Neurotic* anxiety involves intense exaggerated feelings of helplessness and dread even when the danger is mild or nonexistent. It cannot be faced squarely and dealt with rationally, perhaps because it arises from unconscious inner conflicts (which is what Freud believed). To quote Rollo May's precise but technical description, neurotic anxiety "is disproportionate to the objective danger because some intrapsychic conflict is involved."[2]

Anxiety can vary in its intensity. *Moderate* anxiety can be desirable and healthy. Often it motivates, helps people avoid dangerous situations, and leads to increased efficiency. *High* anxiety can shorten one's attention span, make concentration difficult, adversely affect memory, hinder performance skills, interfere with problem solving, block effective communication, arouse panic, and sometimes cause undesirable physical symptoms such as paralysis or intense headaches.

The Bible and Anxiety

In the Bible "anxiety" is used in two ways, as fret or worry and as healthy concern.

First, let us consider *anxiety as fret and worry*. In his Sermon on the Mount, Jesus taught that we should not be anxious (worrying) about life's basic needs, such as food and clothing or about the future. We have a heavenly Father, Jesus said, who knows what we need and will provide.[3] In the New Testament Epistles, both Peter and Paul echoed this conclusion. "Stop perpetually worrying about even one thing," we read in Philippians. Instead, Christians are to bring their requests to God, with an attitude of thanksgiving, expecting to experience the "peace of God which surpasses all comprehension."[4] We can cast our anxieties upon the Lord knowing that he cares for us.[5]

> Anxiety as fret and worry comes because of a sinful turning from God. Instead of acknowledging His sovereignty and preeminence we have shifted the burdens of life onto ourselves and assumed that we alone can handle the problems that we face. When man turns from God and becomes his own god increased anxiety is inevitable. Perhaps it is not surprising, then, that in an age of increased godlessness there is also increased anxiety.[6]

In contrast, *anxiety in the form of a realistic concern* is neither condemned nor forbidden. Although Paul could write that he was not anxious (that is, worried) about the possibility of being beaten, cold, hungry or in danger, he said that he *was* anxious (that is, concerned) about the welfare of the churches. This sincere care for others put a "daily pressure" on Paul[7] and made Timothy "genuinely anxious" (that is, concerned) as well.[8]

According to the Bible, therefore, there is nothing wrong with realistically acknowledging and trying to deal with the identifiable problems of life. To ignore danger is foolish and wrong. But it is also wrong, as well as unhealthy, to be immobilized by excessive worry. Such worry must be committed in prayer to God, who can release us from paralyzing fear or anxiety, and free us to deal realistically with the needs and welfare both of others and of ourselves.

Admittedly, however, it isn't always easy to "stop perpetually worrying." It is difficult for people to "cast their burdens on the Lord," to trust that God will meet their needs, to wait for his help and to know when they should take some responsibility for meeting a difficult situation. Anxious people often are impatient people who need help in handling their pressures realistically and within God's perfect time schedule. The counselor can help such people to see God's promises, to recognize his power and influence in our daily lives, and to take action when appropriate. For many counselees it is also helpful if they can understand the causes and effects of the anxiety which may be persisting in a troublesome way.

The Causes of Anxiety

For a condition so widespread as anxiety, it should come as no surprise that numerous causes have been identified. For example, in a little book titled *The Problem of Anxiety*,[9] Freud discussed this condition in terms of his view that human personality has three parts: the *id* which consists of instincts that demand immediate gratification, the *ego* which is aware of the external world and keeps the personality in contact with reality, and the *superego* which is the moral sense of right and wrong. Anxiety arises, Freud wrote, (a) when the ego recognizes a clear threat to the person (this was called "realistic anxiety"); (b) when the id begins to get too powerful, so that it threatens to overwhelm the ego and cause the person to act with socially aggressive or sexually unacceptable behavior (neurotic anxiety); or (c) when the superego gets too powerful, so that the person is overwhelmed by guilt or shame (moral anxiety). Later writers shifted away from this Freudian view and described anxiety as being less an internal instinctual struggle and more the result of cultural pressures or threats from the world in which we live. Then came an emphasis on learning, with the proposal that anxiety is a condition that we acquire through conditioning.[10]

Sifting through these and other theories we might conclude that anxiety arises as the result of threat, conflict, fear, unmet needs, and individual differences.

1. *Threat.* Following an in-depth survey of the literature, psychologist Rollo May concluded that anxiety is an apprehension that is always

> cued off by a threat to some value that the individual holds essential to his (or her) existence as a personality. The threat may be to physical life (the threat of death), or to psychological existence (the loss of freedom, meaninglessness). Or the threat may be to some other value which

one identifies with one's existence: (patriotism, the love of another person, "success," etc.).[11]

Threats, therefore, can be of different kinds including those which come from perceived danger, a threat to one's feelings of self-worth, separation and unconscious influences.

(a) Danger. Crime, war, violent weather, unexplained illnesses, even visits to the dentist, can be among those events which threaten individuals and cause anxiety. The anxiety arises because the individual feels uncertain about what is coming and helpless to prevent or reduce the threat. At times, most people are anxious about applying for a job, giving a speech or taking a test. Often this apprehension comes because of our uncertainty and feelings of helplessness.

(b) Self-esteem. Most people like to look good and to perform competently. When anything comes along to threaten our image or to imply (to others or to ourselves) that we are not competent, then we feel threatened. On a simple level, self-conscious people often sense a mild anxiety in new social situations because they are threatened by the reactions of others. On a more serious level, some people avoid taking exams or risking failure because the failure which might come would be too threatening to their self-esteem.

(c) Separation. It is never easy to be separated from significant other people. It can be confusing to be on our own and painful to realize that an important person in our life has left or rejected us. Concerned about the uncertainty of the future, faced with a gaping inner void, and sometimes wondering "What do I do now?", individuals often feel threatened and saddened when losses occur through moves, death, divorce, or other separations. So significant is this in explaining anxiety, that a psychologist named Otto Rank once proposed that all anxiety arises from separation, beginning with separation from the mother's womb at the time of birth and ending with the separation from human existence at death.

(d) Unconscious Influence. Even counselors who reject many of Freud's theories often agree that unconscious influences may be at the basis of at least some anxiety. There are so many (real and imagined) dangers in our society that to keep free from immobilizing fear most people have to ignore some potential stresses and push these out of their minds. This is not necessarily bad if done deliberately and temporarily, but according to Freud, when threats and concerns are pushed into the unconscious they may fester away from our conscious awareness. Later these unconscious ideas move toward becoming conscious and that can be threatening because we are then forced to face difficult problems which we don't understand or know how to solve.

Consider, for example, the case of a young man who was seized with intense anxiety one evening while watching a ballet. He felt better upon leaving the theater but subsequently decided to go for counseling. As the incident was discussed, the counselor concluded that this man had strong unconscious homosexual tendencies which he was struggling to keep from becoming conscious. During the performance, he was attracted unconsciously to the male ballet dancers. The anxiety which followed was thought to be in reaction to the threat that his defenses might break down and that his homosexual tendencies might become apparent to himself or to others.[12]

Such an interpretation is difficult for the counselor to see at first, but the man's panic is a good example of anxiety which arises in response to a specific situation. By considering the times and places when anxiety was aroused, the counselor often is able to get a clue concerning the specific danger which threatens the counselee.

2. *Conflict.* Another cause of anxiety is conflict. When a person is influenced by two or more pressures there is a sense of uncertainty which often leads to anxiety. Most general psychology books suggest that conflicts come from two tendencies: approach and avoidance. To approach is to have a tendency to do something or to move in a direction which will be pleasurable and satisfying. To avoid is to resist doing something, perhaps because it will not be pleasurable or satisfying. There are three kinds of conflicts: approach-approach, approach-avoidance, and avoidance-avoidance.

(a) Approach-approach conflict. Here is a conflict over the tendency to pursue two desirable but incompatible goals. We may be faced with two dinner invitations on the same night, either of which would be pleasant. Often making such a decision is difficult and sometimes it is anxiety arousing.

(b) Approach-avoidance conflict. Here there is a desire both to do something and not to do it. For example, a person may grapple with the offer of a new job. To accept might bring more pay and opportunity (approach), but it also may bring the necessity of a move and the inconvenience of a training program (avoidance). Making such decisions can involve considerable anxiety.

(c) Avoidance-avoidance conflict. Here there are two alternatives, both of which may be unpleasant: like having pain versus having an operation which might in time relieve the pain.

Most conflicts involve a struggle between two or three alternatives, each of which may have both approach and avoidance characteristics. A young person may wonder, for example, whether to stay in the present job, shift to another job, or return to school. Each of these alternatives has both positive and negative aspects, and anxiety persists until the choice is made (and sometimes, lasts after the decision while we ponder "did I make a mistake?").

3. *Fear.* As we indicated earlier, some counselors would distinguish fear from anxiety. Let us recognize, however, that the same inner apprehension which characterizes anxiety can also come in response to fear.

Fear and anxiety, therefore, are similar, even though they may not be identical.

Fears can come in response to a variety of situations. Different people are afraid of failure, the future, achieving success, rejection, intimacy, conflict, meaninglessness in life (sometimes called existential anxiety), sickness, death, loneliness, and a host of other real or imagined possibilities. Sometimes these fears can build up in one's mind and create extreme anxiety—often in the absence of any real danger.

4. *Unmet needs.* For many years psychologists and other writers have tried to identify the basic needs of human beings. Cecil Osborne, for example, has concluded that six needs are fundamental: [13]

> survival (the need to have continued existence)
> security (economic and emotional)
> sex (as an expression of love; as a sexual being)
> significance (to amount to something; to be worthwhile)
> self-fulfillment (to achieve fulfilling goals)
> selfhood (a sense of identity)

If we fail to meet these or other needs, Osborne believes, we are anxious, "up-in-the-air," afraid, and often frustrated.

But what if all of these needs are met? Would life be complete and satisfying? Probably not! There still would be questions that transcend life on earth: Where will I go after death? Does existence consist of only a few short years on earth? One writer [14] has lumped these and related questions into something called *finite-eschatological anxiety* and paired this with *the anxiety of sin*—that which comes when our thoughts and actions have violated divine commandments and broken our communication with God and others. We can have no real freedom from anxiety until we are at peace with God, resting in his promises for eternity, and know the stability of sins confessed and completely forgiven.

5. *Individual Differences.* It is well known, of course, that people react differently to anxiety-producing situations. Some people are almost never anxious, some seem highly anxious most of the time, many are in between. Some people are made anxious by a variety of situations; others find that only one or two issues trigger anxiety. Free-floating anxiety—the kind with no clear cause—characterizes some; others are made anxious by clearly identified dangers. Then there are those with claustrophobia, hydrophobia and the other phobias—irrational fears of enclosed spaces, water, heights, or additional circumstances most of which are not in themselves dangerous.

Why are there differences like this? Perhaps the answer comes in terms of the person's psychology, personality, sociology, physiology or theology.

(a) Psychology. Most behavior is learned as a result of personal experience or teaching by parents and other significant persons. When we have failed and must try again, when we have been hurt in the past, when others have demanded more than we could give, when we have seen anxiety in other people (e.g., the child who learns to be anxious in thunderstorms because his mother was always anxious), when we have developed the capacity to think of the potential dangers in a situation, when our perception of a situation gives us reason to suspect danger—all of these are psychological reactions which arouse anxiety. Since we each have different experiences and different ways of viewing the world, we differ in our intensity and frequency of anxiety.

(b) Personality. It may be that some people are more fearful or "highstrung" than others. Some are more sensitive, self-centered, hostile, or insecure than others. These personality differences arise from a combination of inherited and learning influences which, in turn, create individual differences in anxiety.

(c) Sociology. A past president of the American Psychological Association once suggested that the causes of anxiety rest in our society: political instability, mobility which disturbs our sense of rootedness, shifting values, changing moral standards and religious beliefs, and so on.[15] While these are not the only reasons for anxiety, it surely is true that the culture and subcultures stimulate anxiety in some people but give others such a secure environment that anxiety is much less prominent.

(d) Physiology. The presence of disease can stimulate anxiety, but so can dietary imbalance, neurological malfunctioning and chemical factors within the body. Anxiety, of course, can trigger physiological reactions, but physiology can also contribute to increased anxiety.

(e) Theology. Beliefs have a great bearing on one's anxiety level. If God is seen as all-powerful, loving, good, and in ultimate control of the universe (which is the biblical teaching), then there can be trust and security even in the midst of turmoil. If we believe that God forgives when we confess our sin, that he promises life eternal, and that he meets our needs on earth, then there is less cause for anxiety.

It should not be assumed, however, that nonbelievers necessarily are more anxious than believers. (Some Christians, for example, are so worried about pleasing God that their theology increases anxiety.) Nor should it be concluded that anxiety always reflects a lack of faith. The causes of anxiety are too complex for such a simplistic explanation. Nevertheless what we believe or do not believe does contribute to individual differences in the extent to which we experience anxiety.

The Effects of Anxiety

It should not be assumed that anxiety is always bad. When anxiety is nonexistent, life can be boring, inefficient, and unsatisfying. A moderate amount of anxiety (not too little, not too much) motivates us and adds zest to life. When anxiety is great, however, we begin to experience crippling physical, psychological, defensive, and spiritual reactions.

(a) Physical Reactions. It is common knowledge that anxiety can produce ulcers, headaches, skin rashes, backaches and a variety of other physical problems. Almost everyone has experienced stomach discomfort ("butterflies"), shortness of breath, an inability to sleep, increased fatigue, loss of appetite, and a frequent desire to urinate during times of anxiety. Less conscious are changes in blood pressure, increased muscle tension, a slowing of digestion, and chemical changes in the blood. If these are temporary they cause little, if any, harm. When they persist over time the body begins to break under the pressure. This is the origin of the psychosomatic (psychologically caused) illnesses.

(b) Psychological Reactions. Everyone who has taken an examination knows how anxiety can influence psychological functioning. Research has shown that anxiety reduces one's level of productivity, stifles creativity and originality, hinders the capacity to relate to others smoothly, dulls the personality, and interferes with the ability to think or to remember.[16] It is interesting to notice Rollo May's conclusion that people with higher intelligence and originality likewise are more inclined to be anxious. At the same time, intelligent persons also are able to develop more effective ways of managing and controlling their anxiety.[17]

(c) Defensive Reactions. When anxiety builds up, most people unconsciously rely on behaviors and thinking which dull the pain of anxiety and enable us to cope. These defensive reactions, which are well-known and often seen in counseling, include denial of the anxiety, pretending the anxiety-producing situation does not exist, blaming others for a fault which really is our own, rationalizing by logically explaining away the symptoms and their causes, slipping back into childish ways of reacting, and so on. Sometimes people escape through alcohol, drugs, a host of hypochondriacal complaints or even withdrawal into bizarre behavior and mental illness. These are all ways of trying to cope.

(d) Spiritual Reactions. Anxiety can motivate us to seek divine help where it might be ignored otherwise. But anxiety can also drive us away from God at a time when he is most needed. Fraught with worry and distracted by pressures, even religious people find that there is a lack of time for prayer, decreased ability to concentrate on Bible reading, reduced interest in church worship services, impatience and sometimes bitterness with heaven's seeming silence. The Christian counselor may be welcomed as a spiritual minister, or rejected because he or she represents a God who has permitted the stresses and left the impression that he doesn't care.

Counseling and Anxiety

It is not easy to counsel anxious persons, partially because it can be very difficult to uncover and cope with the causes of the anxiety and partly because anxiety is psychologically contagious. Anxious people often make others anxious—including the counselor who is trying to help. To counsel anxious people, therefore, the counselor first must be alert to his or her own feelings.

1. *Recognizing the Counselor's Own Anxieties.* When a counselor feels anxious in the presence of an anxious counselee, it is well to ask oneself several questions: What in this situation is making me anxious? Is the counselee anxious about something which makes me anxious too? What does my anxiety tell me about the counselee? By considering one's own anxiety it is sometimes possible to gain insight into the counselee's anxiety. By asking these questions, counselors are able to learn about themselves and about the counselee. These questions also enable the counselor to keep from confusing his or her anxieties with those of the counselee.[18]

2. *Demonstrating Love.* Love has been called the greatest therapeutic force of all,[19] but nowhere is this more true than in the reduction of fear and anxiety. The Bible states that "perfect love casts out fear"[20] and while this statement concerns fear of future judgment it surely demands a broader application. One writer has suggested that "the enemy of fear is love: the way to put off fear, then, is to put on love. . . . Love is self-giving; fear is self-protecting. Love moves toward others; fear shrinks away from them. . . . The more fear, the less love; the more love, the less fear."[21] To show love, especially mixed with patient understanding, to introduce counselees to the love of Christ,[22] and to help them experience the joy of loving others, can all help to cast out fear and anxiety.

3. *Identifying Causes.* Of course it would be unrealistic and inconsistent with both biblical exegesis and sound psychology if we were to assume that anxious people should simply experience and show love without ever attempting to identify the causes of their anxieties. Fear and anxiety are God-created emotions. They warn of danger of internal conflict and the sensitive, loving counselor does not tell the counselee to "buck up" or "stop being anxious." Instead the counselor seeks to assist the counselee in the difficult task of uncovering the sources of anxiety. This can be done in several ways.

(a) Observation. In counseling, does the counselee show evidence of added anxiety (shifting position, deep breathing, perspiration) when certain topics are discussed? What are these topics?

(b) Reflection. Can the counselee suggest circumstances which have raised or currently raise anxiety? It might be helpful to ask, "When are you most anxious?" "When are you not anxious?" "When was the last time you felt really anxious?" "What was happening in your life then?"

(c) Contemplation. As a counselor, remind yourself of the previously listed causes of anxiety. Ask yourself if any of these might be creating the counselee's anxiety. Raise some of the issues and as the counselee talks about them watch for signs of anxiety. Then discuss your hunches.

In all of this, remember the need for patience and understanding. By its very nature, anxiety often arises in response to threats which are vague and difficult to identify. By pushing the counselee to "snap out of it" or to "hurry and tell me what is wrong," we increase the anxiety, create more confusion, and risk losing or alienating the anxious person. Once again it is important to emphasize loving patience.

4. *Encouraging Action*. The goal in counseling is not to eliminate all anxiety. Instead the goal is to help counselees become aware of the sources of anxiety and then learn how to cope. To do this, the counselee can be helped to identify some specific actions to be taken, goals to be achieved, and skills to be learned. The counselee must be helped to confront the anxiety-producing situation directly, admitting his or her apprehensions, but moving ahead (with the counselor's support) in spite of the anxiety. "Courage consists not of the absence of fear and anxiety but of the capacity to move ahead even though one is afraid." The counselee is helped to take action and to move *through* the anxiety-producing situations rather than moving *around* them or *retrenching* before them.[23] The counselee must be helped to see that there is more to be gained by facing and trying to overcome the anxiety—even though this can be risky—than by wallowing in a state of anxiety which may be painful but also familiar. In all of this be careful to avoid intellectual discussions which may sound reassuring but which do nothing to help one take action to deal with the anxiety.

5. *Giving Support*. As we have seen, anxious counselees can get little help from tense, impatient counselors. The helper, therefore, must be calm, supportive, and patient as he or she watches progress which may, at times, be very slow in coming. There may be times when there really is nothing that a counselee can do to take action against the source of his or her anxiety. At such times it is of special importance to feel the caring support of a warm relationship with an understanding counselor.

6. *Encouraging a Christian Response*. The Bible gives an unusually specific and clear formula for overcoming anxiety. In Philippians 4:6 we are instructed to stop being anxious about anything. As we have seen, however, it is practically impossible to simply stop worrying. Such deliberate effort directs our attention to the problem and can increase anxiety rather than decrease it. A better approach is to focus on activities and thoughts which indirectly reduce anxiety. The Bible describes how this can be done and in so doing gives a formula to be shared with counselees:

(a) Rejoice. This is a command, repeated twice in Philippians 4:4. When the world is dark and dreary, the Christian still can "rejoice in the Lord." This is because of Jesus' promise that he would never leave us, that he would give us peace, and that he would come again to take believers into a place prepared for us in heaven. With this knowledge we can believe in God and not let our minds be troubled or fearful.[24]

(b) Forbear. "Let your forbearing spirit be known to all," we read in Philippians 4:5. It has been said that the Greek word translated "forbear" has no real equivalent in English. It means: let everybody see your kind, sweet, gentle, considerate, gracious attitude.[25] These qualities do not come naturally. They come with God's help and as we work to control our tendencies to condemn or demand our rights. A negative condemning outlook on life builds anxiety; a gracious forbearing attitude reduces it.

(c) Pray. Philippians 4:6 gives several instructions about prayer in times of anxiety. Such prayer should be about everything (even small details), should include definite and precise petitions, should involve thanksgiving for divine goodness, and should be accompanied by the expectation that supernatural peace will be forthcoming.[26] A major cure for anxiety, therefore, is prayer.

(d) Think. Anxiety surely arises when we think about injustice, problems, human weakness and what might go wrong. Philippians 4:8 instructs us, instead, to let our minds dwell on positive things such as that which is honorable, right, pure, lovely, good, excellent, and praiseworthy. Here is evidence for the power of positive, biblically based thinking.

(e) Act. The Apostle Paul sets himself up as a model for action. "The things you have learned and received and heard and seen in me, *put into constant practice.*" [27] The Christian's task is to *do* what the Bible teaches and not simply to sit listening.[28] Anxiety reduction involves godly behavior even in the midst of the anxiety.

Preventing Anxiety

The previous paragraphs, which comment on Philippians 4, give a formula for preventing anxiety as well as an approach to counseling. When people can be helped to rejoice, forbear, pray, think and act in accordance with scriptural teachings, there is progress toward anxiety control.

Studies of military personnel in combat situations reveal other ways in which people defend themselves against anxiety.[29] First there is the development of self-confidence—a belief in one's ability to meet the challenges of life (see chapter 24). Second, there is involvement in work and other activities which presumably expends nervous energy and distracts one from the anxiety-producing situation. Work has been described as one of the handiest ways of preventing and relieving anxiety, but work can become compulsive and be a way to keep from dealing with the causes of one's anxiety. Third, there is faith in the ability and confidence of leaders who can deal with dangers. Then, these military studies showed, there is belief in God.

1. *Trust in God.* The person who learns to walk in daily contact with God comes to agree with the hymnwriter who wrote, "I know not what the future holds, but I know who holds the future." This conviction can bring great security when others are inclined to be anxious.

At times, however, such trust leads to a blind denial of reality, to a refusal to accept responsibilities, or to a rigidity of thinking which ultimately prevents the person from adapting to changing circumstances. In contrast, the Bible encourages realistic confrontation with problems and flexible decision-making. This enables people to grow and adapt to change or danger, while they maintain an underlying confidence in the sovereignty and wisdom of an all-powerful God.

2. *Learn to Cope.* Coping with the causes of anxiety, when and before they arise, can prevent the development of anxiety. Such coping involves the following, each of which can become part of a person's life style:

—admitting fears, insecurities, conflicts, and anxieties when they arise;
—talking these over with someone else—on a regular basis if necessary;
—building self-esteem;
—acknowledging that separation hurts, attempting to maintain contact with separated friends, and building new relationships with others;
—seeking help from God and others in meeting one's needs;
—learning to communicate;
—learning some principles and techniques of relaxation;
—periodically evaluating one's priorities, life goals, and time management.[30]

Conclusions about Anxiety

Writing about physicians, psychiatrist O. Quentin Hyder summarized much of what we have said about anxiety.

> Patients who do not get well quickly sometimes become very impatient at their apparent lack of progress. . . . The fact is, however, that the patient's feelings of helplessness, apprehension, imminent danger, loneliness, and frustration would be far worse if he did not during the crisis period have the security of knowing that at regular intervals he could unburden his thoughts and feelings to someone who he believed really cared and was equipped by training and experience to help him. The doctor on his part must convey understanding, sympathy, confidence, ability to help, and genuine concern. Once the patient is sufficiently confident in his doctor's ability and care he can pour out his fears and admit to other emotions that are troubling him such as depression, hostility, anger, and guilt. As the patient does this, the doctor uses a skillful blend of authoritative persuasion, suggestion, and directive advice with supportive reassurance and nondirective sympathetic listening and understanding.[31]

That blend of skills enables the counselee and counselor to face and deal with the problem of anxiety.

Suggestions for Further Reading
* Collins, Gary R. *Overcoming Anxiety.* Santa Ana, CA: Vision House, 1973.
Levitt, Eugene E. *The Psychology of Anxiety.* Indianapolis: Bobbs-Merrill, 1967.
Marks, Isaac M. *Living with Fear: Understanding and Coping with Anxiety.* New York: McGraw-Hill, 1978.
May, Rollo. *The Meaning of Anxiety.* Rev. ed. New York: Norton, 1977.
Oates, Wayne E. *Anxiety in Christian Experience.* Waco, TX: Word, 1955.
* Osborne, Cecil. *Release from Fear and Anxiety.* Waco, TX: Word, 1976.
* From this point on, those books in the "Suggestions for Further Reading" lists which are particularly well suited for counselees to read will be marked with an *.

Footnotes

1. Rollo May, *The Meaning of Anxiety*, rev. ed. (New York: Norton, 1977), p. ix.
2. Ibid., p. 214.
3. Matt. 6:25–34.
4. Phil. 4:6, 7.
5. 1 Pet. 5:7. See also Ps. 55:22.
6. Gary Collins, *Overcoming Anxiety* (Santa Ana: Vision House, 1973).
7. 2 Cor. 11:28.
8. Phil. 2:20. The RSV uses the words "genuinely anxious." The NASB states "Timothy . . . will genuinely be concerned for your welfare."
9. S. Freud, *The Problem of Anxiety* (New York: Norton, 1936).
10. See Eugene E. Levitt, *The Psychology of Anxiety* (Indianapolis: Bobbs-Merrill, 1967). See especially chapter 3, "Theories of the Basis of Anxiety."
11. May, *Meaning of Anxiety*, pp. 205–206.
12. George W. Kisker, *The Disorganized Personality* (New York: McGraw-Hill, 1964), p. 267.
13. Cecil Osborne, *Release from Fear and Anxiety* (Waco, TX: Word, 1976).
14. Wayne E. Oates, *Anxiety in Christian Experience* (Waco, TX: Word, 1955).
15. Ernest R. Hilgard, quoted in Levitt, *Psychology of Anxiety*, p. viii.
16. Cited in May, *Meaning of Anxiety*, pp. 382–88.
17. Ibid., pp. 386–87.
18. Eugene Kennedy, *On Becoming a Counselor* (New York: Seabury, 1977), pp. 142–43.
19. Gordon W. Allport, *The Individual and His Religion* (New York: Macmillan, 1950). In this book Allport writes: "Love—incomparably the greatest psychotherapeutic agent—is something that professional psychiatry cannot of itself create, focus, nor release . . . By contrast . . . the Christian religion—offers an interpretation of life and a rule of life based wholly upon love" (pp. 90, 92).
20. 1 John 4:18.
21. Jay E. Adams, *The Christian Counselor's Manual* (Nutley, NJ: Presbyterian and Reformed, 1973), pp. 414–15.
22. Note Heb. 13:6.
23. May, *Meaning of Anxiety*, pp. 377, 376.
24. John 14:1–3, 18, 27.
25. William Hendriksen, *Philippians* (Grand Rapids: Baker, 1962), p. 193.
26. Phil. 4:7.
27. Phil. 4:9.
28. James 1:22.
29. May, *Meaning of Anxiety*, pp. 366–67.
30. Relaxation methods, priority evaluation, and time management are all discussed on the cassette tape made to accompany this chapter. See also Gary R. Collins, *You Can Profit From Stress* (Santa Ana: Vision House, 1977).
31. O. Quentin Hyder, *The Christian's Handbook of Psychiatry* (Old Tappan, NJ: Revell, 1971), pp. 108–09.

6
Loneliness

LONELINESS IS A COMMON PROBLEM WHICH HAS BEEN DESCRIBED AS "one of the most universal sources of human suffering."[1] It has been called an "almost permanent condition for millions of Americans . . . . knowing no limits of class, race, or age."[2] It hits everyone periodically and may persist for a few moments or for a lifetime.

Loneliness is the painful awareness that we lack meaningful contact with others. It involves a feeling of inner emptiness which can be accompanied by sadness, discouragement, a sense of isolation, restlessness, anxiety and an intense desire to be wanted and needed by someone. Lonely people often feel "left out," unwanted, or rejected, even when they are surrounded by others. There is sometimes a sense of hopelessness and a strong desire for almost any kind of a relationship which would end the awful pain of involuntary aloneness. It should not be surprising that many lonely people also feel a sense of worthlessness and a conviction that "since nobody wants to be with me, I guess I'm not worth anything." To avoid facing the fact that they may be unwanted or worthless, many people deny their loneliness and rush to bars, encounter groups, or church meetings in a vain attempt to escape from their isolation. But such people often remain isolated and unattached. They appear to be unable to build significant relationships or to gain emotional satisfaction from the relationships which they do have.

Christian psychologist Craig Ellison has suggested that there are three kinds of loneliness: emotional, social, and existential.[3] *Emotional loneliness* involves the lack or loss of a psychologically intimate relationship with another person or persons. The emotionally lonely person feels utterly alone and can only recover by establishing new in-depth relationships with others. *Social loneliness* is the feeling of aimlessness, anxiety and emptiness. The person feels that he or she is "out of it" and on the margin of life. Instead of an in-depth relationship with a specific companion, the socially lonely person needs a supportive group of accepting friends and skill in relating to others. *Existential loneliness* refers to the sense of isolation which comes to the person who is separated from God and who feels that life has no meaning or purpose. Such persons need a committed and growing relationship with God, preferably within the confines of a concerned community of believers.

Before continuing, it is important to distinguish solitude from loneliness. Solitude is a voluntary withdrawal from other people; loneliness comes when we are forced to be alone. Solitude can be refreshing, rejuvenating and enjoyable; loneliness is painful, draining and unpleasant. Solitude can be started and terminated at will; loneliness sweeps over us and hangs on in spite of our best efforts to cast it off.

The Bible and Loneliness

Shortly after God created Adam, he declared: "It is not good for the man to be alone; I will make him a helper suitable for him."[4] Adam and God had talked together in the garden, but the Creator knew that human beings need other humans if they are to get along effectively. So God created Eve and instructed the couple to "be fruitful and multiply and fill the earth." In fellowship with God and with each other, Adam and Eve were neither alone nor lonely.

When they fell into sin, Adam and Eve broke their communion with God and a wedge was driven between husband and wife. Selfishness and interpersonal tension came into their relationship and feelings of loneliness must, at that point, have entered the human race.

Loneliness is rarely discussed in the Bible, but it is seen repeatedly, even in the lives of such giants of the faith as Jacob, Moses, Job, Nehemiah, Elijah and Jeremiah. David once complained that he was lonely and afflicted.[5] Jesus, who knows all of our "infirmities," surely was lonely in Gethsemane. John ended his life alone on the Isle of Patmos, and the Apostle Paul apparently spent his last days in prison. Writing to Timothy, the aging Paul noted that his friends had left, that some had forsaken him, and that he needed his young colleague to "make every effort to come to me soon."[6]

The entire Bible focuses on our need for communion with God and for people, especially Christians, to love, help, encourage, forgive, and care for one another. A growing relationship with God and with others becomes the basis for any solution to the problem of loneliness. But how do individuals build a relationship with God or with others?[7] To begin, it is helpful to consider the causes of alienation and loneliness.

The Causes of Loneliness

Loneliness can have a variety of causes which we might group into five categories: social, developmental, psychological, situational and spiritual. Any combination of these can create loneliness in an individual.

1. *Social Causes.* "Loneliness," writes Paul Tournier, "results from the spirit of our age." [8] Most observers agree that rapid social changes in our era of history have isolated people from close contact with each other and have made loneliness more widespread. The social influences which increase our loneliness include the following:

(a) Technology. As government, business and education get "bigger" and more impersonal, people feel smaller and less needed. As efficiency and convenience have become more important, there is less time for developing deep, satisfying relationships. Complex technology increases the need for specialists, and these people sometimes have neither the time nor ability to communicate with nonspecialists. As a result, relationships are shallow, understanding decreases, and loneliness becomes more prevalent.

(b) Mobility. Modern transportation which makes moving easier, the development of large corporations, and perhaps the lure of a better life elsewhere have contributed to widespread mobility, especially in the United States. This tears up friendships, separates families, eliminates neighborhood or community spirit, and causes people to avoid close friendships which would end later in painful separations.

(c) Urbanization. As people have moved close together, especially in cities, there apparently has been a tendency to withdraw from others. Often there is a fear of strangers which leads to suspicion and withdrawal. There is a discomfort in the midst of crowded conditions, and a desire to avoid the noise and commotion. As a result, thousands of people can live in close proximity to each other, but with intense isolation and loneliness.

(d) Television. This modern invention enhances separation both by the program content, which seems to promote superficiality, and by the viewing habits of people who sit in front of the screen, seldom communicating directly with each other. Caught up in the unreality of television productions, it is easy to live one's life through the people on the screen instead of interacting with neighbors and relatives.

The list could go on, but I hope a point has been made. Along with its many benefits, our changing, dehumanizing, technological society has disrupted people, shattered our traditional sources of security, and created the potential for greater isolation and loneliness.

2. *Developmental Causes.* In his perceptive survey of the literature on loneliness, Ellison concluded that there are three basic developmental needs which must be met if loneliness is to be avoided. These are the needs for attachment, acceptance, and the acquiring of social skills.[9]

(a) Attachment. An impressive body of literature [10] has supported the conclusion that people, especially children, need to feel close bonds with other human beings. When children are separated from their parents there is anxiety and an emotional aloofness. If one parent remains, or if the separated parents return, the child clings to the mother or father, apparently afraid that separation will occur again. When we consider the increasing divorce rate and the alarming prevalence of child abuse, it is easy to recognize why many young people feel alienated and unattached. These people often grow up feeling lonely.

(b) Acceptance. Parents communicate acceptance in a variety of ways; by touching, by spending time with their children, by listening, by disciplining, by showing affection. When these clues are missing, or when children are ignored or excessively criticized, they begin to feel worthless. They conclude that they don't belong and they either withdraw from others or force themselves onto others in a way which brings more rejection. It becomes difficult to trust people and this inability to trust prevents the forming of close relationships. Low self-esteem and a feeling that one is unaccepted are at the basis of much loneliness.

(c) Acquiring Skills. All of us know people who are social misfits. They are insensitive to the needs or attitudes of others, and they do not know how to build smooth interpersonal relationships. They may try to manipulate or force themselves on others but this only brings rejection, frustration and increased loneliness. Such people have never learned how to get along. They keep trying, fail continually, and remain in their loneliness.

3. *Psychological Causes.* Closely connected with the above are psychological tendencies within the individual which create and maintain loneliness. These include low self-esteem, inability to communicate, self-defeating attitudes, hostility and fear.

(a) Low self-esteem. This refers to the opinion we have of ourselves. If it is low, we underestimate our value and withdraw or, if it is too high, we exaggerate our value to the point of conceit. Both reactions hinder closeness with others. When we have little confidence in ourselves it is difficult to build friendships. The person is unable to give love without apologizing; neither can he or she receive love without cutting oneself down. According to one writer,[11] good self-esteem helps in forming close relationships which in turn build good self-esteem and a resulting decrease in loneliness. In contrast, low self-esteem makes the person feel weak or shy and there is an excessive need to depend on others. When others are not available there is intense insecurity and deep loneliness.

(b) Inability to Communicate. Communication breakdowns are at the root of many, perhaps most, interpersonal problems. When people are unwilling to communicate, or when they don't know how to communicate honestly, there is a persisting isolation and loneliness even though individuals may be surrounded by others.

(c) Self-defeating Attitudes. Shortly after World War II, Paul Tournier, the Swiss counselor, wrote a penetrating book on loneliness.[12] Its message is surprisingly relevant today. Loneliness comes, Tournier wrote, because we have developed

—parliamentary attitudes in which we see life as a big tournament with success as the winner's prize and competition as a way of life;

—independent attitudes which cause us to act as if we were each rugged individualists, absolutely autonomous, independent of God and of others;
—possessive attitudes by which we are driven to get what we can for ourselves; and
—demanding attitudes which cause us to fight for our rights and demand "fairness."

All of this implies something which has not yet been mentioned. Loneliness, at least to some extent, may be one's own fault. People increase the potential for loneliness when they are caught up in intense competition, struggling for self-sufficiency, self-centered in a preoccupation with themselves and their success, critical or intolerant of others, holding onto grudges or demanding attention from others. Such attitudes often lead us to use other people to meet our own needs or satisfy our own egos. Nothing drives others away more quickly, and this creates loneliness.

(d) Hostility. Have you ever noticed how some people appear to be innately angry? Even when they smile, there is an underlying attitude of vengeance and hostility. The causes for this are complex [13] but sometimes angry people feel thwarted, frustrated or resentful because of real or imagined injustice. On occasion the anger comes from self-hatred which is turned outward to others. When such thinking is accompanied by negative attitudes and constant complaining, others are driven away and this creates both loneliness and continuing unhappiness.

(e) Fear. In my office there hangs a plaque which reads, "People are lonely because they build walls instead of bridges." Of course, this isn't the only reason for loneliness, but sometimes individuals do erect barriers to keep others out. Often this is done because of fear of intimacy, fear of being known, fear of rejection or fear of being hurt—as we may have been hurt in the past. The loneliness is painful but for such people it is no less painful than the fear and insecurity of reaching out to others.

4. *Situational Causes.* Sometimes people are lonely because of the special circumstances in which they find themselves. Surveys have shown, for example, that the most lonely people of all are those who are single or widowed, living alone, grieving, and/or elderly.[14] People in leadership positions are sometimes lonely because they have moved ahead of and away from the group. University students who are away from home, affluent people who seem to be in a financial class all by themselves, foreigners and newcomers to an area, extremely talented people, homosexuals —all have been identified as people who are especially prone to loneliness.[15] Then there are those people whose bodies are deformed or diseased. In our society such persons are rejected by healthy people who say in effect, "You're different," or "I don't know how to act around you." As a result of this rejection, handicapped people tend to withdraw. Their physical condition often prevents easy access to others and a self-centered loneliness can result.

5. *Spiritual Causes.* In a famous prayer Augustine once expressed our need for God: "Thou hast formed us for Thyself and our hearts are restless till they find rest in Thee." God created human beings for himself, but he respected us enough to let us rebel. This, of course, is what we have done, and ever since our hearts have been restless because we have been cut off from our Creator. Rather than turning to God in repentance, thousands of lonely people have sought meaning in drugs, sex, encounter experiences, work, sports, or a host of other activities which fail to remove the inner restlessness.

Loneliness, especially existential loneliness, comes because of sins which we have not acknowledged or confessed, guilt for which we feel no forgiveness, rebellion against God, or sometimes a convenient casual ignoring of God's concern for us or his claims on our lives.

The Effects of Loneliness

What does loneliness do to people? What are its symptoms? How can it be spotted by a counselor? Because of human uniqueness each person will exhibit loneliness in a different way, but some combination of the following is likely to be seen.

First there is the *isolation* from others which often, but not always, indicates loneliness. This is often accompanied by periodic but frequently futile attempts to reach out for contact with others.

Poor *self-esteem* and feelings of worthlessness can be a symptom as well as a cause of loneliness. *Failure,* in relationships or in activities, further lowers self-esteem and creates greater loneliness. Unable to relate to others, such lonely people sometimes withdraw into *discouragement, self-centeredness,* a "poor-little-me attitude," and a belief that no one understands.

Hopelessness, which sometimes leads to *despair* and even thoughts of *suicide,* can all characterize loneliness. When loneliness is too great, suicide becomes a "way out" which also gives a clear message to the people who didn't seem to care.

Alcoholism and drug abuse often are ways of escape, and people often turn to these in an attempt to avoid isolation or to find friends in other drinkers.

Then there are those who lash out in *violence.* Backed by research reports,[16] one author has suggested that "further investigations will bear out this tentative conclusion: very lonely people, who get angry rather than depressed, will be prone to express their lonely frustration in destructive ways. I do not think it is mere coincidence that we are witnessing an unequalled rise in violence and at the same time loneliness is so pervasive and intense."[17] Apparently loneliness can be expressed in violence and delinquency, which become a release from pain and a cry for attention.

Counseling and Loneliness

Richard Wolff has summarized some of the suggestions which have been given to help people deal with their loneliness:

> Change jobs, join a club, be positive, become aggressive, get married, get remarried, travel, move, have fun, never be alone, use the record player, listen to the radio, watch television, enjoy the movies, read a good book, take up a hobby, pursue cultural interests, expand your horizons, play, increase leisure, develop hobbies, renew goals, volunteer—and all of these activities may temporarily remedy the pain of loneliness but they fail to meet the problem on the deepest level and do not produce the desired lasting results.[18]

How, then, do we help lonely people "meet the problems on the deepest level" and experience "the desired lasting results"?

1. *Admitting the Problem.* Loneliness has a somewhat negative connotation in our society. For many people, admitting that they are lonely is like admitting that they are social misfits, unattractive, or unable to relate to others. Counselees can be reminded, however, that everyone is lonely at times. When people feel lonely the first steps toward recovery are to admit the loneliness, to acknowledge that it is painful and to decide to do something about the problem.

2. *Considering the Causes.* Loneliness, as we have seen, can arise from a variety of causes. If these causes can be identified (through discussion with the counselee and through probing questions), then it is possible to work on the source of the loneliness rather than trying to eliminate the symptoms. Prior to counseling, the counselor might wish to review the causes of loneliness listed earlier in this chapter. By keeping this information in mind, the counselor can be alert to similar causes in the counselee's life and thinking.

3. *Accepting What Cannot Be Changed.* In considering the causes, it is important to recognize that while some things can be changed (such as a poor self-concept or self-defeating attitudes which produce loneliness) there are other issues that are unchangeable. The lonely widow, for example, cannot bring back her husband; neither can we stop the modern tendency of people to move frequently—with the alienation and loneliness that this produces.

Even when circumstances cannot be changed, however, counselees still can be helped to change their attitudes toward loneliness. In his book *Loneliness: Understanding and Dealing with It,*[19] Harvey Potthoff suggests that there are three major resources for dealing with loneliness. Each of these involves the counselee's attitude, and each could help even when loneliness-producing circumstances cannot be changed.

First, people can be encouraged to develop "an inner life" of positive interests, appreciation for what *is* good in life, and a sense of humor. This is more than an attempt to muster up the "power of positive thinking."

It involves a rejection of self-pity and a willingness to see the bright side of life, even in the midst of disturbing social change, loneliness and discouragement.

Second, Potthoff emphasizes the development of "a life style of keeping in touch." If people avoid relationships with others or withdraw into a life of inactivity, then loneliness is intensified. In contrast work, play, involvement in creative activities, awareness of the daily news, worship—all these can keep counselees in contact with those people and events which can pull them out of loneliness and a tendency to brood.

Third, Potthoff writes about a religious faith which helps people see life in its wholeness, which helps all of us find purpose or meaning, and which undergirds individuals with the assurance of God's presence and sovereignty even when surrounding circumstances seem to be unchangeable and defeating. Lonely people cannot always change their environments but they can change their attitudes with God's power and often with the counselor's gentle encouragement.

4. *Altering What Can Be Changed*. Although some causes of loneliness cannot be changed, other casual situations can be altered, corrected or removed. People can, for example, watch less television, spend more time in family activities, or move into useful church activities. All of this involves reaching out to others, but for some people this is very difficult because they lack the self-esteem, lack the courage and/or lack the social and communication skills.

(a) Developing Self-esteem. Lonely people must be helped to see and acknowledge their strengths, abilities, and spiritual gifts, as well as their weaknesses. According to one psychologist [20] many people go through life talking to themselves (not out aloud) and convincing themselves that they are not good-looking, are incompetent or disliked by others. Often we compare ourselves with people who are more popular or successful and in so doing, we convince ourselves of our inferiority. As a result we develop a low self-esteem and lack the confidence which enables us to tackle new situations. Counselees must be reminded that in God's sight every human being is valuable and loved,[21] that every sin can be forgiven,[22] that each of us has abilities and gifts which can be developed, and that all people have weaknesses which can be lived with and for which we can compensate. Counselees can be helped to see that no one ever attains perfection in what he or she does, so we should quit trying. We must learn to do the best we can with God's supernatural help and with the abilities and circumstances that we have been given. Self-esteem is considered more fully in chapter 24. If this is a problem for the lonely counselee, it might be good to work on the self-esteem problem as an important way of tackling loneliness.

(b) Taking Risks. Even when people do have a positive self-image, it sometimes takes great courage to reach out to others. What if others criticize or reject us, or fail to respond? That can be embarrassing and threatening.

It is here that a counselor can provide the encouragement and support which the counselee needs as he or she reaches out to make contact with others. There can be ongoing consideration of questions such as "To whom can you reach out?" "How specifically can you reach out, to contact others?" "What have you done (or failed to do) in the past to prevent close contact with others?" As counselees risk "getting involved," the counselor can give encouragement and provide opportunities to discuss how this social outreach is working and where it might be failing.

(c) Learning Skills. As we indicated previously, some people are social cripples. They are insensitive to others and lack basic communication skills. Counselors can point out social errors, teach counselees how to relate to others, and evaluate the effectiveness of the individual's attempts to interact. Chapter 23 of this book discusses interpersonal relationships and may be of further help to counselors who are working with lonely people who lack basic communication skills and social finesse.

5. *Meeting the Spiritual Need.* A popular Christian song once began with the words: "Why should I be lonely? I have Jesus only." As we have seen, God himself declared that people really need each other if they are to avoid loneliness. Regretfully, however, some writers have concluded that human contact is the only solution to loneliness. They have failed to realize that loneliness never disappears completely until, in addition to human companionship, an individual is introduced to Jesus Christ. He loves each of us unconditionally,[23] died for us, makes it possible for us to come to him by confession of our sins, welcomes us as adopted children,[24] and becomes a friend who sticks closer than a brother.[25] His Holy Spirit lives inside of every believer,[26] helps us, prays for us, and makes us more Christlike.[27]

God is very real and his presence can be sensed. He communicates through his Word even though we cannot hear him with our ears. But God also is intangible—he cannot be touched or seen with the eyes. This is where his tangible body, the church, enters the picture. The church should be a healing, helping community which radiates love, acceptance and support. As a member of this community and a follower of Jesus Christ the counselor should radiate this loving acceptance and point the counselee both to Christ himself and to the local church—which the Bible calls the "body of Christ" here on earth.

Preventing Loneliness

The local church can and should be the best antidote to loneliness that individuals ever encounter. But this is only one of several ways by which the causes of loneliness can be attacked and the experience of loneliness reduced.

1. *Building the Local Church.* To prevent loneliness, individuals can be encouraged to worship in the church, to get involved in church activities, and to accept the fellowship of church members. Regretfully, not all

church members are open to receiving new people and some churches are cold and indifferent. In preventing loneliness, therefore, the church leader must stimulate individuals to be involved with the church, and must stimulate the church members to love, accept, forgive, care for and welcome individuals in the fellowship. There must be opportunity for meaningful activities, especially on weekends, when lonely people so often rush to bars, encounter groups, casual sexual experiences, and intimate experiences with strangers, all in an effort to find love and companionship.

2. *Coping with Change.* In his book, *We, the Lonely People,* Ralph Keyes writes that most of us want a sense of community with others, but there are three things which we want more—mobility, privacy, and convenience, "which are the very sources of our lack of community."[28] Is it possible to be people-centered and intimate with others in an age which prizes technology, mobility, urbanization, television, and other dehumanizing influences? Probably the answer is "yes—with qualifications." We can get really close to only a few people, and to do so we must make up our minds to give the time and effort needed for building relationships in an era where superficiality is more convenient. Seminars, sermons, classroom presentations, and counseling sessions can all be used to help people manage their time or relationships, and thus prevent loneliness.

3. *Instilling Acceptance and Competence.* From the public platform, but even more in family settings, people must be taught that they are valuable, worthwhile and able to relate to others. As indicated above, when children feel attachment and acceptance, they are less inclined to be lonely. In like manner, when children and adults learn social skills, communication ability, and healthy, realistic attitudes toward life, they are better able to relate to others and avoid loneliness. These things should be taught in the home but they also can be taught in churches, schools, counselors' offices and through books, articles and tapes.

(a) Strengthening Family Ties. Since loneliness so often begins in the home, it is at home where the problem can be most effectively attacked and prevented. Teaching family members to communicate openly, to respect and care for one another, to play, worship, and eat together—these are among the ways in which counselors and church leaders can stimulate loneliness-prevention at home.

4. *Counseling and Prevention.* Loneliness, as we have seen, sometimes arises because people are hostile, afraid, or self-defeating in their attitudes or actions, and immobilized by a poor self-concept. By working on these problems, the counselor and counselee not only reduce loneliness, they prevent its increase or reoccurrence.

5. *Growing Spiritually.* Once again we return to the basic spiritual issue. Loneliness is reduced or prevented when individuals are helped to build intimate relationships with God as well as with other humans. Helping people to grow spiritually, therefore, becomes a significant way to prevent loneliness (see chapter 29).

Conclusions about Loneliness

It may be that we live in a loneliness-producing society where rapid change and modern technology discourage intimacy and stimulate loneliness. Even in homes and churches, people avoid each other, only to throw themselves blindly into open sharing with strangers (other students, casual sexual partners, fellow drinkers or seat-mates on airplanes, for example) in the hope of finding closeness and escaping their inner sense of isolation.

But human togetherness, per se, is not the solution. We need to help people develop an intimate relationship with God and build strong involvements with at least a few people, including family members, where there can be mutual openness, acceptance and respect for each other's uniqueness.

Suggestions for Further Reading

* Ford, Edward E., and Zorn, Robert L. *Why Be Lonely?* Niles, IL: Argus Communications, 1975.
* Gordon, Suzanne. *Lonely in America.* New York: Simon & Schuster, 1976.
* Potthoff, Harvey H. *Loneliness: Understanding and Dealing with It.* Nashville: Abingdon, 1976.

Tanner, Ira J. *Loneliness: The Fear of Love (An Application of Transactional Analysis).* New York: Harper & Row, 1973.

Tournier, Paul. *Escape from Loneliness.* Philadelphia: Westminster, 1962.

Footnotes

1. Henri J. M. Nouwen, *Reaching Out* (Garden City, NY: Doubleday, 1975), p. 15.

2. Suzanne Gordon, *Lonely in America* (New York: Simon and Schuster, 1976), p. 15.

3. Craig W. Ellison, "Loneliness: A Social-Developmental Analysis," *Journal of Psychology and Theology* 6:3–17 (1978). See also R. S. Weiss, ed., *Loneliness: The Experience of Emotional and Social Isolation* (Cambridge, MA: The MIT Press, 1973).

4. Gen. 2:18.

5. Ps. 25:16.

6. 2 Tim. 4:9–12.

7. Chapters 23 ("Interpersonal Relations") and 29 ("Spiritual Problems and Spiritual Growth") both address this issue in more depth.

8. Paul Tournier, *Escape from Loneliness* (Philadelphia: Westminster, 1962), p. 20.

9. Ellison, "Loneliness." See also Craig W. Ellison, "The Roots of Loneliness," *Christianity Today,* 10 March 1978, pp. 12–16.

10. See, for example, R. A. Spitz, "Hospitalism: An Inquiry into the Genesis of Psychiatric Conditions in Early Childhood. A Follow-up Report," *Psychoanalytic Study of the Child* 1 (1945): 53–74; J. Bowlby, *Attachment* (New York: Basic Books, 1969).

11. Elizabeth Skoglund, *Loneliness* (Downers Grove, IL: Inter-Varsity Press, 1975).

12. Tournier, *Escape.*

13. See chapter 8.

14. Cited in Ruby Abrahams, "Mutual Help for the Widowed," *Social Work* 17 (September, 1972): 54–61; J. H. Sheldon, *The Social Medicine of Old Age* (London: Oxford University Press, 1948); and Robert S. Weiss, ed., *Loneliness* (Cambridge, MA: MIT Press, 1974).

15. Helen Adams, "Loneliness in the Church," *Eternity* 24 (July, 1973): 19, 25.

16. See, for example, Joseph Moore, "Relationship Between Loneliness and Interpersonal Relationships," *Canadian Counselor* 8 (April, 1974): 84–89.

17. W. A. Sadler, "Cause of Loneliness," *Science Digest* 78 (July, 1975): 58–66.

18. Richard Wolff, *The Meaning of Loneliness* (Wheaton, IL: Key Publishers, 1970), p. 45 (this book is no longer in print).

19. Harvey H. Potthoff, *Loneliness: Understanding and Dealing with It* (Nashville: Abingdon, 1976).

20. A. Ellis, "Rational-Emotive Therapy," in *Four Psychotherapies,* ed. Leonard Hersher (New York: Appleton-Century-Crofts, 1970), pp. 47–83.

21. John 3:16.

22. 1 John 1:9.

23. John 3:16; Rom. 8:35–39.

24. Rom. 8:14–17.

25. Prov. 18:24.

26. Rom. 8:9; 1 Cor. 6:19; 1 John 4:13.

27. Rom. 8:26–31.

28. Ralph Keyes, *We, the Lonely People* (New York: Harper & Row, 1973).

7

Depression

FOLLOWING THE DEATH OF HIS WIFE, A WELL-KNOWN SOUTHERN Baptist preacher named Vance Havner published a diary of his experiences as he walked "through the valley of the shadow of death."[1] Christian experience has three levels, Havner concluded. First there are "mountaintop days" when everything is going well and the world looks bright. But it is unrealistic to expect—as many people do—that we can spend life leaping from one mountain peak to another as if there were no plains or valleys in between. "Ordinary days," therefore, are those when we work at our usual tasks, neither elated nor depressed. Then, thirdly, there are the "dark days" when we trudge heavily through discouragement, despair, doubt and confusion. Sometimes these days string out into months or even years before we begin to experience a sense of relief and victory. When they persist, dark days are days of depression.

Depression (or melancholia, as it was once known) has been recognized as a common problem for more than 2,000 years. Recently, however, it has come so much into public attention that some are calling our era the "age of melancholy," in contrast to the "age of anxiety" which followed World War II.[2] Depression is something which everyone experiences in some degree and at different times in life. An article in the *Journal of the American Medical Association* once suggested that more human suffering has resulted from depression than from any other single disease affecting mankind.[3] Depression has been considered as "by far the commonest psychiatric symptom," and one which is found both as as temporary condition "in a normal person who has suffered a great personal disappointment" and as "the deep suicidal depression of a psychotic."[4]

The signs of depression include sadness, apathy and inertia which make it difficult to "get going" or to make decisions; loss of energy and fatigue which often are accompanied by insomnia; pessimism and hopelessness; fear; a negative self-concept often accompanied by self-criticism and feelings of guilt, shame, worthlessness and helplessness; a loss of interest in work, sex, and usual activities; a loss of spontaneity; difficulties in concentration; an inability to enjoy pleasurable events or activities; and often a loss of appetite. In some cases, known as "masked depression," the person denies that he or she feels sad, but sad events in one's life accompanied by some of the above listed symptoms lead the counselor to suspect that depression is present behind a smiling countenance. In many cases the symptoms of depression hide anger which has not been expressed, sometimes isn't recognized and—according to traditional psychiatric theory—is turned inward against oneself.

Depressions can occur at any age (including infancy) and they come in various types. *Reactive* depression (sometimes called exogenous depression), for example, comes as a reaction to some real or imagined loss or other life trauma. *Endogenous* depression seems to arise spontaneously from within and usually is found in the elderly. *Psychotic* depression involves intense despair and self-destructive attitudes, often accompanied by hallucinations and loss of contact with reality. *Neurotic* depression is mixed with high levels of anxiety. Some depressions are *chronic*—long-lasting and resistant to treatment. Others are *acute*—intense but of short duration and often self-correcting. Many professionals would distinguish all of these from *discouragement,* which is a mild, usually temporary and almost universal mood swing which comes in response to disappointments, failures and losses.

All of this implies that depression is a common but complicated condition, difficult to define, hard to describe with accuracy and not easy to treat.

The Bible and Depression

Depression, per se, is a clinical term which is not discussed in the Bible. The psalmists, however, cried out in words which implied depression and there are several biblical descriptions which suggest depression.

Consider, for example, Psalms 69, 88, or 102, but notice that these songs of despair are set in a context of hope. In Psalm 43 King David proclaims both depression and rejoicing when he writes:

Why are you in despair, O my soul?
And why are you disturbed within me?
Hope in God, for I shall again praise Him,
The help of my countenance, and my God.

Elsewhere in the Bible it appears that Job, Moses, Jonah, Peter and the whole nation of Israel experienced depression.[5] Jeremiah the prophet wrote a whole book of lamentations. Elijah saw God's mighty power at work on Mt. Carmel, but when Jezebel threatened murder, Elijah fled to the wilderness where he plunged into despondency. He wanted to die and might have done so except for the "treatment" that came from an angel sent by God.[6]

Then there was Jesus in Gethsemane, where he was greatly distressed, an observation which is poignantly described in the words of the Amplified Bible: "He began to show grief and distress of mind and was deeply depressed. Then He said to them, My soul is very sad and deeply grieved, so that I am almost dying of sorrow. . . ." [7]

Such examples, accompanied by numerous references to the pain of grieving, show the realism that characterizes the Bible. But this realistic despair is contrasted with a certain hope. Each of the believers who plunged into depression eventually came through and experienced a new and lasting joy. The biblical emphasis is less on human despair than on belief in God and the assurance of abundant life in heaven, if not on earth. [8] Paul's confident prayer for the Romans will someday be answered for all Christians:

> Now may the God of hope fill you with all joy and peace in believing, that you may abound in hope by the power of the Holy Spirit. [9]

The Causes of Depression

According to one psychologist, "the prevalence of depression in America today is staggering. . . . Depression is the common cold of psychopathology and has touched the lives of us all, yet it is probably the most dimly understood and most inadequately investigated of all the major forms of psychopathology." [10] Nevertheless, investigators have identified a number of causes for this common condition—causes which, when understood, can facilitate counseling.

1. *Physical-Genetic Causes.* Depression often has a physical basis. Lack of sleep and improper diet are among the simplest physical causes. Others, like the effects of drugs, low blood sugar and other chemical malfunctioning, brain tumors, or glandular disorders, are more complicated. Then there is research which has stressed the importance of the hypothalamus in producing depression.

> No matter how good one's philosophy, no matter how well adjusted one has been, and no matter how ideal the environment may be, when there is a loss of hypothalamic energy, the person is depressed, feels helpless, and has no energy. . . . Only a return of normal neurohormonal energy in the hypothalamus can effect a resolution of the depressive mood. [11]

Although it is not conclusive, there is some evidence to show that severe depression runs in families. This has led to the conclusion that some people innately may be more *prone* to depression than others, [12] although it must be emphasized that depression in itself is not inherited like blue eyes and black hair.

2. *Background Causes.* Do childhood experiences lead to depression in later life? Some evidence would say "yes." Many years ago, a researcher named Rene Spitz published a study of children who had been separated

from their parents and raised in an institution.[13] Deprived of continuing warm human contact with an adult, these children showed apathy, poor health, and sadness—all indicative of depression which could continue into later life. In addition, depression is more likely when parents blatantly or subtly reject their children or when status-seeking families set unrealistically high standards which children are unable to meet. When standards are too high, failure becomes inevitable and the person becomes depressed as a reaction to the marked discrepancy between goals and achievements.[14] Such early experiences do not always lead to depression but they increase the likelihood of severe depression in later life.

3. *Learned Helplessness.* A more recent theory [15] maintains that depression comes when we encounter situations over which we have no control. When we learn that our actions are futile no matter how hard we try, that there is nothing we can do to relieve suffering, reach a goal or bring change, then depression is a common response. It comes when we feel helpless and give up trying. This might explain the prevalence of depression in the grieving person who can do nothing to bring back a loved one, for example, or in the student who is unable to relate to his peers or succeed academically, or in the older person who is powerless to turn back the clock and restore lost physical capacities. When such people are able to control at least a portion of their environment, depression subsides and often disappears.

4. *Negative Thinking.* It takes almost no effort to slip into a pattern of negative thinking—seeing the dark side of life and overlooking the positive. But negative thinking can lead to depression and when the depressed person continues to think negatively, more intense depression results.

According to psychiatrist Aaron Beck depressed people show negative thinking in three areas.[16] First, they view the world and life experiences negatively. Life is seen as a succession of burdens, obstacles, and defeats in a world which is "going down the drain." Second, many depressed people have a negative view of themselves. They feel deficient, inadequate, unworthy and incapable of performing adequately. This in turn can lead to self-blame and self-pity. Third, these people view the future in a negative way. Looking ahead they see continuing hardship, frustration and hopelessness.

Is such negative thinking a cause of depression or is it a result of depression? The answer is probably both. Because of past experiences or previous training we begin to think negatively. This leads to depression which, as we have seen, can lead to more negative thinking.

Such negative thinking sometimes can be used to control others. If there are people who think everything is bleak, others try to "back them up." A comment, "I'm no good," often is an unconscious way of getting others to say, "Oh, no, you really are a fine person." Self-condemnation, therefore, becomes a way of manipulating others to give compliments. But such comments aren't really satisfying so the negative thinking and depression goes on. And if you keep thinking negatively, you are less likely to be hurt or disappointed if some of your thinking comes true.

5. *Life Stress.* It is well known that the stresses of life stimulate depression, especially when these stresses involve a loss. Loss of an opportunity, a job, status, health, freedom, a contest, possessions or other valued objects can each lead to depression. Then there is the loss of people. Divorce, death, or prolonged separations are painful and known to be among the most effective depression-producing events of life.

6. *Anger.* The oldest, most common, and perhaps most widely accepted explanation of depression is that it involves anger which is turned inward against oneself. Many children are raised in homes and sent to schools where the expression of anger is not tolerated. Some attend churches where anger is condemned as sin. Other people become convinced that they shouldn't even feel angry so they deny hostile feelings when they do arise. A widow, for example, may be angry at her husband who died leaving her to raise the children alone, but such anger seems irrational and is sure to arouse guilt in the person who thinks such thoughts about the dead. As a result, the anger is denied and kept within.

What happens, then, when one is frustrated, resentful and angry? If the anger is denied or pushed out of our minds, it festers "under cover" and eventually "gets us down." The following diagram illustrates this process.

```
                                            → DESTRUCTIVE ACTION
                                          ↗          or
HURT ———→  ANGER ———→   REVENGE ———→ PSYCHOSOMATIC SYMPTOMS
(The first   (The second    (The third    ↘          or
emotion to   emotion to     emotion and   → DEPRESSION
be felt.)    be felt.       thought to    (The fourth emotion to
             This hides     be felt.      be felt. This hides
             the hurt.)     This hides    the hurt, anger, and
                            the hurt      revengefulness.)
                            and anger.)
```

Perhaps most anger begins when we feel hurt, because of a disappointment or because of the actions of some other person. Instead of admitting this hurt, people mull over it, ponder what happened, and begin to get angry. The anger then builds and becomes so strong that it hides the hurt. If the anger is not admitted and expressed and dealt with, it then leads to revenge. This involves thoughts of hurting another person—either the one who caused the original hurt, or someone else who is nearby.[17]

Revenge sometimes leads to destructive violent actions, but this can get us into trouble, and violence is not acceptable, especially for a Christian. As a result, some people try to hide their feelings. This takes energy which wears down the body so that the emotions eventually come to the surface in the form of psychosomatic symptoms. Others, consciously or unconsciously, condemn themselves for their attitudes and become depressed as a result. This depression may be a form of emotional self-punishment which sometimes even leads to suicide. It is easy to understand why such people feel that they are no good, guilty and unhappy.

Some people use their depression as a subtle and socially acceptable way both to express anger and to get revenge. Psychologist Roger Barrett describes this clearly.

> Resentment . . . is the accumulation of unexpressed anger. And, resentment . . . is the most destructive emotion in human relationships and in personal well-being . . . . Some depressed clients . . . wallow in depression as a means of hurting others, as if the depression itself becomes an indirect expression of hostility. It's almost as if they were saying, "I'm depressed and there's nothing you can do about it, but it's all your fault, and if you don't give me attention and sympathy, I may get even more depressed or do something desperate." It's a kind of psychological blackmail.
>
> Suicide attempts (which most often occur in depressed people) not infrequently have this characteristic. There's a kind of "see what you made me do" or "now you'll miss me" quality to the notes or communications surrounding the tragedy. They blame others for their bad feelings.[18]

As the diagram shows, depression often hides underlying hurt, anger and resentment which then are often forgotten. It should be emphasized that this explanation does not account for all depression, but undoubtedly it explains some.

7. *Guilt*. It is not difficult to understand why guilt can lead to depression. When a person feels that he or she has failed or has done something wrong, guilt arises and along with it comes self-condemnation, frustration, hopelessness and other symptoms of depression. Guilt and depression so often occur together that it is difficult to determine which comes first. Perhaps in most cases guilt comes before depression but at times depression will cause people to feel guilty (because they seem unable to "snap out" of the despair). In either case a vicious cycle is set in motion (guilt causes depression which causes more guilt, and so on).

The Effects of Depression

No one really enjoys having problems, but problems sometimes can serve a useful purpose. When we are physically sick, for example, we are excused from work, people shower us with attention or sympathy, others make decisions for us, or take over our responsibilities, and sometimes we can enjoy a period of leisure and relaxation. The same is true when we are emotionally down or distraught. Neurotic behavior, including depression, may not be pleasant, but it does help us to avoid responsibilities, save face, attract attention, and have an excuse for inactivity. Eventually, however, emotionally hurting people realize that the benefits of depression are not really satisfying. Such people begin to hate what they are doing and, in time, they often end up hating themselves. This, as we have seen, creates more depression.

Depression leads to any or all of the following effects. In general, the deeper the depression the more intense the effects.

1. *Unhappiness and Inefficiency.* Depressed people often feel "blue," hopeless, self-critical and miserable. As a result they lack enthusiasm, are indecisive, and sometimes have little energy for doing even simple things (like getting out of bed in the morning). Life thus is characterized by inefficiency, underachievement and an increased dependence on others.

2. *Masked Reactions.* In some people, the depression is hidden even from themselves, but it comes out in other ways including physical symptoms and complaints (hypochondriasis); aggressive actions and angry temper outbursts; impulsive behavior, including gambling, drinking, violence, destructiveness or impulsive sex; accident proneness; compulsive work; and sexual problems, to name the most common. These symptoms of "masked depression" [19] occur in children and adolescents as well as in adults. The person is smiling on the outside but hurting on the inside and expressing this hurt in ways which hide the real inner despair.

3. *Withdrawal.* When a person is discouraged, unmotivated, bored with life and lacking in self-confidence, there is often a desire to get away from others (since social contacts may be too demanding), to daydream, and to escape into a world of television, novels, alcohol or drug use. Some people dream of running away or finding a simpler job and a few even do this.

4. *Suicide.* Surely there is no more complete way to escape than to take one's own life. Suicide and suicide attempts are especially prevalent in teenagers, people who live alone, the unmarried (especially the divorced), and persons who are depressed. Of course, not all depressed people attempt suicide but many do, often in a sincere attempt to kill themselves and escape life. For others, suicide attempts are an unconscious cry for help, an opportunity for revenge, or a manipulative gesture designed to influence some person who is close emotionally. While some suicide attempts are blatantly clear (as when a man leaves a note and shoots himself), others are more subtle and are made to look like accidents. While some people carefully plan their self-destructive act, others drive recklessly, drink excessively, or find other ways to flirt with death.

All of this illustrates the pervasive and potentially destructive influence of depression. It is certain to appear repeatedly in the experience of every Christian counselor, and it is not the easiest condition to counsel successfully.

Counseling and Depression

Depressed people are often passive, nonverbal, poorly motivated, pessimistic and characterized by a resigned "what's the use?" attitude. The counselor, therefore, must reach out verbally, taking a more active role than he or she might take with most other counselees. Optimistic reassuring statements (but not gushiness), sharing of facts about how depression affects people, patiently encouraging counselees to talk (but not pushing them to talk), asking questions, giving periodic compliments and gently sharing Scripture (without preaching) can all be helpful. Confrontation, probing questions, demands for action, and nondirective approaches should all be avoided, especially in the beginning, since these techniques often increase anxiety and this creates more discouragement and pessimism.

It does not follow, of course, that the counselor talks and does not listen. As the counselee becomes more comfortable and begins to talk, the counselor should listen attentively. Watch for evidences of anger, hurt, negative thinking, poor self-esteem, and guilt—all of which might be discussed later. Encourage the counselee to talk about those life situations that are bothersome. Avoid "taking sides," but try to be understanding and accepting of feelings. Watch, especially, for talk about losses, failures, rejection, and other incidents which may have stimulated the current depression.

As this occurs, counselors should be aware of their own feelings. Are you impatient with this negative counselee? Are you inclined to let your mind wander or to be pulled into depressed negative thinking yourself? Awareness of these dangers often can keep the counselor from losing interest. Depressed people provide a demanding test for our counseling skills and the counselor must see this kind of counselee as one whose problems demand special effort and attention.

In counseling the depressed, be aware of their special need to be dependent. Ask yourself, "Am I encouraging dependence in an already depressed dependent person, so that I can build my own feelings of power or importance?" "Am I encouraging anger or negative thinking?" "Am I making so many demands that the counselee feels devastated and thus needs to cling?" Unaware of these tendencies, counselors sometimes increase the depression inadvertently instead of contributing to its relief.

Counseling the depressed can take different directions, many of which you may want to use with each counselee.

1. *Medical Approaches.* Psychiatrists and other medical doctors often use antidepressant drugs to help change the counselee's mood and make him or her more amenable to therapy. More controversial is the use of electroconvulsive (shock treatment) therapy in which a pulse of electrical energy is passed through the brain. This leads to convulsions, and a period of confusion, followed by a brightening of mood. Although widely criticized, this remains a popular form of treatment for the severely depressed, the actively suicidal, and those people who, for medical reasons, cannot take drugs. All of this helps with symptom relief but such techniques are only temporary if they are not followed or accompanied by counseling which deals with the sources of the depression.

Nonmedical counselors may want to contact a psychiatrist or other physician who could prescribe drugs for the temporary relief of a depressed counselee. Also, if a counselee has physical symptoms, referral to a psychologically astute physician is extremely important. The non medical counselor is not qualified to decide whether or not a counselee's physical symptoms are psychologically induced, and neither should the nonphysician make evaluations about whether or not the depression itself has physical causes.

2. *Evaluating Causes.* Counseling is always easier if we can find the psychological and spiritual causes which produce the symptoms. Prior to the counseling session, or shortly thereafter, review the causes of depression listed earlier in this chapter and then try to discover—through questioning and careful listening—what might be producing the depression.

Is there low self-esteem with which you could help the counselee (see chapter 24)? If so, counseling may involve identifying, discussing, evaluating and challenging ideas and attitudes which counselees have learned about themselves and about the world in early childhood.

Is there learned helplessness? If so, you can help counselees learn how to accomplish things—beginning with small tasks and moving on to the more difficult. You can discuss the inevitability of uncontrollable events, and can help counselees to see that God is always in control, even when we are not.[20]

Is there negative thinking? Ask the counselee to state some of these thoughts. Then ask, "Is this a valid conclusion? Could there be another way of viewing the situation? Are you telling yourself things about the world, yourself, and the future, which really are not so?" All of this is designed to challenge the counselee's thinking and to teach him or her a habit of evaluating negative ideas and learning to think more positively. The truth of Philippians 4:8 must become the theme of both counselee and counselor: "whatever is true . . . honorable . . . right . . . pure . . . lovely . . . of good repute, if there is any excellence and if anything is worthy of praise, let your mind dwell on these things."

Is there stress, especially that which concerns a loss? Encourage the counselee to share his or her feelings about this and discuss the practical details of how life can go on.

Is there revenge covering anger; anger covering hurt? If so, these emotions must be discussed and expressed—even if they seem irrational. Hurt can be deeply embedded and sometimes is uncovered only after considerable probing and a lot of careful listening. Perhaps you will want to draw the diagram presented a few pages back to show how hurt can lead so easily to depression.

Is there guilt? What is its cause? Has the counselee confessed the problem to God and perhaps to others? Does he or she know about divine forgiveness? What about forgiving oneself? (See chapter 9.)

In discussing these issues, the counselee often gains insight into the problem. At other times the counselor may, in a tentative way, want to give some of his or her own insights and observations. If there is time to discuss these and to get the counselee's reactions, this can contribute to a better understanding of the problem and of the depression-producing influences in the counselee's life and thinking. Such understanding often leads to change and improvement.

3. *Stimulate Realistic Thinking.* Most people do not "snap out" of depression. The road to recovery is long, difficult, and marked by mood fluctuations which come with special intensity when there are disappointments, failures or separations.

At such times, counselees should be encouraged to ponder their "automatic thoughts." When problems or disappointments come, what does the counselee think? Often he or she thinks "this is terrible," "this proves I'm no good," "nobody wants me now" or "I never do anything right." These are self-criticisms which most often are not based on solid fact. If a person fails, for example, it does not follow that he or she is "no good" or unwanted. Failure means, instead, that we are not perfect (nobody is), that we have made a mistake and should try to act differently in the future. Effective counseling must encourage counselees to reevaluate depression-producing thoughts and attitudes toward life.

Writing in a popular magazine, one writer suggested that her depression came from an attitude which said, "I should be a perfect hostess, parent, wife, and friend. I should not fail. I should contribute to the community by serving on committees and making contributions to everyone who asks." This lady had set up high expectations which were impossible to reach. When she failed, she became depressed.

A similar attitude permeates Christianity. We convince ourselves that we must always be spiritually alive and enthusiastic but never angry or discouraged. As a result of these expectations we can be crushed when failure comes, as it does inevitably.

Counselees must be helped to accept human frailty. "We all need to make a list of our priorities and then figure out how much we can do without becoming angry, frustrated, exhausted or sorry for ourselves" when we fail.[21]

The counselor tries to help counselees evaluate attitudes, expectations, values and assumptions. We should help ourselves to see which of these ideas are unrealistic, nonbiblical and harmful. Since such thoughts are often well entrenched, sometimes resulting from a lifetime of thinking, it may take repeated efforts to help people reevaluate and change their attitudes toward life and themselves.[22] When people are depressed they want to *feel* better. But feelings by themselves are difficult, if not impossible to change. Telling a person "You shouldn't feel depressed," does nothing to relieve the depression and often adds guilt since most of us cannot change our feelings at will.

To change feelings we must change thinking (this we discussed in the previous section) and/or we must change actions. Inaction is common in depressed people, who find it easy to stay in bed or to sit alone brooding and thinking about the miseries of life. But this doesn't help with the depression. Gently, but firmly, therefore, depressed people must be pushed to take actions—to get involved in daily routines, family activities and recreation. Start by encouraging activities in which the counselee is likely to succeed. This increases optimism and interrupts the tendency to ruminate on negative ideas. When the counselee does take action, do not be reluctant to give encouragement and compliments.

4. *Change the Environment.* Counselors cannot do much to change the depression-producing circumstances in a person's life, but it is possible to encourage counselees to modify routines, reduce work loads, or take periodic vacations. Family members can also be urged to accept the counselee, to stimulate realistic thinking, to challenge negative thinking, to encourage action in place of inactivity, and to include the depressed person in family activities. When the family is accepting, interested, and involved, counselees improve more quickly. Counselors can stimulate this supportive environment.

5. *Protect the Counselee from Self-harm.* People can harm themselves in many ways—by changing jobs, for example, by quitting school or by making unwise marriage decisions. The counselor must be alert to a tendency for people to make major long-lasting decisions when they are in the grip of depression. Helping counselees decide if they "really want to do" what they are proposing, helping them to see the possible consequences of the decision, and urging them to "wait a while," can all prevent actions which could be harmful.

Suicide is one action which is contemplated by many depressed people. Since most of these people give prior clues about their intentions, the counselor should be alert to indications that suicide is being considered. Be alert, for example, to any of the following: [23]

- —talk of suicide,
- —evidence of a "thought-out" plan of action for actually killing oneself,
- —feelings of hopelessness and/or meaninglessness,
- —indications of guilt and worthlessness,
- —recent environmental stresses (such as job loss, divorce, or death in the family),
- —an inability to cope with stress,
- —excessive concern about physical illness,
- —preoccupation with insomnia,
- —evidence of depression, disorientation, and/or defiance,
- —a tendency to be dependent and dissatisfied at the same time,
- —a sudden and unexplainable shift to a happy, cheerful mood (which often means that the decision to attempt suicide has been made),
- —knowledge regarding the most effective methods of suicide (shooting, drugs, and carbon monoxide work best; wrist slashing is least successful), and

—history of prior suicide attempts. (Those who have tried before, often try suicide again.)

Counselors should not hesitate to ask whether or not the counselee has been thinking of suicide. Such questioning gets the issue into the open and lets the counselee consider it rationally. Rather than encouraging suicide (as is commonly assumed), open discussion often reduces its likelihood.

Periodically, most counselors are involved in potential suicide situations. At such times, take the threat seriously, be supportive and understanding, and try to be available at least by telephone. At times you may need to take direct and decisive action, like taking the person to the psychiatric ward of a hospital, contacting the family doctor or contacting relatives. If someone calls to report that he or she has taken a drug overdose, or is about to commit suicide, find out the person's location and then call the paramedic rescue squad. Police departments, suicide "hot line" counselors, psychiatric hospital units, and emergency wards are all listed in the phone book and usually are prepared to deal with suicide emergencies. If a drug has already been taken or if other physical self-harm has occurred, such medical intervention is essential.

In all of this, expect failure. If a person is really determined to commit suicide the counselor may delay his or her action but there is little that can be done to prevent suicide. Sometimes there is value in sharing this fact with counselees. Even the most dedicated helper cannot take responsibility to prevent suicide forever. It is well to remember this when a suicide does occur. Otherwise the counselor may wallow in guilt because he or she was unable to prevent the counselee's death.

Preventing Depression

Can depression be prevented? The answer probably is "no, not completely." We all experience disappointments, losses, rejections and failures which lead to periods of discouragement and unhappiness. For some people, these periods are rare and brief. For others, the depression is more prevalent and long-lasting. It may not be possible or even desirable to prevent times of discouragement, but long-lasting depressions are preventable. There are several ways in which this can be done.

1. *Trust in God.* Writing from prison, the Apostle Paul once stated that he had learned to be content in all circumstances. Knowing that God gives us strength and can supply all of our needs, Paul had learned how to live joyfully, both in poverty and in prosperity.[24] Through his experiences, and undoubtedly through a study of the Scriptures, Paul had learned to trust in God and this helped to prevent depression. As in the time of Paul, a conviction that God is alive and in control can give hope and encouragement today, even when we are inclined to be discouraged and without hope. If modern people can learn this lesson, and if church lead-

ers and Christian counselors can teach it, then discouragements need not hit as hard as they might hit otherwise.

2. *Expect Discouragement.* The second verse of a famous hymn proclaims that "we should never be discouraged" if we take things to the Lord in prayer. This is a popular view for which there is no scriptural support. Jesus warned that we would have problems and the Apostle James wrote that trials and temptations would come to test our faith and teach us patience. It is unrealistic to smile and laugh in such circumstances, pretending that we're never going to be discouraged.

Consider our Lord at the time of the crucifixion. He was "deeply distressed" and openly acknowledged his agony. One can hardly imagine him smiling in Gethsemane or on the cross, trying to convince everyone that he was rejoicing and "bubbling over" with happiness. Jesus trusted in his Father, but he expected pain and wasn't surprised when it came.

When we are realistic enough to expect pain and informed enough to know that God is always in control, then we can handle discouragement better and often keep from slipping into deep depression.

3. *Learn to Handle Anger and Guilt.* Some people slide into depression because their minds dwell on past injustices or past failures. This may sound simplistic, but we must ask God to help us forget the past, to forgive those who have sinned against us, and to forgive ourselves. When people dwell on past events and wallow in anger, guilt, and the misery of discouragement, one wonders if such thinking serves some useful purpose. Churches can teach people to admit their anger or guilt and to show how these can be overcome (see chapters 8 and 9). If people can learn to handle their anger and guilt, much depression can be prevented.

4. *Challenge Thinking.* If it is true, as some have suggested, that we each silently talk to ourselves all day, then people should be encouraged to notice what is being said. If I decide, for example, that I am incompetent, then I need to ask, "What is the evidence for this? In what areas am I incompetent? Is it bad to be incompetent in some things? How can I become more competent?" When we learn to challenge our own thinking, and that of others, this can also prevent or reduce the severity of depression.

The Bible also talks about meditation on the Word of God and on things which are good, positive and just. Such meditation directs our minds away from thinking which is negative and inclined to produce depression.

5. *Teach Coping Techniques.* In somewhat formal language, one writer has compared those who resist depression with those who succumb:

> The life histories of those individuals who are particularly resistant to depression, or resilient from depression, may have been filled with mastery; these people may have had extensive experience controlling and manipulating the sources of reinforcement in their lives, and may there-

fore see the future optimistically. Those people who are particularly susceptible to depression may have had lives relatively devoid of mastery; their lives may have been full of situations in which they were helpless to influence their sources of suffering and relief.[25]

Children and adults can be overprotected. This interferes with their ability to learn how to cope or to master the stresses of life. If people can see how others cope, and learn how to cope themselves, then circumstances seem less overwhelming and depression is less likely.

6. *Provide Support.* Émile Durkheim, who wrote a classic book on suicide,[26] discovered that religious people were less suicide-prone than those who were nonbelievers. The reason for this, Durkheim believed, was that religion integrated people into groups. Less lonely and isolated, these people are less inclined to get depressed or to attempt suicide. The church, and other social institutions, can become therapeutic communities where people feel welcome and accepted.

A concerned group of people who have learned to be caring can do much to soften the trauma of crises and provide strength and help in times of need. Aware that they are not alone, people in crises are able to cope better and thus avoid severe depression.

7. *Reach Out.* Alcoholics Anonymous has demonstrated conclusively that needy people help themselves when they reach out to assist others. This is known as the "helper-therapy" principle.[27] In its simplest form it states: those who help are the ones who benefit and are helped the most. When we reach out to help other people, including depressed people, this does wonders to keep ourselves from being depressed.

Of course, the motive for helping is important. Healing is unlikely if someone concludes selfishly, "I don't care about others but I'll help if this is the only way for me to get better." But when there is a joyful reaching out, everyone is helped and depression is reduced. The stimulation of a helping community, therefore, is one indirect way to prevent depression.

8. *Encourage Physical Fitness.* Since poor diet and lack of exercise can make people depression-prone, people should always be encouraged— by word and by example—to take care of their bodies. A healthy body is less susceptible to mental as well as physical illness.

Conclusions about Depression

Vance Havner, the preacher who was mentioned in the first paragraph of this chapter, once hoped that his dying wife would be healed through some miracle. But she died and Havner was plunged into grief. Although he did not understand why this happened, he concluded that God makes no mistakes.

Whoever thinks he has the ways of God conveniently tabulated, analyzed, and correlated with convenient, glib answers to ease every question from aching hearts has not been far in this maze of mystery we call life and death. . . . He has no stereotyped way of doing what He does. He delivered Peter from prison but left John the Baptist in a dungeon to die. . . . At this writing I never knew less how to explain the ways of Providence but I never had more confidence in my God. . . . I accept whatever He does, however He does it.[28]

This man was deeply saddened when his wife died, but probably he never became depressed. He had a realistic perspective on life and death. This is a perspective which can help both counselors and counselees to deal effectively with the problem of depression.

Suggestions for Further Reading

* Barrett, Roger. *Depression: What It Is and What to Do About It*. Elgin, IL: David C. Cook, 1977.

Beck, Aaron T. *Depression: Causes and Treatment*. Philadelphia: University of Pennsylvania Press, 1967.

* Lloyd-Jones, D. Martyn. *Spiritual Depression: Its Causes and Cure*. Grand Rapids: Wm. B. Eerdmans, 1965.

Lum, Doman. *Responding to Suicidal Crisis*. Grand Rapids: Wm. B. Eerdmans, 1974.

Seligman, Martin E. P. *Helplessness: On Depression, Development and Death*. San Francisco: Freeman, 1975.

Footnotes

1. The title of Vance Havner's book, *Though I Walk Through the Valley* (Old Tappan, NJ: Revell, 1974) is taken from Ps. 23:4. See pages 102–104.

2. Gerald L. Klerman, "Affective Disorders," in *The Harvard Guide to Modern Psychiatry*, ed. Armand M. Nicholi, Jr. (Cambridge, MA: Harvard University Press, 1978), pp. 253–281.

3. N. Kline, "Practical Management of Depression," *Journal of the American Medical Association*, 190:732–40.

4. Quentin O. Hyder, *The Christian's Handbook of Psychiatry* (Old Tappan, NJ: Revell, 1971), p. 77.

5. Job 3; Num. 11:10–15; Jon. 4:1–3; Exod. 6:9; Matt. 26:75.

6. 1 Kings 19.

7. Matt. 26:37, 38.

8. See, for example, Pss. 34:15–17; 103:13, 14; Matt. 5:12; 11:28–30; John 14:1; 15:10, 11; Rom. 8:28.

9. Rom. 15:13.

10. Martin E. P. Seligman, *Helplessness: On Depression, Development, and Death* (San Francisco: Freeman, 1975), pp. 77, 76.

11. Samuel H. Kraines and Eloise S. Thetford, *Help for the Depressed* (Springfield, IL: Charles C. Thomas, 1972).

12. Klerman, "Affective Disorders."

13. Rene Spitz, "Anaclitic Depression," *The Psychoanalytic Study of the Child* 2 (1946): 313–42.

14. Roger Barrett, *Depression: What It Is and What to Do about It* (Elgin, IL: David C. Cook, 1977).

15. Seligman, *Helplessness*.

16. Aaron T. Beck, *Depression: Causes and Treatment* (Philadelphia: University of Pennsylvania Press, 1967), pp. 255 f.

17. The diagram is adapted from Paul Welter, *How to Help a Friend* (Wheaton: Tyndale House, 1978), pp. 108, 244, and attributed to G. B. Dunning, a psychologist living in Greenwood, Nebraska.

18. Barrett, *Depression,* pp. 64, 70.

19. Stanley Lesse, ed., *Masked Depression* (New York: Jason Aronson, 1974).

20. Heb. 1:3; 13:5; Col. 1:16, 17; John 14:1–4, 26, 27.

21. Eda LeShan, "Pulling Out of a Depression," *Woman's Day* 42 (November, 1978), pp. 50–54, 246–48.

22. See Beck, *Depression,* for a further discussion of "cognitive psychotherapy" with depressives. The concepts are built on the work of psychologist Albert Ellis.

23. This list is adapted from N. L. Farberow and E. S. Shneidman, eds., *The Cry for Help* (New York: McGraw-Hill, 1965); and E. S. Shneidman, *On the Nature of Suicide* (San Francisco: Jossey-Bass, 1969).

24. Phil. 4:11, 19, 13, 12.

25. Seligman, *Helplessness,* p. 104.

26. Emile Durkheim, *Suicide* (Paris, 1897; Glencoe, IL: Free Press, 1951).

27. F. Reissman, "The 'Helper-Therapy' Principle," *Social Work* 10 (1965): 27–32.

28. Havner, *Though I Walk Through the Valley,* pp. 66, 67.

8

Anger

ANGER IS AN EMOTIONAL STATE, EXPERIENCED AT TIMES BY EVERYONE but impossible to define precisely. It occurs in varying degrees of intensity —from mild annoyance to violent rage. It begins in infancy and continues through to old age. It may be hidden and held inward or expressed openly. It can be of short duration, coming and going quickly, or it may persist for decades in the form of bitterness, resentment or hatred. Anger may be destructive, especially when it persists in the form of aggression, unforgiveness, or revenge. But it can also be constructive if it motivates us to correct injustice or to think creatively. Anger is aroused when our progress toward some desired goal is blocked. It involves a physiological reaction as well as a feeling which usually is conscious but sometimes is buried behind a calm and smiling façade.

Early in their careers, most counselors encounter people who are angry. Anger, openly expressed, deliberately hidden from others, or unconsciously expressed, is at the basis of a host of psychological, physical and spiritual problems. Anger, along with hostility, has been called "the chief saboteur of the mind," "a significant factor in the formation of many serious diseases," and "the leading cause of misery, depression, inefficiency, sickness, accidents, loss of work time and financial loss in industry. . . . No matter what the problem—marital conflict, alcoholism, a wife's frigidity, a child's defiance, nervous or physical disease—elimination of hostility is a key factor in its solution."[1] These are strong words but probably not an overstatement. An understanding of anger, including the counselor's own anger, is one of the basics for effective Christian counseling.

The Bible and Anger

Divine wrath and human anger are mentioned repeatedly in the Bible. In the Old Testament alone there are almost six hundred references to wrath or anger, and this theme continues into the New Testament as well.[2] Anger clearly is an attribute of God and a common, probably universal, experience of human beings.

100

Since anger is a part of God's nature, we cannot conclude that anger, per se, is bad. Indeed, since God is completely good and holy, we must conclude that divine wrath is also good. This divine anger is vigorous, intense, consistent, controlled, and invariably an expression of indignation at unrighteousness. According to Leon Morris, the biblical writers "habitually use for the divine wrath a word which denotes not so much a sudden flaring up of passion which soon is over, as a strong and settled opposition to all that is evil arising out of God's very nature." [3] Divine anger is directed not only at sin but at individual sinners as well. Repeatedly he was angry with the unfaithful Israelites, and his son Jesus, whose wrath clearly is identified in Mark 3, was angry at "the hardness" of the religious leaders in his day. [4] It should be added that divine wrath is always justified and completely consistent with God's love and mercy. [5] Boice writes that

> On the basis of Christ's death, in which he himself received the full judicial outpouring of God's wrath against sin, those who believe now come to experience not wrath (though we richly deserve it) but grace abounding. This is the day of God's grace.
>
> Grace does not eliminate wrath; wrath is still stored up against the unrepentant. But grace does eliminate the necessity for everyone to experience it. [6]

God is forgiving and compassionate. For this reason he at times restrains the full expression of his wrath to give human beings time and opportunity to repent. [7] Romans 1:18 speaks of a divine wrath that is revealed *at present* "from heaven against all ungodliness and unrighteousness of men, who suppress the truth in unrighteousness," but the Bible also speaks of a wrath to come in the future. [8]

An understanding of the divine wrath of God is necessary if we are to comprehend the biblical teachings about human anger. The Bible never criticizes the anger of God but it warns against human anger repeatedly. [9] This is not evidence of a double standard. Anger against injustice is right and good in both God and human beings. Because God is wise, sovereign, powerful, perfect, and all-knowing, he never misinterprets a situation, never feels threatened, never loses control, and is always angered by sin and injustice. In contrast, we humans misinterpret circumstances, make mistakes in judgment, react quickly when we feel threatened or hurt, and sometimes respond with vengeance and vindictiveness. As a result, human anger can be harmful and dangerous. It provides an opening for Satan, [10] and is something against which we are cautioned. "Be angry," we read in Ephesians 4:26, "and yet do not sin; do not let the sun go down on your anger." From these and similar scriptural passages we can reach several conclusions about human anger:

1. *Human Anger Is Normal and Not Necessarily Sinful.* Human beings, created in the image of God, were given emotions, including anger. Such anger is a necessary and useful reaction which was seen in Jesus [11] and is not sinful in and of itself.

2. *Human Anger Can Be Harmful.* Like other emotions, anger can be destructive if it is not expressed in accordance with biblical guidelines. According to Jay Adams:

> Paul distinguishes between sinful and holy anger, he warns: "Be angry *and* sin not." Righteous anger can become unrighteous anger in two ways: (1) by the *ventilation* of anger; (2) by the *internalization* of anger. These two opposite extremes are known more popularly as *blowing up* and *clamming up*. When one blows up, his emotional energies are aimed and fired at someone else. When he clams up, bodily tensions are released within oneself. In both cases, the emotional energies of anger are wasted. In both they *are* used "destructively." In neither instance are they used constructively to solve problems.[12]

Because of its harmful potential, anger is often condemned in the Bible.[13] Anger, we are warned, rests in the bosom of fools. We should, therefore, "cease from anger," or at best "be slow" in getting angry.[14] In the Book of Proverbs alone, anger is accepted with qualifications in one reference, but soundly condemned nine times. Anger isn't wrong, but it can get out of control and cause problems.[15]

3. *Human Anger Often Results from Distorted Perception.* In a stimulating article,[16] one Christian psychologist has suggested that "every instance of God's anger is a reaction of righteous indignation at some form of unrighteousness." Likewise "every man's anger is righteous indignation in his own eyes." The difference between divine and human anger rests in the words, "in his own eyes." Because people are imperfect we see each situation from our own perspectives. We are not able always to judge between real injustice (as perceived accurately by an omniscient God) and apparent injustice. As a result we become angry over things which we think are wrong but which, in fact, would not be considered wrong if we had all of the facts. It doubtless is true that "the fall of man into sin produced multiple sources for distortion. . . . Most of the distortion wrought by sinful desires can be subsumed under a heading of selfishness, or narcissistic self-interest. Accurate (or righteous) perception is distorted to fit more closely with self-interest."[17] Because we feel vulnerable, threatened or inclined to be critical, we misperceive the actions of others and jump to angry, perhaps unjustified conclusions.

4. *Human Anger Often Leads to Sin.* This is implied in Paul's previously quoted warning: "Be angry, and yet do not sin." Such sin can be expressed in a variety of ways.

(a) Vengeance. Bitterness, hatred, revenge, and an attitude of judgment all result from anger and all are condemned in Scripture.[18] Vengeance is God's responsibility alone. There can be no scriptural justification for human revenge or lashing out in anger.

(b) Verbal Abuse. Christians are responsible for controlling their words, but this is especially difficult when we are angry. In the Old Testament the person who ventilates verbally and loses his or her temper is described as a fool.[19] In the Book of James, the dangers of verbal abuse are clearly outlined and in the same sentence readers are urged to be "slow to speak and slow to anger." [20]

(c) Dishonest Sharing. The Bible teaches that there is value in expressing anger if it will lead another person to repent and change for the better.[21] That is a proper use of anger. But what if we pretend to be concerned about the other person's own good but use this as an excuse for expressing our own hostility? That is dishonest—a form of subtle and sinful vengeance.

(d) Refusal to Share. Since we are instructed to express anger when it is for the good of another, then it is wrong to deny, ignore, distort, or refuse to share our feelings because this is more convenient. It is not easy to express anger in a way that lets others know that we feel hurt. As a result, some people gloss over their feelings in an attempt to maintain peace. The motivation may be commendable, but the result can be harmful. The other person never realizes that he or she made someone angry and why. Thus there is no opportunity to change for the better. In turn, the person who represses anger is more open to a growing bitterness and to depression.[22] The Bible even calls such repression a form of lying.[23]

5. *Human Anger Can Be Controlled.* It is unlikely that God would have instructed us to control anger if human anger-control is impossible. Several Bible passages imply that control *is* possible and indicate how this can be done.

(a) Anger Must Be Acknowledged. Before we can "put away" our bitterness, wrath, anger and malice, we must admit, at least to ourselves, that such feelings exist.

(b) Outbursts Must Be Restrained. The man or woman of God thinks before acting. There is quiet meditation before verbal explosions.[24]

Sometimes there is value in sharing one's burden of anger with a friend. Always there is value in pouring out one's feelings to God. Such activities often lead to new perspectives which dissipate anger before it is expressed and allowed to harm others or damage relationships.

This is seen clearly in Psalm 73. The writer gets angry and "embittered" because the wicked seemed to be so happy and successful while the godly were having trouble. Instead of exploding in anger the psalmist came into the presence of God and began to get a fresh new perspective on the apparent injustice in the world. His anger, as a result, subsided and was replaced by praise.

(c) Confession and Forgiveness Must Be Utilized. This involves confession to God, confession to others, and a willingness to both forgive and to receive forgiveness—repeatedly if necessary.[25]

(d) Ruminating and Revenge Must Be Resisted. It might be assumed that when Jesus was persecuted he had every right to become angry. But notice that "while being reviled, He did not revile in return; while suffering, He uttered no threats, but kept entrusting Himself to Him who judges righteously." [26] People who are angry often enjoy ruminating on their difficulties, thinking vengeful thoughts and pondering ways to "get even." This tendency must be resisted and replaced with an attitude of entrusting oneself to God.

In summary, therefore, anger is seen as a universal emotion which is good when expressed against real injustice, harmful when expressed for self-centered motives, and clearly an emotion to be controlled. Wise King Solomon stated the issue concisely: "He who is slow to anger is better than the mighty, and he who rules his spirit, than he who captures a city." [27]

The Causes of Anger

Over half a century ago, one researcher asked a group of college students to keep a record of the things which made them angry during the course of one week.[28] The resulting lists included a sampling of irritations and frustrations such as being scolded or criticized, not getting work done, losing money or being awakened at an awkward time. Almost 80 percent of the anger came because of the actions of other people rather than because of circumstances or events. People were especially inclined to become angry when their self-expression was thwarted and their self-esteem was threatened or attacked. All of this would suggest that anger is a reaction of indignation in response to some person or situation.[29] The Bible gives several illustrations of this. Herod, for example, became indignant and angry when he saw that the wise men had tricked him; [30] the ten disciples "began to feel indignant toward James and John" when they asked for a special place of prominence in the kingdom; and Jonah became indignant and angry when God spared Nineveh—largely through Jonah's reluctant preaching.[30]

Perhaps there are as many causes of anger as there are situations and human actions that make people angry. Nevertheless, most of these causes could be summarized under a few headings.

1. *Injustice.* This, as we have seen, is the reason for divine wrath and should arouse anger in believers. Consider, for example, the actions of Jesus when he drove the money-changers from the temple. The Bible does not state that he was angry, but his overturning their tables and his criticisms of their disrespect for God's house surely imply anger. And it was anger because wrong was being done. Undoubtedly this is one of the most valid reasons for anger (perhaps it is the *only* valid reason), yet it probably is one of the least common causes of anger.

2. *Frustration.* Several years ago some researchers at Yale University concluded that anger and aggression arise primarily in response to frustration.[31] A frustration is an obstacle (an event, person, or physical barrier) that hinders our progress toward a goal. How much we feel frustrated depends on the importance of the goal, the size of the obstacles, and the duration of the frustration. When we are late for church because of a flat tire, we are mildly frustrated; when we fail an important exam, are de-

nied a promotion, or have an illness which does not get better, the frustration is greater. It does not follow that anger increases automatically as one's frustration level goes up, but the *potential* for anger probably increases as frustrations increase.

3. *Threat and Hurt.* When a person is rejected, "put-down," humiliated, unjustly criticized, or otherwise threatened, anger often is aroused. Threats challenge our self-esteem and make us feel so vulnerable that anger and aggression become ways to fight back. Sometimes when we are threatened and made aware of our own imperfections we respond in anger toward those who fail to meet our expectations of them. This directs attention away from ourselves, hides the fact that we are hurt or threatened, and lets us feel better at someone else's expense. According to one psychologist, hurt and anger almost always go together. "Seconds after the event which arouses the hurt feeling, another feeling skyrockets into awareness — anger." [32] The anger comes so quickly and is so apparent that it is easy to miss the hurt which comes first.

4. *Learning.* To some extent, anger may be a learned response. Most people have had the experience of being aroused to anger by the speech or actions of someone else and it is widely accepted that television violence increases the tendency of viewers to tolerate and often engage in aggressive acts. By watching or listening to others, people learn to become more easily angered and more outwardly aggressive.

The Effects of Anger

All people do not respond to an anger-producing situation in the same way. Our reactions depend on such issues as:

—The attitudes and example of parents. Mothers and fathers teach their children how to act in response to anger. If parents explode in rage, or express their anger mildly, children learn to respond in a similar way. In Ephesians 6:4 fathers are instructed not to discipline in a way that provokes anger in the children.

—Family status. Children from lower socioeconomic levels, only children, and the youngest children in large families all tend to express anger openly and more violently. [33]

—Personality. For reasons which are not completely understood, it may be that some people are more sensitive to frustration or injustice, more inclined to get angry and less able to control their reactions. To some extent this relates to maturity level. As maturity increases, uncontrolled angry outbursts become less frequent.

—Perception. How we view a situation largely determines how we react. It is probable that stressful events in the environment are less likely to arouse anger than are our perceptions and interpretations of these events. This explains why the same situation can make one person very angry and hardly ruffle another person. Differences in perception can also explain both why one person can calm another or why one angry person can arouse another's anger. If we can persuade someone else to change his or her interpretation of an event or situation, we can often change the other person's emotions.

—Religious experience. This can affect the experience and expression of anger in three ways. First, there is the issue of one's past background. People with extensive religious training tend to repress rather than express anger.[34] Second is the influence of *present* religious beliefs. While these do not appear to be as influential as some might hope,[35] it is true that many people try to act in accordance with their moral standards. For the Christian it should be remembered that one of the fruits of the Spirit is self-control. Third, people tend to adopt the opinions of their *religious group*. Quakers, for example, believe that violence is wrong and this influences how a Quaker might respond to an anger-arousing stimulus.

One writer has suggested that people have four basic ways of dealing with anger.[36] They can repress it (refusing to admit its presence), suppress it (deliberately keeping it hidden from others), express it (in either destructive or relatively harmless ways), or confess it to God and others. Perhaps another way to summarize the effects of anger is to suggest that we can withdraw from an anger-producing situation, turn our feelings inward, attack a substitute, or deal directly with the source of the anger. These four approaches overlap and each of us may shift from one to the other, depending on the individual and the anger-producing situation.

1. *Withdrawal*. Perhaps this is the easiest but least effective way to deal with anger. Withdrawal can take several forms:

—leaving the room, taking a vacation, or otherwise removing oneself physically from the situation that arouses anger;

—avoiding the problem by plunging into work or other activities, by thinking about other things, or by escaping into a world of television or novels;

—hiding the problem by drinking or taking drugs—behavior which also could be used to "get back at" a person who makes us angry; and

—denying, consciously or unconsciously, that anger even exists. With people who believe anger is wrong, such denial helps them, at least temporarily, to withdraw from both the anger and its resulting guilt.

2. *Turning Inward*. Problems are not solved by denying them or by withdrawing. At best, the relief is only temporary and in time the pressure builds until it bursts out to create more difficulties.

This often happens when anger is held in and not expressed. There may be calmness and smiling on the outside but boiling rage within. This internal anger is a powerful force which may express itself in:

—physical symptoms ranging from a mild headache to ulcers, high blood pressure or heart attacks;

—psychological reactions such as anxiety, fear, or feelings of tension, and depression (which, as we note in chapter 7, often results from held-in anger);

—unconscious attempts to harm ourselves (seen in accident proneness, in a tendency to make mistakes or even in suicide);

—thinking characterized by self-pity, thoughts of revenge, or ruminations on the injustices that one is experiencing; and

—spiritual struggles which come because we wallow in bitterness, wrath, anger, clamor and slander, thus "grieving the Holy Spirit of God" by ignoring his spiritual guidance and direction in our lives.[37]

3. *Attacking a Substitute.* Introductory textbooks in psychology often describe the common human tendency to blame innocent people when things are not going well. The man who is angry with his boss may stifle his anger at work (lest he be fired), but he "takes it out" on his wife or children at home in the evening because this is a safe place to ventilate. The family may not have caused the anger but they bear the brunt of the angry person's feelings.

Anger is especially difficult to handle when we cannot identify who is to be blamed or when we cannot reach the person who created the situation. If inflation decreases our spending power, who do we blame? The grocer or drugstore manager may be charging higher prices but they alone are not responsible for inflation. If we decide that the real source of the problem rests with some government leader, this may be an aloof, distant person who is difficult to contact and never available to hear our anger and criticism. As a result, we verbally, physically, or cognitively attack some largely innocent but accusable person. Sometimes there may even be an illegal or criminal "acting out" against innocent victims who nevertheless are part of the society. Angry revolutionaries who burn and loot stores in an attempt to bring down a political leader, often do nothing to change the leader but, in giving vent to their anger, they destroy the innocent store owners.

4. *Facing the Sources of Anger.* This can be done in either a destructive or a constructive way. Regretfully, the destructive approach probably is more common and clearly is less effective.

Destructive reactions, which are directed toward the person or situation that causes the anger, may include verbal and physical aggression, ridicule, cynicism, refusal to cooperate, or involvement in things which will hurt or embarrass someone else. Drinking, failing in school, or having an extramarital affair, for example, sometimes are really subtle ways to attack and get even with parents, a mate, or some other person who has made us angry. In all of this, the person is engaging in the "eye for an eye, tooth for a tooth" philosophy of vengeance which Jesus clearly condemned.[38]

Much more helpful is an approach which admits that there is anger, which tries to see its causes, and then does what is possible to change the anger-producing situation or perhaps to see it in a different way. This is a constructive, anger-reducing approach, which some people only learn with the help of a counselor.

Counseling and Anger

As we have seen, anger can be a sin and it can harm a person physically, psychologically, spiritually and socially in the form of strained interpersonal relations. But if anger is so harmful, why do so many people seem to take delight in hostility and persist in harboring grudges? Anger often makes people feel powerful, superior and right. Handling the anger maturely and "turning the other cheek" seem to imply that we are weak, inclined to back down, and willing to be "pushed around." Therefore, in the guise of maintaining our self-esteem or standing up for our rights, we often refuse to take those actions which will change situations and eliminate misunderstanding. Stated briefly, many people apparently enjoy being angry. Counseling won't help much because there is little real desire for change. When such an attitude is encountered there can be value in stating your suspicion that the counselee really does not want to change. Be prepared for the counselee to disagree, but this can open further discussion about the counselee's desires and motives for changing.

When there is a desire for change, however, counseling can take several forms:

1. *Helping Counselees Admit Anger.* Anger that is denied will never be eliminated, but sometimes the most difficult goal in counseling is to help people see and admit that they are angry. Such an admission can be threatening, especially for people who are angry at a loved one or who believe that all anger is wrong. It may help to point out that anger is a common, God-given emotion which, for most people, gets out of control periodically. Point out some of the previously mentioned signs which often indicate hidden anger (e.g., depression, physical complaints, criticism, impatience, and so on). If the counselee persists in denying the anger, even after hearing the evidence, perhaps he or she will admit the *possibility* that anger is present.

2. *Considering the Sources of Anger.* Even when denial of anger persists there can be value in asking, "What kinds of things make you angry?" From this general beginning, move to the specifics: "I'd like you to think of a time when you were really mad. Tell me about it." In discussing concrete examples, the counselee can begin to see what caused the angry feelings, and can understand why he or she reacted in anger. In considering the sources of anger with a counselee, watch for attempts to make excuses. Comments like "I am Irish, so how can I help being angry?" or "My father had ulcers from being angry so I guess it runs in the family" are often attempts to excuse the anger and to avoid facing its real source. As a result, the anger persists.

3. *Teaching Counselees the Art of Evaluation.* When we begin to feel

angry, there is value in asking ourselves some questions.

—What is making me feel angry?

—Why am I feeling anger and not some other emotion?

—Am I jumping to conclusions about the situation or person who is making me angry?

—Is my anger really justified?

—Is it right for me to feel inferior or threatened in this anger-arousing situation?

—How might others, including the person who is angering me, view this situation?

—Is there another way in which I could look at the situation?

—Are there things I could do to change the situation in order to reduce my anger?

Recently, following a winter ice storm, a friend of mine lost control of his car, slid into a ditch, and hit a fence which dented a fender. Although the driver was not hurt he was angered by the inconvenience, the damage to the car, and the towing expense of having the vehicle pulled back on to the road. As the tow truck jerked the car out of the snow and my friend walked over to scan the damage, a car horn sounded and the well-dressed middle-aged driver of a big car began shouting from his window. "Hurry up, son," he demanded in an annoyed tone of voice. "You're holding up traffic. I can't sit here all day!"

My friend, who doubtless showed more patience and control than the shouting driver, said nothing, but got into his car and drove away. "But I was really mad," he reported later. "The man put me down and ordered me around—which wasn't what I needed, especially when I was so frustrated already."

Here is an example in which anger was acknowledged. My friend pondered what was really making him angry (and discussed this with his wife), and later evaluated the situation in terms of the questions listed above. The anger did not dissipate immediately, but neither did it persist or erupt in physical symptoms or in impatience at home. Anger which is acknowledged and evaluated loses much of its power.

4. *Emphasizing Humility, Confession and Forgiveness.* Anger, as we have seen, often leads to sinful thoughts, desires, words and actions. Teaching people to admit and evaluate their anger can be a first step in dealing with sin, but this is not a permanent solution. Humility, confession, and forgiveness also are of basic importance.

(a) Humility. It is a humbling experience to admit that we are or have been angry, or that we have lost self-control. Some people apparently prefer to remain angry rather than to risk admitting weakness or failure. Others, however, are willing to acknowledge the reality of their anger along with any accompanying sinful side effects. This attitude must come before confession.

(b) Confession. The Bible emphasizes the importance of confessing

to God and the value of confessing to others.[39] When we confess to God
we can know for certain that we are forgiven.[40] If we confess to one or
more fellow believers, they can support, encourage and pray for us.

(c) Forgiveness. Some people know intellectually that they are forgiven, but since they don't "feel forgiven," they continue in their guilt.
Perhaps one way to feel forgiveness is to meditate repeatedly on 1 John
1:9. An additional technique is to be sure that we consistently forgive
others.

When Jesus was asked about this one day, he said that we should forgive repeatedly. Then he told a story about forgiveness and anger, concluding that people who refuse to forgive others, in turn will not be
forgiven. This has great relevance for those who hold grudges. Their
anger is certain to continue, with all of the accompanying misery and
tension. In the final analysis, "forgiveness seems to be the chief precedent
set in Scripture for the ultimate disposition of angry feelings. . . . Forgiving can be extremely difficult, especially when the situation remains
unjust, but it can be done if responsibility for the situation is abdicated
to God."[41] He can give us the ability to forgive and forget.

5. *Teaching Self-control.* When a person gets angry, reason often gives
way to feeling, and something is said or done which might be regretted
later. There are at least four ways which can help counselees to gain
greater self-control when they are inclined to become angry.

(a) Slowing One's Reactions. The old idea of counting to ten before
speaking sometimes helps one to gain control before reacting in rage.
Others have suggested the value of speaking slowly, not raising one's
voice, pausing periodically (if possible), flexing the muscles (so they
relax), and mentally telling oneself to relax. Certainly "a gentle answer
turns away wrath, but a harsh word stirs up anger."[42]

(b) Dealing with Feelings of Inferiority. Hostility and anger, including prolonged hostility, often indicate that a person feels inferior, insecure, and lacking in self-esteem or self-confidence. If someone is made to
feel inferior, he or she often reacts with anger and an attempt to assert
his or her superiority. This is seen in arguments which frequently consist
of two people trying to bolster themselves and each trying to make the
other feel inferior. As a result there is anger and sometimes a loss of
self-control.

Counselees are better able to control their anger when they are helped
to develop a healthy self-esteem, based on their value as God's special
creatures.[43] In addition, there can be value in the practice of asking oneself, "Am I really as inferior as this situation might suggest?" Then learn
to think of the other person's feelings of inadequacy. One psychiatrist has
suggested, for example, that "whenever anyone belittles, acts superior, or
is hostile to you, think of who or what's been bugging *him*. No matter how
great the provocation or how obnoxious a person seems, your awareness

of the forces responsible for any person's behavior will help you feel less inferior—and thus, less hostile." [44]

(c) Avoiding an Angry Mind-set. Some people look for the worst in almost every situation. They are perpetually critical, always negative, and invariably hostile.

Most people find themselves slipping periodically into a negative mind-set, and unless this is resisted, we get caught in what has been called a "hostility trap." [45] The Scriptures instruct us to think about things which are right, pure, good and praiseworthy.[46] Surely it is impossible to think such thoughts repeatedly and, at the same time, to wallow in anger, bitterness and hostility. The Apostle Paul had a positive mind-set and an attitude of thanksgiving and praise to God. As a result he avoided anger, even when circumstances were difficult.[47]

(d) Growing Spiritually. Self-control is not something which must be done completely on our own. Self-control is listed in Galatians 5 as a fruit of the Spirit. Believers who sincerely desire to be led by the Holy Spirit will discover a slow decline in strife; jealousy, outbursts of anger, disputes and other "deeds of the flesh." With God's help we can learn love, patience, gentleness and self-control.[48] Only the Christian counselor can share such teaching and model it in his or her own life.

6. *What about Catharsis?* In the preceding paragraphs little has been said about the popular idea that "letting off steam" or venting one's hostility will decrease feelings of anger. There is no clear research to support this idea and it is never suggested in Scripture. In contrast, some writers have concluded that intense expressions of anger *increase* instead of decrease hostility.

Acknowledging and dealing with anger is different from venting it, in hopes of "clearing the air." The former can be an effective approach to the problem. The latter is of questionable value and may intensify the very feelings that the counseling is attempting to control.

Preventing Anger

Anger is a God-given emotion which in itself cannot and should not be eliminated or prevented. There are several ways, however, in which the unhealthy, destructive, and nonbiblical aspects of anger can be prevented.

1. *Biblical Teaching.* The Bible, as we have seen, says a great deal about anger, both human and divine. But how often are these teachings shared in a theologically clear and practically relevant way? In the absence of such instruction Christians are confused by the seeming contradictions between the anger of Jesus and the biblical admonitions to control anger. On a practical level there is an uncertainty about one's own anger and how it can be handled. Repeated teaching about anger and self-control can help individuals to better understand these concepts, to

distinguish between righteous anger and personal reactions, and to avoid the long-lasting destructive effects of anger and hostility.

2. *Avoiding Anger-arousing Situations and People.* Problems are never solved if we avoid them in an attempt to maintain peace. Sometimes duty or wisdom demand that we squarely face frustrating situations or deal directly with difficult people. But there are times when one can stay away from situations, events or people which are likely to arouse unnecessary anger. The Book of Proverbs states the issue concisely:

> Do not associate with a man given to anger;
> Or go with a hot-tempered man,
> Lest you learn his ways,
> And find a snare for yourself.[49]

3. *Learning to Evaluate Situations.* It is difficult to control emotions, but we can control the thoughts which give rise to feeling.[50] In the home, but also in the church and school, people can be taught—by words and by example—to evaluate the anger-arousing situation, to realize that they are hurt or disappointed as well as angered, and to respond calmly—without blaming or making statements which will be regretted later. All of this is not something which will be learned completely by hearing a lecture or reading a book. Nevertheless, instruction can be helpful if it gives guidelines for evaluation and self-control. Further learning then will come slowly and by experience, interspersed with failures, which, in turn, can teach more about ourselves and about anger-control.

4. *Building Self-esteem.* It is true that "we can no more insulate ourselves from irritating remarks, attitudes, and actions than we can hide from germs. But we can protect ourselves by maintaining a healthy resistance: a healthy level of Self-Respect."[51] Anger is less destructive and more easily controlled when a person is secure as an individual and not plagued by excessive feelings of inferiority or self-doubt. Chapter 24 discusses inferiority and self-esteem, including ways to prevent a poor self-concept. When Christians have a realistic picture of their value as persons, there is less need or inclination to get angry.

5. *Avoiding Ruminating.* Here again is the issue of thought-control. When people get angry they often go through the day meditating on the cause of their anger. As this ruminating continues, the original causes are blown up into false proportions and anger increases, especially when critical people associate with other critical people and share their criticisms. In this way, some people develop a whole mind-set of negativism and bitterness which grows worse as they get older.

This kind of thinking can be fun, at first, because it lets the thinker fantasize about his or her own superiority. But since this thinking is destructive and harmful it must be resisted and replaced with thinking which is positive and less critical.[52] This message should be taught and modeled in the church and at home. Such teaching can prevent the harmful build-up of anger.

6. *Learning to Confront.* Conflict and disagreement are a part of life which cannot be avoided. But people can be encouraged and taught to tell each other how they feel, what they want and what they think. This can be done in a critical confrontation which stimulates anger, but truth may also be spoken in love. This is biblical,[53] and when people learn to communicate honestly and effectively there is a prevention or reduction of destructive anger.

7. *Spirit Control.* As indicated earlier, uncontrolled anger is listed in the Bible as one of the deeds of the flesh, but self-control is one of the fruits of the Spirit. As believers in Jesus Christ seek to avoid sin and sincerely desire to be led by his Holy Spirit, there can be a slow but predictable growth in self-control and a steady decline in anger and hostility. Committing one's life to the Spirit's control on a daily basis can be an effective approach to the prevention of destructive anger.

Conclusions about Anger

Within recent years, Christian psychologists have had an increasing interest in the integration of psychology and the Bible. Books and articles have been written to discuss integration on the theoretical level,[54] but there is also interest in more practical integration. Can biblical teachings and psychological insights combine to help people cope more effectively with the problems of life?

The answer surely is yes. In this chapter, our discussion of anger has shown that the Bible and psychology can combine to increase our understanding of anger, and can help counselors to be more effective in working with people who struggle with anger and self-control.

Suggestions for Further Reading

* Augsburger, David. *Caring Enough to Confront: The Love-Fight.* Glendale, CA: Regal, 1973.

Layden, Milton. *Escaping the Hostility Trap.* Englewood Cliffs, NJ: Prentice Hall, 1977.

Southard, Samuel. *Anger in Love.* Philadelphia: Westminster, 1973.

* Wright, H. Norman. *The Christian Use of Emotional Power.* Old Tappan, NJ: Revell, 1974.

Footnotes

1. Milton Layden, *Escaping the Hostility Trap* (Englewood Cliffs, NJ: Prentice Hall, 1977), p. 2.

2. James M. Boice, *God the Redeemer* (Downers Grove, IL: Inter-Varsity Press, 1978), p. 95.

3. Leon Morris, *The Apostolic Preaching of the Cross* (Grand Rapids: Wm. B. Eerdmans, 1956), pp. 162, 163. Examples of God's righteous wrath include Nah. 1:2, 3, 6–8; Ps. 2:5–9; Amos 5:18–20; Rom. 1:18.

4. Ps. 95:11; Mark 3:5.

5. "Wrath and love are mutually inclusive, not exclusive in God . . . , the wrath of God arises from his love and mercy," writes G. Stahlin in *Theological Dictionary of the New Testament,* ed. Gerhard Friedrich (Grand Rapids: Wm. B. Eerdmans, 1967), 5:425. See also John E. Pedersen, "Some Thoughts on a Biblical View of Anger," *Journal of Psychology and Theology,* 2 (Summer 1974): 210–15.

6. Boice, *God the Redeemer,* p. 105.

7. Isa. 48:9; Ps. 130:3, 4; Dan. 9:9; 2 Pet. 3:9. See also Pss. 10 and 73 where God's justice against the wicked is withheld temporarily.

8. Rom. 2:5; 1 Thess. 1:10, 2:1b. See also Revelation, especially chapter 6 and following.

9. For example, Eccles. 7:9; Prov. 16:32, 22:24, 25; Matt. 5:22; Gal. 5:20; Eph. 4:26, 31; Col. 3:8; James 1:19, 20.

10. Eph. 4:27.

11. Mark 3:5.

12. Jay E. Adams, *The Christian Counselor's Manual* (Nutley, NJ: Presbyterian and Reformed Publishing Company, 1973), pp. 349–50.

13. Eccles. 7:9.

14. Ps. 37:8; Prov. 16:32.

15. Charles E. Cerling, Jr., "Anger: Musings of a Theologian/Psychologist," *Journal of Psychology and Theology* 2 (Winter, 1974): 12–17. See also the response to this article by Pederson (cf. footnote 5 above), and Cerling's reply: "Some Thoughts on a Biblical View of Anger: A Reply," *Journal of Psychology and Theology* 2 (Fall, 1974): 266–68.

16. John T. Hower, "The Misunderstanding and Mishandling of Anger," *Journal of Psychology and Theology* 2 (Fall, 1974): 269–75.

17. Ibid., p. 272.

18. Rom. 12:19; 14:4; Eph. 4:31; Heb. 12:15; Matt. 7:1–5.

19. Prov. 14:29; 15:18; 29:11, 20, 22.

20. James 1:19; 3:3–14; 4:1; 5:9.

21. Prov. 27:5, 6; 2 Tim. 4:2; Luke 17:3, 4. See also Paul's sharing which produced sorrow followed by change (2 Cor. 7:8–10).

22. Anger held within is one of the major causes of depression. This is discussed in chapter 7.

23. Prov. 10:18; 26:24.

24. Prov. 15:28.

25. 1 John 1:9; James 5:16; Matt. 6:12; 18:21, 22, 33–35.

26. 1 Pet. 2:23.

27. Prov. 16:32.

28. G. S. Gates, "An Observational Study of Anger," *Journal of Experimental Psychology* 9 (1926): 325–26.

29. Hower, "Misunderstanding Anger," p. 270.

30. Matt. 2:16; Mark 10:14; John 4.

31. L. Dollard et al., *Frustration and Aggression* (New Haven, CT: Yale University Press, 1939).

32. Paul Welter, *How to Help a Friend* (Wheaton: Tyndale, 1978), p. 109.

33. R. M. Goldenson, *The Encyclopedia of Human Behavior,* vol. 1 (New York: Doubleday, 1970), p. 82.

34. Mildred M. Bateman and Joseph S. Jensen, "The Effect of Religious Background on Modes of Handling Anger," *Journal of Social Psychology* 48 (February, 1958): 140.

35. L. Berkowitz, *Aggression* (New York: McGraw-Hill, 1962), p. 103.

36. H. Norman Wright, *The Christian Use of Emotional Power* (Old Tappan, NJ: Revell, 1974).
37. Eph. 4:30, 31.
38. Matt. 5:38–44.
39. 1 John 1:9; James 5:16.
40. 1 John 1:9.
41. Hower, "Misunderstanding Anger," p. 274.
42. Prov. 15:1.
43. See chapter 24.
44. Milton, Layden, *Escaping the Hostility Trap* (Englewood Cliffs, NJ: Prentice Hall, 1977), p. 33. Reprinted by permission.
45. Ibid.
46. Phil. 4:8.
47. Phil. 4:4–11.
48. Gal. 5:18–25.
49. Prov. 22:24, 25.
50. 1 Pet. 1:13; Phil. 4:8.
51. Layden, *Escaping the Hostility Trap,* p. 34.
52. Phil. 4:8.
53. Eph. 4:15. In an excellent discussion of Christian confrontation, see David Augsburger, *Caring Enough to Confront: The Love-Fight* (Glendale, CA: Regal, 1973).
54. See, for example, Gary R. Collins, *The Rebuilding of Psychology: An Integration of Psychology and Christianity* (Wheaton: Tyndale House, 1977).

9

Guilt

GUILT HAS BEEN DESCRIBED AS THE PLACE WHERE RELIGION AND psychology most often meet.[1] Probably there is no other topic which is of equal interest to both theologians and professional counselors, and perhaps no other issue so consistently pervades all of the problem areas discussed in this book. Talk with people who are depressed, lonely, struggling with marriage problems, homosexual, alcoholic, grieving, dealing with middle age, or facing almost any other problem and you will find people who experience guilt as part of their difficulties. One writer has even suggested that guilt in some way is involved in *all* psychological problems.[2]

Guilt is so prevalent in our society that several types have been identified. These can be divided into two categories: objective guilt and subjective guilt. Objective guilt exists apart from our feelings. It occurs when a law has been broken and the lawbreaker *is* guilty even though he or she may not *feel* guilty. Subjective guilt refers to the inner feeling of remorse and self-condemnation which comes because of our actions.[3]

Objective guilt can be divided into four types. First, there is legal guilt. This refers to the violation of the laws of society. The person who drives through a red light or steals from a department store is guilty before the law, whether or not the person is caught and regardless of whether the person feels any remorse.

Social guilt comes when we break an unwritten but socially expected rule. If a person behaves rudely, gossips maliciously, criticizes unkindly or ignores a needy individual, no law has been broken and there may be no feelings of remorse. Nevertheless, the guilty person has violated the social expectations of the other people in his or her society.

A third type of objective guilt is personal guilt. Here the individual violates his or her own personal standards or resists the urgings of conscience. If a father determines to spend each Sunday with the family, for example, he experiences guilt when business keeps him away from home

116

over a weekend. Since personal standards frequently parallel the standards of our neighbors, social and personal guilt often are similar.

Theological guilt, sometimes called true guilt, involves a violation of the laws of God. The Bible describes divine standards for human behavior and when we violate these standards by our actions or thoughts, we are guilty before God whether or not we feel remorse. The Bible calls this condition sin and since all of us are sinners,[4] we are all guilty before God.

Most psychiatrists and psychologists do not admit the existence of theological guilt. To do so would be to admit that there are absolute moral standards. If there are absolute standards there must be a standard-setter; that is, a God. For many, it is easier to believe that right and wrong are relative—dependent on one's own experiences, training and subjective values. This, as we shall see, has great implications for counseling.

Most people feel uncomfortable when they break a civil law (legal guilt), act in contrast to social expectations (social guilt), violate a personal standard (personal guilt) and/or deliberately ignore God (theological guilt). It is possible to do all of these, however, and never feel guilty. The hardened criminal may murder and feel no sadness or remorse. Millions of people, including professed Christians, forget God every day and thus sin against him. These people *are* guilty before God but they do not *feel* guilt because of their actions. This brings us to the second major category of guilt.

Subjective guilt is the uncomfortable feeling of regret, remorse, shame and self-condemnation which often comes when we have done or thought something which we feel is wrong, or failed to do something which should have been done. Often there is discouragement, anxiety, fear of punishment and a sense of isolation, all tied together as part of the guilt feeling. According to Narramore, these subjective feelings fall into three categories: a fear of punishment, a loss in self-esteem, and a feeling of loneliness, rejection or isolation.[5] Such guilt feelings are not always bad. They can stimulate us to change our behavior and seek forgiveness from God and others. But guilt feelings can also be destructive, inhibitory influences which make life miserable.

Subjective guilt feelings may be strong or weak, appropriate or inappropriate. Appropriate guilt feelings arise when we have broken a law or violated the dictates of our conscience and feel remorse in proportion to the seriousness of our actions. Inappropriate guilt feelings are out of proportion to the seriousness of the act. Some people, for example, can steal and murder but feel very little guilt while others may be immobilized with guilt in response to some minor act or unkind thought.

All of this emphasizes that guilt is a big subject. In counseling it is important to distinguish objective from subjective guilt, although most counselees will be concerned about the latter. It also is important to understand the biblical teaching about guilt.

The Bible and Guilt

When modern people speak about guilt they usually are referring to subjective guilt feelings, but the Bible never uses guilt in this way. The words which usually are translated "guilt" or "guilty" refer to the theological guilt which was described above. A person is guilty, in the biblical sense, when he or she has broken God's law. In the Bible, therefore, there is little difference between guilt and sin.[6]

This has significant implications for Christian counselors. The Bible does not talk about guilt feelings and in no place does it even imply that we should try to motivate people by making them feel guilty. But this is exactly the approach used by many speakers and preachers who sincerely want to help people change. Non-Christian counselors have been critical of such tactics, arguing with considerable validity that Christianity arouses unhealthy guilt feelings.

But how can we lead people to a place of repentance without creating considerable guilt feelings? To answer we must understand the concepts of constructive sorrow and divine forgiveness.

Constructive sorrow is a term suggested by Bruce Narramore[7] and based on 2 Corinthians 7:8–10. In that passage, Paul contrasts "worldly sorrow," which seems equivalent to guilt feelings, and "sorrow that is according to the will of God." This latter sorrow is "constructive sorrow" because it leads to constructive change.

Narramore illustrates this by describing a situation in which two people are having coffee and one accidentally spills coffee in the other person's lap. A typical guilt feeling reaction would be, "How stupid of me. Look at the mess I've made. I'm sorry." The offender feels foolish and is self-critical. Constructive sorrow is different. The offender might say, "I'm sorry. Here are some napkins to clean up," and later offer to pay the cleaning bill. Table 9-1 contrasts psychological guilt with constructive sorrow. The former is self-condemning and nonbiblical; the latter is scriptural and healthy.

Divine forgiveness is a major biblical theme, especially in the New Testament. Jesus Christ came to die so that sinful human beings could be forgiven and restored to complete fellowship with God.[8]

While some passages of Scripture mention forgiveness without discussing repentance, other passages imply that at least two conditions must be met before God forgives. First we must repent. "For Him to forgive without requiring repentance would be like condoning sin or being indifferent to it."[9] Secondly, we must be willing to forgive others.[10] Jesus mentions this at least three times in the Bible. A man or woman, "must forgive others to be forgiven by God. This requirement evidently rests on the genuineness of one's repentance. A person who seeks forgiveness but does not forgive others hardly knows what he is asking for and is not worthy of it."[11]

TABLE 9-1
Comparison of Psychological Guilt and Constructive Sorrow *

	Psychological Guilt	Constructive Sorrow
Person in primary focus	Yourself	God or others
Attitudes or actions in primary focus	Past misdeeds	Damage done to others or our future correct deeds
Motivation for change (if any)	To avoid feeling bad (guilt feelings)	To help others, to promote our growth, or to do God's will (love feelings)
Attitude toward oneself	Anger and frustration	Love and respect combined with concern
Result	a) External change (for improper motivations) b) Stagnation due to paralyzing effect of guilt c) Further rebellion	Repentance and change based on an attitude of love and mutual respect

* From Narramore, S.B., "Guilt: Christian motivation or neurotic masochism." *Journal of Psychology and Theology,* 1974, vol. 2, p. 188.

The emphasis on constructive sorrow and the promise of divine forgiveness have relevance for the counselor who seeks to help both those who have objective guilt and those who experience subjective guilt feelings.

The Causes of Guilt

Objective guilt comes because we have violated legal, social, personal, and/or theological laws and moral standards. It is rare that anyone comes for counseling solely because of objective guilt. Either the guilty person has been caught and thus fears punishment, or the person is experiencing subjective feelings of guilt.

Why do people feel guilty? There can be several reasons.

1. *Past Learning and Unrealistic Personal Expectations.* Individual standards of what is right and wrong, or good and bad, usually develop in childhood. For some parents the standards are so rigid and so high that the child almost never succeeds. There is little if any praise or encouragement because the parents are never satisfied. Instead the child is blamed, condemned, criticized and punished so frequently that he or she is made to feel like a constant failure. As a result, there is self-blame, self-criticism, inferiority and persisting guilt feelings, all because the child has learned a set of standards, sometimes impossible to reach. While parents most often express these standards, sometimes they come

from churches which believe in the attainment of "sinless perfection."

As they grow older, children take over parental and theological standards. They expect perfection in themselves, set up standards which never can be reached, and slide into feelings of guilt and self-blame following the inevitable failures. Guilt feelings are one of the ways in which we both punish ourselves and push ourselves to keep trying to do better. The "workaholic," for example, often is influenced by feelings of guilt. Convinced that he or she is not producing enough or not "redeeming the time," the workaholic keeps working in an attempt to accomplish more and to keep from feeling guilty.

The answer to the problems of unrealistic standards is the adoption of realistic standards. God expects us to keep pressing on toward the goal of Christian maturity,[12] but surely he whose Son came to give us abundant life does not want us always to wallow in self-condemnation and guilt feelings. Such an attitude has no biblical basis. Love should motivate us—not guilt.

2. *Inferiority and Social Pressure.* It is difficult to determine whether a feeling of inferiority creates guilt feelings, or whether the guilt feelings produce inferiority. In his widely influential book *Guilt and Grace* Paul Tournier titles the first chapter "Inferiority and Guilt." He argues that there can be no clear line of demarcation between guilt and inferiority since "all inferiority is experienced as guilt." [13]

But why do people feel inferior? This is discussed more fully in chapter 24, but clearly our self-concept is greatly influenced by the opinions and criticisms of others.

> In everyday life we are continually soaked in this unhealthy atmosphere of mutual criticism, so much so that we are not always aware of it and we find ourselves drawn unwittingly into an implacable vicious circle: every reproach evokes a feeling of guilt in the critic as much as in the one criticized, and each one gains relief from his guilt in any way he can, by criticizing other people and in self-justification. . . . Social suggestion is then the source of innumerable feelings of guilt.[14]

3. *Faulty Conscience Development.* "Let your conscience be your guide" is a popular ethical principle, but it fails to recognize that consciences differ greatly from person to person. Although the word "conscience" does not occur in the Old Testament, it is used frequently in the writings of Paul, who notes that consciences are built on universal, divinely given moral principles which are "written in" human hearts,[15] and probably placed in us by God before we are able even to think about right or wrong. But the conscience can be "seared"—dulled into insensitivity by persistent involvement in sin.[16] Consciences can be weak, and they can be strengthened.[17] Clearly, therefore, the conscience can be altered by the actions [18] and teachings of others.

Beginning with Freud, psychologists and psychiatrists have maintained that the conscience is molded early in life by the prohibitions and expectations of parents. The child learns how to act in ways which will bring praise and avoid punishment.

At this early stage in life, the child also learns about guilt.[19] When parents are good models of what they want to teach; when the home is warm, predictable and secure, and when there is more emphasis on approval and giving encouragement than on punishment and criticism— then the child knows what it means to experience forgiveness. But when there are poor parental models, and/or moral training which is punitive, critical, fear-ridden or highly demanding, then the child becomes angry, rigid, critical and burdened by a continuing sense of guilt.

As children grow older there comes a shift away from the belief that something is right or wrong simply "because my parents and church said so," and a move toward a personal commitment to ideals which "I believe, in my own heart, to be right." Such maturing, according to psychologist Lars Granberg,

> is not a matter of ridding oneself of his childhood conscience, which usually contains much of real value. Parental instruction instills the practical morality of the family and society along with moral principles and ideals. Conscience maturity begins in earnest in adolescence and is furthered by a climate that encourages both (1) personal commitment to Christ and to His moral priorities and (2) reflection upon one's experience and motives so as to build a personal hierarchy of Christian values and goals. Reflection is stimulated when one's moral habits or values are challenged by competing values, provided the person is not fear-ridden and merely avoids the issues through automatic response. . . . A mature Christian conscience is furthered by sound instruction in the Bible, an open and supportive climate of inquiry which encourages honest expression of opinion and thoughtful appraisal of experience, good adult models after whom to pattern oneself, and a grasp both of the reality of forgiveness and the proper fruit of repentance: getting up and going on without wallowing in self-recrimination.[20]

This is an ideal which many people do not experience. Trained to think rigidly about right and wrong, convinced of one's own imperfections and incompetence, fearful of failures or punishment, and lacking in the awareness of God's complete forgiveness, these people are constantly plagued with guilt feelings. These guilt feelings come not because of sorrow for sin or regret over law-breaking. They are signs that the person is preoccupied with a fear of punishment, isolation, or lowered self-esteem. To bolster oneself, such people often are rigid, critical of others, unforgiving, afraid of making moral decisions, domineering, and inclined to assert an attitude of moral superiority. They are difficult people to have in the church, but often they are angry, unhappy people who need help and understanding more than criticism.

4. *Supernatural Influences.* Prior to the Fall it appears that Adam and

Eve had no conscience, no knowledge of good or evil, and no sense of guilt.[21] Immediately after their disobedience, however, they realized that they had done wrong and tried to hide from God.[22] Objective theological guilt and subjective guilt feelings had entered God's creation.

As the rest of the Bible shows, God's standards are high and people fool themselves if they pretend to be without sin.[23] An awareness of guilt, therefore, can come from the promptings of the Holy Spirit.[24] Such an awareness is for our own cleansing and growth.

Might it be that Satan also creates guilt feelings? The Bible states that he accuses God's followers, at least before God,[25] and we know that he tempts us, and tries to make us stumble. Adam and Eve would not have known guilt if Satan had left them alone, and it is surely probable that he stimulates believers to feel guilty and unforgiven, even when we have done nothing wrong.

The Effects of Guilt

Objective guilt can have a variety of consequences. As stated previously, breaking the law can create subjective guilt feelings but this does not always happen. Evil disobedience can lead to arrest and conviction, but when the offender is not caught, he or she is still guilty even though there never is a trial. Social guilt may bring criticism from other people but little else. Theological guilt, however, is not so easily dismissed. God, who is just and holy, does not wink at sin or miss seeing acts of disobedience. The ultimate punishment for sin is death—although God pardons and gives eternal life to those who put their faith in Jesus Christ, who died to pay for our sins.[26] Sometimes it appears that lawbreakers will avoid punishment, but God will bring justice in the end.[27]

Most counselors see the effects not of objective guilt, but of subjective guilt feelings. These influence people in several ways.

1. *Defensive Reactions.* General psychology books often describe "defense mechanisms." These are ways of thinking which most people use to avoid anxiety, and it may be that, to some extent, all defense mechanisms protect us from feelings of guilt.[28] If we blame others (projection), for example, or withdraw, we can avoid facing our own responsibility for guilt-arousing thoughts or actions. Sometimes when guilt feelings begin to arise, we get angry at others, try to justify our behavior, deny our responsibility, or even apologize profusely.

2. *Self-condemnation Reactions.* Guilt feelings almost always stimulate self-condemnation in the form of anxiety; feelings of inferiority, inadequacy, weakness, low esteem, pessimism and insecurity. Sometimes there is self-punishment: the person acts like a martyr pushed around by others. Sometimes there is a "poor-little-me-I-don't-deserve-to-be-treated-well" attitude. For others there is an inability to relax, a refusal to accept compliments, a sexual inhibition, an unwillingness to say "no" to the demands

of others, or an avoidance of leisure activities—all because the person feels guilty and unable to accept forgiveness. Often there is anger which is held within and unexpressed. This can lead the person into depression, sometimes with thoughts of suicide. Even accident-proneness can accompany guilt feelings. Some believe that this is an unconscious attempt at self-punishment.

3. *Social Reactions*. All of these self-condemning thoughts and actions alienate the guilt-plagued person from others. None of us enjoys being with people who wallow in self-condemnation. For a while we try to argue and prove that the self-critical person is not as bad as stated. When our arguments fall on deaf ears, however, we tend to give up. This moves the guilt-bothered person into loneliness and alienation from people, and this in turn stimulates a tendency to criticize the actions of others.

4. *Physical Reactions*. Whenever tension builds in a person and is not released, the body weakens and eventually breaks down. Some psychiatrists view this as a form of self-punishment. Psychologically and emotionally it is easier to tolerate physical pain than the burden of guilt that would otherwise attract our attention.[29]

5. *Repentance and Forgiveness*. The effects of guilt feelings are not all negative. Some people have learned to accept mistakes, to grow from them, to confess to God and others, and to rest content in the assurance that "if we confess our sins, He is faithful and righteous to forgive us our sins and to cleanse us from all unrighteousness."[30]

Counseling and Guilt

In dealing with guilt the Christian counselor has an advantage over the nonbeliever. Guilt is a moral issue and guilt feelings arise from moral failures. Few secular counselor training programs discuss morals and the counselor who does not believe in God must somehow deal with values, forgiveness, atonement and related theological issues about which there is little understanding and no formal training. Psychological approaches have centered around helping people express anger, make restitution, lower their standards or expectations, improve their performance and get insight into their behavior. Regretfully these are stopgap efforts at best, and it is probable that they rarely bring permanent change.

Several years ago, a highly respected psychologist wrote a controversial book which argued that "man sickens in mind, soul, and perhaps even body because of unconfessed and unatoned real guilt."[31] Mental illness, this author proposed, is really moral illness that can only be cured by confession to significant other people and by the making of restitution. The writer, O. Hobart Mowrer, did not claim to be a Christian and his book attacked some basic Christian doctrines (such as the substitutionary atonement and the concept of original sin) but he challenged counselors and pastors alike to acknowledge the central place of sin and forgiveness in counseling. A decade later, psychiatrist Karl Menninger expressed similar ideas in a book with the intriguing title, *Whatever Became of Sin?* [32]

Regretfully, these books were written from a humanistic perspective, and although they used theological language they failed to acknowledge the biblical truths about confession, forgiveness and justification. These concepts must be in the thinking of every Christian counselor who attempts to help those with guilt feelings.

1. *Understanding and Acceptance.* People with guilt feelings often condemn themselves and expect to be condemned by others. As a result they sometimes come to counseling with either a self-defensive or a self-blaming attitude.

The attitude of Jesus must have surprised the woman who had been caught in the act of adultery.[33] She was objectively guilty and perhaps feeling guilty, but Jesus was not like the others who wanted to condemn her. He did not condone her sin—it clearly was wrong—but he talked kindly to her and told her to sin no more.

One of the most important things to remember in reducing guilt is never to minimize or criticize the feeling.[34]

Guilt feelings hurt, and the counselor should show a willingness to understand without condemning or expecting that the feelings can be stopped at will.

2. *Insight.* People often can be helped if they have some understanding of the forces which are influencing them within. You might discuss issues such as the following with the counselee, trying to find specific examples for each conclusion.

—What were parental expectations of right and wrong?
--Were standards so high that the child could never succeed?
—What happened when there was failure?
—What is the counselee's experience with forgiveness?
—Were blame, criticism and punishment frequent?
—What did the church teach about right and wrong?
—Was there biblical basis for these teachings?
—Was the counselee made to feel guilty?
—What makes the counselee feel guilty today? Be specific.
—Does the counselee show any of the defensive reactions, self-condemnation, social reactions, or physical reactions described above?

The purpose of such discussion is to help the counselee recognize how his or her guilt feelings arose from past moral training. It often will be true that the counselee has the fear of punishment, low self-esteem and feelings of rejection mentioned earlier. He or she may be striving to act in ways or accomplish goals which are impossible. At times you may wish to ask, "Who says you have to accomplish the goals or meet the standards you have set for yourself? What will happen if you don't reach these goals? Is there evidence in the Bible that God will not forgive?" It is here that insight merges into spiritual teaching.

3. *Education*. This has been called "re-educating the conscience"[35]—
a process which may take a long time. First, the counselee must be helped
to reexamine his or her standards of right or wrong. Often people feel
guilty about things the Bible doesn't say are sin. Second, counselees must
learn to ask, "What does God *really* expect of me?" He knows us per-
fectly. He knows that we are merely dust and he recognizes that we will
sin so long as we are on earth.[36] He expects not perfection, but a sincere
attempt to do God's will as we understand it and as best we can. God
is not so much interested in what we are doing, but in who we are and
what we are becoming. He who is compassionate, also loves unconditionally and will forgive our sins without demanding atonement and
penance. Atonement and penance are no longer necessary because Christ
has already paid for human sins "once for all, the just for the unjust, in
order that He might bring us to God."[37]

This is basic theology which is so relevant and practical that it can
revolutionize and completely free human thinking. The ultimate solution
to guilt and guilt feelings is to honestly admit guilt, confess sin to Christ
and at times to others,[38] and then to believe with divine help that we are
forgiven and accepted by the God of the universe. It is he who in turn
helps us to accept, love and forgive both ourselves and others.

4. *Repentance and Forgiveness*. It is possible to understand biblical
teachings but to never act on the knowledge. It is not the counselor's task
to force people to pray, to confess, and to ask God to forgive. For some
counselees it may take awhile to reach that point and the counselor must
be content to pray privately for the counselee and continue to work at
accepting and helping the guilt-ridden person to understand these principles more clearly. The view that we earn divine favor by good works and
that we pay for our sins by undergoing punishment is so widespread that
it dies slowly. But the Bible teaches that repentance and confession are
all we need to obtain forgiveness. Failure to understand this basic tenet
of Christianity has caused countless people, including Christians, to experience unhealthy guilt feelings which lead to worry, depression, loss of
inner peace, fear, low self-esteem, loneliness, and a sense of alienation
from God.[39]

Preventing Guilt

For many years counselors have emphasized and perhaps overempha-
sized the importance of early experience on later behavior. In this chapter
we have seen how early moral teaching and parental expectations can have
profound influence on the child's later thinking about right and wrong.
The place to start the prevention of unhealthy guilt feelings, therefore,
is with parents.

In the church we can teach the biblical doctrine of forgiveness. Help
Christians to realize that God understands our weaknesses, that he forgives freely and lovingly helps us to grow and mature as we walk through

life. Show the difference between guilt feelings and constructive sorrow. Then encourage people to examine their own self-expectations and standards of right and wrong. Are these unrealistic and unbiblical? Remember that two good ways to learn about forgiveness are to practice it and to experience it. If church people can seek God's help in forgiving one another [40] there can be a reduction in bitterness and in the refusal to understand or accept forgiveness from God.

Next, teach parents that children learn not only what we teach; they also learn from the climate in which the teaching occurs. If we are rigid, condemning, demanding and unforgiving, the children feel like constant failures. This does much to instill prolonged guilt feelings. Parents can prevent unhealthy guilt feelings and encourage conscience development in their children, if the parents have some understanding of conscience development as outlined in this chapter. Teach them to instill in their children a commitment to Scripture, and stress discipline which points out failure but also includes abundant love, encouragement and forgiveness.

Teaching the doctrine of forgiveness and teaching the principles of conscience development—these are two ways to prevent unhealthy guilt feelings. Since guilt feelings are tied so intimately with self-esteem, it also can be helpful to follow the prevention guidelines listed in chapter 24.

Finally, there is the issue of obedience. When we attempt to obey the law, meet social expectations, and do what God wants, we are less likely to experience objective guilt. This in turn prevents the development of many subjective guilt feelings.

In all of this it must be remembered that guilt feelings in themselves are not all bad. Sometimes they stimulate us to confess sin and to act more effectively. When they persist as paralyzing influences, however, they are harmful. It is such harmful guilt feelings that we seek to prevent and eliminate.

Conclusions about Guilt

When Jesus talked to the woman caught in adultery he never relaxed his standards. God's standards are perfect and he never settles for imperfection. The woman was told to sin no more and hopefully her life style changed radically.

But she surely never reached perfection. None of us do. Nevertheless we are accepted completely by God, forgiven unconditionally, and assured that someday we will reach divine standards because of the work of Christ.

Throughout the pages of this book the biblical teachings on human problems are discussed. Perhaps in no chapter, however, is Christian theology more relevant. Because God forgives, we are forgiven, our guilt is removed, and a way is provided to deal with guilt feelings.

Suggestions for Further Reading

Belgum, David. *Guilt: Where Religion and Psychology Meet.* Minneapolis: Augsburg, 1963.
Knight, James A. *Conscience and Guilt.* New York: Appleton-Century-Crofts, 1969.
* Narramore, S. Bruce, and Counts, Bill. *Guilt and Freedom.* Santa Ana: Vision House, 1974.
* Tournier, Paul. *Guilt and Grace.* New York: Harper & Row, 1962.

Footnotes

1. G. Belgum, *Guilt: Where Religion and Psychology Meet* (Minneapolis: Augsburg, 1970).
2. S. Bruce Narramore, "Guilt: Where Theology and Psychology Meet," *Journal of Psychology and Theology* 2 (1974): 18–25.
3. This discussion of objective and subjective guilt is adopted from an earlier work by the author: Gary R. Collins, *Overcoming Anxiety* (Santa Ana: Vision House, 1973), pp. 63–66.
4. Isa. 53:6; Rom. 3:23.
5. Narramore, "Guilt: Where Theology and Psychology Meet," p. 22.
6. L. R. Keylock, "Guilt," in *The Zondervan Pictorial Encyclopedia of the Bible,* ed. Merrill C. Tenney (Grand Rapids: Zondervan, 1975), 2:852.
7. S. Bruce Narramore, "Guilt: Christian Motivation or Neurotic Masochism," *Journal of Psychology and Theology* 2 (1974): 182–89.
8. 1 Pet. 1:24.
9. 1 John 1:9. The quotation is from P. H. Monsma, "Forgiveness," in *The Zondervan Pictorial Encyclopedia of the Bible,* ed. Merrill C. Tenney, 2:599.
10. Matt. 6:12, 18:21f.
11. Monsma, "Forgiveness."
12. Phil. 3:12–16.
13. Paul Tournier, *Guilt and Grace* (New York: Harper & Row, 1962), p. 24.
14. Ibid., pp. 15, 16, 18.
15. Rom. 2:18.
16. 1 Tim. 4:2.
17. 1 Cor. 8:10–12.
18. 1 Cor. 10:28, 29.
19. Much of the following discussion is adopted from L. I. Granberg, "Conscience," in *The Zondervan Pictorial Encyclopedia of the Bible,* ed. Merrill C. Tenney, 1:943–45.
20. Ibid., p. 941.
21. Gen. 2:17; 3:4, 5, 22. See S. Bruce Narramore, "Guilt: Its Universal Hidden Presence," *Journal of Psychology and Theology* 2 (1974): 104–15.
22. Gen. 3:8.
23. 1 John 1:8–10.
24. John 16:8, 13; 14:26.
25. Job 1:9–11; Rev. 12:10.
26. Rom. 6:23.
27. Ps. 73.
28. Narramore, "Guilt: Its Universal Presence."
29. O. Quentin Hyder, *The Christian's Handbook of Psychiatry* (Old Tappan, NJ: Revell, 1971), p. 114.
30. 1 John 1:9.
31. O. Hobart Mowrer, *The Crisis in Psychiatry and Religion* (Princeton: Van Nostrand, 1961), p. 82.

32. Karl Menninger, *Whatever Became of Sin?* (New York: Hawthorn, 1973).

33. John 8:3–11.

34. S. Bruce Narramore, "Guilt: Three Models of Therapy," *Journal of Psychology and Theology* 2 (1974): 263.

35. S. Bruce Narramore and Bill Counts, *Guilt and Freedom* (Santa Ana: Vision House, 1974), p. 154.

36. 1 Sam. 16:7; Pss. 103:14; 139:1–4; 1 John 1:8.

37. 1 Pet. 3:18.

38. 1 John 1:9; James 5:16.

39. Hyder, *Christian's Handbook,* p. 104.

40. Eph. 4:32.

Part III
Singleness-
Marriage
Issues

10
Singleness

QUOTING STATISTICS OFTEN CAN BE DANGEROUS. THE FIGURES ARE quickly outdated and sometimes they are biased—depending on who presents them. It is safe to state, however, that the number of single adults is astronomical. In the United States alone, roughly forty-three million people, one out of three adults, are unmarried. This includes those never married (twenty-two million at last count) and those formerly married who have lost a spouse through death or divorce. It includes parents without partners, ten million widows, people who have chosen not to marry and others whose lives are spent waiting for the day when they will walk to the altar. These figures say nothing about the number of single people in other parts of the world. And they do not include husbands and wives whose marriages have grown so cold and distant that the spouses live isolated lives which could almost be classified as single.

Singleness sometimes is seen as a swinging, no-strings-attached, carefree life style. For many singles nothing could be further from the truth. In our society people walk in pairs. If you're alone, you're seen as a misfit, an oddball, an embarrassment to married friends who don't always trust you and aren't always sure how or whether to include you in their activities. Plagued by loneliness, insecurity, low self-esteem, and sometimes rejection, singles face frequent reminders that they are out of step with society. Single people pay higher taxes, and often have difficulty getting credit, insurance, loans, job promotions or even decent seating in a good restaurant.[1] Meeting other singles is a problem. Contacts in singles bars or night spots can be fleeting and destructive, so some people turn to the church. Many singles find, however, that they are unwelcome, or at best tolerated by church members who don't understand, don't know how to relate to singles, and sometimes blatantly reject unmarried people—especially if they are divorced. Of course many singles live fulfilled, meaningful, productive lives. Consider Jesus, for example. But many others find it difficult to be single and for them counseling can often be helpful.

131

The Bible and Singleness

In the world's history, Adam was the first person to experience single-ness, but it didn't last long. God declared that it is "not good for the man to be alone," [2] so woman was created and Adam became the first married man. Clearly, marriage was God's intention for the human race. He expected that a man and woman would unite together for companionship, sexual fulfillment, perpetuation of the human race, and partnership in using and controlling the environment.

But God knew that in our sinful state, a happy blissful marriage would not be the experience of everyone. The tendency for males to die earlier than females and the influence of wars which often reduce the male population both insure that there never will be enough men for all of the women in the world. In addition, many people fear intimacy with the opposite sex, some lose spouses in death, others experience marital breakups and still others—like Jesus—choose not to marry. Surely these people are not "unnatural" because they are unmarried.

Two passages of Scripture support this conclusion and indicate that the single state is a special gift which God bestows on selected people—including some who aren't too enthusiastic about receiving the present.

In Matthew 19, Jesus was asked about marriage and divorce. He emphasized God's high view of marriage, but he realistically acknowledged that marriages sometimes end in divorce. Then he pointed out that single-ness is a gift [3] given only to certain people.

The Apostle Paul elaborated on this in more detail in 1 Corinthians 7. This chapter talks about sex and presents a high view of marriage, but the writer also considers singleness. Once again there is the implication that singleness is a gift [4] and then Paul writes in positive terms about the single life style. Marriage, he says, is fine but singleness is even better:

> If you should marry, you have not sinned; and if a virgin should marry, she has not sinned. Yet such will have trouble in this life, and I am trying to spare you. . . . I want you to be free from concern. One who is unmarried is concerned about the things of the Lord, how he may please the Lord; but one who is married is concerned about the things of the world, how he may please his wife, and his interests are divided. And the woman who is unmarried, and the virgin, is concerned about the things of the Lord, that she may be holy both in body and spirit; but one who is married is concerned about the things of the world, how she may please her husband. And I say this for your own benefit; not to put a restraint upon you, but . . . to secure undistracted devotion to the Lord. [5]

Free of the greater responsibilities and financial pressures that often come with marriage, Paul here elevates the single life as a way of living where the person can give undivided devotion to Christ.

But how many Christian singles view life like this? Instead of "undistracted devotion to the Lord," many (not all) put a major emphasis on bemoaning their fate, wondering where they fit in society, struggling with feelings of inadequacy, and/or trying to find a mate. This gets us to the problems of singleness.

The Causes of Singleness Problems

Why are people single and what causes singleness problems? To answer these questions we might look at the major groupings of single people. While every single adult has either never married or was formerly married, we can identify five categories of singles, each of which has a somewhat unique set of challenges connected with being single.

1. *Some Have Not Yet Found a Mate.* Apparently within recent years there has been a growing trend for young adults, especially women, to postpone marriage until there has been opportunity to travel, to get established in a career, or to otherwise experience the freedom of adulthood before settling into the married state. Students in long training programs, young military personnel, individuals whose work involves traveling, or people getting started in the business world are among those who have every intention of getting married but who decide to "wait a few years." These singles face many of the problems that concern all unmarried people, but often there is a healthy outlook because singleness is more a result of choice than of circumstances.

Nevertheless, there is the danger of slipping into a waiting mentality which says, "I can't make any plans on my own or shouldn't make major decisions because I might have to change if I get married to someone whose ideas and goals are different." Such an attitude may be strengthened by well-meaning friends who imply that life isn't complete until one is married. This is an attitude which can immobilize single people into always living in the future, waiting for the time when marriage will come to somehow make life complete.

2. *Some Choose Not to Marry.* This may be a deliberate decision to remain single or it may come as a gradual awareness and acceptance of the fact that marriage is unlikely. Often there are very good reasons for choosing to remain single: a conviction that this is God's calling, a realization that "the right person hasn't come along," a desire for continuing freedom, a sincere lack of interest in marriage or a shortage of eligible marriage partners. Others may conclude that singleness is preferable because they fear intimacy, have had bad experiences with marriage, or feel shy and self-conscious.

That one should choose singleness, however, is often not understood by onlookers, including church members, who sometimes conclude either that the single person must have problems (e.g., "He's probably gay" or "She's afraid to leave her mother"). At times single persons feel pressured to change their decision and to enter into a relationship which they might not want and for which they may feel unsuited. Even without such pressures, singles-by-choice usually wonder, at times, if the conclusions of others might be true. "Perhaps I *am* afraid, gay, too choosy, or a social misfit," such people may think. These possibilities must be considered honestly and evaluated realistically. Otherwise they can quietly plague the unmarried person for years.

3. *Some Have Had Marriages Break Up.* These, of course, are the separated and divorced. If the marriage has been unhappy for a long time, its ending may bring at least a temporary sense of relief. But there are also problems, most of which are discussed more fully in chapter 14. These include loneliness, a sense of failure and guilt, struggles with the transition from marriage back to singleness, difficulties with self-image, bitterness, and frequently criticism or social ostracism from others, including intolerant nonforgiving church members.

4. *Some Have Lost a Mate.* This can bring pain, loneliness and so great a sense of loss that only those who have had similar experiences can really understand. When death occurs, relatives and friends reach out to offer support and sympathy (which is something that divorced people often do not get), but the grief persists long after the funeral is over, the flowers have wilted and the friends have gone back to their regular routines. There is continuing sadness, emptiness, and the pressures of learning to live alone or to make decisions that previously were shared. Grief is discussed in detail in chapter 28.

5. *Some Have Other Reasons for Singleness.* Overlapping with the above categories are those situations which reduce the likelihood of marriage and thereby contribute to singleness. These include:

—illnesses and handicaps, both physical and mental, which greatly reduce the person's potential for marriage and which would hinder a satisfying relationship with some person of the opposite sex;

—fears of intimacy, including unrealistic views of what members of the opposite sex are like;

—immaturity, including an inability to give, and an unwillingness to accept responsibility;

—homosexuality, real or imagined, which sometimes motivates people to spend life alone and at other times leads them into same-sex relationships that have no legal or economic ties, little social sanction, and great potential for breakup with subsequent pain and loneliness.

The Effects of Singleness

It is important to emphasize that singleness in itself is not a problem for all unmarried people. Just as some married people have marriage problems while others do not, so some singles have singleness-related problems which do not concern every unmarried person. The difficulties which do arise include the following, all of which may come up in counseling sessions with singles.

1. *Problems with Loneliness.* In preparing this chapter, I consulted numerous articles and over twenty books on the subject of singleness.

The loneliness of singles is the one topic discussed in every one of these references. While some writers argue that singles, as a group, are no lonelier than unhappily married people, there is general agreement that intense feelings of aloneness frequently engulf single people. This is especially true of persons who have lost or been rejected by mates, and people who live alone.

John R. W. Stott was once asked about the problems of being single. He replied that the first problem is "the tendency to personal loneliness. Any single person knows more about loneliness than somebody who is sharing his life with a wife and family. This has meant that I have needed to cultivate friendships and force myself to spend time in the company of others." [6]

Stott went on to identify another difficulty: "Singleness limits one's ministry in terms of acceptance. There are some people who distrust one's ministry because they feel you don't understand their problems if you're not married." [7] This brings us to a second problem for singles.

2. *Problems of Self-worth.* If other people don't accept you, distrust you, dismiss your opinions, or do not want you for a marriage partner, it is easy to conclude, "I guess I'm not worth much." This idea was reinforced several years ago in a popular song which proclaimed, "You're Nobody 'til Somebody Loves You." Its concluding line, "so find yourself somebody to love," is a philosophy which has led many singles into transient relationships, often sexual in nature, which frequently end in further rejection and lowered self-esteem. Little wonder that a sense of failure, guilt over broken relationships, self-pity, discouragement, and sometimes a tendency to rush into heavy dating (and sometimes into an ill-advised marriage) all can come in an attempt to bolster one's sagging self-worth.

3. *Problems of Identity and Direction.* When we are young and growing up, most of us identify with the family. That is where we belong. It is where we have our economic and emotional needs met. As we grow up, we sever some of these ties. Young adults begin to ask, "Who am I?" "Where am I going?" "What is my purpose in life?"

In a society which assumes that people travel in pairs, it is easy to conclude that life can have no purpose for the person who is alone. Some develop the previously described attitude of doing nothing significant because they are awaiting a hoped-for marriage partner with whom they can plan for the future.

Marriage, however, involves the exchange of one set of challenges and problems for another. Disappointment is likely to come to the single person who is unhappy with life, has no direction and who is waiting to build his or her identity on someone else. Whenever our happiness, purpose in life and self-worth depend almost completely on some one other person, a dependency relationship has developed which can be dangerous and destructive should that other person ever fail, die, or leave. It is healthy, of course, to build mutual relationships and interdependency between people, including a husband and wife. But our identities are formed as we determine our God-given purpose in life, develop our abilities and gifts, and build relationships with a variety of other people. To remain self-centered or to wait inactively for a marriage which will give life a purpose is to insure continued lack of identity or direction.

4. *Problems with Sex.* When God created male and female, he made us with hormones. He made sex a part of human experience and planned that men and women, within marriage, would enjoy each other's companionship and bodies.

But what does the single person do with these God-given sexual urges? In her book on the single life, Margaret Evening writes that "next to the problem of inner loneliness comes the problem of how to cope with sexual gifts and energies, and the finding of a proper outlet for them. No one can presume to give all the answers for no one knows them!" [8]

Some people engage in promiscuous relationships in an attempt to find instant intimacy, to feel loved, to bolster their self-esteem and sometimes to express their anger, especially toward the opposite sex.[9] Others move into homosexual relationships. Undoubtedly many singles, including Christians, fantasize and masturbate at least periodically. Such behaviors often are followed by guilt which complicates but does little to solve the problem of sex for singles.

5. *Problems with Emotions.* Whenever people have problems which cannot be solved to their satisfaction, there is a tendency to become angry. Sometimes the *hostility* is directed toward God, "fate," or other people who may be innocent bystanders. According to the Bible, such bitterness can cause trouble and lead to impure actions.[10] But for many singles the bitterness persists as an angry response to the question, "Why is it that I'm not married?"

Along with the anger there often comes *guilt* over one's thoughts, attitudes, hostilities and actions.

Then there is *fear:* fear of being alone, fear of rejection, fear that one is somehow being punished by God, fear of making unwise decisions.

Once again it is emphasized that these emotions, while common, are not limited to singles, and neither are they characteristic of all unmarried persons.

6. *Miscellaneous Problems.* To this point, nothing has been said about the unique problems of being a single parent who must make the decisions about raising children without the help and support of a mate. We have not stressed the pressures that singles sometimes feel from married people who become matchmakers, who criticize or envy the single life style, and who at times are threatened and unsure how to act in the presence of a single adult, especially a single person of the opposite sex. There are the unique problems of older singles whose social life is constricted by a loss of friends or a failure in health. Then there are the previously mentioned

problems of social prejudice which make it difficult for singles to get housing, insurance, credit, or job promotions.

Counseling Singles

Some of the problems which singles face have been discussed elsewhere in this volume. Loneliness (chapter 6), anger (chapter 8), guilt (chapter 9), choosing a mate (chapter 11), sex (chapter 20), homosexuality (chapter 22), interpersonal relations (chapter 23), and self-esteem (chapter 24) are among the issues which face singles and which may come up in counseling. At such times, counselors are encouraged to consult the appropriate chapter for assistance in meeting the single counselee's needs. In addition, the counselor can consider each of the following:

1. *Evaluate Your Attitude toward Singles.* The counselor is unlikely to be effective if he or she has a negative attitude toward singles, thinks that they are in some way inferior, or feels either envy or threat in the presence of single people. Singles often feel like misfits in the church. They feel unwanted and at times are the objects of a subtle prejudice or not-so-subtle pressures. It must be remembered, therefore, that it is *not true* that all single adults are excessively lonely, frantically looking for a mate, bad credit risks, afraid of intimacy or responsibility, spiritually immature, angry, or wallowing in self-pity. Each single, like every married person, is a unique human being with individual strengths and needs.

2. *Help with Acceptance.* Single counselees need supportive acceptance, a listening ear which will hear their story, and someone who can understand the pain and bitterness without condemning. When a single counselee experiences such acceptance, he or she may be able to honestly face the pain of singleness, to express the frustrations, and to seriously ponder the biblical teaching that the single life is God's special calling for some people. Help the counselee to see that to be single is not necessarily to be second-best or to be doomed to a life of misery and incompleteness. Be realistic enough to acknowledge that loneliness and single-person frustrations are likely to persist, but remind the counselee that the single individual also avoids some of the equally frustrating problems that are faced by married couples. As these issues are discussed be sure to give the counselee ample time to express his or her feelings and ideas. Remember, we don't solve problems *for* people; we solve problems *with* them.

3. *Stimulate Realistic Life Planning.* In addition to facing problems and dealing with them honestly, singles can learn to make some clear plans for the future. There is nothing wrong with a recognition that future marriage could be a real possibility, but it is not healthy to build our lives around events which might occur. Instead, individuals, especially Christians, must learn both to prepare for the future and to live fully in the present. For singles, this involves facing the fact that marriage (or remarriage) may or may not be a possibility. It involves a consideration

and development of one's abilities and gifts, a prayerful pondering of God's will for one's life now, the formulating of long-range and short-term goals, and movement into a plan of action which will make these goals attainable. The counselor can help with these deliberations, challenging the counselee's thinking and encouraging realism. At times singles will need help with such tangible issues as finding a job, balancing a budget, or running a household. This may be a special need for young adults and people who have recently lost a mate. In all of this the goal is first to accept and deal with the problems, then to move in the direction of helping people to be "single and satisfied."

4. *Guide Interpersonal Relationships.* Since the single person has no mate, he or she must be helped to build intimate relationships apart from marriage. On paper this looks easy. In practice it is very difficult.

In an insightful talk on the single person's identity,[11] John Fischer once spoke about two principles for building close relationships: accepting other people as they are without trying to change them, and committing oneself to others in an attempt to learn from and share with one another. When a single male and female communicate like this, however, something soon develops which Fischer calls "weirdness." This is a pressure which creeps in and hinders the relationship because the people involved begin to wonder, "Is this the one? Is this 'That Relationship'?" Without discussing such thinking openly both people get uncomfortable and one person—usually the man—backs away. To avoid this, Fischer suggests that the fears be acknowledged, that the couple openly agree to forget worrying about marriage and that they go on with their nonromantic friendship.

One of the people who heard this suggestion was a woman named Del Fuller. She suggested that for a woman there is a very thin and easily crossed line between *phileo,* the deep but unromantic feelings of a woman for a man, and *eros,* the compelling, dramatic, romantic love. It is hard for a woman to repress or deny the eros but often the situation becomes threatening to the man who is not ready to be involved romantically. According to Fuller,

> . . . the key to the solution of this problem lies not in a woman's fighting the fact that she loves a man, not in trying to love *less* in order to get back to *phileo,* but in trying to love *more,* to get *beyond eros* to *agape,* the kind of love the Lord has for us. The exciting and beautiful thing about *agape* love is finding out that you truly can love someone very deeply and yet allow them complete freedom to respond to you in whatever way God leads them to respond. . . .
>
> What it comes down to, then, is first of all, How much does she really love that man? Does she love him to the point that she wants him to be part of her life, that she needs him in order to be fulfilled and happy? Or does she love him enough that she wants *him* to be happy, even if it means *without* her??

So the next concern is, How much does she trust God? Does she *really* trust him to "supply *all* her needs"? Does she trust his love for her, and his knowledge of what the absolute best is for her, as well as for the one she loves? Because to the degree that she trusts God and yields her heart to him, to the degree that she chooses to be a servant and a vessel of the Lord, and to let him direct her relationships, she can be free from the leech of expectations, and free to let the Lord love that man through her.[12]

This is a high view of love, one that is rarely expressed in books for singles. Counselors must help singles deal not only with "weirdness" but with the challenges of getting along effectively with a variety of people in different situations.

5. *Assisting with Special Singles Problems.* Space permits us to mention only three of the unique problems that singles may bring to a counselor.

(a) Single Parenting. Most parents, at times, feel overwhelmed and frustrated in the task of child-rearing, but singles must experience the frustrations and make the decisions alone.

The single parent needs to express and understand his or her feelings about coping alone. There should be someone against whom decisions can be checked. There must be an awareness that life with only one parent can be difficult for the children, too, so the single parent must try to understand and meet the children's needs. These children should have opportunity to meet adults of each sex and to have contact with two-parent families in order to get a broader perspective on adult and family life. Then there should be honest, open, genuine, loving communication within the home. Insofar as it is possible, the missing parent should be described realistically—not put on a pedestal and not torn down.

All of these suggestions apply equally to the parent in the home and to the parent who has "visiting rights." The children can be enjoyed, but try to avoid frequent weekend fantasy trips, overpermissiveness or overindulgences, all of which can be designed to buy affection or to create a contrast between the two parents. Such activities deny reality and create further tensions. The counselor can help the single parent with these issues.

One effective way is to refer the single parent to other parents who can engage in parent-to-parent counseling. In all of this, the goal is to help single parents put their confidence in God, meet their own needs effectively, and learn to raise their children with love, discipline and understanding.

(b) Meeting Friends. It is well known that singles often find it difficult to meet new friends. Christians (and many nonbelievers as well) are inclined to avoid the search for friends at singles bars, encounter groups or even at many singles clubs. A better alternative is to seek friends in the church, even though many church members tend to reject single adults. Singles, however, can be helped to break down some of this resistance by establishing roots in their communities. This involves becoming established in a home or community (developing an interest in community affairs, and so on), volunteering for activity and responsibility in the church, showing a sincere interest in others of all ages (rather than talking constantly about one's own concerns or interests), and remembering that it is best to develop a variety of friendships, rather than searching for a "one-and-only best friend."

(c) *Waiting on God.* Waiting is not easy, especially in this era of speed, efficiency, and impatience with inconvenience. When things are not happening quickly it may seem easiest to dash out, make decisions, and take action on our own. But the Christian has volunteered to be under the Lordship of Christ and he, who is in no hurry, often makes us wait for our own good. In waiting we can learn patience, can deal with unconfessed sin or with personal problems, and can work to change our attitudes. Waiting does not imply that we sit and do nothing. We act carefully and in accordance with his will so far as this can be determined now. Then we trust that in God's timing, his plans for us will become apparent.

But how does this apply to singles? Some sit around waiting for God to provide a mate, assuming that if they clear away all obstacles and please God enough, then he will provide a reward in the form of a perfect husband or wife. God does not conform to that thinking, however. Single counselees, like married people, must be encouraged to trust God's providence, to wait on him daily and to seek his help in accepting his best for each of our lives.

Preventing Singles Problems

Within recent years, several helpful books have been published dealing with the church's ministry to singles.[13] Such ministries not only meet the needs of singles but help prevent singleness-related problems from developing. Before such an outreach can begin, however, the attitudes of established church members must be challenged.

1. *Focus on Church Attitudes.* As discussed above, single adults sometimes are misfits in the church. There is no place for them, no unique programs to meet their needs, and often no understanding of their struggles—especially if the single person is divorced. These attitudes can be challenged from the pulpit. Married persons can be encouraged to welcome singles into the church and into their homes. It is helpful to remind people that Jesus and Paul were single. They might not be welcome in some churches today and certainly would be unacceptable to many pulpit committees who maintain a strong prejudice against single pastors.

Speaking at the Continental Congress on the Family, Nancy Hardesty argued that a single person must find his or her family in the church.

> As Christians, our sense of security is to be found in our faith in God, not in any temporal, cultural social institution. Our home is the church,

our family the body of believers. No definition of "family" can be called Christian which does not include single people . . . an addition to the twentieth-century, post-Victorian suburban American nuclear family.[14]

There is a place in the church, perhaps, for sweetheart banquets, couples clubs, and family-related church programs, but these too often exclude or "put down" singles. Such an attitude is wrong and should be challenged. Single people are significant members of the body of Christ and should have full acceptance in the church community.

2. *Stimulate Ministries to Singles.* While single adults should be integrated into the mainstream of the church, there also can be value in ministering to their specific needs. Singles groups in the church (or groups combining the singles from several smaller churches) should stimulate a friendly spirit which reaches out to newcomers, avoids an emphasis on matchmaking or dating, at times involves the children of singles in social gatherings, is sensitive to the needs of group members, and is led by mature, sensitive, preferably unmarried leaders.[15] Programs must appeal to the interests and needs of singles, must recognize individual differences (older singles such as widows, for example, do not have the same needs as unmarried college students), and must focus on teaching discipling, worship, fellowship and service. Such an outreach has potential for preventing many singles problems and providing a way for developing or recurring problems to be handled before they get worse.

3. *Encourage Singles to Action.* Active people with meaningful lives often have little time or reason to dwell on problems. Singleness problems can be prevented when unmarried people are helped to trust God for their present and future needs, to honestly face the personal problems and struggles, to reach out to others in a spirit of giving and friendship, to evaluate their life goals, and to work on developing a balanced life which combines worship, work, play, rest, and periods of both socializing and solitude.

Conclusions about Singleness

Millions of adults in the world today are single—never married and formerly married—and many will remain that way until the end of their lives. These people face many of the same problems encountered by married persons, but in addition there are unique challenges which result from being single. To help singles, these problems must be understood and faced honestly—both by married and by single individuals.

Within recent years, many churches have come alive in their concern for accepting and ministering to singles. This is an encouraging sign, especially in view of the scriptural teaching which elevates singleness. To be single is not to be second-class or second-best. Singles have every potential for developing full, meaningful, Christ-centered life styles. The church and individual counselors can make this possibility a reality.

Suggestions for Further Reading

* Andrews, Gini. *Sons of Freedom: God and the Single Man*. Grand Rapids: Zondervan, 1975.

Collins, Gary R., ed. *It's O.K. to be Single*. Waco, TX: Word, 1976.

Edwards, Marie, and Hoover, Eleanor. *The Challenge of Being Single*. New York: Signet Books, 1974.

* Evening, Margaret. *Who Walk Alone: A Consideration of the Single Life*. Downers Grove, IL: Inter-Varsity, 1974.

Towns, Elmer. *The Single Adult and the Church*. Glendale, CA: Regal Books, 1967.

* Watts, Virginia. *The Single Parent*. Old Tappan, NJ: Revell, 1976.

Footnotes

1. Marie Edwards and Eleanor Hoover, *The Challenge of Being Single* (New York: Signet Books, 1974).

2. Gen. 2:18.

3. Matt. 19:11, 12

4. 1 Cor. 7:7.

5. 1 Cor. 7:28, 32–35.

6. "A HIS Interview with John R. W. Stott," *HIS* 36 (October, 1975): 19.

7. Ibid.

8. Margaret Evening, *Who Walk Alone: A Consideration of the Single Life* (Downers Grove, IL: Inter-Varsity, 1974), pp. 23, 24.

9. Edwards and Hoover, *Challenge*, pp. 166–68.

10. Heb. 12:15, 16.

11. John Fischer, "A Single Person's Identity," *Discovery Papers*, no. 3154 (1973). (Available from Peninsula Bible Church, Palo Alto, CA, 94306.)

12. Del Fuller, "On the Pursuit of Love—As a Woman," in Fischer, *Discovery Papers*.

13. These include: Bobbie Reed, *Developing a Single Adult Ministry* (Glendale, CA: International Center for Learning, 1977); Robert A. Dow, *Ministry with Single Adults* (Valley Forge: Judson Press, 1977); Elmer Towns, *The Single Adult and the Church* (Glendale, CA: Regal Books, 1967).

14. Nancy Hardesty, "Being Single in Today's World," in *It's O.K. to be Single*, ed. Gary R. Collins (Waco, TX: Word, 1976), p. 18.

15. *Richard L. Strauss*, "The Family Church: Any Place for Singles?" *Christianity Today*, 29 July, 1977, pp. 12–14.

11
Choosing a Mate

WHAT ARE THE MOST IMPORTANT DECISIONS THAT WE MAKE IN LIFE? At the top of the list, most Christians probably would put the decision to reject or accept Jesus Christ as Savior and Lord of our lives. Next would come the choice of a life partner.

In our period of history, marriage no longer has the sacred character that was common even half a century ago. Living together out of wedlock, entering marriages casually and dissolving marriages freely are all accepted parts of our Western way of life. For many people, the careful choice of a life partner and the commitment to live with one's chosen mate "for better or worse" has been replaced with a self-centered attitude which sees marriage as a convenient living arrangement which always can be terminated if love grows cold.

For Christians, however, the permanence of marriage is still acknowledged, at least in theory if not in practice. Divorce, while common, is not encouraged and single people take the choice of a mate very seriously. In an effort to be sure that they are making the right choice, many unmarried people seek the counsel of a Christian friend, pastor, or professional counselor. These counselors have an important but difficult task in helping counselees choose a mate.

The Bible and Mate Selection

The Bible says little about mate selection. Jesus gave his sanction to marriage and so did Paul, but neither discussed how a marriage partner should be chosen.

In all probability, this silence reflects the fact that in biblical times choosing a mate was not a responsibility for the persons involved. Consider, for example, the choice of a wife for Isaac. His father sent a servant on a long journey to find a suitable candidate. When Rebekah was chosen, her parents were consulted and they asked the girl if she was willing to leave her family and travel to marry a man whom she had never met. It

143

was assumed that the Lord guided this choice [1] but love, personality, compatibility or the bride and groom's wishes had little to do with the choice.

With Jacob the situation was different. He fell in love with Rachel and in the absence of his parents the groom dealt directly with Rachel's father, although not with the bride.[2]

Isaac and Jacob married later in life but it appears that in biblical times both boys and girls married very young—sometimes as early as age 12 or 13. The parents usually made the decision—just as they do in parts of the world today—but the young person could make his or her wishes known and sometimes even refused to go along with the parental choice. After a marriage had been arranged there often was a period of unbreakable betrothal or engagement followed by a ceremony of marriage.[3] It appears that sometimes the groom didn't even see the bride's face until they were in bed together after the marriage. Such a prospect would send shivers of anxiety up and down the spines of contemporary single people.

Do we have biblical guidelines for choosing a mate today? Perhaps there are two. First, it is clear from Scripture that believers are not to marry non-Christians. "Do not be bound together with unbelievers," Paul wrote, "for what partnership have righteousness and lawlessness . . . or what has a believer in common with an unbeliever?" [4] This is a clear warning that the Christian and non-Christian cannot "pull together" either as business partners or as marriage partners. The idea is emphasized in 1 Corinthians [5] and specifically applied to marriage when Paul states that the unmarried woman is free to marry whomever she wishes "but only if she marries a Christian." [6] In choosing a mate, therefore, the believer must choose another believer.

A second principle concerns divine guidance. Just as Abraham's servant expected and experienced divine leading in selecting a wife for Isaac, so we today can expect that God will lead in mate selection. In writing about marriage, Paul instructed his readers to "be sure . . . that you are living as God intended, *marrying or not marrying in accordance with God's direction and help*. . . . " [7] This may apply more to life style in general than to mate selection in particular, but several other biblical passages [8] teach that Christians can expect divine leading—even though this may not come in dramatic or seemingly miraculous ways.

Causes of Good and Poor Mate Selection

"I'd rather be single and wish I were married than to be married and wish I were single." This opinion, stated by a single woman, expresses a concern held by many unmarried people: if one gets married to the wrong person, life can be miserable. Because of this, some people are afraid or unwilling to take the risks of choosing a mate and building a marriage.

To help people choose wisely and lessen the risk of making a mistake, counselors might consider answers to five important questions.

1. *Why Do People Choose a Mate?* It is commonly accepted that people marry because they are "in love." Love, however, is one of the most confusing and ambiguous words in the English language. To "fall in love" is to feel an exhilarating, exciting closeness and intimacy with another human being. But this emotional "high" cannot last by itself forever. For deep love to persist and grow there must be a giving, other-centered relationship similar to that described in 1 Corinthians 13. It is probable that in most cases this deep love comes after marriage rather than before. To *be in love,* therefore, is to experience a state of emotion; *to grow in love* is to deliberately involve oneself in acts of giving. A feeling of being in love is not in itself a solid basis for marriage (and neither is the fact that "we don't love each other any more" a basis for divorce). The biblical marriages, like marriage in many countries today, were based on issues other than feelings, and even in our society it is probable that people really marry for reasons other than love.

These other reasons may be diverse, but they probably center around the idea of needs.[9] People marry because this enables them to meet their own needs more effectively and to fulfill the needs of others. There are, for example, the needs for mutual companionship, security, support, intimacy, sex, and service to others. In addition, some writers have assumed that we seek mates who have strengths where we are weak. A dominant person, therefore, might select someone less dominant, or an introvert may choose someone who is more extroverted. In each case, one's needs are being met in marriage.

In addition there are those who marry because of premarital pregnancy, a yielding to social pressure, the desire to escape from an unhappy home environment, a fear that one will be left alone, or a compulsion to rescue some unfortunate single person. Each of these reasons for marriage meets some need, although none in itself can be the basis for a mature and stable marital relationship.

It should be clear that some of these reasons for selecting a mate are immature and self-centered; others are more rational and the result of mutual deliberation and respect. In all of this it is wise to remember that people marry, ultimately, because God created us male and female, instituted marriage for companionship, mutual support, and sexual expression, and declared in his Word that marriage is honorable.[10] This must not be forgotten as we help people select a mate.

2. *Why Do Some People Not Choose a Mate?* The same God who created marriage apparently did not expect that everyone would find a mate. God's Son, Jesus Christ, never married and the Apostle Paul wrote that singleness could be a superior state since the unmarried person can be free for "undistracted devotion to the Lord." [11] Some people remain single, therefore, because they believe that this is the will and calling of God for their lives.

There are at least six other reasons why some people do not marry.[12] First, there is the failure to meet eligible prospects. There can be various reasons for this. More women than men are alive so it follows that there simply are not enough potential husbands to go around. In addition, since most people want a mate who has similar interests or education, many women and men desire marriage but may not be able to find compatible prospects. Consider, for example, the Christian who wants a Christian mate but who lives in an area where there are few eligible Christians present. The desire for marriage is present but the prospects are not.

Second, some people fail to take advantage of the opportunities that are available. Busy with education, building a career, travel, or other activities, these people decide to postpone marriage and eventually the prospects disappear. Others, with high expectations, keep "waiting for someone better" and discover too late that they have disregarded some excellent opportunities for marriage.

Third, some people are unattractive to the opposite sex. This may result from mental or physical defects but more often psychological characteristics drive others away. People who are excessively timid, afraid of the opposite sex, anxious, aggressive, insensitive, or self-centered often cannot relate well in dating. The person who is overly concerned about getting married can also drive away potential mates.

Fourth, there is a failure in some people to achieve emotional independence. An unusually strong dependence upon one's parents or guilt over leaving a parent can cause some to remain single. In addition, there are responsible people who make a mature and deliberate choice to remain single because of their duty to needy family members. Sometimes, however, this can be an excuse to keep from taking the risks involved in entering a marriage and building intimacy.

Fifth, some people today prefer to find intimacy apart from traditional marriage. Living together secretly or openly as in common-law marriages, joining a commune, participating in a trial marriage or group marriage, or forming homosexual relationships—all are alternatives to marriage which lead some people to remain single.[13]

Finally, some persons simply do not want to marry. This group includes homosexuals, those who have been "burned" in previous relationships, and people who are afraid of the opposite sex, of sexual relationships, of intimacy, and/or of losing independence. But there are others, mature well-adjusted people, who decide that they would prefer to remain single in spite of the social pressures which might push them toward marriage.

3. *Where Do People Find Mates?* Several decades of research have confirmed the fact that most people select mates from similar social classes, economic and educational levels, occupations, age groups, race, religious backgrounds, and areas of residence.[14] There are many people who cross some of these barriers, of course, but such crossovers put strain on a marriage and often make adjustment more difficult.

In finding a mate, therefore, people usually look for someone who is of a similar background and social-religious-educational level. Within this broad category the choice is often narrowed by parental standards and approval or disapproval, and by the single person's mental image of an ideal mate. Since few people can measure up to one's great expectations, there must be a relaxing of one's standards, an accepting of the negative characteristics in a potential mate, or a decision to remain single while waiting for the ideal person to come along.

All of this—background, socioeconomic level, parental and personal expectations—resides in the minds of single people who contemplate marriage. With the entire opposite-sex population thus narrowed, the unmarried person keeps alert to the people who are seen, met, or befriended at school, work, church, social and athletic gatherings, conferences, or in the neighborhood. It is well known that one person often may be attracted to another who has no desire to respond romantically. When there is mutual interest, however, a relationship begins to build. If it is to be a strong relationship it may start with feelings of sexual attraction but must develop on both a similarity of viewpoints and on a mutual meeting of each other's needs. For the Christian there is, in addition, the absolute essential that the two persons be believers.

4. *Why Do Some People Choose Unwisely?* Although choosing a mate is one of life's most important decisions, rarely is it done in a logical, analytical manner. Subtle influences, including parental-social pressures and unconscious desires often push people into unhealthy relationships. In addition there are unrealistic expectations about the ways in which needs might be met in marriage.

Several years ago, one survey cited the most common needs that unmarried people hoped for in marriage. They were hoping to find someone to "love me, confide in, show affection, respect my ideals, appreciate what I wish to achieve, understand my moods, help make my decisions, stimulate my ambition, look up to, give me self-confidence, back me in difficulty, appreciate me just as I am, admire my ability, make me feel important, and relieve my loneliness." [15] While each of these is realistic and most are found in mature marriages, the satisfaction of these needs only comes when each mate gives to the other. When people expect to receive without giving they are headed for disappointment. When single people choose a mate solely on the basis of what one can receive from marriage, they are preparing for marital tensions.

A lopsided desire to receive, without giving, is a mark of immaturity and sometimes of neurosis. Other issues that reflect immaturity and lead to unwise choices are a desire to prove one's adulthood, to escape from a difficult home situation, to rebel against parents or a former partner, to escape the stigma of being single, to find a substitute for a previous relationship (marrying on the rebound), to get a sexual partner, to improve one's economic-social status or to bolster one's self-esteem and masculinity or femininity. Marriage can accomplish all of these goals, but when these are the motives for choosing a mate, the choice is likely to be regretted later.

5. *Why Do People Choose Wisely?* Clearly, in spite of the difficulties, some people make a wise choice of a marriage partner. What are the reasons for this?

(a) Christian Convictions. Since the Bible clearly teaches that Christians are to marry Christians, it is wise for a believer to seek a mate only from among other believers. In Western cultures, most mates are known first through dating. Since one never knows when a dating relationship may lead to marriage it is a wise policy for unmarried Christian persons to limit their dating to other Christians. Christians who choose wisely often pray about their mate selection, at first alone and later as a couple.

(b) Similar Backgrounds and Complementary Needs. Christians, like nonbelievers, are unique and it does not follow that a marriage will be successful and stable simply because both people are followers of Jesus Christ. As indicated previously, marriage selection is best when the man and woman are similar in such variables as age, interests, values, socio-economic level and education. In addition it is helpful if the couple can meet each other's needs.

It is important, however, to distinguish between complementary and contradictory needs.[16] Complementary needs fit so well together that a relationship is smooth and compromise is rarely needed. Contradictory needs clash and require frequent resolution. If both people enjoy social contacts but one person is outgoing and the other a little shy, this can be complementary. If, in contrast, one person loves parties and the other is a recluse, these contradictory needs make conflict almost inevitable.

(c) Emotional Resonance. As single people many of us have had the experience of asking, "How can I know when 'the right one' comes along?" To hear someone reply, "You'll just know!" isn't a very satisfying answer but it reflects a common observation. Some relationships are felt to be harmonious and "right." With others, the "spark just isn't there." To choose a mate on the basis of such feelings alone would surely be unwise, but to ignore such feelings or to overlook their absence would also be a mistake.

(d) Marriageability Traits. In his book on premarital counseling, Norman Wright has identified several basic elements which, when present, increase the likelihood of wise mate selection and of marital satisfaction and stability.[17] These traits include:

—adaptability and flexibility—the ability and willingness of persons to adjust to change, to accept differences in a partner, and to adapt if necessary;

—empathy—a sensitivity to the hurts and needs of others and a willing attempt to see and experience the world from the other person's perspective;

—ability to work through problems—the recognition of emotions and a willingness to define the issues and work toward solutions;

—ability to give and receive love—elements which are both necessary;

—emotional stability—accepting one's emotions, controlling them, and expressing them without "tearing down" a partner;

—communication ability—learning to talk frequently to one another about a wide range of subjects, to convey the feeling that one understands and is sensitive to the other, to keep communication opportunities open, and to express oneself personally, clearly, and at times nonverbally; and

—commitment—the willingness to yield oneself to a lifetime of adventure including the risks, joys, and sorrows, plus a commitment to work together even when difficulties, obstacles, and challenges interfere with a smooth relationship.

The reading of this list of characteristics could be discouraging to a single person or to a counselor. Hardly anyone can meet these expectations. The list shows, however, that for best mate selection, a feeling of love is not enough. The outside perspective and guidance of a friend or other counselor is very important if one is to attain subsequent marital stability and happiness.

Effects of Good and Poor Mate Selection

Making a wise choice does not insure the development of a good marriage, but it certainly is a solid foundation on which to begin building. Marriage involves effort, risk, and sometimes disappointment. These never are easy experiences, but it is more pleasant and motivating to work with a compatible teammate in life than with someone who apparently was a wrong choice.

There are many people, however, who believe their marriage choice was a mistake but who determine to build the best relationship possible considering the circumstances. These people discover that acts of love often build feelings of love and relatively good marriages result.

Others, however, never recover from a poor mate selection. Unhappiness and conflict characterize the marriage and the relationship is dissolved emotionally and/or legally through separation and divorce. Counseling people in mate selection is designed to help in the prevention of such an unhappy end to marriage.

Counseling and Mate Selection

The selection of a mate is one of life's most important decisions, but seldom is it made carefully, objectively and logically. When people fall in love they have a tendency to overlook faults in each other, to ignore danger signals, and to dismiss the counsel of more objective persons. It should be expected, therefore, that many people will not seek counsel (if they seek it at all) until after a potential mate has been chosen. Nevertheless, the counselor can help by offering unsolicited counsel, by talking with young people before they fall in love, and by counseling with the never-married and formerly married people who do come for help in evaluating the wisdom of their mate choices. There are several goals for such counseling, goals which apply equally to young unmarried persons and to older individuals, including widows and divorced persons, who would like to get married or remarried.

1. *Spiritual Evaluation.* Since the Bible is so clear in its teaching that believers must marry believers only, this must be emphasized repeatedly. Even when people believe this, they are inclined to find excuses by which they justify their dating of non-Christians. "We don't plan to get serious" or "If we date, I may lead my friend to Christ," are statements which can signal a desire to sidestep the biblical teaching about the "unequal yoke." Although Christians do sometimes lead potential mates to Christ, the reverse is also true—non-Christians can cause believers to tumble spiritually. This needs to be stated clearly at some time in counseling. Dating non-believers is risky and, in general, should be avoided.

When a potential mate is found, encourage the counselee to ask such questions as the following; and to discuss the answers with the counselor:
—Is my potential mate a believer?
—Does his or her life show evidence of the fruits of the Spirit (Gal. 5:22, 23)?
—Have my partner and I ever discussed our spiritual lives with their struggles and goals?
—Have we ever prayed together? If not, why not?
—Do we agree on a church, on our basic standard of living, on our views of right and wrong and on our perspectives about a Christian home?

2. *Reassurance.* Sometimes people come to a counselor with the fear that they will never get married. They may wonder if "something is wrong" or if God has "let them down" by allowing them to remain unmarried.

With such persons it is helpful to encourage the expression of feelings—including anger and frustration—and to give the reassurance that God always cares and wants the best for us. Openly discuss the realities and discouragements of the single life; but point out, too, that singleness can be a special calling. Is the counselee willing to remain single? If not, why not? [18] By observing and by asking, seek to determine (a) if the person does show traits—like overeagerness, timidity, or insensitivity—which drive away members of the opposite sex, and (b) if the counselee's life is so bound up in the desire for marriage that nothing else seems to matter. Many people live in the future. They assume that life will be better when they earn more money, graduate from college, or find a mate. While they wait, their lives are meaningless and nonproductive. Such persons should be encouraged to "live life to its fullest now." If a mate is found this will be great. If no mate is found life can be great as well.

3. *Direction in Mate Selection.* Some people need practical guidance in finding eligible partners. This involves two issues—finding places where there are other single people and learning how to relate.

It is an obvious but frequently overlooked fact that you don't find a mate by sitting home watching TV and waiting for God's gift of marriage to arrive at the door. To meet people, we must go where others are. For some, this means singles bars, but for believers this is hardly a suitable place to find a mate. More desirable are churches, study courses, vacation trips, sports events, Christian single adult groups, and Christian conferences. If one goes to these places only to find a mate, this soon becomes apparent to everyone. It is better to get involved in groups that are interesting, knowing that in so doing one may or may not find a potential partner.

Sometimes, potential partners are driven away by the single person's overanxious attitude or desire to "latch on" to someone. Counselees should be encouraged to look neat and attractive, to learn how to ask questions about the other person and then to listen, to try to understand the other person's perspective, and to work at "being oneself"—not pretending to be something we aren't.[19] Gently point out failings in these areas and, if necessary, do some role playing in which the counselor and counselee practice situations in which they pretend to meet as strangers.

4. *Evaluation of Motives, Ideals, and Maturity.* Why does the counselee want to find a mate (or why does he or she not want to marry)? As a counselor you may think you know, but you also may be wrong. It is helpful to ask, therefore, "Why do you want to get married?" Try to determine, by asking tentatively, when necessary, if there are unhealthy reasons for wanting marriage—like social and family pressures, the desire to escape from a difficult home situation, the need to prove that one is an adult, or the feeling that it is "marriage now or never." If the person has chosen to remain single, ask yourself if there are also unhealthy reasons for this. For example, is there a fear of marriage, of sex, or of the opposite sex; homosexual tendencies; or rebellion against traditional forms of marriage? Ask the counselee to discuss these attitudes, indicating the possible reasons for their presence. If there is a desire to change, discuss how this might be done. Be specific and encourage the counselee to take actions to change.

At some time it may be good to ask the counselee to describe his or her "ideal mate." Then, discuss this expectation. Is it unrealistic? Is it causing the counselee to overlook or reject potentially good marriage partners who do not fit the ideal? Can parts of the ideal be changed without lessening one's moral standards?

As these issues are discussed, try to assess the counselee's level of maturity. Immature single people make immature marriage partners and this can lead to problems in dating and marriage.

The spiritually maturing Christian shows a desire to be like Christ, accompanied by some evidence of the fruits of the Spirit in his or her life.[20] As one matures there is:
- —a tendency to behave according to one's age (and not like someone younger or older);
- —a capacity to assume responsibility;
- —an ability to look at oneself and one's problems objectively;
- —an ability to acknowledge but to control emotions;
- —an understanding of other people's feelings and a sensitive ability to respond to these emotions;
- —a growing independence from the control of family or friends;
- —a willingness to postpone immediate gratification so that greater satisfaction can be attained in the future;
- —a responsible attitude toward sex;
- —a realistic and essentially positive self-image; and
- —an ability to make choices and live with the consequences of one's decisions.[21]

In your counseling, these issues might be discussed. In which of these does the person succeed and where does he or she fail? How could these skills be developed? The more these are present, the greater the likelihood of successful mate selection and marital stability.

5. *Teaching about Mate Selection.* In many respects, counseling is a specialized form of education. Nowhere is this more true than when one is being helped to choose a mate. Several pages back, we discussed "Why do people choose wisely?" The contents of this section could be shared with the counselee but do this slowly and perhaps at different times throughout counseling if you feel there is too much information for the counselee to assimilate all at once.

6. *Patience.* In all of this, encourage counselees to be patient, to trust in God's leading and timing, to be alert for opportunities to meet a potential mate, and to pray. Pray with the counselee for patience, for a willingness to accept God's will in the area of mate selection, for the purity and protection of one's potential mate, and for the willingness to accept singleness joyfully if this is God's plan for the counselee.

Preventing Poor Mate Selection

Here is another situation where forewarning is the best protection against error. A great deal is known about mate selection and much of the information presented in the first two-thirds of this chapter could be presented to singles privately or in singles groups, Sunday school classes, special interest groups or weekend conferences. If such material is presented, be sure that there is ample opportunity for people to discuss what they hear, to ask questions, and to apply this learning to their own lives.

The sooner such information is presented and discussed, the better.

Previously in this chapter we have noted that facts about mate selection tend to lose significance and influence after one has fallen in love. If facts and warnings can be given *before* emotional bonds are allowed to develop, it is more likely that error will be avoided. Thus, single people should learn to evaluate relationships intellectually before letting themselves fall romantically and emotionally. When this point is understood and practiced, much progress has been made toward the prevention of poor mate selection.

With some counselees, prevention will start long before a prospective mate appears. Immature or self-centered people, for example, can often profit from individual or group counseling which helps them to cope more effectively with life in general. This can help prevent them from choosing mates for unhealthy reasons.

Conclusions about Mate Selection

Erich Fromm, the famous psychoanalytic writer, once described mate selection as an exercise in bargaining. He wrote:

> Our whole culture is based on the appetite for buying, on the idea of a mutually favorable exchange. Modern man's happiness consists in the thrill of looking at the shop windows, and in buying all that he can afford to buy, either for cash or on installments. He (or she) looks at people in a similar way. For the man an attractive girl—and for the woman an attractive man—are the prizes they are after. "Attractive" usually means a nice package of qualities which are popular and sought after on the personality market. What specifically makes a person attractive depends on the fashion of the time, physically as well as mentally. During the twenties, a drinking and smoking girl, tough and sexy, was attractive; today the fashion demands more domesticity and coyness. At the end of the nineteenth and the beginning of this century, a man had to be aggressive and ambitious—today he has to be social and tolerant—in order to be an attractive "package." At any rate, the sense of falling in love develops usually only with regard to such human commodities as are within reach of one's own possibilities for exchange. I am out for a bargain, the object should be desirable from the standpoint of its social value, and at the same time should want me, considering my overt and hidden assets and potentialities. Two persons thus fall in love when they feel they have found the best object available on the market, considering the limitations of their own exchange values.[22]

This is a blunt analysis but it contains a large element of truth. "Striking a marriage bargain" [23] may be more overt in other cultures where dowries and bride prices are part of the deal, but it surely is true that mate selection in our society also includes some exchanges.

The Christian, however, recognizes that marriage involves more. It is the joining of two individuals so that the two become one and yet retain two unique but interlocking personalities. It probably is untrue that there is only one "perfect" person in the world for each of us, but it surely *is* true that God leads us to someone who will meet our needs and with whom we can blend our lives. Often he leads through counselors who are willing to guide single people in their choice of a mate.

Suggestions for Further Reading

* Andrews, Gini. *Sons of Freedom: God and The Single Man,* chapters 6, 7, 8. Grand Rapids: Zondervan, 1975.

McDonald, Cleveland. *Creating a Successful Christian Marriage,* chapter 7. Grand Rapids: Baker, 1975.

Scanzoni, Letha, and Scanzoni, John. *Men, Women, and Change,* chapter 4. New York: McGraw-Hill, 1976.

* Trobisch, Walter. *Love Is a Feeling to be Learned.* Downers Grove, IL: Inter-Varsity, 1971.

Wright, H. Norman. *Premarital Counseling,* chapter 2. Chicago: Moody, 1977.

* Wright, Norman, and Inmon, Marvin A. *A Guidebook to Dating, Waiting, and Choosing a Mate.* Irvine, CA: Harvest House, 1978.

————. *Preparing Youth for Dating, Courtship and Marriage.* Irvine, CA: Harvest House, 1978.

Footnotes

1. Gen. 24:48.
2. Gen. 29.
3. Merrill C. Tenney, ed., *The Zondervan Pictorial Encyclopedia of the Bible Vol. IV* (Grand Rapids: Zondervan, 1975), 4:96–97.
4. 2 Cor. 6:14, 15.
5. 1 Cor. 5:9 f.
6. 1 Cor. 7:39, *Living Bible.*
7. 1 Cor. 7:17, *Living Bible,* italics added.
8. Ps. 32:8; Prov. 3:5, 6; 16:3, 9.
9. Swiss psychiatrist Bernard Harnik wrote about this in a book titled *Risk and Chance in Marriage* (Waco, TX: Word, 1972).
10. Gen. 1:27; 2:18; 1 Cor. 7:9; Heb. 13:4.
11. 1 Cor. 7:35.
12. Judson T. Landis and Mary G. Landis, *The Marriage Handbook* (New York: Prentice-Hall, 1948).
13. See chapter 5, "Alternatives to Marriage," in Letha Scanzoni and John Scanzoni, *Men, Women and Change: A Sociology of Marriage and Family* (New York: McGraw-Hill, 1976); also John Scanzoni, "A Christian Perspective on Alternative Styles of Marriage," in *Make More of Your Marriage,* ed. Gary R. Collins (Waco, TX: Word, 1976), pp. 157-68.
14. David M. Moss, III, "Three Levels of Mate Selection and Marital Interaction," *Journal of Religion and Health.* 16 (41), (1977): 288–303.
15. Ernest W. Burgess and Harvey J. Locke, *The Family* (New York: American Book Company, 1945), p. 420.
16. Adapted from Robert Blood, Jr., *Marriage* (New York: Free Press, 1969), and reported in Norman Wright, *Premarital Counseling* (Chicago: Moody, 1977).
17. Wright, *Premarital Counseling,* pp. 28–34.
18. 1 Cor. 7.
19. See chapter 23 for suggestions on getting along with people.

20. Gal. 5:22, 23.

21. This list is adapted from chapter 7, "Maturity in Mate Selection," in Cleveland McDonald, *Creating a Successful Christian Marriage* (Grand Rapids: Baker, 1975), pp. 123–41.

22. Erich Fromm, *The Art of Loving* (New York: Bantam, 1956), pp. 2, 3.

23. This is the title to a chapter on mate selection in Scanzoni and Scanzoni, *Men, Women and Change.*

12
Preparing
for Marriage

"IF 50–75 PERCENT OF FORD OR GENERAL MOTORS CARS COMPLETELY fell apart within the early part of their lifetimes as automobiles," the public outcry would be overwhelming and drastic steps would be taken to correct the situation. So wrote psychologist Carl Rogers in a book considering the current state of marriage.[1] It is well known, of course, that marriages are falling apart all around us. Fewer than 50 percent are successful and yet we seem unable and often unwilling to do much to correct the situation.

There are numerous reasons for the present instability in marriages, but undoubtedly one source of the problem concerns the lack of care with which many marriages are put together. Built primarily on sexual attraction, the desire to escape from a difficult home situation, a vague feeling of love, or some equally fleeting motive, many marriage relationships are too flimsy to survive the pressures, challenges and storms of daily living. Unprepared for the stresses of marriage or for the effort and determination required to make marriage work, many people prefer to give up and "bail out." That which could be meaningful and fulfilling thus becomes frustrating and personally devastating.

Unlike most of the other issues discussed in this book, premarital counseling primarily is preventive. It is less concerned about healing existing wounds than about building a union which will survive future attacks. In general, people are not enthusiastic about preventive counseling. It is assumed that the "problems which happen to others will never happen to me," so there is a tendency to resist and sometimes resent such help. This attitude has led many counselors to become disillusioned with premarital counseling. Cecil Osborne, for example, once wrote that he

> long ago abandoned as futile the effort to instruct young couples in these matters before marriage. They tended to look at me through star dust, with amused tolerance. . . . Finally I have come to the point where I ask only one thing of them: a solemn agreement that they will seek a compe-

156

tent marriage counselor or minister at the first sign that they are not com-municating well.[2]

When a couple resists premarital counseling, however, it is unlikely that they will seek counseling "at the first sign" of marital difficulty. Wisely, therefore, many churches and religious leaders insist on premarital coun-seling, and the benefits have been acknowledged subsequently by numer-ous grateful and happily married couples. Many more probably never think back to their premarital counseling, but nevertheless experience marital fulfillment at least partially because of the premarital counseling which came formally or informally before their wedding.

The Bible and Premarital Counseling

The engagement of Mary and Joseph is well known.[3] If they acted ac-cording to the custom of their time, a written contract of engagement was signed under oath and then the bride went home to learn the duties of a good wife and mother. If she was unfaithful during that time, the husband-to-be could have her stoned to death or he could give her a bill of di-vorce. When Joseph learned that Mary was pregnant, he decided to divorce her quietly, until an angel appeared to announce that Mary was to be the mother of the Messiah.[4]

What did Mary and Joseph learn about marriage during their period of engagement? Was there any premarital counseling? The Bible does not say and neither does it give any directions on how people can prepare for marriage today.

In all of Scripture the closest thing we have to premarital counseling is Paul's advice in 1 Corinthians 7. He encourages people to remain single, but acknowledges that it is better to marry than to burn with lust.[5] He warns that marriage will bring challenges and difficulties, and he points out that it is difficult for married people to serve the Lord wholeheartedly.[6] Elsewhere in the New Testament we read what an ideal marriage should be like, what roles the husband and wife should fulfill, and how they should function as parents.[7] In summary, therefore, the Bible warns of marital stresses and gives God's portrait of ideal marriage as a goal toward which every couple can strive. Beyond that, there are no specific instructions for premarital guidance.

Reasons for Premarital Counseling

In our society we tend to spend a lot more time getting ready for the wedding than preparing for marriage. As a result many beautiful wed-dings are followed by a lifetime of misery or, at best, minimal happiness. Premarital preparation is important, therefore, for at least six reasons:

1. *Unrealistic Expectations Which Lead to Disillusionment.* As they approach marriage, perhaps most couples assume that their relationship is unique and invulnerable to the threats which destroy so many other re-

lationships. Coupled with this assumption is our modern belief that marriage will be blissful and pleasure-centered. In his book on premarital counseling, Aaron Rutledge writes that modern couples expect marriage to provide self-development and fulfillment; mutual expressions of affection; satisfaction of sexual urges; a sharing of child-rearing responsibilities; a mutual experience of status, belongingness and security; and shared interests in friends, recreation, worship, and creative work. In the history of mankind, Rutledge writes, never have "so many expected so much from marriage and family life." [8]

Unlike previous generations, people today expect a high degree of satisfaction in all of these areas at the same time. However, there is no realization that meaningful marriages grow slowly and only with effort. Often there is impatience, insensitivity, self-centered attitudes, inadequate skill in relating and great disappointment or disillusionment when one's expectations for marriage are not met quickly.

Premarital counseling lets couples express, discuss and realistically modify their expectations for marriage. Conflicting expectations can be seen and hopefully resolved. With the counselor's help the couple also can learn that expectations can only be met by mutual giving and effort. Such learning comes slowly, but it can help couples anticipate and sometimes avoid the disillusionment that comes to so many marriages.

2. *Personal Immaturity Which Leads to Insensitivity*. What comes out of a marriage depends primarily on what is brought into the relationship. If one or both of the participants is self-centered, hypercritical, impatient, competitive, or striving for status—that is, immature—these characteristics will put a strain on marital stability. During the time of dating there often is high anticipation about the future. Differences are overlooked as the couple plans for the future. Following marriage, however, there is a settling in to daily routines and troublesome characteristics; conflicts and attitudes begin to surface. If these are expressed sometimes with emotion, discussed, understood and in some way resolved or accepted, then the marriage builds and grows. When these differences are ignored or denied the foundation under the marriage begins to crumble.

Immature people are usually self-centered. At different times such persons may be manipulating (actively or passively), exploiting or competing with their mates all in an attempt to satisfy their own neurotic needs. These tactics place a strain on marriage and the partners become insensitive both to each other and to the ways in which their relationship is being destroyed.

Among the important but difficult goals in premarital counseling is to uncover and discuss any self-centered tendencies which might put stress on a marriage. The couple must be taught how to resolve their differences, and to develop an appreciation for each other's needs and individuality. [9] Marriage is a relationship in which needs are met, but for this to happen, each partner must want to meet the needs of one's mate and each must learn to give unconditionally—as Christ gave everything to us.[10]

3. *Changing Roles Which Lead to Confusion*. There was a time when the roles of husband and wife were clearly defined and widely accepted in our society. Within recent years, however, the roles have been changing and this has caused many marriages and families to be confused, since "nobody seems to know who is to do what." [11] When a man and woman each come to marriage with unclear roles and vague expectations about their own and each other's responsibilities, then the stage is set for both confusion and conflict.

In their widely acclaimed book on marriage, Lederer and Jackson write that marriage disintegration does not usually begin with "consciously malevolent behavior, but by what the spouses neglect to say and do. The first steps toward destruction result mostly from omissions, failures to bring the spouse's untested expectations into conformity with reality." Of these failures the two most common both relate to roles. There is, first, "the failure of spouses to identify, determine, and mutually assign areas of competence and responsibility, of who is in charge of what." Second, there is "the failure of spouses to evaluate their differences as being only differences—not marks of inferiority." [12]

Premarital counseling provides opportunity for a couple to discuss their views and expectations about male and female roles in marriage. Together they can learn to accept their different abilities and decide on areas of responsibility. "It is imperative that the spouses deliberately and mutually develop rules to guide their behavior," Lederer and Jackson write. "Omission of this procedure can destroy a marriage. Husband and wife should operate in ways which mutually assist each other—regardless of custom or tradition." [13]

Such role clarification must not ignore biblical teaching. According to the Scriptures, both the Christian husband and wife must be "filled with the Spirit"—daily confessing sin, "giving thanks for all things" and praying for the Holy Spirit to control each life.[14] Then there must be an attitude of mutual submission to each other. Within the home, the husband has major responsibility. He must love his wife unselfishly, discipline his children fairly, and lead the family wisely. The wife, in turn, is instructed to submit to her husband and respect him.[15] This in no way implies an inferiority of women. The husband and wife are equally valuable and equally important in the building of a good marriage, but they do have different responsibilities. Certainly, these scriptural roles for husbands and wives cannot be changed or ignored in order to accommodate the trends in a culture. Nevertheless there is room for variation as individual couples decide on their specific duties and behaviors—but only within the broader guidelines outlined in the Bible.

4. *Alternative Styles of Marriage Which Lead to Uncertainty*. During

the past two decades there has been an increasing tendency for people to challenge and criticize the traditional family structure of one husband, who is the primary provider, legally married to one wife who in turn bears one or more children. Criticisms of the traditional family are sometimes bombastic, hostile, more emotional than logical and certainly contrary to biblical teaching. But the arguments can also be persuasive and convincing. The traditional family *does* have problems and our rigid attitudes may be one of the causes. Some of the alternatives to traditional marriage—like marriages in which the couple decides not to have children, or communal living in which everything is shared—can be fully consistent with biblical teaching. Other alternatives—like trial marriage, open marriage, mate swapping or gay marriages—are unbiblical and cannot be condoned by Christians.[16]

All of this can leave a young couple confused and uncertain. Can there be alternatives to traditional marriage that might be healthy for their relationship? Is trial marriage really wrong? Is traditional marriage unrealistic in the twentieth century? The counselor may have no problem in answering these questions, but many couples need to think them through carefully, in light of the Scriptures, and in the presence of a counselor who is patient and not inclined to lecture.

5. *Changing Sexual Standards Which Lead to Immorality*. Sex before marriage is nothing new—even in Christian circles. What is new is the increasing approval of premarital sex, the upsurge in premarital sexual intercourse,[17] and the flood of arguments that are used, often in a casual way, to justify behavior which clearly is condemned in the Scriptures.[18] Parents and church leaders often look on in dismay and repeat scriptural injunctions as the sexual revolution floods over the land, but the injunctions go unheeded, even by many Christians, and there is continued involvement in sexual activity which "can't be wrong because it feels so right" and so pleasant.

As a result of these trends, dating and the months before marriage have become, for many, a time for exploring each other's bodies instead of each other's minds, feelings, values and expectations. Love is reduced to sex and there is a de-emphasis on respect, responsibility, understanding, care, and continuing interpersonal relationships with people other than one's partner. What is assumed to be increasing sexual freedom is really increasing bondage to one's physiological drives. By ignoring divine standards which free us for maximum satisfaction on earth, we instead have cast away our freedom and settled for biological enslavement.

Since the issue of premarital sex and self-control is discussed more fully in chapter 20, it will not be considered here. Nevertheless, it is an issue which must be talked about honestly, faced compassionately, and examined biblically. Religious commitment does limit premarital coitus [19] but it would be naïve and inaccurate to conclude that premarital sex among

Christians is rare. Sexual standards are loosening, premarital intercourse among evangelicals probably is becoming more prevalent, but the Bible still calls this immorality—a violation of God's best for our lives.

6. *Increasing Divorce Rates Which Lead to Unhappiness.* Statistics about the divorce rate are outdated almost before they appear in print. We do not need statistics, however, to support the conclusion that marriages are breaking up with alarming frequency. The causes for this have been elaborated elsewhere;[20] the effects in terms of pain and unhappiness are widely recognized. Through premarital counseling, the church, more than any other social institution, can work to build stable foundations to undergird new marriages which will endure.

The Effects of Premarital Counseling

Does premarital counseling really improve marriages and reduce the incidence of family disintegration and divorce? Our tendency is to answer "yes, premarital counseling really is effective," but there is little research evidence to indicate whether or not this conclusion is, in fact, true. What is perhaps the most widely consulted textbook in this area assumes that premarital counseling is effective but the author never asks the question.[21]

In his study of 151 Christian couples, Herbert J. Miles concluded that premarital counseling was followed by good sexual adjustment in marriage.[22] But how can we know that it was the premarital counseling which contributed to sexual happiness in marriage? Without a comparison group who had no premarital guidance, how can we be sure that counseling really made a difference?

Married individuals often report that their premarital counseling was beneficial, but can we reach solid conclusions based on personal testimonies? If so, what do we do about those couples who are unhappy in spite of premarital counseling, or about those who never had premarital guidance but who, nevertheless, have happy marriages?

In spite of these questions, there is some scattered research to show that premarital counseling is helpful to the couples involved and apparently it doesn't do any harm. In counseling, many engaged couples are confronted with problems that they had not noticed previously. Such knowledge leads some to work on the problem issues, or to get further counseling. Others are encouraged either to break the engagement or to delay marriage until the difficulties are resolved. In the absence of definitive data, therefore, we may assume that premarital counseling can be helpful and effective even though, at present, nobody can be certain.

Premarital Counseling

Couples often approach premarital counseling with mixed feelings. While many recognize its potential value, there is also the feeling that "our love is so unique that we really don't need this—especially now when we are so busy." Others may come with trepidation and defensiveness, fearing that the counselor might suggest that marriage is unwise. The counselor should be alert to these attitudes and must be convinced of the value of counseling if the sessions are to be alive and helpful.

1. *Purposes.*[23] Premarital counseling seeks to help individuals, couples, and groups of couples to prepare for and build happy, fulfilling and successful marriages. At least seven goals are basic.

(a) Assessing Readiness for Marriage. This involves observation and discussion of the following issues: Why does the couple really want to get married? What do they expect from marriage? How similar are their backgrounds (education, area of residence, religious beliefs, age, race, socioeconomic level)? Have they discussed their different roles in marriage? In discussions of these and other issues the counselor can watch for signs of immaturity, tension and communication breakdown.

(b) Learning the Biblical Teaching about Marriage. The Bible contains a number of statements about marriage and the God-ordained roles of the husband and wife. The family is modeled after the relationship which Christ has with his church, and although no two marriages are alike (since people are so unique) each marriage should reflect the influence of Christ in the home. Scriptural passages such as 1 Corinthians 13, Ephesians 5:21–6:4; Colossians 3:16–21; 1 Corinthians 7 and 1 Peter 3:1–7 should be read, discussed, understood, and applied to the couple's relationship.

(c) Guiding Self-evaluation. Marriage sometimes causes people to grow up quickly, but it is best if there is a strong element of psychological and spiritual maturity prior to the wedding. With the counselor's encouragement, couples should consider their own and each other's strong and weak points, values, prejudices, beliefs, attitudes about the husband-and-wife role in marriage and expectations or plans for the future. During the engagement period there often is a tendency to camouflage injured feelings and hide differences of opinion to keep the relationship running smoothly. These differences need to be acknowledged and discussed as the counselees learn better to understand themselves and each other.

(d) Stimulating Effective Communication Skills. It is widely recognized that failure or inability to communicate is one of the most fundamental problems in troubled marriages. Before marriage, couples must be shown the value of spontaneous, honest, sensitive communication. As they are encouraged to discuss their feelings, expectations, differences, attitudes and even their personal hurts, they can learn to communicate about significant issues, to listen carefully in an attempt to understand each other, and to "talk through" problems without hiding what they feel or "putting down" each other.

(e) Anticipating Potential Stress. When two people of different sex and family backgrounds come together to share life intimately there are certain to be adjustment problems. How does a couple handle finances, different values, in-law pressures and expectations, differences in interests, conflicts over choice of friends and preferences concerning recreation, vocational demands, political differences and variations in spiritual beliefs or maturity? Then there is the issue of sex. Is there misinformation, fear, different expectations for the honeymoon, unhealthy attitudes? All of these potential stress issues should be discussed and, whenever necessary, accurate information should be given.

(f) Planning the Wedding. The counselor, especially the pastoral counselor, may play a major role in the wedding by performing the ceremony. Premarital counseling can be a time (i) for making sure that all legal requirements are met (such as obtaining a license and getting blood tests), (ii) for going over details of the service, and (iii) for urging the participants to "take it easy" in the expense and activities of the wedding. There may be limited success with this latter goal since families in our culture often use weddings to impress others with their status and financial success. It is important to help people recognize that for Christians a wedding can be a service of praise and witness to the couple's mutual commitment to Christ. Too often this message gets lost in the midst of flowers, attendants, photographers, lengthy guest lists and expensive refreshments.

(g) Giving Experience with Counselors. For many people there still is an anxiety about counselors and a reluctance to seek counseling help. Premarital counseling provides a relatively nonthreatening situation in which problem issues are discussed and counselees get an exposure to the counseling process. Hopefully this experience will make it easier for individuals to return if they have difficulties in the future.

2. *Format.* It should be obvious that a counselor cannot accomplish all of these purposes in one brief interview. Most writers recommend that there be five or six one-hour sessions prior to the wedding and at least one session three to six months later. This, of course, can be demanding and it is easy for time pressures and counselee busyness to combine in convincing the counselor that a briefer period of premarital counseling would suffice. This temptation should be resisted. There is much to be discussed if a marriage is to be built on a solid foundation. One way to meet the time pressures is to meet first with the couples alone and then to see several couples together for group premarital counseling.

Each counselor should plan his or her own format in talking with couples, but the following is a suggested approach.

Session one. Encourage the couple to talk about themselves, their backgrounds and interests. Listen carefully and resist the tendency to begin dealing with problem areas. Ask why they want to get married and listen to their expectations about their marriage.

Discuss the premarital counseling. What would they like to accomplish?

Share your policies about this kind of counseling—its purposes and goals, its benefits, its length, and how you will proceed. If you plan to give homework assignments talk about these and the importance of this work being done.

Ask about their spiritual growth and relationship to Jesus Christ. Are they both believers? Does Christ have a central place in their relationship? What are they doing alone and together to build their Christian lives? Do they pray together?

Session two. Discuss the biblical view of marriage: its origins (Gen. 2:18–24); its purposes (such as companionship, sexual union, child rearing, or a reflection of God's dealings with the church); its permanence (Matt. 19:3–9). Look at the major biblical passages which deal with marriage and discuss how these apply to the counselees. Be practical and specific. Do not let this become a lecture but include the counselees, getting their observations, questions, and discomforts.

Sessions three and four. Consider some of the practical issues of day-to-day living:

—What do they expect to get out of marriage that single life would not provide?

—In what ways are they different from each other? How are they the same? How can they live with the differences?

—What are the parents' attitudes toward the marriage? How do the man and woman each anticipate dealing with in-laws after marriage? What are some good and bad things about the in-laws? Where will the couple spend Christmas?

—Do they like each other's friends? How will they form friendships after marriage?

—What do they like to do for recreation, hobbies, vacations?

—Where will they live? How will they make decisions about furniture and housing?

—Do they have a budget? How will they decide on major purchases? Who will buy what?

—What is their attitude toward children? How many do they want and when?

These issues may take more than two sessions to discuss, especially if you are meeting in a group in which each member is encouraged to answer some of these questions. The discussions can continue apart from the counseling, however, and any major differences can then be considered in later counseling sessions.

As these issues are discussed, you can point out and have counselees practice the principles of good communication. Can they listen and express their feelings or ideas honestly and without being hostile and critical? Communication is an art to be learned. It is learned by discussing sensitive and important issues. A counselor can facilitate this process.

Session five. Discuss the meaning of love (see 1 Corinthians 13:4–8) and its relationship to sex. What questions and concerns do they have about sex? If questions are slow in coming, you might raise the following issues which one study of Christian couples found to be of major importance.[24] The issues are listed in decreasing order according to the number of times each was mentioned by the couples surveyed.

—How to stimulate and arouse a wife to orgasm
—The use of contraceptives
—The detailed processes of sexual intercourse
—Suggestions on what to do and expect on the honeymoon
—The nature of the clitoris
—The different sexual timing of men and women
—How to meet the husband's sexual needs
—The spiritual and moral interpretation of the sexual relationship in marriage
—The elimination of fears and misconceptions
—The responsibility of husband and wife in meeting each other's sexual needs
—How to purchase contraceptives
—The discussion of the hymen
—The amount of time necessary for good sexual adjustment

Two tangential issues are related to this discussion of sex. First, the counselor must be well-informed, comfortable in discussing sex, and able to get further information if necessary. In some cases, a physician may be of more help in answering these questions than a nonmedical counselor. Second, remember that the couple may be (a) more naïve than you think or (b) more experienced sexually than you might think. Rather than launching into a lecture, it is more important to find out "where they are." This may involve asking embarrassing personal questions—but be sure that you are not asking to satisfy your own curiosity.

Session six. This involves discussion of the wedding ceremony, the legal requirements, the reception and its costs, and plans for a honeymoon. Remind the couple of their postmarital session when you will discuss with them "how things are going," including the problems and joys of their young marriage.

3. *Variations.* Premarital counseling must not become rigid. Some couples are older, are more mature, have been married previously, have read several books on marriage, and are spiritually alert. These men and women may need a different number of sessions and may be concerned with different issues than those which interest a young couple in their early twenties.

Throughout the counseling, you should be alert to the counselees' readiness for marriage and, at times, you may want to help them see that the proposed marriage is a poor risk. Some will resist this idea, while others will consider breaking their engagement. In either case there needs to be support and encouragement.

Many counselors prefer to give paper and pencil tests which a couple can complete apart from counseling and discuss with the counselor.[25] This is highly recommended, especially since some of these tests are easily obtained. In addition, you may want to encourage counselees to read and discuss some books [26] or to listen to cassette tapes [27] which can become the basis for further discussion. At times there may be value in referring counselees to a doctor or to a financial expert who can give specialized information. For group counseling, such resource people can be invited to share their expertise with the group members. Each of these approaches supplements the counseling and stimulates couples to communicate with each other about important issues.

Prevention

Each of the issues discussed in this book has been presented in the form of a problem which can be caused, understood, counseled, and prevented. In a real sense, however, this chapter deals exclusively with prevention. Its major emphasis is the prevention of marital problems and difficulties which could make life miserable, difficult, unfulfilled and unproductive after marriage. We have assumed that good marriages start before the wedding.

It is also true that good marriages start before a couple comes for premarital counseling. By observing parents and other adults, young people learn what to expect in marriage, what they want in their own marriages, and what they do not want. Their reading and television viewing can give a distorted view of marriage which sometimes leads to unrealistic expectations followed by abrupt reevaluations later in life.

The church leader can correct many of the popular misconceptions about marriage and can build a realistic and biblical view of the family long before marriage becomes a possibility. Sometimes entire families can attend conferences or discuss the contents of a family book.[28] Youth and singles groups, Bible studies, talks, discussions, and the reading of good articles or books are common ways for instilling healthy attitudes toward marriage. High school students may have little interest in housing, finances within marriage or in-law relationships, but they are interested in sex, male-female roles, home life, and ways in which they can evaluate themselves and improve themselves as potential mates. College students should be encouraged to take a course in marriage and the family, recognizing, however, that some professors and textbooks will fail to take the biblical view into account.[29] In the church, discussions of dating can point out that each date is a learning experience which helps unmarried people respect, communicate with, and relate to the opposite sex.

The building of better marriages and families is a lifelong process. It begins in the home, continues in the church and society, is emphasized in premarital counseling, and must be practiced daily as a man and woman build their relationship together.

Conclusions about Premarital Counseling

Counselors usually are busy people. They have a demanding and difficult job, helping people get untangled from problem situations and teaching them how to function more effectively. Surrounded by so many cries for help, it is easy for the counselor to ignore or casually dismiss those who do not have pressing problems. As a result, prevention is overlooked and new problems continue to develop—problems which later must be solved.

In medicine there has been a new interest in preventing disease or injury and helping people maintain their health. This interest in prevention began to seep into the field of counseling several years ago and now has become a rushing force. In no area is preventive counseling more possible, more accepted by the society, and more important than in the area of preparation for marriage. In no counseling area is the church more experienced and more respected than in this same area. Christians can show *that* premarital counseling really works, and we have a responsibility to show *how* it works—by helping people to anticipate difficulties in marriage and family living, by teaching them how to communicate and resolve problems effectively, and by building marriages that are lived according to God's plan as revealed in the Bible.

Suggestions for Further Reading

Dicks, Russell L. *Premarital Guidance*. Philadelphia: Fortress Press, 1963.
*Fryling, Robert, and Fryling, Alice. *A Handbook for Engaged Couples: A Communication Tool for Those About to be Married*. Downers Grove, IL: Inter-Varsity, 1977.
* Phillips, Bob. *How Can I Be Sure?* Irvine, CA: Harvest House Publishers, 1978.
* Roberts, Wes, and Wright, H. Norman. *Before You Say 'I Do'*. Irvine, CA: Harvest House, 1978.
Rutledge, Aaron L. *Pre-Marital Counseling*. Cambridge, MA: Schenkman, 1966.
* Thompson, David A. *A Premarital Guide for Couples—And Their Counselors*. Minneapolis: Bethany Fellowship, 1979.
* White, John. *Eros Defiled: The Christian and Sexual Sin*. Downers Grove, IL: Inter-Varsity, 1977.
Wright, H. Norman. *Premarital Counseling*. Chicago: Moody, 1977.

Footnotes

1. Carl Rogers, *Becoming Partners: Marriage and Its Alternatives* (New York: Delacorte, 1972), p. 11.
2. Cecil G. Osborne, *The Art of Understanding Your Mate* (Grand Rapids: Zondervan, 1970), p. 13.
3. Matt. 1:18–25.
4. Cleveland McDonald, *Creating a Successful Christian Marriage* (Grand Rapids: Baker, 1975).

5. 1 Cor. 7:8, 26, 27, 29.

6. 1 Cor. 7:28, 33.

7. Eph. 5:22–6:4; Col. 3:18–21; 1 Pet. 3:1–9.

8. Aaron Rutledge, *Pre-Marital Counseling* (Cambridge, MA: Schenkman, 1966), p. 25.

9. Ibid., p. 36.

10. Eph. 5:25.

11. E. E. Masters, *Parents in Modern America* (Homewood, IL: Dorsey, 1970), p. 51.

12. William J. Lederer and Don D. Jackson, *The Mirages of Marriage* (New York: W. W. Norton, 1968), pp. 247, 248, 251.

13. Ibid., p. 249.

14. Eph. 5:18–20.

15. Eph. 5:21–6:4.

16. John Scanzoni, "A Christian Perspective on Alternative Styles of Marriage," in *Making More of Your Marriage,* ed. Gary R. Collins (Waco, TX: Word, 1976), pp. 157–68.

17. See for example, Kenneth L. Cannon and Richard Long, "Premarital Sexual Behavior in the Sixties," in *A Decade of Family Research and Action,* ed. Carlfred B. Broderick (Minneapolis: National Council on Family Relations, 1971), pp. 25–38.

18. Eph. 5:3.

19. Cannon and Long, "Premarital Sexual Behavior," p. 33.

20. See chapters 13 and 14 of this book.

21. Rutledge, *Pre-Marital Counseling.*

22. Herbert J. Miles, *Sexual Happiness in Marriage* (Grand Rapids: Zondervan, 1967).

23. This section is adapted from Gary R. Collins, *Effective Counseling* (Carol Stream, IL: Creation House, 1972), pp. 72–73.

24. Miles, *Sexual Happiness,* pp. 133, 134.

25. Consider using "The Marriage Expectation Inventory—Form I" for engaged couples, and "A Sex Attitude Survey and Profile" both available from Family Life Publications, P.O. Box 427, Saluda, North Carolina, 28773. See also the "California Marriage Readiness Evaluation Profile," available from Western Psychiatric Services, 12031 Wilshire Blvd., Los Angeles, California, 90025.

26. Highly recommended is Robert Fryling and Alice Fryling, *A Handbook for Engaged Couples* (Downers Grove, IL: Inter-Varsity, 1977). This book contains a number of "fill in the blank" questions. If a man and woman each get a copy they could fill in the blanks one chapter at a time and discuss their answers later. Also helpful is Dwight Hervey Small, *Design for Christian Marriage* (Old Tappan, NJ: Revell, 1959); H. Norman Wright, *Communication—Key to Your Marriage* (Glendale, CA: Regal, 1974); Tim LaHaye and Beverly LaHaye, *The Act of Marriage* (Grand Rapids: Zondervan, 1976).

27. Consider, for example, the tape by Wesley Roberts made to accompany this book (available from Word, Inc., Waco, Texas), and Dr. Ed Wheat's two tapes on "Sex Technique and Sex Problems in Marriage" (available from Bible Believer's Cassettes, 130 N. Spring, Springdale, Arkansas, 72764).

28. For a book written *about* the family and *for* family reading, see Gary R. Collins, *Family Talk* (Santa Ana: Vision House, 1978).

29. McDonald, *Successful Christian Marriage,* is a college level text written from a biblical perspective.

13

Marital Problems

SEVERAL YEARS AGO, A GROUP OF RESEARCHERS INTERVIEWED PEOPLE who had sought help for some kind of a problem. About one-fifth of the problems centered around "personal adjustment difficulties," 12 percent of the counselees had problems with their children, but a whopping 42 percent—almost half of those surveyed—reported that the problems centered around their marriages.[1]

Marital conflict is almost universal. Before marriage, people in love have a tendency to emphasize their similarities and overlook their differences. There often is a belief that "our love will be different," but tensions become more apparent when two people, with different backgrounds and personalities, begin living together in the most intimate of human relationships. Mutual efforts to adjust, a willingness to compromise and the experience of learning conflict resolution all help couples to get along and to mold a loving, relatively smooth marriage. But this often is difficult. Friction and tensions frequently burst into explosions which in turn can create more tension.

In our modern society the problems are accentuated by the prevailing views of marriage. At a time when divorce was rare and often condemned socially, it is probable that couples were more inclined to work out these differences. Today, in contrast, marital separation is common and there is a widespread belief that divorce can always be used as a fire escape should marital conflicts get too hot to handle. "Irreconcilable differences" or "irretrievable breakdowns" become causes for divorce and there even are places where marriages can be terminated legally when one or both of the spouses simply decide that there no longer is any desire to stay married.[2] With the exception of one or two brief leveling-off periods, the divorce rate has increased steadily since the turn of the century.[3] Marriage, the permanent union created by God, is treated less and less seriously and more as a temporary arrangement.

These social attitudes, coupled with the pressures of modern marriage,

create problems which frequently come to the counselor's attention. It is
not easy to help couples resolve marital conflict and build better marriages, but this can be one of the most rewarding of all counseling experiences.

The Bible and Marital Problems

Marriage is one of the first topics to be discussed in the Bible.[4] It is
mentioned frequently throughout the pages of Scripture, and considered
in depth in the New Testament. The purposes of marriage, the roles of
husband and wife, the importance of sex and the issue of parenting are
all discussed,[5] sometimes more than once. Marriage failure is mentioned
in the Old Testament law and treated in more detail by Jesus and Paul
in their discussions of divorce.[6] Since each of these marital issues is considered elsewhere in this volume, it is not necessary to repeat the discussions in a chapter on marital problems.[7]

What does the Bible say about marriage problems? Almost nothing!
Believers are encouraged to enjoy interpersonal and sexual relationships
with their mates,[8] and the finding of a mate is described as a good thing.[9]
In contrast, the Book of Proverbs picturesquely decries the difficulties of
living with a contentious, vexing spouse: "A constant dripping on a day
of steady rain and a contentious woman are alike; He who would restrain her restrains the wind."[10] There is evidence that Lot, Abraham,
Jacob, Job, Samson and a number of others had marital tensions at least
periodically. These are acknowledged honestly but marital problems, per
se, are not analyzed.

It should be remembered that marital conflict is often a symptom of
something deeper, such as selfishness, lack of love, unwillingness to forgive, anger, bitterness, communication problems, anxiety, sexual abuse,
drunkenness, feelings of inferiority, sin and a deliberate rejection of God's
will for his creatures. Each of these can cause marital tension, each can
be influenced by husband-wife conflict and each *is* discussed in the Bible.
Thus, while the Scriptures deal with marital conflict only indirectly and
in passing, the issues underlying marriage problems are considered in
detail. Many of these issues are discussed elsewhere in this book.

The Causes of Marital Problems

In Genesis 2:24, we read that in marriage "a man shall leave his father and his mother, and shall cleave to his wife; and they shall become
one flesh." Three verbs in this verse—leaving, cleaving, and becoming
one—indicate three purposes of marriage.

Leaving involves a departure from parents and implies a legal union
of husband and wife into a marriage. Walter Trobisch argues that couples
who ignore this legal element have a "stolen marriage." There may be
love and sex but there is no real responsibility to give marriage its proper
balance.[11]

Cleaving comes from a Hebrew word which means to stick or glue together. "A husband and wife are glued together like two pieces of paper. If you try to separate two pieces of paper which are glued together, you tear them both." [12] Ideally, the couple is dedicated to loving, drawing together, and remaining faithful to each other. When such cleaving is absent, they have an "empty marriage" which may be legal but is devoid of love.

Becoming one flesh involves sex but it goes beyond the physical. It means, writes Trobisch, "that two persons share everything they have, not only their bodies, not only their material possessions, but also their thinking and their feelings, their joy and their suffering, their hopes and their fears, their successes and failures." [13] This does not imply that two personalities are squelched or obliterated. The uniquenesses remain and are combined with those of one's mate to make a complete relationship. When the one-flesh relationship is lacking the couple has an "unfulfilled marriage."

Marriage problems arise because a husband and wife have deviated in some ways from the biblical standards outlined in Genesis 2:24 and elaborated in later portions of Scripture. Modern psychology, sociology, and related disciplines have clarified some of the ways in which people deviate from the biblical standards for marriage.

1. *Faulty Communication.* Within the professional literature, this is probably the most commonly mentioned cause of marital discord. Miscommunication occurs when the message which is sent is not the message which is received. In a perceptive little book, Judson Swihart has identified eight ways in which people say "I love you." [14] If a husband says "I love you" by buying presents, but the wife wants to hear these three little words expressed verbally, then there is miscommunication. The message sent is not the message received.

Messages are sent verbally (with words) and nonverbally (with gestures, tone of voice, facial expressions, and so on). When the verbal and nonverbal contradict, there is a "double message" which leads to confusion and communication breakdown. Consider, for example, the woman who says verbally, "I don't mind if you go on the business trip," but whose resigned tone of voice and lack of enthusiasm say, "I *really* don't want you to go." In good communication the message sent verbally is consistent with the message sent nonverbally, and the message sent is the message received.

It has been suggested that occasional miscommunication between spouses is inevitable—perhaps as much as 20 percent of the time. [15] "But when miscommunication begins to overpower clear communication," the marriage is in trouble, and probably will get worse "because poor communication tends to breed more of the same." [16] It should be added that communication is a learned interaction. That which is not good can be made better.

2. *Defensive Self-centered Attitudes.* Getting close to another person is risky. We open ourselves to criticism and possible rejection when we let another person know us intimately, become aware of our insecurities and see our weaknesses. Since most of us have learned the value of "fending for ourselves" it is not easy to trust ourselves to another. Stubbornness, an unwillingness to share confidences, a tendency to blame others and defend ourselves—these are all evidences of what has been called "our fear of love." [17] Sometimes people express these fears by remaining distant emotionally. Sometimes they criticize and thus drive others away. Then there are times when, unconsciously, they reach the conclusion that "sooner or later I'll probably get hurt even by this person I love, therefore I must hurt first." [18] In an attempt at self-protection and with a desire to maintain a dominant position, one's mate is constantly "put down" verbally or manipulated subtly. This creates tension and marital discord. Regretfully the husband and wife often fail to see what is happening and do not recognize the defensive, self-centered attitudes that are creating the tension.

3. *Interpersonal Tension.* When two people marry, each comes to the marriage with approximately two or more decades of past experiences, training and ways of looking at life. Often these differences are resolved through compromise and synthesis, but sometimes there is an unwillingness to change. The differences become rallying points and rigid battle lines are drawn. On other occasions there may be sincere desire for conflict resolution but the couple isn't sure how things can be improved. These tension points may concern any of the following.

(a) Sex. At times, most couples have sexual problems. Sometimes these cause other problems; at times these are the result of other marital tensions. The causes of sexual problems have been discussed elsewhere,[19] but these include lack of accurate knowledge, unrealistic expectations, fear of not being able to perform adequately, differences in sexual drive, inhibiting attitudes about sex, and insufficient opportunities for privacy. Impatience, frigidity and infidelity—perhaps the three most common sex problems—in turn create more tension which further hinders smooth sexual functioning. When sexual problems are not resolved, marriages almost always suffer.

(b) Roles. In this age of women's liberation and the reevaluation of traditional sex roles, there often is conflict over what it means to be a man or woman. The society gives little guidance because opinions seem to be changing so rapidly. The Bible is much more explicit,[20] but Christians differ in their interpretations of these Scriptures. As a result there is disagreement, and sometimes threat, accompanied by competition. Often it appears that the tension arises over the nature and extent of the wife's work.

(c) Religion. The Bible warns of problems when a believer and unbeliever try to live together in marriage.[21] Numerous counselors have observed tensions when there are differences in degree of religious interest or commitment, denominational preferences, and expectations for the religious education of children. Sometimes these differences create tension is other areas such as the choice of friends, views of ethics, whether and to whom charitable donations will be given, or the use of time on Sundays. Religion can be a binding, strengthening force in a marriage but it can also be destructive.

(d) Values. What is really important in life? How should we spend our time? What are our goals? These questions concern values and value conflicts are at the heart of many marital tensions.

Consider, for example, how some of the following value alternatives could create potential for conflict.

—Credit cards can get us over a financial crisis, or credit cards should never be used.

—Divorce is never right, or sometimes divorce is the best solution to marital problems.

—TV is good entertainment, or TV is harmful and best avoided.

—Religion should be the center of one's life, or religion is best left to Sunday.

—Succeeding in one's vocation is of major importance in life, or the most important thing in life is building one's family.

—Working wives are more balanced, better mothers, or working wives are really abandoning their family responsibilities.

Many of these view are held firmly. Even in the home people act in accordance with their values and fight for their beliefs, if these beliefs are attacked or challenged by their mates.

(e) Needs. For almost a century, psychologists have debated about the existence of human needs. Most agree that we each need food, rest, air, and freedom from pain, but there also are psychological needs such as a need for love, security, and contact with others. In addition, might there be unique personal needs—such as the need to dominate, to control, to possess, to achieve, or to help? If one spouse has a need to dominate while the other wants to be controlled, then there can be compatibility. But if both husband and wife have a need to dominate, this creates the potential for conflict.

(f) Money. How are the family finances to be earned? Who controls the money? How is it to be spent? What things are needed and what are merely desirable? Is a budget necessary? How much should be given to the church? What happens when there is a shortage of money?

The answers to these questions reflect one's financial values and attitudes. When a husband and wife have different answers to these questions, there is potential for conflict. Once again it is difficult to determine whether financial tensions cause other problems or whether the reverse is true. It does appear to be true, however, that a harmonious financial relationship is essential if there is to be a harmonious marriage.

4. *External Pressures.* Sometimes marital tensions are stimulated by people and situations apart from the couple. These external sources of pressure include:

—in-laws who criticize or otherwise make demands on the couple;

—children whose needs and presence often interfere with the depth and frequency of husband-wife contacts, and sometimes drive a wedge between the spouses;

—friends, including opposite sex friends, who make time demands on the couple and sometimes involve one or both spouses in infidelity;

—crises which disrupt family relationships and create stress for all who are involved;

—vocational demands which put pressure on the husband and/or wife, create fatigue, and take time from the marriage.

Most of these pressures can be resisted but each can be powerful and a threat to marital harmony.

5. *Boredom.* As the years pass by, husbands and wives settle into routines, get accustomed to each other and sometimes slip into self-absorption, self-satisfaction or self-pity, each of which can take the excitement out of marriage and make life boring. When marriage is dull and routine, couples begin to look elsewhere for variety and challenge. This, in turn, creates further marital tension.

The Effects of Marital Problems

As indicated above, it is difficult to separate the effects of marital problems from the causes. For example, sexual and financial difficulties, as we have seen, may cause marital tension, but marital tension can also cause problems in bed or in balancing the checkbook. Although there is this circular relationship between cause and effect, the counselor also can observe several specific effects of marital tension.

1. *Confusion and Despair.* Caught in the middle of conflict, and watching one's marriage disintegrate, the husband and/or wife often feels overwhelmed and confused about what to do next. Sometimes there are frantic, often futile, attempts to make amends. Sometimes there comes despair and a resigned attitude which says, "Things will never get better so why try?"

2. *Withdrawal.* It is impossible to estimate the number of people who are legally married, living together and sometimes sleeping in the same bed, but who are emotionally and psychologically divorced. The husband and wife may each engage in their own activities but there is little warmth, concern, communication, intimacy or love for one's mate. By withdrawing emotionally the couple avoids the pain and social stigma of divorce. Conflicts remain and although there is no peace treaty, there are few

battles. Instead the marriage exists as a truce which may extend for a lifetime.

3. *Desertion.* When the marital and family pressures get too intense, some people simply leave. It has been suggested that the number of desertions probably equals the number of legal divorces.[22] While this may be too high an estimate (it is difficult to compile statistics on desertion), it is clear that thousands of mates desert their families every year and leave hurt feelings, confusion, uncertainty, and one-parent families behind. The courts can require that a deserting spouse return, but such people are difficult to find, and many ignore the court orders. Since most deserters are from lower-class families, the deserted mate often cannot afford the legal costs of starting court action against the deserter.

4. *Divorce.* This, the most radical and permanent effect of marital problems, is the route being taken by increasing numbers of couples. Divorce is the legal termination of a once promising and satisfying relationship that has been coming apart socially and emotionally. Divorce is never a happy solution to marital problems. Undoubtedly it is used too frequently and often it ignores the biblical guidelines for divorce.[23] Nevertheless it must be recognized that there are times when divorce may be the most feasible alternative to a problem-plagued marriage.

Counseling and Marital Problems

Counseling one person is a difficult task. Counseling a husband and wife is even more difficult and requires special skill and alertness on the part of the counselor. Frequently one or both of the spouses come with skepticism about the value of counseling and sometimes there is an attitude of resistance or hostility. Marriage counseling has been called "one of the most difficult and sensitive of therapies. . . . filled with psychological traps and surprises." Thus, before starting (and frequently thereafter), counselors should look to themselves to clarify some of their own attitudes, prejudices and vulnerabilities.

1. *Be Alert to Yourself.* What is your attitude toward marital problems? Are you critical, inclined to condemn, prone to take sides, afraid that marital counseling might arouse anxieties about your own marriage? Are you nervous lest your counseling be a failure? Remember that your job is to be available to the couple and to the Holy Spirit as an instrument of healing. Your reputation as a counselor never rests on one case. Your help will be most effective if you can commit the counseling to God, relax, and try to provide an atmosphere where constructive discussion is possible. In addition, try to understand both sides of the situation from the perspective of the people involved.

Intimate discussions about marriage can arouse sexual and other feelings in the counselor—feelings which must be admitted to oneself and dealt with perhaps in the ways discussed in chapter 3. Sometimes the counselees remind us of other people and marriages that we have known elsewhere. Unless he or she is extremely careful, the counselor's feelings, attitudes, and prejudices about these outside situations may become imposed on the counselees. This can create great confusion. Recognize too that counselees may cast you into a role that you may neither recognize nor want. A woman, for example, might see her male counselor as "a kind, understanding man—so different from my husband." The husband, in turn, may think of the male counselor as a threat to the marriage and one who doesn't really understand the wife. When a counselor is admired or rejected, one must be careful not to react in accordance with one's feelings.

2. *Be Alert to Special Issues.* Marriage counseling raises some procedural questions which may not be present in other types of counseling.

(a) Should the Couple Be Seen Alone or Together? Many counselors would answer "both." Sometimes, after an initial joint session, counselors will see the husband and wife separately for a few minutes or a few sessions. Often this gives different perspectives on the problem and there will be times when one or both spouses have separate problems which may benefit from individual counseling. Marriage, however, is a relationship and marital problems involve conflicts between two people. If these can be observed and discussed together (sometimes even with the children present), progress may be greater and faster. The counselor, however, must be careful to be impartial in counseling couples. Taking sides could be disastrous.

(b) Is Group Counseling Desirable? Sometimes couples with similar problems can benefit from counseling that takes place in a group with other couples. In general this should not be considered or suggested until the counselor has had time to get some perspectives on the major issues involved in the marital disputes.[24]

(c) Should the Counselor Work Alone or with Another Counselor? Sometimes a man and woman, perhaps a husband and wife, can work together as a counseling team. This lets the couple have a male and female perspective and the co-counselors can model good communication and interpersonal relationships. Such an arrangement can be time-consuming, however, and can put pressure on the counselors, especially if they are married and subject to the same pressures that face the counselees. Nevertheless, mature couples who work together smoothly often counsel other couples effectively.

(d) Are There Marriage Personalities? It has been suggested that marriages, like individuals, have unique personalities. They are not all the same and neither can they be treated alike. At the time of marriage, the husband and wife each bring a unique set of values, beliefs, expectations, past experiences, personality characteristics and "ways of doing things." These must be merged into some kind of a working relationship which also considers social issues such as in-law influences, vocational demands, level of income and economic conditions or minority biases in the society. Although some writers have given creative descriptions of marriage types,[25] it probably is as difficult to categorize marriages as it is to categorize individuals. No person, and no marriage, really fits the "type" category. Each is unique and this uniqueness must be remembered in counseling.

3. *Determine Counseling Goals.* The counselor, the husband, and the wife each approach marriage counseling with expectations and goals. These goals may be either vague or clearly defined. Some will be realistic; some will not. When the goals are clear, realistic, and accepted by everyone, marriage counseling starts with a high potential for success. When the goals are vague or in conflict (e.g., the husband wants a smooth separation, the wife wants a reconciliation), then counseling will be more difficult.

(a) Recognizing Counselor Goals. At the beginning, let us recognize that the Christian counselor does not approach marriage counseling with complete neutrality. He or she is likely to have specific goals which will give direction to the counseling. These goals may include:

—identifying and understanding the specific issue which are creating the marital problems;

—teaching the couple how to communicate constructively;

—teaching problem-solving and decision-making techniques;

—helping the counselees understand the counseling relationship;

—helping them to express their frustrations, disappointments and desires for the future;

—keeping the husband and wife together; and

—teaching the couple how to build a marriage based on biblical principles.

What are your goals in marriage counseling? When these are recognized clearly, counseling can be more effective. The counselor knows where he or she is going and, with one's own goals in mind, it is easier to concentrate on counselee goals.

(b) Determining Counselee Goals. Sometimes the counselees' goals are similar to those of the counselor, but often there is a discrepancy. Questions like "What would you hope to get out of counseling?" or "How would you like your marriage to be different?" often can initiate discussion which clarifies, for the counselees as well as for the counselor, what the husband and/or wife hope to achieve through counseling.

(c) Setting Mutually Acceptable Goals. Many people have vague and distant goals (e.g., "To have a happy Christian marriage"), but these are reached best through a series of more specific, more attainable, more immediate goals. Some counselors work on a contract approach in which the husband and wife each agree to change behavior in some specific way during the periods between counseling sessions. He, for example, agrees to take out the garbage nightly; she agrees to let him read the paper alone before dinner.[26] When a couple sets such goals with the counselor's help, there is increased motivation to attain these goals and the couple can learn about communication and problem-solving in the process. As goals are reached, the couple is encouraged because they see specific progress.

Regretfully, however, not everyone agrees on the goals. Counselees sometimes want help in attaining goals which counselors consider unrealistic or immoral. If, for example, a married male wants help in maintaining an erection during extramarital sexual contacts, the Christian counselor is faced with a goal conflict. To help the counselee reach his goal is to encourage behavior which is sin, according to the Bible. In a noncondemning but honest way these differences in goals and values must be discussed. The counselor's goal is not to manipulate or to force people to change, but neither should people be helped to act in ways which the counselor considers morally wrong, psychologically harmful or detrimental to the marriage. If counselor-counselee goal conflicts persist, even after continued discussion, then withdrawal from the counseling and referral may be the best options.

Also difficult is the situation in which husband and wife have conflicting goals. Such conflicts must be discussed openly if counseling is to be successful. Usually there are at least some common goals, and it is possible to start with these. Sometimes as goals are clarified, it becomes apparent that these are not as divergent as it first appeared.

(d) Reaching the Goals. Since each marriage is unique and since each marital problem is different from all others, it is not possible to give a step-by-step recipe for successful marriage counseling. Table 13–1 summarizes some general guidelines but within this framework counselors must focus on the persons, problems, and processes in counseling.

4. *Focus on Persons.* Books on marriage adjustment often give practical advice on issues such as handling money, dealing with in-laws, changing abrasive personal habits, or resolving sexual problems. Many of these suggestions are practical and helpful but it does not follow that marriage counseling is completed when the practical problems are solved. Such a belief has been called the "fallacy of the reasonable solution." Reasonable solutions often fail, even when presented to reasonable counselees. This is because many problems are more emotional than rational. Logic and rational analysis fail to help because emotional and personality factors get in the way and prevent people from taking action to reach practical conclusions.[27]

The counselor's first task is to understand persons—with their feelings and frustrations—rather than to understand problems. Sometimes, counselors are so intent on solving problems and finding "how-to-do-it" answers that they become insensitive to the people with whom they are

Table 13–1
The Process of Marriage Counseling

STAGE I: *The Beginning*

The Counselor seeks to establish rapport through warm, accepting, trusting, uncritical, understanding attitudes; and to help the counselees overcome initial fears.

The Counselee must share his or her initial reasons for seeking help, and must overcome initial fears and doubts related to seeking help.

STAGE II: *Emergence of Basic Problems*

The Counselor encourages detailed discussions of specific conflict situations and expressions of feelings; raises questions or makes comments to stimulate further thought and to clarify both issues and feelings; continues to give support and encouragement.

The Counselee gives more details; expresses feelings and frustrations; learns to build a trusting, secure relationship with the counselor

STAGE III.   *Developing and Trying Tentative Solutions*

The Counselor continues to be supportive and alert to new information, but encourages and guides in the consideration of tentative solutions such as attitude change, behavior change, confession, forgiveness, reexamination of perceptions, etc.; guides and encourages as solutions are attempted, evaluated, and tried again (both in the counseling sessions and at home).

The Counselee learns how to formulate, act on, and evaluate solutions; expresses frustrations and fears as they arise; experiences some victories.

STAGE IV.   *Termination*

The Counselor encourages the counselees to launch out without the counselor; reviews past progress; expresses the counselor's continued availability if needed.

The Counselee expresses doubts and fears in going out from counseling, but reevaluates progress and examines one's spiritual and personal resources for getting along without counseling.

working. As with all helping, empathy, genuineness and warmth are basic to successful marriage counseling.

5. *Focus on Problems.* It does not follow, however, that problems should be ignored. On the contrary, problems are the major symptoms which indicate that something is wrong. By asking the husband and wife to describe specific incidents of conflict, the counselor is enabled to understand not only the sources of dissension, but also the accompanying feelings of rejection, anger, hurt, frustration, and fractured self-esteem.

The problems vary considerably, of course. They may concern money, sex, husband-wife roles, religion, conflicting values or a host of similar issues. Counselees can be asked how they feel about each problem, how they have tried to solve the problems in the past, what has worked and what has not. Discuss alternative courses of action for the future, encourage and teach counselees how to try out these solutions, and take time to evaluate what works and what does not.

6. *Focus on Processes.* According to the dictionary, *process* refers to the changes or continuous actions which are taking place during a period of time. In counseling, the word *process* often is used to describe the continuous ways in which people relate to one another during the counseling sessions.

How does the couple communicate?

How do they interact in public or in private?

How do they handle disagreements?

How do they react when each perceives a problem in a different way?

Do they criticize each other? Do they build up one another?

These issues, and the warning signals presented in Table 13–2, are so important in marriage counseling that much of the counseling procedure will involve teaching people to relate better.

How does this teaching occur? It begins by careful observation of the couple as they interact in counseling. Listen, then, to their descriptions of how they relate to each other elsewhere. Discuss these styles of relating with the counselees. Can you think of better ways to communicate and interact? Encourage counselees to try these out between counseling sessions.

As with all other types of counseling, the ultimate purpose in marriage counseling is to help counselees grow personally, interpersonally and spiritually. Our greatest success comes when couples learn to build marriages that are yielded to Jesus Christ, based on biblical principles, characterized by a commitment to each other, and growing as the husband and wife constantly work at skillful communication, goal attainment and conflict resolution.

7. *Theoretical Issues.* Within recent years, marriage counseling has developed as a major specialty with its own professional journals, training programs and licensing laws. As the field has grown, so have the theo-

Table 13–2
Marital Problem Warning Signals *

Early Warning Signals

1. Denial—A tendency to ignore, or explain away evidences of tension.

2. Avoidance—A decision to avoid or postpone indefinitely any discussion of tense issues or concerns about the relationship.

3. Repetition—Discussions, including arguments, which bring up issues repeatedly but which never solve problems. This is a "here we go again" attitude.

4. Detachment—A self-defensive attitude which says in words or attitude, "I really don't care about the problem."

More Serious Warning Signals

1. Complete Communication Breakdown—Nevertheless one or both spouses tries to do things (like improving oneself, buying presents, and so on) that will improve the situation.

2. Attacks on Each Other's Integrity—This involves subtle and/or overt, private and/or public, verbal and/or nonverbal attacks on the sexuality, appearance, achievements, intentions or efforts of the other.

3. Withdrawal—An attitude which says "I'll take care of things myself and do my own thing."

4. Lack of Self-worth—A self-evaluating, despondent attitude which asks, "What is wrong with me? What did I do to get us into this mess?"

5. Looking for Consolation—Finding someone inside the family or without to give support, help, love, or affirmation. This is at the basis of many affairs.

6. Giving Up—An "I've had it; things will never get better" attitude.

7. Ambivalence—A pattern of confusion in which the person doesn't know what he or she wants or what to do.

*Adapted with permission from William V. Arnold, Dixie McKie Baird, Joan Trigg Langan, and Elizabeth Blakemore Vaughan, *Divorce: Prevention or Survival* (Philadelphia: Westminster Press, 1977).

retical approaches. While discussion of these is beyond the scope of this book, some of the major approaches are summarized in Table 13–3.

Preventing Marital Problems

The spiraling divorce rate and the increasing public awareness of marital tension have opened this topic for discussion both outside of the church and within. Once again, the Christian community is in a crucially important position for the prevention of marital problems. Teaching young people about marriage and sex, followed later by premarital counseling, can help to prevent marriage problems.[29] Crisis intervention, which often involves the church, can help people to deal with problems as they arise and to avoid long-term destructive patterns of problem solving. A perusal of the chapter titles in this book will reveal a number of problem areas, any one of which could create marriage problems. Dealing with these problems as they arise and working to prevent them can in turn prevent their becoming a cause for marital tensions.

In addition to the above, there are several preventive actions that may be taken, especially by church or parachurch groups—including discussion groups and Sunday school classes.

1. *Teach Biblical Principles of Marriage.* Christians believe that God, who created both male and female and who initiated marriage, also has given guidelines for marriage in the pages of Scripture. These need to be taught clearly at home and church, and modeled consistently by Christian leaders. Since we live in a society which propagates different values, the biblical values—including the biblical teachings about sex and the meaning of love—must be reinforced frequently.

Several years ago, two thousand Christian leaders gathered in St. Louis where they participated in a week-long Continental Congress on the Family. At the conclusion of this conference, the participants issued an "affirmation on the family" which was distributed widely. This could be the basis for sermons, group discussion, and family consideration.[30] Such interaction teaches the biblical views on families and can stimulate marital and family communication.

2. *Stress the Importance of Marriage and Marital Commitment.* For most people life consists of a number of demands, commitments and responsibilities. Often, in the midst of these pressures, one's marriage and family are slowly shunted to a lesser order of priority. Work, church, community responsibilities and other activities take precedence over time spent with one's spouse. Marriage takes time, effort and commitment if it is to grow and develop. This needs to be emphasized in churches and elsewhere. Encourage people to make marriage a high priority item in terms of the expenditure of time and effort. Encourage couples to do things together, and for each other, to establish priorities, to work toward mutual goals, and to think of ways to bring variety into their marriages. (Reading may help in this.)

Table 13–3
Theoretical Approaches to Marriage Counseling [28]

Approach	Special Features
Classical	This is the traditional psychoanalytic approach. The mate who is designated as the patient enters long-term counseling with the therapist who uses psychoanalytic methods to treat individual problems. As the individual improves, this is assumed to affect the marriage positively.
Collaborative	In this approach, each spouse is seen individually by a different counselor. Counselors confer periodically, comparing notes and sharing information that may be mutually beneficial.
Concurrent	Here the husband and wife are seen separately but by the same counselor. This gives one counselor both the husband's and the wife's perspectives, but some critics have raised questions about favoritism and the counselor's inability to refrain from taking sides. A variation of this is consecutive counseling, in which one mate is seen for counseling and then, following termination, the other mate is seen.
Conjoint	Here the husband and wife are seen together, sometimes with other family members present. It is assumed that the family operates as a social system. Counseling teaches everyone in the system to act differently so there is greater understanding, better communication, and less harmful behavior.
Changed Behavior	These are the learning approaches to counseling. Marital problems are defined in terms of behavior that either mate would like terminated, decreased, increased, modified, or developed. Separately or together these new behaviors are learned (or unlearned).
Crisis	This assumes that each family has a developmental history of its own, characterized by a number of crises. When these occur the family is seen together and helped in several ways: —Giving immediate aid—the counselor is available when needed; —Defining the problem as a family need, rather than as an individual problem, even though one family member may be showing the symptom; —Focusing on the present, rather than analyzing the past; —Reducing family tensions by psychological and pharmacological means; —Helping to resolve the precipitating stress: this also teaches families how to solve problems; and —Identifying sources of referral where families can be helped in the future.
Conflict Resolution	Working with whole families, the counselor attempts to teach conflict resolution and problem-solving skills. Sometimes there is an attempt to change the entire family structure by assigning new tasks, changing roles, teaching new communication skills, etc.
Contract	Here married couples, and families, are helped to make and keep family agreements in which there are agreed-upon *performances* which lead either to special *privileges* (as reward for something accomplished) or to *punishment*. This is a form of behavior change therapy in which all participants agree on the behavior to be changed and the consequences of change or no change.
Covenant	This is a form of contract theory described as being conjoint, behavioral change, and biblical in its orientation. Here a marital relationship is treated "through attaining and experiencing an explicit, mutually agreed upon, and satisfactory relational covenant, mediated through the sources of a third person."
Combined	This is a combination of two or more of the above. It is a "catch-all" technique which may be difficult to apply in practice.

3. *Teach Principles of Communication and Conflict Resolution.* Married people should be shown the importance of listening, self-disclosure, acceptance, and understanding. Empathy, warmth and genuineness need not be limited to counseling sessions. These are attributes which can be learned and practiced in a marriage. Chapter 23 outlines some principles which can help with this teaching.

4. *Stimulate Marriage Enrichment.* All marriages, even good marriages, have room for improvement. Couples or groups of couples can be encouraged to read and discuss books which help them improve their marriage relationships.[31] Churches may also wish to sponsor marriage enrichment seminars or encourage couples to attend such meetings.[32]

5. *Encourage Counseling.* Couples, like individuals, often are reluctant to seek counseling, lest this be seen as an admission of failure. From the pulpit and elsewhere it should be emphasized that going for counseling is a sign of strength. The sooner one goes for help, the greater the likelihood of counseling effectiveness. The material presented in Table 13–2 may help couples with their decision to seek counseling.

Conclusions about Marital Problems

Marriage is the most intimate of all human relationships. When this relationship is good and growing, it provides one of life's greatest satisfactions. When it is poor or even static and routine, it can be a source of great frustration and misery. God surely wants marriages to be good—a model of the beautiful relationship between Christ and his church.[33] The Christian counselor who understands biblical teaching and who knows counseling techniques is best qualified to help couples attain the biblical ideal for marriage.

Suggestions for Further Reading

* Clinebell, Howard J., and Clinebell, Charlotte H. *The Intimate Marriage.* New York: Harper & Row, 1970.
Collins, Gary R., ed. *Make More of Your Marriage.* Waco, TX: Word, 1976.
Johnson, Dean. *Marriage Counseling: Theory and Practice.* Englewood Cliffs, NJ: Prentice-Hall, 1961.
Lederer, William J., and Jackson, Don D. *The Mirages of Marriage,* New York: Norton, 1968.
Martin, Peter A. *A Marital Therapy Manual.* New York: Brunner/Mazel, 1976.
Stewart, Charles William. *The Minister As Marriage Counselor.* Rev. ed. Nashville: Abingdon, 1970.

Footnotes

1. Joint Commission on Mental Illness and Health, *Action for Mental Health* (New York: Science Editions, 1961), p. 103.

2. Norman N. Robbins, "Have We Found Fault in No Fault Divorce?" *Family Coordinator* 22 (July, 1973): 359–62.

3. Robert S. Weiss, *Marital Separation* (New York: Basic Books, 1975), p. 11.

4. Gen. 2:18–25.

5. Eph. 5:21–33; Col. 3:18–25; 1 Pet. 3:1–7; Heb. 13:4, for example.

6. Deut. 24:1–4; Matt. 5:31, 32; 19:3–9; 1 Cor. 7:10–16.

7. See chapters 11, 12, 14, 15 and 21.

8. Prov. 5:18; Eccles. 9:9.

9. Prov. 18:22.

10. Prov. 19:13; 21:9, 19; 27:15, 16.

11. Walter Trobisch, *I Married You* (New York: Harper & Row, 1971).

12. Ibid., p. 15.

13. Ibid., p. 18.

14. Judson J. Swihart, *How Do You Say 'I Love You'?* (Downers Grove, IL: Inter-Varsity Press, 1977).

15. William J. Lederer and Don D. Jackson, *The Mirages of Marriage* (New York: Norton, 1968).

16. Ibid., p. 103.

17. M. B. Hodge, *Your Fear of Love* (Garden City, NY: Doubleday Dolphin, 1967).

18. Ibid., p. 8.

19. See chapter 21.

20. Eph. 5:21–33; Col. 3:18–25; 1 Pet. 3:1–7.

21. 1 Cor. 7:12–16; 2 Cor. 6:14–16.

22. André Bustanoby, "When Wedlock Becomes Deadlock: Biblical Teaching on Divorce, Part 1," *Christianity Today* 20 June, 1975, p. 4. Citing government statistics, Stewart estimates that there is one desertion for every 4 or 5 divorces. See C. W. Stewart, *The Minister as Marriage Counselor.*

23. See chapter 14.

24. For a special consideration of group marriage counseling see Richard B. Wilke, *The Pastor and Marriage Group Counseling* (Nashville: Abingdon, 1974).

25. A. L. Rutledge, *Pre-Marital Counseling* (Cambridge, MA: Schenkman, 1966), pp. 39–48; and P. A. Martin, *A Marital Therapy Manual* (New York: Brunner/Mazel, 1976).

26. A. Bustanoby, "Rapid Treatment for a Troubled Marriage," in *Make More of Your Marriage,* ed. Gary R. Collins (Waco, TX: Word, 1976), pp. 108-21.

27. Kennedy, Eugene, *On Becoming a Counselor* (New York: Seabury, 1977), pp. 219, 220.

28. This table is adapted from Bernard Green, *Psychotherapies of Marital Disharmony* (New York: Free Press, 1965); Martin, *A Marital Therapy Manual;* and D. G. Langsley, "Three Models of Family Therapy: Prevention, Crisis Treatment or Rehabilitation," *Journal of Clinical Psychiatry* (November, 1978): 792–796. See also G. D. Erickson and T. P. Hogan, *Family Therapy: An Introduction to Theory and Technique* (New York: Jason Aronson, 1976).

For further information on conjoint therapy see Virginia Satir, *Conjoint Family Therapy* (Palo Alto: Science Behavior Books, 1964); and R. V. Fitzgerald, *Conjoint Marital Therapy* (New York: Jason Aronson, 1973).

For a concise discussion of behavior change see David Knox, *Marriage Happiness: A Behavioral Approach to Counseling* (Champaign, IL: Research Press, 1971).

Contract and Covenant therapy are discussed in Donald F. Tweedie, Jr., "A Model for Marital Therapy," in *Make More of Your Marriage,* ed. Gary R. Collins, pp. 122–33. See also C. J. Sager, *Marriage Contracts and Couple Therapy* (New York: Brunner/Mazel, 1976).

29. See chapters 11, 12, 21.

30. For a reprint of the statement and a devotional-study guide for use by both churches and families, see Gary R. Collins, *Family Talk* (Santa Ana: Vision House, 1978).

31. See for example, Howard J. Clinebell and Charlotte H. Clinebell, *The Intimate Marriage* (New York: Harper & Row, 1970); Gary Demarest, *Christian Alternatives Within Marriage* (Waco, TX: Word, 1977); Lederer and Jackson, *The Mirages of Marriage* (New York: Norton, 1968); David Mace and Vera Mace, *We Can Have Better Marriages If We Really Want Them* (Nashville: Abingdon, 1974); Sven Wahlroos, *Family Communication* (New York: Signet Books, 1974); and H. Norman Wright, *Communication—Key to Your Marriage* (Glendale, CA: Regal, 1974).

32. Especially recommended is Christian Marriage Enrichment, 8000 East Girard, Suite 602, Denver, Colorado, 80231. Family Concern, Inc., 1415 Hill Avenue, Wheaton, Illinois, 60187, also conducts marriage seminars. See also, H. Norman Wright, "The Church and Marriage Enrichment," in *Make More of Your Marriage,* ed. Gary R. Collins, pp. 144–56.

33. Eph. 5:23–30.

14

Divorce
and Remarriage

MODERN MARRIAGE IS A HIGHLY UNSTABLE INSTITUTION.

That sentence could not have been written 100 years ago and there are parts of the world where it would not apply today. But in many nations, including the United States, Canada and some countries in Europe, the divorce rate has been increasing steadily. If to this we add the number of desertions (called the "poor person's divorce") and separations, it is clear that a large percentage of all marriages will fall apart. The size of that "large percentage" will vary, not only with the latest government statistics, but also with individual attitudes toward separation and divorce.

And the attitudes appear to be changing. After viewing a large number of television dramas and soap operas, a Cornell University sociologist concluded that these programs portray a world of "disposable fly-apart marriages," "throw-away husbands, throw-away wives" and "disposable children." [1] Certainly these television dramas are "only stories," but they reflect and influence the thinking of millions of people, including Christians, who may not approve but nevertheless accept infidelity, illegitimacy and divorce as a way of life in our society. Commitment is giving way to an attitude of self-centered "freedom," and "till death do us part" is being replaced by a belief that divorce can always provide an escape hatch if difficulties arise following the wedding.

It is easy to read about statistics and impersonal attitude changes in the society, but it is much more difficult to help "real live" hurting people whose marriages have disintegrated. Guilt, anger, resentment, fear and disappointment burst into life accompanied, at times, by loneliness, confusion, a sense of rejection, and the haunting concern about who was at fault. Sermons and intellectual discussions about divorce often are informative but rarely do they convey the pain that so often accompanies a broken marriage.

187

The Bible and Divorce

The pain of divorce has led some compassionate Christians to reinterpret, "water down" or even de-emphasize biblical teachings to make divorce and remarriage seem easier and more acceptable theologically. But to ignore or de-emphasize biblical teaching is neither compassionate nor helpful. Helpful Christian counseling on divorce must begin with a clear understanding of the Scriptures.[2]

1. *The Teachings of the Old Testament.* The Bible clearly presents marriage as a permanent, intimate union between a husband and a wife.[3] This is God's unchanging ideal, but since the fall, human beings have lived on a subideal level. The Bible recognizes this, and so in Deuteronomy 24:1–4 there are some brief guidelines which govern the practice of divorce—a practice which is tolerated but never commanded or divinely endorsed.

According to the Old Testament, divorce was to be legal (with a written document), permanent and permissible only when "indecency" (presumably of a sexual nature) was involved. Regretfully, the meaning of "indecency" became a subject for debate among Jewish leaders so Jesus clarified the issue both in the Sermon on the Mount and later.[4]

2. *The Teachings of Jesus.* In the New Testament, Jesus reaffirmed the permanent nature of marriage, pointed out that divine permission for divorce was only given because of human sinfulness (and not because it was God's ideal), stated that sexual immorality was the only legitimate cause for divorce, and clearly taught that the one who divorces a sexually faithful spouse and marries another commits adultery (and the new mate also is committing adultery).

Like the ancient Jewish leaders who questioned the meaning of "indecency," some more modern scholars have debated the meaning of "except for immorality." The Greek word for immorality is *porneia,* which refers to all sexual intercourse apart from marriage. Such behavior violates the "one flesh" principle which is so basic to biblical marriage.

But even when immorality is involved, divorce is not commanded; it merely is permitted. Forgiveness and reconciliation still are preferable to divorce. In the opinion of many evangelical biblical scholars, when divorce does occur the innocent party is free to remarry.

3. *The Teachings of Paul.* In responding to a question from the Corinthians, the Apostle echoes Christ's teaching and then adds a second cause for divorce: the desertion of a believer by an unbelieving mate.[5]

This same passage also deals with religious incompatibility—when a believer and an unbeliever are married. This is not cause for divorce, even though it might create tension in the home. Indeed, Paul writes, the believing mate "sanctifies" the marriage and may be instrumental in bringing the nonbelieving spouse to Christ.

4. *The Teachings Summarized.* With his usual clarity, John R. W. Stott summarizes the biblical view which is commonly held by evangelicals:

First, God's intention in creating mankind male and female and in ordaining marriage is clear. Human sexuality finds fulfillment in marriage, and marriage is a permanent and exclusive union. This is the divine purpose and ideal.

Second, divorce is nowhere commanded nor even encouraged in Scripture.

Third, nevertheless, divorce (and remarriage) is permissible on two grounds. First, an innocent person may divorce his/her partner if the latter has been guilty of immorality. Secondly, a believer may acquiesce in the desertion of his/her unbelieving partner, if the latter refuses to go on living with him/her. In both cases, however, the permission is granted in negative (that is reluctant) terms: only if a person divorces his partner on the ground of unchastity is he not committing adultery. Only if the unbeliever insists on departing is the believer "not bound." [6]

To this must be added two additional comments. First, the Bible says nothing about the divorce of two nonbelievers. Clearly this is undesirable since it violates God's "one flesh" ideal and since it often involves adultery, a behavior which is always wrong, regardless of the person's beliefs. Nevertheless, there are no specific divine guidelines for non-Christian divorce.

Secondly, we must emphasize the importance of forgiveness. God hates divorce [7] and forbids adultery,[8] but these are not unpardonable sins. God forgives and expects his followers to do the same [9]—and then to live lives that are pure and free of further sinning.[10]

The Causes of Divorce

There is no one cause of divorce. Every marriage is different, and each that ends in divorce is terminated because of a unique combination of causes and circumstances. Chapter 13 listed some causes of marital problems. When these problems are not resolved, divorce is more likely. In addition, the following specific influences sometimes motivate one or both spouses to initiate divorce action.

1. *Sexual Unfaithfulness.* As we have seen, this is mentioned by Jesus as a legitimate reason for divorce. Although both parties usually contribute to the adultery, one partner frequently is involved in the actual offense. Such adultery

... has the effect of aborting or dissolving a marriage union in the eyes of God. Though the marriage was designed by God to be permanent or lifelong, the act of adultery breaks the one-flesh union of husband and wife in defiance of the will of God. ... This being true, the other partner is not guilty of adultery when getting a divorce. Adultery in that case has already been committed, and has severed the union by the breach of faithfulness and a new physical union.[11]

While divorce is permitted biblically under such circumstances, forgiveness and reconciliation are to be preferred. This is difficult because the "innocent" partner often feels betrayed, rejected and hurt. It becomes more difficult to believe that one's spouse can be trusted in the future and often there is anger and a feeling that one's self-esteem has been injured. But separation and divorce can be even more painful and the believer knows that all things are possible with God—even the restoration and growth of a marital relationship that has been broken by infidelity.

2. *Desertion.* To the words of Moses and Jesus, Paul added this as a second legitimate reason for divorce. When an unbelieving partner leaves or wants to leave, the believer is under no obligation to prevent the departure.[12]

But what if a believer forsakes the marriage? According to Stanley Ellison:

> Although many have tried to equate the word "depart" (*koridzetai*) with divorce, the conclusion cannot be drawn from the grammar. The thirteen usages of the term in the New Testament indicate it simply means "to depart" or separate.
>
> It should be recognized, however, that . . . if sexual immorality is engaged in or if the desertion is so prolonged as to give no prospect of reconciliation, a *de facto* divorce will have taken place, whether or not it has been sought or granted. . . . Although God's desire is always for reconciliation, where that is impossible because of the partner's recalcitrance, there is no useful purpose served in refusing to acknowledge dissolution. Desertion in that sense becomes divorce.[13]

3. *Immature Attitudes.* Immaturity on the part of one or both persons is at the basis of many divorce decisions, although there is no biblical support for this view. "Immaturity," of course, is difficult to define, but it includes such characteristics as an unwillingness to make and keep commitments or to assume responsibility, a tendency to dominate, a demanding that one be indulged or cared for, and a self-centered view of life which insists on "freedom to do my own thing whenever and wherever I want." Such attitudes stimulate conflict and work against attempts both to resolve difficulties and to avoid divorce.

4. *Social Sanctions.* Recent changes in social attitudes and values appear to have made divorce easier and more acceptable. Legal barriers to divorce have been lowered, the church has become more permissive, the women's liberation movement has become more influential, the media have become more supportive of infidelity, and many people have become less inclined to accept the sanctity or permanence of marriage. Some people, both men and women, have come to accept the view that self-realization and personal fulfillment are such major goals in life that everything else—including marriage—must take second place.[14] These social attitudes combine to make divorce a more viable option when marital tensions arise.

5. *Physical and Psychological Abuse.* Within recent years considerable media attention has been given to the problems of physical violence within

the family. Child abuse, mate beating, sexual abuse within marriage and harmful treatment of aged relatives all appear to be more prevalent than had been thought previously. Such physical harm, with its accompanying fear and mental anguish, can make home a hell rather than a heaven. Within marriage the violence can originate with either spouse, but it more often happens that men beat their wives. Many women defend themselves as best they can, and then stay with the marriage believing that their husbands will reform and that home violence is better than trying to survive and raise children alone in a hostile world.[15] Often there comes a time when the victim either responds with violence in return, or decides to separate from the marriage.

Some Christians maintain that such separation is wrong. Clearly, when a Christian and non-Christian are married, the believer has no freedom to leave or to send away the non-Christian mate simply because of theological differences,[16] but this says nothing about violence and mate beating. Such aggression can do incredible physical, psychological and spiritual damage to an abused mate or to abused children. To submit to such attacks is neither right nor healthy. A mate beater is psychologically and spiritually unhealthy. He or she also is sinning and, while such behavior must be forgiven, it cannot be condoned by a mate who meekly stands by and says nothing. Mate beating in and of itself is not an accepted biblical cause for divorce (although some divorces occur because of this), but it does give the victim reason to separate from a mate, at least temporarily.

6. *Other Stresses*. Almost any stress, when it is severe enough, can put sufficient pressure on a marriage to stimulate divorce. The demands of a time-consuming vocation, the alcoholism or drug abuse in a mate, the instabilities of middle age, the pressures of insufficient money, the boredom, rigidities and resentment that can build over the years—each of these has led to divorce, especially when the spouses have also seen their parents' marriages end. It is difficult to be the first one in a family to get a divorce, but when other family marriages have broken up, there is less resistance to subsequent divorces when stresses arise elsewhere in the family.[17]

The Effects of Divorce

Divorce is painful—very painful. It can thoroughly disrupt one's life, routines, feelings of self-worth, and sense of security. It can affect people physically, psychologically and spiritually. It can lead to emotional upheaval, irrational decisions and interpersonal tensions. It affects the two people involved but its influence can extend to children, parents, other family members, fellow employees, friends, neighbors, and people in the church.

Based on his contacts with hundreds of divorced people, Jim Smoke has identified three overlapping stages through which people go when they face divorce.[18] First, there is the *shock stage* in which the person recog-

nizes that "it really is happening to me." The marriage that began with
optimism, hope and happiness has been replaced with dazed feelings of
emptiness, resentment and confusion. As with all other shock, people
facing the shock of divorce react in a variety of ways. Some withdraw
from social contact; others talk about the details with everyone. Some
retreat within themselves; others get busy in a frantic round of activities
which might help them forget. Some feel guilt and failure; others feel
smug and bitter. Regardless of the reaction, before there can be growth
there must be an admission that "this really is happening to me."

Stage two is the *adjustment stage*. This includes "positive mourning"
(which involves the experience of remembering the good and happy times
in the marriage), "negative mourning" (which involves the experience of
swimming in a sea of self-pity and guilt), and "assembling the pieces"—
slowly picking up the demands of life and learning to live without a mate.

The *growth stage* comes next. Here people honestly face the reality of
their new status in life; set time aside for meditation, reading, prayer and
personal reflection; get involved with other people, deliberately resist
blaming others or themselves; fight self-pity; and seek God's guidance in
making realistic plans for the future.

In each of these stages, the counselor often will observe emotional,
behavioral and social effects of the divorce.

1. *Emotional Effects.* Divorce is accompanied by an almost endless
range of emotions, including: anxiety, guilt, fear, sadness, depression
(sometimes accompanied by thoughts of suicide), anger, bitterness and
frustration. Often along with the distress, there is a sense of euphoria and
relief but this sometimes stimulates more guilt. Most couples experience
periods of indecision, confusion or vacillation and sometimes there is a
hyperalertness, as if the person is waiting expectantly for something else
to go wrong. The body, of course, cannot maintain a continuing state
of tension and vigilance, so often psychosomatic illnesses result.

Divorce involves the loss of a love and the death of a relationship. The
divorce reaction, therefore, is a grief reaction with all of the emotions
that grieving involves. And like all grief reactions, the pain seems greater
at Christmas, Thanksgiving, anniversaries and other special times of the
year.

2. *Behavioral Effects.* Divorce not only affects how one feels; it influences what one does. Eating, paying the bills, solving daily problems,
taking care of one's property—these and other routine activities must continue; but they are continued without the help or influence of a mate. If
there are children, the divorced person must adjust to becoming a single
parent either living apart from the children, or with the children present
in a one-parent family. Preoccupied with these problems, one's work often
suffers. Quality and quantity decline, efficiency drops, and sometimes there
is high accident proneness.

3. *Social Effects.* Divorce involves people and whenever separation occurs, numerous persons are affected. These include:

—family—children, parents and other relatives whose reactions range from shock, rejection and fear to support and encouragement;

—allies—including personal friends, lawyers, and supportive relatives who encourage but sometimes complicate the situation with their advice and opinions;

—critics—(some of whom are in the church) who reject, condemn, blame and sometimes treat the divorced person judgmentally;

—married friends—some of whom feel threatened and many of whom are not sure how to react in the presence of the newly divorced person;

—other single people—many of whom are very understanding; some of whom are potential dating partners.

Divorced people often experience loneliness, insecurity, confusion about whether they should date or remarry, and concerns about identity or self-confidence. Most struggle with the issue of sex and self-control. In a minority of cases the divorced person reacts to people as he or she has done in the past, remarries into a similar situation, repeats the same mistakes, and experiences another divorce. More often the difficulties of a disastrous first marriage are avoided in a subsequent marriage,[19] but many newly divorced people fail to realize this. Since at first they did not succeed, they are afraid to try again.

Counseling and Divorce

At the risk of oversimplification, we might conclude that Christian marriage counseling (as discussed in chapter 13) attempts to keep marriages together and to help couples develop smoother, more fulfilling, Christ-centered marital relationships. In contrast, Christian divorce counseling attempts to help an individual or couple separate from a marriage in a way that is consistent with biblical teachings and with (a) a minimum of pain or destruction to themselves and to others, including their children, and (b) a maximum of growth and new learning.

1. *Clarify Counselor Attitudes.* Divorce counseling is never easy. If the counselor feels frustrated, saddened and angry, he or she may not be able to listen carefully, to understand, to avoid condemning, or to resist the pressures and inclination to take sides.

The effective helper must give personal reflection on his or her attitude toward divorce, divorced persons, and people who are going through divorce. Can you in conscience help people to face a divorce which is acceptable biblically? What if the proposed divorce has no biblical justification? Can *you* forgive, support, and help even those who are clearly in the wrong? As a follower of Jesus Christ, what is your responsibility to people who are frustrated, confused, angry and despondent because of marital breakdown? No one can answer these questions for another.

Each counselor must consider them before God, and before getting en-
meshed in the demanding and heartrending work of divorce counseling.

2. *Determine Goals.* In divorce counseling, goal setting is not easy.
Reconciliation and the development of a fulfilling, Christ-honoring marriage certainly are to be preferred, but what if the couple has no such desire? A logical, mutually agreeable resolution of problems is desirable,
but what if the counselees have little desire to be logical? Psychologist
James Framo once described a couple who fought so vociferously that he
had difficulty restraining them.[20] "There is something you don't understand about divorce," the wife exclaimed. "You are trying to be logical,
but divorce is neither a civilized nor logical matter." When such an attitude appears, the counselor also may be tempted to respond with irrational, emotional responses.

Not all divorce counseling is like this, however, and it is possible to
reach a number of goals which might include the following:

—helping counselees realistically evaluate their marital situation including prospects for avoiding divorce;

—discussing biblical teachings on divorce and remarriage, and helping counselees make application of these teachings to their own marital
situation;

—discovering and discussing the counselees' expectations and desires
for counseling, and evaluating whether these are (a) feasible and (b)
consistent with the counselor's own moral and ethical standards;

—assisting those who need help in finding competent legal assistance;

—assisting counselees to reach mutually acceptable agreements concerning such practical issues as the division of property, alimony, child
custody and support, and so on;

—encouraging couples to "calm down" from vindictive or self-centered
hostile ways of relating, and to go through the divorce in a way that will
be as rational and as well handled as possible—especially where the divorce concerns children;

—helping counselees formulate a way of explaining the situation to
children;

—encouraging them to avoid belittling, blaming, and criticizing each
other, especially in the presence of children;[21]

—helping them to understand the effects of divorce on children (even
grown children) and encouraging them not to use children in manipulative
ways either to force children into taking sides or to get messages to one's
ex-spouse;

—helping them, together or separately, to adjust to the difficulties of
post-divorce single life; and

—encouraging counselees in their spiritual growth and in their involvement with other people, ideally including church people, who can give
support, encouragement and friendship.

3. *Decide on One's Approach.* Chapter 13 raised several special issues concerning marriage counseling: Should a couple be seen alone or together? Is group counseling desirable? Should the counselor work alone or with another counselor? These same questions must be asked in divorce counseling.

Two issues make divorce counseling unique, however. First, it is possible that for many couples marriage counseling will have preceded divorce counseling. If so, the decisions in the above paragraph will have been made previously. Second, when divorce is being discussed, couples are less likely to come together for counseling. Although it is preferable to see both husband and wife, this will not always be possible.

4. *Work on Practical Issues.* Divorce is a crisis, and counselors must seek to give the support, guidance and practical help which people in crisis need.[22] In addition, there must be practical consideration of several important issues.

(a) Handling Emotions. It is difficult to make an emotional break, even from a relationship which no longer is intimate. Anger, anxiety, frustration, depression and a host of other feelings flood the counselee, sometimes when they are least expected. Often there is a vacillation of feelings. A relief at being free and a weight of loneliness, for example, can occur at the same time.

Such emotions should be acknowledged and expressed but counselees must be helped to grow beyond the emotional expression stage. There are several guidelines which might help counselees with this growth:

—Express emotions honestly as they arise.

—Ask God to help you avoid hate, resentment and bitterness. In a farewell address to his staff, Richard Nixon made a powerful statement: "Those who hate you don't win until you hate them back—and that will destroy you." No matter how much one has been hurt, nothing is gained by revenge.

—With God's help, practice forgiveness, praying for those "who despitefully use you."

—Deliberately avoid what have been called the "emotional traps of the past."[23] These include: making sweeping and unwarranted generalizations about oneself or others; developing unrealistic expectations; self-fulfilling prophecies (like deciding, for example, that "life will now be miserable"—an attitude which, in turn, will make life miserable); disastering (always being on the defensive and expecting the worse); wallowing in your problems; blaming others perpetually—especially one's mate; running to new jobs, new locations or new churches in an attempt to "start fresh"; living through others (finding satisfaction only in the achievements of others); and assuming that life can only be meaningful again when there is another marriage.

Feelings often follow thinking. To change feelings, counselees must be

helped to accept what may not be changeable (in this case, divorce), and
then learn to resist those thoughts that can arouse painful feelings.

(b) Selecting a Lawyer. Counselors are not always qualified to know
how a lawyer can be chosen and evaluated, although in time the names
of competent lawyers become known. Encourage counselees to select at-
torneys carefully, to hire someone who specializes in divorces (the local
bar association often can make recommendations), to refrain from signing anything until one's own attorney is consulted, and to avoid "do-it-
yourself" divorce. If possible, select a Christian lawyer. Such men and
women should have an appreciation for the sanctity of marriage and be
less inclined to stimulate hostility between the husband and wife.[24]

(c) Finding a New Identity. Divorce plunges one from a married state
into singleness again. The divorced person is now a single, alone, a parent
without a partner, and labeled with the term "divorced." It is easy to live
in the past, to pretend that one is still married, to yield to someone else's
expectations of what one should be like. Counselees must be helped to
accept themselves as God accepts them.[25] They must be encouraged to
talk about, accept and determine their own identity.

(d) Building New Relationships. One major task facing divorced persons is the forming of new relationships. Although this involves finding
new friends, it is more concerned with redefining the nature of one's relationship with the former spouse, the children, friends and relatives, and
church people.

The Former Spouse. When a couple has shared the same goals, joys,
trials and hopes, it is difficult to separate, to watch a former mate remarry,
to be the object of hostility, to deal with one's own feelings of anger, to
be comfortable in talking to one's former mate and to avoid striking out
or showing excessive curiosity about the ex-spouse's life. Getting along
with a former mate requires patience and understanding especially at the
beginning when feelings are running high. Later, as time passes and new
relationships are formed, the conflict level subsides, but this may take a
long time.[26] There is value in discussing one's feelings and discomforts
with a counselor or friend. It also helps if the break can be made as cleanly
as possible. Seeing an ex-mate reminds one of a past which is gone and
delays both healing and the development of a new beginning.

The Children. Children often become unwilling weapons used by the
husband and wife to attack each other, or prisoners of war to be lured
into one's own camp and brainwashed against the enemy. These same
children are often confused, afraid and insecure. The parent who is given
custody of the children often feels overwhelmed with the responsibility
to care for the children alone and to meet their needs at a time when
everyone is vulnerable emotionally. The other parent may feel guilty,
lonely, sad, but sometimes happy to be relieved of the responsibility.

Based on his work with divorced couples, Smoke has suggested some
guidelines for single parents. These can be shared with counselees.

1. Don't try to be both parents to your children.
2. Don't force your children into playing the role of the departed parent.
3. Be the parent you are (Don't try to be a buddy, big brother or big sister).
4. Be honest with your children.
5. Don't put your ex-spouse down in front of your children.
6. Don't make your children undercover agents who report on the other parent's current activities.
7. The children of divorce need both a mother and a father. Don't deny them this right.
8. Don't become a "Disneyland Daddy" or a "Magic Mountain Mommy" (one who becomes an entertainer). Children need to see the departed parent in a real life setting.
9. Share your dating life and social interests with your children.
10. Help the children keep the good memories of your past marriage alive.
11. Work out a management and existence structure for your children with your ex-spouse. . . . Two adults should be able to sit down together and work out things that will lead to the best growth and development of the children.
12. If possible, try not to disrupt the many areas in your children's lives that offer them safety and security.
13. If your child does not resume normal development and growth in his life within a year of divorce, he may need . . . a professional counselor.[27]

Other Adults. Friends can be supportive in a crisis, but some people don't know how to help, others are threatened by the divorced person's new status and some simply withdraw. How does a single divorced person now relate to the couples with whom the husband and wife formerly had a relationship? The counselor can provide encouragement and guidance as new relationships are formed and old relationship styles are readjusted.

The Church. Here is the one place where there should be support, caring and love. Regretfully, however, church members often show criticism, subtle rejection, and sometimes avoidance of the divorced persons. Counselors can help as these attitudes are faced and discussed.

(e) Facing the Future. The divorced person cannot live in the past or bemoan the future. Bills must be paid, work must be completed, life must go on. The counselee can be helped to identify and learn from past mistakes, make immediate decisions about such practical issues as housing and finances, reestablish life priorities, establish goals for the future and move ahead to accomplish God's purpose for one's life. Within recent years a number of practical books have been written to help divorced individuals "rebuild a broken life."[28]

(f) Considering Remarriage. The Christian must determine whether or not remarriage is permitted biblically. Christian counselors will differ in their response to the question, but perhaps most would at least agree that remarriage is permissible if the departing spouse has deserted the mate and/or been unfaithful sexually. This issue must be discussed with counselees.

Divorced persons often resent the need to start dating "like teenagers"; some fear that they will never find another spouse, and others wonder if they will make the same mistakes again. The counselor can help with these fears. Discourage people from marrying too quickly and help them to choose a mate wisely—according to the principles outlined in chapter 11. Before remarriage, divorced persons should be encouraged to ponder what they have learned from the previous marriage and divorce. Premarital counseling should be considered essential.

In all of this, remember that God wants the best for his children. He forgives those who confess, and guides those who want his leading. Divorced persons and their counselors are not left alone to fend for themselves. The Holy Spirit is the constant guide and companion of divorced believers and their Christian counselors who want divine leading as they face the pain of divorce.

Preventing Divorce

The most obvious way to prevent divorce is to build stronger marriages —marriages based on scriptural principles and characterized by love, commitment and open communication. This has been discussed in several previous chapters and will not be repeated here.[29]

Let us assume, however, that a couple is contemplating divorce. How can this be prevented?

1. *Counseling.* Before a couple decides to separate they have a responsibility before God, to themselves and to their families to do whatever is possible to avoid divorce and build a fulfilling marriage. If both husband and wife are sincerely willing to work at resolving conflicts and building a relationship, there is a very high possibility that divorce will be prevented.

2. *Self-examination.* With or without counseling, each spouse must ask, "What am I doing (or failing to do) which contributes to the problems in my marriage?" Often there is bitterness, refusal to forgive, unrealistic expectations, constant criticism, sexual infidelity, unwillingness to work at building the marriage, or some equally harmful attitude which is contributing to the marital tension. Jesus told his followers to look at (and presumably remove) the faults in themselves before criticizing others.[30] Of course, it isn't always possible to see ourselves clearly. If we ask God to enlighten our understanding, he surely will—perhaps through the observations of a counselor or through the insights of one's mate. Then couples should seek divine and human help to forsake harmful behaviors.

3. *Reconciliation.* It has been found that only about one couple in eight tries reconciliation after filing for divorce,[31] but such reconciliations are permanent in about half the cases.[32] Reconciliations come only after hours

of discussion and a realistic evaluation of the problems involved. But reconciliation surely is the desire of a God who hates divorce.

4. *Divine Guidance.* It probably is true that only God can really mend and bind a broken marriage. Separately and together, couples must seek divine wisdom, strength, and guidance as they grow spiritually and work to prevent divorce. Daily Scripture reading and prayer are more than ideological gimmicks. They are powerful forces which open couples up to the healing power of God.

This brings us to the influence of the church—the body of Christ. Believers are instructed to bear one another's burdens, care for one another, and pray for each other. Samuel of old concluded that failure to pray for the needy was a "sin against the Lord." [33] Christians today must realize that prayer, concern, caring, and support are not options. They are commanded by God. To prevent divorce, therefore, believers should be instructed to pray for married couples and to care, recognizing that such caring and effective prayer can accomplish much—including healing,[34] perhaps even the healing of a marriage.

Conclusions about Divorce

Several years ago, a psychiatrist made the controversial suggestion that divorce is never necessary. When people complain of irreconcilable differences and personalities they are resorting to a "cop-out used by couples who are too proud and too lazy to work out their own hangups. Instead of facing them, they run away by divorcing and remarrying. Then there are four miserable people instead of two." [35]

Surely this is an overstatement but it does contain an element of truth. Many people do look to divorce as an easy escape from marital difficulties. Building a marriage is not easy and it surely is true that "When a couple is motivated to have faith that God can and will heal their marriage, followed by their own hard work, divorce is *never* necessary." [36] The Christian counselor, backed by a body of supportive praying believers, can often help to restore broken marriages and insure that divorce will not be necessary.

Suggestions for Further Reading

Arnold, William V.; Baird, Dixie McKie; Langan, Joan Trigg; and Vaughan, Elizabeth Blakemore. *Divorce: Prevention or Survival.* Philadelphia: Westminster, 1977.

* Ellison, Stanley A. *Divorce and Remarriage in the Church.* Grand Rapids: Zondervan, 1977.

* Galloway, Dale E. *Dream a New Dream: How to Build a Broken Life.* Wheaton, IL: Tyndale, 1975.

Krantzler, Mel. *Creative Divorce: A New Opportunity for Personal Growth.* New York: M. Evans and Company, 1974.

* Smoke, Jim. *Growing Through Divorce.* Irvine, CA: Harvest House, 1976.

Weiss, Robert S. *Marital Separation.* New York: Basic Books, 1975.

Footnotes

1. Rose K. Goldsen, "Throw-away Husbands, Wives and Lovers," *Human Behavior* 4 (December, 1975): 64–69.

2. For detailed discussions see Stanley A. Ellison, *Divorce and Remarriage in the Church* (Grand Rapids: Zondervan, 1977); Guy Duty, *Divorce and Remarriage* (Minneapolis: Bethany Fellowship, 1967); and John Murray, *Divorce* (Philadelphia: Presbyterian and Reformed, 1961).

3. Gen. 2:18–25; Matt. 19:5; Mark 10:2–12; 1 Cor. 7:39.

4. Matt. 5:31, 2; 19:3–9.

5. 1 Cor. 7:10–16.

6. John R. W. Stott, *Divorce* (Downers Grove, IL: Inter-Varsity Press, 1973), pp. 27, 28.

7. Mal. 2:16.

8. Exod. 20:14; Matt. 5:27, 28.

9. 1 John 1:9; Matt. 6:14, 15.

10. Rom. 6:1, 2; 12:1, 2; 13:14; 1 Pet. 2:11.

11. Ellison, *Divorce and Remarriage,* p. 52.

12. 1 Cor. 7:10–15.

13. Ellison, *Divorce and Remarriage,* pp. 57–58.

14. Robert S. Weiss, *Marital Separation,* pp. 5–10.

15. Joseph N. Bell, "Rescuing the Battered Wife," *Human Behavior* 6 (June, 1977): 16–23.

16. 1 Cor. 7:12–16.

17. James L. Framo, "The Friendly Divorce," *Psychology Today* 11 (February, 1978): 79.

18. Formerly the Minister to Single Adults at Garden Grove Community Church in California, Jim Smoke conducts divorce adjustment seminars across North America. See his *Growing Through Divorce* (Irvine, CA: Harvest House, 1976).

19. Weiss, *Marital Separation,* p. 309.

20. Framo, "The Friendly Divorce," p. 77.

21. R. V. Fitzgerald, *Conjoint Marital Therapy* (New York: Jason Aronson, 1973), p. 97.

22. See chapter 4.

23. From Mel Krantzler, *Creative Divorce,* pp. 103–16.

24. For the names of Christian lawyers contact the Christian Legal Society, 1122 Westgate, Oak Park, Illinois, 60301.

25. See chapter 24.

26. Smoke, *Growing Through Divorce,* p. 38.

27. Ibid., pp. 60–66.

28. In addition to the books listed at the end of this chapter, see also Norman Sheresky and Myra Mannes, *Uncoupling: The Art of Coming Apart* (New York: Viking Press, 1972); and Luciano L'Abate and Bess L'Abate, *How to Avoid Divorce* (Atlanta: John Knox Press, 1977).

29. Chapters 11, 12, 13; see also chapter 23.

30. Matt. 7:3.

31. Weiss, *Marital Separation,* p. 121.

32. Ibid., p. 123.

33. 1 Sam. 12:23.

34. James 5:16.

35. Paul D. Meier, "Is Divorce Ever Necessary?" *Christian Medical Society Journal* 8 (Winter, 1976): 2–8.

36. Ibid., p. 8.

Part IV
Developmental
Family Issues

15

Child-Rearing and Parental Guidance

IN OUR SOCIETY, PEOPLE ARE EXPECTED TO HAVE SEVENTEEN YEARS of education before they can teach in public schools. Medical doctors have twenty or more years of schooling. Plumbers and carpenters go through years of apprenticeship. But for the work of raising a child, we give or require no formal training.[1] God entrusts tender young lives to the guidance of adults (including some very immature adults) who have little or no experience in child-rearing, but who face a variety of challenges and perhaps even a greater variety of child-rearing books. Some parents devour these books in an attempt to be better mothers and fathers. Some ignore the advice and try to "do what comes naturally." Others would agree with the psychologist who wrote that "being a good parent isn't just difficult, it is impossible. Anyone who isn't bewildered by child rearing and doesn't find it an extremely formidable and trying experience probably isn't a parent."[2]

At times the Christian counselor will be involved in counseling with children directly, but more often the emphasis will be on *parental guidance*. This has been defined as the task of offering parents such information, clarification, advice, support, counsel or other help as a counselor can give for the purpose of indirectly helping the child. Parental guidance recognizes that parents can influence children more profoundly than can any counselor. It assumes a cooperative working alliance between the parents and the counselor, who are all interested in the welfare of the child.[3]

Literally thousands of books have been written about children and child-rearing. Freud, Erickson, Piaget, Sears, Dreikurs, Gesell, Spock and numerous others have produced theories of child development. Christian writers like James Dobson, Bruce Narramore, Paul Meier and others have produced books designed to help parents with their child-rearing problems. Innumerable studies have investigated the abilities and psychological maturation of developing children, while other research has studied

203

physical malfunctioning, psychological retardation and childhood pathology. Pediatrics, the well-known medical speciality, has been paralleled by child psychiatry, child psychology and related specialties. Clearly then, in one chapter it is not possible to summarize the massive literature which has built up in this field, but some general principles are identifiable and potentially helpful to the Christian counselor.

The Bible and Child-Rearing

Shortly after the creation, God instructed Adam and Eve to "be fruitful and multiply, and fill the earth." Unlike most divine commands, this one was obeyed and the world quickly filled with people. In Old Testament times a large family was considered a source of special blessing from God and childlessness was regarded with reproach.[4] In more modern times, in an era of overpopulation, many people have limited the size of their families, but children are still important. Jesus showed them special attention and he lauded their simplicity and trust.[5]

Biblical teachings on children and child-rearing can be divided into two categories: comments about children and comments about parents and parenting.

1. *Children.* In the Bible, children are seen as gifts from God and can bring both joy and sorrow. They are to be loved, honored and respected as persons; they are important in God's kingdom and they are not to be harmed.[6] Children also are given responsibilities: to honor and respect parents, care for them, listen to them and be obedient.[7] This is stated most concisely in Ephesians 6:1–3:

> Children obey your parents in the Lord, for this is right. Honor your father and mother (which is the first commandment with a promise), that it may be well with you, and that you may live long on the earth.

Earlier in his writings Paul had strongly criticized childhood disobediences [8] and in this passage he is speaking to children who must have been old enough to understand and follow such directives. It does not follow that children must obey forever. If parents require compliance to something unbiblical it should be remembered that God's laws always take a higher priority than human instruction.[9] It would seem, further, that adults who leave parents to cleave to a spouse have moved to establish new families—but such families must still honor older parents.

2. *Parents.* Mothers and fathers have a responsibility to love their children, to model mature Christian behavior, to care for their needs, to teach the children and to discipline fairly.[10] "Do not provoke your children to anger," we read in Ephesians 6:4, "but bring them up in the discipline and instruction of the Lord."

Commenting on this verse, Gene A. Getz notes that parents "bring up" children by example, direct instruction and encouragement. We "provoke children" to bitterness and discouragement when we abuse them physically, abuse them psychologically (by humiliating them and failing to treat them with respect), neglect them, don't try to understand them, expect too much from them, withhold our love unless they perform, force them to accept our goals or ideas, and refuse to admit our mistakes.[11]

Training a child in the way he or she should go is more easily discussed than accomplished. Children, like parents, have different personalities and the biblical directives for child-rearing are not as specific as many people might like. But there is one section in the Old Testament which puts the principles together. Ray Stedman calls it the "Magna Carta" of the home —a choice summary of the great principles which are developed later in Scripture and which give an overview for Christian child-rearing.[12] Although this was written for the Israelites prior to their entrance into the promised lands, it has practical relevance for modern child-rearing and parental guidance—Deuteronomy 6:1–8:

> Now this is the commandment, the statutes and the judgments which the Lord your God has commanded me to teach you, that you might do them in the land where you are going over to possess it, so that you and your son and your grandson might fear the Lord your God, to keep all His statutes and His commandments, which I command you, all the days of your life, and that your days may be prolonged.
>
> O Israel, you should listen and be careful to do it, that it may be well with you and that you may multiply greatly, just as the Lord, the God of your fathers, has promised you, in a land flowing with milk and honey.
>
> Hear, O Israel! The Lord is our God, the Lord is one! And you shall love the Lord your God with all your heart and with all your soul and with all your might. And these words, which I am commanding you today, shall be on your heart; and you shall teach them diligently to your sons and shall talk of them when you sit in your house and when you walk by the way and when you lie down and when you rise up. And you shall bind them as a sign on your hand and they shall be as frontals on your forehead.

Christian parenting involves the following:

(a) Listening. The good parent seeks to hear God's commandments and to understand them so well that they become "on the heart"—a part of one's being. This learning comes through regular study of God's Word, the Bible, interpreted to us by the Holy Spirit.

(b) Obeying. Knowledge is not enough. In addition to hearing there must be a doing of what God has commanded. When parents fail to obey God it is more difficult for children to obey parents.

(c) Loving. We are to love the Lord and give ourselves to him wholeheartedly—heart, soul and strength. Notice that the emphasis here is on parental behavior. In spite of their importance, children are not prominent in the Bible. Although we read that Jesus grew psychologically (in wis-

dom), physically (in stature), spiritually (in favor with God) and socially (in favor with men),[13] we know very little about his childhood.
Childhood is important, but children are only with us temporarily and then
they leave—as God intended. It would seem to be true, therefore that
parents are not to exist primarily for their children. Parents exist first as
individuals before God. Raising children is part of our purpose in life, if
God gives us children, but this is not our only purpose.[14]

(d) Teaching. There are four ways by which this teaching is done:

—Diligently. Even though child-rearing is not a parent's sole task in
life, it is an important task, not to be taken lightly.

—Repeatedly. The passage indicates that teaching was not a one-time
effort. It was to concern parents repeatedly through the day and night.

—Naturally. When we sit, walk, lie down and rise up we are to look
for teaching opportunities. Daily family devotions are fine, but parents
teach whenever an opportunity arises.

—Personally. What one says is rarely as influential as what one does.
This returns us to the first part of the passage. When parents listen, obey,
and love they provide a model for children which reinforces what is being
said in the home.

Notice these words "in the home." Peers and teachers are important,
but the most significant teaching and child-rearing occurs at home.

Causes of Child-Rearing Problems

Children and parents do not always agree on what constitutes a problem. A parent, for example, may view disobedience as a problem, but the
child may not see this as a problem at all. Then, when problems *are* recognized, the causes may be as varied as the numerous theories of child
development. In spite of this, several themes appear repeatedly in the literature.

1. *Instability in the Home.* When parents are not getting along with
each other, children feel anxious, guilty and angry. They are anxious because the stability of the home is threatened, guilty because they are afraid
that they may have caused the strife, and angry because they often feel
left out, forgotten, and sometimes manipulated into taking sides—which
they do not want to do. Sometimes there also is a fear of being abandoned.
Unstable homes, therefore, often (but not always) produce unstable children.

2. *Parental Failures.* Within recent years the problem of physical child
abuse has attracted considerable attention in the media. This will be discussed more fully in chapter 31. But what about those parents who never
hurt their children physically but abuse them psychologically? When
children are rejected subtly or overtly, nagged and criticized excessively,
punished unrealistically (or not at all), disciplined inconsistently, and
shown love spasmodically (if at all), then children often experience per-

sonal problems or show disruptive behaviors which in turn are annoying to the parents. Child development books often discuss the harmful effects of parental overprotection, overpermissiveness, overrestrictiveness and overmeticulousness—all of which can arouse anxiety and create insecurity in children.

3. *Unmet Needs.* Psychologists do not always agree on what should be included in any listing of basic human needs, but some needs come up repeatedly. In a recent book, John Drescher identified "seven of the most basic needs of the growing child (and of all of us throughout life)" [15] —the needs for significance, security, acceptance, love, praise, discipline, and the need for God. When these are not met, maturation is hindered and problems frequently result.

4. *Neglect of the Spiritual.* Although the Bible does not say a great deal about children, it does emphasize the importance of teaching children about God.[16] Psalm 78:1–8, for example, emphasizes that children should receive spiritual instructions so that they will put their faith in God, remember his faithfulness, and not become unruly, stubborn, or rebellious. Perhaps there is no well-designed spiritual research comparing the adult behavior of children who had religious training with those who did not, but the Scriptures clearly teach that biblical education is beneficial to children; its absence is surely harmful.

5. *Other Influences.* Physical illnesses and handicaps, the serious illness or death of significant persons (including a parent), traumatic early experiences (such as accidents, a serious fire in the home, a near drowning, and so on), peer rejection, and the experience of failure can each create problems in later life. As a result of these events, children can develop unhealthy self-concepts, preoccupations with danger and fears of failure, hurt or criticism.

These past several paragraphs could be discouraging to counselors and parents who might wonder if it is ever possible to raise a child successfully and without the development of problems. Two facts need to be remembered as this question is considered. First, it should be noted that most children grow up normally in spite of parental mistakes and failures. Even when the home has "abusive, psychotic, or desperately poor parents," some children (often called "invulnerables" or "superkids") respond by developing extraordinary competence.[17] Poor homes do not always produce problem children.

Second, there are times when problems arise which are independent of parental actions.

> Many parents are burdened with the assumption that any problems manifested by the child are a result of some parental mishandling or are seen as such by the child. Such a parent may have a hard time realizing . . . that the child's autonomous mental life can occasionally manifest problems that have nothing to do with the parent. The child may even

engage in activity apparently hostile towards the parent as a convenient means of acting out or resolving a problem that basically has little or nothing to do with the parent and is not accompanied by any real hostility for the parent. It is important to help parents realize at such times that there is "nothing personal" in the child's attitude or behavior. This can free the parent to be more objectively emphatic and helpful to the child.[18]

Even if the parents were to be perfect there is still a possibility of rebellion and problems because children have minds and wills of their own. No one could be more perfect than God, and yet Isaiah's prophecy begins with these words: "The Lord speaks: Sons I have reared and brought up, But they have revolted against Me." [19] Many times parental failures lead to child problems, but this does not always happen. This realization can be a source of encouragement and a challenge to the parents of problem children.

The Effects of Child-Rearing Problems

Most Christians will remember the story of Samuel, the Old Testament prophet, who as a boy one night received a message from God concerning Eli the priest. "I am about to judge Eli," God said "because his sons brought a curse on themselves and he did not rebuke them." [20] Eli had failed to discipline his sons even though God had warned him about this previously. Soon Eli and the sons died and Samuel grew to a position of leadership, but his sons were also a source of embarrassment. They did not walk in the way of God, "but turned aside after dishonest gain and took bribes and perverted justice." [21] One does not get the impression that Samuel had neglected his parental duties, but the children still turned from God and behaved dishonestly. When parent-child problems occur, this can influence both the parents and the children—and sometimes childhood pathology results.

1. *Parental Effects*. It isn't easy to have children "turn out" differently than parents had hoped. Fathers and mothers sometimes feel—with or without good supportive evidence—that childhood problems are a monument to the parents' incompetence. This can lead to inner frustration, hostility between husband and wife, anger expressed toward the children, guilt, fear of what might happen next, and sometimes frantic attempts to assert authority and regain control. On occasion there may be an attempt to defend or protect the child, but often this is mixed with anger because the child needs defending or protection. Then, there are parents, perhaps like Eli, who feel unwilling or perhaps powerless to do anything about a deteriorating situation—so they watch as things grow worse.

2. *Child Effects*. When there are parent-child problems, the children sometimes act in ways similar to the parents. Anger, hostility directed to parents or brothers and sisters, guilt and fear can all occur. Unlike parents who can express themselves verbally, children often resort to nonverbal means of expression. Temper tantrums, rebellion, underachievement (es-

pecially in school), delinquency, fighting—even excessive crying, silliness, dawdling, and other attention-getting behavior can be ways of saying non-verbally, "Notice me, I'm hurting too!" Of course none of this is conscious or deliberate, and we cannot always assume that such behaviors mean that the child senses something is wrong. Neither does the absence of such behavior mean that the child is oblivious to the problem. Some children are afraid to express themselves. They may attempt to deny reality or they may quietly conclude that they are incompetent failures. The seeds of inferiority and low self-esteem are getting started early in life although they may not become apparent to others until much later.

3. *Pathological Effects.* Sometimes young people develop more severe emotional disturbances, all of which indicate the existence of problems within the children, and some (but not all) of which imply that there are problems in the home. Even when the parent-child relationships are good, these pathological conditions put a strain on the family and as a result counseling often can be helpful.[22]

(a) Psychophysiological Disorders. These physical reactions include asthma, ulcers, bed-wetting and headaches—all of which may have either strict physical causes—or psychological causes including severe stress, rigid discipline, disappointments, loss of family members or a smothering mother-child relationship. Such children, of course, should be seen by a physician but often counseling can help both parents and children to learn how to handle stress better.

(b) Developmental Disorders. Sometimes speech, motor, social, think-ing or other abilities are slowed by family pressures, numerous moves, and other stresses. In time children catch up, but the developmental slowdown can be difficult for both child and parent.

(c) Psychoneurotic Disorders. When conflicts and aggressive or sexual impulses are "held within" and denied or suppressed, they eventually hinder smooth psychological functioning. Anxiety, irrational fears, ex-cessive guilt reactions, sleeping or eating disturbances, and compulsive behavior may all indicate the presence of underlying struggles.

(d) Personality Disorders. Sometimes the child senses no conflict or tension but develops a personality that is high-strung, overly inhibited, isolated, excessively independent, or distrustful. All of this can reflect in-ner tension.

(e) Sociopathic and Delinquent Disorders. When the child is frustrated by the environment, he or she sometimes "acts out" in delinquent, aggres-sive, sometimes sexually impulsive behavior. Here the person reacts to frustration by "lashing out" at others, often with no feelings of remorse or desire to change. Society, including parents, is burdened with the effects of the aggression, and with the responsibility to rehabilitate the aggressor.

(f) Childhood Depression. Children do not get depressed in the same way that adults are depressed, but they nevertheless struggle with feelings of sadness, deep disappointment and loss. These feelings are expressed by withdrawal, refusal to eat, apathy, running away, physical complaints, sullenness, and sometimes aggression or immobility. Of course, all children show each of these attitudes periodically, but their prolonged appearance indicates more troublesome underlying problems.

(g) Psychotic Disorders. This is the severely disturbed behavior which requires professional treatment. Psychotic children, like psychotic adults, may show bizarre behavior, severe fears, extreme withdrawal, lack of self-control and irrational thinking, to list a few of the symptoms. Sometimes very young children develop "infantile autism," a widely studied condition characterized by withdrawal, emotional blandness, repetitious behavior, and fascination with inanimate things (such as a chair) instead of with people.

(h) Brain Damage and Mental Retardation. These are seen in slow physical development, learning disabilities, memory problems and similar disabilities that might be expected when the brain is not functioning normally. While brain damage and mental retardation do not come as effects of faulty child-rearing, these conditions greatly influence parents who often have difficulty adjusting to the reality and challenge of raising a mentally handicapped child.[23]

(i) Hyperactivity. This common condition, characterized by excitability, short attention span, destructiveness, sleep disturbances, and poor impulse control, may have a physical or a psychological cause. Physicians frequently use drugs to help such children, but this does not solve the problem unless there is counseling with parents, special attention given to children, and treatment of medical problems.

(j) Learning Disabilities. These are widespread and are not necessarily the result of low intelligence or poor schooling. Sometimes the cause is physical but often learning problems are the effect of hearing or visual difficulties, problems with speech, poor memory ability, or tensions at home. When they learn slowly, children often experience ridicule by peers, criticism by parents, and pressure by teachers—each of which damages the child's self-concept and increases the learning disabilities. If these children grow older without improvement, there can be school failures, truancy, delinquency and subsequent unemployment.

Each of the ten pathological conditions described above can greatly concern parents and can adversely affect child development. Usually such conditions are treated by physicians, psychologists, educators and others who are specially trained in the problems of children. Unless the Christian counselor is a specialist in these areas, he or she should seek professional consultation if available, or should refer the child and parents to some person or persons who specialize in the disorders of children.

Counseling and Child-Rearing Problems

Christian counselors have three responsibilities in working with the problems of children: counseling the children, counseling the parents, and making referrals. In some cases you will do only one of these; in some situations you will do all three.

1. *Counseling Children.* Unlike adults, who use conversation to discuss their feelings and frustrations, younger children, as we have seen, often communicate nonverbally. Observing children at home, asking them to make up stories or play with doll families, watching as they draw pictures, model with clay, or "play house" are among the techniques used by child specialists to elicit information and uncover childhood problems. These methods, along with the use of psychological tests, usually require special training, but they might give general counselors some helpful insights, and it should not be assumed that talking is never helpful. Children are spontaneous and sometimes share their worries and concerns openly. Also helpful are questions about what makes the child most happy or unhappy, what is the funniest or saddest thing he or she can think of, what would be granted if the child had three wishes, or similar questions which have potentially revealing answers.

Although the goals of child counseling depend largely on the stated and identified problems, counselors often seek to reduce irrational fears and disturbing behavior, resolve conflicts, increase the child's ability to express feelings, improve interpersonal relationships at home or school, and teach skills. Counseling may involve instruction, play therapy, the demonstrating of compassion and structured conversation, and the giving or withholding of reinforcement.

In counseling children, the counselor should be kind but firm; compassionate, but not easily manipulated. In all of this, remember the obvious but easily forgotten fact that children are people. They have feelings, needs and insecurities. They respond to love and firmness, but they also must be treated with sensitivity, empathy, warmth, consideration and a respect which does not treat them with disdain or adult superiority. Remember too that the counseling of children almost always occurs in conjunction with the counseling of parents.

2. *Counseling Parents.* At times the Christian counselor will first come in contact with a "problem child" and then make contact with the parents. More often, it is the parents who come seeking help and the child is seen either later, with the parents, or not at all. When counseling children it is extremely important that parents be seen as well since the counseling can be undermined quickly by uncooperative or uninformed parents. When counseling parents it also is helpful to see the child, but especially with more minor problems, helping the parents may be the best way to help the child, and influence the family indirectly.

(a) General Issues. There are several general guidelines for working with parents regardless of the specific problem. These include the following: [24]

Appreciate the parents' position. Child-rearing can be frustrating, and in spite of their mistakes and failures it can be assumed that most parents really want to succeed in this task. It doesn't help, therefore, to blame, criticize, or demean parents. Assume that the parents have tried to improve the child's situation. Try to understand the parents' perspective and express a desire to work together cooperatively with parents, in helping them to help their children.

Use different approaches. Some parents need simple information or a clearer understanding of the situation. Others may need advice, cautioning, support, encouragement, and/or suggested alternatives for dealing with a problem. Some parents have a good idea about what to do, but they need a counselor to give a little push and offer "back-up support" from an authority as action is taken. At times it will be necessary to gently challenge parental myths (for example, "all adolescents are rebellious," "children should never get angry at parents," or "boys are harder to raise than girls"). Frequently it will be helpful to break down a problem into smaller issues which can be dealt with more easily, one at a time. It is only after listening and observing for a while that counselors can decide on suitable guidance tactics.

Be sensitive to parental needs. As they raise their children parents may feel self-doubt, a sense of being overwhelmed, competition (with the child or with the spouse over the child's affection), jealousy, a fear of losing one's children, or a need to be in authoritarian control of the family. When these needs are intense or when they are unmet, tensions often result. In counseling, such needs should be identified, discussed and reevaluated.

Model the parental role. The counselor does not treat parents like they are children, but the counselor nevertheless models a willingness to understand, communication skills, and sometimes a kind firmness. If the counselor talks to the children in the parent's presence, this interaction can be an example of adult-child respect and interaction.

Recognize that you are expendable. The ultimate goal of counseling is to promote the building of maturing, Christ-centered relationships between family members. The counselor is a facilitator of this process. His or her ultimate goal is to withdraw from the situation. To this end, one psychiatrist recommends a "twofold approach." [25] When advising parents to do something the child won't like, such as being stricter or less inclined to give in to the child's demands, state this to the parents with the children present. This lets the counselor "take the blame," helps the parents feel less guilty, and hooks them into carrying out the recommendation. In contrast, when advising parents to do something the child will like, such as relaxing restrictions or spending more time together, tell the parents privately, without the children present. This lets the parents take full credit for the pleasant changes and does not put them in a position to be criticized by their children when the counselor's recommendations are forgotten or rejected.

It has been said that an effective parent is the child's most important counselor.[26] If this is true, then one very effective way to help children is to teach parents how to help their sons and daughters. This teaching is known as filial therapy. The counselor meets regularly with the parents, applies the principles described in this section and serves as a consultant and coach. This works best when at least one parent is relatively well-adjusted and when the children are free of severe internal conflict.

(b) Theological Issues. In a perceptive observation, Getz has noted that the Bible says relatively little about the family, compared to what it teaches about the church. This is because "the Christian home in the New Testament world was almost synonymous with the Church. . . . What was written to the Church was also written to individual families. . . . The family is really the *Church in miniature*." [27] Thus, evangelism, Christian education, the teaching of moral standards, or helping children learn about death and the meaning of life are among the challenges that parents face. The Christian counselor must be willing to discuss theological and moral issues. Parents who are failing in these areas must be challenged and helped to make their homes more alert to the presence and guiding power of Jesus Christ. This is a crucial aspect of effective Christian counseling with parents and children.

(c) Psychological Issues. Four psychological issues commonly arise as parents are counseled.

First, there is *understanding*. How can a parent understand the challenging world of children? Encourage parents to think of the world and the family from the child's perspective. Remind parents that children have feelings and the need for significance, security, acceptance, love, praise, discipline and faith in God. It helps to discuss specific examples of conflict or misunderstanding. What happened? Why? How could the situation have been handled better? Be careful to acknowledge that parents need understanding too. It also helps, at times, to suggest books which can help parents understand childhood behavior. Since readers sometimes tend to see and remember what they want to remember, it is wise to discuss such readings and correct misinterpretations after parents have had opportunity to read.[28]

Second, families should be helped with *communications*. The principles discussed in chapter 23 can apply within the family and can be shared, modeled, and practiced in counseling sessions. If they want to communicate with their children, parents should model good husband-wife communication. The family should establish a time for communication, perhaps over dinner.[29] Let the children know that their opinions, gripes and experiences are of interest to you. In turn let them know your ideas, experiences, frustrations and dreams. Although there should be no limits on subject matter to be discussed, parents can expect that there be no disrespectful language or long "nagging." Encourage children to talk, but let them know that they have a right to privacy and personal opinions. Sometimes the family must agree on rules such as "no interruptions until the person talking has finished." [30] When questions are raised they should be answered honestly and fully. All of this takes time to learn but it is an important part of counseling.

Third, *behavior management* is of concern to many parents. Punishment, perhaps, is the most common approach to behavior change. This can be helpful in curbing undesired behavior, and it may instill some respect for authority, but punishment tends to lose its effectiveness if it is repeated too often, and although it curbs undesirable actions, it rarely brings about desired behavior. More efficient is the rewarding of desired behavior and the nonrewarding of undesired behavior. If the child's whining and temper tantrums are ignored, for example, they usually disappear quickly. In contrast, little things such as words of approval, stars stuck on a chart, the reading of a story, or other "reinforcers" can help to mold a child's behavior. Parents can be taught how to give such reinforcements immediately after desirable behavior. With the counselor's help, parents can decide what behavior they want to instill. Then, they decide on the steps necessary to bring this about, and reinforce each specific behavior which helps move the child toward the desired goal. Such a program sometimes can be taught by counselors who have only a small knowledge of reinforcement principles,[31] but for more extreme cases there is value in making referrals to a specialist.

Fourth, *teaching skills* is a common issue of parental concern. Some may wonder, "Will my child ever learn to talk properly, to develop athletic skills, to be polite, to close the door?" These behaviors (or lack of behaviors) are clearly more of a concern to parents than to children. Sometimes parents can be helped to understand that many of these childhood actions are common. Gentle reminders, praise for desirable behavior, and sometimes the avoidance of nagging accompanied by a slight lowering of parental expectations, can all be helpful.

(d) Special Problem Issues. Parents often express concern about special problems such as autism, bed-wetting, stuttering, school phobia, aggressive behavior, excessive nightmares, intense fears, or reactions to traumas such as accidents, deaths or hospitalization. Many of these problems are transitory and often they are evidences of anxiety. Overstimulation from books or TV programs at bedtime, for example, can lead to nightmares or expressions of terror during the night. The fear and anxieties of the day or bedtime stimulation come out during the night. Fear of hospitalization or worry over death reflects an anxiety over the unknown or the possibility of being rejected. Bed-wetting and stuttering often indicate that the children feel pressures from parents and others— pressures which sometimes increase as the enuresis and stuttering persist. Parents should be helped to give reassurance, greater acceptance, approval and support. Fears can be discussed openly and overstimulation with anxiety-arousing movies and stories should be avoided. If these simple tactics do not relieve the symptoms, counselors should consult some of the books which deal in depth with these special problems of children.[32]

(e) The Issue of Disturbed Parents. Sometimes parents bring their children for counseling as a way of getting help for themselves when they are too embarrassed to seek help directly. At other times parents are less aware of their own problems but it becomes clear to the counselor that the child's symptoms largely result from parental problems. When parents are helped to deal with their own "hang-ups" and insecurities, children often improve spontaneously as a result. The counselor must not impose counseling on parents who do not want it, but whenever children are brought for help it is important to be alert to parental problems, many of which can be dealt with in the context of discussing the child. For example, parents can be asked, "What could you do differently to help solve this problem?" From this there is opportunity to talk about parental frustrations, fears and actions.

At times it will appear that parents are severely disturbed or so concerned with personal problems and difficulties that they are unable to meet their children's needs effectively. The counselor's task is to provide a place of stability and strength while helping parents deal with the conflicts in themselves and in the home. This is difficult since

> counseling the very disturbed . . . parent requires experience and resilience from the counselor and the capacity for endless patience that can put up with interminable recitals of petty resentments, trivial preoccupations, obsessive questioning, repeated recriminations, the breaking of appointments without warning, prolonged telephone calls, unexpected disappearances from the therapeutic scene, and clamorous demands for help at all times of day and night. Such parents have a poor parental concept of themselves and are beset with fears that they have harmed their children who will be taken away from them as a safeguard. Thus, they will resist any attempt on the part of the counselor to "help with the children" as this would at once imply that the children were in need of help and that this was the result of the care they were receiving.[33]

All of this implies that the counselor must be flexible and at times inclined to make referrals to more specialized counselors.

3. *Counseling Referrals*. Child counseling is a speciality within the helping professions. The Christian counselor who mostly works with adults may wish to refer children and their parents, especially disturbed parents, to counselors who are more skilled or experienced in the treatment of children, families, or adult psychopathology.

Preventing Child-Rearing Problems

In all of society there is no institution that can match the church in its potential influence on childhood and family development. Entire families come to church. They bring their infant children for dedication or christening and often return for church services and Sunday school classes. The church, therefore, can influence child-rearing in a variety of ways.

1. *Spiritual Training.* Earlier in this chapter we discussed biblical teachings about the home and child-rearing. Through sermons, Sunday school classes, seminars and retreats, the church can teach parents how to build Christian homes. Parents can be helped to be example believers. They can teach their children in accordance with the approach outlined in Deuteronomy 6, making spiritual issues a normal part of family discussions. The home is the backbone of society, and stable Christian homes are built on the guidance that comes from the Bible, often through the church.

2. *Marital Enrichment.* When marriages are good and growing, this influences the children positively by creating stability and security at home. Problems with children can put a strain on the parents' marriage. It helps if mothers and fathers can discuss the child problems together without having to face marital difficulties as well. Stimulating good marriages, therefore, is one way to prevent child-rearing problems.[34]

3. *Parental Training.* Becoming a parent can be an overwhelming responsibility. At times almost all parents feel that they have failed, and most have periods of discouragement and confusion. At such times parents need understanding, encouragement and guidance concerning the needs and characteristics of children. Christian leaders can give such help. Show parents where to get valid information about child-rearing.[35] Alert them to the child's need for security, love, discipline, self-esteem, acceptance and an awareness of God's presence. Point out the dangers of overprotection, overpermissiveness, overrestrictiveness and overmeticulousness. Then, as part of the training of parents, it may be helpful to consider principles of effective parent-child communication,[36] to teach ways to discipline,[37] to talk about behavior management, and to discuss how children's needs can be met. All of this may be discussed in church settings where parents can share with one another.

Be careful to emphasize that while child-rearing is a serious responsibility, everyone makes mistakes and parents who are too rigid or "uptight" probably create problems because of their anxiety and inflexibility. Child-rearing can be difficult and challenging, but it also can be fun—especially when parents can discuss their mutual concerns informally with other parents, including Christian counselors.

4. *Encouragement.* The story is told of a preacher who, when invited to speak at a meeting of preteenagers, asked his daughter what he should say. "Tell them, Dad," the daughter replied, "that they should be patient because their parents are just learning how to raise kids."

Perhaps this message, though simple, should be sounded to both parents and children. It is biblical to encourage one another,[38] and there are times when family members should be encouraged, prayed for, and given verbal emotional support.

One recent report describes the establishment of "The Parent Place," a parent-operated center where other parents can call or visit for help with their child-rearing problems.[39] The idea is new and community sponsored, but it is a concept which could be used by church groups to help other parents both within the body of believers and without.

Conclusions about Child-Rearing and Parental Guidance

It has been suggested that many people find it easy to talk about parenting—until they have children. Then the favorite child-rearing theories are quickly discarded as mothers and fathers begin an occupation for which they are largely unprepared and which they rarely master.

Having raised his children, one former college president shared his "homemade, groping, amateur rules on how to learn to be a parent in this bewildering age." These rules are worth remembering and sharing as we help parents to deal with the challenges of parenthood.

—Accept the fact that being a parent is one of the most important tasks you will ever undertake—and budget your time and energy accordingly.

—Think long and hard about the particular parental role you have to play now.

—Don't regard your child as an extension of yourself.

—Enjoy your children.

—Love and believe in them.

—Expect something of your children.

—Be honest with them.

—Let them go. We do not own our children. In the end, the best we can do for them is free them into the hands of God.[40]

Suggestions for Further Reading

Arnold, L. Eugene., ed. *Helping Parents Help Their Children*. New York: Brunner/ Mazel, 1978.

*Dobson, James. *Dare to Discipline*. Wheaton, IL: Tyndale House, 1970.

* ———. *Hide or Seek*. Old Tappan, NJ: Revell, 1974.

* ———. *The Strong Willed Child*. Wheaton, IL: Tyndale House, 1978.

* Getz, Gene A. *The Measure of a Family*. Glendale, CA: Regal, 1976.

* Ginott, Haim G. *Between Parent and Child*. New York: Avon Books, 1965.

* Narramore, S. Bruce. *Help! I'm a Parent*. Grand Rapids: Zondervan, 1972.

Footnotes

1. S. Bruce Narramore, *Help! I'm a Parent* (Grand Rapids: Zondervan, 1972), p. 11.

2. The quotation by Richard Farson appears in Eleanor Links Hoover, "Far Out: Richard Farson" *Human Behavior* (July, 1976): 11.

3. L. Eugene Arnold, ed., *Helping Parents Help Their Children* (New York: Brunner/Mazel, 1978).

4. Ps. 127:3–5, Jer. 22:30, Gen. 30:22, 23; Rachel, Sarah, Hannah, Michal and Elizabeth were among biblical women whose childlessness caused considerable distress.

5. Luke 18:15–17.

6. Ps. 127:3; Prov. 10:1; Matt. 18:10; Ps. 103:13; Titus 2:4; Matt. 18:1–6.

7. Exod. 20:12; Mark 7:10–13; Prov. 1:8, 4:1, 13:1; 23:22; Eph. 6:1.

8. Rom. 1:30, 31. See also 2 Tim. 3:1–5.

9. Acts 5:29.

10. Titus 2:4; Deut. 6:1–9; Prov. 22:6; 2 Cor. 12:14; Col. 3:21.

11. Gene A. Getz, *The Measure of a Family* (Glendale, CA: Regal, 1976), pp. 83–94.

12. Ray C. Stedman, "Parents Are People," *Journal of Psychology and Theology* 1 (1973): 57–65.

13. Luke 2:52.

14. These ideas are developed more fully by Stedman, "Parents Are People."

15. John M. Drescher, *Seven Things Children Need* (Scottdale, PA: Herald Press, 1976).

16. See Deut. 6:1–9; Prov. 22:6; Ps. 78:1–8.

17. Maya Pines, "Superkids," *Psychology Today* 12 (January, 1979): 52–63.

18. Arnold, *Helping Parents,* p. 10.

19. Isa. 1:2.

20. 1 Sam. 3:13.

21. 1 Sam. 8:3.

22. This section is adapted from Group for the Advancement of Psychiatry, *Psychopathological Disorders of Childhood: Theoretical Considerations and a Proposed Classification* 6, no. 62 (New York: Mental Health Materials Center, 1966); and Elinor Weeks and John E. Marks, "The Child," in *The Harvard Guide to Modern Psychiatry,* ed. Armand M. Nicholi, Jr. (Cambridge, MA: The Belknap Press of Harvard University Press, 1978), pp. 495–518.

23. Child handicaps are discussed more fully in chapter 30.

24. This section is adapted from chapters 1 and 2 of Arnold, *Helping Parents.*

25. Ibid.

26. Ibid.

27. Getz, *The Measure of a Family,* p. 13.

28. Among the recommended books, consider Francis L. Ilg and Louise Bates Ames, *Child Behavior* (from birth to ten) (New York: Harper & Row, 1966); and A. Gesell, F. L. Ilg, and L. B. Ames, *The Years from Ten to Sixteen* (New York: Harper & Row, 1956).

29. In the author's home we talk over the dinner table. Several rules guide our conversation: no answering of the phone during dinner, no one leaves the table without being excused, and there is no "putting down" of each other, or name-calling. One other rule which we each break at times (sometimes together): no singing at the table when others are talking. And the radio does not play rock music when we are trying to communicate.

30. Joseph Bird and Lois Bird, *Power to the Parents* (Garden City, NY: Image Books, Doubleday, 1972), chapter 6.

31. The interested reader might want to consult two books by Gerald R. Patterson, *Families: Applications of Social Learning to Family Life,* rev. ed. (Champaign, IL: Research Press, 1975); and *Living with Children: New Methods for Parents and Teachers,* rev. ed. (Champaign, IL: Research Press, 1976).

32. See, for example, Arnold, *Helping Parents,* and B. Wolman, *Manual of Child Psychopathology* (New York: McGraw-Hill, 1972).

33. E. James Anthony and Manon McGennis, "Counseling Very Disturbed Parents," in *Helping Parents,* ed. Arnold, pp. 339–40.

34. Marital issues are discussed in chapters 12, 13, and 14.

35. See footnote 28. Groups may wish to consider Wayne E. Rickerson, *Getting Your Family Together: A Guide to Christian Parenting* (Glendale, CA: Regal, 1977).

36. See chapter 23.

37. See, for example, James Dobson, *Dare to Discipline* (Wheaton, IL: Tyndale, 1970).

38. 1 Thess. 5:11; Heb. 3:13; 10:25.

39. Jerry Richard, "The Parent Place, For the Besieged, Some Comfort and Counseling," *Human Behavior* (September, 1978): 36, 37.

40. Landrum Bolling, "Relaxing with Parenthood: Guidelines from a Veteran," *Eternity* (August, 1975): 11, 23.

16
Adolescence and Youth

THE CHAPTERS IN THIS BOOK DEAL WITH PROBLEMS WHICH MANY of us have never experienced. But we've all been adolescents and most of us can remember those stressful but exciting years when we were moving through that part of life which one psychiatrist has called "the most confusing, challenging, frustrating, and fascinating phase of human development."[1]

The word *adolescence* means "the period of growth to maturity." The adolescent is in an ill-defined period of life which begins prior to the teenage years and extends into the late teens or early twenties. During this time the young person changes physically, sexually, emotionally, intellectually and socially. He or she moves away from dependence and the protective confines of the family and toward relative independence and social productivity. The changes sometimes come quickly, and immature young people do not always adjust efficiently. This has led some people to conclude that adolescence is a highly disruptive period characterized by rebellion and perpetual turmoil. Such a view, however, is not supported by the professional literature. There still is much that we do not know about adolescence, but in spite of the rapid growth and changes during this time of life, it probably is true that "taken as a whole, adolescents are *not* in turmoil, *not* deeply disturbed, *not* at the mercy of their impulses, *not* resistant to parental values, *not* politically active, and *not* rebellious."[2] They *are* going through a significant change period, characterized first by a need to adjust to physical changes, second by the influence of great social pressures, and third by the challenge of making life-determining decisions about values, beliefs, identity, careers, and one's relationships with others, including those of the opposite sex.

Adolescence is often divided into three periods: early adolescence (sometimes called "pubescence" or "preadolescence") which begins around age ten or eleven and continues through the junior high school years; middle adolescence, which comprises those years from about age

220

fifteen to eighteen when the young person is in high school; and late adolescence (sometimes called the period of "youth") which begins approximately at age eighteen and extends into the twenties.

Early Adolescence. This period begins with a bursting of biological changes which can evoke simultaneous feelings of anxiety, bewilderment and delight. In both sexes there is a spurt of growth, especially in the limbs (this creates awkwardness and a gangly appearance), a change in body proportions (boys wider in the shoulders and develop thicker muscles, girls expand in the hips and develop breasts), a lowering of the voice in males, an enlargement of sexual organs, an increase in sex hormones, the growth of pubic hair, the increase in size of skin pores with more active glandular activity (which leads to acne), and the appearance of hair on the face and body which, of course, is generally heavier in boys. The beginning of menstruation in girls and the occurrence of seminal emissions in boys both appear at this stage and bring the need for new emotional adjustments. It is interesting to note that over the past hundred years there has been a steady decline in the age of first menstruation and first emission of semen. This means that the onset of adolescence has been getting earlier and earlier in life.

These physical changes have social and psychological influences. Most adolescents have times of feeling awkward, self-conscious and dissatisfied with their physical appearance. Often there is difficulty in handling the new sexual urges, and people who develop quickly or slowly often feel embarrassed, especially in the locker room where their peers can easily observe the differences. Girls who feel awkward about using sanitary pads or young males who have erections at the most unexpected and potentially embarrassing times are bothered by these preadolescent influences, especially if they were not anticipated.

Peer influences and pressures, the insecurities of shifting into junior high school, the development of close "chumship" relationships, hero worship and "crushes" on people of the opposite sex all indicate social adjustments during this period. There is, in addition, a new spirit of independence from parents, including parental values, and the development of more abstract, self-critical and reflective thinking—all of which increase the ability to worry and be anxious.

Middle Adolescence. This period has fewer physical changes, but the adolescent must adapt to his or her new identity as a person with an adult body. Sexual urges remain intense and difficult to control in the face of peer pressures and the values of a hedonistic society which no longer considers self-control to be of importance. (Within recent years there has been a staggering increase in the number of births to teenagers, most of whom are unmarried.)

Peers who were important in early adolescence now become of even greater significance as adolescents seek to break away from parental influences, values and controls. Teenagers often do not want to accompany their parents to church, on vacations, or on shopping trips. Communication at home may be minimal, but daydreaming is common and long hours are spent talking with friends on the telephone. There is a great desire to be accepted and to identify with the current teenage language, heroes, style of dress, and forms of entertainment. Dating and other relationships with the opposite sex become of extreme importance and "breakups" are very painful.

It is during this period that three influences can become extremely important: sex, drugs and motor vehicles. Each of these relates to the peer pressures, physical changes, insecurities, and adolescent struggles for identity. The need for love and acceptance, the influence of sexual hormones, the sexual openness in our society, and the relative ease of finding privacy (often in a car) make sexual intercourse a common experience for adolescents, even though this often arouses guilt, self-criticism, and sometimes the pregnancies mentioned above. The use of drugs, including alcohol,[3] has always characterized adolescence, especially those who are seeking an unusual experience, escape from anxiety and boredom, or acceptance with drug-using friends. Cars and motorcycles also give acceptance and provide a way to express power and bolster feelings of insecurity. In a fascinating study, Armand M. Nicholi reached some conclusions about motorcycle use which reveal a great deal about the needs of middle adolescents.

> Charging through the streets on a motorcycle (or in a car) gives the adolescent a sense of moving ahead, of doing, and of exerting himself; but it is finally a false sense and a poor substitute for concentrated effort. Racing a motorcycle into the middle of the night relieves the anxiety of rejection or failure, but it effects little change in the conditions causing the anxiety. A fast, noisy, breathtaking ride tends to relieve apprehension over exams, but it helps little in preparing for them. The cycle stimulates sexual feeling and even helps the adolescent approach a girl, but it contributes little to forming a meaningful relationship with her. The cycle helps express anger, but the destructive tendencies of these adolescents make a machine that can travel 125 miles an hour, a less than adaptive means of doing so.[4]

As they move into late adolescence this interest in sex, drugs and vehicles continues. There is a vacillation between maturity and immaturity, but young people also face the serious challenges of choosing a college or finding a job, leaving home, shifting responsibility onto themselves, and coping with the subtle, often unconscious attempts of parents to keep them dependent and close to home.

Late Adolescence. To most people, this period begins at the time of graduation from high school. Neither adolescent nor adult, the young person in this period is faced with the task of moving comfortably into adult society, assuming adult responsibilities, shifting to an independent status, and formulating a distinct life style. Planning for the future, including the challenge of choosing a mate and moving into a career, occupies considerable time and energy.

All of this may be secondary, however, to the "three crucial questions" of late adolescence: Who am I? (the question of identity), how do I relate to others? (the question of interrelationships), and what should I believe? (the question of ideology).[5] As they attempt to answer these questions, many young adults struggle with feelings of inner emptiness, confusion, interpersonal tension and anxiety. Some of the idealism of the early teens is replaced by the realism of adulthood and the challenge of beginning to find one's place in life.

The Bible and Adolescence

The concept of adolescence, as we know it, did not appear in the literature on child-rearing until late in the nineteenth century.[6] It was not until 1904 that the term *adolescence* was first used—by G. Stanley Hall, the first president of the American Psychological Association.

With this historical background it should come as no surprise that the word *adolescence* does not appear anywhere in the Bible. The biblical writers probably did not think of adolescence as a separate period of human development. As we noted in chapter 15, however, childhood was mentioned with some frequency and the fact that instructions are given directly to children would imply that these children were old enough to understand and comply. Biblical teachings on children,[7] therefore, undoubtedly apply to "children" of adolescent age.

The Bible also speaks to "young men" and "young women." The writer of Ecclesiastes, for example, tells young men to rejoice:

> Young man, it's wonderful to be young! Enjoy every minute of it! Do all you want to; take in everything, but realize that you must account to God for everything you do. So banish grief and pain, but remember that youth, with a whole life before it, can make serious mistakes.[8]

Young people are portrayed in Scripture as visionaries who are strong, able to incorporate the Word of God into their beings, overcome Satan, expected to be submissive to elders, told to love their mates and instructed to humble themselves "under the mighty hand of God, that He may exalt you at the proper time, casting all your anxiety on Him, because He cares for you."[9] These few phrases give considerable guidance to adolescents and, of course, the teachings of the entire Bible can be helpful to young people struggling with adolescence, just as the Scriptures are helpful to those who are older.

The Causes of Problems in Adolescence

The problems of adolescence are well known. Although the adolescent society changes quickly, and adult memories tend to fade, most of us can recall our own struggles. At least partially we can appreciate the problems of the growing-up years of life. Several issues create these problems for adolescents.

1. *Physical Changes.* The growth spurt, skin problems, excess fat, periodic decrease in energy, changes in body proportions, development of body hair, lowering of voice pitch and other physical changes can each influence adolescents psychologically. At a time when it is important to look attractive, these changes can bring embarrassment and dissatisfaction, especially if the changes are slow in coming. Late maturers are treated as children by both peers and adults. While girls are able to overcome this rejection, late maturing boys are more inclined to show personal and social adjustment problems even into adulthood.[10]

2. *Sexual Changes.* Even when they are expecting the sexual changes of adolescence, most young people struggle with embarrassment and anxiety over the physical changes in their bodies and the erotic impulses within. Sexual fantasies, masturbation and adolescent intercourse can all produce guilt. Crushes on people of the same sex can lead to fears of homosexuality. Physical growth can create confusion over one's identity and a desire to act appropriately as an adult male or female. Dating can be both desired and feared. While the sexual freedom in our society does nothing to bolster sexual self-control, impulsive sexual experimenting often leads to guilt and pregnancies, with the emotional trauma that follows.

3. *Interpersonal Relations.* Adolescence is a time when the person is changing in his or her relationships with parents, peers, and others in the society. It is important to be liked and accepted by peers, especially of the opposite sex, but even as he or she turns away from parents the adolescent needs to feel that the environment has stability. When both the inner and outer worlds seem to be changing and unstable, the adolescent begins to challenge adult authority. When there are little certainty and no clear parental guidelines, the young person feels anxious and sometimes hostile.

4. *Values, Morals and Religion.* Prior to adolescence, the young person accepted parental standards and beliefs with little question or challenge. The adolescent, however, must learn to control and live with heightened impulses. As parental restraints are thrown off and peer attitudes are exchanged, there develops a personal set of values and beliefs. Often, young people get no help with this process of value clarification, except from equally confused and struggling peers. Doubt, a decrease in religious activities, and turning to some other faith are all common in adolescence, much to the distress of parents and church leaders. Later, it often happens that young people adopt values similar to those of the parents, but when these values and beliefs are accepted they are what the young person really believes and not simply what he or she has been taught.

At a denominational conference, a layman once sat in on a meeting to discuss "the problems of today's teenagers." The topics for discussion were selected by adults and proved to be of little interest to the adolescent participants. When urged to express their real concerns, the young people expressed resentment at the standards and life styles which were imposed on them by adults;

—noted that Christian parents and church leaders fail to realize the intense pressures and problems facing teenagers today—including the pressures to "turn on" with drugs and sex;

—complained that outward conformity to adult standards often is taken as evidence of spiritual maturity when in fact, it may show a desire to not "rock the family boat" by asking questions or expressing doubts;

—indicated that Christian parents don't instill healthy and realistic attitudes toward sex;

—asked that adults show confidence in adolescents by letting them undertake some *real* responsibilities;

—resented the lackadaisical attitude that many church people take toward important economic, health, social and political issues; and

—recognized a disparity between the pat answers and the day-to-day Christian lives of their elders.[11]

While these conclusions are not based on a scientific study, they do demonstrate some of the moral struggles of adolescents, and alert older Christians to the fact that we may be ignoring pressing adolescent issues while we seek to answer questions that nobody is asking.

5. *Independence*. By definition, adolescence is the period of growth into maturity. Aware that they are no longer children, adolescents seek freedom. They want it in large doses, but handle it better in small and ever-increasing amounts. Often what the young people want and think they can handle differs from what parents are willing or think it wise to give. This can create considerable tension, frustration, power struggles and even rebellion.

6. *Identity and Self-esteem*. According to James Dobson there are three things that teenagers feel they need in order to feel good about themselves: physical attractiveness, intelligence (which often translates into academic ability), and money.[12] Rarely are these all present and frequently there are feelings of self-condemnation, social incompetence, academic and athletic ineptness, and spiritual failure—feelings which are emphasized whenever there is criticism, social rejection, or the inability to succeed in some important task.

The well-known "identity crisis" comes as the growing teenager begins to wonder, "Where do I fit?," "What am I worth as a person?," "Who do I follow?," and "What will be my purpose in life as I move into adulthood?"

7. *The Future*. The time when people are in college or job training has been called a period of "psychosocial moratorium" when young adults

are free to "regroup" psychologically and socially and to find their niche in society.[13] But even during this moratorium there is pressure from older adults and from within, as adolescents seek to determine who or if they will marry, how they will plan for a career, what they will do with their lives, and how they will live in terms of values and life styles. While one can change later, especially in our society, decisions made in early adulthood can have lifelong implications. This can create a pressure to choose wisely and an anxiety as decisions are made.

The Effects of Problems in Adolescence

In spite of all that is written and discussed about the problems of adolescence, it is important to note that most teenagers *do* grow up into a relatively normal adulthood, sometimes to the amazement of their beleaguered parents. But the pressures of adolescence do take their toll. Teenage insecurities, feelings of guilt, inferiority, loneliness and rejection can persist far into the adult years, and for many young people the problems of adolescence make their presence felt long before adulthood.

1. *"Holding in" the Problems.* Some adolescents struggle with their problems alone. There may be loneliness, daydreaming, alienation or withdrawal from friends, apathy, a forsaking of usual interests and activities, or perpetual inner turmoil which sometimes comes out in the form of psychosomatic illnesses, anxiety, scholastic failure, or more serious emotional and behavioral disorders.[14] Depression, anxiety and unexplainable changes in mood or behavior often indicate serious disturbance in adults, but unless these are prolonged or intense they are not considered pathological in adolescence.[15] More common are the "adjustment reactions of adolescence" which come in response to stress and are characterized by irritability, depression (often associated with school failure), brooding and temper outbursts.[16]

2. *"Acting out" the Problems.* Adolescents often "act out" their problems in socially disapproved ways. Excessive drinking, drug abuse, lying, stealing, violence, crime, "gang" behavior and other forms of delinquency or rebellion give the adolescent a sense of power, a feeling of independence, a way of "bucking the system" (including one's parents), and a means for gaining and retaining the acceptance of one's friends—most of whom also may be acting out.

But there are other ways to resist parents, assert independence, and gain peer acceptance. There is, for example, failing in school subjects or rejecting parental religious beliefs and moral standards. Adolescent sexual activities, especially sexual intercourse, sometimes become another way of acting like adults and asserting one's independence.

Teenage sex, however, is not always rebellious. Often there are intense social pressures to experiment and yield to sexual impulses. Nicholi's observations of these people are worth considering at length:

Many who have worked closely with adolescents over the past decade have realized that the new sexual freedom has by no means led to greater pleasure, freedom, and openness, more meaningful relationships between the sexes, or exhilarating relief from stifling inhibitions. . . . A recent study of normal college students . . . found that, although their sexual behavior by and large appeared to be a desperate attempt to overcome a profound sense of loneliness, they described their sexual relationships as less than satisfactory and as providing little of the emotional closeness they desired. They described pervasive feelings of guilt and haunting concerns that they were using others and being used as "sexual objects." . . . Clinical experience has shown that the new permissiveness has often led to empty relationships, feeling of self-contempt and worthlessness, an epidemic of venereal disease, and a rapid increase in unwanted pregnancies.[17]

The increase in teenage pregnancies has become one of the "most serious complex challenges" facing the country today. Not only is there concern for the care and welfare of the babies, but there is clear evidence that when compared to their classmates, teenage parents get less education, earn less money in life, hold lower prestige jobs, experience less job satisfaction, and have a higher than average rate of divorce and remarriage.[18] Of course these unhappy results may not be due to teenage pregnancy alone, but the contrast between adolescent childbearers and nonchildbearers is sharp enough to strongly suggest that teenage childbearing can radically change a young person's whole educational, occupational, social and marital future.[19] This clearly is a long-term effect of adolescent "acting out" in response to sexual impulses.

3. *"Running from" the Problems.* Every year large numbers of adolescents, mostly females between the ages of fifteen and seventeen, run away from home. Many of these people are frustrated at home and school, lacking in self-esteem, subject to depression, unable to communicate with parents, and sometimes impulsive or having problems with peers.[20]

But leaving home is not the only way to escape. Some withdraw from the world psychologically with or without the help of drugs and alcohol. (Drinking and taking drugs, as we have seen, can also be a way of "acting out.") Then there are those who attempt to take their own lives. Within recent years, there has been a sharp rise in the suicide rate among adolescents, and suicide has become one of the leading causes of adolescent death. Suicide attempts often indicate a real desire to die, but invariably there is also a cry for help, indicating how much the young person really is hurting.

4. *"Sticking with" the Problems.* Not all adolescents hold in, act out, or run from their problems. Many face the challenges squarely, talk them over with friends or trusted adults, read (if they can find something relevant), react to failures by trying harder next time, learn from their mistakes, and move through the era of adolescence in a relatively smooth

fashion. Such young people or their parents could benefit from preventive, educative and supportive counseling, but more often the Christian counselor is called to help those whose adjustment problems are more disruptive to individuals, families and society.

Counseling and the Problems of Adolescents

Adolescent problems can be approached in two ways, by counseling the adolescent and by helping the parents. In both cases, the counselor must begin with a broad understanding of the struggles of adolescents and of the kinds of tensions which build up both inside the counselees and within their homes. Often, parents and teenagers are confused, disappointed and hurt over the interpersonal tensions and adolescent pressures which have developed. Frequently there is anger, a loss of self-esteem, anxiety about the future, and feelings of guilt over the past.[21] The counselor who understands and accepts such problems without taking sides can have a significant impact on both parents and teenagers. The impact can be even greater if the counselor is sensitive, calm, compassionate and secure enough to tolerate criticism and adulation—sometimes in the same interview. Adolescents and their parents need a caring, wise, self-confident person who provides a haven of calm guidance in times of strong upheaval.

1. *Counseling Parents.* In chapter 15 we considered a number of ways by which parents can be helped to cope with the problems of their children. Since most of these principles apply equally to the problems of adolescents, we will refer the reader back to the previous chapter and to the section headed "Counseling Parents." In counseling the parents of adolescents, however, there are additional guidelines which might be kept in mind.

(a) Support and Encouragement. When adolescent problems arise, parents often conclude that they are to blame, that they are not "good" parents, or that their children are headed for certain disaster. Counselors do not help if they ignore or explain away such feelings, but there is value in reassuring and encouraging parents. Almost all children—even the children of effective parents—go through periods of anger, rebellion and criticism. God, the only perfect parent, once stated that even the sons which he "reared and brought up" had "revolted" against him.[22] Young people have been given the freedom to think independently and this often puts them in conflict with their parents. The reasons for adolescent behavior are complex and although parental influence is extremely important, it is not the sole determinant of teenage and young adult actions. At home parents need to relax and do the best job they can, seeking the daily help and guidance of a God who understands.

(b) Limit Setting. Many of the home conflicts in adolescence come because young people push for more freedom than the parents are willing to give, at least initially. When adolescents react adversely to the setting of limits, parents begin to wonder if they are being rigid and unreasonable. Convinced that the well-adjusted, well-run household is a neat, quiet, tranquil, strife-free place to live, parents begin to doubt their competence when there is the usual turmoil.

Instead of giving in to adolescent demands (an action which often produces anger followed by even more demands), parents can be helped to recognize that all family members have rights in the household. To insure these rights, some limits must be set and maintained, regardless of adolescent and neighborhood pressures. This is not meant to advocate a rigid conformity to inflexible rules. As adolescents grow older, they must be given greater freedom, but at all times there must be respect for the rights and interests of each other. Counselors can help parents to set limits which respect the individual family members and which conform to biblical teachings.

> The maturing young person will find the world with its many demands an overpowering experience if he does not have the security of strong, loving parent figures on whom to rely. When a parent finds that he himself cannot stand for what he believes, because of social pressures from his neighbors or psychological pressures from his child, then his ability to provide stability for his offspring is measurably diminished. Guidance by example is still the most effective kind. If a parent has a healthy self-image based on integrity in dealing with others, then his children will learn values which no amount of advice, nagging or correction could possibly communicate. If a parent is able to help his teenager set limits on the youngster's own impulsive, egocentric behavior in a firm, but loving way, then the young person will learn to respect himself as well as others.[23]

(c) Spiritual Guidance. Commenting on a massive research study of evangelical youth,[24] one writer has made a strong case for the conclusion that adolescents forsake their religious heritage and are alienated from parents when the parental faith is based on rules, rather than on the Christian virtues of acceptance and forgiveness.[25] When the family is concerned about status, competition and legalism, the young people are more likely to rebel. At times it may appear that parental rigidity and legalism really are a cover for some underlying anxiety. If so, there is a need for counseling in this area. Helping parents to grow spiritually, to develop biblical values and to live a consistent Christian life style is both a therapeutic and a preventive counseling technique.

2. *Counseling Adolescents.* Perhaps the most difficult task involved in counseling adolescents is to establish a trusting relationship and to help the counselee recognize the need for help. Some counselees come voluntarily for help, but often the adolescent sees no need for counseling and is sent by a parent, teacher, or judge. In such cases the counselor is seen as the parent's ally and resistance is present from the beginning.

(a) Rapport-building. Honesty and respect, mixed with compassion and gentle firmness, can be the best point to begin adolescent counseling. If there is resistance, deal with it directly and give the counselee opportunity for self-expression. For example, you might ask, "Could you tell me what brought you here?" and if the counselee doesn't respond, ask, "Well, somebody else must have wanted you to come. I'm sure you must have some ideas why." Remember to keep this on a conversational level. Show respect for the counselee, and avoid asking questions in a way that implies judgment or criticism, since this will only serve to arouse resistance and defensiveness. Try to focus the discussion on specific concrete issues and periodically take the time to point out what is happening emotionally within the interview.

(b) Transference. This term refers to the tendency of individuals to "transfer" feelings about a person in the past to a person in the present. For example, a young counselee who hates his father may transfer this hatred to the male counselor. The counselor must recognize that he or she will often be treated with hostility, suspicion, fear, or praise primarily because of the counselor's appearance or position which resembles some other adult. Counselors may want to discuss such feelings with counselees, being careful not to respond like the counselee's parent, hero or other individual with whom the counselor is being compared. At times there can be value in observing and discussing the counselee's attitude toward the counselor.

(c) Problem Identification. It is difficult to help if you cannot identify the problem, and since adolescent counselees sometimes deny that they have problems, the counselor is in a challenging position. Instead of trying to classify or diagnose the counselee's difficulties, it is helpful to encourage adolescents to talk about such issues as school, leisure activities, home, parents, religion, plans for the future, dating, sex, likes and dislikes, worries, and similar issues. Start with relatively nonthreatening items (e.g., "Tell me about your school or family"; "What has happened recently that interests you?") and try more sensitive areas later. In all of this you should try to be a friend instead of an interrogator, and show that your desire is to listen. Some general questioning may be needed to get the process started, but once the counselee starts talking be alert in your listening.

(d) Goal Setting. Once you begin to identify the problems, there is value in determining what you want to accomplish in counseling. In chapter 2 we considered the goals of stimulating self-understanding, building better communication with others, helping people acquire skills and change behavior, stimulating self-actualization, and giving support. These apply to adolescents as well as to adults.

But the overarching goal of adolescent counseling is to help young people grow into maturity and become adults who honor Christ with their life styles, beliefs, inner serenity, and interpersonal relationships. To help people reach such a goal it is necessary to focus on present, more immediate problems. Help people reach solutions and change behavior, thinking and perceptions about present problems. This frees them to move on to larger problems and teaches problem-solving methods.

(e) Counseling Variations. Individual, one-to-one counseling is not the only approach to helping adolescents. Family counseling, in which the entire family is seen together, can be helpful, and other adolescents respond well to group counseling. This is true especially when the group members have problems with interpersonal relations, a tendency to withdraw, or a problem which they all share—such as an alcoholic parent or a terminally ill relative. The relationships that are built in such counseling sessions can give support and teach adolescents an important lesson—how to relate to others effectively.

Preventing the Problems of Adolescence

It is well known that baby chicks struggle to peck their way out of the shell of the egg. If a sympathetic observer helps by breaking the shell, the chick gets out of the egg faster, but without the strength to get free of the shell and face the stresses of life.

Adolescents are somewhat similar to those baby chicks. It can be painful and difficult to break out from the restraints of childhood, but with each challenge the adolescent can gain in confidence, competence, and knowledge, even when there is failure. Parents and other sympathetic adults sometimes try to prevent all problems and protect teenagers from the stresses of life, but this is both impossible and poor child-rearing. Instead, we should seek to help young people mature without the painful and unnecessary consequences that come when there is a breaking of the law, sexual immorality, severe emotional disturbance, inability to succeed academically, interpersonal conflict, or loss of faith. As Christian counselors, how can we help adolescents mature and prevent undesirable problems?

1. *Spiritual Foundation.* It has been said that the best time to begin preparing for adolescence is at least ten years before it begins. By building communication skills, mutual respect, concern for others, and an open attitude about problems, parents help children learn how to deal honestly and immediately with issues when they arise.

In no area is this early training more important than in the spiritual realm. Adolescents are not impressed by theological legalism and religion that is all talk but little action. They are much more impressed when they see a live faith in their parents, characterized by worship, sincere commitment to Jesus Christ, and a daily willingness to serve him. When parents can be taught to grow spiritually, there is greater love, stability, acceptance and forgiveness in the home. This creates a firm foundation on which adolescents can build lives, formulate values, solve problems and plan for the future.

2. *Education.* Within recent years, schools have become interested in

giving education about the dangers of teenage drinking, drug use, sex, and related issues. But information-giving, while helpful, does not seem to be enough. Adolescents often know more about drugs and sex than their teachers, and frequently, factual knowledge fades in the face of peer pressure and the excitement of "taking a chance."

Drug, sex, and health education must not be abandoned. Some have suggested that this is more effective if given not by professional teachers, but by people who have experienced the pain of chemical abuse or sexual promiscuity. Even more effective is the discussion of moral standards, values, and biblical teachings about right and wrong. These issues must be discussed openly and honestly, preferably at home and before they arise in adolescent experience. In addition, adolescents must be helped to find love and acceptance in life so there is less need to escape into chemical euphoria or intimate sex.

For many years it has been the attitude of Christian parents and church leaders to assume that God will protect our children if we pray for them regularly. This is a valid conclusion, but surely he protects, at times, by giving forewarning and teaching principles for morality through parents and Christian teachers. Such learning does not occur if issues like sexual intercourse, birth control, drinking, masturbation, teenage pregnancies and drug abuse are never mentioned. When these are discussed openly before they arise, they can be discussed again when the temptations abound.[26]

3. *Family Example and Stability.* Parental example is one of the most effective preventive influences in the adolescent's life. How do the parents cope with stress, resolve differences, or respond to temptation? Is their marriage stable and the family able to provide a haven in times of stress and a place of certainty when the world around seems to be in turmoil? Stimulating better marriages is one crucial way in which the church can prevent teenage problems. Parents can also be encouraged to love their kids, to accept them as they are, to try to understand, to point out their good points, and to avoid constant nagging.

4. *Interpersonal Support.* Most churches are aware that peer support and encouragement is crucial in adolescence. The church can stimulate such friendships and group support. Of course, rebellion, drug abuse, and immorality occur in church and parachurch groups, too, but when sensitive, concerned leaders are available to give direction and spiritual teaching, help the participants have fun, build self-esteem, provide a place to discuss real problems, and give emotional and social support, then the church can have a tremendous positive and preventive impact on young people. Modeling is one of the most important means of teaching adolescents. If the model can get to know the adolescents and gain their respect, this can have a significant influence on teenage development. Churches should not underestimate the importance of such youth leaders and youth organizations.

5. *Guidance.* Choosing a career, finding one's place in life, learning to date, developing an identity, formulating values, deciding what to believe —these are among the decisions that adolescents must face. No one else can make these decisions for them, although parents, Christian counselors and leaders in the church can give guidance and encouragement as the decisions are being made. Sunday school classes, youth groups, and retreats can stimulate discussion and thinking about these issues—and so can parents.

Conclusions about Adolescence

It is not easy to be an adolescent or to help young people through their adolescent years, but surely the crisis nature of this period in life has been overrated. Considering the changes which occur and the adjustments which are required, most young people reach adulthood in remarkably good shape.

Immediately before his ascension into heaven, Jesus told his followers that they had one basic responsibility to complete in his absence: to make disciples.[27] Where could this be done more effectively than in the home? As children become teenagers, parental discipline should move into parental discipleship, teaching by word and example how to be a follower of Jesus Christ. Teenagers are "too big to spank,"[28] but they are old enough to respond to logic, persuasion, fairness, interest, positive reinforcement, love, parental example and the power of prayer. Rather than trying to force adolescents into some parental mold, our task as counselors and parents is to help them grow into Christian personal maturity. Few tasks could be more challenging or fulfilling.

Suggestions for Further Reading

Blees, Robert A., and Staff of First Community Church of Columbus, Ohio. *Counseling with Teenagers*. Philadelphia: Fortress Press, 1965.

Brandes, Norman S., and Gardner, Malcolm L., eds. *Group Therapy for the Adolescent*. New York: Jason Aronson, 1973.

* Dobson, James. *Preparing for Adolescence*. Santa Ana: Vision House, 1978.

Gallagher, J. Roswell, and Harris, Herbert I. *Emotional Problems of Adolescents*. Rev. ed. New York: Oxford University Press, 1964.

Kemp, Charles F. *Counseling with College Students*. Philadelphia: Fortress Press, 1964.

Malmquist, Carl P. *Handbook for Adolescence*. New York: Jason Aronson, 1978.

Narramore, Clyde M. *Counseling Youth*. Grand Rapids: Zondervan, 1966.

Schneiders, Alexander A., ed. *Counseling the Adolescent*. San Francisco: Chandler Publishing Co., 1967.

Footnotes

1. Armand M. Nicholi, Jr., ed., *The Harvard Guide to Modern Psychiatry* (Cambridge, MA: The Belknap Press of Harvard University Press, 1978), p. 519.

2. Joseph Adelson, "Adolescence and the Generalization Gap," *Psychology Today* 12 (February, 1979): 33–37.

3. See chapter 26; also Tom Alibrandi, *Young Alcoholics* (Minneapolis: CompCare Publications, 1978).

4. Nicholi, *The Harvard Guide*, p. 532.

5. Donald Williamson, "Later Adolescence," in *Youth Education in the Church*, eds. Roy B. Zuck and Warren S. Benson (Chicago: Moody Press, 1978), pp. 143–62.

6. J. Demos and V. Demos, "Adolescence in Historical Perspective," *Journal of Marriage and Family* 31 (1969): 632-38.

7. See the section entitled "The Bible and Child-Rearing" in chapter 15.

8. Eccles. 11:9, 10, *Living Bible, Paraphrased*.

9. Acts 2:17; Prov. 20:29; 1 John 2:13, 14; Titus 2:4; 1 Pet. 5:5–7.

10. M. C. Jones, "Psychological Correlates of Somatic Development," *Child Development* 36 (1965): 899-911.

11. Don Booth, "What Christian Kids Don't Tell Their Parents," *Eternity* (November, 1976): 32, 33.

12. James Dobson, *Preparing for Adolescence* (Santa Ana: Vision House, 1978).

13. E. H. Erikson, *Identity: Youth and Crisis*. (New York: Norton, 1968).

14. For further information on adolescent psychopathology see J. Roswell Gallagher and Herbert I. Harris, *Emotional Problems of Adolescents* (New York: Oxford University Press, 1964); and Carl P. Malmquist, *Handbook of Adolescence: Psychopathology, Antisocial Development, Psychotherapy* (New York: Jason Aronson, 1978).

15. Nicholi, *The Harvard Guide*, p. 532.

16. Ibid, p. 533.

17. Ibid, p. 530.

18. Charlotte MacDonald, "The Stunted World of Teen Parents," *Human Behavior* (January, 1979): 53–55.

19. Ibid.

20. Hershel D. Thornburg, *You and Your Adolescent* (Tucson, AZ: H.E.L.P. Books, 1977).

21. These issues are considered in other chapters. See especially 5, 7, 8, 9, 23, and 24.

22. Isa. 1:2.

23. Robert A. Blees and staff of First Community Church, Columbus, Ohio, *Counseling with Teenagers* (Philadelphia: Fortress, 1965), p. 133.

24. Merton P. Strommen, *Five Cries of Youth* (New York: Harper & Row, 1974).

25. Philip Yancey, "How Your Faith Affects Your Teenager," *Moody Monthly* (December, 1975): 57–62.

26. The author has written a book designed to stimulate such discussion in the church and family. See Gary R. Collins, *Family Talk* (Santa Ana: Vision House, 1978).

27. Matt. 28:19, 20.

28. This is the title of a book by the president of Youth for Christ: Jay Kesler, *Too Big to Spank* (Glendale, CA: Regal Books, 1978).

17

Vocational Counseling

CHOOSING A CAREER OFTEN IS SEEN AS A ONCE-IN-A-LIFETIME EVENT which occurs in late adolescence or early adulthood, at the time when a young man or woman picks an occupation. Little children are prepared for this ominous choice whenever they are asked, "What will you be when you grow up?" College students frequently are asked about their majors and often it is assumed, especially by parents, that the primary purpose of education is to help with vocational choice and prepare students for a career.

Almost everyone makes vocational decisions. These choices are crucially important, frequently difficult, and rarely "once-in-a-lifetime events." They are important because career choices largely determine one's income, standard of living, status in the community, general satisfaction with life (it is hard to be happy if one hates one's job), social contacts, emotional well-being, feelings of self-worth and use of time (how we will spend at least one-third of our waking hours as adults). Career choices are frequently difficult because of the many available careers, the staggering array of jobs and the great potential for making mistakes. Then, as most people learn through experience, career choices are rarely once-in-a-lifetime events. Beginning in high school, or even before, people start making decisions about work. These decisions come as educational courses, college majors and further training are all considered. Vocational decisions also come whenever one applies for a job, is offered a position, is promoted or not promoted, changes work, is fired or laid off, reevaluates a career, or faces retirement. For the Christian, all of these are influenced by the belief that one's vocational choices should be in accordance with God's will.

The Bible and Vocational Choices

The Bible does not say much about what Adam did between the time of his creation and the time of the fall. We know that he communicated

235

with God, slept, and became a husband, but it also appears that he worked. He was given the job of naming all living creatures and he was instructed to subdue the earth and rule over it. After the fall, Adam, with his wife, was sent "out from the garden of Eden, to cultivate the ground . . . in toil" by the sweat of his brow.[1]

Throughout the Bible other examples of work appear frequently. Cain, the first child of Adam and Eve, was a "tiller of the ground." His brother Abel was "a keeper of flocks." For at least part of his life Noah was a ship-builder who later turned to farming. Abraham was a wealthy livestock owner and David was a shepherd who later changed careers and became a king. Prophets, priests, tentmakers, hunters, political leaders, salespersons, homemakers, real-estate dealers, carpenters, fishermen—all of these, and more, are mentioned in the Bible as occupations for both men and women. It appears, therefore, that from the beginning work was part of God's plan for the human race. After the fall it became harder, but it has always been God-ordained and a human responsibility.

Biblical descriptions of work lead us to several conclusions:

1. *Work Is Honorable; Laziness Is Condemned.* The early church was instructed to give suitable wages and honor, especially to those who *work hard* at preaching and teaching.[2] The "excellent wife" is pictured as one who works diligently and is praised as a result.[3] In contrast, wise King Solomon warned of poverty and foolishness that would come to those who were lazy.[4] The Apostle Paul is even more blunt: "If anyone will not work, neither let him eat."[5]

2. *Work Is to Be Interspersed with Rest.* The Bible approves of diligence and quality in work, but it gives no sanction to the workaholic who never rests or takes a vacation. God rested after creating the world, and in the Ten Commandments he instructed human beings to rest one day out of every seven. Many modern believers do not regard one day as being any more special than another,[6] but we each have a biblical precedent to follow the example of Jesus and the spiritual leaders in Judeo-Christian history who set aside one day each week for worship, rest and relaxation.

3. *Work Is to Be of High Quality.* Employees and other workers have a responsibility to work honestly and diligently, not merely to please men, but to honor Christ. Employers are to be fair and just, recognizing that they too have a Master in heaven.[7] Poor quality and dishonest workmanship are clearly unbiblical.

4. *Work Is Unique and for the Common Good.* Like modern vocational counselors who emphasize the differences in human interests and abilities, the Bible points out that we each have unique capabilities and responsibilities When a person becomes a Christian, he or she is given one or more spiritual gifts. These are to be developed, used "for the common good," and applied to the building up of other believers in the body of Christ.[8] Our

differences in abilities and success come from God, however, and provide no reason for self-centered boasting.[9]

5. *Work and Vocational Choice are Guided by God.* Some historical people in the Bible had their life work selected by God before birth. Isaiah, David, Jeremiah, John the Baptist and Jesus are the clearest examples of this.[10] Is it not possible, therefore, that God still chooses men and women to accomplish special tasks for him? Is it not probable that he guides in the selection of careers? James I. Packer answers this with his characteristic depth and clarity.

> Has God a plan for individuals? Indeed He has. He has found an "eternal purpose" (literally, a "plan of the ages"), "a plan for the fulness of time," in accordance with which he "accomplishes all things according to the counsel of his will" (Ephesians 3:11; 1:10, 11, RSV) . . . God has a plan for each of his children.
>
> But can God communicate His plan to us? Indeed He can. . . . He made known His will to and through the Old Testament prophets. He guided Jesus and Paul. . . . God has no difficulty in making His will known to His servants.
>
> Moreover, Scripture contains explicit promises of divine guidance, whereby we may know God's plan for our action. "I will instruct you and teach you the way you should go; I will counsel you with my eye upon you," says God to David (Psalm 32:8, RSV). Isaiah 58:11 contains the assurance that if the people repent and obey "the Lord will guide you continually." Guidance is a main theme in Psalm 25, where we read, "Good and upright is the Lord; therefore he instructs sinners in the way. He leads the humble in what is right, and teaches the humble his way. . . . Who is the man that feareth the Lord? Him will he instruct in the way that he should choose" (verses 8, 9, 12, RSV). So in Proverbs 3:6, "In all thy ways acknowledge him, and he shall direct thy paths."
>
> In the New Testament, the same expectation of guidance appears. Paul's prayer that the Colossians "might be filled with the knowledge of his will in all wisdom and spiritual understanding," and Epaphras' prayer that they might "stand perfect . . . in all the will of God" (Colossians 1:9; 4:12), clearly assume that God is ready and willing to make His will known. "Wisdom" in Scripture always means knowledge of the course of action that will please God and secure life, so that the promise of James 1:5—"if any of you lacks wisdom, let him ask of God who gives to all men generously and without reproaching, and it will be given him" (RSV) —is in effect a promise of guidance. "Let your minds be remade and your whole nature thus transformed," counsels Paul. "Then you will be able to discern the will of God, and to know what is good, acceptable and perfect" (Romans 12:2, NEB).[11]

The Christian vocational counselor uses modern techniques to help people choose and change careers. But the Christian counselor goes about this work convinced that a sovereign God can and will guide the counselor and counselee who want divine leading in the making of vocational decisions.

Causes of Good and Poor Vocational Choices

Traditionally, vocational counseling has consisted of three parts: learning about the person, learning about vocations, and matching personal talents with job requirements. Sometimes the match is good, appropriate training and job openings are available, and the counselee is helped to find a meaningful and satisfying career.

Often, however, such a smooth process does not occur. High status, high prestige and high-paying jobs are relatively scarce but they are sought by numerous people. Many of the more attractive professional and entertainment careers require intellectual ability and special aptitudes which few people possess. Because of high demand, intense competition and limited opportunities, many people are disappointed in their career choices and are forced to settle for a less desirable alternative.

Others never have the opportunity to plan careers. In need of work, they skim the "help wanted" advertisements and slip into jobs which provide a paycheck and some security but are neither satisfying nor personally fulfilling. Some people stay in these jobs for their entire lives, comprising that large segment of our population who are dissatisfied and unhappy at work. Others are laid off or shift from one job to another, none of which they enjoy or do well.

Even people who enjoy their work often make changes as they go through life. Government estimates have shown that ten years from now nearly half of the working population will be in jobs that have not yet been invented. People who enter the job market in the 1980s can be expected to change jobs twelve to fifteen times during their working lives, and change careers four or five times.[12] Clearly vocational guidance must be an ongoing process that involves everyone—not just professional counselors.

With or without such guidance, some people make good vocational decisions while others decide unwisely. There are several reasons for this:

1. *Social Pressure.* In our society, parents, teachers and friends expect career decisions to be made early. Thus at a time when they are immature, idealistic, inexperienced, and struggling with the problems of late adolescence, young people have the added responsibility of choosing from an almost unlimited number of career possibilities. If one quits or is forced to leave a job there is financial and social pressure to find another job as quickly as possible. All of this prevents careful planning and leads to vocational choices which can be frustrating and disappointing.

2. *Personality Influences.* An individual's personality influences both the selection of a vocation and the success or satisfaction that is experienced within one's career. One of the leading writers in the psychology of career choice has suggested that most people can be categorized into

six general personality types: realistic (the person who prefers tangible, practical, skill activities); investigative (the one who is methodical, intellectual, curious and scientific); artistic (the creative, aesthetically oriented person); social (he or she who is friendly, sensitive, and interested in people); enterprising (the aggressive, energetic, self-confident problem-solver); and conventional (the person who prefers routine and orderly, practical, somewhat inflexible activities).[13] It is never possible to fit people into rigid categories, but this general organization suggests that there are individual differences which have a bearing on one's work.

According to this same theory, jobs can also be divided into six categories: realistic, investigative, artistic, social, enterprising and conventional. If investigative type people enter investigative jobs (like scientific research) or if artistic people enter artistic occupations (such as writing, painting or acting), there will be a high degree of satisfaction. In contrast, if a socially inclined person gets into a realistic type of job, or if an enterprising person enters a conventional occupation, there is certain to be frustration and unhappiness.

3. *Interests.* In the field of vocational counseling there is an old saying that people do best in those activities and occupations which interest them most. If a job is boring, it isn't likely to bring much personal fulfillment, even if the salary is high.

Why would someone choose a vocation in which there is no interest? Sometimes in their need and desire to find employment, people take what is available whether or not they find it interesting. Often these people expect to change jobs later, but frequently, because of insufficient training or lack of opportunities, they do not or cannot change. Others take a boring job because of the salary or fringe benefits. It would appear that many of the least desirable jobs in our society have a high level of remuneration in order to attract workers. Since many of these workers have little interest in their work, they must find fulfillment and satisfaction in leisure-time activities—including sports, social clubs, lodges and church work.

4. *Aptitudes or Abilities.* A large commercial airline used to have the slogan: "We're American Airlines—doing what we do best!" When people have jobs "doing what they do best" there often is great vocational fulfillment, but workers feel frustrated when they are unable to do what the job requires or when the job does not give them opportunity for achieving their greatest potential.

Technically, there is a difference between an aptitude and an ability. Aptitude refers to the potential that one has for learning something in the future. Ability refers to skills or other learning which has taken place in the past. A young student, for example, may have an *aptitude* (good potential and capacity) for learning music. Then, after years of study, he or she may demonstrate great *ability* as a musician.

Careers are most satisfying when one's aptitudes and abilities relate to one's work. According to one report, however, approximately 80 percent of working people are underemployed, that is, working below their capacity and ability levels.[14] People submit to this because they consider underemployment preferable to unemployment. As a result they go through life unhappy with their work. Once again, however, lack of training and the need to find employment quickly lead some people into jobs or careers where they feel mismatched with their capacities. Hence, they are dissatisfied.

5. *Values*. What is most important in life? One early study found that three values influence the career choices of college students: helping people, earning money or attaining status, and having opportunity to be creative.[15] Others want to change society, attain maximum independence, find the best working conditions, or have the greatest possible influence for Christ.

How people spend their money and their spare time is a good indication of their values. While such values do not greatly influence career choice,[16] they can be important at times. For example, the worker who values honesty but is employed in a dishonest business is likely to be dissatisfied until he or she can change positions.

6. *Divine Leading*. Most Christians believe that God personally guides in the lives of his children. Some people want and seek this guidance; others do not. When an individual seeks divine leading in career decisions, he or she can rest in the confidence that God is guiding. Often this makes a job more satisfying or at least more tolerable.

Jonah, for example, had it both ways. When God said "go to Nineveh the great city, and cry against it," Jonah went elsewhere instead and the results were almost fatal. When Jonah "arose and went to Nineveh according to the word of the Lord," the results were more satisfying. Instead of rejoicing, however, Jonah was displeased, angry and apparently depressed.[17] His obedience had been less than enthusiastic and he was not happy in his work. Contrast this with the Apostle Paul. His work involved many hardships, but he enjoyed his labors and ended life with a feeling of vocational satisfaction.[18]

It is probable that no one influence alone contributes to good or poor vocational choice. Social pressures, personality interests, aptitudes, abilities, values, and sensitivity to divine leading all combine with job availability and training opportunities to influence the nature of an individual's career. The possibilities are great that one will choose unwisely or find oneself in a career that is not satisfying. When this happens, one's whole life is affected.

The Effects of Good and Poor Vocational Choices

Whenever we meet strangers, one of the first questions we ask concerns the nature of their work. This reflects more than personal interest or curiosity. When we learn about another person's work we are often able to make accurate assumptions about his or her education, social status and economic level. One's income is largely determined by one's work, and income in turn can influence the person's life style, place of residence, choice of friends, leisure activities, feelings of self-worth, and general satisfaction with life. People who like their work are often happy with life in general. When a person is not happy at work, this unhappiness can permeate his or her whole life.

Of course, there are exceptions to this general rule.[19] Some people are able to divorce their work from the rest of their lives and find fulfillment in one area if not in the other. But such a separation is difficult to accomplish. The nature of our work and the degree of our success affects many areas of life and even has an impact on our spiritual development. When we believe that God is leading in a vocation, we can be more content on the job and better able to handle the complexities of life. Vocational counseling, therefore, is more than an important responsibility for all counselors, it is an issue of special importance for those counselors and counselees who are Christians.

Counseling and Vocational Choices

Within the counseling profession, career counseling has become a specialty with several theoretical approaches and a variety of vocational guidance techniques.[20] In general, however, the goal of these approaches is the same—helping people find fulfilling, satisfying jobs which they can do well.[21] In the past it often was assumed that career guidance occurred early in life when young people were helped to find the one vocation in which they would work for a lifetime. More recently, vocational counseling has come to be seen as part of a broader lifelong process of "career education and development."[22] Vocational choices—which include decisions about training, accepting or retaining jobs, making changes and facing retirement—are made throughout life. The career educator exposes people to information about vocations, teaches them to evaluate themselves and their careers continually, and provides special support or guidance at those times when career changes are being contemplated.

1. *Vocational Counseling Principles.* Career education, including vocational counseling, requires a knowledge of the world of work, a knowledge of the counselee, and the giving of guidance to those who are making specific decisions.[23] All of this must be within the confines of finding and knowing God's will.

(a) Knowing the World of Work. Unless he or she is a specialist in vocational guidance, it is unlikely that a counselor can keep abreast of the literally thousands of available job opportunities. Nevertheless, there are two ways in which any Christian counselor can help: sharing where to get information and suggesting ways in which such information can be used.

Public and college libraries often keep vocational information on file in the form of books, brochures, catalogs and government publications such as the *U. S. Dictionary of Occupational Titles* (DOT). Unions, professional organizations, businesses, and insurance companies often publish vocational information which is available free or at nominal cost. The local library often can give the desired addresses. In addition, the yellow pages of a telephone book can put you in touch with local persons in specific vocations. Such persons may know where to write for further information and often can give vocational information themselves. Many people are busy in their work, however, and there is a limit to the time available for information-giving interviews. More readily available, therefore, are the resources of government and private employment agencies.

When one locates a source of information several questions can be asked, including the following:

What is the nature of the work?

What personal qualifications are needed (in terms of skills, abilities, interests, experience or physical requirements)?

What training is required, where is it available, how long does it take, and what does it cost?

Can everyone enter the occupation or are there educational, age, sex, religious or other restrictions?

What are the working conditions?

What is the starting and potential salary, including fringe benefits?

How will it influence one's personal life in terms of need for travel, overtime, Sunday work or geographical location?

Will it require the compromising of one's ethical principles and religious beliefs?

What is its potential for the future in terms of its continuance as a vocation, available openings, opportunities for advancement, and preparing people to move on to other satisfying work?

How does this fit with the Christian's desire to serve Christ and to utilize one's God-given abilities and gifts?

In all of this, recognize that God calls some, but not all, people into positions of full-time Christian ministry. It should not be assumed that the committed missionary or pastor is necessarily more spiritual or more within God's will than the committed scientist or salesman. Recognize, too, that when a person wants data about church-related vocations, the Christian counselor is often an excellent source of relevant information.

(b) Knowing the Counselee. Professional guidance counselors usually give a battery of psychological tests which can provide concise information to help counselees in two ways: to increase self-understanding and to make predictions about the future. These assessment tools include *mental ability tests* (which can measure both general intelligence, and competence in special areas such as abstract reasoning, mathematical capability and verbal ability); *achievement tests* (which measure skills and the amount of material which the counselee has learned); *aptitude tests* (which measure one's potential for learning in such areas as music, art, manual dexterity, or skill acquisition); *interest tests* (which measure not only expressed interests, but whether or not the counselee's general interests are the same as those of successful people in specific occupational groups[24]); *personality inventories* (which can identify a variety of personality traits); and *special tests* (which can measure such diverse traits as creativity, flexibility, mental stability, and one's potential for learning a foreign language). The use and interpretation of such tests usually require special training which some Christian counselors may not possess. It can be helpful, therefore, to refer counselees for testing at psychological clinics, college counseling centers, private employment offices, government employment agencies and Christian vocational guidance services.[25] Before making such referrals be certain to check the costs of such services since these vary widely.

Even without testing skills or test results the counselor can give useful information from counselees themselves—information which can be supplemented and confirmed through observation and consultation with others who know the counselee. Through interviews it is possible to get accurate information about the counselee's general mental ability, specific skills and abilities, educational level and potential for further training, personality traits, mental and physical health, personal appearance, interests (including those which are stated and those that are reflected in his or her leisure-time activities), level of spiritual commitment or maturity, and (for older counselees) dependability and efficiency as an employee. Of course, the counselor's observations may not always be accurate, but these observations can be discussed with counselees and sometimes altered as the vocational counseling process continues.

(c) Guiding the Vocational Decisions. It is not the counselor's job to tell the counselee what to do vocationally. Instead, the counselee must be helped to make and evaluate his own decisions based on the available information. It should not be expected that counseling will reveal the "one true job" for the counselee. Instead, such counseling will narrow the career opportunities down to a few categories of potentially satisfying kinds of work. Educational opportunities, counselee desires and motivation, job availability, and similar circumstances then determine the type of work that may be chosen.

Remember that vocational education and counseling is a lifelong process. As a worker learns more about a vocation, he or she may then see a need to change emphasis or even careers. Most vocational theorists assume that there are stages of vocational development.[26] In the *earliest stage,* which lasts for the first twelve or fourteen years of life, the child thinks about many glamorous types of work, most of which will be abandoned later as being unrealistic. In high school, the *tentative-exploratory* stage begins in which there is a more realistic self-appraisal and narrowing of career possibilities. Often there is considerable vacillation and floundering as the young person selects, and discards, a number of occupational plans. Beginning in early adulthood, the *realistic* stage comes next. Here the individual seriously considers vocational possibilities and makes choices as to training and job choice. The *establishment-maintenance* stage comes next and occupies most of adult life. There may be job changes but only a few people make radical changes to something new. If a person reaches his or her vocational goals at this time, life can be very satisfying. It can also be a time of great frustration if goals are not reached and the person feels "locked into" a disappointing "dead end," a boring vocation. In the final *termination* stage, many major vocational activities are terminated, to be replaced by meaningful work and nonwork retirement activities, it is hoped. There are no clearly identifiable times when one stage ends and the next begins. The career-educator, including the personal counselor, can provide information and guidance at any one of these stages in life.

How do we help people make decisions? First, the counselee must decide what he or she wants to accomplish. On paper, ask counselees to write down their vocational goals and objectives. If the goals seem unrealistic, suggest this and discuss it together. Then gather information about the counselee and about potential job or career possibilities. Third, ask counselees to write down specific possibilities, based on the accumulated information. Then, try to evaluate the positive and negative aspects of each choice and, based on that evaluation, choose one alternative. This will be difficult for some counselees because decisions involve both commitment and the risk that one might fail. Counselors must then encourage counselees to (a) act on the decision by moving into a specific training program, seeking a job, or accepting an offer of employment; (b) periodically evaluate the job and, at times, repeat the whole process again. This process is illustrated in Figure 17–1.

In conclusion it would appear that vocational guidance can occur throughout life and be centered in at least four overlapping areas.[27]

Job or career placement. This involves helping people get information and training, helping them find positions, and sometimes helping potential employers find people.

. .*Job or career preparation.* Prior to entry, counselees can be helped to ponder the good and bad aspects of the job. This can occur whenever a job change is anticipated, and it includes preretirement counseling.[28]

Job or career adjustment. Sometimes people believe that they have found a desirable career but they are having difficulties adjusting. Consider, for example, the missionary who believes he or she is called to the mission field, but has trouble adapting. Sometimes crisis counseling, as-

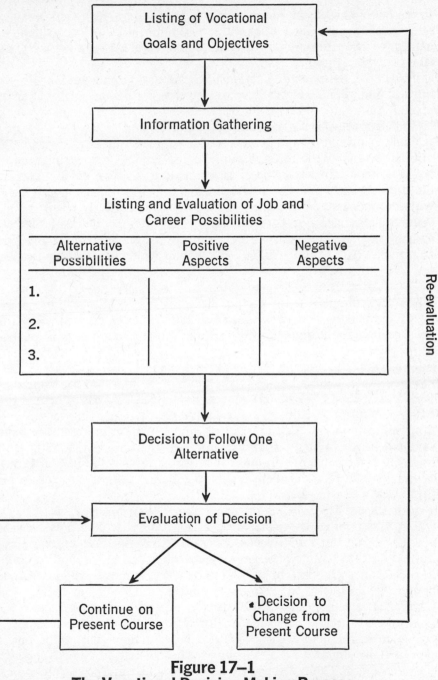

Figure 17–1
The Vocational Decision-Making Process

sisting such people with interpersonal relations, or dealing with loneliness may be among the ways of helping these counselees adjust to their new career.[29] Such counseling can mean the difference between vocational satisfaction or stagnation.

Job or career change. This includes discussion and guidance before, during, and after a forced or voluntary change, including the offer of a promotion.

(d) Knowing God's Will. Several years ago an article appeared in *HIS* magazine, written by a man with advanced academic degrees who could not find a suitable job but was employed, instead, as a tool salesman in a neighborhood hardware store.[30] In evaluating his own disappointments, the man realized that he "had been holding a grudge against God for withholding . . . the gift of appropriate employment." He tried to understand the reasons for his frustrating job situation but concluded that "wish as I might, I was not able to find a portion of Scripture that absolutely guaranteed God would give me employment which allowed the extensive use of my talents."

How do we counsel someone like this? As a committed believer, the man wanted God's will for his life, including his vocational life. But how do we help counselees (or counselors) determine God's will? Much has been written about divine leading but perhaps there are only a few basic principles.

(a) Want It. Does the counselee *really* want God's leading or is he or she seeking, instead, a divine "rubber stamp" of approval for some previously devised plan? For God to guide "we must of necessity have a prior willingness to obey Him. . . . The Holy Spirit is not going to waste His time indicating God's will to a person who is uncertain about the matter of obedience." [31] When a counselee does not want God's leading it would be helpful to discuss the reasons for this, to confront the person with his or her attitude of disobedience, and to encourage the counselee to pray for a change in attitude.

(b) Expect It. God has promised to show us his way when we are willing to trust him completely, when we attempt to live holy lives and when we keep our minds focused on God-pleasing thoughts.[32] He does not play a game of hide and seek, deliberately trying to confuse his followers. He has promised to lead—and believers can rest confidently in the knowledge that he or she who really desires God's will (including God's timing) is certain to find it. Of course, each of us can turn away from God and fall into our own paths. But when we want it and expect it, God will enable us to find his will, one day at a time. This truth must be shared with counselees.

(c) Seek It. There are no pat formulas which automatically indicate God's will, and rarely does he lead in dramatic, miraculous ways. Throughout the centuries he has led most often through the Holy Bible and the Holy Spirit. Once again James Packer writes clearly on this issue:

> Earnest Christians seeking guidance often go wrong about it. Why is this? . . . Their basic mistake is to think of guidance as essentially *inward prompting by the Holy Spirit, apart from the written Word.* . . . Two features about divine guidance in the case of "vocational choices" are distinctive. . . . First, these problems cannot be resolved by a direct application of biblical teaching. All one can do from Scripture is circumscribe the lawful possibilities between which the choice has to be made. . . . Second, just because Scripture cannot decide one's choice directly, the factor of God-given prompting and inclination . . . becomes decisive.[33]

The Holy Spirit leads sometimes through the Bible directly and always in ways consistent with biblical teachings. The person who either ignores the Scriptures or discounts the Spirit's inner presence and influence is unlikely to know God's will.

From this it does not follow that counselees should refuse to use their God-given brains. Psychological testing, job analysis, the completion of application forms, vocational counseling, discussions with friends, and prayers for guidance can all help counselees find God's will as they make career decisions. Trusting that God will lead, they move forward confidently, making the wisest decisions possible in light of available evidence.

(d) "Cool It." But what if the counselee makes an apparent mistake? What if he or she cannot find a suitable job but becomes, for example, a tool salesman with graduate college degrees?

Counselees must be reminded, first, that everyone makes mistakes but God forgives and restores. Like Jonah who tried to go his own way, and Peter who denied Christ, individuals today can know that God always restores those who come back to him asking for further guidance.

Then, remind counselees that God, in his wisdom and timing, puts us where he wants us. He expects us to serve diligently, wherever and whatever the circumstances. When there is anger or anxiety (both of which are common), believers should admit these feelings, bring them to God in prayer and ask that they be removed. In this way counselees can be helped, like Paul, to be content whatever the circumstances.[34]

Preventing Poor Vocational Choices

Almost always, prevention is a specialized form of education. In no place is this truer than in the prevention of poor career choices and vocational unhappiness. From the pulpit, in church classes and small groups, on retreat weekends, in Christian colleges and elsewhere, people can be taught and encouraged to apply some of the material presented earlier in this chapter. This Christian career education should be directed to people of all ages and could include consideration of:

—biblical teachings about work;
—the causes of good and poor vocational choices;
—how to find God's guidance (want it, expect it, seek it, and cool it);
—how to get information about vocations and the world of work; and

—how to know oneself better (including a knowledge of where to take psychological tests).

In this educational process, emphasize that vocational choice is not a once-in-a-lifetime decision. Most adults, including housewives, struggle at times with career dissatisfaction and this should be acknowledged. Encourage people to be open to further training and to evaluate their priorities, life goals and job situations periodically, perhaps in accordance with Figure 17-1. Point out that as one gets older, it becomes increasingly more difficult and risky to change vocations. Nevertheless, there are things which can be done: changing employers or careers (the most risky); changing jobs within the same company or vocation; and/or changing one's attitude towards work. Even if little can be done to change the job situation, it is possible to stay with the present job (trusting that God either wants this and/or will bring a change in time), to do one's best "as to the Lord" [35] without complaining, and then to look for greater satisfaction in avocational, leisure time activities which probably will occupy greater amounts of time as one gets older.

Conclusions about Vocational Choice

In this chapter, nothing has been said about some of the unique and difficult aspects of *vocational counseling* and career education. These include helping such people as the mentally retarded, psychologically unstable, physically handicapped, terminally ill, minimally educated, elderly, and non-English speaking immigrant. All of these people can benefit from meaningful, satisfying work which is within their capabilities. If the *Christian counselor* is unable to help, referral to a government agency or private counseling facility may be the best help you can give.

Vocational choices are among the most crucial decisions in life. To help people make these decisions wisely can be among the most satisfying and rewarding tasks in the Christian counselor's own work.

Suggestions for Further Reading
* Bolles, Richard Nelson. *What Color Is Your Parachute? A Practical Manual for Job-Hunters & Career Changers*. Berkeley, California: Ten Speed Press, 1978.
Haldane, Bernard; Haldane, Jean; and Martin, Lowell. *Job Power Now: The Young People's Job Finding Guide*. Washington, D.C.: Acropolis Books, 1976.
Holland, John I. *Making Vocational Choices: A Theory of Careers*. Englewood Cliffs, N.J.: Prentice-Hall, 1973.
Kemp, C. F. *The Pastor and Vocational Counseling*. St. Louis: Bethany, 1961.

Footnotes
1. Genesis 3:17, 19, 23.
2. 1 Timothy 5:17, 18.
3. Proverbs 31:10–31.
4. Proverbs 6:6–11; 10:26; 13:4; 20:4; 26:16.
5. 2 Thessalonians 3:10.

6. Romans 14:5.

7. Ephesians 6:5–9; Colossians 3:22—4:1.

8. Romans 12:3–8; 1 Corinthians 12:4–31; Ephesians 4:7–13.

9. Romans 12:3; Jeremiah 9:23, 24.

10. Isaiah 49:1, 5; Psalm 139:13–16; Jeremiah 1:5; Luke 1:13–17, 30–33.

11. James I. Packer, *Knowing God.* Downers Grove: Inter-Varsity, 1973, pp. 210–11.

12. Bernard Haldane; Jean Haldane; and Lowell Martin. *Job Power Now! The Young People's Job Finding Guide.* Washington, D.C.: Acropolis Books, 1976, p. 2.

13. John I. Holland. *Making Vocational Choices: A Theory of Careers.* Englewood Cliffs, N.J.: Prentice-Hall, 1973.

14. Reported in R. N. Bolles, *What Color Is Your Parachute? A Practical Manual for Job Hunters and Career Changers.* Berkeley, Calif.: Ten Speed Press, 1978, p. 15.

15. Samuel H. Osipow. *Theories of Career Development,* 2d ed. Englewood Cliffs, N.J.: Prentice-Hall, 1973, p. 179.

16. Ibid., p. 183.

17. Jonah 1:2; 3:3; 4:1, 3.

18. Philippians 4:10–13; 2 Timothy 4:6–8.

19. Benjamin Iris and Gerald V. Barrett, "Some Relations Between Job and Life Satisfactions and Job Importance." *Journal of Applied Psychology* 56, 1972, pp. 301–304.

20. For a summary of these approaches see Osipow, *Theories of Career Development* and John O. Crites, "Career Counseling: A Review of Major Approaches." *The Counseling Psychologist,* 4(3), 1974, pp. 3–23.

21. Holland, *Making Vocational Choices,* p. 85.

22. Harold L. Munson. "Career Education Reconsidered: A Life-Experiences Model." *Personnel and Guidance Journal* 57, November, 1978, pp. 136–39.

23. Much of the material in this section is adapted from the author's chapter on vocational counseling in Collins, Gary R. *Effective Counseling.* Carol Stream, Illinois: Creation House, 1972.

24. It may be discovered for example, that successful men in occupation X also enjoy sports, reading novels, and yard work. If a test taker scores high on these extra-curricular interests, it is clear that he likes the same things that are liked by successful people in occupation X.

25. A vocational counseling service is operated by Like a Mighty Army, Inc., IFMA Building, 370 Schmale Road, Carol Stream, Illinois 60187. This organization provides testing and test interpretation by mail. Persons seeking long or short term positions with Christian organizations should contact Intercrista, Box 9323, Seattle, Washington 98109.

26. J. C. Hansen, R. R. Stevic, and R. W. Warner, Jr. *Counseling Theory and Practice,* 2d ed. Boston: Allyn and Bacon, 1977, pp. 467–9.

27. Ibid., pp. 463–4.

28. See Chapter 19.

29. See other relevant chapters in this book, eg. Chapters 3, 23 and 6.

30. Meredith W. Long, "God's Will and the Job Market." *His.* 36: June, 1976, pp. 1–4.

31. C. Stacey Woods. "No Flip Answers: A Brief (and Realistic) Guide to Christian Guidance." *Eternity,* January, 1976, pp. 24–25, 61–63

32. Proverbs 3:5, 6; Romans 12:1, 2.

33. Packer, *Knowing God,* pp. 212–213.

34. Philippians 4:11.

35. Ephesians 6:7.

18

Middle Age

THERE WAS A TIME, NOT MANY YEARS AGO, WHEN UNDERGRADUATE college courses in "human development" began their discussions at the point of conception and ended with considerations of adolescence. Apparently it was assumed that most human development stops when our bodies reach their adult size and when young people graduate from high school. Of course Carl Jung, the famous Swiss psychiatrist, had challenged this view many years ago, and so had a Harvard professor named Eric Erikson.[1] Nevertheless, widespread interest in the growth and problems of adults were lacking until recently. Then, popular books like *Passages*[2] and *Transformation*[3] captured public attention, and researchers began to report on their efforts to understand and help individuals move through adulthood.[4]

This increasing interest in adulthood can have great relevance for Christian counseling. In churches, as in the society, middle-aged adults make most of the decisions, earn and disperse most of the money, fulfill most leadership positions, and appear to have most of the power. But middle-aged people also struggle with boredom, declining vitality, marriage disintegration, and shifting values. Middle age has been called a "second adolescence," or time for "self-examination, discontent, and rebellion" and, according to one lady, "the cruelest joke in life so far." When one considers the prevalence of middle-aged people, and the preponderance of middle-aged problems both in the community and in the church, then it becomes clear that middle age concerns are at the basis of much Christian counseling.

What is middle age? Many people answer in terms of years: "It is a period of life which covers the years between 35 and 55," or "It is a time of which begins when one turns 40." Others might agree with Jung who described middle age as the time when we are free to move on to other things because we have pretty much completed such tasks as the "begetting of children ... protecting the brood" and the "gaining of money and social

250

position."[5] Another writer humorously defined the middle years as a "state of mind" which, at least in America, comes to people who can remember *Collier's* magazine, Harry Truman, Fibber McGee's closet, Baby Snooks, a song called "Jeepers Creepers," and a time when "a five dollar bill bought two bags of groceries, cars had running boards, all movies were rated G, and a 'going out of business' sign meant the shop was going out of business."[6] In a more serious vein, the same author defines the middle years as a time when one can say "I'm responsible . . . Most goals have been reached," or when there is the growing realization that goals will not be reached, that time is running out, and that one must decide whether to keep life moving in the same direction, or to make changes before it is too late.

Middle age, therefore, can mean different things to different people. Beginning in the late '30s or early '40s it is a period of life characterized by self-examination, reevaluation of beliefs and values, readjustment to physical change and reconsideration of one's life style and priorities. For many men and women, it is a time of crisis—crisis which can be met alone or with the help of concerned friends and counselor. And for many it is a "wonderful crisis" which launches us on to "the best half of life."[7]

The Bible and Middle Age

The Scriptures say little about middle age, perhaps because relatively few people lived that long in Bible times in spite of the famous people who lived into old age.[8] It has been estimated that the life expectancy of people in the Bronze Age was 18 years. In Greece it wasn't much longer and by medieval times the average life span had risen to only 37 years. Even in 1900, life expectancy was a relatively low 50 years, so there is little historical precedent or theological insight to guide modern people through the middle years.

Within the Bible, however, there are historical accounts which portray individuals whose actions suggest middle age struggles. David, for example, struggled through his younger years until he was firmly established as king. Then he had a mid-life affair which brought great agony, remorse and self-examination.[9]

More helpful for Christian counselors are those biblical passages which speak to the major problems that middle-aged people encounter—problems of good and bad marriages, self-esteem, life purpose, work, grief, interactions with children and older parents, spiritual maturity, impatience, physical illness, disappointment, and so on. When these and similar issues are discussed in Scripture, there rarely is reference to age. Biblical teachings and principles for living apply universally, but individuals—including middle-aged persons—sometimes must be helped to see how the Scriptures can be helpful in meeting one's unique personal needs.

The Causes of Middle Age Problems

What does it mean to be an adult? What are the basic issues, the major problems, satisfactions, disappointments and sources of fulfillment that adults face as they go through life? Questions such as these led Yale psychologist Daniel Levinson to initiate a ten-year in-depth study of forty men who were all adults but diverse in terms of social class, religion, educational level and ethnic background.

Levinson began his work before the current upsurge of interest in adulthood. Middle age, he discovered has been a taboo subject. Hoping that life would begin at 40, many people instead were found to fear that it might begin to fall apart after the first decade. As a result there has tended to be an unwillingness for adults to share their insecurities and struggles. Levinson's comments about this reveal much about the causes of mid-life problems:

> Middle age activates our deepest anxieties about decline and dying. The most distressing fear in early adulthood is that there is no life after youth. Young adults often feel that to pass 30 is to be "over the hill" . . . . The middle years, they imagine, will bring triviality and meaningless comfort at best, stagnation and hopelessness at worst.
>
> Middle age is usually regarded as a vague interim period, defined primarily in negative terms. One is no longer young and yet not quite old . . . . The connotations of youth are vitality, growth, mastery, the heroic, whereas old connotes vulnerability, withering, ending, the brink of nothingness. Our overly negative imagery of old age adds greatly to the burden of middle age. It is terrifying to go through middle age in the shadow of death, as though one were already very old; and it is a self-defeating illusion to live in the shadow of youth, as though one were still simply young.[10]

Instead, Levinson and his research colleagues came to see adulthood as a series of phases, each with its own values and liabilities. These are shown in Figure 18–1.

In the early adult era the individual emerges from adolescence, finds a place in adult society, selects an occupation, frequently chooses a marriage partner, and settles down both to establish one's niche in society and to work in building a fulfilled useful life.

Then comes the middle life transition—roughly at age 40 to 45. For 80 percent of the men in Levinson's study this was a time of crisis. It became a period of reexamination and internal struggles which persisted until about age 45.

Then there is movement away from self-examination into a period of making choices and living with them. The individual often settles down in the fifties to a time of great fulfillment which terminates as there is movement into the preretirement and then the late adult era.

With this overview of adulthood, let us focus attention on the middle

Figure 18–1
Developmental Periods
Over the Life Course*

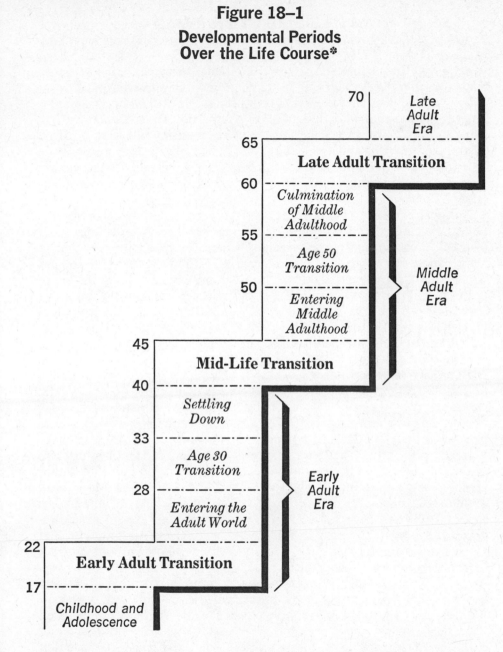

Reprinted with permission from Levinson, Daniel J., et. al. *The Seasons of a Man's Life*. New York: Knopf, 1978, p. 57.

adult era, and especially on the "mid-life transition." A variety of internal and environmental changes combine to make this a crisis time especially in the lives of men.[11] For example, there is:

Boredom. In the middle years, the excitement and challenge of establishing a career and launching a marriage give way to what have been called "middle-age blahs." Everyday routines at work, home, or church, duty-motivated visits with dull relatives, the perpetuation of daily frustrations (e.g., a house that always needs work, monthly bills that must be paid, bosses that must be pleased)—all of these merge into a routine of boredom. In an attempt to escape this boredom, some people "break out" into extramarital affairs, sudden job-changes, and unconventional or outlandish dress.

Fatigue. The early adult era is a time for vigorously establishing oneself, building a career and sometimes developing a family. After twenty years of this it is easy to feel tired, especially when we ponder the fact that at least twenty more years must pass before retirement. Some men and women have not accomplished much so they push themselves at this point to prove their worth. Others have begun to succeed and must exert extra effort to keep up. This extra effort is required at a time when physical vitality is beginning to slip. Little wonder that some people collapse physically or emotionally, while others began to think of ways to withdraw or escape to get some rest.

Physical Changes. In a society which values *youth,* there is resistance to the physical changes of middle age because these show—where all the world can see—that we are aging. Gray hair, baldness, coarser skin, bags under the eyes, stiffening of joints, less resiliency in movements and changes in body-build all occur in mid-life. Few people take these changes as lightly as the middle-aged movie actress who remarked that her bust and hip measurements were the same as ever except for the fact that within recent years "everything has slipped down about six inches." More often middle-aged people recognize that they are developing a "middle-age spread." Whereas body fat is only 10 percent of body weight in adolescence, it is at least 20 percent by middle age, and most of this settles around the waist. As the bust or chest gets smaller, the abdomen and hips get larger. All of this can lead appearance-conscious people, to diet, exercise, and place special emphasis on clothing and cosmetics. At times there also can be discouragement about the perceived loss of youthfulness and attractiveness.[12] In women, all of these physical changes can be complicated by the anticipation and experience of menopause with the hormonal and emotional changes which come as a result. Some researchers believe that a similar, though less noticeable change occurs in men.

Fear. As the middle-aged person experiences physical changes, watches aging parents, and observes the struggle of middle-aged friends, a number of fears begin to arise. For some there is a first encounter with the fear of death. Many are afraid of losing their attractiveness, authority over children, health or desirability as a mate. Some fear that younger people will replace them at work or that life will become meaningless. Others wonder if they will become rigid, and unable or unwilling to change with the times. Then there is a fear of one's ability to be sexually active and attractive. At times this fear creates tension in bed and the feared inability to perform becomes a reality.

All of this can stimulate the middle age reevaluation, dissatisfaction and search both for purpose and self-esteem. In addition there are two issues which create the major problems for the middle-aged. These are one's vocation and one's marriage. According to one writer,[13] a person must "work through" these issues if there is to be a successful resolution of mid-life problems.

1. *Vocational Issues.* Whatever one's vocation, and whatever one's degree of success or failure, it is good to remember that every line of work has its less attractive features. These become more obvious the longer we work at a job. If we feel, no longer challenged, taken for granted or afraid of failure, it is easy to look towards problems at work and to become angry. This anger (with accompanying disappointment, disillusionment and defeat) is directed toward the job because of its weaknesses or toward oneself for being in such a position.

Many individuals begin to feel inadequate and self-critical even when they have been vocationally successful. As one moves up the ladder of success, responsibilities become greater and competition may become stronger at the time when physical energies are declining. Some people are asked to train new workers who, in time, could take one's job. Homemakers, whose lives may have been busy and productive, discover that the nest is emptying and there is less need for their services at home. All of this can lead to cynicism, self-pity and sometimes a temptation to leave everything and run away.

2. *Marriage-Family Issues.* Freud once said that the need of every person is *leben und arbeiten*—to live and to work. If we don't find fulfillment in these areas, our lives are incomplete. Work has been discussed above, but what about middle-aged love? Let us consider four aspects of this issue: love as it relates to children, parents, spouse, and sex.

(a) *Children.* When children leave home, mothers especially can feel depressed, sad, empty, and inclined to grieve. For some there is guilt over past failures, loneliness, a tendency to cling, and for a feeling that one is no longer needed or useful. The departure of children does not seem to affect fathers to the same extent that it affects mothers. (Fathers often find greatest satisfaction outside of the home.) Nevertheless the "empty nest" forces both parents to reexamine their roles in the home. Sometimes there is a sense of relief and renewed vigor, but with the children gone both parents must face each other and more realistically evaluate the status of their marriage.

(b) *Older Parents.* Caught up with the challenges of raising a young family and then starting a career, young adults often fail to notice that their own parents are growing older. When we reach middle age, these parents often begin to lose their health, their freedom, their financial stability and, at some time their spouse. Parents, therefore, become more dependent— often at the time when their grandchildren are becoming independent. Aging parents want attention from their middle-aged children, and the infirmities of old age serve as a reminder of the fleeting nature of life.[14]

(c) *Marriage*. Bored with the family routines of middle life, well aware of the weaknesses in one's mate, no longer held together by dependent children, and tired of routine sex, many mid-age husbands and wives discover that their marriages are very unstable. Often there is a lack of intimacy, similarity of interests, or ability to communicate. As a result the couple may resign themselves to a divorce or one of the partners may slip into a mid-life affair. This gives temporary excitement, the experience of being cared for, and some proof both of one's sexual prowess and of one's continuing attractiveness to the opposite sex. But affairs also put strain on a marriage, arouse guilt, create tension, in time become monotonous, and frequently lead to divorce.[15]

(d) *Sex*. An article in *Psychology Today* magazine once asked an interesting question: Is there sex after 40? When several hundred university students were asked about this, most responded that probably their parents rarely had intercourse and never had oral-genital sex.[16] Aware of their declining vigor and loss in attractiveness, many middle-aged people begin to wonder if their children are right. Perhaps there will not be sex, at least satisfying sex, after 40. Conway expresses these fears concisely:

> During the mid-life crisis, a man's sexual capacity is his single greatest concern. Often he is afraid he is losing his sexual ability. The drama goes something like this: a man is overextended at work. He is running out of energy. Younger men seem eager to take his place. He is on innumerable boards and committees for the community and the church. His family has giant financial needs, and there never seems to be enough money to go around. With that as a background, he crawls into bed at night. His wife is experiencing a new sexual awakening. Instead of being passive, she begins aggressive sexual moves on him. To his amazement, he finds he is extremely slow in being ready for the sex act. Partway through intercourse, he may lose his erection, and at that moment, he suddenly believes life is all over. He is no longer a man. It's exactly as he had heard—the middle years mean the end of sex.[17]

Such an attitude can lead people to "give up" on sex or to plunge into an affair in order to prove one's attractiveness and virility. The prevalence of such affairs should demonstrate that "sex after 40" and after menopause is not only possible—it can be better and more satisfying than it was in the earlier years. Middle-aged people need to hear this and to learn how sexual intercourse can be better.

With this emphasis on marriage and family relationships it would be easy to forget that single people reach middle-age too. Many of the special challenges of singleness, divorce and grief come into the unmarried person's life and intensify his or her middle life struggles. The middle adult era, therefore, influences each person—married or single—in unique ways.

The Effects of Middle Age

In a book dealing with counseling and problems it is easy to stress what is wrong with life and never to mention what is good. Our consideration of middle age thus far has focused on the negative and failed to acknowledge that many people are able to get through this period without undue distress. Nevertheless, almost everyone is affected in some way by middle age and its pressures. These effects of middle-age change are sometimes hidden internally, sometimes shown in outward behavior, and often most apparent in one's vocation and marriage.

1. *Internal-emotional Effects.* Aware of the changes in one's body and the reality of one's middle-aged status, many people experience anger, bitterness, frustration, a sense of failure, boredom, self-pity and discouragement. Sometimes these come and go—one or two at a time—to swell up with brief intensity but then recede to a place where they are ever present and waiting for the opportunity to swell up again. There may be disenchantment with life, periods of sadness, a sense of futility and an envy of the freedom or exuberance of young people including, perhaps, one's children. In addition, there are the inner fears that were mentioned earlier. For many people, this turmoil and emotional conflict may have been present for years, but the long hidden problems come into focus when we encounter the realities of middle life.

Even in mid-life, these inner emotional struggles can be hidden from outsiders, at least for a while; but they are apparent to one's family and usually to oneself. Often, there is a tendency to blame one's problems on others and a failure to see that many of the difficulties come from within.

2. *Behavioral Effects.* Even when we try to keep feelings hidden, they "spill out" in other ways. We can become irritable, impatient, complaining, preoccupied with things other than our work or family, inclined to blame others for our problems, less efficient, restless and sometimes prone to overactivity. Some people escape by drinking, or preoccupation with hypochondriacal physical symptoms. Many withdraw from contact with friends and other people.

In addition, there sometimes is the previously mentioned attempt to break out of one's routine by changing jobs or residence, by altering one's life style, or by changing one's mode of dress in order to create a new image.

3. *Vocational Effects.* There are three ways in which a man or woman can react to the disillusionment with work which so often comes at mid-life.[18] First, one may push harder in an attempt to succeed and demonstrate one's value. Since many people measure their worth in terms of

work, it becomes critically important to succeed at the job even if this means becoming a workaholic.

A second reaction is to give up in discouragement. Sometimes there is anger, resistance in the form of lowered productivity, and an attitude of resignation which says, "Why work hard; I'll never be appreciated or get anywhere here." Basically the reason for this dissatisfaction can be stated briefly—the person's interests, values, goals, and abilities to not match what is required in the job. This can apply to the frustrated employee and to the frustrated housewife who is tired of her job as homemaker.

A third reaction is to use one's dissatisfaction as a springboard to change. This may mean a risk and it may require courage, but some people change jobs, change vocations to fit one's abilities and personality, or reorganize their lives so that there is more fulfillment in general even though work at times may not be satisfying.

Of course, some people lose their jobs. This is especially devastating at mid-life when financial and family responsibilities are great, but when there are few good-paying satisfying jobs available to middle-aged women and men.

4. *Marriage-Family Effects*

> It is extremely difficult to live with a man who is going through the mid-life crises. Some days he may act like an adolescent, with great outbursts of anger, or deep depression, or withdrawal. He clearly presents a picture of instability. He doesn't know who he is, where he is going, what he is doing. His values are confused.[19]

Probably men respond differently to mid-life than do women. For both men and women, however, it is the family, including one's spouse, who is closest to the middle-aged person and thus most immediately affected by the vacillating emotions and changing attitudes. It is the family which suffers most when there is an affair, an abrupt change in life style or the loss of work with its resulting influence on family finances and on the unemployed person's self-esteem.

Counseling the Middle Aged

Within recent years a number of popular self-help books have been published to help people cope with middle age.[20] These books have attempted to increase the reader's understanding and have offered a number of common sense suggestions which might be shared, at times, by a counselor:

—get periodic physical check-ups;
—get into the practice of regular exercise and consistent rest;
—work to keep down one's weight;
—get into the habit of saying "no" to the outside demands which come with such frequency in middle age;

—consider which activities could be eliminated and how one could be freed for more contemplation time;

—think about taking on some new challenges which could add variety and change from regular routines;

—listen to music or make time for other activities which can be relaxing;

—postpone any major decisions, especially about one's job, residence and marriage, until there is time for reflection and discussion with a sympathetic friend or counselor.

Using his or her knowledge of counseling techniques, the Christian counselor can also help middle-aged persons in the following ways:

1. *Build an Understanding, Accepting Relationship.* This, of course, is basic to all counseling but especially is it important in working with someone who feels inadequate, unaccepted, and no longer valuable to family members or to the society. The counselor-counselee relationship provides the emotional support which enables the middle-aged person to express his or her frustrations and to slowly regain self-esteem and the courage to go out into the middle adult era. At times, there may be strong dependency on the counselor. This may be needed for a while, but the middle-aged counselee must be helped to make decisions and to take responsibilities which eventually will lead to great self-reliance.

In all of this, remember that the counselor needs to show tolerance, patience, interest, and acceptance mixed with a strong dose of realistic thinking so that the counselee can keep things in perspective. What is *not* needed is an attitude of criticism, moralizing or condemnation. It is not helpful to imply that Christians should never have mid-life problems (such an assertion has no biblical justification), neither is it helpful to avoid facing the practical but sometimes difficult decisions that must be made in middle life. It is good to remind the counselee that problems of mid-life are temporary. Most people come through this period with no permanent damage and many find that the mid-life crisis leads to greater fulfillment later. This is encouraging and needs to be stated periodically. The prognosis for improvement usually is excellent.

2. *Work on the Specific Problems of Middle Age.* By careful listening and periodic questioning seek to determine exactly what is bothering the middle-aged counselee. What are his or her feelings and what specifically is causing unhappiness? How much clear evidence is there to support the complaints? In practical ways, what can be done about the mid-life problems?

It has been suggested that the real problems of middle age come not because of hormone defects or glandular secretions. Problems come because individuals have failed to admit and satisfactorily deal with the threats and emotional strains of the mid-life transition.[21] If this is true, then the counselor's task is to stimulate discussion of the specific mid-life complaints and to help counselees reach realistic solutions. There will be times when counselees must be guided as they make important decisions about life, values, vocation, marriage and family issues. The counselor may need to help a counselee develop the willingness to slow down, to modify one's life goals, to talk about physical changes or the inevitability of death, to let the grown children develop their own lives and to discuss better ways to use one's time.

The preceding paragraphs on the causes and effects of mid-life problems can alert counselors to specific issues which might concern the mid-life counselee. In addition, some of the other chapters in this book give information which can be helpful in meeting such common mid-life problems as anxiety (chapter 5), marital problems (chapter 13), sex (chapter 21), and low self-esteem (chapter 24).

3. *Work with the Family*. An understanding, supportive and interested family can do much to help an individual through middle life. The Christian counselor can help the family, especially the spouse, understand the problems of middle age, give support or encouragement in the home, participate in decisions, and help the middle-aged person to discuss and do something about his or her boredom, fatigue, changing self-image, fears, vocational frustrations and marital tensions. The spouses can help each other to work on maintaining and building better sexual relationships. Sometimes the counselor can suggest books which family members or the counselee might read to increase understanding.[22]

It should not be assumed that the family members will have an easy task as they try to help someone face middle age. Since husbands and wives often face middle life together, it may be difficult for one to help the other. Patience, an attempt to understand and a willingness to challenge at times, are all part of the family treatment. Since the counselee may be critical, moody and not easy to live with, the family members may need periodic encouragement and coaching from a friendly counselor.

4. *Encourage Spiritual Awareness*. The Bible was written to teach us about God and ourselves. Its pages bring comfort and direction to anyone who takes the time to read carefully. Such comfort and direction don't always come quickly and neither are they regularly experienced as an "emotional high." Regular communion with God, however, leads to the realization that God is present with us and ministering through his Spirit.

As he went through a mid-life crisis, one pastor explained his feelings in a way that might be an encouragement to other middle-aged Christians:

> Early in the crisis I became deeply aware that God was my ally. I could tell him anything, even share with him the contradictory motives within my personality, and he would still love and accept me. As the crisis deepened and I came into the depression and withdrawal stages, I knew intellectually that God was still my friend, even though I did not feel it emotionally.[23]

Preventing Problems of Middle Age

Many years ago Carl Jung noted that we have schools and colleges to help people prepare for young adulthood but there are no colleges for forty-year-olds who need to be educated into the intricacies of living as older adults.[24] If there were such colleges, most people in middle age would be too busy to attend. However, community institutions, especially the churches, can give the preparation and help that is needed to prevent serious mid-life problems. This can be done in two ways.

1. *Anticipation.* When serious storms are approaching an area, there is less damage and loss of life if the weather bureau issues a prior warning in time for the residents to get ready and take cover. It can also be helpful if people in their mid-thirties are warned that the mid-life transition is coming. Such warnings need not be frightening; but they need to be mentioned periodically and in conjunction with a positive attitude toward middle age.

Middle age is a time of problems, especially during the early forties, but middle age is also a period filled with rewards and challenges. There is a sense of being settled, of having found one's place in life, and of being freed from the demands and responsibilities of raising small children. When compared with younger adults, middle-aged people often have more financial security, positions of prestige and leadership in the community, more opportunity to travel, and increased wisdom. Some of the striving and financial struggles of the twenties and thirties have passed and often there is the greatest opportunity for significant Christian service in the church. It should not be assumed or implied, therefore, that there is nothing to live for after thirty-nine. People can be helped to anticipate both the positive and negative aspects of this period in life.

2. *Education.* Family conferences, couples' retreats, discussion groups, Sunday school classes, and occasional sermons can and should deal with the major issues of middle age. In many churches the pews are filled with middle-aged people and their families who fail to understand the turmoil that is building within and who do not recognize the universality of mid-life crisis. When the problems are identified and acknowledged they can be faced and discussed often among friends in an atmosphere of acceptance. One more time, let us turn to the perceptive observations of Pastor Jim Conway:

> Over the years I have watched scores of people in mid-life quietly slip out the back door of the church. Each one felt he was a failure—morally, and spiritually—and most of all, emotionally. He had been taught all his life that being a Christian would guarantee that no problem would ever defeat him. When the mid-life crisis hit, he was literally flattened as if in a boxing match. As he lifted his head from the canvas and staggered to his feet he looked at the church filled with people who seemed to be so suc-

262 PART IV DEVELOPMENTAL FAMILY ISSUES

cessful and cocksure of themselves. He saw people with whom he was afraid to speak, people who would have only compounded his guilt. He saw a church speaking about forgiveness, love, and acceptance, but he didn't experience any of that. So, disillusioned, he quietly walked away to his dressing room and out into the night in a different direction.[25]

This can be prevented when mid-life crises are anticipated, accepted and faced in an educated manner. Employers, book writers and magazine editors, government leaders, teachers, and broadcasters can all contribute to this preventive effort. But the church can be most helpful of all. Its members know the healing power of divine love and can demonstrate the burden bearing which should characterize Christians. This can bring both support and guidance to people facing middle age.

Conclusions about Middle Age

Readers of this book might see themselves in its pages at times, but so does the writer. In preparing this chapter, for example, I have been acutely aware of my own struggles and victories upon entering middle adulthood. It has been encouraging for me to realize afresh that the emotions and struggles of middle age are common, temporary and ultimately contributing to one's spiritual growth and personal maturity. With God's help, we can guide ourselves or our counselees through the mid-life crisis. It is possible to face middle age realistically and to move on to a fuller "middle adult era" in which our lives can honor God and fulfill his purposes. That should be a goal for all of us—the writer of this book, the readers and the people to whom we minister and offer counsel.

Suggestions for Further Reading

Conway, James. *Men in Mid-Life Crisis.* Elgin, Ill.: David C. Cook, 1978.
Gould, Roger L. *Transformations: Growth and Change in Adult Life.* New York: Simon & Schuster, 1978.
LeShan, Eda. *The Wonderful Crisis of Middle Age.* New York: McKay, 1973.
Ortlund, Ray, and Ortlund, Anne. *The Best Half of Life.* Glendale, CA: Regal, 1976.

Footnotes

1. See, for example, Erikson's view of "Eight Ages of Man," at least three of which refer to post-adolescent development: Erik H. Erikson, *Childhood and Society,* 2d ed. (New York: Norton, 1963).
2. Gail Sheehy, *Passages: Predictable Crises of Adult Life* (New York: Dutton, 1974).
3. Roger L. Gould, *Transformations: Growth and Change in Adult Life* (New York: Simon & Schuster, 1978).
4. One of the most complete and widely reported research reports is that of: Daniel J. Levinson, Charlotte N. Darrow, Edward B. Klein, Maria H. Levinson, and Braxton McKee, *The Seasons of a Man's Life* (New York: Knopf, 1978).
5. C. G. Jung, *Psychological Reflections,* ed. Jolande Jacobi (New York: Harper Torchbooks, 1961), p. 125.

6. Robert Taylor, *Welcome to the Middle Years* (Washington, DC: Acropolis Books, 1976).

7. These phrases are taken from two books dealing with middle age: Eda LeShan, *The Wonderful Crisis of Middle Age* (New York: McKay, 1973); and Ray Ortlund and Anne Ortlund, *The Best Half of Life* (Glendale, CA: Regal, 1976).

8. Reported in Gordon MacDonald, "The Middle Years—Why Do We Resist?" *Eternity* (July, 1976): 40.

9. For a further discussion of David as a man in mid-life see James Conway, *Men in Mid-Life Crisis* (Elgin, IL: David C. Cook, 1978).

10. Levinson et al., *Seasons of a Man's Life*, pp. ix, x.

11. Levinson's study dealt with men. His research team believes that women go through similar stages of adult development but with some changes due to "differences in biology and social circumstances." A study of women is now underway. For a female perspective, see Judith Viorst, *How Did I Get to be 40 and Other Atrocities* (New York: Simon & Schuster, 1973).

12. Lillian E. Troll, *Early and Middle Adulthood: The Best is Yet to Be—Maybe* (Monterey: Brooks/Cole, 1975).

13. Conway, *Men in Mid-Life*, p. 105.

14. The issue of older parents is discussed in chapter 19, and in Arthur N. Schwartz, *Survival Handbook for Children of Aging Parents* (Chicago: Follett, 1977).

15. For a further discussion of affairs in mid-life see Conway, *Men in Mid-Life;* and Morton Hunt, *The Affair* (New York: New American Library, 1969).

16. Ollie Pocs, Annette Godow, William T. Tolone, and Robert H. Walsh, "Is There Sex After 40?" *Psychology Today* 11 (June, 1977): 54.

17. Conway, *Men in Mid-Life*, p. 124.

18. *Ibid.*, pp. 137 f.

19. *Ibid.*, p. 90.

20. See, for example, the preceding references to books by Conway, Gould, Ortlund and Ortlund, LeShan, and Taylor. In addition, see John C. Cooper and Rachel Conrad Wahlberg, *Your Exciting Middle Years* (Waco, TX: Word, 1976); and John Davitz and Lois Davitz, *Making It from 40 to 50* (New York: Random House, 1976).

21. Dana L. Farnsworth and Francis J. Braceland, *Psychiatry, The Clergy and Pastoral Counseling* (Collegeville, MN: St. John's University Press, 1969), p. 161.

22. If you only want to recommend one book, the volume by Conway (*Men in Mid-Life*) is suggested. This primarily deals with men, but it does discuss women in mid-life as well.

23. Conway, *Men in Mid-Life*, p. 188.

24. Jung, *Psychological Reflections*, p. 121.

25. Conway, *Men in Mid-Life*, p. 174.

19
The Later Years

Grow old along with me!
The best is yet to be,
The last of life, for which the first was
made. . . .

THUS WROTE ROBERT BROWNING OVER A CENTURY AGO, BUT HIS optimistic approach to the later years has not been shared by many other writers. The Egyptian philosopher Ptah-hotep wrote in 2500 B.C. that "old age is the worst of misfortunes that can afflict a man." Emerson described the elderly as "rags and relics," while Shakespeare said that the twilight years usher in "a second childishness and mere oblivion. Sans [without] teeth, sans eyes, sans taste, sans everything."

More modern views are not much better. Surveys have shown that old people often are regarded as tired, ugly, "old fogies" who are rigid, old-fashioned, resentful of the young, disinterested in sex, and declining in health.[1] Sometimes an old person is respected as a sage, but more often he or she is viewed as a doddering, rigid old fool—a view which is reinforced by television comedy shows. Little wonder that many old people conceal their ages, maintain that they are still middle-aged, and frequently look at themselves in a negative light which thereby perpetuates the modern stereotype that "old is ugly."

It is widely assumed that old age begins when one is in the 60 to 65-year-old period. People age at different rates, however, both physically and psychologically, so it is important to remember that among 65-year-olds there may be wide differences in health, attitudes, ability and physical appearance. Some people seem old at 40 while others appear to be youthful and vigorous even when they get into their 80s.

The percentage of older people in the population has been increasing within recent years. In the United States alone, the over-65 population increases at a rate of 1600 people per day. Advances in medicine and public health are insuring that many people will live longer, but with longer

264

life comes a new source of problems and challenges—the challenges of adjusting to the realities of old age. These challenges often can be met more efficiently with the help of a Christian counselor.

The Bible and Old Age

Old age, of course, is not something new. Life expectancy has increased over the centuries but there always have been aged people. Although Methuselah's 969 years clearly is unusual, many of the Old Testament patriarchs lived until they were well past the age of 100.

Even in Bible times older people apparently faced rejection and frustration. While it was recognized that wisdom often increased with age,[2] it is interesting to note that the psalmist prayed, "Forsake me not, O God, when I am old and grey."[3] Apparently he knew that older people were sometimes rejected.

Perhaps Ecclesiastes 12 is the clearest biblical picture of old age. Near the turn of the century, psychologist G. Stanley Hall called this the most pessimistic description of old age ever written,[4] but it also is realistic. People in the later years do not delight in their age, we read. Days can be cloudy, strength fails, often there is nothing to do, sight and hearing decline, fears increase and there is a new realization of the nearness of death.

But all is not "vanity of vanities." Everyone, including the aged, can find meaning in life when one fears God and keeps his commandments.[5] Old people can expect to be respected and honored; while young people have strength, the elderly should be respected for their wisdom and experience.[6] In turn they are to be temperate, dignified, sensible, sound in faith, love and perseverance, teaching what is good, and not malicious gossips or excessive drinkers.[7] This clearly presents a picture of hope, and nowhere should this be more apparent than in the community of believers. We are commanded to honor our parents "that you may live long on the earth"—an injunction which clearly is meant to be something positive.[8]

The Bible, therefore, is realistic in its portrayal of the problems of old age, positive in its attitude toward the value of old age, and specific in its commands concerning how we should treat persons in old age. Clearly older persons are to be respected, cared for and loved as human beings. Christians have no other options.[9]

The Causes of Problems in Old Age

Before we begin discussion of the problems of old age, it should be emphasized that for millions of people this *is* a happy and meaningful time of life. Not all persons over 65 are lonely, in failing health, bored, poverty-stricken, or exploited. This obvious fact must be stated lest the following paragraphs are taken to imply that the later years are always plagued by problems.

Of course it is true that many difficulties do arise as one advances in years. There are physical, mental, economic, interpersonal, self-esteem, and spiritual-existential causes of problems among the aged.

1. *Physical Causes.* As one gets older the body runs down. This is an aging process which differs from person to person. Some of our bodies decline sooner and more quickly than others, but for everyone, the aging process is speeded up when we are under stress. The physical changes might be classified in three ways.

(a) Physical appearance. Graying and thinning hair, loss of teeth, decreasing height, wrinkling skin, darks spots on the hands and wrists, sagging skin on the face—these changes begin long before a person turns 65, but in the later years they can no longer be ignored or hidden. In a culture which prizes youth and physical attractiveness these evidences of age can influence one's self-esteem and sense of security.

(b) Sensation and movement. It is well known that older people cannot see or hear as well as they once could. In addition there is a degeneration in the senses of taste and smell, a stiffness of joints which hinders movement, a declination in strength and energy level, a slower reaction time, a poorer circulation which makes it more difficult to keep warm and a lower ability to tolerate pain. Although these changes come slowly and are not recognized in one "jolt" they can interfere greatly with one's ability to get along and to get around.

(c) Sexual changes. Reproductive capacities diminish as one grows older but it is not true that sexual interest and activity diminish as well. Older people need physical proximity and human contact, just like the young. And it is now known that pleasurable sexual experiences are possible for both sexes well into the later years.[10]

It is true that older couples take longer to achieve orgasm, that the sexual organs change size, and that there is a declination in such functions as the amount of vaginal lubrication produced or the volume of semen ejaculated. But these changes need not detract from sexual appreciation or enjoyment. Indeed, for some couples, sexual activity and satisfaction increase as they grow older.

Regretfully, there is a commonly held misconception that old people have no sexual interest, drive, or ability to experience orgasm. Jokes about "dirty old men," about old age as "a time when a man flirts with girls but can't remember why," or about sex in adulthood as a progression from "tri-weekly, to try-weekly, to try-weakly" are all a mixture of humor with an attitude which implies that sex in the elderly is somehow wrong or lecherous. Such attitudes are believed by many older people, who then withdraw from sexual involvement, physical closeness and physical expression of love with one's mate.

(d) Illness and disease. "Only a minority of old people are infirm, but approximately three fourths of those who are over 65 have one or more chronic conditions that place restrictions on their activities."[11] Of these chronic diseases, arthritis, heart disease, hypertension and diabetes are most common,[12] but many people also suffer from cancer and from the breakdown of internal organs. All of these can arouse anxiety, diminish mobility, and create discouragement. It doubtless is true, as one author has written, that "if one is healthy, old age can be another interesting period of life; if one is ill, it can be terrifying and depressing." [13]

2. *Mental Causes.* Hundreds of research projects [14] have attempted to determine the extent to which older people decline in terms of creativity, memory, intellectual ability or capacity to learn new things. It is widely recognized that older persons take longer to respond, think more slowly, are distractible, are less able to understand new ideas or develop skills and have difficulty with short-term memory. But old people often can rely on their wisdom and appearance to make up for these declining abilities. With a little extra effort they can continue to be creative, intellectually astute and able to learn even in the later years.

The declination in mental ability is most apparent when one has to make a quick decision—like stepping on the brakes or jumping out of danger. Aware of their slower reaction time, many people learn to act cautiously—as many younger drivers have discovered when they get behind an older person who is driving.

It isn't always possible to compensate for declining mental abilities, however, and some people give up trying. Bored by the inactivity of retirement, the death of friends and the inability to move about, it is easy for an older person to daydream about the "good old days." The present is uncomfortable and the future offers little hope so there is an escape into past memories which have become distorted both by the passage of time and by the human tendency to forget that which was painful or unpleasant. Such a retreat contributes to confusion and senility that may be more psychological in origin than it is physiological.

3. *Economic Causes.* Retirement brings a departure from work, but for many it also brings a low income, a reduced standard of living and adjustment to a retirement pay scale which often fails to keep pace with the rate of inflation.

This economic situation creates a host of problems: finding an affordable place to live, meeting medical expenses, maintaining a balanced diet, being able to afford transportation costs to continue contact with friends, or facing the self-esteem problems which may come when one goes on public welfare—to name a few. Little wonder that aging has been called "one of life's most difficult adjustment problems." Economic problems do much to create the difficulties.

4. *Interpersonal Causes.* To function adequately as human beings, we need people with whom we can socialize and exchange ideas. Other people challenge us, encourage us, keep us in contact with reality, and enable us to feel useful.

For many older people there is a devastating loss of such social contact. Retirement isolates one from the occupational world. Friends and relatives, including one's spouse, often die and leave surviving old people without peers to bolster their morale. Declining health limits one's ability to get away from home, friends may change residence or move away, and adult children are sometimes too busy, too far away or too critical to provide contact. All of this can contribute to the older person's withdrawal from social contact, to the feeling that he or she is no longer useful or needed, and sometimes to a self-centeredness which can contribute to premature death.

5. *Self-esteem Causes.* The self-confidence and self-esteem of older people frequently are undermined by the misconceptions and prejudices of those who allege that the elderly are too old to make decisions, do useful work, create new things, accept responsibilities or go out alone. When everyone else seems to accept these conclusions, it is easy for an old person to feel useless and unimportant. Little wonder that many older persons have a poor opinion of themselves and of their value as persons.

For many people, one of the most influential blows to self-esteem is the reality of retirement. Eagerly anticipated and enjoyed by many people, retirement can also be a stark reminder that society considers us too old to work—and one's income and sense of self-worth often drop substantially.

According to Mildred Vandenburgh [15] there are three stages in retirement. *The get-up-and-go stage* is a time for enthusiastic involvement in the activities, projects and travel that one has long wanted to do but which work and other responsibilities have prevented. Without realizing it, people gradually slide into a *why-bother stage* in which comfort is important and there is a declining willingness to exert unnecessary effort. Then, writes Vandenburgh, "unless you pull up your bootstraps or someone rescues you from apathy and lethargy, you are on your way to the third and final stage: the *my-get-up-and-go-has-gone stage.*" [16]

This more popular analysis points to a well documented conclusion that there are great individual differences in the way people adjust to retirement and the self-esteem changes it brings. Depending somewhat on one's health, financial security, attitudes and degree of life success, some people welcome retirement as a time to sit back, relax and enjoy old age. Other people are active retirees who fill their lives with useful and meaningful activities. Then there are those who adjust poorly. Some, unable or unwilling to face the realities of old age, react with anger and blame others for their miseries and failure to achieve life goals. In contrast, others blame themselves and become self-haters.[17] Such persons have an especially low self-concept and often slide into long periods of depression.

It is well established, therefore, that the pressures of the later years can adversely influence one's self-concept. Even here, however, there are individual differences. The people who adapt best to old age are those who are well-adjusted before retirement, who have a realistic view of their strengths and weaknesses, and who had a positive self-concept during the younger years. It surely is true that one's adjustment, attitudes and self-concept at forty or earlier are good predictors of what one will be like decades later.

6. *Spiritual and Existential Causes.* Old age, declining health, and the passing of friends all bring us face-to-face with the reality and inevitability of death. For many there is a fear of pain, deterioration, dependence on others and helplessness. For many there also is a fear of death itself and a painful uncertainty about the existence or nonexistence of life after death. Some people reach old age with a burden of guilt and a sense of failure which they do not know how to handle. This is a time when the church could help, but many older people are unable to attend worship services. When they do attend, they sometimes feel unwanted and unwelcomed in congregations which emphasize youth programs, family ministries and the activities of couples clubs. Even the design of church buildings, with high stairs, no railings and basement washrooms, can subtly imply that older people—especially those with problems—are not welcome. Clearly "the church has a significant task to perform in resolving spiritual problems and lifting spiritual burdens of older persons." [18]

The Effects of Old Age

Researchers at the University of Michigan recently developed a creative method for helping students understand how it felt to be old. Nose plugs to stifle smell, ear plugs to reduce hearing, coated lenses over the eyes to limit clear vision, gloves to make hands slow and insensitive, and splints to limit leg and arm movement were all used to give students the experience of going about their daily activities with the sense organs dulled. "Nothing tasted right," complained one student and another observed, "Like everybody else, I used to call old people Sunday drivers and tell them to get off the road, but this program has helped me to understand why some old people don't dare go over 20 miles an hour." [19]

One good way for a counselor to understand the aged person is to put oneself in his or her place. Ask yourself how it would feel to have declining health, no useful work, limited income, a loss of friends and a declining ability to think or act quickly. Ponder how it would feel to be lonely, rejected by a society which has little respect for the elderly, and living in a neighborhood where the crime rate is high, but you have neither the strength nor the agility to protect yourself.[20] To imagine how an older person might think enables us to better understand the effects of aging and should enable us to be more sympathetic and effective counselors.

The effect of aging on one's self-concept, emotions, interpersonal relations, life style and intellectual capabilities has already been mentioned.

With aging there also may come slowness, new anxiety over the future, self-pity, depression and sometimes attempted suicide. In the United States, for example, 50 percent of all suicides are committed by people over 45 and 25 percent are committed by people—especially men—over 65. As one gets older, therefore, suicide rates increase significantly.[21]

> Old age in and of itself is not a social problem, for it is natural and inevitable. Old age is also a glorious occasion which is—and should be—looked upon as a significant accomplishment. Even so many older persons do have problems that are at least in part due to their growing old. ... The lack of respect for our senior citizens, the growing emphasis upon youth, and the substitution of technology for manpower has left tens of thousands of older Americans with no role in society. These, along with the numerous other problems alluded to in this book and elsewhere, contribute to the despair that is found so frequently among the elderly. Faced with disappointment and disillusionment at reaching the "harvest years"; finding the "golden years" to be a period of relative poverty; feeling themselves to be on the shelf and not permitted to make the contributions they still are able to make to the economic life of our nation; frustrated with the reduction of income which usually comes with retirement, and living in unpleasant, inconvenient, and unhealthful dwellings; it is no wonder that so many older persons are seriously maladjusted. The church has a tremendous challenge to face in the problems related to the economic plight of so many of our older citizens.[22]

Counseling and Old Age

As we move through life, each of us develops personal methods of coping with stress and pressure. These coping techniques extend into the later years and it probably is true that those who coped effectively in the past will do so again in the future. Nevertheless, the crises of later years bring unique pressures, and often, even among the well-adjusted, there is a need for continuing help and counseling assistance. This help can take several forms.

1. *Counselor Self-examination.* What is your attitude toward the elderly? Do you harbor some of the common stereotypes which see old people as incompetent, useless, childish, rigid, cranky and preoccupied with physical aches and pains? Do you resent old people, look down on them or attempt to avoid them? These are common reactions which must disappear before a counselor can be helpful. If you hold these negative attitudes, ask God to make you more compassionate and loving. Then spend some time talking with a few old people about their lives, problems and needs. It is probable that your attitudes will change and you will begin to see the elderly as worthwhile human beings who are loved by God. It is only then that you will be able to counsel successfully with those who are old.

2. *Physical Examination and Counseling.* Many of the problems in old age come or are accentuated because of physical deterioration. It is im-

portant, therefore, that older people be encouraged to have regular physical checkups by a competent physician. Such physicians can also give general advice on health care to the aged. This is an important issue that is beyond the training and expertise of nonmedical counselors. When medical treatment helps people feel better, some of their psychological problems disappear and others can be dealt with more efficiently.

3. *Preretirement Counseling.* Just as there are myths about old age in general, there are false ideas about retirement. Some dread it. Others see it as a time of constant loafing, of waiting for death or of perpetual work on hobbies. Some resent retirement because it implies that one is no longer useful.

The place to start counseling is with persons in their late forties or fifties. Clear up some of their misunderstandings about retirement—perhaps through a workshop or Sunday school class discussion. The years after sixty-five can be, and often are, a time of productivity and personal satisfaction, especially if there is prior planning.

Then as retirement approaches, encourage people to read some of the books written to help individuals face old age.[23] Remember that people often resist the fact of aging. As long as they feel physically well, they may not even notice the gradual changes which are evidence of advancing age.

In discussing retirement, ask the person to consider the following questions:

> When will I retire?
> What is God's will for me after retirement?
> Where will I retire?
> Where will I live in retirement?
> How will I spend my time after retirement?
> How will I keep healthy after retirement?
> What will I do to keep my mind alert and active?
> How much money and financial resources do I have?
> What will I need after retirement?
> What are my pension and Social Security benefits and when am I eligible to receive them?
> Will I have enough health insurance?
> Is my will complete and up-to-date?
> Specifically, what can I do now to prepare for retirement?

Discussion of such questions prevents future problems and helps with old age concerns in the present.[24] Since few people are likely to come for a discussion of these questions, you might encourage their consideration in informal groups, perhaps at a retreat or discussion time in the church.

4. *Individual Counseling.* This, of course, will depend on the needs of the counselee, but there can be several overlapping types of individual counseling with the aged.

(a) Supportive Counseling. This involves sensitive listening, reassurance, encouragement and attempts both to motivate the older person and to help him or her accept the realities of advanced age. Such counseling can help people feel worthwhile and accepted. It can help people forgive themselves and know that God forgives and cares. This can and should emphasize the love of God, and there should be a discussion of God's plan of salvation, of his justice and his provisions for "believers" after death. At times there will be a need to help the older person face the realities of sickness (see chapter 27) or to deal with the pain of grief (see chapter 28). An individual can do such counseling but it is best accomplished not by an occasional pastoral call, but by a group of believers, including the counselor, who consistently show care, support, and acceptance. Often the face-to-face contact can be supplemented by periodic telephone calls or cheerful notes.

(b) Educative Counseling. Old people, like those who are younger, have many misconceptions about aging. These can be discussed and true facts about aging can be taught. Such discussion can give reassurance and reduce anxiety.

Consider, for example, the issue of sex after sixty. It is helpful for older people to recognize that this is not wrong, that physical satisfaction is both possible and common, that problems like impotence can be temporary, and that sexual stimulation does not stop on the day of retirement.

A very different subject is that of living accommodations in old age. What are the costs, advantages, and other relevant issues involved in living alone, moving to a retirement village or home, moving in with one's children, and so on? The counselor may have to consult with several senior citizens and community leaders to get accurate information which might be shared with the counselee.

(c) Life Cycle Counseling. At times it can be helpful for older people to review their lives and plan realistically for the future. This type of counseling involves preparing a complete biography of the counselee (sometimes on paper). Ask him or her to bring photographs, diaries and other memorabilia, and it may be good to talk with family members. The goals of these activities are to help counselees express and confess tensions about the past, discuss and accept failures, get rid of guilt feelings, look at life realistically, solve conflicts and behavior patterns that cause trouble, learn new ways to cope with problems and prepare realistically for a smooth transition to the coming years.[25] This review must include discussions of the older person's spiritual life, relationship with Jesus Christ, and expectations about life after death. In addition, consider the person's marital and family history, earliest memories, education and work history, happiest and saddest memories, and plans for the future.

(d) In-depth Counseling. This involves more long-term involvement with people who are depressed, withdrawn, or otherwise inclined to show more severe mental problems. In general such persons should be referred to more experienced counselors. Sometimes there is a professional reluctance to work with the elderly because it is assumed that they are beyond help. This is a stereotype. At present, there is little evidence to suggest that older people are more difficult to treat than younger patients. This is especially true when the counselee wants to get better.

Counselors sometimes emphasize a reaction called *transference*. This is the tendency for a counselee to have feelings toward the counselor that originally were directed toward someone else. Consider, for example, a situation in which a young counselee meets with an older male counselor. If the counselee hates his or her father, this hatred may be "transferred" to the counselor. If the counselor, in turn, begins treating the counselee like his grown son or daughter, we have a reaction termed *counter-transference*.

In counseling with the elderly, the counselor is often younger than the counselee. This can create awkwardness, since young people usually are not thought of as counselors to the elderly. Sometimes the younger counselor treats the counselee like a father or mother. The older counselee, however, often thinks of the counselor as a peer or even a parental figure.[26] These perceptions must be recognized, especially by counselors, when they work with older counselees.

5. *Group Counseling.* Often there is reluctance for people to discuss their problems in groups and this can be especially true for older persons who are less accustomed to being open about themselves before others. Groups, however, can be helpful to the elderly who need contact with others, acceptance, and assurance that their problems are not unique or abnormal. Such groups can consider adjustment problems, life crises, prejudice against the aged and most of the other issues that concern the elderly. Helpful books are available for the counselor who wants to conduct group counseling.[27]

6. *Milieu Counseling.* It has long been realized that one good way to change a person is to change his or her environment. Attractive accommodations, adequate meals, recreational opportunities, and the presence of cheerful, encouraging people can all help to alter the older person's outlook and adjustment to later life. One research study with hospitalized geriatric patients showed that simply being around younger people can alter the older person's negative self-concept and improve his or her behavior.[28] This has great implications for church youth groups whose members can serve a useful role by brightening the lives of older people in the church or community.

Preventing Old Age Problems

It is not always possible to delay the aging process, but it is possible to prevent the negative attitudes which accompany old age and which can, in turn, hasten the process of physical deterioration. Prevention of old age problems involves motivating people in four areas:

1. *Stimulating Realistic Attitudes.* From the pulpit, through small

groups, and in other church meetings, the stereotypes and myths about aging must be attacked. The Bible clearly respects the aged and followers of Christ are expected to do the same. If the whole church can develop a positive attitude about aging, the older person will do the same.

One way to develop such an attitude is to get the congregation in contact with the elderly and involved with helping. Gray and Moberg have listed some of the things that a church can do for older people.[29] Included in the list are the following. A church can:

—plan specific programs for senior citizens;
—speak to the spiritual needs of the elderly—including their feelings of insecurity, insignificance, alienation from God, regret over past failures and fear of death;
—educate people to better cope with life's problems;
—stimulate social, spiritual and recreational contact with same age and younger persons;
—help solve personal problems before they escalate;
—help meet physical and material needs;
—meet with people in nursing homes;
—influence civic affairs and government programs for the elderly;
—adapt its physical facilities so people can come to church; and
—create opportunities for older people to be involved in useful service—teaching, visiting, praying, or doing clerical, maintenance, and a host of other useful service activities.

A program such as this shows everyone that the aged are important among younger persons, especially, and this eliminates some of the fears and facilitates a smoother adjustment into the later years.

2. *Stimulating Realistic Planning.* The problems of age sometimes hit with spiraling intensity because they were unexpected and come without any prior preparation. Within the church we can encourage people to evaluate their attitudes toward aging, to discuss how to use leisure time, to ponder relationships with aging parents or grown children, to talk about death and to plan for retirement. Such discussions need not be morbid. Instead they can be positive, pleasant and presented as a healthy, wise exercise. While this planning for the future could take place in a one-to-one counseling situation, it probably is done better in groups, such as a Sunday school class. Such group discussions can serve as an innoculation against the psychological traumas of aging.

3. *Stimulating Education and Activity.* People can avoid some of the problems of aging if they can be encouraged to use their minds, to exercise their bodies, to plan their diets, to make good use of their leisure time and to find creative ways of serving others. This conclusion is based on the assumption that mental and physical activity will do much to keep one from becoming apathetic, lethargic and senile.

4. *Stimulating Spiritual Growth.* No one is ever too old to come to

Christ and to grow spiritually. Such growth enables us to cope more successfully with the problems of life, and it lets us learn more about the One with whom we will be spending eternity. This is a message which must be proclaimed to people of all ages. Then believers must be shown how they should pray, read the Bible, worship regularly, fellowship with other believers and become involved in active service. It is well known that spiritual growth does not prevent life's problems, but the committed believer should be able to deal with stress more effectively because he or she has confidence in an all-powerful, sovereign God. The believer who, with God's help, is able to rejoice in the earlier years, will carry that same joyful attitude into adulthood.

Conclusions about Old Age

It has been estimated that one-fifth of the American population suffers from *gerontophobia*—the fear of growing old.[30] Perhaps the figure would be different in other parts of the world but one conclusion is clear—many people recoil from thoughts of their own old age, and attempt both to deny aging in themselves and to avoid others who are older. Perhaps to justify their disinterest in old people, young persons tend to perpetuate myths about the disadvantages of the later years. These myths are widely held, even by the aged, and hence contribute to the problems of the elderly. But such myths are neither biblically nor scientifically supportable. The place to start in helping the elderly is with the exposure of untrue stereotypes.

Preparations for becoming elderly begin with attitudes, life style, activities and spiritual maturing while one is younger. Inactive, critical, bitter, nervous, self-centered young people most often carry these characteristics into old age. This was a truth recognized by Plato many years ago when he wrote, "He who is of calm and happy nature will hardly feel the pressure of age, but to him who is of opposite disposition youth and age are equally a burden."[31]

Suggestions for Further Reading

Aiken, Lewis. *Later Life*. Philadelphia: Saunders, 1978.
Birren, James E. *The Psychology of Aging*. Englewood Cliffs, NJ: Prentice-Hall, 1964.
Gray, Robert M. and Moberg, David O. *The Church and the Older Person*. Rev. ed. Grand Rapids: Wm. B. Eerdmans, 1977.
* Tournier, Paul. *Learn to Grow Old*. New York: Harper & Row, 1972.
* Vandenburgh, Mildred. *Fill Your Days With Life*. Glendale, CA: Regal, 1975.

Footnotes

1. Summarized in Lewis Aiken, *Later Life* (Philadelphia: Saunders, 1978), pp. 13–16.
2. Job 12:12.
3. Ps. 71:18.

4. Reported in C. Gilhuis, *Conversations on Growing Older* (Grand Rapids: Wm. B. Eerdmans, 1977), pp. 19–21.

5. Eccles. 12:13.

6. Lev. 19:32; Prov. 16:31; 20:29.

7. Titus 2:2, 3.

8. Eph. 6:3.

9. See Robert M. Gray and David O. Moberg, *The Church and the Older Person*, rev. ed. (Grand Rapids: Wm. B. Eerdmans, 1977).

10. W. H. Masters and V. E. Johnson, *Human Sexual Inadequacy* (Boston: Little, Brown and Co., 1970); and Morton Puner, "Will You Still Love Me?" *Human Behavior* 3 (June, 1974): 40–48.

11. Aiken, *Later Life*, p. 31.

12. U. S. Department of Health, Education and Welfare, *Health in the Later Years of Life* (Rockville, MD: National Center for Statistics, 1971), p. 20.

13. Aiken, *Later Life*, p. 28.

14. See for example, James E. Birren, ed., *Handbook of Aging and the Individual* (Chicago: University Press, 1959).

15. Mildred Vandenburgh, *Fill Your Days with Life* (Glendale, CA: Regal, 1975).

16. Ibid., p. 95.

17. S. Reichard, F. Livison, and P. G. Peterson, "Adjustment to Retirement," in *Middle Age and Aging*, ed. B. L. Neugarten (Chicago: University Press, 1968).

18. Gray and Moberg, *The Church and the Older Person*, p. 49.

19. L. A. Pastalan, "The Simulation of Age-related Sensory Losses: A New Approach to the Study of Environmental Barriers," *The New Outlook for the Blind* (October, 1974): 356–62.

20. According to Aiken, *Later Life*, in the United States nearly 20,000 Social Security checks are stolen each year in purse-snatchings, burglaries and muggings.

21. James E. Birren, *The Psychology of Aging* (Englewood Cliffs, NJ: Prentice-Hall, 1964).

22. Gray and Moberg, *The Church and the Older Person*, pp. 55, 35. Used by permission.

23. See, for example, Gilhuis, *Conversations on Growing Older;* Olga Knopf, *Successful Aging: The Facts and Fallacies of Growing Old* (New York: Viking Press, 1975); Jeanette Lockerbie, *Fifty Plus* (Old Tappan, NJ: Revell, 1976); Sam C. Reeves, *The Bright Years: How to Make Your Retirement the Best Time of Your Life* (Old Tappan, NJ: Revell, 1977); Paul Tournier, *Learn to Grow Old* (New York: Harper & Row, 1972); and Vandenburgh, *Fill Your Days with Life.*

24. A complete and exceptionally helpful guidebook gives worksheets and practical guidelines to help people face retirement: Mark J. Staley, *Dynamic Retirement: How to Retire and Love It* (Cleveland: Uniline Co., 1976). (Uniline Co., 23632 Mercantile Road, Cleveland, Ohio, 44122.)

25. R. J. Butler, "Age: The Life Review," *Psychology Today* No. 5, (7), (1971): 49–51 ff.

26. Martin A. Berezin, "The Elderly Person," in *The Harvard Guide to Modern Psychiatry*, ed. Armand M. Nicholi, Jr. (Cambridge, MA: Harvard University Press, 1978), pp. 541–49.

27. See especially Wilma H. Klein, Eda J. LeShan, and Sylvan S. Furman, *Promoting Mental Health of Older People Through Group Methods: A Practical Guide* (New York: Manhattan Society for Mental Health, Inc. [11 West 42nd St., New York, NY, 10036], 1965); and Clyde Reid, *Groups Alive-Church Alive: The Effective Use of Small Groups in the Local Church* (New York: Harper & Row, 1969).

28. B. Kahana and E. Kahana, "Changes in Mental Status of Elderly Patients in Age-Integrated and Age-Segregated Hospital Milieus," *Journal of Abnormal Psychology* 75 (1970): 177–81.

29. Gray and Moberg, *The Church and the Older Person,* chapter 8.

30. Joseph H. Bunzel, "Note on the History of a Concept—Gerontophobia," *The Gerontologist* No. 12, (2), (Summer, 1972) : 116, 203.

31. *The Dialogues of Plato,* vol. 2, *The Republic,* trans. Benjamin Jowett (New York: National Library Co., n.d.).

Part V
Sex and
Interpersonal
Issues

20

Sex Apart from Marriage

SEX APART FROM MARRIAGE IS BECOMING MORE COMMON AND MORE widely accepted as we move toward the end of the twentieth century. Cohabitation, the practice of an unmarried male and female living together with full sexual relations but with no intention of getting married is increasing in popularity.[1] The hedonistic playboy-playgirl philosophy has become more and more accepted, while both premarital and extramarital sexual intercourse appear to be increasing.[2]

But coitus apart from marriage is not the only sexual behavior apart from marriage. Homosexuality, a sexual orientation that has been practiced for centuries, recently has increased in prominence as gay liberation groups have become more visible and more active. Masturbation, probably the most common sexual behavior apart from intercourse, is so prevalent that it hardly concerns sexual researchers, although the practice brings guilt and anxiety into many lives, especially among boys and young men. Then there are the more pathological forms of sexual expression like exhibitionism, rape, transvestism, child molesting, or bestiality, each of which continues to attract the periodic attention of reporters and psychiatrists.

Our society, it would seem, is obsessed with sex. It is a central issue of concern on college campuses and television, in magazines, advertisements of all kinds, literature, music, the theater, movies, art, popular conversation and even in business, politics and the church. One would have to be a hermit to avoid the sexually arousing stimuli in our day. That which God created for enjoyment and intimacy has become perverted—*the* prime example of the sin and moral sickness which characterizes modern human beings.

In this chapter we will limit our discussion to three of the four most common examples of sex outside of marriage: masturbation, premarital sex and extramarital sex. Homosexuality is considered in chapter 22.

The Bible and Sex Apart from Marriage

Sex, according to one dictionary definition, is an instinct which draws one sex toward another; the sum total of all those physical and anatomical differences which distinguish the male from the female. But sex, as everyone knows, is more than a physical instinct and biological creation. Sex involves sensual lovemaking and stimulating orgasms, but it also involves in-depth intimacy and intense communication even in the absence of physical contact. Sexuality, writes Lewis Smedes, "throbs within us as movement toward relationship, intimacy, companionship." It is "an exciting desire, sometimes a melancholy longing, to give ourselves in trust to another."[3] Karl Barth even called sexuality the "God-like within us." It is an urge toward closeness and the expression of a deep personal relationship with someone else.[4]

The Apostle Paul was unmarried and inclined to favor singleness,[5] but this did not mean that he was unfulfilled or nonsexual. He understood lust and the passions of sexuality,[6] but surely he also appreciated his maleness and experienced both intimacy and personal wholeness without physical sex. Sexuality, therefore, includes but involves much more than genital contact.

Psychiatrist Judd Marmor once described the difference between healthy and unhealthy sexuality:

> Healthy sexuality seeks erotic pleasure in the content of tenderness and affection; pathologic sexuality is motivated by needs for reassurance or relief from nonsexual sources of tension. Healthy sexuality seems both to give and receive pleasure; neurotic forms are unbalanced towards excessive giving or taking. Healthy sexuality is discriminating as to partners; neurotic patterns often tend to be nondiscriminating. The periodicity of healthy sexuality is determined primarily by recurrent erotic tensions in the context of affection. Neurotic sexual drives, on the other hand, are triggered less by the erotic needs than by the nonerotic tensions and therefore more apt to be compulsive in the patterns of occurrence.[7]

Unhealthy sexuality distorts God's perfect plan for human beings. It destroys intimacy and communication, is self-centered, and often expresses a desire to manipulate, control, or hurt another person. The experience is pleasurable; it dulls one's sense of loneliness, and it gives a feeling of intimacy, but all of this is temporary, dehumanizing, and ultimately unfulfilling.

Perhaps this is why the Bible writers so soundly condemned fornication (which usually refers to premarital sex), adultery (sexual relations with someone other than one's spouse), and other forms of sex outside of marriage.[8] These are deviations from God's plan and commands; hence they are sinful. While sinful pleasures are enjoyable, the pleasure is only "for a season." [9] Within marriage (as we will see in the next chapter), sexual intercourse is good—created by God for reproduction, intimacy and pleasure, but sexual abuse is condemned with great vehemence.

Consider, for example, what the Bible says about fornication and adultery. In the New Testament alone, the word *fornication* occurs forty-seven times.[10] In several passages it refers to general immorality,[11] and twice it means voluntary sexual intercourse of an unmarried person with someone of the opposite sex (in premarital sex).[12] Although it is used sometimes as a synonym for adultery,[13] the word *fornication* more often is set apart from adultery.[14] Since sexual adultery only includes the behavior of married people, fornication would have to mean (among other things) sexual intercourse and other misuses of sex among single people.[15] A reading of these references clearly shows that fornication is condemned as a sin.

Adultery is used in two ways in the Bible. One meaning refers to idol worship and unfaithfulness to God;[16] the other concerns sexual intercourse by a married person with someone other than one's mate (i.e., extramarital sex). In both cases, adultery is forbidden and strongly condemned.[17] Several times in the writings of Paul, lists of evil behavior are given—lists which include adultery and fornication, along with "immorality," "impurity," "sensuality" and "homosexuality." [18] It is significant to note that the wrath of God will come upon those who engage in such behaviors. Clearly God does not take a light view of physical sexual intimacies apart from marriage.

What, then, can we conclude from our discussion thus far?

1. *Sex Is Created by God and Is Good.* This is discussed more fully in chapter 21, but it is the place to begin all considerations of human sexuality. God created the human race with male and female bodies capable of sexual intimacy including genital orgasm. As with other parts of his creation, God called sexual human beings "very good," and undoubtedly wanted us to "multiply" and enjoy our bodies within the confines of his will.[19] When the human race fell into sin, God's creation was marred, the potential for unhealthy sexuality came into being, and Adam and Eve, who previously were "not ashamed" of their nakedness, suddenly became self-conscious about their bodies.[20]

2. *Sex Apart from Marriage Involves Behavior Which Is Sinful.* This is stated most firmly in 1 Corinthians 6 where we read that,

> I can do anything I want to if Christ has not said no, but some of these things aren't good for me. . . . Sexual sin is never right: our bodies were not made for that, but for the Lord, and the Lord wants to fill our bodies with himself. . . . That is why I say to run from sexual sin. No other sin affects the body as this one does. When you sin this sin it is against your own body. Haven't you yet learned that your body is the home of the Holy Spirit God gave you, and that he lives within you? Your own body

does not belong to you. For God has bought you with a great price. So use every part of your body to give glory back to God, because he owns it.[21]

Repeatedly, the Bible warns against the enslaving influence of sexual behavior apart from marriage.[22] And there is nothing to even hint that sexually aroused persons are free to engage in sexual intercourse, even if they intend to marry. If you cannot restrain yourselves, the Apostle Paul wrote, then get married, since it is better to marry than to burn with passion.[23]

3. *Sex Apart from Marriage Involves Thinking Which Is Sinful.* Legalists, back in the time of Jesus and in our own day, have maintained that there is no adultery so long as the man does not let his penis, enter the woman's vagina. Such a legalistic view was challenged by Jesus in the Sermon on the Mount. "You have heard that it was said, 'You shall not commit adultery,'" he stated, "but I say to you that every one who looks on a woman to lust for her has committed adultery with her already in his heart."[24] Clearly adultery, lust, and undoubtedly fornication can all take place in the mind without genital contact at all.

It is difficult to give an accurate definition of *lust*. Surely it does *not* refer to normal God-given sexual desires, or feelings of attraction toward sexually stimulating people. God has not given us sexual needs or interests which he then condemns as lust. Lust is a specific desire for the body of some other person. "When the sense of excitement conceives a plan to use a person, when attraction turns into scheme we have crossed beyond erotic excitement into spiritual adultery."[25]

In a controversial book, one Christian writer has suggested that sexual fantasies, excitement in the presence of a sexually stimulating person, and even the viewing of sexual pictures is not necessarily lust, unless the excitement leads our minds to imagine or plan sexual involvement with the people we are thinking about.[26] Not all Christians would agree with this opinion, however, since mental fantasies can be so dangerous. Often they are a first step leading to subsequent genital contact and they do, at times, substitute for intimacy when the fantasizing person is unable or unwilling to engage in sexual communication with a real person.

Engaging in sex apart from marriage leaves at least two people abused. Mental lusting primarily influences the one who lusts. But according to Jesus both are wrong.

4. *Sex Apart from Marriage Involves Talk Which Is Sinful.* The Bible warns against the dangers of saying things which can create conflict and misunderstanding,[27] but it also condemns loose sexual talk: "Let there be no sex sin, impurity or greed among you. Let no one be able to accuse you of any such things. Dirty stories, foul talk and coarse jokes—these are not for you. Instead, remind each other of God's goodness and be thankful."[28]

5. *Sex Apart from Marriage Involves Masturbation.* Unlike fornication and adultery, masturbation (the self-stimulation of one's genitals to the point of orgasm) is never mentioned in the Bible. Some have argued that the sin of Onan, described in Genesis 38, is a form of masturbation because "he spilled his semen on the ground." However, even a casual reading of the text indicates that Onan's sin involved his disobedience to God by refusing to impregnate the wife of his deceased brother.

Is masturbation wrong? According to Jay Adams, "masturbation is clearly wrong since it constitutes a perversion of the sexual act." [29] In sharp contrast Charlie Shedd calls masturbation a "gift of God . . . a blessing" which helps people maintain self-control and avoid immoral sexual intercourse.[30] In between is the view of James Dobson, who believes that masturbation is not much of an issue with God "since it isn't even mentioned in the Bible." [31] Although their views of masturbation differ, all of these writers would agree that masturbation often is accompanied by lusting thoughts. Such thoughts, as we have seen, are wrong whether or not they are accompanied by genital stimulation.

6. *Sex Apart from Marriage Restricts Freedom.* At the beginning of his discussion on immorality, Paul writes about freedom. We are free to do anything, he writes, but all things are not wise.[32] In this world, everything has a design and function and we get along best when we stay within these guidelines. The fish, for example, is designed to swim in the sea, and although it is free to jump up on the shore, this would not be wise. In the same way, the Bible states that the human body is created for sex within marriage. We are freest and most fulfilled when we stay within that divine guideline. We are free, of course, to engage in immorality, but such actions ultimately are enslaving. The person who cannot resist sexual temptation is not free. He or she is caught in the strangling hold of uncontrolled impulses.[33]

The Causes of Sex Apart from Marriage

Beginning with the work of Kinsey, various researchers have reported a disturbing increase in the number of persons, both male and female, who report that they have been involved in premarital or extramarital sexual intercourse. There can be a variety of overlapping reasons for this, including environmental stimulation and internal pressure.[34] Many of these same influences lead others to masturbation, homosexual involvements, or other sexual practices apart from marriage.

1. *Environmental Stimulation.* Our sex-saturated society stimulates people to think about sex and encourages us to seek hedonistic physical sexual gratification.

(a) Social Atmosphere. Modern society emphasizes the value of immediate, physical sexual gratification. Most popular magazines and modern films, numerous television programs, and many commercial advertisements are blatantly designed to arouse and "play on" our sexual urges and desires. Citizen attempts to "clean up" the media and reduce pornography are often met with resistance in the form of a compelling argument: Although the media stimulate sexual (and violent) urges, the media also reflect what most readers, listeners and viewers want.

This sexually supercharged atmosphere is soaked up by the populace (including Christians) who in turn exude a powerful peer pressure. This is seen with special clarity in the young. At a time when sexual urges are most intense, and the need for peer approval most pressing, adolescents often succumb to social pressures and enter into sexual encounters in an attempt to find acceptance and status. But social pressure can also influence adults, including traveling business people, entertainers, speakers (even Christian speakers), and others whose work draws them away from home and repeatedly puts them into motel rooms.

(b) Sexual Convenience. A newspaper report recently described the difficulties faced by Russian couples who want privacy. Cars are scarce, motel rooms are difficult to rent, and apartments are usually crowded with relatives. Such is not the case in our culture. As mobile people with cars, we can get to private locations more easily. As affluent people with money, we can pay for secret lunches and motel rooms. As freedom-loving people with less social and parental surveillance, we can be less anxious about sexual experimentation. As sophisticated people with contraceptive devices, we can avoid the worry about pregnancy. "Convenient adultery" is becoming more and more accessible both to teenagers and adults.

(c) Changing Values. Sex apart from marriage is no longer a taboo subject. Our generation probably knows more about birth control, sexual intercourse and masturbation than any previous generation. Cohabitation, mate swapping, unfaithfulness, and similar behaviors are openly discussed and widely tolerated, if not accepted. Sexual restrictions have lessened, sexual standards have loosened, and sexual expectations have become more liberal. Marriage, which once was thought to bring security, status and responsible parenthood, now is entered by many for personal and sexual fulfillment. When the "thrill is gone," adultery and divorce are seen as alternatives. Of course, openness about sex is not necessarily bad, and some Victorian inhibitions are best changed. But the changes have become a stampede to license and licentiousness. These changes are hard for sexually vulnerable people to resist.

(d) Inappropriate Education. Many people, especially young people, enter sexual relationships with inaccurate or inadequate knowledge of the consequences. Novels and films often give a distorted picture of sexual love, and sex education classes teach the facts of biology without the stabilizing influence that comes with a knowledge of the principles of morality. For many people the basis of their behavior is the new Western ethic: if it feels good, do it!

2. *Internal Pressure.* The environment makes it easier to yield to sexual temptations, but the real source of the trouble rests inside the individual's mind. Jesus indicated this clearly during one of his talks with the pious Pharisees. "The things that proceed out of the mouth come from the heart, and those defile the man. For out of the heart come evil thoughts . . . adulteries, fornications. . . ." [35] What are some of these internal "heart" pressures?

(a) Curiosity. With all of the present emphasis on sex, it is easy for anyone, married or single, to conclude: "I must be missing something which I'd like to try." Bored, perhaps, with one's current sexual behavior (or lack of behavior), there is a desire to try something new and different. This increases the likelihood that we will take advantage of sexual opportunities when they become available.

(b) The Search for Identity and Self-esteem. Many modern people feel inferior, insignificant, insecure and lacking in any real life purpose. For such people, sex apart from marriage often is seen as a way to be accepted, to prove oneself, to feel needed, and to bolster self-esteem. Many middle-aged and older people, fearing a loss of virility and attractiveness, have an affair in an attempt to convince themselves that they still are desirable sexually. Masturbation, accompanied by fantasies of sexual exploits, can give a passing feeling of self-acceptance and sexual capability, without the risks of real intimacy with another person. Regretfully, the transitory nature of such sexual behaviors often leaves the participants more rejected and self-condemning than before. As a result, some run from relationship to relationship in an attempt to fill the emptiness and find a more stable self-identity.

(c) The Search for Intimacy and Closeness. Sexuality, as we have seen, involves more than genital contact. It involves deep communication, acceptance and sincere love. When people feel lonely, unwanted, unloved and emotionally deprived, they often seek intimacy, tenderness, excitement and fulfillment in sexual relationships apart from marriage.

(d) Escapism and Rebellion. Sexual behavior, including masturbation, can sometimes be a way to escape boredom, relieve tension, and temporarily avoid the pressures of life. At other times, this sexual behavior is an indication of rebellion against parental or church authority, a declaration of independence from one's past, or an expression of anger and defiance against one's mate or some other person.

(e) Sexual Deviations. The prevalence of sexual deviation is better documented than the causes of such disorders. Past learning, failures in earlier sexual encounters, fears that one is "different," neurotic and psychotic misperceptions, twists in mental thinking, failure to anticipate the consequences of one's actions, an unconscious desire to be caught and punished, excessive curiosity or daring—these are among the many reasons people involve themselves in perverse sexual activities.

(f) Satanic Influence. The Scriptures state clearly that Christians especially are in a spiritual battle against the forces of evil and the "schemes of the devil." [36] Satan is alert and very wise. By masquerading as an "angel of light," [37] he "prowls about" trying to devour and lead people into darkness. Since many people appear to be vulnerable in the area of sexual temptation, it is here that the attack often comes, and it is here that many fall. In a desire to be sexually liberated and free of "hang-ups," we allow ourselves to enter potentially disastrous, compromising situations. Even Christians fail, at times, to rely on the protective power of the Holy Spirit. Satan is successful because believers try to fight the battle alone, failing to appreciate the truth of 1 John 4:4: "Greater is He who is in you than he who is in the world." It is the Holy Spirit within believers who alone can give us power to resist satanic influences.

The Effects of Sex Outside of Marriage

It is impossible to understand or describe adequately the effects of sex apart from marriage. Much of this sexual activity is sin and, according to the Bible, all sin which is not forgiven will be punished in a time of future judgment. But the effects of sin often come much sooner. For a while there is pleasure but the harmful influences of nonmarital sex quickly become apparent to many people.

It would be inaccurate to imply, however, that sex outside of marriage always (or even frequently) leads to immediate guilt and remorse. A perusal of the research in this area [38] indicates that many persons report little or no guilt following nonmarital sex—especially if the participants feel a genuine affection for each other. And as sex apart from marriage continues, initial qualms and insecurities often disappear—at least temporarily.

But a lack of remorse does not make such sexual activity morally right. Nonbelievers often develop an attitude which is "hardened" to biblical teaching and they are unable to sense or understand the inner promptings of the Holy Spirit.[39] In time, such people—who may be highly respected and educated members of the church and society—"do not see fit to acknowledge God," so he leaves them to their lust, impurity, "depraved minds," improper behavior, and tendency to give "hearty approval" to others who practice immorality.[40] The Christian counselor cannot ignore such biblical statements. The modern world, having rejected biblical teaching, largely is insensitive to the ultimate dangers and harms of the debauchery in which we live. Like the proverbial frog in the water pot whose temperature rises slowly as the surrounding water approaches the boiling point, many people are blithely unaware of the consequences of their attitudes or behavior—until it is too late to jump.

Most believers and many nonbelievers would agree that sex apart from marriage can have harmful effects in several areas.

1. *Emotional Effects.* Emotional turmoil, guilt, jealousy, fear, anxiety,

insecurity, self-condemnation, anger and depression are among the reactions that have been known to follow in the wake of sex apart from
marriage. One study of adolescent sexual experiences concluded that the
new attitudes of "freedom" have created "a psychological disaster" in
which young people "suffer from emotional deprivation and a kind of
deadening, as a result of their so-called free and unlimited sexual excitement." [41] Similar conclusions might be applied to adult sexual "freedom."

2. *Interpersonal Effects.* How does nonmarital sex (including masturbation and heavy petting) influence one's dating, family, marriage and
other relationships? To some extent the answer depends on one's sex,
educational level, income and ethnic group.[42] A so-called "double standard" still exists in which women tend to be more severely criticized for
nonabstinence than men. This is true especially at lower income and
socioeconomic levels. It probably is true, also, that men are more tolerant
of nonmarital sex than women, and this in turn may influence how males
and females are affected by sex outside of marriage. Although there is
some evidence to suggest that premarital and extramarital sex do not
influence marriages adversely,[43] there are other examples of situations in
which marriages have disintegrated, careers (and ministries) have been
wrecked, families have been broken up, and personal relationships have
been destroyed because of nonmarital sexual actions.

3. *Spiritual Effects.* As we have seen, fornication, adultery, lust and
other forms of nonmarital sex are condemned in Scripture and described
as sin. The Christian is obligated to forsake sin and follow the teachings
of Christ. Attempting to maintain a Christian witness while engaging in
sinful sexual practices is a contradiction. If the sexual immorality continues, one's spiritual vitality and influence are certain to decline. Sin
must be confessed and forsaken if one is to expect spiritual growth and
avoid spiritual deadness.

4. *Physical Effects.* It is well known that sex apart from marriage
increases the prospects of illegitimate pregnancies and venereal disease—
both of which are increasing at a currently alarming rate. There is also
evidence that sexual intercourse within marriage is influenced by nonmarital sex. Some popular viewpoints maintain that the influence is
usually good, others say the effects are neutral, some say the influence is
harmful—and each view has research evidence to support its claim. The
Christian counselor must accept the biblical teaching on the ultimate
harmfulness of nonmarital sex. This harmfulness is most apparent when
guilt, mistrust, emotional involvements in other relationships, comparisons with other partners, anger, anxiety, or insecurity are brought to the
marriage bed. In such circumstances or when at least one partner finds
major sexual fulfillment apart from marriage, it is difficult for a married
couple to attain maximum satisfaction and fulfillment.

As sexual standards continue to change it is probable that the debate about "effects" will continue. It is difficult for any researcher or writer to maintain complete neutrality in evaluating such a sensitive and important issue as the influences of sex apart from marriage. Although the Christian counselor should be alert to these studies, he or she must recognize that our ultimate authority is not scientific data or cultural mores—important as these are. The Christian's ultimate authority is the Bible, God's Word.

Counseling and Sex Apart from Marriage

Several years ago, two counselors suggested why "sex talks with adolescents go wrong." [44] Too often, they said, counselors fail to listen, take a condemning, moralizing attitude, transmit inaccurate information, show shock or excessive curiosity, fail to keep confidentiality, or are too quick to give "easy answers." More effective is sexual counseling which accomplishes the following.

1. *Look at Your Own Attitudes.* Someone once defined counseling as a relationship between two anxious people. Perhaps this is never more true than with sexual counseling. Embarrassed, ill-at-ease, and uncertain how to proceed, counselors sometimes show shock, discomfort, or a tendency to provide pat answers which may do nothing to help anxious, searching counselees.

Much more helpful is an understanding, informed, compassionate attitude which acknowledges the reality of sin, the power of temptation, and the healing of forgiveness. To be outraged, embarrassed, vindictive, or condemning does nothing to help. Instead, such attitudes alienate the counselee when help is most needed, and create more anxiety or anger. Even worse, a nonunderstanding counselor can batter self-esteem and communicate hopelessness. This, in turn, can drive the counselee back into further immorality.

When we learn of sexual involvement apart from marriage, it is easy to feel angered and threatened. Showing a realistic, understanding attitude is not easy, especially if we know the persons involved. Here we need divine help to show love without compromising our biblical standards, compassion without denying reality, and directness without becoming vindictive. If sexual counseling is too threatening or too difficult, we must evaluate our attitudes (perhaps with the help of another counselor), and possibly avoid this kind of helping until our attitudes become more therapeutic to others.

2. *Listen with Sensitivity.* This is a basic starting point for all counseling but sometimes it is forgotten when we are presented with sexual issues. By listening, we convey our desire to understand and our willingness to help with the counselee's real problem. It is quite appropriate to ask clarifying questions (provided that these are intended to increase our understanding and not to satisfy our curiosity). Try to avoid giving advice,

preaching, expressing opinions, or even quoting Scripture, at least until you have a clear perspective on the problem.

At times during the course of counseling, you will hear about the sexual exploits of some person who is respected, even in the church. Initially this will come as a shock but instead of reacting with anger or gossip, try to verify whether or not the information is correct (sometimes informers make allegations which are untrue and arise out of the counselee's own insecurities). If the information does, indeed, appear to be valid, it is appropriate to approach the accused person, first alone and then, if necessary, with one or two brothers.[45] An attitude of concern and understanding, coupled with a willingness to listen sensitively, provides the accused person with an opportunity to talk, a chance to experience divine forgiveness, and possibly a willingness to take responsibility for getting further help. An attitude of confrontation and condemnation, without sensitive listening, creates resistance, defensiveness, and sometimes anger, which make confession and restitution much more difficult.

3. *Examine Attitudes.* As we listen, we begin to understand the counselee's values and attitudes toward sex. Such attitudes often determine sexual behavior, and before there can be changed actions, there must be changed values. Be alert, also, to the counselee's knowledge about sex. Misinformation and misunderstanding frequently contribute to sexual behavior which the counselee later regrets.

4. *Help with Practical Issues.* Counseling always is most effective when we deal with specifics. Sometimes counselees need support and practical suggestions for resisting sexual approaches, fleeing temptation,[46] terminating sexual relationships, or informing a mate or parents about illicit sex or an illegitimate pregnancy. It also may be helpful for counselees to discuss their feelings about masturbation, premarital or extramarital intercourse, homosexuality, abortion, or related issues. Once again, it is not helpful to give advice too quickly, but neither is it helpful to maintain a consistent "nondirective" approach which gives little practical guidance and ignores the clear teachings of the Bible.

In dealing with practical issues, remember that people always respond best when the desire and motivation for change come from within. Instead of telling counselees what to do, encourage them to think of different courses of action which might work. Point out dangers or problems which counselees might not see, and then encourage commitment to one of the alternatives which does not violate biblical teaching. If such action fails to resolve or reduce the problem, help the counselee find another alternative and keep giving guidance, support and encouragement until the situation improves.

5. *Demonstrate Forgiveness.* At the heart of the Christian message is the issue of forgiveness. Because God forgives, we can have freedom from guilt, abundant life on earth and eternal life in heaven.[47] It is inconsistent

and confusing to preach forgiveness but never to show it. As believers, we experience God's forgiveness but we are expected to forgive others.[48] If we model forgiveness, we help some counselees recognize the reality of God's forgiveness in their own lives, we help others forgive people who have participated in sexual acts apart from marriage, and we encourage counselees to forgive themselves, just as God and the counselor forgive.

6. *Stimulate Sound Attitudes, Christian Behavior, and the Securing of Accurate Information.* Counseling is often a specialized form of Christian education. At times the counselor must give accurate information— hence it is important that such information be available for references.[49] Many counselees also need help in learning self-control, evaluating current sexual standards, forming a personal set of values which is consistent with biblical truth, determining appropriate dating behavior, evaluating the moral issues surrounding masturbation, and understanding biblical teachings on sex. Often these will be discussed openly, especially if counselees are encouraged to ask questions which are answered candidly and without shock or condemnation. Often, too, the counselor's behavior and general comments will model an accurate and consistent picture of sex as God intended.

7. *Be Alert to the Need for Referral.* Counselors frequently face situations in which they must decide if referral to another counselor would be more helpful to a counselee. Referral should be considered when counselees appear to have more complicated sexual problems than the counselor can handle, when their sexual problems are accompanied by considerable depression and/or anxiety, when there is great guilt or self-condemnation, when there are extremely disturbed behavior and thinking in the counselee, when sexual perversions are involved, when counselees need detailed information which the counselor cannot give, when the sex problem appears to have physical or legal implications, when the counselor is too shocked or embarrassed to continue counseling, or when he or she feels a strong and persisting sexual attraction to the counselee. Sometimes other help is not available and at times the counselee may refuse to see another counselor. At such times the counselor must decide whether to continue counseling, to terminate the relationship, or to insist on referral. Remember that referral can be threatening to many people. Such individuals need to be shown that referral is common, is not an indication of rejection by the present counselor, and ultimately is for the greatest benefit of the counselee.

Preventing Sex Apart from Marriage

While fornication, adultery, lust, and other forms of immorality clearly violate scriptural teaching, it should be emphasized that not all sexual behavior apart from marriage is wrong. Dating, for example, is sexual activity which we do not want to prevent, although the Christian counselor does want to help people avoid the immorality which sometimes comes with dating relationships.

1. *Sex Education.* Where should people learn about sex? At school? At home? At church? Most educators and many parents would agree with the first two answers, but there still is controversy concerning the church's role in sex education.

The church can influence sex education in two ways—*indirectly*, by encouraging and instructing parents about what and how to teach at home, and *directly* through sermons, classes, discussion groups and retreats. This teaching must include giving factual information, but of equal importance is teaching biblical morality (see the earlier section in this chapter). Such teaching must be in good taste, honest and practical. To be sure it is accurate, do not hesitate to bring in resource persons such as a physician or psychologist who can give specialized information. To be sure it is relevant, encourage honest questioning and try to avoid pat answers. With younger people, written questions submitted anonymously may be the best way to uncover real issues. With older students and adults there may be value in reading or discussing some of the available books in this area.[50]

2. *Consideration of Practical Issues.* In a sense, this really is a variation of sex education. Although issues such as premarital and extramarital sex are clearly discussed in the Bible, other practical sexual matters are not even mentioned. Let us consider two of these.

(a) Dating and Petting. Dating has changed radically in the past several decades. Chaperones are a thing of the past and so, for many people, are church socials and dates without heavy petting or sexual intimacies.

Dating, the relationship between two people of the opposite sex, provides mutual human companionship, better understanding of the opposite sex, greater self-understanding, sexual stimulation and sexual fulfillment. The rules and practices of dating vary geographically and change frequently. Often dating involves little physical contact except for "healthy touching" which conveys concern, interest, compassion, empathy and affection. In many cases, however, touch is much more sensual in nature and intended to bring sexual arousal. This is known as *petting*, a conscious mutual body stimulation and exploration designed to bring erotic arousal through the fondling of sexually excitable areas.

Considerable debate and confusion surround the issue of petting. For those who see no harm in nonmarital sex, petting is no problem. If it leads to sexual intercourse, this is acceptable to the parties involved. But what if the couple believes that intercourse should be confined to marriage? Can there be such a thing as "responsible petting," which exists for mutual discovery and sexual gratification apart from intercourse?[51] While many Christian leaders would say "no," and argue for total abstinence, most young Christian singles show by their actions that their answer is "yes." Often young people look to the church for guidance in this most significant area of prevention. In helping, several guidelines should be kept in mind and communicated, perhaps in public lectures followed by discussion. These are listed in Table 20–1.

There are no easy answers to the questions of dating and petting. But even difficult questions are better discussed than ignored or dismissed with a few pious, insensitive admonitions.

(b) Masturbation. The stimulation of one's own genitals to the point of orgasm is a very common form of sexual arousal apart from marriage.

Table 20–1
Some Principles for Dating and Sexual Involvements Apart from Marriage *

1. God made us sexual beings. Sexual attractiveness and sexual feelings are good, not sinful.

2. Because all persons, male and female, are created in the image of God, we should have a deep respect for the personhood of each one. *Persons* are to be loved; *things* are to be used. To use another person is to violate his/her personality by making that person an object.

3. Christians must take seriously God's directions for expressing sexuality. Anything done contrary to God's will as it is specifically revealed in Scripture is sin. The Bible gives us many strong, stern warnings about the misuse of sex: Prov. 5:1–20, Eph. 4:19, 20, Col. 3:5, 1 Cor. 6:9–11. Yet in the right context physical love is a beautiful thing.

4. God intends his people to live holy lives. They must be a reflection of his perfect character. The guiding principle in every Christian's life should be, "Whatever you do, do all to the glory of God" (1 Cor. 10:31b).

5. Sexual sins—be they lustful actions or fantasies, sexual arousal that is defrauding another person, or extramarital sex of any kind—can be forgiven when the person turns to Christ in repentance. God does not want his people to be burdened with guilt. He freely forgives us on the basis of our faith in Jesus and his redemptive action for us on the cross.

6. God, through his Holy Spirit, is the source of personal, practical power to help us guide and control our sexuality. Sex is not a *drive* that we are enslaved to. Instead, it is an *appetite* we can feed, either illicitly or spiritually (in the context of marriage). The choice is ours and God helps us along the way by cleansing us on a moment-by-moment basis from wrong attitudes and actions (1 John 1:9; 1 Cor. 6:11).

7. From God's perspective the only proper place for sexual intercourse is within the context of a mutual, lifelong commitment of a man and a woman, in the form of marriage. God has his people's best interests in mind when he commands them to "wait until marriage."

8. Petting is a common activity among nonmarried people. Unlike foreplay which is a tender preparation for sexual intercourse, petting is a tender exploration of one another by two people who do not intend to have intercourse.

9. Petting has many risks, spiritual and psychological. One of the

first adverse effects of heavy petting is illustrated by the "Law of Diminishing Returns." This psychological and biological principle holds that with constant repetition over a period of time, the effect of a stimulus on an individual tends to decrease. To keep the same effect the stimulus must later be increased. Petting is physical stimulation of this variety. After reaching a certain point of intimacy, a couple almost always finds it difficult to retreat to a less intimate level of involvement. Petting also may create the desire for more intimate sexual union. In advanced stages, petting is especially difficult to stop and may result in frustration, tenseness and irritability. The lack of release may unleash bitterness against the other partner as well.

*Adapted from Joan Barlett, Marty Hansen, Isolde Anderson, and Jay Terbush. "Dating and Heavy Petting," unpublished paper, Trinity Evangelical Divinity School, 1977.

Research studies generally conclude that about 95 percent of all males, and a lower percentage (50 percent to 90 percent) of all females have masturbated to the point of orgasm at least some time in their lives. The frequency of masturbation declines following adolescence and after marriage, but it does not disappear. Apparently most married men and many married women continue to masturbate at times throughout their lives— and regular church attenders masturbate as much as the nonattenders.[52]

But many of these church attenders are greatly bothered by their masturbation behavior. There is no medical evidence to indicate that the practice is harmful to the body or that it interferes physically with subsequent sexual intercourse. The myths surrounding masturbation (e.g., it produces insanity, pimples, or increased genital size; it will prevent enjoyable sexual intercourse in later life; it indicates a dirty mind; it can be controlled by cold showers or athletics) have proven to be false, and professional counselors rarely consider it an abnormality. Nevertheless, masturbation often is accompanied by guilt, frustration, feelings of inferiority, and anger over its compulsive grip. Unaware that the practice is so prevalent, and afraid of condemnation, many people—including Christians—struggle with the problem alone and without noticeable improvement. All of this has led one observer to conclude that masturbation is the most frequently discussed, most roundly condemned and most universally practiced form of sexual behavior.

Should the church say anything about masturbation? It should if it is concerned about the personal and spiritual problems of its members— especially young males. Can the Christian counselor help people who struggle with masturbation and prevent its start, continuance or increase? This is a more difficult question to answer, but the following observations can be helpful if shared, perhaps in small, same-sex groups.

—Masturbation is very common and of no harm physically.

—Masturbation is never mentioned in the Bible. This does not make it right, but it does show that masturbation is not a major sin—otherwise the Bible surely would have mentioned it.

—Masturbation can be helpful in relieving sexual or other tensions, and it is a substitute for sexual intercourse apart from marriage. Many singles and married people away from their spouses masturbate as a sexual release.

—Christian counselors differ in their view of masturbation. It has been called "sin," "a gift from God," and an issue which is "no big deal . . . on God's list of priorities."

—Masturbation clearly has some potentially harmful influences. It can produce intense guilt; can be a means of escaping from loneliness and interpersonal (including sexual) relationships with others into a world of fantasy; can increase self-centeredness and lowered self-esteem; and can stimulate and be stimulated by lust—in which case it clearly is wrong.

—Masturbators should understand the biblical perspective on sex and marriage. Masturbation clearly is a substitute activity.

—Masturbation is rarely helped by a direct determination to quit. This focuses attention on the issue, increases anxiety, and makes failure more incriminating.

—Masturbation can be reduced by prayer, a sincere willingness to let the Holy Spirit control, involvement in busy activities involving others, an avoidance of sexually arousing material (such as erotic pictures or novels), a practice of not dwelling on harmful sexual fantasies, and a recognition that sin (including lust) will be forgiven when it is confessed with sincerity and with sorrow.

Any person who writes or speaks about masturbation is certain to be criticized. In the absence of clear biblical guidance on this issue we are left with a variety of conflicting opinions, often given by sincere, compassionate counselors whose views we should understand and respect. Surely masturbation is a sin when it is accompanied by a lusting for sexual relations which God forbids, when it masters us, and when it hinders our relationship with Christ. Masturbators need to know that others accept them, that God helps and forgives, and that open communication about masturbation helps to diffuse its destructive impact. Creating guilt and worry over masturbation may be one of Satan's major ways of attacking Christians and thus the church should not ignore this issue. But the writer of this book agrees with David Seamands, who once wrote:

> When there is open communication on the subject of sex, including masturbation . . . it will . . . not become a major problem. . . . It's high time we stop making such a "big deal" out of masturbation and give it the well-deserved unimportance it merits.[53]

3. *Providing Realistic Alternatives.* Sex, as we have seen, involves more than genital stimulation. It involves and pervades the whole issue of intimacy, communication and interpersonal relationships. Like all of the

issues discussed in this book, sex is best considered in the context of a caring, supportive Christian community. It is here that people can feel accepted and loved; that healthy and meaningful activities can be provided especially for young people and those adults who otherwise might find themselves bored, lonely or lured into morally dangerous situations; that problems and questions can be discussed; that values and sexual ethics can be formulated through counseling or group interaction; and that dating can be considered along with the issues of petting and the importance of dating other believers only. If, as some have suggested, the devil attacks us most strongly in the area of sex, it is here that he can be resisted—through the provision of honest, sensitive help, the support of a caring body of believers, and the power of the Holy Spirit who lives within every believer.

Conclusions about Sex Apart from Marriage

There are times when every Christian counselor faces conflict between social pressure and the Bible, or between scientific data and Scripture. What does one do in such situations?

Most of us, perhaps, would examine the scientific, social and scriptural data to see if the conflict can be resolved. If we assume that all truth is consistent and comes from God, then the wisdom of this world, if it is *really* true, cannot be in conflict with the truth that comes via written revelation. If conflict persists, however, many Christians, including the author of this book, would agree that the Word of God must be accepted as the final authority to which other findings must be submitted.

This is not a popular view but it raises questions which must be considered whenever sex outside of marriage is discussed. Society's values, and even some scientific data, contradict biblical teachings. Where, then, do we find the principles which will guide our counseling and our own moral behavior? The Bible isn't always explicit on these issues but the Christian people-helper sees the Word of God as the only source of stability and certainty on morals. This, then, must be our guide in all counseling, not just in dealing with the issue of sex apart from marriage.

Suggestions for Further Reading
Collins, Gary R., ed. *The Secrets of Our Sexuality*. Waco, TX: Word, 1976.
Kennedy, Eugene. *Sexual Counseling*. New York: Seabury, 1977.
* Miles, Herbert J. *The Dating Game*. Grand Rapids: Zondervan, 1975.
* ———. *Sexual Understanding Before Marriage*. Grand Rapids: Zondervan, 1971.
* Scanzoni, Letha. *Sex Is a Parent Affair*. Glendale, CA: Regal, 1973.
* ———. *Why Wait? A Christian View of Premarital Sex*. Grand Rapids: Baker, 1975.
Smedes, Lewis B. *Sex for Christians*. Grand Rapids: Wm. B. Eerdmans, 1976.
* Stafford, Tim. *A Love Story: Questions and Answers on Sex*. Grand Rapids: Zondervan, 1977.

Wheat, Ed, and Wheat, Gaye. *Intended for Pleasure*. Old Tappan, NJ: Revell, 1977.
* White, John. *Eros Defiled: The Christian and Sexual Sin*. Downers Grove, IL: Inter-Varsity, 1977.

Footnotes

1. Eleanor D. Macklin, "Going Very Steady: Cohabitation in College," *Psychology Today* 8 (November, 1974): 53–59; James Hassett, "A New Look at Living Together," *Psychology Today* 11 (December, 1977): 82–83.

2. This is true especially among women. See David E. Shape, *Interpersonal Sexuality* (Philadelphia: Saunders, 1975), pp. 239–257.

3. Lewis B. Smedes, *Sex for Christians* (Grand Rapids: Wm. B. Eerdmans, 1976), p. 20.

4. Ibid., p. 42.

5. See 1 Cor. 7.

6. Rom. 13:14; 1 Cor. 7:9.

7. Judd Marmor, in *Journal of the American Medical Association* 217 (July 1971). Copyright 1971, American Medical Association.

8. Exod. 22:16–19; Lev. 18; Matt. 5:27; 1 Cor. 6:9; Heb. 13:4.

9. Heb. 11:25, KJV.

10. H. J. Miles, "Fornication," in *The Zondervan Pictorial Encyclopedia of the Bible*, ed. Merrill C. Tenney (Grand Rapids: Zondervan, 1975), 2: 601–602.

11. John 8:41; Acts 15:20, 29; 21:25; Rom. 1:20; 1 Cor. 5:1; 6:13, 18; 2 Cor. 6:17; 12:21; Eph. 5:3.

12. 1 Cor. 7:2; 1 Thess. 4:3.

13. Matt. 5:32; 19:9.

14. Matt. 5:19; Mark 7:21; 1 Cor. 6:9; Gal. 5:19.

15. Herbert J. Miles, *Sexual Understanding Before Marriage* (Grand Rapids: Zondervan, 1971), p. 205.

16. Isa. 57:3; Jer. 3:8, 9; Ezek. 23:43; James 4:4; Rev. 2:20, 23.

17. Exod. 20:14; Lev. 18:20; Deut. 5:18; 22:22–24; Matt. 9:3–12; John 8:4.

18. 1 Cor. 6:9, 10; Gal. 5:19, 20; Col. 3:5.

19. Gen. 1:27, 28, 31.

20. Gen. 2:25; 3:9–11.

21. 1 Cor. 6:12, 13, 18–20, *Living Bible*.

22. Prov. 5:1–8; 1 Cor. 6:8; 1 Thess. 4:3; Eph. 5:3–7; Col. 3:5, 6.

23. 1 Cor. 7:9.

24. Matt. 5:27, 28.

25. Smedes, *Sex for Christians*, p. 210.

26. Ibid., pp. 210–13.

27. James 3:1–12.

28. Eph. 5:3, 4, *Living Bible*.

29. Jay E. Adams, *The Christian Counselor's Manual* (Nutley, NJ: Presbyterian and Reformed, 1973), p. 401.

30. Charlie W. Shedd, *The Stork Is Dead* (Waco, TX: Word, 1968), pp. 70–73.

31. James Dobson, *Preparing for Adolescence* (Santa Ana: Vision House, 1978), p. 87.

32. 1 Cor. 6:12.

33. This appears to be the message of 1 Cor. 6, 7.

34. This distinction is made by Smedes, *Sex for Christians*, pp. 190–200. Some of the discussion which follows is drawn from Smedes's analysis.

35. Matt. 15:18, 19.

36. Eph. 6:10–13.

37. 1 Pet. 5:8; 2 Cor. 11:14, 15.

38. Some of this research is summarized in Shape, *Interpersonal Sexuality;* Macklin, "Going Very Steady"; and Ira L. Reiss, *Premarital Sexual Standards in America* (New York: The Free Press, 1960).

39. John 12:35–40; 1 Cor. 2:14; Heb. 13:3.

40. Rom. 1:24, 28–32.

41. H. Deutsch, *Selected Problems of Adolescence* (New York: International Universities Press, 1967), p. 102.

42. Reiss, *Premarital Sexual Standards.*

43. Shape, *Interpersonal Sexuality.*

44. Gordon Jensen and Myra Robbins, "Ten Reasons Why Sex Talks with Adolescents Go Wrong," *Medical Aspects of Human Sexuality* (July 1975): 7 ff.

45. Matt. 18:15, 16.

46. 1 Tim. 6:9–11.

47. John 10:10; 3:16.

48. Matt. 6:12–15; Mark 11:25 (26).

49. A good source is Ed Wheat and Gaye Wheat, *Intended for Pleasure* (Old Tappan, NJ: Revell, 1977).

50. Please note the "Suggestions for Further Reading." Stafford's book is for young people. The books by Miles and Scanzoni are for older teens. More sophisticated are the books by White and the Wheats. The book by Smedes, *Sex for Christians,* is more controversial and best reversed for more mature and thoughtful readers.

51. This view is argued persuasively in Smedes, *Sex for Christians,* pp. 152–60.

52. These statistics, with supporting studies, are reported in James Leslie McCary, *McCary's Human Sexuality,* 3d ed. (New York: Van Nostrand, 1978), pp. 262-64.

53. David A. Seamands, "Sex, Inside and Outside of Marriage," in *The Secrets of our Sexuality,* ed. Gary R. Collins (Waco, TX: Word, 1976), p. 156.

21

Sex within Marriage

SEX HAS BEEN DESCRIBED AS "ONLY ONE STRAND" IN THE CABLE THAT ties a husband and wife together. But sex is a central strand, intimately tied in with other aspects of a relationship. According to Masters and Johnson, at least 50 percent of marriages are flawed by some form of sexual maladjustment or dysfunction.[1] Sometimes the sex problems come first and produce marital discord. In other cases, the marital conflict comes first and generates such anger, disappointment, resentment, fear and tension that mutually satisfying sex is no longer occurring and perhaps no longer possible. In each case sex and marriage are so closely interwoven that problems in one area invariably influence the other.

In reading this chapter, two limitations should be kept in mind. First, in spite of the close relationship between sexual and marital adjustment, this chapter will focus primarily on sex. Marriage problems are considered in chapter 13. Second, the following pages are restricted to discussions of sex between a husband and wife within marriage. In our age of sexual promiscuity many people, including scientific writers, have come to see sex as little more than flesh rubbing on flesh for the purpose of achieving erotic experiences. Warmth, concern, love, trust, and especially commitment are all relegated to a position that is of secondary importance to the sensations that come from foreplay and orgasm. Although these pages will draw on the research of writers who study sex between "partners," the emphasis here will be on sex between "marriage partners" who have committed themselves to one another in a marriage relationship.

There still are some people, including pastors, who believe that sex and sex problems are topics for physicians to discuss with patients, but not issues for the Christian counselor. This narrow viewpoint is fading. God created sex when he made the world and created human beings. Sex was part of his plan, something to be enjoyed by the human race but something marred and disfigured by the Fall. Helping people deal with sex problems is an important and significant responsibility for any Christian counselor.

The Bible and Sex within Marriage

Sex is not a taboo subject in the Bible. Almost every Book says something about sex and some of the descriptions (as in Song of Solomon, for example) are explicit and even sexually arousing. Not all of these references can be considered here, but several are major and represent clear biblical teaching about sex within marriage.

1. *Sex Was Created by God and Is Good.* When he created human beings, God made us male and female and declared that his creation was good. He instructed the first husband and wife to "be fruitful and multiply" —instructions which clearly involved nakedness and sexual intercourse.[2] Centuries later, the divinely inspired writer of Hebrews proclaimed that "coitus in marriage is honorable in all and undefiled."[3] It is not something shameful or, at best, tolerated by God. Sex is an evidence of God's goodness. It is something for which we can express praise and gratitude.

2. *Sex Is for Propagation and Pleasure.* The first birth recorded in the Bible is described as a result of sexual intercourse plus "the help of the Lord."[4] Obviously sex is involved in the conception of children and in the divine command to multiply, but is sex also intended for pleasure?

Perhaps the clearest answer comes in the Song of Solomon. In vivid poetic language, this little book describes the pleasures of physical sex between married lovers. The descriptions are explicit but never offensive.[5]

The same is true of Proverbs. "Rejoice with the wife of thy youth," we read.

> As a loving hind and a graceful doe,
> Let her breasts satisfy you at all times;
> Be exhilarated always with her love.[6]

In the New Testament, we read that a husband and wife actually deprive one another when they refuse to give physical pleasure and satisfaction to each other. The only exception to this is when a married couple agrees to abstain from sex temporarily and for the purpose of retreating spiritually for a special time of prayer.[7]

3. *Sex Is for Marriage.* Whenever the Bible speaks approvingly about sex, it refers to married couples. Quoting Genesis, Jesus spoke with favor about the permanence and "one flesh" nature of marriage. Paul noted that marriage (not intercourse outside of marriage) is the desirable answer for a person who is struggling with sexual self-control. When such marriage occurs, however, the husband and wife are to give their bodies freely to each other and not to hold back sexually.[8]

4. *Sexual Abuse Is Condemned Strongly.* Modern readers, accustomed to a widespread looseness of sexual standards in the society, might be amazed at the vehemence with which sexual promiscuity is condemned in the Bible. Adultery is pictured as something very attractive but ultimately destructive and foolish.[9]

The language sounds outdated to more modern ears, but the words of a post-World-War-II writer are undoubtedly true: "Out of sex, rightly used, arise some of the most profound satisfactions, most meaningful human relationships, richest beauty of which man is capable. Out of sex misused arise some of the profoundest disappointments, most tragic interpersonal relationships, grossest ugliness known to man." [10]

Many people do not believe these conclusions which, however, are consistent with biblical teaching. God, who created sex, commands us to abstain from sexual immorality. This is not because God is determined to take away our fun. It is because he knows the dangers of sexual abuse and wants to protect us from the misery which comes when we give in to "lustful passions" and accept the sexual values of people who do not know God.[11]

In summary, therefore, the Bible is very honest about sex and intercourse. Sex was created by God for procreation and pleasure within marriage, but it can be misused and abused. When that happens, problems, difficulties, and regrets arise later, if not immediately.

The Causes of Sexual Problems within Marriage

Many people approach marriage with anticipation of the sexual freedom to follow. But many of these same people are disappointed when they discover (sometimes as early as the honeymoon; sometimes later) that sex within marriage is not as exciting and consistently pleasurable as they had hoped or expected. There are numerous causes for this.

1. *Misinformation.* In spite of the modern openness about sex, counselors often are amazed at the ignorance and lack of accurate knowledge that characterize many couples. "Within any marital unit," wrote sex researcher William Masters, "one can anticipate that the couple has a vast amount of misinformation, misconception, and quite simply, inadequate knowledge of sexual physiology." [12]

This ignorance may come from any or all of the following: lack of accurate sex education, misinformation acquired from peers, inhibitions which prevent people from asking questions, unrealistic expectations gleaned from movies, books or one's own fantasies, and failure to realize that male and female sexual responses differ from each other. Sexual instinct and urges are inborn but a knowledge about love-making must be learned. When the learning is inadequate, sexual adjustment problems often arise.

2. *Fatigue, Haste, and Lack of Opportunity.* Fatigue has been described as the most common cause of unsatisfactory sex. Mutually pleasurable sexual intercourse takes physical and mental energy. It also takes a relaxed, unhurried attitude which is not greatly concerned about time.

When a young couple is first married, they can sleep late on weekends, and have no children to demand their attention or to interfere with sexual spontaneity. Such couples also have a great deal of vigor and natural energy. As they grow older, however, added responsibilities at home and work create physical and mental fatigue. The husband and wife may have an undiminished desire for sex but they also have less energy and need more sleep. Growing children demand time. Their presence prevents sexual spontaneity in the parents and often interferes with privacy. As a result of these influences many couples are forced to reduce the frequency of sexual intercourse. And when they are able to get alone in bed, there often is a desire to "hurry so we can get some sleep," or to "keep very quiet so the kids won't wake up." Such common concerns interfere with free, relaxed sex and create sexual tensions within the marriage.

3. *Boredom*. After a couple has been married for a while, they get accustomed to each other. They run out of novel ways to have sex, foreplay becomes shorter, and coitus becomes routine. After several years, the sexual activities which once were so exciting have become monotonous. Partners spend little time stimulating one another sexually and sometimes there is a lack of interest in one's appearance. Sex under such circumstances is not very fulfilling and the stage has then been set for an extramarital affair with someone who is more exciting and novel than one's own mate.

Some couples cope with their boredom by fantasy. During the act of intercourse they fantasize about previous, desired, or exotic sexual involvements. Fantasies, of course, are common and not always wrong. Sometimes they add variety to sex and increase its pleasure. But they also can be guilt-inducing for Christians who are seeking to avoid lust and who fear that their fantasies border on the lustful. In addition, fantasies can hinder intimacy and sharing if one individual can reach orgasm only by thinking of some person other than one's mate.

4. *Cultural Attitudes and Past Experience*. The society in which one lives often influences sexual attitudes and behavior. In past years, at least in our culture, sex was not discussed openly but marital fidelity was the expected norm. Men were assumed to be the sex experts whose virility was acknowledged and whose occasional extramarital experiences were "winked at," at least in some circles. Women were assumed to be passive and lacking in sexual interest or arousal. Some people considered sex to be dirty and a taboo subject for polite society. Such attitudes may have contributed to a relatively low frequency of intercourse outside of marriage, but they also may have led to misunderstanding and sexual frustration.

Then things began to change. Sex became a subject which could be discussed more openly. Old taboos began to break down, sexual intercourse outside of marriage became more accepted and frequent, and the media—especially television and popular magazines—began the long, continuing process of blatantly challenging the Christian based ethic of marital fidelity and sexual responsibility. This prevalence of sexual discussion has created great public awareness about sex, has elevated our expectations about sexual enjoyment, has made us less tolerant of sexual problems within our own lives and marriages, has given cultural sanction to extramarital sex, and has led to a belief that sexual awareness, fulfillment and participation are *the* signs of healthy adult maleness and femaleness.[13]

Such cultural expectations can generate anxiety and feelings of insecurity in people who do not conform. Young people, whose sexual urges are especially difficult to control, frequently slip into a pattern of sexual experiences where there often is the fear of getting caught and a pressure to experience orgasm as quickly as possible. When intercourse is hurried, primarily self-centered, or lacking in relaxed tenderness, sexual fulfillment is often diminished so that people feel cheated and disappointed. Many feel guilty and somehow "different" because their virginity, which can never be regained, has been lost forever. In reaction to this, some people move into a life style of seeking sexual satisfaction with a variety of partners, some of whom are left feeling guilty and debased. Still others maintain that their sexual freedom is liberating and free of harmful consequences, but others struggle with guilt and feelings of self-criticism.

Often, however, these early experiences have adverse effects on later marriages. When initially high expectations have not been met, there is less of a willingness to work at solving sexual problems and more of an inclination to seek satisfaction elsewhere in a society which sanctions promiscuity. Later sexual problems, such as premature ejaculation or impotency, have been found to be more related to ingrained attitudes and to early experiences than to physiological malfunctioning. Cultural standards, unrealistic expectations, earlier unfulfilling sexual experiences, and previously learned attitudes, therefore, can all contribute to later sexual problems.

5. *Physical Causes.* Sometimes sexual problems have physical origins such as endocrine disturbances, obesity, diabetes, low energy level, or the weakening of vaginal muscles in women who have given birth. While psychological causes are most often at the bases of sexual problems, physical causes are always a possibility. Sometimes physiological malfunctioning—real or imagined—is used as an excuse for sexual difficulties. Almost always, when physiology creates sexual problems, psychological tensions come along as well and a vicious circle develops: the physiological problem creates psychological tension which in turn hinders physical functioning.

Perhaps the most influential physical hindrance to sexual fulfillment is the use of drugs, including alcohol. Since alcohol relaxes people, minimizes anxiety and makes them less inhibited, some couples drink before intercourse. In quantity, however, alcohol dulls sensations. It is one of the principle causes of impotence in males. Such impotence creates anxiety and a fear that one is sexually inadequate. These anxieties hinder further attempts at intercourse, especially if the man has a few more drinks to relax before "trying again."

6. *Psychological Blocks.* Some people approach marriage with the belief that sexual adjustment and fulfillment will be easy, automatic, fast in coming, and permanent. Most often, this does not happen, sometimes because of fears, guilt feelings, anxieties, anger or other psychological blocks to satisfying sex. Several of these are very common.

(a) Doubts about One's Masculinity or Femininity. Perhaps many people go through life, especially early adulthood, wondering if they are *really* masculine or feminine. This concern is a special problem in our society where traditional male and female roles are breaking down and where there is confusion over the meaning of masculinity and femininity.

One place where these roles are clear is in bed. It is the male penis that enters the female vagina. If a couple, especially the male, cannot perform in bed, this is a great threat to his sexual adequacy. For this reason, books on sex emphasize the psychological trauma that often accompanies impotency in males. Female hysterectomies also are difficult psychologically since women who know that they can no longer bear children sometimes feel, unconsciously, that a part of their femininity has gone.

When there are problems in the genital area, one's masculinity or femininity is threatened. When there are doubts about one's maleness or femaleness, the anxiety often hinders sexual functioning and another vicious cycle begins.

(b) Fear. Sexual fears are of various types. There can be fear of being interrupted in the midst of intercourse, fear of pregnancy, fear that sex will hurt, fear of not being able to perform adequately, fear of being compared with previous sexual partners, fear that one's sexual advances will be rejected, fear of being ridiculed, fear that one's penis is too small, fear of losing self-control, and fear of intimacy. Each of these can be sexually inhibiting since fear and love (including sexual love) are mutually exclusive.[14]

(c) Embarrassment. In spite of our cultural openness about sex, some people are embarrassed about their own bodies and about sex. They are concerned that sex is dirty—even within marriage—and as a result they are unwilling or unable to relax sexually.

(d) Differences in Sexual Preferences. Sometimes there are differences in the frequency with which a husband and wife desire sexual intercourse (one wants it more frequently than the other), differences in preferred time for intercourse (one person wants it in the morning; the other wants it at night), and differences of opinion concerning what is appropriate for a couple (e.g., one wants oral-genital sexual contact, the other does not; one likes to try a variety of positions or locations for sex, the other does not); these differences of opinion are many and can create serious blocks to sexual satisfaction.

(e) Guilt. This is one of the most common psychological blocks to sexual fulfillment. Guilt over past sexual misconduct, present extramarital activities, homosexual tendencies, masturbation, or recurring fantasies can create sexual problems in marriage. When one attains sexual satisfaction apart from the marriage bed, sex with one's spouse will be less satisfying.

(f) Anger. It is difficult to enjoy sex if one is angry, resentful, bitter, or feeling that he or she has been manipulated into bed. Sexual intercourse is an expression of love, but real love cannot coexist with bitterness and continuing anger.

Such anger is not always directed at one's mate. Previously unresolved conflicts with parents or other persons, and an unwillingness to forgive others, can create sexual tensions at home.

7. *Marital Conflict.* Sex is a powerful weapon in marriage. Withholding sex, or demanding it, are ways in which some couples assert their authority and get favors or decisions from a partner. Sometimes this is discussed openly. More often sex is a passive way to react. "I'm too tired for sex" or "I don't feel well" may at times be ways of saying, "I'm going to get even with you by withholding sex."

It is difficult to determine which comes first—sexual problems or marriage problems. Sometimes one exists without the other. More often they go together, each hindering the other in a recurring fashion.

8. *Miscellaneous Causes.* Fatigue, fear of homosexual tendencies, worry about nonsexual issues such as finances or family tensions, environmental stress, inhibiting religious beliefs, overinvolvement in a career or other activities—these are among the other causes of sexual problems. For most people, sex occupies only a part of their thinking and energy. But sex is an important part of life. Sexual problems can arise from a variety of circumstances and can have profound influence on individuals and marriages.

The Effects of Sexual Problems within Marriage

When sexual problems come, some people simply "give up" and avoid trying to solve their difficulties. There may be a fear of discussing the frustration within or a resigned acceptance of the belief that things will never be better. Some get busy with other things and sincerely lose interest in sex. Others develop physical symptoms—like headaches, abdominal pain, fatigue, insomnia, or emotional distress [15]—all of which hide the sexual problem and provide an excuse for abstinence. In a surprisingly large number of young marriages, there is no sex at all, primarily because of the bride's fears and attitudes.[16] All of this can be very difficult for a mate who wants sexual fulfillment.

In addition to the avoidance of intercourse, sexual difficulties in marriage can lead to five major effects:

1. *Inability to Perform.* Within recent years numerous books and research reports have described some of the more common sexual problems within marriage. These include frigidity or "preorgasmic dysfunction" (the inability or unwillingness of a female to experience full sexual pleasure including orgasm), impotence (the inability of a male to achieve or maintain an erection for purposes of sexual intercourse), premature ejaculation (the ejaculation of semen, with a resulting loss of erection, immediately before, just at, or shortly after insertion of the penis into the vagina), and dyspareunia (painful intercourse). While each of these may have a physical basis, the cause more often is psychological.

Here is a classic example of the vicious cycle that has been mentioned earlier in this chapter. Psychological blocks to sexual fulfillment usually come first. Because of these fears and attitudes, sex is not satisfying. The realization that intercourse is not satisfying then intensifies the fears and creates stronger psychological blocks. This, in turn, makes sexual fulfillment even more unlikely. It then becomes difficult to distinguish the causes from the effects.

2. *Lowered Self-esteem.* Self-esteem and sexual capability often go together, especially in men. If intercourse is not mutually satisfying, the husband and wife may both have doubts about their sexual competence—doubts which sometimes are accentuated by the jokes of one's mate. If a man cannot maintain an erection or arouse his wife, he is likely to experience a loss in confidence about his sexual and manly capabilities. If his wife jokes about the fact that he must be losing his virility, this is an even greater blow to his self-esteem, and further hinders his ability to perform sexually.

3. *Selection of Substitutes.* When sex within marriage is not satisfying, husbands and wives often turn to substitute activities. These include the following:

(a) Masturbation. Stimulating one's own genitals to the point of orgasm is a common form of sexual behavior both among the unmarried and in married people, especially males, when intercourse is not possible. If sexual intercourse is not satisfying, it should come as no surprise that one or both of the partners may turn to a practice that depends only upon oneself and that has proven to be pleasurable in the past. The accompanying fantasies help bolster one's sexual self-esteem and remove any pressure to respond in bed with one's mate.

(b) Fantasies. These often accompany masturbation but also occur alone. If actual sexual intercourse is unpleasant, some people find that imagined sex in the form of increased fantasies becomes a "second-best" substitute.[17] However, like masturbation, such a substitute interferes with intimacy and ultimately creates more problems than it solves.

(c) Extramarital Sex. Infidelity—sex with someone other than one's mate—can cause sexual problems, but often it comes as a result of sexual problems in a marriage. According to Virginia Johnson, when sex within marriage is not satisfying, is threatening or otherwise distressful, thoughts of sex become very important in one's life.[18] There is a preoccupation with sex-for-the-sake-of-sex and this leads people into extramarital affairs, homosexual liaisons and/or group sexual experiences. But such affairs do little to give security, clarify identity, create feelings of competence, or provide permanent sexual satisfaction. Guilt, concerns about secrecy, and further frustration often result.

4. *Deteriorating Relationships.* Sexual problems often bring anger, resentment, interpersonal tension, communication breakdowns, and sometimes divorce. It would be overly simplistic to conclude that sexual problems cause divorce, but it is accurate to conclude that sexual tensions, coupled with other marital pressures, contribute to marriage breakups. It is possible, perhaps, but rare to have a really good marriage which also has sexual incompatibility.

5. *Increased Motivation.* Some couples, undoubtedly fewer than we might wish, face their sexual problems with a new determination to make sex better. Open to suggestions, disinclined to blame each other, and willing to work on the problems, these couples invariably see improvement both in their sexual relationships and in their marriages. These are the people with whom a counselor most likes to work.

Counseling and Sexual Problems within Marriage

Some counselors feel uncomfortable and embarrassed when discussing sex. There is no theological reason for this. Sex was created by God and is discussed frequently in his Word. Nevertheless, some may feel that sexual counseling violates the counselee's privacy and there is fear that sexual discussions will be stimulating or otherwise harmful to the counselor. In such cases, it is quite acceptable to refer counselees to another counselor. But for those who choose to counsel people in the area of sex, several suggestions can be helpful.

1. *Listen with Acceptance and Understanding.* It isn't easy to talk about one's sexual problems and failures. Embarrassment, shame, guilt, and anxiety all accompany such discussions and the sensitive counselor can help by showing an attitude of understanding. He or she can gently encourage the individual or couple to talk openly, can compliment them for doing so, and can state (if you feel this would help) that difficulty in talking about sexual issues is common.

This is not to imply that counselors should be "gushy" or that they should treat sexual problems in a hushed manner. Sexual problems are really no different than any others and they should be discussed in a relaxed, straightforward way. Counselees are more likely to do this when they observe that the counselor is relaxed, accepting and wanting both to understand and to help.

In discussing these issues, remember that one reason for the awkwardness and embarrassment is the counselee's difficulty in finding words to describe genitals and sexual activities. He or she may prefer pet terms or even "gutter language" which is not easy to express to a counselor, especially to one who is a Christian. You, as a counselor, should be accepting of such language but in general should use correct terminology (e.g., penis, vagina, intercourse, masturbation), making sure that the counselee knows what you are talking about. Recognize that there will be times when you may have to use terms which are more familiar to the counselee. For example, technically it is correct to ask, "Do you have problems with premature ejaculation?" but it may be clearer for you to ask, "Do you come too fast?"

2. *Be Aware of Counseling Dangers.* Earlier in this book we discussed the subtle sexual implications that sometimes occur in counseling.[19] These include undue sexual curiosity on the part of the counselor, feelings of sexual attraction for a counselee, seductive behavior in the counselee, or the counselee's falling in love with the counselor. Such issues are especially prevalent in sexual counseling where overt discussions of sex are acceptable and, as a result, potentially erotic for both counselor and counselee. The counselor constantly must be alert to these issues. He or she must maintain an impersonal distance from counselees who are seductive or sexually arousing. In no case will the counselor be effective if there is erotic involvement with a counselee. Acting out one's sexual impulses with a counselee is both bad morals and bad therapy.[20] If the counselor continues to feel attraction for a counselee this should be pondered carefully and perhaps discussed informally with another counselor. If the counselee is seductive, this should be raised in counseling and discussed directly. How a counselee acts toward the counselor may be a good indication of how the counselee responds to his or her mate or to others apart from marriage.

3. *Gather Information.* It is easier to help when you understand the nature of the problem. By questioning and careful listening try to determine the following:

—What are the sexual problems that a couple may be having? Ask them to be specific and honest.

—What did they expect from sex and how have they been disappointed?

—How do they feel about such issues as oral-genital sex, masturbation, frequency of sex, using a variety of sexual positions and locations, and so on?

—Who initiates sexual activity and how is this done?

—How do they communicate about sex?

—Where did they first learn about sex?

—What are their attitudes about sex now?

—What do they think might be causing their sexual problems?

—Apart from sex, how does the couple get along with each other?

—What stresses are they currently facing as a couple?

The purpose of these and similar questions is to discover the details and the causes of the problem. Prior to counseling you might want to review the section of this chapter titled "The Causes of Sexual Problems within Marriage," then try to determine if any of the listed causes are creating the counselees' problems.

It is best if you can counsel with both the husband and wife although this is not always possible. Many counselors prefer to see the couple together. Do they answer questions in the same way? Does one partner condemn, dominate or "put down" the other? Periodic private interviews with each may add additional information.

As information is gathered you might form some hunches about the cause of the problem. Probing in these areas will give further information and help to confirm or disprove your guesses. These hypotheses can later be shared with the counselees.

4. *Suggest a Physical Examination.* Although most sexual problems arise from psychological causes, one should not overlook the possibility of physiological malfunctioning. For this reason, couples with sexual problems should be urged to get a physical examination as soon as possible. If physical problems are found, the counselor should seek to work with the counselees in conjunction with the physician.

5. *Give Accurate Information.* While this may not be the only or best solution to a sexual problem, information-giving is often very important. Such information can be of several types. The counselor, for example, can:

—Answer questions with factual information. This rests on the debatable assumption that counselees know what to ask.

—Explain details of physiology and the techniques of foreplay or intercourse. Such lectures can be helpful but they often are difficult for counselees to remember.

—Give counselees helpful books or articles to read at home and discuss later.[21]

—Encourage counselees to listen to cassette tapes dealing with sex within marriage.[22]

—Instruct counselees in sexual exercises which they can do at home. Premature ejaculation, for example, can be treated with a very high degree of success when couples are taught and encouraged to practice something called a "squeeze technique," in which the woman manipulates the male penis in a way that permits ejaculatory control.[23] A description of these techniques is beyond the scope of this book, but detailed information is easily available to counselors.

—Provide information about the biblical teaching on sex and sexual fulfillment.

Some counselors may wish to administer a sexual knowledge inventory to discover areas of misinformation.[24] Such misinformation should then be discussed and corrected. In doing so be sure that counselees understand. As information is shared, attitudes also can be uncovered and reevaluated.

6. *Deal with Related Problems*. As indicated earlier, psychological blocks (fears, embarrassment, guilt, anger, and so on); marital conflicts (including power struggles, disagreements and communication breakdowns); inhibiting attitudes and memories of past sexual experiences; guilt over past or present sexual thoughts and actions; beliefs that sex is bad, dirty, or un-Christian; unrealistic expectations about sex, and a variety of other issues can hinder sexual satisfaction. When such problems are present the counselor must do more than give factual information. These sex-related issues must be considered fully.

The counselee must be encouraged to describe the problem fully. Its origins should be discussed, if possible, and strategies should be worked out so the counselees can take practical steps to resolve the problems with the counselor's guidance and encouragement. At times counselees will have to face previous sexual sins and learn to experience the liberation of knowing that sins are forgiven when we confess to our loving Savior. When marital conflict is apparent, counselors must be careful not to take sides but to apply the principles discussed in the chapter on marriage counseling (chapter 13). Then, as these problems are resolved, sexual relations often will improve.

7. *Be Alert to the Need for Referral*. Sexual counseling and the treatment of sexual dysfunction are parts of a highly skilled specialty for which some professionals have unique training.[25] When counselees do not respond to counseling, when there continue to be sexual problems and dissatisfaction, when medical issues are involved, when a counselee is consistently seductive, or when it appears that there will have to be prolonged training and sexual exercises, then referral to an expert in sexual counseling is recommended. Remember that this is not an admission of counseling failure; it is a recognition of the need for more specialized attention.

Preventing Sexual Problems within Marriage

Sexual problems can be prevented both prior to marriage and before they arise within marriage.

1. *Premarital Counseling*. When sexual issues are discussed as part of premarital counseling, there is more accurate information about physiology or love-making techniques, more realistic expectations about sex in marriage, and less likelihood of sexual problems, especially at the beginning of marriage. When a good counseling relationship has been established before the wedding, couples are more inclined to return for help if problems arise after the marriage begins. This is especially true if premarital counselors encourage such postmarital "checkups." And when sexual problems or frustrations are discussed early, before they become complicated, then serious difficulties are less likely to develop.[26]

2. *Sex Education.* Since misinformation is at the basis of many sexual problems it would appear that giving accurate information can do much to prevent sexual difficulties. This information can be in four areas: what the Bible teaches about sex, basic data about male and female physiology, information about techniques of intercourse, and teaching healthy sexual attitudes.

Ideally, this information should be given by parents in the home, long before marriage is ever contemplated. It is well known, however, that for many people there is no sex education at home—not even in Christian homes. The church, therefore, can encourage and instruct parents in giving sex education, and can provide this information directly to young people including young married persons. This can be done through church meetings (including youth meetings), small group discussions of printed materials,[27] and the presentation of some information from the pulpit.

3. *Communication.* When people cannot communicate in general, it is not likely that they will be able to communicate about sex. Teaching people, especially couples, to communicate, therefore, is one way to prevent sexual problems.[28]

Then couples must learn to talk about sex. This is not easy. Some people find it embarrassing and fail to realize that males do not know automatically how to stimulate a female; neither do females know how to "turn on" a man. It surely is true, however, that honest husband-wife communication about feelings, physical sensations and attitudes is the best possible sex education. Such communication should be honest, gentle, and nonverbal as well as verbal. Taking the hand of one's mate and showing him or her how to stimulate can be an excellent communication technique.

Writing from a female perspective, one person commented that "it is amazing how silent we women are on something as important as the sex act in marriage. We *wish* in silence or we *suffer* in silence or we *hope* that this time will be different, that this time he will think of doing that which we long for him to do. Why not just tell him?"[29] Why not show him? Why not recognize, also, that men need to communicate just as much as women? When a couple is encouraged to communicate like this, many subsequent sexual problems will be prevented.

4. *Work and Cleanliness.* Good sex, like a good marriage, requires time, effort, and a willingness to work at making things better. An old song once proclaimed the value of "doing what comes naturally"—but in marriage this is not enough. If sex is to be satisfying and if serious sexual problems are to be prevented, a couple must always be alert to ways in which they can build a better relationship. This may involve reading about sex and trying new positions. It also involves an attitude which says, "I will try to keep myself as attractive as possible, as clean, and at least as concerned about my mate as I was when we were first married."

Married people who get lax about personal hygiene, weight control, and physical appearance find that sex is less satisfying as they grow older.

A young woman, for example, who once enjoyed sex with her clean-shaven, freshly bathed husband, is not going to enjoy sex more if her middle-aged husband is sloppy in appearance, not inclined to shower before sex, and unwilling to shave on weekends. Cleanliness and dedication to improving sex, therefore, are both preventive measures.

5. *Marriage Enrichment.* Within recent years, marriage enrichment and marriage encounter programs have been developed for the purpose of improving marriage (including sex within marriage) and preventing marital and sexual problems.[30] While some of these programs are based on humanistic values, others have a Christian orientation and can be recommended to couples.[31]

Conclusions about Sex within Marriage

Is sexual counseling appropriate for Christians? Some counselors and counselees might say "no." They are skeptical of counseling which is aimed toward individual fulfillment and appears to be selfish and narcissistic. In a professional journal, two Christian sex counselors have challenged this view.[32] Persuasively they argue that sexual fulfillment not only is God's plan for married people but that it teaches us about intimacy and about closeness to him.

> The theological and psychological parallel between letting go sexually, as in orgasmic release, and in accepting one's dependence upon God is quite apparent. . . . We go on to say that it appears that the finest, most sublime foretaste of heaven (overcoming separateness and attaining oneness) lies in sexual intercourse and that God wants us to experience this joyful foretaste of heavenly unity.[33]

Helping people deal with sexual problems in marriage is not advocating a self-centered hedonism. It is helping a husband and wife to relate more effectively to each other, to experience the marital closeness that God intended, and to be so free of hang-ups that they can reach out more effectively in loving service to others.

Suggestions for Further Reading

Kennedy, Eugene. *Sexual Counseling.* New York: Seabury Press, 1977.
* LaHaye, Tim, and LaHaye, Beverly. *The Act of Marriage: The Beauty of Sexual Love.* Grand Rapids: Zondervan, 1976.
* Miles, Herbert J. *Sexual Happiness in Marriage.* Grand Rapids: Zondervan, 1967.
Rice, F. Philip. *Sexual Problems in Marriage: Help from a Christian Counselor.* Philadelphia: Westminster Press, 1978.
* Wheat, Ed, and Wheat, Gaye. *Intended for Pleasure: Sex Technique and Sexual Fulfillment in Christian Marriage.* Old Tappan, NJ: Revell, 1977.

Footnotes

1. William H. Masters and Virginia E. Johnson, *Human Sexual Inadequacy* (Boston: Little, Brown, 1970).
2. Gen. 1:27, 28; 2:24, 25.

3. This translation of Heb. 13:4 is suggested by Tim LaHaye and Beverly LaHaye, *The Act of Marriage* (Grand Rapids: Zondervan, 1976), p. 13.

4. Gen. 4:1.

5. See, for example, Song of Sol. 7:1–10.

6. Prov. 5:18, 19.

7. 1 Cor. 7:2–5.

8. Matt. 19:4–6; 1 Cor. 7:1–9; 1 Thess. 4:1–8.

9. Prov. 5:1–11, 20, 23; 6:23–33; 7:5–27.

10. Henry A. Bowman, *A Christian Interpretation of Marriage* (Philadelphia: Westminster Press, 1952), p. 15.

11. 1 Thess. 4:1–8; 2 Tim. 2:22.

12. Quoted in Ronald M. Deutsch, *The Key to Feminine Response in Marriage* (New York: Random House, 1968), p. 5.

13. These ideas are discussed more fully in Eugene Kennedy, *Sexual Counseling* (New York: Seabury Press, 1977). See especially chapters 1–4, 13.

14. 1 John 4:18.

15. Group for the Advancement of Psychiatry, *Assessment of Sexual Function: A Guide to Interviewing* (New York: Jason Aronson, 1974), p. 57.

16. J. A. Blazer, "Married Virgins—A Study of Unconsummated Marriages," *Journal of Marriage and Family* 26 (1964): 213–14.

17. For a discussion of sexual fantasies see E. Barbara Hariton, "The Sexual Fantasies of Women," *Psychology Today* 6 (March, 1973): 39–44; and Daniel Goleman and Sherida Bush, "The Liberation of Sexual Fantasy," *Psychology Today* 11 (October, 1977): 48–52, 104–107.

18. William H. Masters, Virginia E. Johnson, and Robert J. Levin, *The Pleasure Bond: A New Look at Sexuality and Commitment* (Boston: Little Brown, 1970), pp. 137–38.

19. See chapter 3.

20. Charles L. Rassieur, *The Problem Clergymen Don't Talk About* (Philadelphia: Westminster, 1976).

21. Most highly recommended are the books by LaHaye and LaHaye, *The Act of Marriage;* and Ed Wheat and Gaye Wheat, *Intended for Pleasure: Sexual Technique and Sexual Fulfillment in Christian Marriage* (Old Tappan, NJ: Revell, 1977).

22. Consider, for example, the tape by David and Helen Seamands designed to accompany this book. A more detailed treatment is given on two highly recommended tapes by Ed Wheat, M.D. Totaling three hours of sexual counseling, the tapes are entitled "Sex Problems and Sex Problems in Marriage." They are available from Bible Believer's Cassettes, 130 No. Spring, Springdale, Arkansas, 72764. It is recommended that Christian counselors keep a copy of these two cassettes available for loan to counselees—including those who are preparing for marriage.

23. These techniques are described on the above tapes and discussed in detail in the book by Wheat and Wheat, *Intended for Pleasure.* See also LaHaye and LaHaye, *The Act of Marriage;* and F. Philip Rice, *Sexual Problems in Marriage: Help from a Christian Counselor* (Philadelphia: Westminster Press, 1978).

24. Consider, for example, the Sex Knowledge Inventory, Form X Revised, developed by Gelolo McHugh and available from Family Life Publications, Box 427, Saluda, North Carolina, 28773.

25. See for example, W. E. Hartman and M. A. Fithian, *Treatment of Sexual Dysfunction* (New York: Jason Aronson, 1974).

26. Premarital counseling is discussed more fully in chapter 12.

27. Denominational groups sometimes produce such materials. The author recommends the following: for a discussion of sex education in general, see Letha

Scanzoni, "Sex Education in the Home," in *The Secrets of our Sexuality,* ed. Gary R. Collins (Waco, TX: Word, 1976), pp. 132–48; and Letha Scanzoni, *Sex is a Parent Affair* (Glendale, CA: Regal, 1973). For high school students, see Charlie W. Shedd, *The Stork Is Dead* (Waco, TX: Word, 1968). College age people and young adults may want to study the books and tapes mentioned above in footnotes 20 and 21.

28. This is discussed more fully in chapter 23.

29. Wheat and Wheat, *Intended for Pleasure,* p. 130.

30. For an evaluation of these programs see Joanne Koch and Lew Koch, "The Urgent Drive to Make Good Marriages Better," *Psychology Today* 10 (September, 1976): 33–35, 83–85, 95.

31. Especially recommended is the Christian Marriage Enrichment program developed by H. Norman Wright and Wesley Roberts, both of whom have produced some of the tapes made to accompany this book. For further information write Christian Marriage Enrichment, 8000 East Girard, Suite 602, Denver, Colorado, 80231.

32. James R. David and Francis C. Duda, "Christian Perspectives on Treatment of Sexual Dysfunction," *Journal of Psychology and Theology* 5 (Fall, 1977): 332–36.

33. Ibid., pp. 335, 334.

22

Homosexuality

Homosexuality.

THERE PROBABLY IS NO OTHER WORD IN THE ENGLISH LANGUAGE WHICH is so symbolic of controversy and which so quickly triggers emotional reactions. Several decades ago homosexuality was rarely mentioned in polite society. Looked upon as something sinful, sick and illegal, it was ignored by most heterosexuals (including church members), "treated" by psychiatrists, and hidden by perhaps millions of persons who wanted to keep their homosexual tendencies from becoming known.

Then things began to change. In 1948 researcher Alfred Kinsey estimated that 4 percent of the American population was homosexual and reported that in the United States "37 percent of the male population had committed at least one homosexual act and 50 percent had responded at some time in their lives to a homosexual motivation." In 1954 a government-sponsored report on homosexuality rocked Britain and before long homosexuality had become a topic of government and media debate. Great numbers of homosexual persons who previously had been silent about their sexual orientation began to "come out of the closet" to declare their homosexuality, to form gay organizations, and to demand a stop to government, cultural and media persecution. Controversy over homosexuality soon invaded virtually every part of society: the military, local elections, government, the courts, schools, sports, science, professional societies, the entertainment world, business and industry, the media and, of course, the church. Heated debate over the ordination of homosexuals has characterized several denominations, a string of gay churches has been established, and within recent years there has been an increasing stream of articles and books on homosexuality, written by both Christian and non-Christian authors.[1]

Some Christians still try to ignore the controversy, some lash out in condemnation and anger against homosexuals, some seem intent on making

316

"Christian homosexuality" a legitimate, God-approved way of life, and others (perhaps most) are confused and not sure what they think.

This confusion is easy to understand. Homosexuality is not easily defined, its causes are not clearly known, and it is difficult for homosexuals to change—even with counseling. There are many unfounded but widely held assumptions about the characteristics of homosexuals. In addition, it is probable that some people are afraid, both of the influence of gays in society and of the possibility that homosexual tendencies might be found within themselves.

Because of the controversy and confusion surrounding this topic, it is almost certain that some readers will object to the author's statements in the paragraphs which follow. Please remember, however, that this chapter is not written to advocate any one theory or to enter into debate. Within our society and our churches there are innumerable people who are sexually attracted to members of the same sex and who sometimes are entwined in erotic homosexual relationships and activities. These people need understanding rather than condemnation, help instead of rejection, acceptance but not debate, compassion in contrast to the horror and attitude of revulsion with which so many Christians recoil from homosexuals. The following paragraphs are written in an attempt to summarize what we know about homosexuality, to pinpoint the areas of controversy, and to cut through the emotional rhetoric so we can understand and help those homosexually inclined persons who seek counsel.

In his book *Eros Defiled,* Christian psychiatrist John White writes that "a homosexual act is one designed to produce sexual orgasm between members of the same sex. A homosexual is a man or woman who engages in homosexual acts." [2] This puts the emphasis on behavior rather than on people. It stresses acts rather than the personalities or life styles of the people who engage in homosexual behavior.

Most writers also use the term *homosexual* to refer to those persons who never or almost never engage in overt sexual acts with same-sex partners, but who are sexually attracted to members of the same sex. To avoid confusion let us distinguish between *overt* homosexuals (who engage in homosexual acts, at least periodically) and latent homosexuals (who have a same-sex attraction but do not act on it and sometimes try to deny that it exists). The professional literature also identifies *circumstantial* homosexuality in which a person (such as a prisoner) temporarily chooses homosexual behavior because opposite sex partners are not available.

There is no such thing as a homosexual personality type (or types), or typical homosexual behavior and mannerisms. Homosexuals are of both sexes (female homosexuals are usually referred to as lesbians). They are of all ages, come from all occupational fields and socioeconomic levels, possess a variety of interests (as do heterosexuals), are inside the church as well as outside, and are not always thinking about sex (any more than heterosexuals think only about sex). While some homosexuals "cruise" in and out of gay bars looking for sexual partners, many more are respected and often married members of the community whose homosexuality is well hidden. While many are lonely and insecure, it cannot be assumed that homosexuals as a group are mentally ill or socially incompetent. In fact, it cannot even be assumed that humans can be divided into two groups—homosexual and heterosexual. The Kinsey report suggested a scale with 7 points in which 0 represents a person who is exclusively heterosexual, 3 is midpoint and 6 represents a person with exclusively homosexual tendencies and actions. The Kinsey researchers concluded that few people are at the 0 and 6 points on the scale.

In helping homosexuals our first goal must be to get rid of stereotypes and misconceptions which so often are imposed upon these people who are attracted to others of the same sex.

The Bible and Homosexuality

The Bible says little about homosexuality. Seven passages mention it and in each case the reference is relatively brief.[3] Clearly, it never is approved but neither is it singled out as being worse than other sins.

In an attempt to clarify the biblical teachings about homosexuality, several Christian writers have written books and articles which sometimes reach conflicting conclusions.[4] At times, it would seem that many of these writers start with an opinion about homosexuality and then interpret the Scriptures in a way which will support their positions. Some, for example, have used the Scriptures to support a sweeping condemnation of homosexuals while others blithely explain away the sinful implications of homosexuality and even conclude that it is a gift from God.[5]

In the Old Testament, overt homosexuality clearly is condemned, but some people argue that this is a part of the ceremonial law which was put aside when Christ came to die for our sins. Within the New Testament, however, there are three references to homosexuality and in two of these (1 Cor. 6:9 and 1 Tim. 1:1) the Greek word means "coitus with other males."[6] Overt homosexuality, therefore, is condemned in these passages, along with idolatry, thievery, lying, murder and other sins.

Romans 1:26, 27 is more explicit in its teachings about homosexuality. Some have argued that this passage only condemns former heterosexuals who have shifted to homosexuality, but this interpretation makes two highly debatable assumptions: (a) that people become homosexual by deliberate choice, and (b) that the verses do not apply to lifelong homosexuals. Others argue that the writer of Romans 1 is concerned not about homosexuality but about idolatry. Clearly the passage condemns people who worship something other than God, but Paul makes no attempt to say here that only idolatrous homosexuality is wrong. Instead, he points out that when people don't care about God he lets them get into all kinds of sinful situations, including overt homosexuality.

Every time homosexuality is mentioned in the Bible it is mentioned in a bad light. It seems clear, therefore, that genital homosexual acts are wrong.

But if overt homosexuality is sinful, what about homosexual thoughts and feelings? What can be said about those persons who have sexual fantasies and impulses which are primarily homosexual, but which are kept well hidden? What can be concluded about people, including Christians, who appear to live normal lives, who have satisfying heterosexual marriages, but who are bothered by recurring homosexual tendencies which threaten one's masculinity or femininity and which might sometime "slip out" and become apparent to others? To have homosexual temptations, feelings and desires, is nowhere condemned in Scripture, but when one dwells on such thoughts and continually engages in sexual fantasy—homosexual or heterosexual—then thoughts become lust and lust clearly is sin.

Jesus is described in the Bible as One who has been tempted in all things as we are.[7] Therefore, Jesus *may have* had homosexual temptations but he did not sin. This can be encouraging to the believer whose homosexual temptations and feelings continue. We have a Savior who knows how we feel because he was tempted too. He also showed that it is possible to avoid "giving in" to sinful temptations of any kind—including homosexual temptations.

The Causes of Homosexuality
There is no clearly identified single cause of homosexuality.

An increasing body of research would seem to support the idea that homosexuality is *not* inherited, or the result of physiological and biological abnormality. Studies of physical build, chromosomes, neurological or biochemical make-up and even hormones have failed to show differences between homosexuals and heterosexuals. It has been found that while some homosexuals have hormone imbalances, many do not, and a similar hormone imbalance is found in heterosexuals.[8] This has led most researchers to conclude that there is no present evidence to support the idea that homosexuality has a physical or biological cause.

We are left then with the conclusion that homosexuality is learned. There are several theories about how this happens.

1. *Parent-child Relationships.* Psychoanalytic theories have maintained that homosexuality comes to males raised in families where there is a weak, passive, ineffective father and a domineering mother. This mother subtly teaches her son to be passive and dedicated to her. He has no strong male example to follow and soon discovers that he is less competent than his peers in relating to girls. The son, therefore, loses confidence in his masculinity and dreads the thought of intimacy with women. Daughters in such families perceive their fathers as being unfriendly or rejecting so the girls have little opportunity to relate to really masculine men. They relate better to women.

This explanation is the most commonly accepted and best documented cause of homosexuality.[9] However, while many homosexuals do experience this kind of family relationship, others do not. Furthermore, children in the same family relationship do not all become homosexual, even though there may be similar parent-child relationships.[10] This has led to additional explanations for homosexuality.

2. *Other Family Relationships.* Homosexuality has been found to result when: [11]

—mothers distrust or fear women and teach this to their sons;

—mothers distrust or fear men and teach this to their daughters;

—a son is surrounded by too many females (mother, sisters, aunts) so that he learns to think and act like a girl;

—parents who wanted a daughter but got a son subtly raise the boy to think and act like a girl. A similar situation arises when parents wanted a son but got a daughter;

—a son is rejected by the father and hence feels inadequate as a male;

—a daughter is rejected by the mother and hence feels inadequate as a female;

—both parents are afraid of sex, silent about it in the home, or strong in their condemnation of sex. In all of this the child gets a distorted view of sex and as a result, struggles with heterosexual adjustment; or

—a mother is so overindulgent that the child is overly attached to the parent, unable to break away, and convinced that no mate could ever compare with mother (especially the son).

It would be possible to continue this list perhaps for several pages, but enough has been stated to show that the roots of homosexuality are most often imbedded in the family setting.

In any society, a child learns what it means to be male or female. If there is no opportunity to learn healthy male or female roles then the child's behavior and attitudes become distorted. Such children reach adulthood not knowing what to expect or how to react to the opposite sex. Sometimes, then, there is a retreat into homosexuality.

3. *Fear.* Some people are afraid of the opposite sex sometimes because of a lack of frequent contact with opposite sex persons and sometimes because of rejection by or traumatic experiences with members of the opposite sex. One book [12] adds that religious groups sometimes promote homosexuality when they prohibit boy-girl social interaction. In these settings, heterosexual contact is so much prohibited that homosexuality becomes a safer, less fearful alternative.

4. *Willful Choice of Homosexual Actions.* It should not be assumed that homosexuality comes as a deliberate and conscious decision. At some time in their lives most homosexuals apparently begin to realize that, through no fault of their own, they are primarily attracted to people of the same sex. Such a realization can be very disturbing and sometimes people try to hide it even from themselves. Since this tendency was not chosen

deliberately, it might have been resisted, at least in the beginning. The individual often assumes that he or she was born with homosexual tendencies. This, however, is not supported by current research. According to the findings of one writer:

> It is more correct to say that humans—and other mammals—have a capacity for heterosexual response and a capacity for homosexual response at birth, but that they do not have an inborn tendency toward either heterosexuality or homosexuality. After the drive has been conditioned one way or the other or both ways—in other words, after the *capacity* for response has been exploited and learning has begun—we may speak of a *tendency* toward heterosexuality and/or a tendency toward homosexuality. But this tendency is acquired and is a product of learning rather than a part of the individual's biological inheritance.[13]

These homosexual tendencies are acquired often before one realizes what is taking place. Just as a predominantly heterosexual person is attracted by the opposite sex, so a predominantly homosexual individual has learned an attraction for the same sex. These attractions are not wrong. What is wrong, according to the Bible, is the willful decision to engage in homosexual *actions*.

Whenever a person experiences pleasure from sexual activities with someone of the same or opposite sex, the sex activities become more appealing the next time. It doesn't really matter how the behavior got started —voluntarily, as a result of seduction from another person, as an expression of curiosity, or as an attempt to release tension while in the military or while confined in jail.[14] What does matter is whether the sexual activities continue. According to one leading writer "lasting homosexual patterns tend to be established by *recurrent homosexual practices* beginning even before adolescence and continuing after it, especially if the homosexual partner—whether a contemporary or an adult—is someone the young person admires." [15] For many young people a passing sexual encounter, even with a same-sex person, isn't especially satisfying and is unlikely to be repeated. But for people whose background and tendencies make them vulnerable, one sexual experience can lead to another and a vicious circle begins. Homosexual acts increase homosexual tendencies which in turn lead to more homosexual acts. Of course a similar cycle can begin when persons with heterosexual tendencies choose to engage in sexual activities with persons of the opposite sex. According to the Bible, this heterosexual cycle isn't wrong within marriage, but outside of marriage such physical involvement, as we have seen, is sinful.

The Effects of Homosexuality

The Gay Liberation movement has emphasized its belief that "Gay is good," but this should not hide the fact that millions of people with homosexual tendencies are extremely unhappy. Their homosexual orientation may cloud every area of life. Of course individuals are affected in uniquely different ways, but homosexuality influences three areas especially: one's life style, self-concept and inner feelings, and interpersonal relationships.

1. *Life Style Effects.* Reports in the popular press and in scientific journals have given a disturbing picture of gay communities and the life styles of homosexuals. A report on "Gay Ghettos," for example, has described the recent emergence of homosexual communities where the shops cater to gays, where the streets are "dominated by pairs of men holding hands or walking with their arms around each other's waists," where women and children are conspicuously absent, and where clothing styles reflect a way of dress currently favored by gays.[16] More prevalent are reports of male school teachers and youth leaders who sexually molest young boys and lure them into homosexual acts.[17] Other writers have described the increasing number of gay bars where both men and women come to seek out other homosexuals with whom they can find acceptance, friendship and perhaps sexual involvement.[18] Such reports have aroused fear and revulsion in the minds of many people, including church members.

It should be remembered, however, that there is no such thing as a typical homosexual life style. It is inaccurate and unkind to conclude that most homosexuals are "bar-hoppers," radicals who march in the streets, child molesters, effeminate (in the case of males), psychologically maladjusted,[19] and constantly preoccupied with sex. Such stereotypes lead Christians to push homosexuals away and deny them the love and acceptance that should be found in the church community. Of course, each of the above characteristics describes some homosexuals, but it is also true that many homosexual persons are law-abiding, accepted members of the community. Some live together in overt homosexual relationships; others, as we have seen, keep their homosexual tendencies hidden and controlled.

Homosexual tendencies, therefore, influence people and their life styles in different ways. Some are open about their sexual preference; others give no hint of their tendencies but many live with a quiet and persisting fear that their homosexual orientation might surface inadvertently and lead to the loss of friends, jobs and acceptance from others.

2. *Self-concept and Emotional Effects.* With the recent openness about homosexuality, some gays have developed an attitude which proclaims not only that "gay is good" but that to be gay is to be superior to others.[20] Far more prevalent is the inner insecurity and lower self-esteem which comes to anyone who is different from the majority. Guilt over homosexual tendencies or actions, loneliness, fear of one's homosexuality being detected, a sense of hopelessness (which leads, at times, to drinking and sometimes to suicide) and an inner anger have all been seen in homosexuals. For many persons, especially those who are unmarried, the flight to gay bars is an attempt to find love and support from understanding people who can bolster individual self-confidence and salve the inner hurt.

3. *Relationship Effects.* While doubtless it is true that numerous homo-

sexuals do build supportive intimate relationships with other people of the same sex, it is also true, first, that such relationships often are temporary and second, that many gays never have such experiences. In a world which highly values youth, virility and good looks, it is difficult to find intimacy and acceptance if you lack these qualities. Some persons whose homosexuality is kept hidden (at times even from their mates) discover that their sexual orientation or fear of rejection can put a strain on their marriages and can prevent them from getting close to others lest the harbored tendencies slip out for others to see.

Then there is one's relationship with God. Since homosexual behavior is sinful, involvement in such behavior puts a barrier between the person and God. Many Christians fail to distinguish between homosexual behavior, which is a sin, and homosexual desires and tendencies, which are not sins. Failure to recognize this distinction can lead to perpetual attempts to squelch one's gay tendencies. When this proves futile, there is often discouragement, guilt, a stifling of spiritual growth, or sometimes a flight to one of the churches which openly accepts homosexuality.

Counseling the Homosexual

The place to begin counseling is with the counselor's own attitudes. If you retain a revulsion about homosexuals, if you joke about them or condemn them, if you uncritically accept stereotypes about "typical homosexuals," and if you are unfamiliar with the complexity of homosexuality and its causes, then you will be ineffective in helping. Jesus loved sinners and those who were tempted to sin. We who seek to follow in his steps should do the same. If we sense no inner compassion for overt homosexuals or for people with homosexual tendencies, then we must ask God to give us such compassion. We must examine our own attitudes toward gay people, we must seek to understand the diversity of homosexuality and we should avoid counseling homosexually oriented persons so long as we are unwilling to learn or our negative attitudes persist.

One common myth which must be changed is the idea that homosexuality is a disease which cannot be cured. Homosexuality is not a disease; it is a tendency which sometimes, but not always, leads to habitual acts of homosexual behavior. Homosexuality is difficult to counsel successfully, but change (even to heterosexual tendencies and behavior) is possible,[21] especially when some of the following are present (the more that are present, the better the chance for help):

—a counselee who honestly faces his or her homosexuality;

—a strong desire to change on the part of the counselee;

—a willingness to break contact with homosexual companions who tempt the counselee into homosexual behavior;

—a willingness to avoid drugs and alcohol which leave one vulnerable to temptation;

—a desire to avoid sin and to commit one's life and problems to the Lordship of Jesus Christ.

These preliminary considerations should be remembered and discussed with the homosexual who seeks help. Then the counselor can help in the following ways:

1. *Determine Counseling Goals.* When someone comes for help, what does he or she want—elimination of homosexual tendencies, knowledge of the biblical teaching on homosexuality, help in stopping gay behavior, sanction for continuing homosexual behavior, or something else? Do not assume that you know what the person wants until you ask and discuss the counselee's answers.

2. *Instill a Realistic Hope.* It is not easy to counsel with homosexuals. Let us be honest enough to recognize, therefore, that while homosexual actions can be stopped completely and unconditionally forgiven by God, homosexual tendencies are much more difficult to eradicate. Sometimes a person may not change to a heterosexual orientation, but he or she can be helped to live a victorious, meaningful life free of homosexual entanglement and activity. There is cause for real hope, especially when the person sincerely wants to change.

3. *Share Knowledge.* Homosexuals who come for counseling may believe some of the greatest myths about their problem. At various times as the counseling progresses, be alert to ways in which these stereotypes can be challenged and replaced by accurate information about homosexuality and human sexuality in general. It can be very encouraging to know, for example, that people with homosexual feelings are not all misfits, incurable, perverted, or unable to function effectively in society. Since homosexuality is learned, there is hope that it can be unlearned. Since homosexual behavior is a sin, it can be forgiven and conquered.

Of special importance is a teaching of the biblical statements on homosexuality—especially the distinction between homosexual tendencies and homosexual actions.

4. *Show Love and Acceptance of the Person.* In a courageous and insightful chapel address, a Christian seminary student once talked of his own homosexual tendencies and his ministry among the gay community.

Come to one of the dozens and dozens of gay bars in Chicago with me tonight and at 3 a.m. I will show you some of the nicest people in the world who are crying out to be loved—hundreds and hundreds of them—and where are we who know the love of Christ? Surely the search for love often takes on twisted and sinful expressions, but the hunger, the heart's cry, the vacuum seeking to be filled with the love of God is there and it is the same as yours and mine. Christian friends need to be there; not tract-wielding preachers, but listening compassionate friends. . . .

More than anything else, a person who struggles with gayness, Christian or non-Christian, has a desperate need for love. He or she has been hurt by pathogenic family patterns, twisted environmental influences, or basically the sin which affects each one of us. More than being a victimizer, the gay person has been a victim of sin. He has been hurt and usually has suffered greatly for his orientation which he did not inherit or choose, but rather learned long before the age of accountability. Often as a last resort in falling into gay sex the person has sought love which becomes eros defiled. So why does he or she need a Christian friend? Because we have Christ in us and we know the love of Christ. Ultimately the only thing that will help anybody is the pure and unadulterated agape love of Christ—the redeeming, sanctifying, healing power of God's incarnate love. Our whole world has a desperate need to see this love of Christ, to feel it, to touch it, to experience it personally, and we are his instruments.[22]

The speaker of these words goes on to maintain that it is the Christian community which should reach out, accept the counselee and give the continuing love which makes the individual counseling effective. Christians can also demonstrate that it is possible to have close friends of both sexes without the necessity of sexual involvement. To break with one's gay friends is threatening and involves a real grief process as one loses the people who to this point have been most supportive and accepting. If there is no supportive community of believers waiting and willing to accept the homosexual, then there can be an easy retreat back to the old life style.

5. *Encourage Behavior Change.* Even with love and acceptance, change will not come to the person who continues his or her sexual involvement with other homosexual persons. If this involvement has gone on for a long time it may be especially difficult to stop overt homosexual actions. After a deliberate decision to change, the counselee may experience some relapses and at times may resist the idea that change is desirable. Such resistance should be discussed in a straightforward, patient, kind and firm manner.

One way to change behavior is to avoid people, publications and situations which are sexually arousing. This may lead to loneliness and a change in life style but this is a price which must be paid. Counselor support and encouragement at such times can be helpful. Remind the counselee that Christ forgives and that the Holy Spirit always is present to help us resist temptation and to forsake sinful behavior.

At this point there also can be value in discussing the counselee's whole life style. Sex is a part of life but so is worship, work, family, recreation, time management, exercise and rest. One does not find fulfillment in life solely through sexual satisfaction and neither do problems all disappear if counseling considers only sex. Unless the counselee finds satisfaction in nonsexual parts of life—such as in his or her spiritual life, work, or recreational activities—there will be a tendency to slip back into homosexual actions when life pressures build. A more balanced life is a common sense remedy, especially for the many minor and fleeting homosexual feelings or actions.[23]

6. *Recognize That Counseling May Be Complex.* Homosexuality is a

complicated problem. While the previously discussed techniques can be effective in dealing with some of the symptoms, and while these methods can bring permanent change, it is also true that for some people the treatment may require more time and more counseling expertise than the church leader may possess. Homosexuality develops over a long period of time. It can be highly ingrained and its treatment may take both a long time and considerable counseling expertise. The professional literature in the area of homosexuality lists a number of counseling approaches, some of which take time to learn and practice to use. This is not stated to discourage the reader. Instead, it should alert you to the complexity of your task and should show that in some cases, referral to another counselor may be the best way to help.

At the risk of oversimplification, let us mention only three of the many approaches to the counseling of homosexuals.

(a) The Psychoanalytic Approaches. Long, expensive and in-depth, this approach aims at helping the homosexual gain insight into the causes of his or her sexual orientation. In spite of occasional success stories it seems unlikely that homosexuals are helped much by this approach. Even if it could be shown that they are helped, it isn't realistic to think that most counselees could afford the 150–350 sessions of individual counseling that would be required for psychoanalytic treatment.[24]

(b) The Behavioristic Approaches. Based on principles of conditioning and learning, these approaches try to help counselees unlearn their preferences for the same sex and relearn a heterosexual orientation. Little or no emphasis is placed on consideration of the family interactions or fears which may have caused the homosexuality. At times there is a use of sexually arousing (some would say pornographic) pictures in an attempt to stimulate heterosexual tendencies and some therapists encourage heterosexual acts outside of marriage. These practices, of course, would have to be avoided by Christians. The behavioristic methods often do change behavior and reduce anxiety, but they may do little to alter homosexual tendencies and there is some question about whether or not the change in behavior is permanent.

(c) The Multiple-phase Approach. As reported by John Powell, an evangelical counselor on the faculty of Michigan State University, this approach has two stages: the premultiple and the multiple. In the premultiple phase the counselee meets for several sessions with a same-sex counselor who shows acceptance, warmth and support, while there is discussion of the possible causes of homosexuality in the counselee's life, the way the homosexuality is expressed and the goals for counseling. Then there is a shift to the multiple-phase. Here a male and female counselor work together with the counselee in an attempt to show how men and women react in mutually satisfying ways, to help the counselee resolve some of his conflicts with parents, and to teach counselees how to relate to males and females in mutually fulfilling ways.[25]

The approach of Powell and his associates emphasizes the value of helping counselees to reexamine the family background and other causes of their homosexuality, and helping them learn how to relate in healthy ways to the opposite sex. Such an approach also permits counselors to discuss the sinful nature of homosexual behavior and to challenge counselees to change their actions with divine help. Since it deals with more than current behavior, however, the approach (or one like it) can also help people to change homosexual tendencies.

Eugene Kennedy, in a book written for Christian counselors, gives some helpful guidelines for counseling homosexuals:

> Ministering to persons with human problems is not the same as taking them on as psychological clients for long-term help. . . . Members of the clergy (and other Christian counselors) have to decide on how they minister religiously in counseling situations with homosexuals. It is probably not by trying to be psychologists who try to go deeper into the emotional material. . . . It is not for amateurs, no matter how concerned they are about their clients, to attempt long-term analytic-like therapy; neither should they try to reproduce some of the behavior modification treatment that has been employed in attempting to change homosexual erotic preferences through conditioning techniques. . . .
>
> If members of the clergy can separate the idea of treating the other from ministering to the other they will carry out their function far more effectively and with greater success in the long run. They will have a better opportunity, for example, to refer the person if additional psychological help seems to be required and they will be able to maintain their own position without confusing their identity or trying to deliver a psychological service that they cannot actually give.[26]

The nonpsychologist, therefore, can have a significant impact in helping homosexuals. But the nonprofessional also can help at times by referring a counselee to a counselor who has more specialized skills in dealing with the common problem.

Preventing Homosexuality

As we have seen, the evidence is strong that homosexuality is a learned condition and not something genetic, glandular or physiological. If this is true, then homosexuality can be prevented by providing learning experiences which stimulate heterosexuality. This does not mean, of course, that we can give a lecture or a reading assignment and expect that this will prevent homosexuality. The learning must start in the home even before the child knows how to read.

1. *Building Healthy Home Environments.* Since homosexuality often develops in homes where there is parent conflict and rejection of the children, the home is where prevention must begin. It is true, no doubt, that no woman who has a satisfying marriage turns to her son or daughter for a

relationship which she should have with her husband. No father rejects or ignores his children if he has a satisfying marriage and feels both secure in his masculinity and adequate as a male.[27] No child becomes homosexual if there has been a warm, emotional relationship with the father.[28]

All of this suggests that the church is preventing homosexuality when it stimulates biblically based family patterns in which the father and mother maintain clearly differentiated roles. The father is a leader in the home, the children are respected and disciplined, and the parents have a mutually satisfying relationship. Stable homes stimulate healthy heterosexual attitudes in the family members.

2. *Giving Accurate Information about Homosexuality.* It is tragic to observe the condemnation and horror with which so many Christians react to homosexuality. Growing up in such an environment, young people learn to fear homosexuals and to suppress any gay tendencies within themselves instead of dealing with them. If these tendencies persist, the young person keeps them hidden. Since he or she cannot get understanding and help from parents or church members, there may be a drift toward homosexual groups who are understanding, accepting and loving. By its condemning attitude, therefore, the church sometimes pushes people into situations in which overt homosexual behavior is encouraged.

The alternative is not the development of liberal attitudes which deny the sinfulness of the homosexual act. The alternative is for churches to teach what the Bible says about human sexuality (including homosexuality), love, friendship and sexual control. Church leaders should demonstrate an attitude of compassion and encouragement rather than one of condemnation. Stereotypes about homosexuality (some of which, regretfully, are taught in popular Christian books about gays) should be exposed for what they are: untruths which alienate people, perpetuate ignorance, stimulate fear, push homosexuals away from Christian fellowship, and serve mainly to boost the critic's own sense of self-righteous superiority. All of this implies that issues like homosexuality should be discussed in the church instead of being denied.

Since overt homosexuality often becomes a habit in response to environmental stimulation, the church should emphasize the importance of sexual self-control. This comes through prayer, meditation on the Scriptures, avoidance of sexually arousing situations or people, deliberate decisions to avoid sinful actions, and the habit of being accountable to an understanding friend or counselor.

3. *Developing Healthy Self-concepts.* In a best-selling book, George Gilder pointed out that "there are millions of males who under the wrong conditions are open to homosexuality. A frequent catalyst is self-abasement. Failure in love or work may so deject a man that he feels incapable of rising to a relationship with a woman. . . . To have a woman, a man

must to some extent feel himself a man."[29] If a male feels inadequate or unmasculine, he may seek for a safe relationship where he does not have to act like a male. Perhaps a similar situation exists in women. A low self-concept stimulates homosexual behavior.

Chapter 24 discusses the development of self-esteem. Churches and homes can help individuals build realistic and positive self-concepts and this, in turn, can contribute to the prevention of homosexuality.

Conclusions about Homosexuality

It is impossible to estimate how many people, including Christians, struggle with homosexual urges. Afraid of rejection and being misunderstood, such people are afraid of admitting their tendencies—sometimes even to themselves. As they ponder this alone, such persons grapple with guilt, struggle with self-condemnation, and find rationalizations to explain or pardon their sexual thoughts or actions. People like this can be helped and the church can be a helping place. Perhaps at no time in history has there been such interest in homosexuality and openness about this condition. At no time has there been such opportunity for church members and Christian counselors to make an impact in both the counseling and the prevention of homosexuality.

Suggestions for Further Reading

* Davidson, Alex. *The Returns of Love: Letters of a Christian Homosexual.* Downers Grove, IL: Inter-Varsity, 1970.
* Enroth, Ronald M., and Jamison, Gerald E. *The Gay Church.* Grand Rapids: Wm. B. Eerdmans, 1974.
Hatterer, Lawrence J. *Changing Homosexuality in the Male.* New York: McGraw-Hill, 1970.
Lovelace, Richard F. *Homosexuality and the Church.* Old Tappan, NJ: Revell, 1978.
Tripp, C. A. *The Homosexual Matrix.* New York: Signet, 1975.
* White, John. *Eros Defiled: The Christian and Sexual Sin.* Downers Grove, IL: Inter-Varsity, 1977.
Williams, Don. *The Bond That Breaks.* Los Angeles, CA: BIM (Box 259995), 1978.

Footnotes

1. One of the most controversial reports is another study by researchers at the Kinsey Institute: Alan P. Bell and Martin S. Weinberg, *Homosexualities: A Study of Human Diversity* (New York: Simon & Schuster, 1978).

2. John White, *Eros Defiled* (Downers Grove, IL: Inter-Varsity, 1977).

3. Gen. 19:1–11; Lev. 18:22; 20:13; Judg. 19:22–25; Rom. 1:25–27, 1 Cor. 6:9; 1 Tim. 1:9, 10. (Five other passages refer to homosexuality in the context of male prostitution: Deut. 23:17; 1 Kings 14:24; 15:12; 22:46; 2 Kings 23:7.)

4. See for example Letha Scanzoni and Virginia Ramey Mollenkott, *Is the Homosexual My Neighbor?* (New York; Harper & Row, 1978) for a liberal view. A more traditional view is taken in the excellent book by Richard Lovelace, *Homosexuality and the Church* (Old Tappan, NJ: Revell, 1978).

5. Reported in Ronald M. Enroth and Gerald E. Jamison, *The Gay Church* (Grand Rapids: Wm. B. Eerdmans, 1974), p. 42.

6. John F. Alexander, "Homosexuality: It's Not That Clear," *The Other Side* 81 (June, 1978): 8–16.

7. Heb. 4:15.

8. Cited in Ted D. Evans, "Homosexuality: Christian Ethics and Psychological Research," *Journal of Psychology and Theology* 3 (Spring 1975): 94–98.

9. This view has been clearly presented and carefully researched by I. Bieber and associates, *Homosexuality* (New York: Basic Books, 1962).

10. Wainwright Churchill, *Homosexual Behavior among Males* (New York; Hawthorn, 1967).

11. These causes are among many listed by Lawrence J. Hatterer, *Changing Homosexuality in the Male* (New York; McGraw-Hill, 1970).

12. Merrill T. Eaton and Margaret H. Peterson, *Psychiatry,* 2d ed. (Flushing, NY: Medical Examination Publishing Company, 1969).

13. Churchill, *Homosexual Behavior,* p. 105.

14. White, *Eros Defiled,* p. 117.

15. Hatterer, *Changing Homosexuality,* p. 45, italics added.

16. See "Gay Ghettos: A Search for Male Communities," *Human Behavior* (September 1978): 41.

17. Kay Oliver and Wayne Christianson, "Unhappily 'Gay': From the Closet to the Front Page," *Moody Monthly* 75 (January 1978): 62, 29. More scholarly reports, such as that of Bell and Weinberg, *Homosexualities,* refute this popular stereotype. They are quoted in Ashley Montagu, "A 'Kinsey Report' on Homosexuals," *Psychology Today* 12 (August 1978): 62–66, 91.

18. For a description and discussion of gay bars, see Wayne Sage, "Inside the Colossal Closet," *Human Behavior* (August, 1975): 16–23.

19. Studies comparing homosexuals and heterosexuals have shown "no difference in degree of adjustment between the two" groups. See Wayne Sage, "The Homosexual Hangup," *Human Behavior* (November/December, 1972): 56–61.

20. See for example, Mark Freedman, "Homosexuals May be Healther than Straights," *Psychology Today* 8 (March, 1975): 28–32.

21. Evidence for this is cited in Hatterer, *Changing Homosexuality,* p. 151; in John E. Powell, "Understanding Male Homosexuality: Developmental Recapitulation in a Christian Perspective," *Journal of Psychology and Theology* 2 (Summer, 1974): 163–73; and in John M. Vayhinger, "Understanding Homosexual Behavior and Life Styles Clinically and Religiously" (Paper presented at CAPS convention, Chicago, 14 April 1978). (Author's address: Anderson School of Theology, Anderson, Indiana 46011).

22. Address by Marty Hansen, Chapel, Trinity Evangelical Divinity School, 2 February 1978.

23. Eugene Kennedy, *Sexual Counseling* (New York: Seabury, 1977).

24. Bieber et al. report that counseling by psychoanalytic methods helped 27% of the bisexuals and homosexuals in treatment to become exclusively heterosexual. The number of sessions ranged from 150 to 350. For an in-depth discussion of the psychoanalytic approach see Charles W. Socarides, *Homosexuality* (New York: Jason Aronson, 1978).

25. This approach is outlined in Powell, "Understanding Male Homosexuality."

26. Kennedy, *Sexual Counseling,* pp. 141, 143.

27. Churchill, *Homosexual Behavior,* p. 290.

28. For an interesting and popularly written book about parental influences

which can prevent homosexuality, see P. Wyden and B. Wyden, *Growing up Straight* (New York: Stein and Day, 1968).

29. George Gilder, *Sexual Suicide* (New York: Quadrangle/The New York Times Book Co., 1973), p. 227.

23

Interpersonal Relations

WHEN GOD CREATED HUMAN BEINGS, HE MADE US SOCIAL CREATURES. He declared that it is not good for people to be alone, he instructed us to multiply, and he has permitted us to expand into the billions of persons who now occupy planet Earth.

Whenever two or more of these people get together there are interpersonal relations. Sometimes these relationships are smooth, mutually supportive and characterized by clear, efficient communication. Often, however, these interpersonal relations are strained and marked by conflict. According to early American psychiatrist Harry Stack Sullivan, all personal growth and healing, as well as all personal damage and regressions, come through relationships with other people. All counseling, and almost all of the issues discussed in this book, deal directly or indirectly with interpersonal relations. Clearly, how people get along with each other, including how they communicate, must be an issue of crucial concern to all Christian counselors.

The Bible and Interpersonal Relations

The Bible is a realistic book which documents the historical existence of interpersonal problems and communication breakdowns. Adam and Eve, the first married couple, had a disagreement about the reasons for their sins in the Garden of Eden. Their first two sons had a conflict which led to murder, and as its population multiplied, the earth became "filled with violence." [1] A few years after the Flood the herdsmen of Abram and Lot began fighting, there were family disputes, and a whole succession of wars which continued "on and off" throughout Old Testament history.

In the New Testament, things were not much better. The disciples of Jesus argued among themselves concerning who would be greatest in heaven. [2] In the early church Ananias and Sapphira lied to their fellow believers, the Jews and Greeks were at odds with each other, and there were disputes over doctrine. [3] Many times in his letters the Apostle Paul

332

commented on the disunity in the church and appealed for peace. In his own missionary activities he was involved in conflict,[4] and on one occasion wrote to the Corinthians expressing the fear that if he came for a visit he might find "strife, jealousy, angry tempers, disputes, slanders, gossip, arrogance, disturbances" and other evidences of interpersonal tension.[5]

Although the Bible records many cases of dissension, such interpersonal strife is never condoned or overlooked. On the contrary, strife is strongly forbidden and principles for good interpersonal relations are mentioned frequently. For example, the Book of Proverbs alone instructs us to refrain from untrue, slanderous comments, to speak softly and pleasantly, to listen carefully, to tell the truth, to resist the temptation to gossip, to confront honestly, and to trust God.[6] Unrestrained anger, hasty words, personal pride and dishonesty, envy, the struggle for riches—these and a host of other harmful attributes are mentioned as sources of tension. Perhaps there is no book in the Bible which equals Proverbs in clear, consistent teaching about good interpersonal relations.

But the teaching does occur elsewhere. Most of the Sermon on the Mount concerns interpersonal relations.[7] Throughout his later ministry Jesus taught about conflict reduction and intervened in several disputes.[8] He instructed people to "be at peace with one another." Paul warned Timothy not to be quarrelsome, especially over unimportant things; and in other Bible passages there are instructions to live in harmony, to demonstrate love, and to replace bitterness and wrath with kindness and a tendency to be tender-hearted and forgiving.[9] After a warning against those who cause trouble because they do not control their tongues, James notes that quarrels and conflicts come because of personal lust and envy.[10] Then, in the midst of an exciting list of practical guidelines for living, we read Paul's instructions to "never pay back evil for evil to anyone. . . . If possible, so far as it depends on you, be at peace with all men." [11] Jesus and the biblical writers were peacemakers who, by their example and exhortation, expect modern believers to be peacemakers as well.[12]

As one ponders the many biblical statements on interpersonal relations several themes are apparent:

1. *Good Interpersonal Relations Start with Jesus Christ.* Every Christmas we are reminded that Jesus Christ is the Prince of Peace.[13] He predicted that there would be tension between his followers and their non-believing relatives and friends,[14] but he also promised to give a supernatural peace which originated with him and was more authentic and longer lasting than the efforts of this world's peace seekers.[15] Jesus himself is described as "our peace" who is able to break down the walls of dissension that divide us.[16] Peace with God comes when we confess our sins and failures to him, ask him to take control of our lives, and expect that he will give us the peace which the Word of God promises. This is not something relegated to the future. A commitment of our lives and differences to Christ brings peace *now*.

2. *Good Interpersonal Relations Start within People*. There is nothing wrong with negotiations between individuals, political factions, protagonists in labor disputes, or between sovereign nations. Such efforts at peacemaking often can be helpful, but the Bible puts a greater emphasis on the attitudes and characteristics of the persons involved in the disputes.

In his first letter to the Corinthians, Paul divides all people into three categories.[17] The *natural people* are nonbelievers who do not accept or understand the things of God. They are characterized by "deeds of the flesh" such as strife, jealousy, outbursts of anger, disputes, dissensions, factions and envy.[18] They may desire and strive for peace but their alienation from God makes peace ultimately unattainable. The second group, *young believers,* have committed their lives to Christ but have never grown spiritually. They are Christians who are "still fleshy" and characterized by strife and jealousy. *Spiritual people,* the third group, are Christians who are yielded to divine control and are seeking to know the mind of Christ. These people are growing in the "fruit of the Spirit" which involves love, joy, peace, patience, kindness, goodness, faithfulness, gentleness, self-control, and a freedom from self-centered boasting and envy.[19]

When people are transformed within, there is a change in their outward behavior. This is an important principle to remember in counseling. For real peace to occur there must be peace within individuals. Then comes peace between people. Both the internal and interpersonal peace must be preceded by a commitment to Christ which is followed by spiritual growth. This growth comes as individuals and groups worship together, pray, and meditate on God's Word.

3. *Good Interpersonal Relations Involve Determination, Effort, and Skill*. Good interpersonal relations do not happen automatically, even among Christians. The Bible and modern psychology agree that conflict reduction demands a desire to get along, accompanied by the consistent development and application of such skills as listening carefully, watching, understanding oneself and others, refraining from unkind comments or emotional outbursts, and communicating accurately. All of this is learned; all of it can be taught by the perceptive Christian counselor.

The Causes of Poor Interpersonal Relations

Why can't people get along with each other? This has been debated for centuries, and although the answers are far from being conclusive, they might be summarized in four general categories:

1. *Personal Attitudes and Actions*. Interpersonal tension begins with people whose attitudes, perceptions, feelings and behavior create conflict and distrust. Jesus once was approached by a man whose simple request was, "Teacher, tell my brother to divide the family inheritance with me." Instead of arbitration; Jesus gave a warning against every form of greed.[20] The man's family conflict came because of his greedy attitude. Elsewhere, Jesus warned about finding fault in others when there are even worse

faults in ourselves.[21] The "faults" which hinder good interpersonal relations include:

—A self-centered need to be noticed, to be in control, to have our own way, or to have money, prestige, and status;

—a nonforgiving, bitter attitude;

—a tendency to be hypercritical, judgmental and angry;

—an insecurity which involves feelings of threat, fear of rejection and a reluctance to trust others;

—prejudice, often unrecognized or denied;

—an unwillingness or inability to "open up" and share one's feelings and thoughts; and

—a failure or unwillingness to recognize individual differences (not everybody thinks and feels and sees situations like I do).

It would be incorrect to assume that all of these are deliberate attempts to hinder smooth relationships. An unwillingness to forgive, holding grudges, or demands to have one's own way are sinful and avoidable. In contrast, fear of getting close, or a reluctance to trust others may be ingrained attitudes which are more difficult to change without help from a friend or counselor.

2. *Conflict Patterns.* Conflict has been called one of the most pervasive and confounding of all human activities. It is a struggle which occurs when two or more people have goals which appear to be incompatible, or want something which apparently is scarce. Stated somewhat formally, people in conflict "face the problem of reconciling their individual needs for power, success, attainment, and winning with their relationship needs for trust, affection, collective benefits, and mutual growth."[22] While conflicts often are destructive and threatening, they also can serve a useful purpose in clarifying goals, unifying a group, and sometimes bringing previously ignored disagreements to a point of discussion and resolution.

It has been suggested that people and groups have their unique conflict styles which sometimes are very rigid and, as a result, contribute to furthering the conflict.[23] Some people throw adult temper tantrums, pouting and stomping away when they are in conflict. Others resort to such conflicting approaches as speaking quietly (using a "soft answer"), shouting, interrupting frequently, attempting to intimidate or attack the opposition, ignoring the other side, trying to manipulate subtly or openly, attempting to bribe, pretending to avoid the situation, openly discussing the issues honestly, attempting to be deceitful, or engaging in "behind the scenes" politics—to name a few.

When there is conflict the counselor should attempt to discover the real issues involved (which may be different from the stated issues), and it will be useful to observe and attempt to understand the approaches or styles of conflict which the participants are using.

3. *Communication Failure.* The essence of good interpersonal rela-

tions is good communication. When communication is inefficient or in danger of breaking down, interpersonal tensions often follow.

But even when two people want to communicate accurately there can be several reasons for failure. At the simplest level a *sender* attempts to communicate a message to a *receiver*. This process is hindered if:

—The sender is unclear in his or her own mind about the message (if the sender doesn't think clearly, communication cannot be clear).

—The sender does not put the message into clearly understandable words.

—The sender says one thing, but conveys a different message by behavior (for example, if the sender says "I'm sad" but at the same time is laughing and joking, the message is confused. When we say one thing with our lips but show something else with our actions we are sending a "double message").

—The sender mumbles the message so it is not sent clearly.

—The receiver doesn't understand the message.

—The receiver adds his or her interpretation to the message, or misses ideas which are too threatening to hear.

Even when the communication process begins clearly, the receiver often begins to respond with facial features, gestures and verbalizations—even before the whole message is sent. This, in turn, can interrupt the sender and cause him or her to change the message before it is completely sent.

When the communicators do not know each other, communication will depend largely on words and widely understood gestures. When the communicators are in intimate contact (like two close colleagues, or a husband and wife) they know each other so well that much is communicated by a facial expression, tone of voice, a half sentence, or even a grunt. These shortcuts speed up communication, but they also create great potential for miscommunication. This is because intimates often are inclined to interpret what is being said, based on past experience, instead of concentrating on the message or the messenger.

4. *Social Irritants*. Sometimes events or conditions in the society prevent or hinder good interpersonal relations. For many years, people have recognized the power of "mob psychology" in arousing people to support or defy well-known individuals or issues of public interest. Lynching, rebellions, racial and labor violence, student unrest, church splits, military uprisings and even wars are examples of interpersonal tensions which arise as a result of social irritants.

Even our closeness to others can have an influence on interpersonal relations.[24] It appears that tensions are more likely to erupt in crowded, uncomfortable urban areas, than in the more spacious suburbs or rural communities. One research study even tested the influence of physical closeness on anxiety. Women, it was found, appreciated being in close contact with others, while men were anxious and felt "fenced in" when they were close enough to touch.[25]

These social influences frequently arouse such emotions as anger, jealousy, frustration, or fear. When there is no opportunity to get away from noise, from the demands of one's work or from other people (including the family), tension frequently builds and interpersonal conflict results. Within recent years human behavior specialists have begun more detailed study of the social influences on interpersonal relationships.

The Effects of Poor Interpersonal Relations

People react differently to interpersonal tension. Some resist it, others avoid it, and there are people who appear to thrive on it. Such tension always is potentially threatening, however, so we often act in ways that protect ourselves. We hide our true feelings and insecurities, for example, subtly try to manipulate others and pretend to be something that we are not. All of these tactics take a toll and influence us physically, psychologically, socially and spiritually.

The *physical* effects of stress and interpersonal tension are well known. Fatigue, tense muscles, headaches, stomach upsets, ulcers—these and a variety of other biological reactions come, especially when tensions are denied or kept hidden. "When I repress my emotions," wrote John Powell, "my stomach keeps score. . . ." [26]

Psychologically, poor interpersonal relations can trigger almost every human emotion, and the actions of people in conflict can range all the way from murder to mild disinclination to cooperation. When there is tension, people sometimes feel depressed, guilty, "put down" or lacking in self-confidence. At times there is anger, bitterness, cynicism, and attempts to dominate, manipulate or get revenge. When they feel threatened or frustrated in their attempts to get along, people don't always think clearly. As a result things are said or done which later are regretted.

This gets us to the *social* effects of interpersonal stress, including verbal aggression, violence, withdrawal from others and the breaking of previously meaningful relationships (as, for example, when two business people impulsively terminate their partnership, a family stomps out of church, an employee quits "on the spot," a couple suddenly decides to separate, or two nations go to war over some minor issue). Such actions escalate or maintain the conflict but they rarely solve anything. They may satisfy one's desire for power and revenge, but these are destructive reactions which often lead to suffering, negativism, loneliness and later feelings of regret.

None of this helps people *spiritually*. When Adam and Eve were tempted, the devil tried (successfully) to create interpersonal tension between the Creator and his creatures. When they ate of the fruit, Adam and Eve alienated themselves from God and soon were at odds with each other. In one broad sense, therefore, all interpersonal tension is a result and a reflection of sin. When they are alienated from God and from each other, people cannot mature emotionally or spiritually.

Certainly the Bible does not talk about peace at any cost. Sometimes there must be conflict and tension so that compromise, understanding and justice can come. But when conflict exists because of the immaturity or self-centered attitudes of the participants, then conflict is wrong and potentially harmful (although the experience may also stimulate growth).

Counseling and Interpersonal Relations

Getting along with people involves the development of personal characteristics like self-awareness, kindness, concern, sensitivity and patience. But good interpersonal relationships also involve skills, such as the ability to listen, communicate and understand. These effective interpersonal skills do not just appear magically. They are learned, often with help from a sensitive counselor.

The counselor's work occurs in four general areas: helping people to know and change themselves, teaching people how to resolve conflict, teaching communication skills, and helping people change their environments.

1. *Changing the Individual.* Love is a word rarely mentioned in psychological literature, but it dominates the New Testament. It was love which motivated God to send his Son into the world to die for lost human beings. It is love which has been called "the greatest" of all attributes and a characteristic so crucial to Christianity that it becomes the distinguishing mark of believers.[27]

One goal in counseling is to help people become more loving. In any counseling situation we begin by listening and trying to understand the problem, but the counselor demonstrates love and at some time talks about this with the counselee. Try to determine if he or she is a natural individual, baby Christian or spiritual person. Discuss the meaning of love and point out that complete yielding to Christ can change our attitudes and hence our relationships with others. It would be wrong to imply that interpersonal problems disappear automatically when one is yielding to Christ. Skill acquisition is also important, but interpersonal skills are more effective when the skill-user is characterized by a spirit of love, patience, self-control, and the other fruits of the Spirit.

Personal changes such as these come when believers want and seek God's leading in their lives. Often, however, the Holy Spirit works through fellow believers, including counselors, to bring about these changes. The counselor can work more efficiently if he or she can encourage the counselee to share strong and weak points, to express feelings and to be honest before God (in confession), before themselves (in self-examination) and before others (in sharing). Several psychologists have written about the importance of sharing and making ourselves known to at least one other significant person.[28] Such sharing can be overdone. We don't reveal intimate details of our lives indiscriminately and with a variety of people. But sharing with one or two others can be tension-relieving and can give the sharer a greater self-understanding. Such understanding often leads to behavior changes, which contribute to smoother relationships with others. When there is better self-knowledge there is greater freedom to look to the needs of others and to work on building interpersonal relations.

"Changing the individual," therefore, is an overlapping two-part process. It involves encouraging openness and self-examination, and it is concerned with helping counselees grow in their relationship to Jesus Christ. It is the approach which Jesus used when he dealt with conflict.[29]

2. *Teaching Conflict Resolution.* According to David Augsburger, conflict is natural, normal, neutral and sometimes even delightful. "It can turn into painful or disastrous ends, but it doesn't need to. . . . It is not the conflicts that need to concern us, but how the conflicts are handled. . . . How we view, approach and work through our differences does—to a large extent—determine our whole life pattern."[30] Augsburger adds that people can be helped to view conflicts as honest differences which can be resolved by those who are willing to treat each other with respect and to confront each other with truth expressed in love.

There can be value in asking counselees to describe specific recent conflicts. What were the issues, who was involved, how was the conflict handled? What are the differences between conflicts that were handled efficiently and those that were not? Can you see conflict styles evolving? Then, one can work on clarifying goals and discussing tactics for dealing with conflicts.

(a) *Clarifying Goals.* When two people or two groups are in conflict, they often share many of the same goals in spite of their differences. A college faculty, for example, may want quality education but be in conflict over how this is attained in a curriculum. A husband and wife may both want a good marriage, but be in conflict over details of life style, handling money, or raising children. In such cases both sides may want to see the conflict resolved in a way that will be mutually agreeable, mutually beneficial and inclined to enhance the relationship so that future communication will be better. When there are similar goals such as these, conflict resolution is easier.

The two sides often differ in their goals, however. If a wife wants the marital tension to be mended but the husband wants a divorce, then conflict resolution is more difficult. Talking about issues such as finances, life style or contrasting views on religion doesn't help to bring peace because the ultimate goals of the husband and wife are different.

One way to clarify goals is to ask people what they really want. "Let's talk about our goals," one might say. "What do you really want to accomplish by this counseling?" Remember that most conflicts involve both issues and relationships. A father and teenage daughter, for example, may argue about the merits of the girl's new boy friend. That is the issue being debated but underneath there may be the more pressing relation-

Table 23–1
The Directions and Tactics in Conflicts *

Direction 1: *Avoiding the Conflict*
Tactics:

(a) Postponement.
(b) Arguments and discussions about *"how to proceed* in resolving the conflict."
(c) Resorting to use of formal rules.
(d) Precueing—giving prior clues about your position so the other person knows what to expect. This defuses the intensity of the issues.
(e) Keeping track of gripes and grievances which later are "dumped" on the other person. The following discussion or arguments concern the gripes rather than the more basic differences.
(f) Coercive, strong-arm tactics—including bribes. These squelch the opposition and hence avoid issues.
(g) Refusal to recognize the conflict.

Direction 2: *Maintaining the Conflict*
Tactics:

(a) Striking a bargain. Each side gives something to please the other and maintain the status quo, but the real issue of conflict is not resolved. (A couple, for example, may decide to live together "because of the kids" but their marital difficulties are not solved.)
(b) Combining escalation and reduction tactics.

Direction 3: *Escalating the Conflict*
Tactics:

(a) Name-calling (describing another person or issue as "communistic" "rigid," etc.).
(b) Issue expansion (pulling in other issues to increase significance of the conflict).
(c) Coalition formation (finding other people to serve as allies which increases your power).
(d) Threatening.
(e) Constricting the other person (frustrating a person by cuting off discussion, announcing time limitation, etc.). This increases the other person's tendency to fight back.
(f) Personal Attack.

Direction 4: *Reducing the Conflict*
Tactics:

(a) Fractionation (breaking the conflict into smaller issues and dealing with these one at a time).
(b) Asking for more information about the other person's point of view and trying to understand.
(c) Talking about what is happening and what each is feeling as you communicate in the conflict.
(d) Stating your own position clearly and concisely.
(e) Compromising—relying on a situation where everyone loses something and everyone wins something.
(f) Resisting tendencies to criticize, attack, or use emotionally loaded words (like "rigid," "unreasonable," "stupid," etc.).

*Adapted with permission from Joyce Hocker Frost, and William W. Wilmot, *Interpersonal Conflict* (Dubuque, IA: William C. Brown Company, Publishers 1978).

ship question of who has more power in this family—the father or the daughter? The goals of these people, therefore, may be considered in terms of issues (to reach some conclusion about the boy friend) or in terms of relationships (to assert and maintain control over the other person). These differences will not always be recognized or stated, so the counselor must observe activities and attitudes in an attempt to determine if the stated goals are the real or most pressing goals.

When goals are identified and clarified, they can be attained, understood and modified more easily. Sometimes, in counseling, two people first can be reminded of the goals which they share. Then there can be discussion of differences.

(b) Identifying and Discussing Tactics. When individuals or groups are in conflict, they have four major choices about the direction they will take. They may seek to avoid the conflict, maintain it at its present level, escalate it, or reduce it. As we have seen, people don't always want conflict reduction, and sometimes the participants may want to go in different directions. One spouse, for example, may want to avoid facing the conflict in hopes that it might go away if it is ignored for a while. The other spouse may want to escalate the conflict, perhaps in an attempt to get power or to "bring things to a head."

Table 23–1 summarizes some of the tactics which people use to move the conflict in the desired direction. As specific examples of conflict are discussed, the counselor can look for the recurring tactics, point out why some of these are avoiding, maintaining, or reducing the tension; and encourage people to use conflict reduction tactics. This is the essence of teaching ways in which conflict can be reduced and prevented.

3. *Teaching Communication Skills.* Entire books have been written about communication, speaking the truth in love, honesty and related issues.[31] Sometimes the books contain rules for communication, similar to those listed in Table 23–2. When these guidelines are followed consistently, communication and interpersonal relations tend to be smooth, differences are discussed honestly, and conflicts can be resolved satisfactorily.

Often, however, people never learn the communication principles, never practice them, forget them in the heat of argument, or choose to cast them aside. The counselor has the responsibility to (a) learn these and similar principles, (b) practice them in his or her own life, (c) model them in talking with counselees, (d) share them with counselees, and (e) discuss how they could be applied to the counselees' interpersonal relationships.

Look, for example, at the first guideline: *Remember that actions speak louder than words; nonverbal communication usually is more powerful than verbal communication. Avoid "double messages" in which the verbal and nonverbal messages convey something contradictory.* Ask counselees to think of a recent specific conflict. Did anyone give a con-

Table 23–2
Guidelines for Communication *

1. Remember that actions speak louder than words; nonverbal communication usually is more powerful than verbal communication. Avoid "double messages" in which the verbal and nonverbal messages convey something contradictory.

2. Define what is important and stress it; define what is unimportant and deemphasize or ignore it. Avoid fault-finding.

3. Communicate in ways that show respect for the other person's worth as a human being. Avoid statements which begin with the words "You never . . ."

4. Be clear and specific in your communication. Avoid vagueness.

5. Be realistic and reasonable in your statements. Avoid exaggeration and sentences which begin with the words "You always . . ."

6. Test all your assumptions verbally by asking if they are accurate. Avoid acting until this is done.

7. Recognize that each event can be seen from different points of view. Avoid assuming that other people see things like you do.

8. Recognize that your family members and close friends are experts on you and your behavior. Avoid the tendency to deny their observations about you—especially if you are not sure.

9. Recognize that disagreement can be a meaningful form of communication. Avoid destructive arguments.

10. Be honest and open about your feelings and viewpoints. Bring up all significant problems even if you are afraid that doing so will disturb another person. Speak the truth in love. Avoid sullen silence.

11. Do not "put down" and/or manipulate the other person with tactics such as ridicule, interrupting, name-calling, changing the subject, blaming, "bugging," sarcasm, criticism, pouting, guilt-inducing, etc. Avoid the "one-upmanship" game.

12. Be more concerned about how your communication affected others than about what you intended. Avoid getting bitter if you are misunderstood.

13. Accept all feelings and try to understand why others feel and act as they do. Avoid the tendency to say "you shouldn't feel like that."

14. Be tactful, considerate, and courteous. Avoid taking advantage of the other person's feelings.

15. Ask questions and listen carefully. Avoid preaching or lecturing.

16. Do not use excuses. Avoid falling for the excuses of others.

17. Speak kindly, politely, and softly. Avoid nagging, yelling, or whining.

18. Recognize the value of humor and seriousness. Avoid destructive teasing.

*Adapted with permission from Sven Wahlroos. *Family Communication: A Guide to Emotional Health* (New York: Signet-New American Library, 1976).

tradictory message? How could this be avoided in the future? As a counselor, look for examples of double messages and point these out to the counselee. Perhaps as an assignment outside of counseling, the counselee could concentrate on avoiding double messages. Discuss this in a later counseling session.

Care should be taken to present these guidelines in small portions, one or two at a time. In this way counselees are less likely to be overwhelmed by the list.

In all of this, emphasize and demonstrate the following basics of communication: express yourself clearly and honestly, listen carefully with a sincere desire to understand, and respect each other as you would want others to respect you. "It is a law of human life, as certain as gravity: to live fully we must learn to *use* things and *love* people . . . not *love* things and *use* people." [32] These principles enable believers to live in peace, as Jesus demonstrated and commanded.

4. *Changing the Environment.* If, as we have indicated, the environment contributes to interpersonal tension, then counselors and counselees should attempt to change the stress-producing conditions. As a start, whenever possible discuss conflict resolution in a quiet, comfortable place, where crowding is minimal and noise is reduced. Some people like to discuss their conflicts in a restaurant while drinking coffee. This can be a nonthreatening, relaxing place except when there is loud music, distracting customers or gaudy decorations. Environment makes a difference!

But the place in which conflicts are discussed can be less important than the environments in which people live. It is not easy to reduce neighborhood noise, eliminate poverty and violence in the street, improve working conditions or decrease crowding and other physical discomforts. The counselor, therefore, must have a concern for more than the counseling process. He or she surely must be committed to the elimination of the social and environmental conditions which stimulate and escalate interpersonal tensions.

5. *Getting Involved.* It may not always be wise to get involved in some other person's conflict even when invited to do so. The intervener will feel pressure to take sides, will be required to make quick analytical decisions, and will be responsible for keeping communication smooth.

If you do choose to get involved, however, as counselors we must try to:
—show respect for both parties;
—understand both positions without openly taking sides;
—reassure people and give hope if you feel free to do so;
—encourage open communication, and mutual listening;
—encourage people to be specific;
—focus on things which can be changed;
—try to keep the conflict from escalating and prevent the communication from breaking down;

—summarize the situation and positions frequently;

—encourage further help if your mediation does not seem to be effective.

Preventing Poor Interpersonal Relationships

Christianity is a religion of relationships. Its founder is the God of love and love is its most distinguishing characteristic. This is not a sentimental, wishy-washy affection. It is a powerful, sacrificial, giving love which involves the characteristics described in 1 Corinthians 13 and reflects the love of God who sent his Son to die for a sinful world. The church is failing in its duty if it does not preach and practice this love which is so central to the Christian message. Whenever such a message is preached and practiced, interpersonal tensions are reduced.

But God has also given us some more specific guidelines for showing this love.[33] Much advice is given in the pages of Scripture and he has allowed us to discover some principles for getting along and communicating effectively. Interpersonal relations can improve when people of all ages are taught and encouraged to practice consistently:

—the biblical teachings about good relationships;

—a daily walk with Jesus Christ; a walk characterized by prayer, meditation on Scripture, confession of sin, and a willingness to seek and obey divine leading;

—a self-examination which leads to the removal, with God's help, of bitterness, cynicism, and other personal attitudes or actions which would stimulate conflict;

—an understanding of conflict and a practice of those tactics which reduce conflict (rather than maintaining or escalating the conflict);

—the guidelines for effective communication listed in Table 23–2; and

—the reduction, avoidance or elimination of conflict-producing environmental stresses.

This is a large task but one which should be emphasized repeatedly, especially in the church. When Christian leaders, including counselors, are involved in preventing interpersonal tension, they are helping individuals to live in peace and harmony with one another, to avoid destructive conflict and to experience something of the peace which comes from God.[34]

Conclusions about Interpersonal Relations

Human beings are complex creatures with individual personalities and strong wills. We are crowded on a planet which seems to be overly populated with individuals whose sinful nature puts them at odds with God and with each other. Many of us want to get along with each other but this isn't easy.

Perhaps the Apostle Paul was thinking along these lines when he wrote the following inspired directive: "If possible, so far as it depends on you, be at peace with all men."[35] These words come near the end of a few paragraphs dealing with practical rules for getting along: "love without hypocrisy . . . be devoted to one another in brotherly love; give preference to one another . . . practicing hospitality . . . do not be haughty . . . associate with the lowly . . . never pay back evil for evil to anyone, respect what is right . . . ."

Surely it is interesting that Paul's instruction to live in peace is preceded by two qualifiers: "If it is possible" and "so far as it depends on you." "If it is possible" implies that sometimes it isn't possible to live in peace. But each person has responsibility for his or her own attitudes and behavior. As much as it depends on each person, we are to live in peace. With the help of the Holy Spirit, Christian counselors try to establish such peace, to teach others how to live in peace, and to prevent the strain which is characteristic of so many interpersonal relationships.

Suggestions for Further Reading

* Augsburger, David. *Caring Enough to Confront: The Love-Fight.* Glendale, CA: Regal, 1973.

Egan, Gerard. *You and Me: The Skills of Communicating and Relating to Others* Monterey: Brooks/Cole, 1977.

Frost, Joyce Hocker, and Wilmot, William W. *Interpersonal Conflict.* Dubuque, IA: William C. Brown, 1978.

Johnson, David W. *Reaching Out: Interpersonal Effectiveness and Self-Actualization.* Englewood Cliffs, NJ: Prentice-Hall, 1972.

* Powell, John. *Why Am I Afraid to Tell You Who I Am?* Niles, IL: Argus Communications, 1969.

Stott, J. R. W. *Christian Counter-Culture: The Message of the Sermon on the Mount.* Downers Grove, IL: Inter-Varsity, 1978.

* Wahlroos, Sven. *Family Communication.* New York: Signet—New American Library, 1974.

Footnotes

1. Gen. 6:11, 13.
2. Luke 22:24.
3. Acts 5; 6:1; 15:2, 7.
4. Acts 15:36–40.
5. 2 Cor. 12:21, 22.
6. Prov. 10:18, 19; 12:22; 13:3; 15:1, 28, 32; 16:24, 28; 17:9; 19:22; 24:26; 26:20; 28:23, 25.
7. Matt. 5, 6, 7 may take on a new perspective if it is read as a commentary on interpersonal relations.
8. Matt. 18:15–35; 20:20–28; 22:36–40; Luke 12:13–15; 22:24–26.
9. Mark 9:50; 2 Tim. 2:14, 24; Phil. 4:2; 1 Thess. 5:13; 1 Cor. 13:4–8; Eph. 4:31, 32.
10. James 4:1, 2.
11. Rom. 12:17, 18.
12. Matt. 5:9; Prov. 12:20; Heb. 12:14.

13. Luke 2:14; Isa. 9:6.
14. Matt. 10:34.
15. John 14:27; Phil. 4:7.
16. Eph. 2:14–17.
17. 1 Cor. 2:12–3:3.
18. Gal. 5:19–21.
19. Gal. 5:22, 23.
20. Luke 12:13–15.
21. Matt. 7:3–5.
22. Joyce Hocker Frost and William W. Wilmot, *Interpersonal Conflict* (Dubuque, IA: William C. Brown, 1978), p. 1.
23. Ibid.
24. Albert Mehrabian, *Public Places and Private Spaces* (New York: Basic Books, 1977).
25. Gregory J. Nicosia and John R. Aiello, "Effects of Bodily Contact on Reactions to Crowding," paper read at American Psychological Association 84th annual meeting, September, 1976, Washington, DC.
26. John Powell, *Why Am I Afraid to Tell You Who I Am?* (Niles, IL: Argus Communications, 1969), p. 155.
27. 1 Cor. 13:13; 1 John 4:8.
28. Sidney M. Jourard and Dan C. Overlade, *Disclosing Man to Himself* (Princeton, NJ: Van Nostrand Reinhold, 1968).
29. Luke 12:13.
30. Reprinted from p. 3 of *Caring Enough to Confront* (Regal Books) by David Augsburger, with permission of Gospel Light Publications, Glendale, CA 91208. © Copyright 1973 under the title *The Love Fight* by Herald Press.
31. See for example, Marjorie Umphrey, *Getting to Know You: A Guide to Communicating* (Irvine, CA: Harvest House, 1976); Sven Wahlroos, *Family Communication* (New York: Signet-New American Library, 1974); Gerard Egan, *You and Me: The Skills of Communicating and Relating to Others* (Monterey: Brooks/Cole, 1977); Donald L. Kirkpatrick, *No-Nonsense Communication* (Brookfield, WI: K & M Publishers [4380 Continental Dr.]); Powell, *Why Am I Afraid?;* and H. Norman Wright, *Communication—Key to Your Marriage* (Glendale, CA: Regal, 1974).
32. Powell, *Why Am I Afraid?* p. 134.
33. 1 John 4:16–19; John 13:35.
34. 2 Cor. 13:11; Phil. 4:5, 6.
35. Rom. 12:18.

24

Inferiority and Self-esteem

IN A WIDELY READ BOOK WHICH APPEARED SEVERAL YEARS AGO, physician Maxwell Maltz estimated that 95 percent of all people in our society feel inferior. He argued that millions of persons are seriously handicapped because they have a strong sense of inadequacy, and he went on to suggest that a more positive self-image is the "key to a better life." [1] Many years before Maltz, psychiatrist Alfred Adler had reached a similar conclusion. To be a human being, he once wrote, "means the possession of a feeling of inferiority that is constantly spurring us on . . . ." Feelings of inferiority, therefore, are very common and likely to be encountered in the work of any Christian counselor.

In discussing the issue of inferiority we must begin with a consideration of three psychological terms: self-concept, self-image, and self-esteem. Self-concept and self-image refer to the pictures we have of ourselves. Ask yourself, or a counselee, "If you were a novelist describing yourself as the chief character in a book, what would you say?" Undoubtedly, such a description would include a listing of character traits, strengths and weaknesses, and physical features. Self-concept and self-image include the thoughts, attitudes, and feelings we have about ourselves. Self-esteem means something slightly different. This term refers to the evaluation that an individual makes of his or her worth, competence and significance. Whereas self-image and self-concept involve a self-description, self-esteem involves a self-evaluation. Clearly these three overlap. They are carried around in our heads, and often change as the result of our experiences. Sometimes they are maintained stubbornly in spite of contrary evidence, and almost always they influence how we think, act, or feel.

The Bible and Self-esteem

Within the Christian community there has been a tendency to emphasize human inadequacy and worthlessness. Consider, for example, a hymn

347

like "Amazing Grace" which speaks of human wretchedness, or the familiar phrase in another hymn: "Would He devote that sacred head for such a worm as I?" In Christian counseling it is crucial to understand and share the biblical teaching about human worth since, as we shall see, the Bible gives us the only real perspective by which we can overcome inferiority and build true self-esteem.

1. *The Biblical Teaching about Human Worth.* Throughout its pages the Bible constantly affirms that human beings are valuable in God's sight. We were created in God's image with intellectual abilities, the capacity to communicate, the freedom to make choices, a knowledge of right and wrong, and the responsibility to administer and rule over the rest of creation.[2] Even after the Fall, we are described as "a little lower than God," and crowned with "glory and honor."[3] Because he loves us, God sent his own Son to pay for our sins and to make possible our redemption and renewed communion with God the Father.[4] He has sent angels to guard us, the Holy Spirit to guide us, and the Scriptures to teach us that we are the salt of the earth, the light of the world, and individuals who, if we trust in God, will spend eternity with him in a place prepared for us in heaven.[5] Bruce Narramore has suggested what this means for human self-acceptance:

> Compared with . . . secular perspectives, the Christian view of self-esteem is in a category by itself. It alone elevates man above the animals. It alone provides a solid foundation on which to build self-esteem. The biblical view of man acknowledges our sins and failures, but it doesn't demean our deepest significance as creations of the living God. . . . Because we are created in the image of God, we possess great worth, significance, and value. We are loved by God and deserving of the love of ourselves and others.[6]

2. *The Biblical Teaching about Human Sin.* The Bible teaches that as a result of Adam's sin, all people are sinners who have become alienated from God and condemned because of their sinful natures and actions.[7] Sin is rebellion against God. It represents a doubting of God's truthfulness and a challenge to his perfect will. Sin leads to interpersonal conflict, attempts at self-justification, a tendency to blame others for our weaknesses, psychosomatic problems, verbal and physical aggression, tension, and a lack of respect for God.[8] All of this surely influences the way we feel about ourselves, often producing guilt and undoubtedly lowering our self-esteem.

But even in our fallen state, God still loves and values us. He hates the sin but loves the sinner. He knows that we are ungodly and helpless but this does not mean that we are unredeemable and worthless. Indeed, because of his love and mercy, he sent his Son to die so that we could be made righteous and be brought back into his family as fully forgiven sons and daughters.[9]

Sin, therefore, breaks our relationship with God, but it does not destroy the fact that in God's sight we still are human beings, at the apex of divine creation, and of immense worth and value.

3. *The Biblical Teaching about Pride.* Some Christians who emphasize human depravity argue that self-esteem is a form of pride. Since pride is greatly abhorred by God,[10] these believers assume that self-condemnation and inferiority are attitudes that keep us humble.

Pride is characterized by an exaggerated desire to win the notice or praise of others.[11] It is an arrogant, haughty estimation of oneself in relation to others. It involves the taking of a superior position which largely disregards the concerns, opinions and desires of other people. In essence, it is an attempt to claim for oneself the glory that rightly belongs to God.

In contrast, humility is characterized by "accurate self-appraisal, responsiveness to the opinions of others, and a willingness to give praise to others before claiming it for one's self."[12] The humble person accepts his or her imperfections, sins, and failures, but also acknowledges the gifts, abilities and achievements which have come from God. Humility is not a self-negation or the rejection of all our God-given strengths and abilities. Humility involves a grateful dependence on God and a realistic appraisal of both our strengths and weaknesses.

The Apostle Paul, for example, was deeply aware of his sinful past and continuing imperfections, but he also acknowledged his considerable achievements.[13] He recognized that he had been redeemed and greatly used by God. His was a realistic self-image. It was characterized not by pride, but by a humble evaluation of what God had done and was doing through him. Self-esteem, a realistic self-appraisal, and humility go together.

4. *The Biblical Teaching about Self-love.* The Bible assumes that we will love ourselves.[14] But this conclusion is difficult for some Christians to accept because they equate self-love with an attitude of superiority, stubborn self-will or self-centered pride. Self-love, however, is not an erotic or ecstatic self-adoration. Self-love means to see ourselves as worthwhile creatures, valued and loved by God, gifted members of the body of Christ (if we are Christians), and bearers of the divine image. We can love ourselves because God loves us, and we do not deny the abilities and opportunities which God has given. This biblical view of self-love must become the basis of self-esteem.

The Causes of Inferiority and Low Self-esteem

We have given an extended consideration to the biblical teachings on self-esteem first because these are so basic to counseling in this area, and second, because departure from these teachings is at the root of many inferiority problems. To be specific, people feel inferior and develop low self-esteem because of faulty theology, sin, past experiences, poor parent-child relationships, unrealistic expectations, faulty thinking and community influences.

1. *Faulty Theology.* This has been considered in the preceding paragraphs. People are inclined to feel inferior when they assume that humans are worthless, that sin makes us of no significance to God, that humility is the same as self-condemnation, or that self-love is sinful. Each of these views is held by sincere people, many of whom apparently assume, incorrectly, that self-esteem is wrong or that feelings of inferiority are desirable for committed Christians.

A variation of this view is held by those sincere Christians who accept a "self-crucifixion" approach to theology. This assumes that humans are worthless; that our desires, thoughts and individual uniqueness should be "crucified," and that we should let Christ's thoughts and actions pass through and control us like water runs through a pipe. Such a view seems to be spiritual but it really squelches the individual gifts, abilities, personalities and creativities that come to each of us from God. It is a view which fails to realize that Christians have been crucified (in the past) with Christ, but that now we are to live as new creatures in vital fellowship with him. This does not mean that we are to reject our individuality, abilities and personalities. Instead we are to submit these to divine control and trust that God will work through the unique individual differences he has given to each person.

2. *Sin.* When God created human beings, he gave us a standard of right and wrong—not because he was interested in spoiling our fun, but because he wanted us to be happy and to experience the well-being that comes when we love in accordance with his universal principles. When we violate these principles we are guilty, and as a result we feel remorse, guilt, and disappointment in ourselves. This contributes to our inferiority and undermines our self-esteem.

3. *Past Experience.* In a society which values success, it is difficult to experience failure, rejection and criticism. When failure and belittling are frequent it is easy to conclude, "I'm no good. Look what people think of me. Look how I mess things up."

At times failure comes because others expect us to fail. We conclude, "Nobody expects me to succeed or be liked so why try?" When we don't try, failure is assured and self-esteem is further eroded.

4. *Parent-child Relationships.* Within recent years numerous books have appeared dealing with the subject of self-esteem. All agree that inferiority and low self-esteem most often arise in the home. A child's self-esteem is formed largely in his or her early years.[15]

Parents are inconsistent in their feelings about children. Even the most patient parent explodes in criticism at times or withholds acceptance and warmth. Children rarely, if ever, are damaged by such minor parental fluctuations, but real feelings of inferiority do come when parents

—criticize, shame, reject, and scold repeatedly (it has been said that we dislike ourselves in direct proportion to the amount of rejection and criticism we experience in childhood);[16]

—set unrealistic standards and goals;
—express their expectation that the child will probably fail;
—rarely give praise, encouragement, compliments, and emotional support;
—punish repeatedly and harshly;
—imply that children are a nuisance, stupid, or incompetent;
—avoid cuddling, hugging or affectionate touching; and
—overprotect and dominate children so that they fail later when forced to be on their own.

5. *Unrealistic Expectations.* As we grow up, most of us develop expectations for the future and ideals that we would like to attain. When these expectations and ideals are unrealistically high, we have set ourselves up for failure and the feeling of inferiority which often follows.

According to Narramore,[17] there are three common "enemies of self-acceptance." These are assumptions which we commonly accept but which undermine self-esteem. The three enemies are the false but widely held beliefs that:
—I must meet other people's standards and expectations if I am to be accepted and loved;
—whenever I fail to reach my goals and expectations (or those of other people) I need to be pressured, shamed, frightened or punished; and
—I must seek to master my world, to be in charge, to be smart, to be the center of my environment, and to make my own decisions.

Each of these beliefs is unrealistic and hence contributes to failure and low self-esteem.

6. *Faulty Thinking.* It is common for each of us to believe and sometimes even make up statements about ourselves which have little or no basis in reality. "Nobody likes me" or "I'm no good" are ideas which may contain more fantasy than realism. If it is not to control us, such thinking must be challenged. Where is the evidence to support such conclusions?

7. *Community Influences.* Society has certain values which are emphasized by the mass media and demonstrated in homes, schools, governments, businesses, and social settings. It is widely assumed that a person's worth depends on his or her intelligence, physical attractiveness, education, money, powers and achievements. People are encouraged to manipulate circumstances and each other to attain and retain these symbols of success. It is assumed that their possession will increase one's self-esteem; that their loss or nonattainment will increase one's sense of inferiority. Nothing could be further from the truth—as many so-called successful people will verify. Self-esteem that is built on status symbols is unstable and nonsatisfying. Nevertheless these cultural myths persist, motivate many people, and lead to a lowered self-esteem when the status symbols are not attained—or attained and then lost.

The Effects of Inferiority and Low Self-esteem

Low self-esteem affects a wide variety of actions, attitudes and emotions. Summarizing numerous research studies, Ellison[18] has reported that people with low self-esteem:

—feel isolated and unlovable;

—feel too weak to overcome their deficiencies, are lacking in drive and unable to defend themselves;

—are angry, but afraid of angering others or drawing attention to themselves;

—have difficulty getting along with others;

—are likely to be submissive, dependent, and inclined to have their feelings easily hurt;

—have lower curiosity and creativity; and

—are less inclined to disclose themselves to others.

Other writers[19] have suggested that low self-esteem contributes to:

—a lack of inner peace and security;

—low self-confidence;

—social withdrawal;

—jealousy and criticism of others;

—interpersonal conflict;

—self-criticism, self-hatred and self-rejection;

—depression;

—a drive to gain power, superiority and control over others;

—a tendency to be complaining, argumentative, intolerant, hypersensitive and unforgiving;

—an inability to accept compliments or expressions of love; and

—an inclination to be a poor listener and a poor loser.

All of this reflects the tremendously extensive influence of low self-esteem. Perhaps all of us feel inferior to some extent. When the inferiority feelings are great, virtually all human actions, feelings, attitudes, thoughts and values are affected.

Counseling People with Inferiority and Low Self-esteem

Feelings of inferiority and low self-esteem build up over many years. It is unrealistic, therefore, to expect that change will come quickly, but over a period of time the following can be done:

1. *Give Genuine Support, Acceptance and Approval.* There is research to support the conclusion that people who feel inferior will "back off" and respond negatively to expressions of approval and affirmation which are unrealistic, abrupt, or not genuine.[20] If we "overdo" the praise and approval, counselees won't believe us and at times will decide to avoid the counselor. It is more helpful to give continuing support, gentle encouragement, and mild but sincere approval for achievements that clearly can be evaluated as good. From all of this it follows that a back-slapping attitude which says, "Buck up, you're really a significant person,"

does almost nothing to help an individual shed feelings of inferiority.

2. *Seek to Develop Self-understanding.* Insight into one's own behavior isn't easy, neither is it always helpful. Sometimes such introspection
causes people to become more self-condemning, to overlook significant
facts and to lose objectivity. A counselor, however, can help a counselee
search out the sources for his or her poor self-concept (perhaps by considering past experiences which were affirming or condemning). But
the counselor also can keep an objective perspective on the situations
being discussed, and can remind the counselee—frequently if necessary—
that we are not prisoners of the past. As we understand the past roots of
behavior and thinking, we can change.

3. *Share the Biblical Perspective on Self-esteem.* Counseling will not
be very successful if the counselee is convinced that inferiority is the
same as humility and that self-esteem is equivalent to sinful pride. Christians must be helped to see the biblical teachings about human worth
and self-esteem. They must be shown that proper self-love is all right and
approved by God. They must be urged to give up self-condemnation and
shown that such condemnation is both destructive and wrong in the sight
of God. It may take a long time before such ideas are accepted, but their
acceptance is a prerequisite for anyone who wants to develop a more
positive self-concept.

4. *Encourage Self-disclosure and a Realistic Self-evaluation.* It is
true, no doubt, that sharing helps build self-esteem. When a person shares
his or her self-concept others can give "feedback" in the form of their
perceptions. As these other people show acceptance, the counselee can
begin self-acceptance.

The counselor must be alert to the fact that such sharing can lead
counselees into a subtle manipulation of others. If I say, for example,
"I'm no good—I'm a failure," other people are made to feel that they
should deny this evaluation with a comment like, "Oh, that's not true!"
Counselees should be shown how their own self-condemning comments
are often used to pull expressions of praise from other people. Praise and
affirmation that come through such manipulation aren't really very affirming. As a result the inferiority feelings persist.

It is better for the counselor to help the counselee list his or her good
traits, strengths and assets, as well as weaknesses, inabilities and less desirable characteristics. As the list is developed, and preferably written on
paper, ask, "What is the objective evidence (in the form of others' opinions, past experiences, and so on) that each item on the list—both positive and negative—should be there?" Remember to emphasize the strong
points, special talents or gifts and show how those can be put to better
use. People often focus so much on their weaknesses that they inhibit or
deny their God-given talents and abilities.

Remember, too, people are reluctant to acknowledge their strengths
because this can be threatening. When a person is convinced of his or

her inferiority, there is no pressure to succeed, and no motivation to risk failure. Some people even bask in their assumed inferiorities. Once they admit that there are strong points, the pressure is on to develop and use these positive traits. That means effort and it also means that individuals must take the risk that they might fail. They must take more responsibility for their actions. For persons with a poor self-concept, the risk may seem too great. It is safer to wallow in one's inferiorities. This brings us to the next two suggestions for counseling.

5. *Stimulate the Reexamination of Expectations, Goals and Priorities.* There can be two kinds of goals—long-range and short-term. Long-range goals are often major (like buying a house, getting a college degree, earning a promotion) while short-term goals are more immediate and more easily attained (like passing a test, finishing a do-it-yourself project, or introducing yourself to a new neighbor). Long-range goals often seem overpowering and unattainable, so the person who feels inferior declines to tackle them.

It is well to remember, however, that long-range goals can be broken down into short-term projects. As each short-term goal is reached, we experience a sense of accomplishment and move slightly toward our long-range aspirations.

Consider, for example, the writing of this book. At first the project seemed overwhelming, but as I write, I am moving to the goal by completing one paragraph at a time. I set up daily goals—to write five or six handwritten pages a day, for example. This is challenging enough to motivate me, but realistic enough to ensure that on most days I will succeed in meeting my expectations.

Counselees should be encouraged to write down their long-range goals and priorities. Then they should be helped to break these down into much smaller, attainable goals. As the smaller goals are reached the individual can experience some kind of success. This leads to a better self-image. In all of this, the counselor can stimulate realistic goal-planning (which will ensure some successes), can give encouragement as the counselee attempts new activities, can help the counselee evaluate what went wrong when there was failure, can encourage the person to "try again," and when necessary, can point out that periodic failure is not proof of one's inferiority.

At times there is also value in examining one's motives. Why does the counselee want to attain certain specific goals? What are his or her motives? Be sure to remind people that it is always important to do what one believes to be right (even if this leads to criticism from others). It is unlikely that one can experience real self-esteem unless this is done.

In all of this, remember that no human being is completely alone. God gives strength and guidance to those who seek his help. He directs individuals in the development of their goals or priorities, and he helps us as we develop new skills.

6. *Teach New Skills.* Sometimes counselees need to learn new skills or improve old ones, all of which can help them attain goals, complete tasks, or reach vocational objectives. As a counselor your task may involve encouraging someone to attend school or enroll in a training program.

There are other skills, however, which can be taught in the counseling sessions and practiced elsewhere. These involve teaching counselees to:

—Avoid dwelling on the negative—the tendency to think hypercritical thoughts and to make negative, argumentative comments which alienate others, arouse hostility within the critic and undermine the critic's own self-esteem.

—Give frequent encouragement, compliments and respect to others. Respecting others whom God has created helps us to respect ourselves.

—Listen and communicate. This builds smooth interpersonal relationships and these, in turn can be supportive.

—Meditate regularly on God's Word. He loves us and communicates with us through the Bible. This Book can help individuals keep a realistic perspective when there is a tendency, instead, to slip into thoughts of one's own inferiorities and incompetence.

7. *Help Counselees Avoid Destructive Influences.* The first of these is sin. Sin ultimately creates guilt, self-condemnation, depression, and a loss of self-esteem. It is impossible to feel good about ourselves while we deliberately disobey God's principles for our lives. Counselees must be helped to honestly face their sin, to confess it to God and perhaps to one or two others, and to remember that God forgives and forgets.[21]

The inability to forgive, especially the inability to forgive oneself, can also undermine self-esteem. There is need to remember that vengeance and the administration of justice are God's responsibilities, not ours.[22] We need to ask him to help us forgive, to give up our grudges, to love and to really accept the fact that wrongs and injustice can be committed to God who will both forgive those who are sorry and will bring justice to unrepentant wrongdoers.

In his book on building an adequate self-concept,[23] Maurice Wagner notes that we all have destructive tendencies which alienate us from people, prevent spiritual growth, and lower self-esteem. These include the tendencies to:

—treat people as objects to be manipulated;

—resent circumstances which are painful or unpleasant;

—become angry and resentful when we lose control of a situation;

—resent humiliating happenings;

—give up when we are proven wrong;

—be paralyzed and unwilling to act when we are afraid; and

—dread problems instead of accepting them as challenges.

When these are seen in a counselee, they should be pointed out, discussed, and changed if possible, since each can hinder self-esteem.

8. *Give Group Support.* Being accepted by a group of people can do much to stimulate self-esteem and help an individual feel worthwhile. Group counseling, therefore, can be helpful, providing group members are supportive, wanting to help, and not inclined to use the group as a vehicle for criticizing and tearing down each other.

Preventing Inferiority and Low Self-esteem

The Christian community can have a powerful influence in changing self-concepts and preventing individual feelings of inferiority. Ideally, the church is a body of valuable people who exist to care for and build up one another, free from the power struggles, manipulation and status-seeking that characterizes so much of our society. Of course, this doesn't always happen, but the church, nevertheless, can strive to build self-esteem and individuals by giving teaching, support, and parental guidance.

1. *Prevention through Teaching.* As indicated earlier, many people have developed a low self-esteem because of religious teaching which says that it is spiritual to feel inferior. Others see God either as a harsh judge who is waiting to condemn our actions, or as a Being who wants to squelch our personalities and take the fun out of life. These views need to be challenged and replaced with the biblical teachings on human worth, forgiveness, pride and the importance of self-love.

Maurice Wagner summarizes this biblical concept in something which he calls the "basic identity equation": [24]

$$\text{God} + \text{Man} = \text{a Whole Person}$$

An individual's self-concept need not depend on human goals and achievements alone. Each person's sense of belonging, worth and competence comes because we are loved and held up by the sovereign, almighty God who accepts us, gives us unique abilities and gifts, makes us into new creatures, forgives our sins and gives real reason for self-esteem. We are whole persons only when we stand not on our own, but with God.

Within the church Christians should learn that we can love ourselves because God loves us and has made us his children; that we can acknowledge and accept our abilities, gifts, and achievements because these come from God and with his permission; that we can experience the forgiveness of sins because God forgives unconditionally; and that we can praise God for what he is doing in and through us. There is no institution that even comes near to the biblical church in educating people toward a more positive self-concept. In addition to biblical teaching from the pulpit and classrooms, this education might include group discussion of the books listed at the end of this chapter.

2. *Prevention through Christian Community.* It is comforting and self-esteem-building to know that one is an accepted, valued member of a group. The church can provide this acceptance and show support especially in time of need. Church members should be encouraged to care for one another [25] without smothering or overwhelming newcomers or reluctant participants.

The church can also help people acquire new practical skills, and within the church we can reject much of the materialism and success-achievement values which are common in society. We can learn to love one another as brothers and sisters, each of whom has important gifts and contributions to make to the body of Christ.[26] Of course this is idealistic in some ways. People's dress, bearing and speech reveal their social status, and the variety of cars in the parking lot show that the congregation is divided economically. Nevertheless, since God is unimpressed with these status symbols, we should attempt to keep them from influencing our interpersonal relationships and values within the body of Christ.

3. *Prevention through Parental Guidance.* Since many self-esteem problems begin in the home, it is there that the problems are most effectively prevented. Surely it is within the confines of Christian education to teach parents how to build a loving Christian home [27] and how to communicate acceptance to their children. With younger children there is need for physical contact, spontaneous expressions of pleasure, and patient periods of interaction such as play. With older children there must be encouragement, consistent discipline,[28] praise, and time spent in communication. Since there is evidence that parents with high self-esteem tend to have children with high self-esteem,[29] it also is important to help mothers and fathers overcome their inferiorities and build more positive self-concepts.

Conclusions about Inferiority and Self-esteem

Problems of inferiority are so prevalent that a variety of books and psychological theories have been produced to help counselors and counselees build self-esteem. For the nonbeliever who sees human beings as little more than well-developed animals, there is no ultimate basis on which to build or a reason for human dignity and worth. The Christian, however, believes that human worth comes from the love, words and actions of God. How sad that many Christians have so misunderstood and misapplied biblical teaching that inferiorities have been built up in themselves and others. How encouraging to realize that the church and church-related counselors can play a vital role in the understanding, counseling, and prevention of self-esteem problems.

Suggestions for Further Reading

Briggs, Dorothy C. *Your Child's Self-esteem.* Garden City, NY: Doubleday-Dolphin, 1975.

* Dobson, James. *Hide or Seek.* Old Tappan, NJ: Revell, 1974.

Ellison, Craig W., ed. *Self-esteem.* Farmington Hills, MI: Christian Association for Psychological Studies, 1976.

* Narramore, S. Bruce. *You Are Someone Special.* Grand Rapids: Zondervan, 1978.

* Osborne, Cecil G. *The Art of Learning to Love Yourself.* Grand Rapids: Zondervan, 1976.

* Wagner, Maurice E. *The Sensation of Being Somebody: Building an Adequate Self-concept.* Grand Rapids: Zondervan, 1975.

Footnotes

1. Maxwell Maltz, *Psychocybernetics* (New York: Essandes Special Edition, 1968), p. 51.
2. Gen. 1:26–28.
3. Ps. 8:4, 5.
4. John 3:16.
5. Ps. 91:11, 12; Heb. 1:14; Luke 12:12; Matt. 5:13, 14; John 14:26, 1–3.
6. S. Bruce Narramore, *You Are Someone Special* (Grand Rapids: Zondervan, 1978), p. 29.
7. Rom. 3:25; 5:12, 17–19; 6:23a; 7:18.
8. Gen. 3:11–13; Ps. 32:1–5; Rom. 3:11–18.
9. See John 3:16; Rom. 5:1, 8–11; 8:1, 14–17.
10. Prov. 16:18; James 4:6; 1 Pet. 5:5.
11. Craig W. Ellison, ed., *Self-esteem* (Farmington Hills, MI: Christian Association for Psychological Studies, 1976).
12. Ibid, p. 5.
13. See the section entitled "Paul's Self-image" in the chapter by Anthony A. Hoekema, "The Christian Self-image," in *Self-esteem*, ed. Craig W. Ellison, pp. 25–39.
14. Eph. 5:28, 29.
15. For discussion of this issue see Dorothy C. Briggs, *Your Child's Self-esteem* (Garden City, NY: Doubleday-Dolphin, 1975).
16. Cecil G. Osborne, *The Art of Learning to Love Yourself* (Grand Rapids: Zondervan, 1976), p. 21.
17. S. Bruce Narramore, *You Are Someone Special*, pp. 85–96.
18. Ellison, *Self-esteem*, p. 17.
19. See especially Narramore, *You Are Someone Special;* and Osborne, *The Art of Learning to Love Yourself.*
20. R. M. Baron, "Social Reinforcement Effects as a Function of Social Reinforcement History," *Psychological Review* 6 (1966): 529–39.
21. John 1:8, 9; James 5:16.
22. Rom. 12:19.
23. Maurice E. Wagner, *The Sensation of Being Somebody: Building an Adequate Self-concept* (Grand Rapids: Zondervan, 1975).
24. Ibid., p. 236.
25. I Cor. 12:25.
26. 1 Cor. 12:4–25.
27. One of the best books concerned with building a Christian home is that of Gene A. Getz, *The Measure of a Family* (Glendale, CA: Regal, 1976). See also Gary R. Collins, *Family Talk* (Santa Ana: Vision House, 1978).
28. For a good discussion of discipline see James Dobson, *Dare to Discipline* (Wheaton, IL: Tyndale House, 1973).
29. Ellision, *Self-esteem*, pp. 13, 14.

Part VI
Other Issues

25
Financial Problems

"THE LOVE OF MONEY IS THE ROOT OF ALL EVIL." THUS WROTE THE divinely inspired writer of Scripture many centuries ago.[1] Although the Apostle Paul didn't say so, it probably would have been equally true to add that "the abuse and mismanagement of money is at the root of all kinds of human problems." Individual tension, family conflict, interpersonal strife, anger, frustration, driving ambition—at times all are related directly or indirectly to the pursuit and management of money.

The existence of money is not, in itself, a problem. We need money to trade and to meet individual needs. What is a problem is our *attitude* toward money, and our *inefficiency* in handling it wisely. The Christian counselor discovers this frequently. Sometimes finances are listed as the basic problem; sometimes financial struggles are presented as a part of some broader problem, such as anxiety, marital conflict, or adjusting to retirement.

The Bible and Finances

Unlike some of the other issues discussed in this book, the Bible says much about the subjects of money, possessions and management of finances. These biblical teachings can be summarized in the form of several principles.

1. *Money and Finances Must Be Viewed Realistically.* In a well-known parable, Jesus once described a man whose whole life was spent in accumulating wealth. Then the man died, unprepared to meet God, and left his precious possessions to someone else. Jesus called this man a fool.[2] He was rich in worldly wealth but poor in his relationship to God.

In modern times there are many similar people whose lives are centered on money. The story is told of several very successful American businessmen who met in 1921. The group included the most successful speculator on Wall Street, a cabinet minister, and the presidents of the New York Stock Exchange, the Bank of International Settlements, the largest

361

steel company in the United States, the largest utility company, and the largest gas company. Twenty-five years later all were dead. Three had died of suicide, three had been in prison, one went insane and two died in bankruptcy. All had been ruined financially by the Great Depression of the 1930s. At a time when millions of common people took in their belts and went on living, these men had been destroyed because their lives centered on money. When the money was gone there was no purpose in living.[3]

According to the Scriptures, money is temporary.[4] Ultimately it does not satisfy or bring happiness and stability.[5] Little wonder that we are warned to "let your way of life be free from the love of money, being content with what you have. . . . If riches increase, do not set your heart upon them."[6] Once again we should emphasize that money is not condemned, but the love of money and dependence on riches are clearly wrong.

2. *Money and Finances Are Provided by God.* He supplies all of our needs, expects us to trust in him for our finances, and has shown that we need not be anxious or worried about having enough.[7] There are people who squander their money through mismanagement and others confuse their real needs with their desired extras, but in terms of basics like food and clothing, God provides—often in great abundance.

Sometimes, however, he chooses to provide only the barest necessities. For reasons known only to him, he permits starving and hardship. Nevertheless he supplies what we need (not always what we want or think we need) when we need it.

3. *Money and Finances Can Be Harmful.* The rich young ruler who came to Jesus asking about eternal life walked away grieving when he heard the command to give to the poor.[8] Apparently a love of money prevented his spiritual growth. It is possible, as Jesus said on another occasion, to gain the whole world and lose one's soul.[9] Elsewhere he taught that it is not possible to love both God and money. Eventually we will come to the point of loving the one and hating the other.[10]

A love of money, therefore, can prevent our turning to Christ and can stifle spiritual growth. Wealth can lead us to forget God, and sometimes a desire for things leads us to steal.[11] Nowhere is this stated more clearly than in 1 Timothy 6:6–11, where the dangers of loving money are contrasted with an emphasis on godliness and a command to flee greedy attitudes:

> But godliness actually is a means of great gain, when accompanied by contentment. For we have brought nothing into the world, so we cannot take anything out of it either. And if we have food and covering, with these we shall be content. But those who want to get rich fall into temptation and a snare and many foolish and harmful desires which plunge men into ruin and destruction. For the love of money is a root of all sorts of evil, and some by longing for it have wandered away from the faith, and pierced themselves with many a pang. But flee from these things, you man

of God; and pursue righteousness, godliness, faith, love, perseverance and gentleness.

The Bible also shows that greed and the overemphasis on money can also lead to interpersonal tension. A man once came to Jesus complaining about a family squabble and the Lord attributed this problem to greed. Then he warned that even when we have abundance, real life consists of more than possessions.[12] The parable of the talents warns about a misuse of our possessions, and ends with the unwise slave being alienated from his colleagues.[13]

4. *Money and Finances Should Be Managed Wisely.* To do this, our resources should be:

—Gained honestly. Trying to make money quickly and dishonestly is condemned in the book written by Solomon—the richest man in the Bible.[14]

—Invested carefully. In the parable of the talents the wise slaves managed their money wisely. Clearly, money is to be used carefully and not hoarded.[15]

—Spent realistically. This means keeping out of debt whenever possible. The Bible gives little sanction for credit-card buying. In Romans we are instructed to pay our taxes honestly and then to "owe nothing to anyone." [16] When we borrow we are slaves to others and this can lead to a number of personal and interpersonal problems.[17]

—Shared joyfully. God loves a cheerful giver and throughout the Bible there is emphasis on giving to God, to the poor, and to each other.[18] There is a strange principle in the Scripture, one which seems to be at odds with the wisdom of the world: "when we give, we get"—material wealth and/or spiritual blessing. "Honor the Lord with your wealth," we read in Proverbs 3:9, "so your barns will be filled with plenty." The same principle was echoed by Paul, who thanked the Philippians for their generosity and then added that God would, in turn, supply all their needs "according to His riches in glory in Christ Jesus." [19]

When we ponder the above paragraphs it is abundantly clear that the Bible speaks again and again about money. Clearly this is an issue which must concern every Christian and which comes up repeatedly in counseling.

The Causes of Financial Problems

Among financial experts there is an old saying that if we are to manage our assets wisely, we must stop asking where the money went and start telling it where to go. Perhaps this is good advice, but many people work on a different principle. They live from payday to payday, financially flush at certain times in the month and "flat broke" at other times. Others manage to get along without great hardship, but saving seems impossible and there is barely enough cash to meet family needs. It might be argued that the reason for this is simply too little income and too many expenses.

But financial difficulties occur at all socioeconomic levels. For the wealthy, the financial problems involve greater amounts of money, but the root causes are similar to those problems facing less prosperous people.

1. *Distorted Values.* The way one handles money probably is an accurate indicator of one's values. Each of us spends money or wants to spend it on things we consider important. Sometimes, however, what we consider important gets us into debt. Even Christians slip into accepting desires and values which are nonbiblical and harmful.

(a) Materialism. The dictionary defines this as an attitude of "devotion to material things rather than to spiritual objects, needs and considerations." Materialism is an attitude which leads us to pursue money, possessions, pleasure and the "good things in life." It leads to impatience, overindulgence, and overspending on luxuries which are nice to have but not really needed. Such an attitude often forgets Jesus' statement that our lives do not consist of the abundance of things which we possess.[20]

Some of the great spiritual leaders in Bible times had considerable wealth. Abraham, Solomon and Job are examples. But these people never gave evidence of pursuing riches. They accepted their wealth as God-given and sought to know and serve him better. Surely today there are wealthy people who have a similar attitude toward their possessions.

More common, perhaps, is an attitude which finds reasons for the accumulation of things. We think, for example, "As long as it doesn't hurt us or control us, why not have the best?" "If we have more, we can give more to missions." Such reasoning can be legitimate but often it is a veil to hide our materialism. Christ, it should be remembered, told the rich young ruler to give to the poor, not to "change your attitude about what you've got."[21]

(b) Covetousness and Greed. These words imply a desire for more, even if others are made poorer as a result. Such attitudes are soundly condemned in Scripture[22] but entrenched in our modern way of life.

Shortly after his move from Russia, Alexander Solzhenitsyn commented that "something which is incomprehensible to the human mind is the West's fantastic greed for profit for gain which goes far beyond all reason, all limitations, good conscience." This has led one commentator to conclude that covetousness and greed cause a variety of problems—inflation, unmanageable debts, and family arguments, to name a few.[23] In Western countries we don't worship idols of wood and stone, but many people, Christians included, seem to worship money and material things.

(c) A Desire to Get Rich Quickly. Perhaps people have always been impressed with the idea that one can earn a lot of money quickly and with little effort. The Scriptures warn against this,[24] but the "itch for more" urges some people to invest hard-earned funds into programs which, more often than not, fail to deliver what is promised.

(d) Pride and Resentment. The church at Laodicea took the proud attitude that it was rich, wealthy and needing nothing.[25] Even today such a superior attitude characterizes some wealthy and successful people who fail to realize that they are poor, needy, "wretched and miserable" if they ignore God, rely on their wealth for security and happiness, or fail to realize that their possessions and success have come as a gift from God.

In contrast to the proud wealthy, we find the resentful poor who are angry at God because of their lack of wealth and envious of those who have more.

All of these values suggest that the possession or nonpossession of material things does less to cause financial problems than does the attitude that we have toward money and finances.

2. *Unwise Financial Decisions.* There are a variety of ways in which people waste money which they cannot afford to lose. Unwise financial decisions include the following:

(a) Impulse Buying. This involves seeing something we want and buying it without checking quality, prices, whether the purchase really is needed, or whether we can afford it.

(b) Carelessness. Without the limiting influence of a budget, some people spend money carelessly and then are surprised when the wallet is empty or the checkbook is overdrawn. At times all of us dream of being rescued by someone who could pay all our bills. When people have inherited large sums of money, however, it has been found that most of the money is gone within a year and there is little to show for the inheritance. Apparently people who are careless with small sums of money are careless, as well, with large sums.[26]

(c) Speculation. There is an old adage which people often ignore: if you can't afford to lose it, don't speculate with it, no matter how bright the prospects. The Bible warns against speculation,[27] and so does common sense, but many people lose money in an attempt to "get rich quick."

(d) Cosigning. This involves signing a statement to say that you promise to pay if someone else fails to remove a debt. This is often done for good motives—to help a friend get a loan—but when the friend doesn't pay, the co-signer is left with the debt and the friendship disintegrates. Little wonder that the wise and wealthy King Solomon, writing under divine guidance, warned against cosigning.[28]

(e) Laziness. When people are too lazy to work or to manage a budget, financial problems almost always follow.[29] Regretfully, in these days of government handouts to deserving people, the undeserving also come for money and thus are encouraged not to work. This creates a financial strain for everyone although often the lazy suffer the most.

(f) Wasted Time. To a large extent we decide how to spend our time. For salaried employees this is less of a financial issue, but for the self-employed or people who are paid according to productivity, time equals money. When one is disorganized, undisciplined, or inclined to waste time, there is a resulting loss of income.

(g) Neglect of Property. When people fail to take care of property, there is faster deterioration, costly repairs, and the need to spend money which might have been used for something else.

(h) Credit Buying. In this day of easy credit and the proliferation of credit cards, buying "on time" is one of the major causes of financial problems.

It is easy for people to fall into the credit card trap. First, we purchase something we need and intend to pay for when the bill arrives at the end of the month. Then we see something we want, or a sale comes along, and we make one or two additional purchases on the assumption that we can spread the payments over a couple of months. If the minimum payment on our bill is, say, $10, we rationalize that an additional purchase will only raise the payment a few dollars, so we buy more.

This is a process of slow financial self-strangulation. Using a credit card often doesn't seem like spending money so we are tempted to buy more things than we might otherwise purchase. Impulse buying is encouraged, we are inclined to buy where we can charge (which may not be where the prices are lowest), and we end up paying a large finance charge which adds to the cost of the item. In summary, credit-card buying becomes a license to spend money we don't have and can't spare for goods we don't need.[30]

All of this leads to increased debt. Besides being wrong and enslaving according to Scripture,[31] the accumulation of debts is financially costly and psychologically binding. Caught in the credit card trap, it is hard to get out. The burden of using a limited salary to pay a high price for something that has been used already puts other stresses on the debtor. As the pressure builds so do family arguments and personal tensions. It doubtless is true that credit cards in our pockets can be time bombs to shatter peace, happiness and mental stability.[32]

3. *Lack of a Budget.* A budget is another term for a "spending plan." When such a plan exists and is followed, there is a control on spending, less impulse buying, and fewer debts. When there is no financial plan there is no control on spending. Spending begins to exceed income and this leads either to a deficit at month's end, or a turning to credit cards to make ends meet.

4. *Lack of Giving.* The Bible teaches that giving and receiving go together. Hoarding is wrong, and the person who refuses to give often runs into financial difficulties. In contrast, the person who gives receives from God in abundance.[33]

Believers are to give in three areas: to God,[34] to other believers[35] and to the poor.[36] Failure to do so is to court financial problems.

The Effects of Financial Problems

The previous paragraphs have mentioned several of the results which come with financial stress. These include:

—worry about one's money or how to pay the bills (one national survey found that 70 percent of all worries concern money);

—family and marital problems which often rise or increase because of financial pressures;

—loss of friends because we become greedy, envious, seek loans, or are embarrassed by debt; then at other times, old friends forsake or reject us if we have an increase of money or an increased debt;

—guilt, envy, jealousy, resentment, or pride, each of which is sinful, and each of which can be stimulated by finances;

—emotional emptiness and unhappiness, which come to those whose main interest in life is the accumulation of possessions; and

—spiritual deadness which follows when we get too concerned about money, have the wrong attitudes and violate biblical principles for handling finances.

Financial problems put us under stress and, as with other stresses, there can be physical illness, anxiety, discouragement, interpersonal tension and inefficiency as a result. At times there also can be uncontrolled, irresponsible spending especially if riches increase suddenly. At times there also is bankruptcy with the resulting psychological trauma.

Counseling and Financial Problems

Several helpful books on financial management have appeared within recent years. These can be loaned to counselees who often are able then to solve many of their own financial problems. Others need counseling, and with them there are several issues to consider as this counseling proceeds.

1. *Help the Counselee Acknowledge the Problem and Determine to Solve It.* It is difficult, if not impossible, to help a person work on a problem when that person fails to acknowledge that the problem exists. It is equally difficult to help someone who claims "it will never be different" and uses this as an excuse to do nothing.

People with financial problems often bring an additional problem of worry. They need to be urged to face the reality of their situation and encouraged emotionally when they do so. Point out that God supplies our needs and that it *is* possible to get out of debt and to manage money efficiently. It should be emphasized, however, that the solution to financial problems depends less on the state of the economy than on the way individuals and families handle their financial resources. Counselees need to experience hope. While this may not eliminate the worry, it gives encouragement and can motivate the counselees to take action to work on their financial problems.

The realistic counselor will recognize, however, that for some there is no hope, because they don't want to change or are unwilling to work on financial problems. Such people may have to experience financial disaster before they are motivated to work on the problem. And for some the motivation may never come.

2. *With the Counselee, Seek Divine Guidance.* In the midst of crises it is easy to be so distracted by circumstances that we take our eyes off God. Counselees should be reminded that God has abundant riches and he knows our needs.[37] He has instructed us to cast our burdens and anxieties on him,[38] and surely this includes financial burdens. If someone asks for divine help and expects it, then God will meet that person's need. He will also help us to be content in any circumstance, including our financial state.

All of this implies that prayer should be an important starting point in financial counseling. Pray with the counselee, asking God to lead as the practical details of financial planning are discussed. Then encourage the counselee and his or her family to pray together about this as they work together on their money problems.

3. *Teach Biblical Principles of Finance.* People with financial problems are in a hurry to get some relief. Often they are not interested in sermons or in Christian education, but it is important, nevertheless, that they understand the biblical guidelines for managing money. These principles must guide the Christian counselor and should be shared explicitly at various times as the counseling continues.

An earlier section in this chapter discussed the Bible and finances. In addition to the concepts presented earlier, counselees should be helped to see the following.

(a) Everything Belongs to God. We are only stewards of God's possessions. In the Psalm where God states "the world is Mine, and all it contains," he also encourages people to "call upon Me in the day of trouble; I shall rescue you, and you will honor Me." [39] A first step in financial planning is to recognize that ownership of everything must be transferred to God, who is the rightful owner.

(b) Stealing Is Wrong. Although God ultimately owns everything, he allows each of us to possess certain things. To take these things from another is to steal from God as well as from fellow human beings. In times of need it is easy to "cut corners" on income tax, to "borrow" supplies that rightfully belong to our employer, or to get money in other ways. This is stealing and does not help with our financial problems.

(c) Coveting Is Wrong. Coveting, like stealing, is forbidden in the Ten Commandments.[40] To covet is to want something which we see others enjoying. It implies a dissatisfaction with the possessions and opportunities which God has given. Regretfully, our entire economy seems geared to helping people violate this principle. We are encouraged to engage in extravagant and wasteful spending even if this creates personal financial crisis, harms our national economy, or hinders the economics of less developed nations. God can help us to be content with what we have and to avoid comparing ourselves with others who seem to have more.

In addition to coveting the goods of another it also is possible to have a clinging, covetous attitude to our own possessions. If we assume that everything comes from God and rightfully is his, then there is no need to cling tenaciously to our goods or to be excessively distraught when something is lost, stolen, or broken. This involves a responsible but realistic attitude toward our possessions.

(d) Giving is Right. This is emphasized throughout the Bible. God expects us to give, even when we own little and have nothing to spare. Of course this does not mean that everything should be given away. In the Old Testament the people gave a portion of their possessions. We need a willingness to give, followed by acts of giving to God and to those in need.

(e) Money Management Is Right. In the parable of the talents,[41] there were differences in the amounts which each person possessed. Nevertheless, two people managed their money carefully while the third did not. It was the poor manager whom Jesus criticized. God expects us to be good stewards of what he has given. He demanded this of Adam[42] and has expected it from people ever since.

4. *Help Counselees Develop and Follow a Financial Plan.* Without a blueprint for money management, it is largely impossible to control one's

Assets (what we own)

Savings	$_____
Checking Account	_____
Value of Car	_____
Value of House	_____
Resale Value of Furnishings	_____
Cash Value of Insurance	_____
Other	_____
Total	_____

Liabilities (what we owe)

Unpaid Balance on Car	$_____
Home Loan	_____
Other Debts (List)	_____
	_____
	_____
	_____
Total	_____
Net Worth (difference between Assets and Liabilities)	_____
Date _____	

Table 25-1

finances. This financial plan involves a variety of elements which can be discussed in counseling. Notice that several of the following steps can be initiated in the counseling session, completed by the counselees at home, and discussed subsequently with the counselor.

(a) Get the Facts. This involves making a list on paper of one's assets and liabilities. Table 25–1 is an example of how this might be done. To get an accurate picture of the current financial situation is an important first step in solving financial problems. When one's net worth is increasing every year the person is moving ahead financially. When the net worth is decreasing the person is declining financially.

(b) Establish Goals. What are the counselee's financial goals? Begin with some general goals—like "getting out of debt," "being able to provide for the family," "doing what we can to advance the cause of Christ," "saving for the education of children and for retirement," "having enough money to travel," "owning a home," and so on.

When these general goals have been written down, it is good to be more specific by listing long-range and short-term goals. What specifically does the counselee hope to have achieved in ten years, five years, and one year from now? Help counselees be realistic in terms of their education, present income and debts. A man who earns $9,000 annually but has a $4,000 debt cannot realistically expect that all debts will be gone within a year, but he can set a goal to have a portion of this debt gone within the next twelve months.

In setting goals remember the biblical teachings about finance. Our goals must fit within the scriptural guidelines. This means that we should seek God's guidance, through prayer and Bible study, as we establish goals; determine to be honest and fair in all financial dealings including the payment of taxes; avoid selfish indulgence; show a concern for others including family, employees and/or employers, and the poor; avoid borrowing—except, perhaps, for major purchases such as a home or car (and on occasion, for a bill consolidation loan).

(c) Set Priorities. Few people can meet all of their financial goals immediately, so there must be decisions about what can be done now and what must wait until later. Tithing, paying off debts, and eliminating the misuse of credit cards must be high on the priority list.

One financial counselor has suggested that we distinguish between needs, wants and desires.[43] *Needs* are the purchases necessary to provide food, housing, clothing, medical care, transportation and other basics. *Wants* involve choices about quality—whether to get a used or a new car, for example, or whether to eat hamburger or steak. *Desires* are choices made out of surplus funds after other expenses are met. To get around in our society most people need a car. A good used car would meet the need, a new car might be wanted, a new Cadillac may be desired. In establishing a financial plan and getting out of debt, needs must be met first;

wants and desires can be met later. Each expenditure should be evaluated in terms of these categories.

In setting priorities remember, once again, that time management often is important financially. In many occupations, to waste time is to reduce one's income.

(d) Set Up a Budget. A budget is a spending plan which enables us to manage and effectively control the expenditures of money. Such a budget includes keeping records which help us determine where the money is going. "By keeping good records, having a plan and being honest with oneself, a person won't get into financial trouble," writes one expert. "I seldom see financially successful people who don't keep good records." [44]

It is not easy to develop and stay within the guidelines of a budget. It probably is true, however, that people who "cannot" keep within a budget really don't want to take the effort to control their money carefully. Most people get along fine without budgeting, but in so doing they waste a lot of money which is spent more on their whims than on their priorities. [45]

One plan for saving and spending has been called the 10–70–20 plan for budgeting. As shown in the following diagram, each dollar is divided into five parts. Ten percent of one's total income goes to God in tithe, a second portion goes to the government, then the remaining portion is "working income" which is divided three ways. Ten percent of this is saved, 70 percent is for living expenses, and 20 percent goes to pay past debts. When the debts are gone, the 20 percent can be used for making purchases on a cash basis.

10% of Gross Tithe	Taxes and Fixed Expenses	Working Income		
		10% Saving	70% Living Expenses	20% Debts
1	2	3	4	5

Table 25–2 gives a sample budget worksheet which counselees could use (with modification for individual differences). This worksheet assumes the 10–70–20 plan and each month allows counselees to plan and evaluate how successful they have been in keeping within the budget.

Remember that budgets should be tools to help manage spending and not strait jackets to bind spenders. If a budget is unrealistic or if one's financial status changes, then the budget should be altered accordingly. This should be done with care, however, and not in an attempt to cover up or justify reckless spending and deviations from the budget plan.

5. *Conclusions.* Counselors who are accustomed to more in-depth

Table 25–2

Budget

Month of _____

Gross Income (before taxes) $ _____ *

Item	A Amount Allocated	B Amount Spent	C Difference (+ or −)
1. *Tithe* (10%)	$ _____	$ _____	$ _____
2. *Fixed Expenses*			
Taxes			
Social Security			
Professional Dues			
Other			
Total	$ _____		
Total Tithe and Fixed Income	$ _____		**
Working Income—Deduct Total Tithe and Fixed Income (**) from Gross Income(*)	_____		
3. *Savings* (10% of Working Income)			
4. *Living Expenses* (70% of Working Income)	_____		
Mortgage or Rent			
Heat			
Electricity			
Telephone			
Water/Sewage/Garbage			
Gasoline			
Car Repairs			
Insurance			
Medical			
Food/Household			

Item	A Amount Allocated	B Amount Spent	C Difference (+ or −)
Clothing			
Home Repairs, Upkeep, Furnishing			
Gifts			
Vacation			
Buffer			
Other			
Total	$ _____	$ _____	
5. *Debts* (20% of Working Income)			
Total			

6. Summary of Allocations

    Gross Income (from * above) $ _____

    Total Allocated (Total of 5 boxes in column A) $ _____

    Difference (Balance or Amount Short) $ _____

7. Summary of Amount Spent

    Gross Income (from * above) $ _____

    Total Spent (Total of 5 boxes in column B) $ _____

    Difference (Balance or Amount Short) $ _____

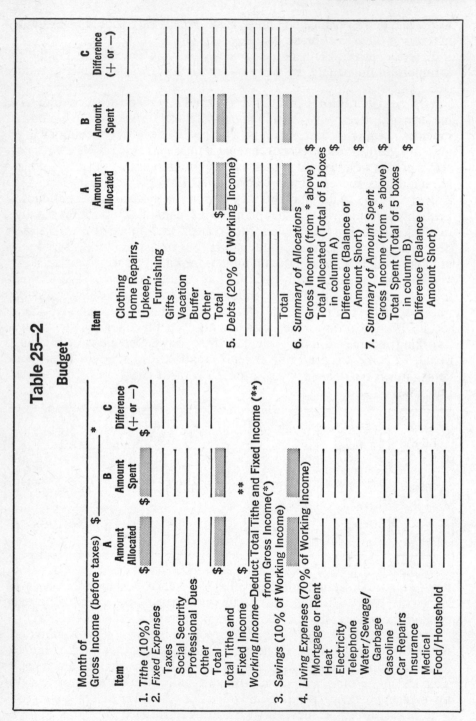

problems may feel that such detailed planning is beyond the scope of Christian counseling. Such counselors may wish to refer their counselees to a banker, accountant or other financial counselor. Helping people manage their money and possessions, however, can be one of the most rewarding and visibly successful aspects of Christian counseling. And a resolution of financial difficulties can have implications for a variety of other counseling problems.

Preventing Financial Problems

Most of the problems discussed in this book apply only to some people. Not everyone, for example, becomes alcoholic, is deeply depressed, or has marriage problems. But everyone handles money and the Christian counselor has a responsibility to help people handle it better.

1. *Teach Biblical Values Concerning Finances.* This can be taught from the pulpit, in group meetings (including youth meetings), in Sunday school classes and in individual conversations. Such instruction should:

—present teaching similar to that summarized in "The Bible and Finances" section of this chapter;

—encourage people to thank God for what they have, instead of making comparisons with others and lamenting their lacks and needs;

—warn people of the dangers of credit buying and encourage them to live within their means;

—emphasize the importance of saving and joyful giving.

2. *Teach Practical Guidelines for Managing Money.* This involves showing people how to budget (including tithing and saving), encouraging them to do so, and urging them to share their experiences with other believers. It is exciting and encouraging to believers to see how God blesses when his guidelines are followed.

The Christian counselor may not be an expert on insurance, banking procedures, the preparation of a will, or the best ways to save and invest money. Nevertheless, the counselor can stress the importance of each of these issues and point Christians either to books or to people who can give practical advice. Within the body of Christ there often are persons with business and financial expertise. These people can be invited to meet with individuals or groups to help with financial planning. This involves the body in practice—people sharing their knowledge and gifts to build up and encourage others.

3. *Emphasize Finances in Premarital Counseling.* When people get married they usually enter an entirely new financial picture. Two incomes often merge into one and there is potential for conflict over money. Premarital counseling can prevent such conflicts.

4. *Raise the Issue of Finances Whenever There Is a Crisis or Life Change.* Major changes in life, for example, starting college, changing

jobs, moving, retirement, operations or other prolonged sickness and death in the family often bring financial struggles. If these financial issues can be raised and discussed informally, problems can often be faced and resolved before they become major difficulties.

Conclusions about Financial Problems

The Bible never condemns the possession of goods and money but it does speak against hoarding, coveting and money mismanagement. Satan has used financial pressures to enslave people in debt and worry and to turn them away both from God and from divine principles for money management. To help people get out of debt and into financial freedom can be a satisfying experience in counseling—an experience which can be even more fulfilling because in a practical way it helps people live more in accordance with the principles of Scripture.

Suggestions for Further Reading

Bowman, George M. *How to Succeed with Your Money.* Chicago: Moody Press, 1974.

Burkett, Larry. *Your Finances in Changing Times.* Arrowhead Springs, CA: Campus Crusade for Christ, 1975.

Galloway, Dale E. *There Is a Solution to Your Money Problems.* Glendale, CA: Regal, 1977.

MacGregor, Malcolm, with Baldwin, Stanley C. *Your Money Matters.* Minneapolis: Bethany Fellowship, 1978.

Footnotes

1. 1 Tim. 6:10.
2. Luke 12:16–21. See also Prov. 28:20.
3. Cited in Malcolm MacGregor with Stanley Baldwin, *Your Money Matters* (Minneapolis: Bethany Fellowship, 1978), pp. 14, 15.
4. Ps. 49:10–12; Prov. 23:4, 5; 27:24; 1 Tim. 6:7.
5. Eccles. 5:10; Ps. 52:5–7.
6. Heb. 13:5; Ps. 62:10.
7. Phil. 4:19; Mark 6:7–11; Matt. 6:25–34.
8. Matt. 19:16–24.
9. Mark 8:36.
10. Matt. 6:24.
11. Deut. 8:11–14; Ps. 52:7; Prov. 30:7–10. See also Luke 16:19 f. and Job 31:24, 25, 28.
12. Luke 12:13–15.
13. Matt. 25:14–30.
14. Prov. 28:20; 15:27; 10:9; 11:1; 17:23.
15. Matt. 25:14–30; Luke 12:16–21.
16. Rom. 13:6–8.
17. Prov. 22:7; see also Matt. 18:23–35, the parable of the unforgiving slave.
18. 2 Cor. 9:7; 8:14, 15; Prov. 3:9; 19:17; 1 Cor. 16:2.
19. Phil. 4:18, 19.
20. Luke 12:15.
21. Interview with Larry Holben, *The Wittenburg Door* 44 (August/September, 1978): 19.

22. Exod. 20:17; Rom. 13:9; Ps. 72:2, 3.

23. Waldo J. Werning, "Family Financial Planning," in *Living and Growing Together: The Christian Family Today,* ed. Gary R. Collins (Waco, TX: Word, 1976), pp. 62–74.

24. Prov. 28:20, 22.

25. Rev. 3:17.

26. Cited in Dale E. Galloway, *There Is a Solution to Your Money Problems* (Glendale, CA: Regal, 1977), p. 84.

27. Prov. 21:5; Eccles. 5:15–17.

28. Prov. 11:15; 17:18; 22:26, 27.

29. Prov. 19:15; 1 Thess. 3:10.

30. MacGregor and Baldwin, *Your Money Matters,* p. 89.

31. Rom. 13.8; Prov. 3:27, 28; 22:7.

32. George Otis, *God, Money and You* (Van Nuys: Bible Voice, 1972), p. 26.

33. Luke 6:38; 12:16–21; Prov. 3:9, 10; 11:24, 25; 19:17; Mal. 3:10.

34. Prov. 3:9; Mal. 3:10.

35. Gal. 6:10.

36. Luke 3:11; Prov. 14:21; 19:17.

37. Ps. 50:10–12; Matt. 6:25–34.

38. Ps. 55:22; 1 Pet. 5:7.

39. Ps. 50:12, 15.

40. Exod. 20:15, 17.

41. Matt. 25:14–29.

42. Gen. 1:28.

43. Larry Burkett, *Your Finances in Changing Times* (Arrowhead Springs, CA: Campus Crusade for Christ, 1975), pp. 83, 84.

44. Quoted in Haddon Robinson, *You Can Budget Your Money Successfully* (Grand Rapids: Baker, 1978), p. 5.

45. Ibid.

46. See chapter 12. The issue of finances in premarital counseling is discussed in Norman Wright, *Premarital Counseling* (Chicago: Moody, 1977). See especially pages 125–28, 198–201.

26

Drugs
and Alcohol

THERE IS NOTHING NEW ABOUT THE PROBLEM OF ADDICTION. SINCE
the beginning of recorded history a certain percentage of people have had
serious trouble with drugs whenever or wherever they have been used. In
some cultures, opium or marijuana have been the problem drugs. In Western societies there have been problems with "hard drugs" like heroin or
cocaine. But the most common addictive drug of all has been alcohol.

Dr. George A. Mann, Medical Director of the Johnson Institute in Minneapolis—a center for understanding and treating chemical addictions—
has written that all addictive chemicals have one thing in common: they
change moods. Some mood changes are very potent and highly addictive;
others are much less powerful. According to Mann, drugs can be placed
on a scale ranging from those with highest potential for addiction to those
with lowest potential: [1]

Highest	Heroin
	Morphine
	Demerol
	Cocaine
	Barbiturates
Addiction	Amphetamines
Potenital	Alcohol
	Tranquilizers—minor
	"sleeping pills"
	Codeine
	Bromides
	Nicotine
Lowest	Marijuana
	Caffeine

Almost any person can become psychologically and/or physically dependent on these drugs if that person is exposed to a high dosage for a long
enough period of time. With a drug like heroin the time need not be long

376

and the effects are both fast and very dangerous; with caffeine the time is longer and the effects are almost negligible.[2]

It is possible to divide our lives into four general categories: family life, social life, vocational life, and spiritual life. When a chemical interferes with the productivity, tranquility, efficiency or well-being of any of these areas; and when we are made aware that this is happening but still persist in using the chemical, then we are addicted, at least psychologically. If we get physically ill when the drug is withdrawn, then we are physically addicted as well.[3]

It is almost impossible to present accurate statistics concerning the prevalence of addictions. Figures change so quickly that they probably are outdated before they appear in print. In the United States alone almost ten million people (including 1.3 million teenagers under the age of 18) have serious drinking problems.[4] This means that of the people who drink, one person in ten will become alcoholic and millions of family members will suffer as a result. Alcoholism is one of the four major public health problems in America (along with heart disease, cancer and mental illness),[5] and costs an estimated $25 billion every year.[6] To this add the millions of persons addicted to other drugs and it is easy to see why addiction has become a problem of crisis proportions. It is a problem which every Christian counselor will encounter at least periodically and probably frequently during his or her counseling career.

The Bible and Addiction

The Bible does not specifically mention drugs in general but it does say some things about heavy drinking and it lays down some principles which could apply to the issue of addiction. Perhaps these can best be listed as a series of "don'ts" and "do's."

1. *The Don'ts*

(a) Don't Break the Law. The Bible instructs us to be law-abiding citizens.[7] It is wrong, therefore, to buy, sell, condone, possess, or use any drug illegally.[8]

(b) Don't Expect to Come to God through Drugs. Several years ago a controversial book argued that psychedelic drugs offered a superior route to discovering truth and entering into meaningful religious experiences.[9] Such a view denies the fact that we come to God only by ways of Jesus Christ,[10] and that we are to come with clear minds,[11] rather than with brains drugged by addictive substances.

(c) Don't Be Mastered by Anything.[12] Surely this includes a prohibition against our being controlled by or addicted to drugs, including alcohol.

(d) Don't Assume That Drugs Resolve Problems or Reduce Tension. As we shall see, stress is one of the major causes of addiction. The alcohol or other drug gives a feeling of euphoria and a sense that all is well. But this serves only to avoid responsible action and ultimately can create addi-

tional problems. The person who escapes through drugs fails to acknowledge the scriptural directive to bring burdens to Christ[13] where we can
face them squarely and deal with them directly.

2. *The Do's*

(a) Do Remember Our Responsibility to Control Creation. God told
Adam to subdue and rule over the earth,[14] but over the centuries we have
abused and misused God's creation. As new creatures in Christ, believers
have a responsibility to take care of the things God created, including their
own bodies. Therefore, "the use of any drug for the purposes of entertainment and escape, mind-control, religious worship, occult experiences,
magic, or murder is a sin against God, the Creation, the Society, and the
Individual."[15]

(b) Do Avoid Drunkenness. This is clearly and explicitly condemned
in Scripture and called a sin.[16] It surely would be consistent with biblical
teaching to extend this clear prohibition beyond alcohol. We should not
become drunk with any chemical substance.

(c) Do Be Filled with the Spirit. "Don't get drunk with wine" (or
with drugs?), we read in Ephesians 5:18, ". . . but be filled with the Spirit."
A life controlled by the Holy Spirit is presented in the Bible as a superior
alternative to life filled with chemical addiction.

(d) Do Keep the Human Body Pure. The Holy Spirit dwells in the body
of each Christian and for this reason we must do whatever we can to keep
our bodies free of pollutants—including drugs and excessive amounts of
food. Every human body was made by God and the Christian body belongs
to him both because of divine creation and because of divine redemption. Scripture and common sense tell us, therefore, that we should take
care of ourselves so that we can "glorify God" with our bodies.[17]

(e) Do Use Moderation, If Not Abstinence. The Bible does not teach
abstinence, although it does teach temperance. In Psalm 104, wine is included among the blessings from God and described as something which
"makes man's heart glad." In his first miracle, Jesus turned water into
wine, wine apparently was taken at the last supper, and it appears that
Jesus himself drank wine.[18]

According to one writer, the wine in first-century Palestine was mixed
with water, probably on an average of three parts water to one part wine.
Translated into modern terms, two present-day martinis would equal
twenty-two glasses of Palestinian wine.[19] Nevertheless, the early wine
could produce drunkenness and the headwaiter at the Cana wedding implied that people drank freely and at the end of the celebration were less
able to tell good wine from bad.[20] Whether the wine was strong or diluted,
however, the drinker had a responsibility to control his or her input.

Although the Bible teaches moderation in drinking, abstinence was also
considered favorably. John the Baptist was a special messenger from God
who "drank no wine,"[21] and when a dedicated person took the Nazarite
vow, "to dedicate himself to the Lord," this was marked by abstinence

from wine and strong drink.[22] Many Christians today would conclude that while moderation is good, abstinence is better—especially in view of the clear dangers inherent in drinking and chemical abuse.

(f) Do Allow for Christian Liberty. While all things may be lawful, including drugs such as alcohol, not all things are wise or profitable.[23] If something like drinking alcoholic substances hurts the body, leads to immorality, or causes another Christian to stumble, then such practices should be abandoned and avoided.[24] Here is a principle of the believer having the liberty to use restraint since this would be for the good and growth of the body of Christ—the church.

(g) Do Allow for Drugs As Medicine. When Jesus was on the cross he refused to take the wine which would have dulled his pain. Elsewhere, however, he spoke approvingly of the Good Samaritan whose art of compassion included pouring wine on the wounds. And it is well known that Timothy was encouraged to use a little wine to help his ailing stomach.[25]

The above paragraphs show that wine is mentioned frequently in the Bible. These scriptural teachings have clear relevance to our present-day era, especially the repeated warnings against chemical addiction. But what about the person who already is addicted? It isn't enough to simply quit drinking or taking drugs; neither is it easy for persons who are in the process of becoming addicted to reverse the process. It is here that the Christian counselor can help.

The Causes of Addiction

It has been suggested that ours is an era of "pill-taking." Early in life, most children become well acquainted with medicines that take away pain and make one feel better. Teenagers watch parents consume aspirin, cold tablets, sleeping medications and a host of other drugs. Millions of people relax with coffee, a cigarette or a drink before dinner, and when problems arise, tranquilizers are available to calm our troubled nerves. Little wonder that young people follow this adult example and, in turn, perpetuate the idea that drugs are the first line of defense against physical and psychological pain.

Of course, few people would assume that drugs in themselves are bad. Their medicinal value is well known and perhaps there is no harm in the occasional use of mild stimulants or relaxation-producing drugs. But many people become dependent both on mild drugs like caffeine or nicotine, and (what is worse) on more harmful and addictive chemicals, including alcohol.

Over the years, massive amounts of research have attempted to discover why some people become addicted while others do not. Some of these research conclusions could be listed under the following categories. Probably no one of these in itself causes drug abuse. (Complex problems rarely have only one cause.) But acting together they make some people especially prone to become addicts.

1. *Personality, Heredity and Physiology.* Are drug abusers unique in terms of personality or physiological characteristics? There are some traits which appear with above average frequency in those who abuse drugs. These include a high level of anxiety, emotional immaturity, problems in accepting authority, a low ability to tolerate frustration, low self-esteem which sometimes is hidden behind grandiosity, feelings of isolationism, perfectionism, guilt and compulsiveness.[26] It might be argued that these characteristics come as a result of drug abuse and not a cause, but Cline-bell reports that, at least with alcoholism, these attributes are present before excessive drinking begins and they persist in diminished form long after sobriety has been achieved.[27] "Impaired personalities" are even more apparent in nonalcoholic drug abusers than in alcoholics.[28]

In spite of these conclusions, not all specialists would agree on the personality characteristics of drug abusers. There is no such thing as a typical alcoholic or drug-abusing personality, and science has not yet discovered any heredity influence or marked physical difference between those who become addicted and those who do not.[29] Personality, heredity, and physiology may make some people more prone to become drug abusers, but in themselves these three factors do not cause drug addiction.

2. *Past Background and Culture.* The family environment and society in which we are raised also can increase or decrease the likelihood of addiction.

(a) Parental Models. How parents behave often influences the subsequent behavior of children. When parents drink excessively or abuse drugs, children sometimes vow to completely abstain. More often, however, they follow the parental example. It has been estimated that "without intervention, forty to sixty percent of children of alcoholic parents become alcoholics themselves."[30]

(b) Parental Attitudes. Parental permissiveness and parental rejection can both stimulate chemical use and abuse. When parents don't care whether or not the children drink, there is no concern about the dangers of drugs or alcohol and misuse often follows. If parents neglect the children or are excessively punitive, the children rebel. Delinquency, excessive drug abuse, and alcoholism often follow.[31]

According to Clinebell, the homes of alcoholics tend to show authoritarianism, success worship, overt rejection and/or a moralism which instills guilt and arouses hostility. While exceptions occur frequently, a majority of those who experience drug abuse problems come from unstable and inadequate homes.[32]

(c) Cultural Expectations. If a culture or subcultural group has clear guidelines about the use of alcohol or drugs, abuse is less likely. Among Italians and Jews, for example, young people are generally permitted to drink but drunkenness is condemned, and the rate of alcoholism is low. In contrast, cultures such as our own are more tolerant of drunkenness. Teenage and college drinking is winked at as a sign of growing up and inebriation becomes a topic for television and cocktail hour jokes. Since "getting high" is the "in" thing to do, conditions are set up which lead many to drug abuse.

These observations overlook the fact of individual differences within the culture. Many people who come from alcoholic prone backgrounds never become addicted; others become addicts even though this would not have been predicted by their backgrounds. The reason for these differences may largely be related to the issue of stress.

3. *Present Stress*. The roots of addiction most often are found in the teenage years. As an example, let us follow the addiction process as it begins in a hypothetical normal teenage male.[33] By "normal" we mean that he likes some things about himself and dislikes others. In some things he feels competent, and in other areas he feels inadequate. Like others of his age, he experiences anxiety, fears, guilt, disappointment and insecurity in certain situations. Even though he may come from a good family there will be times of tension at home. Having been raised in an affluent society and time in history, he may be accustomed to comfort and the immediate meeting of his needs and desires. Because of this comfortable childhood, adolescent stresses may hit him with special intensity.

Let us suppose, further, that this young person has an opportunity to take a drug. He may first be given the drug as part of medical treatment but more likely he takes it deliberately. There can be a number of reasons for this: pressure from friends, a desire to "see what it is like," a search for personal meaning, identification with a group or hero who uses drugs, a belief that drugs (including alcohol) will "prove" one's manhood, or use of drugs and alcohol as a way of "getting even" with parents. Some hope that the chemical will help them escape boredom or loneliness and provide acceptance from friends who are involved with drugs. Others drink or take drugs because it is a socially accepted way for friends to relax together.

When our hypothetical young person takes the alcohol or other drug he has a sense of euphoria. He feels tranquil, less nervous, more adequate and socially at ease. His problems seem less severe and the world looks good to him. There may be periodic hangovers or remorse during times of sobriety, but the drug use continues because the mood-change is so pleasant and the danger seems so minimal.

By the time the young man is in his early twenties he has repeated the drug experience many times. By the time he reaches thirty, the use of alcohol or other drugs has become an integrated part of his life style. He is now addicted psychologically and physical addiction will soon follow. Over the years, drug use has increased because it takes larger and larger quantities to create new euphoria and relieve anxiety. If the drug is withdrawn, sickness results. Thus, by early middle life, acquiring and taking the drug has become so important that his personal, family, social and business life all suffer. The person who began drinking or taking drugs as a way of relaxation now has become an addict.

Examples such as this have led many writers to conclude that stress is a major influence in addiction. To escape pressures temporarily and enjoy a feeling of tranquility or euphoria, the person begins with a limited quantity of the drug and takes it only occasionally. Since nicotine and caffeine do not bring much of a sensation, people turn to something stronger. In our society, the preferred drug is alcohol because of its availability and social acceptance. Later this or some other drug becomes an indispensable crutch by which people deny stress and dull the pains of life. What began in a social setting for relaxation and fellowship becomes a way to escape stress, anxiety and feelings of inadequacy. As the addiction builds, the need for the drug increases, control lessens, work suffers and so does one's health and family and social relationships.

4. *Perpetuating Influences.* In understanding addiction it is important to consider what makes some people vulnerable (including personality, culture, and background), what motivates people to start taking the drug (primarily peer pressures and stresses), and what keeps the addiction going.

At some stage in the addiction process endocrine and biochemical changes occur which make withdrawal very difficult. Even more powerful are the psychological changes which have built up over the years. The drug has become the core around which life is organized. It may be the cause of one's problems, but it also has come to be viewed as the solution —a magic, but tragic answer to the stresses of life.

The members of Alcoholics Anonymous believe that there can be no cure for addiction until a person "reaches bottom," admitting that he or she is "powerless over alcohol" and unable to manage life without the help of "a Power greater than ourselves."

Regretfully, this determination to change often is delayed by the people who most want change to occur—the addict's family. Alcoholism and, to a lesser extent, drug addiction have been described as family diseases. Most of the alcoholics in this country are living, not on skid row, but at home with their families. As one's alcoholism or other addiction gets worse, each member of the household is affected. Often, each tries to deny the reality of the situation, to both protect and criticize the addict, and to hold the family together with as little additional strain as possible. First, there is an attempt to control or stop the family member's drug use. Then there is an attempt to understand it and eliminate the causes.[34] Often there is an effort to hide it from the community while at home the addict is exhorted to quit.

Sometimes the family members slip into "survival roles" which are sincere and sometimes unconscious efforts to keep the family together and to prevent it from buckling under the stress. The "enabler role," for example, is taken on by the person, usually the spouse, who seeks to take responsibility for meeting family needs. The "family hero" tries to make things better for the family and to provide self-worth for its members. The "scapegoat" gets into trouble or withdraws in a way which provides a distraction for the family. In contrast, the "mascot" tries to inject humor into the painful situation, while the "lost child" covers up his or her feelings and tries to be the one person whom the family does not have to worry about.[35] All of this reflects the pain and pathos that infiltrates and characterizes the addict's family.

Roles such as these help the family to keep going but, in turn, can also support the addict in his or her addiction. As long as the family seems to be getting along, there is less motivation for change. The family, therefore, is caught in a trap where winning is impossible. If they adjust to the addict this may perpetuate his or her problem and the pain goes on. If they don't adjust, the family members also are hurt, and the pain goes on as well.

In a hard-hitting book entitled *The Booze Battle: A Common Sense Approach That Works,*[36] one counselor argues persuasively that addicts must be faced with the reality of the situation before improvement can occur. Treatment will be delayed if families or employers perpetuate the problem by denying its reality, hiding it from others, and protecting the addict from facing the consequences of his or her irresponsible and self-centered behavior.

To all of this it may be added that society perpetuates the addiction problem when it overlooks the seriousness of addiction, laughs at inebriation, tolerates drunken driving, excuses crimes committed under the influence of drugs, and portrays chemicals as the ultimate, fastest and most pleasant solution to our problems, stresses and fears of social isolation.

5. *Spiritual Influences.* One Christian writer has emphasized that

> by far the most important cause of drug abuse . . . is the existence of a spiritual, religious, and existential vacuum. It seems that young people today, lacking foundational value systems from stable family units, are constantly looking for meaningful models of identification in other places in society. When they fail to find them, they are left to struggle on their own with an increasing sense of frustration, lack of purpose, and meaninglessness. As materialism has become a god, there has been a simultaneous humanization of God. . . . Such a human production of God, however, will always fail to fill a sense of emptiness and to infuse any sense of value, hope, or meaning in the existence of the young person. Thus, again, adolescents become likely prospects for the psychochemical experience, fascination with the occult, and have all the prerequisites for the development of antiestablishment delinquent activities.[37]

Stated concisely, human beings have an inner need for a real and growing relationship with God. When this craving is denied, unrecognized and unfilled, there is a search for something else which will fill the vacuum. No more clearly is this stated than in the Bible: "Don't drink too much wine, for many evils lie along that path; be filled instead with the Holy Spirit, and controlled by him." [38] Here, in one sentence, is a warning, an implied cause, and an answer to the problem of addiction.

The Effects of Addiction

Addiction can immobilize the addict, ruin his or her family, and create immense social problems. Although the effects of addiction cannot be described adequately within a few paragraphs, it is possible to summarize them under four headings.

1. *Physical Effects.* Whenever a chemical substance is taken into the body there will be a physiological reaction. The nature of this reaction depends on the physical condition of the person, the type of drug taken, the amount, and the frequency with which it is used.

Alcohol, for example, is a toxin (poison) which affects most body cells. If it is taken rapidly, the alcohol content of the blood rises, the brain's functioning is impaired temporarily, and the drinker's balance, motor skills, thinking and emotional responses are influenced. If alcohol is taken consistently and in large amounts, a variety of physical changes can result. These include destruction of brain cells with a resulting change in mental functioning, malfunctioning of the liver and/or pancreas, numbness of the limbs, and a variety of gastrointestinal diseases.[39]

Chemical abuse ultimately can bring death and, in pregnant women, it can affect the health of unborn babies.[40] Because of these physical aspects of addiction, medical intervention is a crucial part of treatment.

2. *Psychological-social Effects.* Since drug abuse, especially alcoholism, is so common, many people are familiar with the most obvious effects: dulled thinking, inappropriate behavior and emotional responses, self-neglect, withdrawal, and loss of social inhibitions. As the condition worsens, psychological defenses begin to build—most noticeably rationalizations (making excuses for drinking or the resulting behavior), repression (a spontaneous forgetting of shameful and painful memories), and projection (blaming others for one's problems and unacceptable thoughts, feelings or actions). Later, life is built around getting enough of the drug; all else is of secondary importance.

While this affects the addict, it influences society as well. It is well known that many crimes are committed by addicts and by people under the influence of alcohol. Every week, drunken driving leads to death, injury, and the destruction of millions of dollars' worth of property. Then, there are the deep family problems, the loss in employee production or efficiency, and the decline of military alertness which come with chemical abuse. All of this represents drug abuse at its worst, but it is surprising that chemicals with such potential for destruction are tolerated openly, used freely and advertised enthusiastically in our public media.

3. *Family Effects.* The family effects of drug abuse have already been mentioned. Families, at first, try to protect, control and blame the drinker

or other addict. Then they take over the addict's responsibilities, all the while living with tension, fear and insecurity. Often there is embarrassment, which leads family members to withdraw and, as a result, to experience loneliness and social isolation.

4. *Spiritual Effects.* It is impossible to grow spiritually when one is dependent on and controlled by a drug. Many addicts know this, but they seem powerless to change. As a result there is greater alienation from God. The drug becomes an idol of worship—the thing that matters most. This can have adverse spiritual influences on one's family as well as on the addict.

Counseling and Addiction

Table 26–1 lists the symptoms of chemical dependency in the approximate order of their appearance. Such a chart can be a helpful reference

Table 26–1
SYMPTOMS of CHEMICAL DEPENDENCY *

Alcoholism	Drug Dependency
I. Signs of:	I. Signs of:
A. Growing preoccupation	A. Growing preoccupation
1. Anticipation of drinking	1. Anticipation of drug usage
a. During daytime activities	a. Keeping track of prescribed times for dosage
b. Vacation times (fishing trips become drinking binges)	b. Growing number of physical complaints which would require more drugs to relieve them
c. Growing involvement in drinking activities (bar building, receipts)	2. Growing need during times of stress
2. Growing need during times of stress	a. Begins to attempt to prevent stress—"It's going to be a rough day so I'll take a couple just in case."
a. On job	b. Minor family and marriage problems
b. Family and marriage problems	c. Emergency situations
c. Emergencies	
B. Growing rigidity in life style	B. Growing rigidity in life style
1. Particular times for drinking during the day	1. Has particular times during day for drug usage—example—can't sleep unless he/she takes a sleeping pill
2. Self-imposed rules beginning to change—Saturday lunch	2. Cannot go anywhere without supply of medication
3. Will not tolerate interference during drinking times	3. Will not tolerate attempts to limit or change medication (drugs) times or amounts
4. Limits "social" activities to those which involve drinking	
C. Growing tolerance	C. Growing tolerance
1. "Wooden leg" syndrome—ability to hold liquor without showing it	1. Increasing dosage and/or number of a different medications (drugs).
2. Ingenuity about obtaining the chemical without others being aware	2. Ingenuity about obtaining the drug without others being aware

a. Gulping drinks
b. Ordering "stiffer" drinks—doubles, martinis, etc.
c. Self-appointed bartender at social gatherings
d. Sneaking drinks
e. Drinking prior to social engagements
f. Purchasing liquor in greater quantities—cases instead of six-packs
g. Protecting supply
   (1) Purchasing more well before current supply is exhausted
   (2) Hidden bottles—at home, car, on the job

a. Seeking out a variety of physicians and dentists for prescriptions but not informing them about each other
b. Attempting to get refillable prescriptions
c. Use of several drug stores
d. Using several drugs in combination for the synergistic effect—i.e., a barbituate and an alcoholic drink
e. Using the drug for longer than the original prescription called for
f. Protecting the supply—
   (1) Purchasing more before current supply is exhausted
   (2) Hiding bottles at home (suitcases), car, at work

D. Loss of control
  1. Increasing blackouts
  2. Unplanned drinking or larger doses and more frequent times
  3. Binge drinking
  4. Morning drinking
  5. Repeated harmful consequences resulting from chemical use

D. Loss of control
  1. Increasing blackouts and memory distortion
  2. Larger and more frequent dosages, than prescription calls for—using another person's prescriptions
  3. Continuous dosages—i.e., red pill every three hours, white pill every two hours, green capsule twice daily, etc.
  4. Repeated harmful consequences resulting from drug usage

    a. Family
       (1) Broken promises involving "cutting down"
       (2) Drinking during family rituals (Christmas, birthdays)
       (3) Sacrificing other family financial needs for chemicals
       (4) Fights (physical) or arguments about drug usage
       (5) Threats of divorce

    a. Family
       (1) Frequent blackouts which lead to many "broken commitments"
       (2) Inappropriate behavior during family rituals (Christmas, birthdays)
       (3) Sacrificing other family needs for doctor appointments and prescriptions
       (4) Changing family duties due to physical incapacity (increase time in bed, lack of motivation and drive)
       (5) Drug-induced mood changes creates uncertainty and suspicion in family members

b. Legal
   (1) Traffic violations—
       DWI, etc.
   (2) Drunk and disorderly
   (3) Suits—result of
       impaired judgment
   (4) Divorce proceedings

c. Social
   (1) Loss of friendships
       because of antisocial
       behavior
   (2) Previous hobbies,
       interests and
       community activities
       neglected as a result
       of increased chemical
       use
d. Occupational
   (1) Absenteeism (hang-
       overs)
   (2) Lost promotions due
       to poor performance
   (3) Threats of termination
   (4) Loss of job

e. Physical
   (1) Numerous hospitaliza-
       tions
   (2) Medical advice to cut
       down
   (3) Using alcohol as
       medication
       (a) To get to sleep
       (b) Relieve stress
f. Growing defensiveness
   (1) Vague and evasive
       answers
   (2) Inappropriate reac-
       tions to consequences
       of drug usage
   (3) Frequent attempts at
       switching to other
       areas of concern
II. Counselor should be:
   A. Direct but not D.A. (District
      Attorney)
   B. Persistent but not threatening
   C. Aware of possible distortions due
      to sincere delusion
   D. Ready to seek out corroborating
      data from concerned person if
      person becomes highly defensive

b. Legal
   (1) Buying and/or selling
       illegal drugs
   (2) Buying from illegal
       sources
   (3) Traffic violations
   (4) Disorderly conduct
       violations
   (5) Suits—result of
       impaired judgment
   (6) Divorce proceedings

c. Social
   (1) Loss of friendships
       because of past anti-
       social behavior
   (2) Previous hobbies,
       interests and com-
       munity activities
       neglected as a result
       of increased drug
       usage
d. Occupational
   (1) Absenteeism
   (2) Lost promotions due
       to poor performance
   (3) Demotions due to im-
       paired and inappro-
       priate behavior
   (4) Loss of job

e. Physical
   (1) Numerous hospitaliza-
       tions
   (2) Increasing number of
       physical complaints
   (3) Physical deterioration
       due to chemical use

f. Growing defensiveness
   (1) Vague and evasive
       answers
   (2) Inappropriate reac-
       tions to consequences
       of drug usage
   (3) Frequent attempts at
       switching to other
       areas of concern
II. Counselor should be:
   A. Direct but not D.A. (District
      Attorney)
   B. Persistent but not threatening
   C. Aware of possible distortions due
      to sincere delusion
   D. Ready to seek out corroborating
      data from a significant other if
      person becomes highly defensive

* Reproduced with permission of the Johnson Institute, 10700 Olson Memorial Highway, Minne-apolis, Minnesota.

for counselors who want to know how far the chemical dependency has advanced. But even if the counselee has not progressed very far or if he or she sees no need for help, there still is a drug problem if the person cannot completely control chemical intake or if the family perceives that a problem exists.

To begin, it might be helpful to list some things that usually do *not* help. These include criticism, coaxing, making the person promise to stop, threats, hiding or destroying the alcohol or other drug, urging the use of will power, preaching, or instilling guilt. Most families try all of these; most discover that they rarely work. What does work successfully?

1. *Get the Addict to a Source of Help.* This is difficult because many addicts, especially alcoholics, deny that there is a problem. Their thinking is dulled and the reality of their condition sometimes is hidden by the actions of well-meaning family members who "cover" for the addict when he or she does something irresponsible.

How, then, can the addict "get the message" that help is needed? In an accepting but firm, factual and nonjudgmental way, point out the nature of one's actions. Present specific examples (e.g., "Last night at 11 P.M. you knocked over and broke the lamp") rather than vague generalities (e.g., "You're drinking too much!"). One writer has suggested that the message may be best conveyed nonverbally. If the addict collapses on the living room floor, for example, leave him or her there rather than helping the person into bed—and thus hiding the fact that the collapse occurred.[41]

Remember that most addicts have high anxiety and low self-esteem. One must be careful, therefore, not to criticize or condemn in a way that arouses anxiety and threatens. Convey acceptance of the person but not of the behavior. Listen to the addict but do not give reassurance. Recognize that addicts are dependent, often childish, manipulative and specialists in evoking sympathy. The counselor must resist the tendency to give advice, preach, or act like a parent. Instead, show a noncondescending, firm, sensitive attitude which implies that responsibility for recovery must remain with the addict. In all of this, remember that the best counselors are gentle, but not soft-hearted, in their approach.

2. *Get the Addict Off the Drug.* This is a medical problem which must involve the intervention of a physician, although medical personnel sometimes work in conjunction with psychologists who use an advanced "relearning" technique known as behavior therapy.

While "detoxification" usually can be accomplished safely and quite quickly, this is only the beginning of treatment. A larger problem is keeping the addict free of drug use. This involves counseling which has at least four goals: (1) repairing medical damage that has come with the addiction, (2) helping the counselee learn how to cope with stress, (3) helping him or her find an effective, nonchemical substitute for the drug,

(4) building or restoring self-esteem and dealing with guilt. The first of these goals involves medical treatment. The others can be goals for non-medical counselors, preferably working with the family, support groups (like Alcoholics Anonymous), and other treatment specialists.

3. *Provide Support.* Drug abusers are lonely, immature people who are being asked to give up a substance which they have come to value and to change a life style which has become well entrenched. This will not be accomplished in one or two hours of individual counseling each week.

Many addicts are best helped within the confines of hospitals or rehabilitation centers where help is available on an "around-the-clock" basis. Some can be assisted through group counseling where recovering addicts can help each other to face the stresses of life, interact with people, and live life without a chemical dependency.

Without doubt the most effective support comes from Alcoholics Anonymous (AA) and related groups (Al-Anon for spouses of alcoholics and Alateen for their children). These organizations meet in cities and towns all over the world, are free of charge, listed in the phone book, and established as perhaps the most effective approach for helping alcoholics and their families. They are based on principles which are consistent with biblical teaching: acceptance of reality; faith in God; commitment of one's life to divine care; honesty with God, self and others; desire and readiness to change one's way of life; prayer; making amends; and sharing with others. Narcotics Anonymous has been less successful but provides, nevertheless, a support group where understanding and care abound. Surely "any treatment that promotes supportive group membership in a drug-free environment is a far more effective means of treating drug addiction than efforts to provide psychological insights or better drugs." [42]

In reading the above paragraphs did it occur to you that the church could also provide such supportive help? This can happen if church members are understanding, familiar with the facts about addiction, available to help and noncondemning. Since many nonaddicts have trouble understanding the addict's struggles, counselees might be encouraged to be involved in AA, plus the broader, more diversified fellowship of a local church.

4. *Help with Stress Management.* In the past, addicts dealt with stress by escaping through the use of drugs. Counseling must show that there are better ways to meet the pressures of life. To show this, the counselee must learn that he or she can trust the counselor who, in turn, must be patient and dependable. Stress in general can be discussed, but a better approach is to take each problem as it arises and help the counselee determine how it can be handled effectively. This will include considerations of interpersonal relations and how to get along with others—apart from drug or alcohol use.

5. *Encourage Self-understanding and a Change of Life Style.* When a

relationship of trust has been established, there can be value in considering some of the reasons for drug abuse. These discussions can lead to insight, but insight in itself is of little value unless it is followed by practical, specific plans for changed behavior.

Sometimes these plans involve vocational counseling (see chapter 17), the consideration and establishment of life goals, an evaluation of self-esteem (see chapter 24), and a discussion of marriage relationships (see chapter 13).

Then there is the issue of life style. Now that he or she is not taking the drug, how will life be different? One's style of life depends on making decisions concerning what will or will not be done. These decisions involve the counselee, but they also concern the family.

6. *Family Counseling.* Drug abuse is a family problem and the whole family must receive support, understanding and help. At times they must be encouraged to not withdraw, but to live life as best as they can despite the circumstances. The family members must be helped to see how they might be contributing to the addiction problem or how their protection of the addict might prolong the condition. They can be given facts to help them understand the addiction, and before the addict comes for help, family members can be encouraged to confront the addict with specific evidences of his or her drug-induced behavior.

Sometimes family members, especially spouses, want to rescue the addict and take responsibility for running the family. When sobriety occurs, the family must readjust to the change and learn to accept the addict as a responsible member of the home. This may be difficult either because of a fear, based on past experience, that the present "dry spell" is temporary, or because the family has grown accustomed to functioning smoothly around the addict. Family change is risky for the family, important for the counselee, and accomplished best when there is encouragement from the counselor or outside support group.

7. *Be Prepared for Relapses.* These are common among addicts, including alcoholics. AA has long maintained that one drink can plunge an alcoholic quickly back into the addiction. The same is true with nonalcoholic drugs. If the relapse is followed by blame and condemnation, the addict is inclined to give up and adopt an attitude which says, "I'll never win, so why should I bother to try?"

It is not easy to work with chemically dependent people. The counselor can expect failures and after a relapse must help the counselee "pick up" and keep working on the problem.

8. *Recognize That Evangelism and Discipleship Are Basic.* If the counselee is to find new meaning and purpose in life, he or she must come to see that true and lasting fulfillment is found only in Jesus Christ. The counselor must depend on the Holy Spirit's guidance to determine when and how to present the gospel. Highly emotional preaching sometimes produces false decisions which later are rejected—although there are many examples

of persons converted to Christ, freed from their addiction, and permanently changed through the preaching of evangelistic messages.

Counselees are most responsive to the gospel when they recognize that they have a need and that Christ can fill that need. Since addicts are masters in manipulating other people, be careful not to fall into the same pattern with an attempt to manipulate them into the kingdom. The counselee should be presented with the facts of the gospel and urged, but not coerced, into making a decision to commit his or her life to Christ.

In all of this, prayer is of central importance. Through the intercession of believers and the availability of concerned human helpers, God works to restore those who are controlled by chemical substances. He also helps to prevent chemical abuse in others.

Preventing Addiction

The prevention of drug abuse begins in the home. When children are respected, loved, disciplined and raised by sensitive, concerned, stable parents, there is greater opportunity for healthy maturing and less likelihood of chemical dependence. When children's emotional needs are met in the home, when they are helped to cope with stress, and when they are taught a clear set of values, there is a greater sense of security and self-esteem, accompanied by a greater ability to handle the problems of life without drugs.

For many people, however, home does not fit this description. Even when it does there can be outside influences which may lead one into drug abuse. To prevent this several additional considerations are important.

1. *Instill a Healthy Religious Faith.* A survey of 5,648 university students revealed that habitual church-goers and those who have a strong religious faith "are far less likely to be taking drugs than classmates who are shifting church affiliations in their search for the divine. And . . . drug use was highest among those for whom there was no spiritual search at all." [43] From this it does not follow that faith in God always prevents drug abuse, but Christian counselors can be aware that when one is "filled with the Spirit" [44] of God, there is less need to depend on chemical substances.

2. *Provide Education on Drug Abuse.* It is true that those who never drink or take a drug will never become addicts. But emotional pleas for abstinence rarely convince or influence people who are curious about drug effects or influenced by peers. Neither is it helpful to ignore the subject of drug abuse on the assumption that discussion will arouse curiosity. When the subject is considered in a frank, open discussion, this weakens the temptation to dabble with the secret and the forbidden.

Education should (a) begin early, since most drug abusers start their long decline in the teenage years; (b) present accurate facts concerning the nature and effects of drugs, including alcohol; (c) avoid emotional appeals which involve "scare tactics" but little factual content; (d) clearly discuss the biblical teachings about wine and drunkenness; (e) make young people aware of why people drink or take drugs, pointing out that "the alcoholic on the road to recovery at 45 years of age has to face, without alcohol, the same feelings and problems he sought to escape through drinking in his teen years"[45]; (f) discuss how one can say "no" in an environment where one's peers may all be drinking or taking drugs; (g) encourage people to make a decision—to drink or not to drink; to take other drugs or to abstain—instead of drifting into the habit; (h) encourage abstinence as the best and most effective means of prevention; (i) describe the warning signs which indicate developing addiction; and (j) alert people to the availability, place and nature of help for those with developing drug-related problems.

One writer has summarized the nature of a truly effective prevention program:

> There is . . . the task of helping the abstinent youngster to understand his behavior in an environment in which most others are drinking. There is the task of making the youngster who drinks aware that alcohol is not just another social beverage, but an intoxicant which in specific amounts for a given individual has specific effects. There's also the task of helping youngsters to understand the alcoholic as a person with a behavior disorder who can be and ought to be helped. . . . What is needed is not less alcohol education, but alcohol education which is realistically supplemented by a broad concern for identifying and helping the youngster with problems of social and personal development, whether or not his problems are alcohol.[46]

This last sentence leads to the next aspect of prevention.

3. *Teach People How to Cope with Life.* If we can assume that drug abuse often reflects a failure in coping, then the approach to prevention is teaching people to openly face, discuss, and deal with the stress-related problems of life. "The key to prevention," concludes one report, "is to reduce exposure to stress where you can and to teach healthy means of coping with stress that can't be eliminated."[47]

4. *Provide Realistic Adult Examples.* In his book on alcoholism, Clinebell reports that parental example is the most influential factor in determining whether or not children will develop chemical dependency. When parents regularly rely on drugs and alcohol, children learn to do the same. When parents rigidly prohibit and condemn the use of chemical substances, children often react by partaking of this "forbidden fruit."

More effective is an open attitude about drugs and alcohol, a recognition of their dangers, an encouragement of moderation if not abstinence, and an example of parents who enjoy life without having to rely on drugs to meet problems or to enjoy fellowship with others.

Conclusions about Addiction

Is drug abuse a sickness or a sin?

Many Christians conclude that it is a sin which must be confronted, confessed, and stopped. In contrast, counselors and former addicts (including AA members) maintain that addiction is a sickness which the addict is powerless to stop and must be treated as such.

Probably it is more accurate to conclude that addiction is both a sin and a sickness. The addict originally chose to subject his or her body to a poison, but the poison then took control and the person became powerless to stop the deterioration without help from others.

Addicts and their families are not helped by moralizing about the sins of drug abuse; neither is it fair to dismiss drug abuse as a sickness, devoid of wrongdoing and for which there is no responsibility. The addict must be helped professionally to overcome the sickness and taught spiritually to live the rest of life in obedience and submission to Jesus Christ. Only then is the difficult problem truly and effectively resolved.

Suggestions for Further Reading

Alibrandi, Tom. *Young Alcoholics*. Minneapolis: CompCare Publications, 1978.
Clinebell, Howard J., Jr. *Understanding and Counseling the Alcoholic*. Rev. ed. Nashville: Abingdon, 1968.
Duncan, Tommie L. *Understanding and Helping the Narcotic Addict*. Philadelphia: Fortress Press, 1965.
Keller, John E. *Ministering to Alcoholics*. Minneapolis: Augsburg, 1966.

Footnotes

1. George A. Mann, *The Dynamics of Addiction* (Minneapolis: Johnson Institute, n.d.).
2. Ibid. See also John Timson, "Is Coffee Safe to Drink?" *Human Nature* 1 (December, 1978): 56–59.
3. Ibid.
4. From a report of the National Institute on Alcohol Abuse and Alcoholism, reported in Tom Alihandi, *Young Alcoholics* (Minneapolis: CompCare Publications, 1978), p. vi.
5. Clarence J. Rowe, "Alcoholism," in *Psychiatry, the Clergy, and Pastoral Counseling,* eds. Dana L. Farnsworth and Francis J. Braceland (Collegeville, MN: St. John's University Press, 1969).
6. "Breakthrough on the No. 1 Drug Problem," *Purdue Perspective* (May/June, 1977). Unsigned article on pp. 1 & 12.
7. Rom. 13:1–5; 1 Pet. 2:13–17.
8. Jay E. Adams, *The Big Umbrella* (Nutley, NJ: Presbyterian and Reformed, 1973), p. 231.
9. Walter Houston Clark, *Chemical Ecstasy: Psychedelic Drugs and Religion* (New York: Sheed and Ward, 1969).
10. John 14:6; 1 Tim. 2:5.
11. This is implied, perhaps, in Col. 3:2; 1 Thess. 5:4–8; 1 Pet. 1:13. Notice also Deut. 6:4. We are to love God with our mind and strength. This clearly is impossible for one who is influenced by drugs. Sorcery is also condemned in Scripture (Gal. 5: 16–21; Rev. 9:20, 21; 18:23; 21:8; 22:15). Sorcery comes from the Greek word *pharmakeia* and refers to one who prepares drugs for religious purposes.
12. 1 Cor. 6:12.
13. 1 Pet 5:7; Ps. 55:22.
14. Gen 1:28.
15. R. A. Morey, *The Bible and Drug Abuse* (Grand Rapids: Baker, 1973), p. 29.

16. Prov. 20:1; 23:29–31; Isa. 5:11; Rom. 13:13; 1 Cor. 5:11; 6:10; Gal. 5:21; Eph. 5:18; 1 Pet. 4:3; 1 Thess. 5:7, 8.

17. 1 Cor. 6:19, 20; Rom. 12:1.

18. Ps. 104; John 2:9; Matt. 11:19; 26:27–29; Luke 7:33, 34.

19. Robert H. Stein, "Wine Drinking in New Testament Times," *Christianity Today*, 20 June 1975.

20. John 2:10.

21. Luke 7:33.

22. Num. 6:2–4.

23. 1 Cor. 6:11.

24. 1 Cor. 6:12; Rom. 14:21.

25. Matt. 27:34; Mark 15:23; Luke 10:34; 1 Tim. 5:23.

26. Howard J. Clinebell, Jr., *Understanding and Counseling the Alcoholic* (New York: Abingdon, 1956), pp. 49–52.

27. Ibid.

28. George E. Vaillant, "Alcoholism and Drug Dependence," in *The Harvard Guide to Modern Psychiatry*, ed. Armand M. Nicholi, Jr. (Cambridge, MA: Harvard University Press, 1978), pp. 567–77.

29. According to a recent report, some people "go berserk" when they drink even a very small quantity of alcohol. These people normally are well adjusted but their brains contain some cells which were damaged earlier in life. Alcohol produces an excessive electrical charge in these damaged cells and this causes rage, violence, destructiveness and amnesia. This condition applies to a very small number of people, however, and describes a physiological basis for *some* violence; not for addiction. See Ronald Kotulak, "Brain Malfunction: Drink Can Fuel 'Jekyll & Hyde,' " *Chicago Tribune*, 2 November 1978.

30. Robert J. Ackerman, *Children of Alcoholics* (Holmes Beach, FL: Learning Publications, 1978).

31. Vaillant, "Alcoholism;" David W. Swanson, Amos P. Bratrude, and Edward M. Brown, "Alcohol Abuse in a Population of Indian Children," *Diseases of the Nervous System* 32 (December, 1971): 835–42.

32. Clinebell, *Understanding and Counseling*, pp. 45–49.

33. Much of the information in this segment is adapted from Mann, *The Dynamics of Addiction*.

34. Ruth Maxwell, *The Booze Battle* (New York: Praeger, 1976).

35. Sharon Wegscheider, *The Family Trap: No One Escapes from a Chemically Dependent Family* (Minneapolis: Johnson Institute, 1976).

36. Maxwell, *The Booze Battle*.

37. Basil Jackson, "Drugs, Adolescence, and the Family," in *Living and Growing Together: The Christian Family Today*, ed. Gary R. Collins (Waco, TX: Word, 1976), p. 116.

38. Eph. 5:18, *Living Bible*.

39. George A. Mann, *Medical Aspects of Intoxication* (Minneapolis: Johnson Institute, n.d.). It is beyond the scope of this book to list specific physical responses to individual drugs. Interested readers may want to consult Eugene Kennedy, *On Becoming a Counselor* (New York: Seabury, 1977), pp. 317–20.

40. For an extended discussion of the effects of drinking and drugs on pregnancy, see Lucy Barry Robe, *Just So It's Healthy* (Minneapolis: CompCare Publications, 1977).

41. Maxwell, *The Booze Battle*.

42. Vaillant, "Alcoholism" p. 577.

43. Samuel Pearlman, "Religious Affiliations and Patterns of Drug Usage in an

Urban University Population," presented to the First International Conference on Student Drug Surveys, and reported in *Human Behavior* (May 1973): 44.

44. Eph. 5:18.

45. John E. Keller, *Ministering to Alcoholics* (Minneapolis: Augsburg, 1966), p. 155.

46. George Maddox, "Community Factors in Alcohol Education," *A Report of the Second Conference on Alcohol Education,* reported in Keller, *Ministering,* p. 146.

47. David F. Duncan, "Life Stress as a Precurser to Adolescent Drug Dependence," *Human Behavior* (February, 1977): 52. For a discussion of stress see Gary R. Collins, *You Can Profit from Stress* (Santa Ana: Vision House, 1977).

27

Sickness

THE HUMAN BODY, AS EVERYBODY KNOWS, IS A REMARKABLE ORGANISM. Comprising billions of cells, numerous chemicals, hundreds of muscles, miles of blood vessels, and a variety of organs, the human body can grow, heal itself, fight disease, adapt to temperature changes, react to environmental stimulation, and survive numerous physical abuses. But the body does not go on forever, at least in this world. Sometimes it is injured beyond repair. It can break down if it isn't cared for and eventually each body wears out.

When we are healthy, we often take the body for granted. Colds and periodic bouts with the flu are annoying but usually only temporary interruptions to the activities of life. When sickness is more serious, painful, or of longer duration, however, we are forced to recognize our own limitations. Sickness, writes one chaplain,[1] is more than a lack of health. It is an expression of our own physical, emotional and spiritual limitations. It is a vivid indication that we are human beings, inhabiting a body which is destined to die.[2] Since most of us try to avoid thoughts of illness, and sometimes even ignore symptoms, it becomes more difficult to tolerate or accept sickness when it does come. Sickness inhibits our activities, slows us down, makes life more difficult and often seems to have no meaning or purpose. If the illness persists, we are inclined to ask hard questions— like, "Why me?" or "Why has this happened now?"—and often the sickness is accompanied by feelings of anger, discouragement, loneliness, bitterness and confusion. Counseling the sick and their families, therefore, becomes a major challenge for Christian counselors.

The Bible and Sickness

Sickness is an issue which runs throughout the pages of Scripture. The illnesses of Miriam, Naaman, Nebuchadnezzar, David's newborn child, Job, and a variety of others are described with clarity in both the Old and New Testaments. When Jesus came to earth in person his concern for the sick was so important that almost one-fifth of the Gospels is devoted to the topic of healing.[3] The disciples were expected to carry on this healing ministry,[4] and the Book of Acts records how the early church cared for those with physical illnesses.

This biblical emphasis on sickness points to at least four conclusions which can be helpful for the Christian counselor.

1. *Sickness Is a Part of Life.* Few people, if any, go through life without experiencing at least periodic illness. It seems likely that sickness entered the human race as a result of the Fall, and since that time people have known what it is like to be unhealthy. The Bible makes no attempt to diagnose, categorize, or systematically list the symptoms of mental and physical illness, but it does mention symptoms in passing and refers directly or indirectly to alcoholism, blindness, boils, deafness, muteness, dysentery, epilepsy, fever, hemorrhaging, indigestion, infirmity, inflammations, insanity, leprosy, palsy, speech impediments, and a number of other illnesses.[5] It is implied that each of these causes psychological as well as physical stress, and all are mentioned in a way which implies that sickness is an expected part of life in this world.

2. *Care, Compassion and Healing Are Important for Christians.* By his words and actions, Jesus taught that sickness, while common, also is undesirable. He spent much of his time healing the sick, he encouraged others to do likewise, and he emphasized the importance of compassionate caring for those who were needy and unhealthy. Even to give someone a drink of water was considered praiseworthy and Jesus indicated that helping a sick person was the same as ministering to himself.[6] Elsewhere, believers are instructed to pray for the sick and to help in practical ways.[7] Clearly, therefore, the Christian has a responsibility to care for those who are not well.

3. *Sickness, Sin and Faith Are Not Necessarily Related.* When Job lost his family, possessions and health, a trio of well-meaning but ineffective comforters argued that all of these problems resulted from sin. Job discovered, however, that sickness does not always come as a result of individual sin—a conclusion which Jesus clearly taught in John 9.[8] All sickness comes ultimately because of mankind's fall into sin, but individual cases of sickness are not necessarily the result of the sick person's sins— even though there may be times when sickness and personal sin *are* related.[9]

This becomes clearer as we examine the healing miracles of the New Testament. Sometimes people improved because they personally believed that Christ would heal. The woman with the issue of blood is a good example.[10] There were other times, however, when a person other than the patient had faith. Several parents came to Jesus, for example, told about their sick children, and saw the children healed.[11] Then, in the Garden of Gethsemane, a servant's ear was healed even though no person had faith except Jesus. In contrast, there was Paul, a man who had great faith in Christ but whose "thorn in the flesh" never left. Still others had no faith and no healing.[12] From these examples it surely is clear that to be sick is not necessarily a sin or evidence of a lack of faith.[13]

The Bible gives no support to those Christians who proclaim that sick people are out of God's will or lacking in faith. God has never promised to heal all of our diseases in this life and it is both incorrect and cruel to teach that instant health always will come to those whose faith is strong.

4. *Sickness Raises Some Difficult and Crucial Questions about Suffering.* In an influential little book titled *The Problem of Pain,* C. S. Lewis summarized two basic questions which face anyone who suffers and which often are raised in counseling. If God is good, why does he permit suffering? If he is all-powerful, why doesn't he stop suffering? Entire volumes have been written to answer these questions and the Christian counselor might find it helpful to read some of these.[14]

It is probable that our finite minds will never fully comprehend the reasons for suffering, but the Bible teaches that suffering keeps us humble, refines our faith, conforms us to Christ's image, teaches us about God and produces patience, maturity, perseverance and character. Suffering also teaches us to become more compassionate and caring.[15] This brings us to the issue of counseling, and points us to the causes of sickness.

The Causes of Sickness and Related Problems

Sickness, as everyone knows, comes from a variety of causes: contact with viruses and disease-carrying plants or animals, poor diet, lack of exercise or good body care, injury, hereditary defects, the ingestion of harmful substances (like drugs or poisons), the wearing out or degeneration of body organs, contact with extreme heat or cold—to name some of the most obvious. These are the causes which physicians seek to discover and treat especially when symptoms are present.

But sickness involves much more than physical malfunctioning. It brings with it a variety of psychological and spiritual reactions which concern both physicians and nonmedical counselors as well. Many of these psychological-spiritual influences accentuate the physical and delay or prevent recovery. Let us consider several of these influences.

1. *The Influence of Pain.* There are great individual differences in how people experience pain, in how they respond to it, and in the intensity and duration of pain. Pain which is intense and brief—such as that experienced in the dentist's chair—is different from the gnawing, never ending pain of a cancer patient. Pain which is understood and known to be short-term—like a headache—is handled differently than pain that is long lasting or undiagnosed.

Medical research has demonstrated that people show differences in their awareness and tolerance of pain, and there is evidence that these psychological responses largely are unrelated to the severity of the illness. Some people feel little pain even with a major injury or sickness; some feel great pain even when there is no discernible organic disease; some deny their pain and pretend it doesn't exist; others almost seem to enjoy the suffering. While these differences, in part, may have biological causes, many of the individual differences in pain tolerance result from one's attitudes about pain, culture, values (some people, for example, stoically believe that pain is a sign of weakness), family background, past experiences with pain, and anxiety (anxieties which come with pain, in turn, may intensify the pain).[16] In addition, it is probable that one's religious beliefs also are related to pain tolerance.

The counselor must recognize and accept these individual differences. They influence a sick person's emotions, reactions and prognosis for recovery. Remember, too, that the differences are not necessarily good or bad. A high ability to tolerate pain is no more a sign of strength—or weakness—than is a low level of tolerance.

2. *The Feeling of Helplessness.* It is not easy to be sick, especially when our routines are disrupted, when we do not understand what is wrong with our bodies, or we don't know when or if we will get better. If we are sick enough to seek medical attention we must submit ourselves to the care of strangers, some of whom are more aloof and scientific than they are compassionate and sensitive. All of this increases our sense of helplessness in the face of illness.

It has been suggested that sick people, especially those who are hospitalized, experience seven categories of psychological stress: [17]

(a) A Threat to One's Integrity.

> Sudden illness, hospitalization, and the threat of death undermine the universal, albeit irrational, beliefs that we are always capable, independent and self-sufficient; that our bodies are indestructible; that we can control the world around us and are the masters of our own destiny. . . . Once he enters the hospital, the patient is expected to passively comply with myriad orders. He is told what medication to take, and when to take it; and, whether he wants to or not, he is expected to submit to a variety of diagnostic and therapeutic procedures. His activities no longer depend on his own whims and desires; they are routinized to conform with established hospital procedures. He is told when to go to sleep, when to wake up, when to eat; he may even have to go to the bathroom on schedule. In short he is treated like an infant, but has none of the normal perquisites of the infant, for example, to behave irresponsibly, make excessive demands on those around him, or just be terribly upset.[18]

(b) A Fear of Strangers. When we are sick, we at times are expected to put our lives and bodies into the hands of strangers with whom we may have no close personal ties and whose competence we may not be able to judge. This can be frightening.

(c) A Separation Anxiety. Sickness separates us from friends and from customary routines. During hospitalization we are separated from familiar people and things at the time when we need them most.

(d) A Fear of Losing Love and Approval. Sickness or injury can leave us physically deformed, forced to slow down, and passively dependent on others. All of these can threaten our self-esteem and lead to the fear that because of these changes, others will no longer love or respect us. Sometimes there is a desire to receive visitors, mixed with the hope that "nobody will come and see me looking like this."

(e) A Fear of Losing Control. It is threatening to experience even a temporary loss of one's physical strength, intellectual alertness, bowel or bladder control, speech, control of limbs, or the ability to regulate one's emotions. It can be even more threatening to realize that these losses most often come when we are on semipublic display in a hospital room.

(f) A Fear of Exposing and Losing Body Parts. Sick people are expected to expose the "hurting" parts of the body and submit themselves to the visual examination and touch of medical personnel. This can be embarrassing and sometimes threatening, especially when it becomes apparent that a part of one's body may be injured, operated on, or removed.

(g) Guilt and a Fear of Punishment. Sickness or accidents often lead people to think that their suffering may be punishment for previous sins or failures. As we have seen, this was the view held by Job's comforters and it has been accepted by thousands of people ever since. Lying in bed for long hours and wondering "Why?" these people can be overwhelmed with guilt, especially if there is no recovery.

Whereas these stresses are common, once again there are individual differences in the way people react. Some feel depressed, guilty, self-condemning, embarrassed, and/or helpless. Others become angry and critical, especially of doctors. Then there are those who cheerfully make the best of a difficult situation and, as a result, often recover faster.

3. *The Experience of Emotion.* It has already been implied that sickness and injury arouse numerous feelings which can in turn influence the speed and likelihood of recovery. Emotions include:

—fear of pain, subsequent diagnoses, physical complications, helplessness, isolation, an uncertain future, nonrecovery, rejection, and/or death (for some there is also fear of what they might say when under the influence of an anesthetic);

—anger at oneself, at the illness, at one's doctors, at others (including the counselor) and sometimes at God;

—guilt, over what one has done or failed to do; one research study found that 93 percent of cancer patients felt their illness was the result of sin or past failure; [19]

—depression, which sometimes leads to suicide or loss of a desire to get better; and

—confusion which comes when one can't determine the prognosis and isn't sure how to evaluate the illness.

4. *The Presence of Family Reactions.* When a person becomes ill, his or her family is affected and the awareness of this, in turn, influences the patient. Changes in family routine as the result of an illness, financial hardships, difficulties in scheduling hospital visits, and even the loss of opportunity for sex between a husband and wife can all create tension which sometimes leads to fatigue, irritability and worry. In an attempt to reassure one another and prevent worry, the patient and family sometimes refuse to discuss their real fears or feelings with each other and as a result, each suffers alone, fearing the worst but pretending that "all is well and recovery is on the way."

The above paragraphs are not designed to paint a bleak picture of sickness. In many cases these problems are not present, but for others they are apparent to the counselor, if not to the patient and patient's family. These fears and threats in turn can affect the course of treatment, influence the patient's attitudes toward the illness, and have a bearing on the speed or likelihood of recovery.

The Effects of Sickness

In one sense it is difficult to separate this section from the preceding paragraphs. Pain, feelings of helplessness, emotions and family reactions to an illness are as much the effects of sickness as they are the causes of additional adjustment problems. Many reactions, such as guilt, complicate the sickness and, as the physical illness gets worse, leads to more guilt. Thus a vicious circle develops.

In addition, there are effects which, once again, appear in some sick people, but not in everyone. To be effective as a counselor we must be aware of these different effects and attempt to deal with them.

1. *Defense and Denial.* Since sickness is so unwelcome, there is a tendency to deny its seriousness and sometimes its presence. This is true especially if the illness is serious or likely to be terminal. At least for a while the attitude of the patient may imply that "It can't be me, I'm sure the diagnosis is wrong. God will surely heal."

Readers of introductory psychology textbooks are familiar with the "defense mechanisms"—ways of thinking which enable us to deny reality and to pretend that a frustration or conflict is of no importance. Such thinking is very common. It is used automatically, usually without prior deliberation, and often without our even being aware that it is taking place. Its purpose is to protect us from anxiety.

Psychologists have identified a number of these defensive ways of thinking, and many are seen in sick persons or their families. *Rationalization,* for example, is the tendency to make excuses which make sense ("They've probably misinterpreted the test results"). *Projection* lets us put our own feelings of anger or fear on to someone else ("My problem is with the doctor who is trying to make my life miserable"). *Reaction formation* is the tendency to display, in excess, the opposite of what one feels ("Look at how well I am and how I'm getting so much better day by day"). *Magical thinking* lets us pretend ("The doctor will surely find a new cure before long"). *Repression* is an unconscious forgetting and *suppression* is a deliberate forgetting, both of which are used to push unpleasant reality out of our minds. Such gimmicks can be helpful if they give us time to gather strength and the knowledge needed to cope more realistically with reality. When the defenses and denial persist, however, the patient or family is being unrealistic and may be rudely awakened later.

2. *Hope.* In her landmark book, *On Death and Dying,* psychiatrist Elisabeth Kubler-Ross reported that whenever a patient stops expressing hope, it usually is a sign of imminent death.[20] Even severely ill people who have a realistic view of their condition find that hope sustains and encourages them, especially in difficult times. Medical and nonmedical counselors have found that patients get along better when there is at least a glimmer of hope. This does not mean that doctors and others must lie about the patient's condition. It means, writes Kubler-Ross, that "we share with them the hope that something unforeseen may happen, that they may have a remission, that they may live longer than expected."[21] For the Christian there is even greater hope in the knowledge that the loving, sovereign God of the universe is concerned about us both now and for eternity.

3. *Withdrawal.* When we are sick, we need to let others help and love us. For many people, however, this isn't easy. They feel threatened by their dependence on others, weak, and not really understood. As a result they withdraw, sometimes in an attitude of self-pity and subsequent loneliness.

4. *Resistance.* Some patients "come out fighting." Since it isn't easy to fight the disease, they direct their anger to doctors, nurses, family and other people, including counselors. Criticism, complaining, noisy protests, and demands for relief often characterize such patients and create frustration in the lives of others.

5. *Manipulation.* Some people go through life attempting to control and manipulate others by subtle or "steam-rolling" means. When such persons become ill, it is not surprising that they use the sickness to control or to get sympathy, attention and favors from others.

6. *Hypochondriasis.* Sickness sometimes brings benefits, like attention and sympathy from others, an opportunity to do nothing, freedom from responsibility, and socially sanctioned permission to stay home from work. Some people enjoy the benefits of being sick and as a result they never get better or they experience a series of physical symptoms for which there is no organic basis and little relief.

One medical team has divided hypochondriasis into two types.[22] The "masochistic-hostile" type characterizes people who tend to be dependent and angry at themselves and others. Some of them have sacrificed themselves to care for another, and when that other dies or leaves, the person can only maintain equilibrium by caring for his or her own illnesses. The "clinging-dependent" type are often isolated, passive people who use symptoms to gain attention, relationships and direction from authority figures. Whether or not we accept this classification, it must be recognized that for some people, sickness becomes a way of life. This may be unpleasant for the patient but he or she finds it easier than living life without physical complaints.

Counseling and Sickness

In counseling with the sick it is good to remember the basic principles which apply to all counseling: the importance of counselor warmth, empathy and genuineness; the value of listening patiently and encouraging the patient (without pushing) to talk about fears, anxieties, anger, the illness, one's family, the future, and so on; the importance of confidentiality; and the need to show acceptance, understanding and compassion—without being gushy or condescending. Sick people sometimes are more sensitive to these counselor characteristics than are people who are physically well.

In addition to these general guidelines there are specific issues to remember when counseling the physically ill person.

1. *Evaluate Your Own Attitudes and Needs.* When a person is found to have a terminal illness, doctors, nurses, clergymen, even family members often withdraw and leave the patient to face the problem alone. It has been found that some of the best counseling in such situations is done by cleaning women who are cheerful, regular visitors, and willing to listen and talk.[23]

This sad situation points to the fact that most of us don't like to face sickness, especially serious illness, so we avoid people who are ill. Perhaps we are threatened by the reminder of our own susceptibility to illness. Perhaps we are uncomfortable or feel helpless because we don't know what to say, are not sure how to react to the patient's anger and discouragement, or feel incapable of dealing with difficult questions—such as "Why me?" or "Do you think I'm going to die?" The sight of severely ill or injured persons, perhaps with physical deformities or tubes and machines attached to the body, can create discomfort in the counselor and sometimes reactions of shock which the patient is quick to detect.

For some counselors, the more they face sickness, the easier it becomes to deal with the sick. If the counselor has been ill in the past, he or she may have greater understanding for patients now. This does not always happen, however, and some of us never become accustomed to hospitals or sickness. If this is so, the counselor should take some time—perhaps

Table 27–1
Guidelines for Visiting the Sick *

For All Patients

Visit frequently but keep the visits brief.

Let the patient take the lead in shaking hands.

Stand or sit where the patient can see you easily.

The side of the bed is more suitable than the foot of the bed.

Give the patient freedom to talk freely, and listen carefully as he does so.

Use your resources as a Christian: prayer, Scripture, encouraging comments, etc. Whether you pray audibly should be determined by the Holy Spirit and the situation—the patient, his spiritual background, the people present, etc. Suggest prayer rather than ask if it is desired, and keep it short.

Take appropriate precautions against contagious diseases.

Leave some devotional material.

Evaluate each visit to determine how they could be improved in the future.

For Patients at Home

Telephone the home before the visit to make sure you call at a convenient time.

Try to call when there will be time for private discussion.

For Hospital Patients

Upon arrival, check at the reception desk, introduce yourself and make sure that a visit at this time is acceptable.

Do not enter a room that has a closed door or a "no visitors" sign.

Try to call when there are not a lot of other visitors present.

Do:

Be friendly and cheerful.

Be reassuring and comforting.

Help the patient relax.

Recognize that anxieties, discouragement, guilt, frustrations and uncertainties may be present.

Give reassurance of divine love and care.

Promise to pray for the patient during his illness—and act on your promise.

Don't:

Speak in an unnatural tone of voice.

Talk about your own past illnesses.

Force the patient to talk. Your silent presence can often be very meaningful.

Promise that God will heal them. Sometimes in his wisdom God permits illness to persist.

Visit when you are sick.

Talk loudly.

Sit, lean on, or jar the bed.

Visit during meals.

Whisper to family members or medical personnel within sight of the patient.

Share information about the diagnosis.

Question the patient about the details of the illness.

Tell the family how to decide when presented with medical options (but help them to decide).

Criticize the hospital, treatment or doctors.

Spread detailed information about the patient when you complete your visit.

*From Gary R. Collins, *Effective Counseling* (Carol Stream, IL: Creation House, 1972), p. 139.

right now if you wish, before reading further—to ponder the reasons for this discomfort in the presence of sick people. An understanding of his or her own attitudes toward sickness and sick people can help the counselor to be more effective. Central to all of this is the issue of prayer and spiritual preparation for counseling. Since Christians are instructed to care for one another,[24] surely we can expect that a compassionate God will give us the ability and sensitivity to be compassionate in turn.

2. *Learn Some Guidelines for Visiting the Sick.* As we have seen, counseling is not limited to a counselor's office; it can take place in a variety of settings. This is true especially when we counsel the sick. Because of physical limitations the counselees cannot always come to us, so counselors must go to the sick person. In visiting these people there are some generally accepted guidelines which the counselor should know and remember. These are summarized in Table 27–1.

3. *Deal with the Specific Feelings and Concerns of the Sick.* When calling on the sick, visitors sometimes avoid sensitive topics on the assumption either that an appearance of cheerfulness will drive away worry or that physically ill persons cannot handle emotional issues. Other visitors take an "isn't it terrible" attitude which turns the visit into morbid introspection. Still others talk enthusiastically of miracles or healing and apparently ignore the realities of the present sickness.

Counselors should avoid all of these extremes. Recognize that patients sometimes want to discuss their feelings and concerns, while at other times they prefer to talk about something else. The counselor should be alert to these differences, but by gentle questioning or tentative mentioning, he or she should give opportunity for the patient to consider sensitive issues such as the following.

(a) Fear. Does the patient experience any of the fears described earlier in this chapter? Are there additional fears that he or she would share? Are the fears based on real facts or are they ill-founded? Fears should be expressed, discussed, evaluated, committed to God in prayer, and not discounted, even when the counselor thinks they are irrational.

(b) Self-pity. When one is sick, forced to slow down and to be alone at times, there is more opportunity to think about one's present circumstances. Often the mind drifts to thoughts of what is bad about the illness or about life in general, and this can lead to self-pity. Some writers[25] would suggest that the potential for even greater distress is initiated at this point: as boredom and loneliness lead to self-pity, self-pity leads to anger, and anger leads to discouragement.

In essence, self-pity is "an angry complaint about one's condition and an attempt to get back at others or to manipulate others into giving sympathy." Brooding can be pleasant for a while, as we ponder the injustice of the world, but ultimately it "churns us up" internally and drives others away.

If a person is entangled in self-pity, this should be pointed out gently. The patient may respond with anger but the counselor must be accepting and understanding, yet firm. Help the counselee think about the positive as well as the negative things in life. Can anything good come from the illness? [26] Can we get a more realistic view of the present situation? Encourage him or her to pray, confessing bitterness and asking for divine forgiveness and direction. Then it may be helpful to ponder what one can *do* to make the best of one's illness. Recognize that the best solution for the present may be to rest, to reevaluate one's life, and to spend time in communication with God.

(c) Anger. As indicated earlier,[27] anger isn't necessarily wrong and neither is it always destructive. Often, however, anger accompanies illness, adversely affects the patient's condition, and sometimes isn't even recognized by the counselee. Questions of "Why me?", criticisms of one's family or the hospital staff, ignoring others, demanding attention or special treatment, depression and refusal to pray are often veiled evidences of intense anger against God, oneself and others. Anger and resentment which is suppressed or denied cannot be resolved. The counselor should seek the Holy Spirit's guidance in helping the angry counselee. Then, encourage him or her to face the anger honestly, to acknowledge its presence, to talk about it, to confess it to God and to ask for his help so that anger can be controlled and not allowed to control the patient.

(d) Discouragement. An old hymn proclaims that "We should never be discouraged" if we "take it to the Lord in prayer." This correctly teaches that discouraging situations are a reason for prayer, but the hymn has also reinforced the questionable conclusion that discouragement is wrong. Many people are unwilling to admit their discouragements and don't want to talk about the things which make them discouraged. Here again, the counselor can show that "it's all right to be discouraged for a while," can help counselees get a realistic perspective on the causes of this discouragement, and can help counselees both to pray and to do what they can to deal realistically with the sources of the discouragement.

(e) Guilt. Patients should be encouraged to express their guilt, to confess their sins or failures to God and to others,[28] and to experience the joy of knowing that God forgives. With some people, it will be necessary for the counselor to show that the guilt feelings, while real, are based on faulty conclusions and assumptions about past behavior or about God's dealings with human beings. These issues are discussed more fully in chapter 9.

(f) Difficult Questions. Although they may not always say so, many sick people struggle with questions like "Why am I experiencing this?"; "Why me and not someone else?"; "How serious is my sickness?"; "Will I really get better?"; "What will happen to me and my family if I don't recover?"

These are questions that counselors and family members tend to avoid.

They are not questions that should be brought up whenever you visit the sick. (Sometimes we all like to push them aside *for a while*.) But if the counselee never mentions such questions, the counselor should—preferably when there is time for discussion without interruptions. Remember, too, that these questions are not always answered easily. The Bible gives some answers,[29] but it also teaches us that God's ways often are beyond the capacity of our human ability to understand.[30]

Sometimes the counselor will be asked whether or not a patient should be told the truth about a serious or terminal diagnosis. This question has been debated endlessly but many doctors would agree with Kubler-Ross that most patients pretty much sense the truth even before they are told. A frank, honest description of the diagnosis does much to retain the patient's trust. When this is followed by unhurried discussions of the situation, the counselee can express his or her feelings, can be helped to put practical and financial affairs in order, can say good-by to loved ones, resolve interpersonal tensions and can insure that there is a peace with God.

4. *Encourage Decisions*. It is possible for sick people to step into a "what's the use?" attitude of inactivity, brooding and self-pity. This hinders recovery and makes life miserable. Such people should be challenged to reexamine their attitudes and to make decisions about the future. They may be faced with permanent limitations, but they can still live life fully with the mental abilities, opportunities and physical capacities which remain.

5. *Instill Hope*. The Christian recognizes that serious illness and even death are not the end of meaningful living. Hope is at the basis of our Christian faith. It is more than the wish that God will perform a miracle. It is the confidence that God, who is living and sovereign, also controls all things and can be expected to bring to pass that which ultimately is best for us.[31] Often that means recovery; sometimes it means long years of incapacity; eventually it means passing through death and, for the believer, into eternal life with Christ. Anger, frustration and disappointment almost always are present with serious illness, but these can be countered by the hope that we have as Christians—not a hope in some emotionally based fantasy of what might happen—but a hope that is based solidly on the Bible's teachings about God and the universe.

6. *Help the Family and Staff*. When an individual has a problem, the family almost always is affected. This is especially true when a family member is ill. Home routines are disrupted, finances are strained, and at times there is the reality of approaching death. Family counseling is discussed more fully in chapter 31 but, for the present, it is sufficient to remember that most of the issues which concern patients also concern their families. Families, therefore, often need counseling, too, and this, in turn, can help the patient to deal with the illness more effectively.

In all of this, it is wise to remember that medical personnel can also profit from periodic counseling. It is not easy to deal with suffering or death—and staff workers, including doctors, can benefit from casual, supportive counseling which helps them deal with their emotions and unanswered questions.

7. *Help the Hypochondriac.* For some counselees the sicknesses will go on in spite of medical treatment. It rarely helps to ignore the symptoms or to confront the patient by stating that the illness has an emotional basis. It has been stated that there is no medication that will cure a psychologically based illness and no surgery that will cut it out. The illness ultimately must be treated at its cause—the underlying anxiety.

Nonmedical counselors must first insure that the illnesses are, in fact, nonorganic. This can be determined only by a physician. If the doctor concludes that there is no physical basis for the symptoms, the counselor can proceed along the lines suggested in the chapter on anxiety. Although the symptoms may have no organic basis, they nevertheless are very real and uncomfortable. The counselor should show an understanding of the discomfort but attempt, in addition, to discover and help the counselee deal with underlying anxieties. Try also to determine what needs are being met by the symptoms (e.g., the needs to be noticed, to control others, and to be dependent). Can the counselee learn to meet these needs in healthier ways?

Prevention and Sickness

Within recent years the medical profession has given considerable attention to the ways in which disease and injury can be prevented or avoided. When people are prevented from getting sick, the problems discussed in this chapter do not arise. But even before or when sickness comes, the illness-related problems can be reduced and sometimes prevented.

1. *Ponder and Discuss One's Attitude toward Sickness and Death.* Since healthy people avoid thinking about these issues, the realities of sickness and death hit with greater force when we are forced to face them. Perhaps this trauma could be lessened if we would (a) not avoid people who are suffering—often they need our help, (b) give deliberate thought to our own possible sickness, death and funeral—this is realistic planning, and (c) openly discuss sickness and death with family members while everyone is well. This need not be morbid or imply "wishful thinking." It is an acknowledgment of our own mortality on earth. It is a way to prepare for the future and to open lines of communication at times when there is no crisis.

2. *Learn to See Meaning in Sickness.* Illness often is seen as something which is harmful and bad, but this isn't necessarily so. Illness can slow us down, bring us face-to-face with our own limitations, give us a clearer perspective on life and eternity, and teach us more fully about the love and forgiveness of God. "Illness," writes a hospital chaplain, "often

becomes the opportunity many people need to stop running long enough to find a happier, more fruitful life. Sometimes a person does have to get sick to get better, at least emotionally and spiritually, if not physically."[32] Such an attitude helps us to see sickness in a more meaningful light.

3. *Face One's Concerns Realistically.* Fear, anger, guilt, confusion, concern about the family—the earlier such issues are raised and discussed, the less they fester and complicate an illness. If people can learn to share and pray about their concerns and emotions as a way of life, these issues will not be hidden when sickness comes.

4. *Acquire Information.* Studies of surgical patients have shown that recovery is faster and pain is less severe when patients are told before treatment what to expect during and after treatment.[33] When the patient and family know what is coming, the discomfort and anxiety can be handled much more effectively.

5. *Strengthen One's Christian Commitment.* Learning to walk with God—through prayer, meditation, Bible study, and worship—can prepare us for the crises of life. The Scriptures never teach that believers are exempt from illness or that suffering will be easy for Christians; neither are we taught that we should bear problems alone. When we are in the habit of "bearing one another's burdens," and casting our burdens on God in prayer, then we are better prepared for facing illness and death when they come. The physical and psychological pain will be present still, but underneath is the assurance that God is in control.

Conclusions about Sickness

Prior to World War II, Dr. Paul Tournier, the Swiss physician, first proposed his concept of medicine of the whole person. When an individual is sick, Tournier believed, his or her whole being is affected—the physical, psychological and spiritual. Jesus demonstrated this concern for whole persons when he ministered to spiritual needs but he also had a deep and practical concern about individual suffering, thinking and sickness. We who are his followers must have an equal and compassionate concern for whole persons. To divorce the physical, psychological and spiritual parts of the person from each other is both impossible and unbiblical.

Suggestions for Further Reading
* Bittner, Vernon J. *Make Your Illness Count.* Minneapolis: Augsburg, 1976.
Havner, Vance. *Though I Walk Through the Valley.* Old Tappan, NJ: Revell, 1974.
Justice, William G. *Don't Sit on the Bed: A Handbook for Visiting the Sick.* Nashville: Broadman, 1973.
Kubler-Ross, Elisabeth. *On Death and Dying.* New York: Macmillan, 1969.
Oates, Wayne E., and Lester, Andrew D., eds. *Pastoral Care in Crucial Human Situations.* Valley Forge: Judson Press, 1969.
* Yancey, Philip. *Where Is God When It Hurts?* Grand Rapids: Zondervan, 1977.

Footnotes

1. Vernon J. Bittner, *Make Your Illness Count* (Minneapolis: Augsburg, 1976).
2. Heb. 9:27.
3. Reported in Morton T. Kelsey, *Healing and Christianity* (New York: Harper & Row, 1963), p. 54.
4. Mark 6:7–13; Matt. 10:5–8; Luke 9:1, 2, 6.
5. Healings of these are reported throughout the four Gospels and Acts.
6. Matt. 25:39, 40.
7. James 5:14–16.
8. See especially John 9:2, 3; also Luke 13:1–5.
9. Matt. 9:2–6; 1 Cor. 11:29, 30.
10. Matt. 9:20, 21.
11. Mark 7:24–30; 9:20–27; Matt. 9:18, 19, 23–26.
12. Matt. 13:58.
13. See E. Margaret Clarkson, "It's No Sin to Be Sick," *Moody Monthly* 79 (November, 1978): 52, 53, 144.
14. See, for example, C. S. Lewis, *The Problem of Pain* (New York: Macmillan, 1962); Philip Yancey, *Where Is God When It Hurts?* (Grand Rapids: Zondervan, 1977).
15. 2 Cor. 2:7–10; 1 Pet. 1:5–7; Rom. 8:28; Heb. 12:11; Ps. 119:71; James 1:2–4; Rom. 5:3–5. In the tape recording made to accompany this chapter, Dr. Stuart Briscoe deals more fully with the problem of pain.
16. James J. Strain and Stanley Grossman, *Psychological Care of the Medically Ill* (New York: Appleton-Century-Crofts, 1975), chapter 8, "The Problem of Pain."
17. Ibid., pp. 24–27.
18. Ibid., p. 25.
19. Nathan Schnaper, "Care of the Dying Person," in *Psychiatry, The Clergy and Pastoral Counseling,* eds. Dana L. Farnsworth and Francis J. Braceland (Collegeville, MN: St. John's University Press, 1969), p. 184.
20. Elisabeth Kubler-Ross, *On Death and Dying* (New York: Macmillan, 1969).
21. Ibid., p. 123.
22. Strain and Grossman, *Psychological Care of the Medically Ill,* pp. 83–91.
23. Kubler-Ross, *On Death and Dying.*
24. 1 Cor. 12:25, 26.
25. See for example, Jay Adams, *The Christian Counselor's Manual* (Nutley, NJ: Presbyterian and Reformed, 1973), pp. 371, 372.
26. This question is the theme of Bittner, *Make Your Illness Count.*
27. See chapter 8 of this book.
28. 1 John 1:9; James 5:6.
29. These are discussed in the books noted in footnote 14. See also the references in footnote 15, above.
30. Rom. 11:33.
31. Heb. 11:1.
32. Bittner, *Make Your Illness Count,* p. 12.
33. Irving L. Janis, *Psychological Stress: Psychoanalytic and Behavioral Studies of Surgical Patients* (New York: Wiley, 1958); L. D. Egbert, G. E. Batit, C. E. Welch, and M. K. Bartlett, "Reduction of Post-operative Pain by Encouragement and Instruction to Patient," *New England Journal of Medicine* 270 (1964): 825.

28

Grief

THE EXPERIENCE OF GRIEF IS UNIVERSAL AND FELT BY EVERY PERSON during the course of a lifetime. Since grief is so common and since it has concerned people for centuries, it might be expected that grief is a well-understood experience. But this does not seem to be true. Death and grief are difficult issues to face. When they come we cope as best we can, but otherwise we prefer not to discuss them. Only recently, therefore, have there been careful studies of the grief process.

In 1917, Freud published one of the first careful studies on grief.[1] Almost thirty years later a Harvard professor named Erich Lindemann wrote about his interviews with 101 grieving relatives,[2] and soon a number of books and articles began to appear. It was in 1969, however, that a previously unknown psychiatrist named Elisabeth Kubler-Ross published her book, *On Death and Dying*.[3] Soon an avalanche of publications appeared and although many of these consist of personal experiences and "sticky-sweet poems," others give excellent helpful insights into the process of grieving. Within a decade, therefore, we have seen the development of a whole new literature and field of study known as *thanatology*—"the branch of knowledge dealing with the dying and the bereaved."

Grief is an important, normal response to the loss of any significant object or person. It is an experience of deprivation and anxiety which can show itself physically, emotionally, cognitively, socially and spiritually. Any loss can bring about grief: divorce, retirement from one's job, amputations, death of a pet or plant, departure of a child to college or of a pastor to some other church, moving from a friendly neighborhood, selling one's car, losing a home or valued object, loss of a contest or athletic game, health failures, and even the loss of confidence or enthusiasm. Doubts, the loss of one's faith, the waning of one's spiritual vitality, or the inability to find meaning in life can all produce a sadness and emptiness which indicate grief. Indeed, whenever a part of life is removed there is grief.

411

Most discussions of grief, however, concern losses which come when a loved one or other meaningful person has died. Death, of course, happens to everyone and the mourners are left to grieve. Such grieving is never easy. We try to soften the trauma by dressing up the corpse, surrounding it with flowers or soft lights, and using words like "passed away" instead of "died," but we cannot make death into something beautiful. As Christians we take comfort in the certainty of the resurrection, but this does not soften the emptiness and pain of being forced to let go of someone we love. When we experience "loss by death grievers are faced with an absolute, unalterable, irreversible situation; there is nothing they can do to, for or about that relationship." [4] Death, says the Bible, is a stinging enemy, [5] and grief can be devastating. Eventually each of us will die [6] and in the meantime most of us will grieve at least periodically. Such grieving gives counselors a difficult but rewarding challenge—to help people deal with death.

The Bible and Grief

The Bible is a realistic book which describes the deaths and subsequent grieving of many people. In the Old Testament, we read of God's presence and comfort as we "walk through the valley of the shadow of death" [7]; we read descriptions of people grieving in times of loss and trouble [8]; we learn that the Word of God strengthens grievers [9]; and we are introduced to the Messiah as "a man of sorrows, acquainted with grief. . . . Surely our griefs He Himself bore, and our sorrows He carried." [10]

In the New Testament, a variety of passages deal with death and grief. These might be grouped into two categories, each dealing with the influence of Jesus Christ.

1. *Christ Has Changed the Meaning of Grieving.* There are many nonbelievers who grieve without any hope for the future. For them, death is the end of a relationship—forever.

But the Christian does not believe that. In the two clearest New Testament passages on this subject, [11] we learn that "if we believe that Jesus died and rose again, even so God will bring with Him those who have fallen asleep in Jesus." [12] We can "comfort one another with these words," [13] convinced that in the future "the dead will be raised imperishable, and we shall be changed. . . . When this perishable will have put on the imperishable, and this mortal will have put on immortality, then will come about the saying that is written, 'Death is swallowed up in victory.' " [14]

For the Christian, death is not the end of existence; it is the entrance into life eternal. The one who believes in Christ knows that Christians will "always be with the Lord." Physical death is still present because the devil has "the power of death," but because of the crucifixion and resurrection, Christ has defeated death and promised that the one who lives and believes in Christ "shall never die." [15]

This knowledge is comforting but it does not eliminate the intense pain of grief and the need for comfort. In a discussion of death, Paul encouraged his readers to take courage and not lose heart since the person who is absent from the body is present with the Lord.[16] Believers are encouraged to be steadfast, immovable and doing the Lord's work since such effort is not in vain [17] when we have assurance of the resurrection.

2. *Christ Has Demonstrated the Importance of Grieving.* Early in his ministry, Jesus preached his Sermon on the Mount and spoke about grieving: "Blessed are those that mourn," he said, "for they will be comforted." [18] Mourning was taken for granted. Apparently it was seen as something positive since it is listed among a group of desirable qualities such as meekness, gentleness, mercy, purity of heart and peacemaking. Might we also assume from this passage that without mourning, comfort cannot be given?

When Lazarus died, Jesus was troubled and deeply moved. He accepted, without comment, the apparent anger that came from Mary, Lazarus's sister, and he wept with the mourners. Jesus knew that Lazarus was about to be raised from the dead, but the Lord still grieved.[19] He also withdrew and grieved when he learned that John the Baptist had been executed.[20] In the Garden of Gethsemane, Jesus was "deeply grieved," [21] perhaps with an anticipatory grief, more intense but similar to that experienced by David as he watched his infant son die.[22]

Even for the Christian, then, grief is normal and healthy. But it also can be pathological and unhealthy. As we shall see, this difference is of special concern to any Christian counselor.

The Causes of Grief

In one sense, the cause of grief can be stated simply: Something or someone has been lost and the griever is faced with the almost overwhelming and time-consuming task of readjusting. According to Lindemann, this grief work following a death involves three big tasks: untangling oneself from the ties that bind one to the deceased, readjusting to an environment in which the deceased person is missing, and forming new relationships. All of this takes work.

> "Grief work" (a term first used by Freud) is just what it says, the task of mourning. And it *is* work—hard, long, painful, slow, repetitive, a suffering through the same effort over and over. It's a matter of rethinking and refeeling, reworking the same long-past fields, the same old emotional material, over and over—breaking through the denial and disbelief that the past and the deceased are both dead; re-examining one's past life repeatedly and seeing each thought, each intimate experience, with and without the deceased, looking at everything that has gone before from a thousand or more points of view until finally the past like the deceased is ready to be buried. Out of this a whole new mourner emerges with new attitudes, new concepts, new values, new appreciations of life itself; and

if these *are* better than the old, then there has been growth and change
and all the suffering has been worthwhile, then the grief has been good.[23]

But the grief isn't always good. It is possible to distinguish normal grief
from pathological grief.[24] Normal grief often involves intense sorrow,
pain, loneliness, anger, depression, physical symptoms and changes in
interpersonal relations, all of which comprise a period of deprivation and
transition that may last for as long as three years—or more. Often there
is denial, fantasy, restlessness, disorganization, inefficiency, irritability,
a desire to talk considerably about the deceased, an unconscious adoption
of the lost person's mannerisms, and a feeling that life no longer has
meaning. In all of this there are great individual differences. How one
grieves depends on one's personality, background, religious beliefs, relationship with the deceased, and cultural environment. Because of the
unique ways in which we grieve, it is difficult to determine when a normal
grief reaction is becoming unhealthy or pathological. Normal grief has
been called "uncomplicated grief." [25] It is a process which runs a reason-
ably consistent course and leads eventually to a restoration of mental and
physical well-being.

Sometimes, however, grief is complicated or pathological. It is grief
that is intensified, delayed, prolonged, or otherwise deviating from normal
grief, resulting in a bondage to the deceased that prevents one from coping
adequately with life.[26] There are no symptoms unique to pathological
grief, but some behavior is seen frequently. This includes a delay in grieving, hyperactivity, a "giving-up" attitude of helplessness and hopelessness,
intense guilt, a strong self-condemnation, extreme social withdrawal or
moodiness, impulsivity, antisocial behavior, excessive drinking, and veiled
threats of self-destruction. Such people seem unable to emancipate themselves from the deceased. Each of these signals may be present in normal
grief, but the symptoms are more intense and of longer duration when the
grief is pathological.

What "causes" grief to be normal or pathological? Among the many
possible influences are the griever's beliefs, personality, social environment, and circumstances surrounding the deceased person's death.

1. *Beliefs.* In an attempt to help others, numerous authors have written of their own grief and struggles with readjustment. Each of these
describes the turmoil and deep pain involved in grieving, but many also
point to the sustaining power of religious beliefs. Often there are periods
of doubt, confusion, and even anger with God, but in time the healing
power of one's faith becomes evident. Religion gives support, meaning,
hope for the future and comfort. Christians believe, in addition, that the
Holy Spirit who lives within each believer gives supernatural comfort and
peace in times of mourning. When the griever has no religious beliefs, he
or she grieves without hope. Thus, the pain is greater, the grieving may

be more difficult, and presumably there is greater potential for pathological grief.

2. *Background and Personality.* Widely accepted in psychology is a rule which states that "the best predictor of future behavior is past behavior." One indication of how mourning will be handled is how the mourner reacted to separations and losses in the past. If such separations were difficult and problem-producing, grieving may be more difficult. In addition, people who are insecure, dependent, unable to control or express feelings and prone to depression often have more difficulty handling their grief.

It must be emphasized, however, that grief is so unique and individualized that it is impossible to list "typical" grief reactions. Grievers differ in their personal needs, closeness to the deceased, typical way of handling feelings, willingness and ability to face the reality of the loss, closeness to others who can give support, personal views about life after death, flexibility and ability to cope with crisis. Grieving is always difficult but for some people it seems to hit harder than for others.

3. *Social Environment.* Most, if not all cultures have socially sanctioned ways of meeting needs at the time of bereavement. These social mores often are built around religious beliefs or practices, and frequently there are wide variations even between communities that are relatively close to each other. Ethnic and racial backgrounds also become important and clearly apparent in times of mourning. In a city like Chicago, for example, Polish Americans may express their grief in ways that differ from the customs in black, latino, Irish or Jewish neighborhoods. Cultural and religious groups also differ in the extent to which they allow, discourage or encourage the overt expression of sorrow. There are differences in practices concerning the wake, and in the social behavior expected from visiting friends and relatives. Even funerals differ, although it appears that in every culture the funeral offers group support to the bereaved, involves some expression of religious values, beliefs and/or rituals, includes some visual confrontation with the dead body, and tends to end in a procession which, in the opinion of some writers, symbolically pictures a "final journey." [27]

In spite of these social, cultural and religious variations, there are some commonly held values. In the American society, for example, there has tended to be an intolerance of prolonged grieving. In a country which values efficiency, intellectualism, rationalism and pragmatism, death often is seen as an inconvenience or embarrassment. Emotional expressions are discouraged and grief is viewed as something which, while inevitable, should end as quickly as possible. Since most Americans die in hospitals, away from their families, and since the society encourages a mobility and independence which separates us from close contact with others, it is easier to deny or ignore the reality of death. This can make the loss more traumatic for close relatives of the deceased, but there are fewer intimate people nearby who can give continual, warm, in-depth support. In our society, instead, we have encouraged ourselves and one another to deny death and to respond to the bereavement of others with little more than a card, a casserole or sending some cut flowers. Of course, such an analysis does not apply to every person or to all communities, but surely many of us will recognize that our modern attitudes toward death greatly influence how mourners are able to experience, express and work through the grieving process.

4. *Circumstances Accompanying the Death.* The death of a revered and respected national leader can bring grief to thousands of people,[28] but this mass grieving surely differs from the grief experienced by a widow or child of the deceased. If the dead person was elderly and sick for a long time the grief of relatives is less likely to be prolonged or pathological than when the loss is sudden or the deceased is a child—especially a grown child. When a brother or sister dies, there often is a sense of personal threat and a "there-but-for-the-grace-of-God-go-I" feeling which can make mourning more difficult.

Closeness to the deceased, suddenness of death, and age of the deceased can each influence the mourner's reaction to the death. But there are other circumstances which can complicate the grieving process. One psychiatrist has listed almost fifty such complicating influences.[29] For example, grieving may be prolonged and more difficult when:

—the death is considered exceptionally untimely, as in the death of a child, adolescent, or successful adult "in the prime of life, at the height of a career";

—the mode of death is considered incomprehensible or tragic, as in suicide or auto accidents;

—there is a sense of guilt at having "participated" in the event which caused the death (e.g., the driver of a car involved in a wreck in which someone else was killed);

—there are ambivalent (both positive and negative) feelings toward the deceased;

—there was so intimate a relationship with the deceased that close relationships with others did not exist;

—there was extreme dependency on the lost person to give the mourner identity, self-confidence and meaning in life;

—the deceased person had been excessively dependent on the survivor;

—the mourner's work, family, or other environmental circumstances disallows the expression of grief;

—the dead person has extracted a promise that the survivor would not grieve, be sad, remarry, move, and so on;

—there is excessive attachment and proximity to the deceased person's possessions, allowing the survivor to maintain a belief that the deceased is still alive;

—there is excessive and premature involvement in life activities to the point that loss is not acknowledged; and/or

—the griever believes, contrary to biblical teaching and the example of Jesus,[30] that Christians should so rejoice that they never grieve. This is the sincere but harmful view that grieving is a sign of spiritual immaturity.

The Effects of Grief

Grief has been described as a deprivation experience in which the griever must adjust to a significant loss.[31] Grief is a searching experience [32] where the survivor searches for new relationships and new ways of living. Grief, as we have seen, is an individual experience in which each person copes in a unique way.

In spite of this uniqueness, there are so many similarities among the grieving that several writers have attempted to identify stages of grief.[33] C. M. Parkes, for example, describes four phases. In the phase of numbness there is shock and a period when the reality of the loss is partially disregarded. In the phase of yearning there is an urge to recover the lost object and the permanence. In the phase of disorganization and despair, both the fact and permanence of the loss are accepted and attempts to recover the lost object are given up. Finally there is a phase of reorganization of behavior.[34]

In an influential little book, Granger Westberg identified several stages of grief: shock, emotional release, depression-loneliness, physical distress, panic, guilt, hostility/resentment, inability to return to usual activities, gradual hope, and struggles to affirm reality.[35] Similar to this are the stages listed by J. R. Hodge: shock and surprise, emotional release, loneliness, anxiety and physical distress, panic, guilt, hostility and projection, suffering silence, gradual overcoming, and readjustment.[36]

Counselors might question whether the identification of stages really is of practical value in their understanding and work with the grieving. In his own grief C. S. Lewis noted how the stages overlap and merge with each other:

> Tonight all the hells of young grief have opened again, the mad words, the bitter resentment, the fluttering in the stomach, the nightmare unreality, the wallowed-in tears. For in grief nothing "stays put." One keeps on emerging from a phase, but it always recurs. Round and round. Everything repeats. Am I going in circles, or dare I hope I am on a spiral?
> But if a spiral, am I going up or down it? [37]

1. *Common Effects of Grief.* Perhaps the three most commonly observed reactions to grief are crying (which expresses deep feelings and releases tension), restlessness (including sleep disturbances) and depression.[38] Also common are physical symptoms such as exhaustion, weakness, headaches, shortness of breath, indigestion, loss of appetite, or sometimes an increase in eating, anxiety, feelings of inner emptiness,

guilt, anger, irritability, withdrawal from others, forgetfulness, declining interest in sex, dreams about the deceased, nightmares, errors in judgment and feelings of loneliness. Often there is a loss of zest, disorganization of routines, and a realization that even the simplest activities which once were done automatically now require great effort and expending considerable energy. Frequently, the survivor takes on and begins to show some of the characteristics of the deceased person. Each of these symptoms, as Lewis observed, comes in waves, and rarely are they all present, all the time. As the months pass they tend to fade, but they come back with renewed intensity sometimes when they are least expected.

Most grievers also experience anniversary reactions. The first Christmas, Easter, birthday or wedding anniversary after the loss can be especially difficult emotionally, as can the anniversaries of the death. Often these anniversary reactions continue for a number of years. On specific significant days, or in the presence of outstanding reminders of the loss (such as on subsequent visits to the hospital where the person died), many of the old grief feelings and reactions sweep over the person with new intensity. If this continues for several years it is probable that there still is uncompleted or perhaps pathological mourning. Sometimes, when people are not free to mourn immediately after the death, a full grief reaction will be triggered by a later anniversary or other reminder of the loss.

2. *Pathological Effects of Grief.* Most grieving begins with a period of shock, numbness, denial, intense crying, and sometimes collapse. It moves into a prolonged period of sorrow, restlessness, apathy, memories, loneliness and sleep disturbances. Then there emerge a slow waning of grief symptoms and a resumption of normal life activities.

Pathological grief reactions occur when this normal grief process is denied, delayed, or distorted. This most often can be expected when the death has been sudden or unexpected; the mourner has been excessively dependent on the deceased; there was an ambivalent relationship (love mixed with hatred) between the mourner and the lost one; there was "unfinished business" between mourner and deceased (such as siblings who hadn't talked for years, family conflicts that hadn't been resolved, confessions that hadn't been made, or love that hadn't been expressed) the cause of death was violent, accidental, or suicidal; and/or the loss left the mourner with practical difficulties such as raising children or making business decisions.[38]

Among the most prevalent indications of pathological grief are the mourner's:

—increasing conviction that he or she is no longer valuable as a person;
—tendency to speak of the deceased in the present tense (e.g., "He doesn't like what you are doing");
—subtle or open threats of self-destruction;

—antisocial behavior;

—excessive hostility, moodiness, or guilt;

—excessive drinking or drug abuse;

—complete withdrawal and refusal to interact with others;

—impulsivity;

—persisting psychosomatic illnesses;

—veneration of objects that remind one of the deceased and link the mourner with the deceased;

—preoccupation with the dead person;

—refusal to change the deceased's room, or to dispose of his or her clothing and other possessions;

—extreme emotional expression;

—a resistance to any offers of counseling or other help;

—stoic refusal to show emotion or to appear affected by the loss (this usually indicates denial and avoidance of grief); and/or

—intense busyness and unusual hyperactivity.

Most writers believe that the most intense portion of grieving will be completed within a year or two. If it continues longer, especially when some of the above symptoms are present, this gives a fairly clear indication that pathology is present.

Counseling and Grief

Pondering the illness and death of his wife, the well-known Southern Baptist preacher Vance Havner wrote that "whoever thinks he has the ways of God conveniently tabulated, analyzed, and correlated with convenient, glib answers to ease every question from aching hearts has not been far in this maze of mystery we call life and death." [39] Havner realized what some well-meaning counselors have failed to realize: the grieving are not looking for pat responses from people who come to talk rather than to listen. Instead, they need understanding, reassurance, and contact with people who care.

1. *Counseling and Normal Grief.* Normal grief is a difficult, long-term process of healing which "needs no special help; it takes care of itself and with time the mourner heals and recovers." [40] The most widely available sources of help are family members, friends, ministers and physicians. These people can help in the following ways:

Encourage discussions about death before it occurs. When dying persons and their families feel free to express their feelings and discuss death before it occurs, there is an anticipatory grief which tends to make grieving more normal after the loss has occurred.

Be present and available. "There is a sort of invisible blanket between the world and me," wrote C. S. Lewis. "I find it hard to take in what anyone says. Or perhaps, hard to want to take it in. It is so uninteresting. Yet I want the others to be about me. I dread the moments when the house is empty. If only they would talk to one another and not to me." [41] Try to be available after the funeral. If the mourner is a special friend, phone periodically to "touch base"—and be alert to giving support or expressing concern on holidays and anniversaries.

Make it known that expression of feelings is good and acceptable—but do not pressure the griever to show feelings.

Expect outpourings of crying, anger, or withdrawal—but still let it be known that you are available.

Be a receptive, careful listener. Recognize that grieving people need, at their own time, to talk about issues such as the feelings and symptoms that are being experienced, the details of the death and funeral, details of past contacts with the deceased, the ultimate reasons for the death ("Why did God allow this now?") and thoughts about the future. Guilt, anger, confusion and despair will all be expressed at times and need to be heard by the helper, rather than condemned, squelched or explained away.

Help the grieving person make decisions.

Gently challenge pathological or irrational conclusions, giving the grieving person opportunity to respond and discuss the issues.

Provide practical help—such as meal preparation or baby-sitting. This frees the person to grieve, especially at the beginning.

Do not discourage grieving rituals. Participation in a wake, funeral, memorial service and religious ritual can help to make the death more real, demonstrate the support of friends, and encourage the expression of feelings and stimulate the work of mourning.

Pray for the bereaved and comfort them with the words of Scripture—without preaching or using religious clichés as a means for stifling the expression of grief.

In all of this, remember that our desire is to support the mourner, and not to build unhealthy dependency, to avoid reality, or to stimulate denial. In time, the support and care of friends will help the bereaved work through the grief process and resume the normal activities of life once again.

2. *Counseling and Pathological Grief.* Counselors are more often called upon to work with people who are showing pathological grief reactions. These people often resist help but the counselor's task is to bring a transformation of abnormal grief into a normal grief reaction. This process has been called "re-grief": a reexperiencing of the grief process in order to free the counselee from his or her bondage to the deceased. [42]

To accomplish this, it can be helpful to discuss, in detail, the counselee's relationship with the deceased.

> The relationship with the deceased needs to be explored in detail, preferably from its inception through its crises, its highlights and its low points, till the time of death. Gentle encouragement and an interest in

knowing of the deceased will promote this. Visits to the home where memories are real, the viewing of photographs and treasured possessions may facilitate this.[43]

The counselor should try to avoid the clichés and exhortations that may have come previously from friends and relatives. Encourage the expression of feelings and gently challenge some of the irrational thoughts and actions which may have developed since the deceased person's time of death. Often it can be helpful if counselees learn about the grief process and discover that their feelings and symptoms are relatively common. Reading books can often help in this learning process, providing the contents are discussed later in counseling.[44] This prevents misconceptions and stimulates discussion about the counselee's own reactions. At times there can be value in raising questions about the future and challenging counselees to make some realistic plans. Encourage discussion of practical issues—such as raising children, meeting financial needs, and dealing with sexual frustrations. In all of this remember that your goal is to help counselees avoid denial and deal with the reality of their loss. As Parkes has noted:

> The treatment of pathological relations to bereavement follows the same principles as those that have been indicated for the support of bereaved people in general. Thus the appropriate treatment for delayed or inhibited grief would seem to be a form of psychotherapy in which it becomes possible for the patient to begin to express his grief and to overcome the fixations or blocks to realization which have prevented him from "unlearning" his attachment to the lost person.[45]

Overcoming "fixations or blocks" may require the expertise of a more specialized counselor, such as a professional clinical psychologist or psychiatrist, and for this reason referral should always be considered as a possibility in working with pathological grief.

Of special interest to Christian counselors is an approach long held in counseling but more recently popularized in a controversial book by Ruth Carter Stapleton.[46] Recognizing that counselors can bring some healing by "probing into the past and bringing understanding of our weak and vulnerable spots and our angry and fearful reactions,"[47] Stapleton argues, nevertheless, that only the Holy Spirit can really remove the scars. Through prayer and discussion of past memories and attitudes, the counselor and counselee "are really asking Jesus to walk back into the dark places of our lives and bring healing to the distressing and painful memories of the past."[48] Some professionals have criticized the Freudian overtones in this approach, the simplicity and the dangers involved when lay people "help people to find and expose repressed painful memories . . . in order that any unhealed, crippling memory can be touched by the Great Healer."[49] Nevertheless, the approach has considerable potential and demonstrates the power of Christ to help people deal (among other things) with the basics of pathological grief.

3. *Counseling When Children Grieve.* In the midst of grieving, relatives sometimes try to protect children from the realities and sadness of death. It should be remembered, however, that children also have a need to grieve and to understand as best they can.

To really understand death, children must be able to distinguish between themselves and others, between living and nonliving, between thought and reality, and between past, present and future. Whether or not the child has this understanding he or she must be helped to comprehend the finality of death, to express emotion and to ask questions. It is important to reassure children (repeatedly by words and actions) that they are loved and will be cared for. Children often interpret death, especially the death of a parent, as a form of rejection. They are sensitive to any signs of adult insecurity and need to know that they will not be forsaken. Many counselors would agree that children also should be present at the wake and funeral since young people need emotional support and opportunity to accept the reality of the loss, just as do adults.[50]

4. *Counseling When Children Die.* Death is always difficult for survivors to handle, but when the deceased is a child, the experience is especially upsetting. Approximately one out of every 350 babies born alive die of something called the Sudden Infant Death (SID) Syndrome. The cause is not completely understood and since the babies are strong and healthy before death, the loss comes as a rude jolt. Even when children are weak or malformed before death, it is difficult for parents to accept the reality of death after so short a time on earth. Guilt, self-condemnation, despondency and unanswered questions abound.

As we have seen, each grief reaction is somewhat unique, although there are similarities in all cases. To a large extent, therefore, counseling following the death of a child is similar to any other grief counseling. Recognize, however, that the loss and grief are as real as the death of a spouse or close adult friend. Comments like "You can always have another child" are not at all comforting. When children die, the survivors must be helped to express their feelings, accept the loss, and learn to readjust. Often this help comes from neighbors and friends, from church leaders, and from the support of other parents who understand because they have experienced similar losses in the past.[51]

Prevention and Grief

Grief, of course, cannot and should not be prevented. When survivors show no sense of grief it is possible that there was no close relationship with the deceased, but it also is possible that the grieving process is being denied or avoided. This can lead to a pathological grieving and it is this abnormal grief that we want to prevent.

1. *Before the Time of Death.* The prevention of unhealthy grief re-actions should begin long before a death occurs. Such predeath prevention can include the following:

(a) Developing Healthy Attitudes in the Home. When parents are open and honest about death, children learn that this is an issue to be faced honestly and discussed openly. Misconceptions then can be corrected and there is natural opportunity to answer questions. It is probably true that a child can never be prepared for death, but an open attitude at home facilitates communication and makes later discussions of death more natural.

(b) Clarifying Family Relationships. Grief sometimes is complicated by guilt, anger, jealousy, bitterness, competitiveness and other issues which never were resolved before the death. This could be prevented and subsequent grief made smoother if, before death, family members could:

—learn to express and discuss feelings and frustrations;

—verbally forgive and accept forgiveness from each other;

—express love, appreciation and respect;

—develop a healthy interdependence which avoids manipulation or immature dependency relationships.

To build better families is an important way to prevent pathological grief. This, of course, is an ideal which many families cannot reach unless they are helped through training and counseling.

(c) Building Friendships. Grief is harder when there is no estab-lished network of supporting friends who can give intimate support in times of sorrow. Each of us needs a group of quality relationships, rather than exclusive dependence on only one or two people. In all of society, the church gives the best example of a community of caring, affirming, ac-cepting friends. Next to the immediate family, the church and its pastor become the first line of support in times of bereavement. When there is involvement in the church before the loss, this community support is more meaningful at the time of a death and afterward.

(d) Activity Development. People who are involved in a variety of recreational and other activities have meaningful and fulfilling involve-ments which help soften the pain of death and other losses.

(e) Stimulating Mental Health. Well-adjusted people who have learned to handle "little crises" successfully usually handle grief with success. Such people have learned to express emotions freely, to face their frustrations openly, and to admit and discuss their confusions and problems.

(f) Anticipating and Learning About Death. Death education is a relatively new but growing emphasis. In schools, churches and other places, people are learning to talk about death (including their own deaths), and to discuss such issues as how the terminally ill face death, how people grieve, and how to make a will and plan for the needs of our families should we die first. It is difficult to talk of one's own death, funeral, place of burial, and afterlife. But it is easier to consider these issues when all those involved are healthy, and this can be very helpful as a survivor makes funeral arrangements in the future.

(g) Anticipatory Grieving. When people develop terminal illnesses, families and friends frequently pretend that all will be well, and there is no talk of "leave-taking." When patients and families can talk about the possibilities of imminent death and can be honest about their sadness, the subsequent grief process is less likely to be pathological.[52] Such honesty, it has been found, is even important in talking with dying children.[53]

(h) Theological Understanding. After the funeral is not the time to begin asking about eternal life and the reality of heaven or hell. The Bible says a great deal about death, the meaning of life, the reality of the promise of eternal life with Christ for believers, and the pain of mourning. These truths should be taught and understood before death occurs. Such teaching is comforting and better understood after the grieving process has begun.

2. *At the Time of Death*. The hours and days following a death can have a strong influence on how grief is handled.

(a) Communicating the News. It is not easy to announce a death and for this reason, medical personnel, policemen and others often carry out this task as quickly and explicitly (and hence as abruptly) as possible.

It is much better to communicate the news gently, somewhat gradually and, if possible, in a location private enough to permit the free expression of emotion. Give the survivor time to respond, to ask questions, and to be surrounded by two or three friends who can be present to give continuing initial support.

(b) Giving Support. Some people face their grief with no one present to give immediate support and help in making decisions. This makes grieving harder. In our society the clergyman is the one designated to give immediate care to the bereaved, but the church leader's task is much easier and more effective if church members give additional support.[54] Perhaps this is especially important when the circumstances of death were unusual or violent, such as a suicide or murder. In such cases, grief is often mixed with shame and fear of social rejection.

When a family recently lost their son, a friend from the church came almost immediately to offer condolences. The grief-stricken family declined the offer of help so the friend went back to his car and sat there. Several hours passed before the family became aware of the friend's continued quiet presence outside. Later they reported that this, more than anything else, sustained them through their subsequent grief.

(c) Planning Funerals. Within recent years, funeral practices have come under considerable criticism, and long-established customs and rituals have been discarded. These changes are not necessarily bad, but it must be remembered that funeral rituals do serve several useful functions: helping the survivors accept the reality of death, the support of friends, the present state of the deceased, the need for readjustment, and the peace and presence of God. Funerals should develop a balance between a realistic acknowledgment of grief, and sincere rejoicing over the fact that believers who are absent from the body are then present with the Lord. A carefully planned, worshipful funeral service can facilitate the grieving process and help prevent pathological grieving.

(d) Using Drugs? In an effort to sedate the grief-stricken, drugs are often given to survivors at the time of the death. Although there may be nothing wrong with this as a temporary measure, there is a real danger that chemicals can dull the pain and inhibit the grief process. In general, therefore, the use of drugs does not contribute to the prevention of pathological grief.

3. *After the Time of Death.* The continuing presence of supportive care-givers, including pastoral counselors, can help the griever during the months following the death. It is during this period that the counseling procedures described earlier in this chapter can help counselees to avoid pathological grief.

4. *The Church and Preparation for Death.* Much of the discussion in the preceding paragraphs has presumed that death preparation and the prevention of pathological grief often take place in the church. Pastoral counseling (including anticipatory grief counseling), the preaching of periodic sermons on the subject of death and related topics, education about death in Sunday school classes and study groups, encouraging church members to read a book or two on dying and bereavement, and stimulating church members to pray and care for the spiritual, emotional and practical needs of the grieving, can all help to prepare people for death.

But there can also be indirect preparation through the strengthening of family communication, the stimulation of loving honesty as well as the open expression of feelings, and the natural talk about death in the church —with the suggestion that such natural talk should also extend to the home. Church members may also be encouraged to develop a philosophy of life which is built on biblical teaching and which incorporates the reality of death both intellectually and emotionally into the person's way of thinking.[55]

Conclusions about Grief

Grief is a universal experience. Few escape it, some are trapped by it, and those who come through it find that they have been through a painful refining process. Perhaps it is true that grief is a gift[56]—not something to be grasped eagerly and used to satisfy our gleeful desires, but a permanent, reluctantly received growth experience from God. To profit from its in-

fluence we must accept it honestly and move through it both with the help
of our friends and the support of our Lord who uses the pain to mature us
and make us holy and fit for the Master's use.

> ..ae thing is certain when your dearest leaves you for heaven and you plod
> on alone—there can be no harder blow . . . . It does no good to continually
> accuse and condemn ourselves. Things might even have been worse if
> we had done some things we think would have been better. Let us put the
> past, good and bad, and whatever might have been into God's hands and
> resume our pilgrimage.[57]

Helping others resume the pilgrimage is the real goal of grief counseling.

Suggestions for Further Reading

Bachmann, C. Charles. *Ministering to the Grief Sufferer*. Philadelphia: Fortress
Press, 1964.
* Bayly, Joseph. *The View from a Hearse*. Elgin, IL: David C. Cook, 1969.
Cutter, Fred. *Coming to Terms with Death*. Chicago: Nelson-Hall, 1974.
Freese, Arthur. *Help for Your Grief*. New York: Schocken, 1977.
Jackson, Edgar N. *Telling a Child About Death*. New York: Channel Press, 1965.
————. *Understanding Grief: Its Roots, Dynamics, and Treatment*. Nashville:
Abingdon, 1957.
* Landorf, Joyce. *Mourning Song*. Old Tappan, NJ: Revell, 1974.
* Lewis, C. S. *A Grief Observed*. New York: Bantam Books, 1961.
Switzer, David K. *The Dynamics of Grief*. Nashville: Abingdon, 1970.

Footnotes

1. Sigmund Freud, "Mourning and Melancholia," in *Collected Papers of Sigmund Freud*, vol. 4, trans. J. Riviere (London: Hogarth Press, 1953). (The papers
appeared originally in 1917; originally published in English in 1925.)
2. Erich Lindemann, "Symptomatology and Management of Acute Grief,"
American Journal of Psychiatry 101 (1944): 141–48.
3. Elisabeth Kubler-Ross, *On Death and Dying* (New York: Macmillan, 1969).
4. W. A. Miller, *When Going to Pieces Holds You Together* (Minneapolis: Augs-
bury, 1976).
5. 1 Cor. 15:55, 56.
6. According to Heb. 9:27 it is "appointed for men to die once." The only exceptions are Old Testament figures like Enoch and those believers who are still living
when Christ returns. "Then we who are alive and remain shall be caught up together . . . in the clouds to meet the Lord in the air" (1 Thess. 4:17).
7. Ps. 23:4.
8. Pss. 6:5–7; 137:1, 5, 6; 2 Sam. 12.
9. Ps. 119:28.
10. Isa. 53:3, 4.
11. 1 Cor. 15 and 1 Thess. 4.
12. 1 Thess. 4:14.
13. 1 Thess. 4:18.
14. 1 Cor. 15:52–54.
15. 1 Thess. 4:17; Heb. 2:14, 15; 2 Tim. 1:10: John 11:25, 26.
16. 2 Cor. 4:14–5:8.

17. 1 Cor. 15:58.
18. Matt. 5:4.
19. John 11.
20. Matt. 14:12–21.
21. Matt. 26:38.
22. 2 Sam. 12:15–23.
23. Arthur Freese, *Help for Your Grief* (New York: Schocken Books, 1977), p. 48.
24. Karen Peterson, "Normal and Pathological Grief" (M.A. thesis, Trinity Evangelical Divinity School, Deerfield, IL, 1978).
25. G. L. Engel, "Is Grief a Disease? A Challenge for Medical Research," *Psychosomatic Medicine* 23 (1961): 18–22.
26. Peterson, "Normal and Pathological Grief," p. 44.
27. V. R. Pine, "Comparative Funeral Practices," *Practical Anthropology* 16 (1969): 49–62.
28. Commenting on Lincoln's death, Jackson suggests that "mass mourning . . . can develop when a person becomes a symbol for the investment of the hopes and fears of many persons. It also indicated the effect . . . when the lost person has held a significant place in the life system of the mourner." See Edgar N. Jackson, *Understanding Grief: Its Roots, Dynamics and Treatment* (Nashville: Abingdon, 1957), p. 29.
29. David Barton, ed., *Dying and Death: A Clinical Guide for Caregivers* (Baltimore: Williams & Wilkins, 1977), pp. 116, 117.
30. John 11:33–36.
31. R. W. Doss, *The Last Enemy: A Christian Understanding of Death* (New York: Harper & Row, 1974).
32. C. M. Parkes, " 'Seeking' and 'Finding' a Lost Object: Evidence from Recent Studies of the Reaction to Bereavement," *Social Science Medicine* 4 (1970): 187–201.
33. See for example, G. C. Bonnell, "The Pastor's Role in Counseling the Bereaved," *Pastoral Psychology* 22 (Fall, 1971): 27–36; M. H. Hecht, "Dynamics of Bereavement," *Journal of Religion and Health* 10 (October, 1971): 357–72; and J. R. Hodge, "They that Mourn," *Journal of Religion and Health* 11 (July, 1972): 229–40.
34. C. M. Parkes, *Bereavement: Studies of Grief in Adult Life* (New York: International Universities Press, 1972).
35. Granger Westburg, *Good Grief* (Philadelphia: Fortress Press, 1962).
36. Hodge, "They that Mourn."
37. C. S. Lewis, *A Grief Observed* (New York: Bantam Books, 1961), pp. 66, 67.
38. V. D. Volkman, "The Recognition and Prevention of Pathological Grief," *Virginia Medical Monthly* 99 (1972): 535–40.
39. Vance Havner, *Though I Walk Through the Valley* (Old Tappan, NJ: Revell, 1974), p. 67.
40. Freese, *Help for Your Grief*, p. 85.
41. Lewis, *A Grief Observed*, p. 1.
42. "Re-grief" is a term suggested by V. D. Volkman, "Normal and Pathological Grief Reactions," *Virginia Medical Monthly* 93 (1966): 651–56.
43. B. Raphael, "The Management of Pathological Grief," *Australian and New Zealand Journal of Psychiatry* 9 (September, 1975): 173–80.
44. Suggestions are given at the end of this chapter.
45. Parkes, *Bereavement*, p. 179.
46. Ruth Carter Stapleton, *The Gift of Inner Healing* (Waco, TX: Word, 1976).

47. Ibid., p. 10.

48. Ibid.

49. Ibid., pp. 68, 78.

50. To help children grieve, the reader may wish to consult one or more of the following books: Edgar N. Jackson, *Telling a Child About Death* (New York: Channel Press, 1965); Janette Klopfenstein, *Tell Me About Death, Mommy* (Scottdale, PA: Herald Press, 1977); and Elizabeth L. Reed, *Helping Children with the Mystery of Death* (Abingdon: Nashville, 1970).

51. For further information see Loren Wilkenfeld, ed., *When Children Die* (Dubuque, IA: Kendall/Hunt Publishing Company, 1977).

52. Freese, *Help for Your Grief,* p. 122.

53. Constance Rosenblum, "Dying Children," *Human Behavior* 8 (March, 1978): 49, 50.

54. Thomas C. Welu, "Pathological Bereavement: A Plan for Its Prevention," in *Bereavement: Its Psychological Aspects,* eds. Bernard Schoenberg et al. (New York: Columbia University Press, 1975), pp. 139–49.

55. David K. Switzer, *The Dynamics of Grief* (Nashville: Abingdon, 1970), p. 213.

56. Ira J. Tanner, *The Gift of Grief* (New York: Hawthorn Books, 1976).

57. Havner, *Though I Walk,* pp. 91, 117.

29

Spiritual Problems and Spiritual Growth

SEVERAL YEARS AGO, A PUBLICITY-SEEKING PREACHER ANNOUNCED that he would preach the shortest sermon in history. On Sunday morning the pews were filled as the preacher stepped up to the pulpit to deliver his "sermon" which had only one word:

"Love."

At a time when the word *love* has so many meanings, it is possible that the congregation and perhaps even the preacher failed to realize the significance of what was being said. The Bible tells us that God is love, that we can only love because he loved us first, and that Jesus came to die for us because of God's love.[1] Love has been called *the* mark of the Christian.[2] The one who does not love "does not know God," but everyone "who loves is born of God and knows God."[3] Clearly love is at the basis of Christianity—not the transient, self-centered sentimentalism that forms the foundation of so many modern love songs, but the giving, patient, other-centered, Christ-honoring, divinely bestowed love which is described in the pages of Scripture.[4]

Regretfully, many Christians do not feel very loving and neither do their words or actions express a loving attitude. Many feel defeated by sin, internal conflicts, and the pressures of life. Some are frustrated because their growth seems to be so slow. Others are concerned because their lives seem so joyless, there is no "sparkle" in their worship, and they are caught in a net of "spiritual dryness."[5] They read the Bible but the words seem dull and irrelevant. They pray, more out of habit than desire, but their prayers seem unanswered. They want to do good and to love, but their actions aren't very loving and their consciences seem insensitive and blunted.

This is not a state which God desires, but it is a common experience, perhaps even in the lives of the counselors or potential counselors who read these words. Counseling those who have spiritual problems is a challenge at any time, but it is even more difficult when the counselor struggles with problems similar to those of the counselees.

429

Periods of spiritual dryness cause a tremendous amount of suffering in the life of a Christian. . . . Inwardly everything is dead in him. . . . But the world around him needs and expects his love. The sick and the dying want to be comforted. Hurt and lonely people want to be understood. His family, students, congregation and fellow Christians want to be ministered to and strengthened. Nobody really knows what desperation is who has never faced another human being craving help when inside he feels completely empty and dry.[6]

Unlike most of the previous chapters, this one can speak to the needs of counselors and counselees alike.

Tnt Bible and Spiritual Problems

In an age when people like to be progressive, successful, and able to get things done quickly and efficiently, it is difficult for many of us to realize that God is never in a hurry. His goal is that each believer will mature into Christlikeness, but he knows that none of us will ever succeed completely, this side of heaven. He wants us to be holy and to follow in Christ's steps, but he knows that none of us will ever do that completely.[7] He wants us to "put on the whole armor of God," but he realizes that we cannot fight life's battles alone.[8] He wants us to present our bodies to him as "a living sacrifice,"[9] but he realizes that this presentation will not be continuing and unselfish. He wants us to stop sinning and to flee from youthful lusts, but he realizes that we are fooling ourselves if we say we have no sin and so he tells us to confess our sins and expect forgiveness when we do fall.[10] He sets up a high standard for our behavior because he is just and holy, but he has provided a Savior to pay for our sins and failures because he is loving and merciful.[11] He has adopted us as his children and requires us to "do justice, to love kindness and to walk humbly" with God, but he is compassionate, gracious, and "abounding in lovingkindness," because he knows that we are nothing but dust so long as we remain in this world.[12]

Clearly God has high standards. To expect anything less than perfection for his human creatures would be to lower his standards and make him less than God. Along with his holiness, perfection and greatness, however, there also are divine attributes of love, mercy and compassion. God is realistic. He knows that we are weak so he has not left us to stand alone. In a spirit of love, he sent his Son to pay for our sins, and his Holy Spirit to live within, guiding, strengthening and teaching us.[13] We may think that he is far away, at times, but he is ever near, sticking closer than a faithful brother.[14]

The goal of the Christian life is to be Christlike in worship, character and service. In the Old Testament, *worship* included the offering of sacrifices to atone for sin Now that Christ has died for our sins, "once for all, the iust for the unjust,"[15] we are to present our bodies as a "living and holy sacrifice, acceptable to God." This commitment of self to God, along with verbal praise, is how we worship.[16]

But such worship also involves a continuing change in *character*. We are not to conform to worldly standards. Instead we are to be "transformed" mentally and in terms of our actions. We are to disentangle ourselves from sin, to be holy as he is holy, to be like Christ, to walk in his steps, and to let the Holy Spirit make us to be people who are characterized by love, joy, peace, patience, kindness, gentleness, fruitfulness and self-control.[17]

The Christian, however, must not be solely God-centered and self-centered. There must also be *service* to others. We please God when we are involved in "doing good and sharing." [18] Indeed, the Christian view of success radically contradicts that of the world in which we live. "If you want to be great," Jesus said, in essence, "be a servant." Humble ourselves, and in due time, he will build us up and give us the acclaim that we need.[19]

Christlike worship, Christlike character, and Christlike service—these are the goals of the Christian life. In one sense we press on to reach these goals, like a runner straining toward the finish line. But in another sense we grow not by effort, but by yielding ourselves completely to his control and direction. Christian growth, writes Richard Halverson, "is not the struggle to become the kind of person we think God wants us to be, but a surrender of our bodies, all our faculties, our right to ourselves, to God —that He may make us and mold us into the image of His Son, that through us His life and love and grace might flow." [20]

In writing this chapter, I was surrounded by literally dozens of books on Christian growth, spiritual maturity, and the struggles of believers. Some of the titles are thought-provoking:

How Come It's Taking Me So Long to Get Better?
What Every Christian Should Know About Growing
Born to Grow: For New and Used Christians
How to Overcome Temptation
My Utmost for His Highest
Lord, Change Me!
The Call to Holiness
A Call to Christian Character
Knowing God
The Cost of Commitment
He That Is Spiritual
Being Human: The Nature of Spiritual Experience
Building Up One Another [21]

The continued publication of such books must indicate a never ending need for help in Christian growth. This need is nothing new. For centuries, believers have struggled with spiritual deadness, periods of stagnation, and the need for help in Christian growth. It could be argued that the entire

Bible is written for such people, teaching us about God, his attributes, and his power to mold believers into clean vessels, ready for the Master's use.[22]

The causes, effects, counseling and prevention of spiritual problems are all discussed in the Bible. No other subjects are more Bible-based and less illuminated by psychology than the subjects of spiritual growth and solving spiritual problems. And the Christian counselor alone can help with such problems since it is only the believer who has "the mind of Christ" to understand and help others comprehend and assimilate "the things of the Spirit of God." [23]

The Causes of Spiritual Problems

It is probably true that most people who have lived an intensely religious life have had to struggle through periods of spiritual dryness and despair. "Often the intensity of such suffering may be in direct relationship to the intensity of a person's life with God, just as deep valleys show up only in the face of high mountains." [24] This realization may be comforting, but it does little to help us solve our spiritual problems unless we can identify some possible causes.

1. *Where We Are.* Let us begin with the recognition that for some people the problem is that they are still nonbelievers: individuals who may attend church and engage in "good" behavior, but who still are outside of God's kingdom.

Christianity is not a matter of goodness or badness, of right actions or wrong. It deals with one's inner nature. It is more concerned about what we *are* than with what we *do.* This is stated repeatedly in Scripture but nowhere with greater clarity than in Ephesians 2.

Prior to conversion we are "dead," controlled by the devil and separated from God, regardless of our deeds. But it is God who saves us and makes us his children. This salvation comes not because of our efforts, but because of his giving us salvation when we completely yield ourselves to him. "For by grace you have been saved through faith; and that not of yourselves, it is the gift of God; not a result of works." [25] When we accept God's gift of salvation, he begins to work, molding us into the kinds of persons he wants us to be. Since he created us and knows us intimately, his plan is the best for our lives.

For some, the chief cause of spiritual struggles is that the individuals are still not believers. For others, there has been a commitment to Christ but there is no real interest in spiritual things and hence there has been no growth. Such persons may be long-time Christians but they are "babes in Christ," not much different from nonbelievers.[26] "Where we are" in terms of our relationship to Christ, therefore, has a major bearing on spiritual problems.

2. *What We Do.* Have you ever considered what most disturbed Jesus during his time on earth? It was not pornography, violence, racism, abor-

tion or the other things which most rankle us today. Jesus reserved his strongest attacks to condemn sin and to fight what perhaps angered him the most—pious legalism. Both of these can cause spiritual problems.

(a) Sin. This involves specific acts such a lying, stealing, or committing adultery, but as used in the Bible sin involves something more. Sin is any action or attitude which violates or fails to conform to the will of God. We can sin by what we think, by what we do or fail to do, and by what we are. Sin is a powerful force which can master and enslave us, especially when we fail to repent, admit sin, or confess our faults. Sin is the major cause of spiritual stagnation and loss of vitality.[27]

(b) Legalism. In Jesus' day, the Pharisees were religious purists who believed that spiritual maturity came as a result of observing rules. Such a view has been common in religious circles for centuries and it is held today by many fundamentalists, evangelicals and liberals. Often seen in people who sincerely want to please God and maintain a "good testimony," this legalistic mentality maintains that there are "rules and regulations" which determine what a good Christian does not do (drink, attend movies, dance, wear certain clothes, and so on) and what the good Christian does do (read a certain number of Bible chapters each day, witness to someone every week, attend a specified number of church services, and so on). The psalmist, prophets, Jesus and Paul all condemned such attitudes.[28] They can lead to sinful pride and they contradict the very heart of the biblical message. The theme of the Bible is redemption, and redemption "is first, last, and always, from beginning to end, from inception to consummation, the work of God."[29] We are saved through faith, plus nothing.[30]

But what about spiritual growth? Does this come by following rules? Jesus' condemnation of the Pharisees clearly indicates that the answer is "no." True spirituality comes when we walk humbly before God with an attitude of thanksgiving and praise, accompanied by an awareness of our weaknesses, our tendency to sin, and our need of his continued grace and mercy. This, of course, does not involve us in a passive "do-nothing attitude." The Christian must be alert to the devil's schemes and, as we shall see, prayer, meditation on the Bible, fellowship, and a sincere attempt to refrain from sin are all important to spiritual growth. But the power and even the desire for such holy living must come from God[31]—not from our determination to follow man-made rules. Clearly the Scriptures condemn both legalism (the strict keeping of rules) and its twin partners: gnosticism (the belief that spirituality is gained by superior knowledge) and asceticism (the conscious denial of pleasures, experiences and material things).[32]

3. *What We Think.* Most human problems, it seems, begin in the mind. It is our thinking that leads us to self-sufficiency, pride, bitterness, and non-Christian values—each of which can create spiritual problems.

(a) Self-sufficiency. This is common in a culture which praises "self-made men" and universally accepts "rugged individualism." Even in the church we advocate "determination" and "possibility thinking," with little or no reference to the will and power of God. Self-sufficiency is the mark of lukewarm Christianity. To the believers who maintained, "I am rich, and have become wealthy, and have need of nothing," Jesus urged repentance and threatened to "spit you out of my mouth." [33] Self-sufficiency is the absolute antithesis of spiritual maturity.

(b) Pride. Self-sufficiency and pride go together. Pride involves a trust in one's power or resources, and a tendency to derive satisfaction from the contemplation of one's own status, capabilities or accomplishments, especially as these are compared with others who appear to have less. It has been suggested that pride is more easily seen than defined, and more easily detected in others than in oneself. Pride is self-centered, self-satisfied and ultimately self-destructive.

(c) Bitterness. According to the writer of Hebrews, bitterness can spring up to cause trouble and create defilement which apparently includes immoral and godless behavior.[34] Anger, including bitterness, was discussed in chapter 8. It is a powerful and subtle source of spiritual problems.

(d) Distorted Values. What is really important in life? The answer to this question is often seen in how people spend their money, their time (including their spare time), and their mental energies—especially when the mind is free to "wander." Often, people value money, selfish pleasures, business success, acclaim and other issues which are important in the society but destructive to Christian growth.[35] Such values are subtle in that they draw us away from God and create a false sense of security.[36]

In contrast to self-sufficiency, pride, bitterness and distorted values, the spiritually maturing person is transformed mentally, so that his or her thinking seeks and intends to do the "good and acceptable and perfect" will of God.[37]

4. *What We Lack.* Both physical problems and deterioration can come when there is a lack of food, air, rest and other physical requirements. In a similar manner, spiritual problems are caused by a lack of those basic ingredients which cause health and growth.

(a) Lack of Understanding. Probably, it would be distressing for us to know how much spiritual pain and turmoil arise because people lack understanding and clear biblical knowledge. Consider, for example, the ideas that we are saved by good works, that God's love and continued approval depend on our personal actions, that Christian growth depends entirely upon ourselves, that doubt or sexual urges will arouse God's wrath, that God punishes acts of disobedience in the Christian's life, or that God doesn't really care about our needs and concerns. These and a host of similar misconceptions can create restlessness, uncertainty, spiritual doubt and apathy.

(b) Lack of Nourishment. Just as a baby never grows without food, so a Christian never develops without continued prayer and reading of God's Word, the Bible.[38] For some, spiritual problems come because they never spend much time "taking in" spiritual nourishment. For others, there is so much "giving out" that the giver runs dry. It is a spiritual law, writes Walter Trobisch, that "the one who gives out much must also take in much.... If he gives out continuously without taking in, he will run dry."[39]

(c) Lack of Giving. People who eat too much become fat and, in time, uncomfortable. A similar condition can occur in our spiritual lives. Over-feeding on sermons, Bible studies, devotional reading, Christian radio programs and weekend retreats can lead to spiritual bloating. Christians are not to be a sponge, soaking up and retaining everything. Instead, we are to be vessels used by God to bring instruction and blessing to others. The essence of Christian love is giving and sharing—so we don't grow fat.

(d) Lack of Balance. During his three-year ministry, Jesus lived a balanced life. He ministered, interacted with individuals, rested, spent time in prayer and worship, and relaxed with friends. He had a purpose in life, sought God's help in daily living, and took care of himself spiritually, physically, intellectually and socially.

Many modern people lack this balance. They "run themselves ragged," fail to get proper exercise or rest, do not eat a balanced diet, and are so busy—even "doing the Lord's work"—that their efficiency and spiritual vitality run down. A balanced life requires planning, discipline and a realization that no person in the body of Christ is so important that he or she is indispensable.

(e) Lack of Commitment. To be a disciple, Jesus taught, one must be willing to take up a cross and follow him. True Christian growth must be preceded by a commitment to let Jesus Christ be Lord and controller of one's life. Any "holding back" interferes with spiritual maturing and contributes to lusterless Christianity.

(f) Lack of the Holy Spirit's Power. The Holy Spirit lives in the life of every believer,[40] but the Spirit can be quenched and pushed aside. When that happens, spiritual lethargy is assured. In contrast, when the Holy Spirit controls a life, that life develops strength, understanding, unity with others, love, joy, peace, self-control and the other spiritual fruit[41]—all of which are designed to bring glory to Christ.

(g) Lack of Body Life. The Christian is part of a group or "body" which consists of other believers, all of whom are important and gifted, all of whom love Christ, and each of whom should seek to know, love, pray for, help, encourage, challenge, exhort, teach and minister to the others. When Christians attempt to grow on their own, to build their Christian "empires" or rise on the Christian status ladder, they are out of God's will. He has placed us in the body and expects us to grow there, not forsaking the other brothers and sisters.[42]

5. *What We Fight.* Whether or not we consciously recognize it, the

Christian is in a battle. Jesus was tempted when he began his ministry—and surely at other times thereafter. The giants of the faith, both those mentioned in the Bible and others, battled the forces of evil, and the struggle continues today. In this continuing world war there are no islands of neutrality. We are either fighting the devil or aligned on his side—in attitude if not in activity.

At times the battle is in the intellectual arena—where confusion, doubts, nonbiblical thinking, and overt heresy are at issue. Sometimes the battle is physical as we struggle with disease and injury. Often the conflict centers around psychological discouragement, anger, anxiety, guilt and other internal conflicts. At times—especially when we are tired, not feeling well, emotionally or intellectually drained, fresh from a spiritual retreat, or basking in the light of success—the attack is more intense. And at times each of us loses a battle.

But to lose a battle is not to lose the war. The Bible already tells us how to prepare, warns us of Satanic tactics, assures us that the Holy Spirit in us is greater than the devil's forces, and declares that Satan in time will be banished forever.[43] In the meantime, the fight continues, and some people crumble spiritually because they are unprepared and not alert.

6. *What We Receive.* The sufferings of Job do not really fit any of the above categories (although it could be argued that Satan was really battling God by trying to bring down Job). Job's struggles came from the devil, with God's permission, for reasons which Job never understood. As we look over the preceding paragraphs perhaps we see most of the causes of spiritual problems. By identifying the causes we can identify the place to focus our counseling. But the ways of God are not always comprehensible by our little human minds. Sometimes we must stand with Job, shake our heads, wonder why, and end with an ultimate trust in the sovereignty of him whose ways are not our ways and whose thoughts are not our thoughts.[44]

The Effects of Spiritual Problems

Spiritual problems create spiral effects. Many of the causes listed above also become effects. An attitude of pride, for example, often leads to more pride. Sin stimulates more sin. Legalism breeds more of the same. Self-sufficiency, distorted values, misunderstandings, selfishness, theological error—these are all like creeping vines which keep getting larger and more able to squeeze out the vestiges of spiritual life that remain.

In addition to the causes which also become effects, there are other results which come from spiritual problems in a person's life.

1. *Spiritual Effects.* When spiritual problems are left unchecked they can lead to compromising behavior, an increasing tendency to miss worship services and personal devotions, spiritual naïveté, a decreasing sensitivity to the Holy Spirit's leading and control, hypocrisy and phoniness, a

boredom with religious activities and a greater tendency to self-reliance. The fruit of the Spirit—love, joy, peace, patience, kindness, goodness, faithfulness, gentleness and self-control—are experienced less and shown to others with decreasing frequency.

These spiritual effects are not evident immediately. Many spiritually dry or dying people are good actors—especially if they know and can use the accepted theological jargon. Even Moses, whose face once shone as it reflected God's glory, tried to hide from his fellow believers. He put a veil over his face so that the Israelites could not see that the spiritual glory was fading away.[45] Many people do the same today. They hide their fading spirituality behind a veil of clichés or pious (but hypocritical) actions. It is not until they turn to the Lord that the veil is taken away.[46]

2. *Physical Effects.* It is well known that psychological tension and conflicts can influence us physically. This is known as psychosomatic illness. Apparently there is also a spiritually produced sickness and even death.[47] Not all sickness results from the sick person's sin, but sometimes sin does lead to illness.

3. *Psychological Effects.* Guilt feelings, self-condemnation, discouragement, anger, fears, defensiveness, insecurities, misplaced values—each of these can have a variety of causes, but each can also be the result of spiritual deadness or waning vitality.

4. *Social Effects.* Christian fellowship can be a beautiful experience, but Christian fights can be vicious. In describing spiritual immaturity, the Apostle Paul listed two characteristics as being of special significance: jealousy and strife. When there is spiritual growing, the barriers between people disintegrate;[48] when there are spiritual problems, then unkind criticism, cynicism and interpersonal tension are among the first and clearest signs of trouble.

5. *Evangelism Effects.* Confined to a Roman prison, Paul once wrote about people who were preaching the gospel, not from motives of good will, but "out of selfish ambitions," hoping to stir up envy and strife.[49] The same situation exists today. Many men and women seem so intent on building followers or converting people to their own point of view, that the Person of Christ is forgotten, even though his name may be mentioned often. The true disciple points people to Christ and seeks to have a part in building a body of believers who are Christ-centered, not man-centered.[50] When Christ is pushed behind the glory of some human leader, even a Christian leader, then we surely have evidence of spiritual insensitivity, distorted values, and deadness in the leader and/or in the followers.

Counseling and Spiritual Problems

The approach and course of spiritual counseling depends largely on the nature of the counselee's problem. If the counselee raises theological questions, for example, the counseling might differ from help given to a

person who is involved in deliberate sin. If a counselee is sincerely concerned about spiritual lethargy, our approach might differ from that taken
with a counselee who is bitter and unwilling to change. As with every other
type of counseling, therefore, it is important for helpers to listen carefully,
to show acceptance and empathy, and to determine—if possible—what
the real problem is, and what are its causes. As you listen and talk with
counselees who have spiritual problems, remember that this type of counseling involves the following:

1. *Prayer*. Before, during and after counseling, the counselor must
seek divine guidance. More than any other form of helping, spiritual counseling can involve us in conflict with satanic forces. For this reason the
counselor needs special strength, wisdom and direction. At times you may
choose to pray directly with the counselee. Always you should spend at
least some time alone in prayer concerning the counselee.

2. *Modeling*. In a thought-provoking book, David McKenna has shown
how the life of Jesus should and can be a model for every believer.[51] But
since Jesus is no longer here in the flesh, the best models that many people
have are Christians in whom Christ lives. On several occasions the Apostle
Paul repeated the theme: "Be imitators of me, just as I also am of
Christ."[52] Peter urged church leaders not to be "lording it over those
allotted to your charge" but instead to "be examples to the flock."[53]
Whether or not we seek or desire the role, Christians—including Christian
counselors—are examples of Christian living. The counselor who is not
seeking to imitate Christ and to grow as a Christian will not be effective
in spiritual counseling. The counselor who wants to be effective in helping
those with spiritual problems must recognize that he or she is a model
which counselees will follow—and occasionally react against.

3. *Exhorting*. As used in the Bible, this word does *not* mean "to preach
at someone," to use sharp words or to demand obedience. Exhortation
involves a God-given ability to come alongside to help, to strengthen those
who are spiritually weak, to reassure those who are wavering in their faith,
to support those who are facing adverse circumstances, and to encourage
those who lack assurance or security. At times the helper will point out
sin, gently challenge the counselee's thinking or conclusions, encourage
the counselee to change, guide as decisions are made, and give support
as new behavior is attempted.

4. *Teaching*. Counselors teach by example but they also teach by instruction. Spiritual counseling is often a gentle, sensitive form of Christian education, frequently conducted on a one-to-one basis. Such teaching
may involve giving information, answering questions, making suggestions,
stimulating thinking, pointing out errors, and sometimes giving advice.
The teaching may concern a variety of issues, often including one or more
of the following.

(a) The Attributes of God. Confusion and spiritual problems often come to those who understand and ponder one or two attributes of God while overlooking or forgetting the others. To emphasize the wrath of God without seeing his mercy is to plunge us into fear and guilt. To stress his mercy and love without his holiness and justice can lull us into a false sense of security and nonconcern about spiritual issues or responsibilities.

> A right conception of God is basic not only to systematic theology but to practical Christian living as well. . . . There is scarcely an error in doctrine or a failure in applying Christian ethics that cannot be traced finally to imperfect or ignoble thoughts about God. . . . Among the sins to which the human heart is prone, hardly any other is more hateful to God than idolatry. . . . The essence of idolatry is the entertainment of thoughts about God that are unworthy of Him.[54]

God wants us to know him.[55] That, writes James Packer, is our main purpose in life. "Once you become aware that the main business that you are here for is to know God, most of life's problems fall into place of their own accord." Knowing God is a continuing challenge which no human mind could ever complete. It is a process which comes first by listening to God's Word, seeking to understand, to obey and to apply it to our lives, through the help and guidance of the Holy Spirit. Secondly, we know God by thinking about his character as revealed in the Bible and in the world, and expressing thanks for his love and fellowship.[56] Third, we know God by obeying his commands. Then, we know God through participation and service in his body, the church.

The counselor has the challenge of helping counselees to know God. Such knowledge rarely comes by hearing lectures about God. The counselee must see God in the counselor's life style, conversation, attitudes and periodic references to Scripture. Such teaching places considerable responsibility on the counselor. We cannot teach others to know God unless we ourselves are growing in this knowledge in the ways mentioned in the preceding paragraph. Helping counselees to know God, therefore, requires a knowledge and spiritual depth that far exceeds the teaching of any book on counseling or psychotherapy.

(b) Christian Love. Love—the giving, sacrificial, unconditional, Christlike love that is described in 1 Corinthians 13—has been called "incomparably the greatest psychotherapeutic agent; something that professional psychiatry cannot of itself create, focus, nor release."[57] It is the attribute of God which led him to care for us and to send his Son to earth so that we might become personally acquainted with the Divine.[58] Counselees need to hear about God's love. Even more, they need to experience and observe this love as it flows from God, through the dedicated counselor (and other Christians), into the lives of counselees who feel unloved, unaccepted, guilty, confused and spiritually needy.

(c) Sin and Forgiveness. The Bible never "covers over" sin or denies its prevalence and destructiveness. God hates sin and eventually punishes unrepentant sinners. In contrast, those who are "in Christ Jesus" are not condemned. God's Son, Jesus Christ, came to pay for our sins. When we sin, therefore, there is a way to be forgiven completely. "If we confess our sins, He is faithful and righteous to forgive us our sins and to cleanse us from all unrighteousness." This can be a liberating realization. God doesn't want sacrifices and penance. He wants confession and a desire to change. When he hears our confession he forgives and completely forgets.[59]

The Bible also instructs us to confess our sins to one another.[60] This is not done to get divine forgiveness, since God alone forgives and only when we confess to him directly. Confession to others can be therapeutic, however. Often it stimulates others to forgive us and sometimes it helps us to forgive ourselves. Confession to others can also be accompanied by the healing power of prayer.

The counselor must share this biblical perspective on sin and forgiveness. At times, it will be necessary to confront counselees with their sin. In so doing, the counselor must show a forgiving, nonjudgmental attitude. We cannot talk about forgiveness, but refuse to demonstrate forgiveness.[61]

(d) Holy Spirit Control. It has been said that the most important thing in the life of any Christian is to be filled with the Holy Spirit.[62] In Ephesians 5:18 Christians are commanded to "go on being filled with the Spirit," a process which involves the following:

—self-examination (Acts 20:28, 1 Cor. 11:28);
—confession of all known sin (1 John 1:9);
—complete voluntary submission to God (Rom. 6:11–13);
—asking in prayer for the Holy Spirit to fill us (Luke 11:13);
—believing that we then are filled with the Spirit, and thanking God for this (1 Thess. 5:18).

Spirit-filling is not a "once-in-a-lifetime" event. It is a daily process of "breathing out" sin through confession, and "breathing in" the fullness of the Holy Spirit. Such repeated filling (which is somewhat equivalent to "walking in the Spirit") is not always accompanied by emotional "highs" or ecstatic experiences (although these do come at times), but it does lead to joyful thanksgiving, to mutual submission, and to the development of love, peace, patience, self-control and the other fruits of the Spirit.[63]

Many of the spiritual problems discussed in this chapter arise and persist because believers attempt to solve the problems and grow on their own. It is the Holy Spirit who teaches, strengthens and empowers us to meet and overcome the spiritual problems of life. Counselees must be aware of this foundational truth.

(e) Discipleship. In the Great Commission, Jesus instructed believers to "make disciples"—a process which involves evangelism and Christian education.[64] At times, the counselor will want to evangelize, sharing the good news of the gospel. At times, the counselor and counselee will discuss the meaning and importance of Bible study, prayer, trust in God, meditation, discipline in our devotional lives, and reaching out to others.

In two sentences, Paul once stated his ultimate purpose in life:

> We proclaim Him, admonishing every man and teaching every man with all wisdom, that we may present every man complete in Christ. And for this purpose I labor, striving according to His power, which mightily works within me.[65]

With qualifications, it might be stated that this is the counselor's ultimate purpose. The qualification comes because some well-meaning but insensitive counselors have been too hasty in presenting the gospel and urging counselees to make a commitment to Christ. To proclaim, admonish, teach and present everyone "complete in Christ" is an ultimate goal, but this can be done too abruptly, too quickly and too enthusiastically. After seeking the Holy Spirit's leading, the effective and sensitive counselor gently moves into discussions of spiritual matters, aware that it is the Holy Spirit who convicts people of sin and brings them to repentance and growth as disciples. We are to be divine instruments in that process.

(f) Balance. Counselees with spiritual problems need to be alerted to the importance of such "nonspiritual" influences as proper diet, rest, recreation and exercise. Help counselees develop a balanced life style which avoids legalism and self-sufficiency; deals with pride and bitterness (through discussion, understanding and prayer); reexamines values, goals and priorities; eliminates theological misunderstanding; and evaluates the problems of spiritual undernourishment and overfeeding (with its accompanying lack of giving).

(g) The Body. Christianity, as we have stated earlier, is not a "do-it-yourself" religion. God made us social creatures and recognized that it is not good for us to be alone. Clearly in the Bible, the church is pictured as a body which has many parts.

Each person in the body is important. Each has been given one or more special gifts (such as teaching, counseling, hospitality or evangelism). Each is expected to develop these gifts in order to serve and "care for one another," [66] and to build up the church, "so that in all things God may be glorified through Jesus Christ, to whom belongs the glory and dominion forever and ever." [67]

Christian counseling can be only minimally effective if it exists apart from the body of Christ, the church. Believers are instructed to help one another and bear one another's burdens. When counselees experience this acceptance and support, they are better able to work on their spiritual and other problems within the confines of the counseling relationship.

(h) The Devil. At times, and in some Christian circles, it seems that Satan gets more credit than he deserves. The devil is blamed for all problems, rebuke and exorcism are the preferred methods of "problem-solving," and there is no place for compassion, understanding and sensitive Christian counseling.

In an overreaction to such distorted teaching, it is possible to forget that Christians are in a battle, that exorcism may be the preferred method of treatment in some rare cases,[68] and that every counselor should constantly be alert to satanic influences in all our lives. Ephesians 6 warns us to "pray at all times in the Spirit, . . . for all the saints." We are to stand firm against the devil, not trying to resist him with our own strength, but "in the strength of His might." [69]

Counselees can misinterpret our comments about Satan and sometimes develop paranoid fears of the demonic. The counselor, therefore, should use discretion in mentioning Satan and should be alert to correct counselee misconceptions about the devil. His influence and power should be clearly understood, alertly recognized, and firmly resisted with determination and the Holy Spirit's power. Most Christian counselees will be able to understand both the devil's influence, and the resounding truth that the Holy Spirit who resides in us is greater than the devil who is in the world.[70]

Preventing Spiritual Problems

The church exists as a company of God's people, called out from the world to live for Christ. According to Ray C. Stedman,

> The supreme thing, the paramount thing, the thing God is after above everything else is to produce in this present world men and women who are like the humanity of Jesus Christ. He does not want white-robed saints, or accomplished churchmen, or religious experts; what he wants is that you and I may be grown up, responsible, well-adjusted, wholehearted, human beings like Jesus Christ! [71]

This task is the responsibility of the church. When the church is doing its job properly, many spiritual problems will be prevented.

It should be noted, however, that the believer can always expect to have some trials, tribulations and temptations. Jesus called us to "take up a cross" in following him. His life on earth was not easy and he never promised that we would be free of problems. Instead, we are told that such difficulties can enable us to grow.[72]

In spite of this, the Christian counselee can be taught, through counseling but especially through the church, how to prevent some of the spiritual problems of life. The preventive measures, surely well known to most Christian leaders, include the following:

—Commit one's life to Christ and accept him as Lord and Savior.
—Develop the practice of regular, consistent prayer and Bible study.
—Practice the regular confession of sin and filling of the Holy Spirit.
—Become involved actively in a local body of believers.
—Reach out to others in evangelism, service and fellowship.
—Be alert to the devil and resistant to his influences.

This is not presented as a simplistic formula to prevent all spiritual problems. It is a basic foundation upon which the church's preventive and discipleship program must build.

Conclusions about Spiritual Problems

Of all the issues discussed in this book, perhaps none is more familiar to Christian leaders and counselors than the spiritual problems considered in this chapter. These problems have concerned godly men and women for centuries, and the Bible deals with these in more detail than any of the other issues considered in this volume.

Since the Bible speaks so frequently about spiritual problems, some believers have concluded that *all* of our problems are really spiritual and that all can be solved through the discovery and application of some biblical principle. While we can admire the theological dedication of many who hold such views, this is not the perspective of the preceding pages.

Spiritual problems have causes and solutions that most often are described in the Bible. The Bible, however, never claims to be a psychiatric diagnostic manual and textbook of counseling. While all problems stem ultimately from the fall of the human race, not all human problems are spiritual in that they involve the counselee's specific relationship with God. For example, problems caused by faulty learning, misinformation, early traumas, environmental stress, physical illness, misperception and confusion over decision-making, may or may not be addressed by biblical writers. Counseling people with these problems may use techniques derived from Scripture. More often they use methods *consistent with the Bible's teachings and values,* but discovered and developed by social science and common sense.

Christian counseling, then, is deeply concerned with the issues discussed in this chapter, but it goes further. It recognizes that all truth, including psychological truth, comes from God—sometimes through secular psychology and psychiatry books. The Christian evaluates such secular findings against biblical teachings and discards what is inconsistent with the Bible. What remains is then used, along with and in submission to biblical teachings. The counselor, so equipped, then seeks to be used by God to touch lives and change them so that people on earth can be helped to live with greater meaning, stability, fulfillment and spiritual maturity.

Suggestions for Further Reading
* Adams, Lane. *How Come It's Taking Me So Long to Get Better?* Wheaton, IL: Tyndale, 1975.
* Getz, Gene A. *Building Up One Another.* Wheaton, IL: Victor, 1978.
* Halverson, Richard C. *Be Yourself . . . And God's.* Grand Rapids: Zondervan, 1971.
* Little, Paul E. *Know Why You Believe.* Downers Grove, IL: Inter-Varsity, 1968.
* Macaulay, Ranald, and Barrs, Jerram. *Being Human: The Nature of Spiritual Experience.* Downers Grove, IL: Inter-Varsity, 1978.

* Maeder, Gary, and Williams, Don. *The Christian Life: Issues and Answers*. Glendale, CA: Regal, 1976.
Packer, James I. *Knowing God*. Downers Grove, IL: Inter-Varsity, 1973.
Schaeffer, Francis A. *True Spirituality*. Wheaton, IL: Tyndale, 1971.
* Stedman, Ray C. *Body Life*. Glendale, CA: Regal, 1972.
* Tozer, A. W. *The Knowledge of the Holy*. New York: Harper & Row, 1961.
* White, John. *The Fight*. Downers Grove, IL: Inter-Varsity, 1976.

Footnotes
   1. 1 John 4:7–11, 16–21; John 3:16.
   2. Francis A. Schaeffer, *The Mark of the Christian* (Downers Grove, IL: Inter-Varsity, 1970).
   3. 1 John 4:8, 7.
   4. 1 Cor. 13; Eph. 5:25–30.
   5. Walter Trobisch, *Spiritual Dryness* (Downers Grove, IL: Inter-Varsity, 1970).
   6. Ibid., p. 6.
   7. 1 Pet. 1:14–16; 2:21.
   8. Eph. 6:10–17.
   9. Rom. 12:1.
   10. Rom. 13:14; 1 Pet. 2:11; 1 John 1:8–2:2.
   11. Eph. 2:4–9.
   12. Rom. 8:15–17; Mic. 6:8; Ps. 103:8, 14.
   13. John 14:16, 17; Luke 12:12; 1 Thess. 4:8; 1 Pet. 5:10.
   14. Matt. 2:8–20; Prov. 18:24.
   15. 1 Pet. 3:18.
   16. Rom. 12:1; Heb. 14:15.
   17. Rom. 12:2; Heb. 12:1; 1 Pet. 1:14–16; 2:21, 22; Gal. 5:22, 23.
   18. Heb. 14:6.
   19. Matt. 20; 26, 27; 1 Pet. 5:6.
   20. Richard C. Halverson, *Be Yourself . . . And God's* (Grand Rapids: Zondervan, 1971), p. 53.
   21. The authors and publishers of these books are Lane Adams (Tyndale), LeRoy Eims (Victor), Larry Richards (Victor), Rick Yohn (Thomas Nelson), Oswald Chambers (Dodd, Mead), Evelyn Christenson (Victor), Martin Parsons (Eerdmans), Bruce Shelley (Zondervan), J. I. Packer (Inter-Varsity), John White (Inter-Varsity), L. S. Chafer (Dunham), Ranald Macaulay and Jerram Barrs (Inter-Varsity), and Gene A. Getz (Victor).
   22. 2 Tim. 2:21.
   23. 1 Cor. 2:14–16.
   24. Trobisch, *Spiritual Dryness*, p. 16.
   25. Eph. 2:8, 9.
   26. 1 Cor. 3:1–3.
   27. Rom. 6:12, 16; Ps. 32:3, 4.
   28. Ps. 50:8–15; Isa. 1:11–17; Hos. 6:6; Matt. 23:23, 24; Col. 2:23; Gal. 3:2; 5:1.
   29. Halverson, *Be Yourself*, p. 49.
   30. Eph. 2:8, 9.
   31. Phil. 2:12, 13.
   32. Col. 2:8, 16–23.
   33. Rev. 3:16–19.
   34. Heb. 12:15, 16.
   35. 1 Tim. 6:10; Heb. 13:5; James 4:3, 13; Matt. 20:25–28.

36. 1 Tim. 6:10–21.
37. Rom. 12:1, 2.
38. John 8:31; 2 Tim. 3:15–17; Heb. 4:12.
39. Trobisch, *Spiritual Dryness,* p. 8.
40. 1 Cor. 6:19.
41. 1 Thess. 1:6; Eph. 1:6; 3:16; 4:3; Gal. 5:22, 23; Col. 1:29; 1 John 2:20, 27.
42. Rom. 12; 1 Cor. 12; Eph. 4; Heb. 10:24, 25.
43. Eph. 6:11–20; 1 Pet. 5:8, 9; 2 Cor. 11:14; James 4:7; 1 John 4:3, 4; Rev. 12:9; 20:3, 10.
44. Isa. 55:8.
45. 2 Cor. 3:7, 12–16.
46. 2 Cor. 3:16–18.
47. 1 John 5:16–17.
48. 1 Cor. 3:3; Eph. 2:14.
49. Phil. 1:17, 16.
50. 1 Cor. 3:4–23.
51. David L. McKenna, *The Jesus Model* (Waco, TX: Word, 1977).
52. 1 Cor. 11:1. See also 1 Cor. 4:16; Phil. 3:17; 4:9.
53. 1 Pet. 5:3.
54. A. W. Tozer, *The Knowledge of the Holy* (New York: Harper & Row, 1961), pp. 10, 11.
55. Jer. 9:23, 24; Hos. 6:6; John 17:3.
56. James I. Packer, *Knowing God* (Downers Grove, IL: Inter-Varsity, 1973), pp. 29, 32.
57. Gordon W. Allport, *The Individual and His Religion* (New York: Macmillan, 1950), p. 90.
58. John 3:16; 1 John 4:7–21.
59. Rom. 6:23; Matt. 13:41, 42; Rom. 8:1; 1 Cor. 15:3; 1 John 1:8–10; Isa. 43:23–25; Jer. 31:34.
60. James 5:16.
61. Matt. 6:14, 15; 7:1–5.
62. The statement is from Tim LaHaye, *Spirit-Controlled Temperament* (Wheaton: Tyndale, 1966), p. 57. Although LaHaye's concept of temperaments is based on Greek philosophy and has virtually no support in contemporary psychology or biblical exegesis, his chapter on "How to Be Filled with the Spirit" is excellent. Much of the discussion in the next paragraph is taken from LaHaye's book.
63. Eph. 5:18–21; Gal. 5:22, 23.
64. Matt. 28:18–20.
65. Col. 1:28, 29.
66. 1 Cor. 12:25. Over sixty times in the New Testament, Christians are instructed to do things for "one another," e.g., pray for, help, encourage, love, strengthen, serve, bear the burdens of one another, etc.
67. 1 Pet. 4:10, 11. Other passages dealing with the body and spiritual gifts are Rom. 12:1–8; 1 Cor. 12–14; and Eph. 4:7–16.
68. Discussion of exorcism is beyond the scope of this book. Interested readers may wish to consult Kurt E. Koch, *Christian Counseling and Occultism* (Grand Rapids: Kregel, 1965). See also John W. Montgomery, ed., *Demon Possession* (Minneapolis: Bethany Fellowship, 1976).
69. Eph. 6:18, 10–17. See also James 4:7, 8 and 1 Pet. 5:8, 9.
70. 1 John 4:4.
71. Ray C. Stedman, *Body Life* (Glendale, CA: Regal, 1972), p. 117.
72. Heb. 12:5–11.

30

Life Traumas

IT DOESN'T TAKE LONG FOR COUNSELORS TO RECOGNIZE THAT EACH counseling situation, each session, and each counselee is in some way unique. Even though there are general principles of counseling the specific techniques and approaches which might be very effective with one counselee may be less effective with someone else. This uniqueness contributes both to the frustration and to the challenge of counseling.

Since each problem is unique and since the number of potential human problems is legion, it is not possible to discuss every counseling situation, especially in the pages of one book. In the first four chapters we described some general counseling guidelines which can apply regardless of the specific counselee program. Chapters 5–29 considered what probably are the most frequently encountered counseling issues. Each of these was viewed from a biblical perspective. The causes and effects of each were discussed and suggestions were given for counseling and prevention. In this chapter we want to give a briefer overview of several less common but nevertheless prevalent problems. We will conclude by looking at a question which Christian counselors hear frequently: "Why?"

Counseling and Childlessness

One of the most poignant pictures in the Bible is that of Hannah "greatly distressed," weeping bitterly and crying out to God because she could not get pregnant.[1] In Bible times childlessness was considered an indication of divine disapproval, and women such as Hannah, Sara, Elizabeth and others were embarrassed and distressed when their marriages were childless.

Although we no longer see childlessness as an indication of God's disapproval, the inability to bear children still is a great stress for many couples—especially wives. Infertility strikes 10 to 15 percent of married couples, and the rate has been increasing within recent years partly because many couples choose to postpone child-bearing until after 30 when

446

fertility tends to be declining. Whenever a couple begins to realize that pregnancy is not forthcoming, even after repeated attempts to get pregnant, or when there is a medical confirmation that the husband (in 40 percent of the cases) or wife is sterile, there first comes a period of surprise. This tends to be followed by grief (similar to that discussed in chapter 28), anger ("Why me?"), and isolation from friends who might ask questions. Later there is denial and a reluctance to admit the problem, followed finally by acceptance and a willingness to find alternative sources of satisfaction (such as a greater devotion to one's vocation, a decision to adopt or become foster parents, or involvement with other people's children).[2]

When their infertility is discovered, women especially feel guilty and inadequate. Many feel family and social pressures to bear children and often there is a sense of failure or a feeling of sexual incompetence when pregnancy does not occur. Sometimes there is constant concern and worry about the problem. According to one counselor, the whole world looks pregnant to the woman who can't conceive. "Everywhere she goes she sees babies and bellies."[3] This creates tension which can disrupt marital stability, throw off the body's cycles and delay conception even further.

Counselors at fertility clinics have noted that many couples are reluctant, even ashamed, to admit their infertility. Perhaps they feel that infertility is an indication of their inadequacy as males or females. Some may feel uncomfortable discussing sex, even with a medical counselor. Others may resist genital examination by physicians, and some may fear that they will be told, "It's all psychological. Go home, relax, and keep trying to get pregnant."

The counselor should be aware of this reluctance to talk about infertility. If a married couple remains childless after several years of marriage you may wish to gently raise the issue, but try not to fall into the pressuring attitude of well-meaning relatives or friends. If the couple does not wish to talk about their childlessness, assure them of your availability to talk at any future time and do not press the issue further.

When you are involved in counseling a childless couple, the following guidelines should be remembered.

—Childlessness may have several causes including physiological sterility, psychological tension, or a deliberate decision to remain childless. Do not assume that you know why the couple has no children.

—If a couple has chosen not to have children try to find the reasons for this. You may wish to talk with the husband and wife together and then separately.

—Recognize that the decision to remain childless may be logical and carefully considered. Both husband and wife may feel called to serve God in special careers, for example. In other cases, the decision not to have children may reflect insecurity, fear of intimacy, a desire to avoid responsibility or some other inner or interpersonal conflict.

—When there is a desire for children but an inability for the wife to get pregnant, referral to a physician is imperative. Begin with referral to the family doctor then, if the problem persists, try (with the help of the local physician) to find a doctor who has special expertise in fertility problems.[4] Both husband and wife should seek the medical consultation.

—Do not condemn, probe into areas of sexual intimacy that may not concern you, assume that all couples should have children, use trite platitudes, or even hint that you find the problem amusing.

—Recognize that many couples need consistent support, especially during times when a new medical or other procedure has been tried and found to fail. Couples may also need opportunity to discuss their guilt, anger (even at God), feelings of inadequacy, fear of the future (including old age with no children), loneliness and frustration. Some of these feelings may create tension which contributes to the psychological causes of sterility.

—Focus on the theological issues involved. These include the common idea that God is punishing the couple by preventing pregnancy, or that he doesn't care. There is no scriptural basis for either view and couples should be helped to discuss these issues, including the question of "Why?" or ethical issues such as artificial insemination. At some time mention that sterility is no reason to abstain from sexual intercourse in marriage, and correct misconceptions about God's will or the purpose of marriage.

—Help the couple find alternatives to bearing children. Realistically discuss adoption, becoming foster parents, becoming involved in vocational activities, and similar issues. If childlessness has become a preoccupation, raise this with the husband and wife. Then discuss other meaningful activities that can give purpose to a life apart from children.

It is estimated that about half of those who are involuntarily childless can have children following medical diagnosis and treatment. Others adopt children, become foster parents, or plunge into a meaningful life and vocation without children. Perhaps 15 percent "remain to mourn," to accept their permanent childless state, and then to accept "indirect" parenthood which comes from contact with the children of others.[5]

Counseling and Illegitimate Pregnancies

A different problem is that of the unwed mother. The number of illegitimate pregnancies, especially among teenagers, has been rising at an alarming rate within recent years. Although sexual intercourse apart from marriage is becoming more and more accepted in our society, this does not make it right. The Bible strongly condemns intercourse apart from marriage, and illegitimate pregnancies still are socially disapproved. Of course the male, whose sperm impregnates the woman, is as much a part of the problem as the unwed mother, but the father's identity is sometimes unknown even to the woman. Males can hide their involvement since they do not show evidence of pregnancy, and sometimes the father "takes off" leaving the unwed mother to face the pregnancy alone.

Unwed mothers often try to keep the pregnancy hidden for as long as possible. Anxiety, fear of parental reaction, concern about social judgment, guilt, self-condemnation and sometimes anger all serve to keep the unwed mother preoccupied and away from sources of help and prenatal care.

When the pregnancy is discovered there are often outbursts of anger, condemnation, fear, panic and general confusion, especially if the pregnancy involves teenagers. All of these emotions may be brought to the counselor's office. Clearly this is not the time for moral exhortations, theological discussions, or intellectual debates about the reasons why the girl became pregnant. Instead, counseling should involve several overlapping goals.[6]

First, allay the initial fears. Do not discourage initial expressions of anger, hurt, guilt and fear, but continue to show acceptance, understanding, and a quiet confidence. Remember that a loving, wise, forgiving God will guide as you counsel.

Sometimes there will be considerable resistance to the counseling. The unmarried girl, for example, may resist because she has been brought or sent for counseling against her will; she may never have learned to trust people; or she may see the counselor as a condemning, unforgiving authority figure. Unwed fathers may have similar insecurities and resistances.

During the first session attempt to give calm reassurance that you will help (but avoid pious clichés). Try to determine what help is needed and what the counselee(s) and the family members see as immediate courses of action. Although you should encourage a physical examination for the mother, try to discourage quick decisions (such as abortion or immediate marriage) at least for a day or two and until initial emotional expression has been vented. Prayer can be especially calming, helpful and reassuring.

Second, help counselees consider practical steps to be taken. The major question to be considered is "What do we do with the baby?" For some, the answer may be abortion. This will be discussed in the next section.

Others may see marriage and parenthood as a possibility, especially if the couple has had a good prepregnancy relationship and shows prospects for a good marriage. If these conditions do not exist, the marriage will have a low probability of success.

Some mothers decide to remain single and bear the child to maturity. Many find maternity homes, move to boarding homes, go to live with distant relatives or foster parents, or stay at home and openly bear the child. Each of these alternatives should be discussed along with the issue of the baby's future.

Keeping the baby or making it available for adoption are alternatives which both should be considered. In deciding on these issues, counselors must draw on the advice and expertise of others in the community, including local physicians, social agencies, adoption agencies and lawyers. Remember that unwed fathers are not always willing to leave the child's future in the hands of the mother or her family. Increasingly, it seems, unwed fathers want to be as involved as the mother in making decisions about the child's and the parents' immediate future.

Third, there can be continuing counsel. After the prenatal decisions have been made, either or both of the unwed parents may experience continuing guilt, insecurity, a lowered self-image, and similar emotional struggles. The counselor can help with these problems, especially if he or she has been accepting, noncondemning, and helpful from the beginning. Early in counseling it should be stated clearly that the counselor would like to see the counselees again—if not before the baby's birth, then shortly thereafter. The unwed mother usually needs someone with whom she can share the details of childbearing and the grief that often comes if a baby is given up for adoption. Ideally the parents of the unwed mother or unwed father are the best people with whom to talk. But such older parents may have their own problems about the out-of-wedlock pregnancy and may be unwilling or unable to listen or discuss anything concerning their new grandchild. The counselor, therefore, can be available to the entire family to discuss feelings, moral implications, and planning for the future. If the baby is stillborn or deformed, this can create additional guilt, grief and confusion—all of which should be talked through.

An unwanted pregnancy out of wedlock is usually a traumatic experience, even for people in an age of sexual laxity and moral decline. The Christian counselor can use this experience to demonstrate and point people to the forgiveness and love to be found in Jesus Christ. The unwed mother and father can be helped to reach some new conclusions about responsibility and moral choice. In the church, the believers can be encouraged to show forgiveness and acceptance, instead of condemnation, gossip and rejection. In these ways, the pain of an out-of-wedlock pregnancy can be turned into a growing, learning experience which can help individuals and couples live more Christ-honoring lives in the future. It can also alert parents to a sexual promiscuity which is increasingly common, even in evangelical church circles, and hopefully prevent further out-of-wedlock pregnancies in the future.

Counseling and Abortion

In January of 1973, the United States Supreme Court granted women an absolute right to abortion on demand during the first six months of pregnancy, and an almost unqualified right to abortion (i.e., for "health" reasons—with "health" including psychological, physical, social and economic well-being) during the final three months. Suddenly abortion ceased to be a crime and became a right. It ceased to be the privilege of the affluent and soon became available to all, sometimes subsidized by taxpayer dollars. The resulting shouts of approval and cries of disapproval have continued to the present and have been heard both in North America and beyond. In the meantime, the number of legal abortions has increased drastically.

Much of the debate about abortion centers on the question of when human life begins. The Supreme Court concluded that it did not need "to resolve the difficult question of when life begins." Since "those trained in the respective disciplines of medicine, philosophy and theology are unable to arrive at any consensus, the judiciary, at this point in the development of man's knowledge, is not in a position to speculate as to the answer." [7] But the answer is crucially important. If life begins at birth, then abortion is not terminating a human being's existence. But if human life begins earlier, perhaps at the time of conception, then abortion is murder. The same legal code which makes it a crime to destroy a baby born prematurely makes it all right to destroy another child of identical age who has not yet been born. The same law which stresses civil rights, denies these rights to the unborn.

The Christian counselor must grapple with these issues preferably before he or she counsels people concerning abortion. Christians differ in their conclusions about these issues, perhaps because the Bible is silent on the topic of abortion. The Bible does make it clear, however, that the developing fetus already is human life in God's eyes.[8] Life, therefore, does not begin at birth. It must start either at conception or at some time during the gestation (prenatal development) period. In the absence of any convincing biblical, physiological, medical or other evidence to support the view that life really begins at some specific time during the nine months before birth, many people conclude that life must start when the male sperm and female egg unite at conception. If this is true, abortion is wrong. It is not simply a medical procedure, legal issue or counseling problem. It is a violation of the commandment, "You shall not murder."

Not all counselors will agree with this conclusion, and the issue is complicated by other ethical concerns such as the rightness or wrongness of abortion when the mother's life and health are clearly in danger if the pregnancy continues, when the fetus is clearly deformed, or when the pregnancy results from rape.

An unplanned pregnancy often stimulates anxiety, anger, fear and discouragement. Abortion, which now is relatively safe, common, easy to obtain, and widely accepted is one way to solve the pregnancy problem efficiently, quietly and quickly. Although many women experience some guilt or sadness and wonder about the moral implications of abortion, there is evidence that these feelings pass quickly and that few women develop postabortion psychiatric problems.[9]

For the Christian, however, there is still the question, "Is it right?" This and related ethical questions are best discussed *before* an abortion. The woman should feel free to discuss her feelings and alternatives openly with a supportive, understanding counselor. If the father is available, he should be involved in the counseling process as well. It may be helpful to discuss how abortions are performed,[10] and questions should be referred to a competent physician—preferably a gynecologist. Alternatives to abortion (such as adoption or keeping the child) should be considered.[11] Counselors may have difficulty hiding their own views on abortion and probably shouldn't try. Ultimately the woman must decide what to do, before God, and the counselor is there to help.

If the woman decides to get an abortion, the counselor can either help her find competent medical care or graciously withdraw from counseling and refer her to a counselor who is not opposed to abortion. Either decision is difficult for the counselor who believes that abortion is sin, but we cannot and should not force a person to act in accordance with our wishes. The best alternative is to express our beliefs, demonstrate our care and concern, and help the counselee find another counselor.

After an abortion, many counselees can profit from individual or group counseling [12] which focuses on issues such as feelings about the surgery, guilt, forgiveness, attitudes toward sex, contraception, the meaning of femininity, and biblical teachings about life, death and sex. The goal here is not to condemn or instill guilt. The goals are to help the counselee to experience God's cleansing and forgiveness; to express feelings and "work through" the grief process that often follows abortion; to reevaluate the meaning of sexuality; to consider biblical teachings about sex, birth, and life before birth; and to help counselees move beyond the abortion and into a future where they can begin or continue serving God and others as true disciples of Jesus Christ.

Counseling and Rape

Rape might be defined as a forced, violent sexual penetration against the victim's will and without the victim's consent.[13] While there can be homosexual and child rape, most rapes involve the actions of males against nonconsenting females. Although rape often involves vaginal intercourse, most experts see it more as an act of violence than as a means of sexual gratification.

There are many myths about rape, including the views that women subconsciously ask to be raped, that they enjoy it, and that they could stop it if they really wished. These myths lead many women to keep a rape secret, lest police, physicians, friends or others assume that they really were "asking for it." Thus the rape victim finds herself revictimized by the people who should be giving help. These people, including some counselors, may also be inclined to believe that rapists are always sick and perverted men, that they cannot control their sex drives, or that they especially prefer victims of another race. None of these myths is supported by evidence. Each is false.

Rape victims may be classified in three ways, depending on how they respond to the rape.[14] The majority show the *rape trauma syndrome*. This begins with acute stress immediately following the rape. There may be fear, anger, anxiety, shock, self-blame and disbelief, often expressed by crying, sobbing, tenseness, nausea or restlessness, but sometimes hidden behind a calm, composed exterior. At this point the victim may be flooded with feelings of terror, concern for her safety, and guilt because she did not struggle more. Some women feel they have been spoiled or "made impure" and often the woman wonders if the myth really is true which says women secretly attract rapists.

At this point the counselee is sensitive to someone who will listen, accept and believe her, especially if she has faced subtle disbelief and rejection from friends, family, police, or medical personnel. The counselor can encourage the expression of feelings, can help the woman find competent medical and legal aid, can give support when she does encounter criticism, can help her and her friends recognize the myths about rape, can encourage the victim to discuss her fears for future safety (and to take action that will increase safety), and can give assurance of continued support especially as the woman faces crisis situations in coming weeks.

Two or three weeks after the rape, many women begin to experience nightmares, irrational fears and restless activity. Often there is a decision to move, change a phone number, or spend more time with close friends. Some women develop a variety of phobias including fear of being alone, in crowds, in places where people are behind them, being indoors, or being outdoors. Some experience a fear of sex and/or a disruption of normal sexual activities and responsiveness. In all of this the victim is in the process of reorganizing her life following an experience which probably has been terrifying. Such women need support, freedom to express feelings, acceptance, an opportunity to talk with someone who considers them "normal," and guidance as they make decisions. Many will want to discuss the issue of "Why me?" and will need to be reassured of God's continued care, love and concern. Sometimes it helps for a counselor to take the initiative in helping these women, instead of waiting for the victim to seek more traditional counseling. It also is helpful to counsel with families and mates, if possible.[15] These people can be very supportive to the victim, but relatives often have feelings of their own which need to be expressed, attitudes which need to be changed, and misconceptions which need to be corrected.

A second general response to rape has been termed the *compound reaction*. Victims with previous physical, psychiatric or social difficulties sometimes develop more intense symptoms such as depression, psychotic or suicidal behavior, psychosomatic disorders, drug use, excessive drinking or sexual "acting out" behavior. Such women often need referral for help that is more in-depth than crisis counseling.

A third response to rape is the *silent rape reaction*. These women, including some who were molested as children or adolescents, have not told anyone about the rape, have never talked about their feelings or reactions, and have carried a tremendous psychological burden. Later in life such women may develop anxiety, fear of men, avoidance of sexual behavior, unexplained fears of being alone or going outside, nightmares, and a loss of self-esteem. If these women are raped again, they often spend more counseling time talking about the pent-up emotions concerning the first rape than they do about the current situation.

Studies of rape victims report that most women are able to reorganize their lives and protect themselves from further assault.[16] Perhaps more than any other influence, the feminist movement has attacked the myths concerning rape and has helped victims get the medical treatment, psychological help and practical guidance they need after rape. Regretfully, some writers in this same movement are in danger of perpetuating the idea that the real cause of rape is the deliberate effort of men to subjugate women.[17] The victimization of women by rape or any other means is a gross deviation from God's intended plan, but there is no evidence to support the myth that rapists are really "front-line masculine shock troops, terrorist guerrillas in the longest sustained battle the world has ever known,"[18] the battle between men and women.

Rapists are rarely militants in the battle against women. Some are men who find themselves in a situation where rape would be convenient, so their action is a spur-of-the-moment decision. More often, rapists are young, married, employed people whose family life is disturbed, who can't relate successfully to women, and who deny that they are a menace to society.[19] In each case, rapists need more than supportive counseling. They need to know God's forgiveness, to experience the power of God to transform a life, and to participate in counseling designed to deal with those underlying issues that caused them to initiate the act of rape.

Counseling and Physical Abuse

Within recent years the media, governmental agencies, medical personnel and professional counselors have given increasing attention to the problem of child abuse. It is difficult to determine if actual child abuse is increasing or if we primarily are increasing our awareness of a longstanding problem. It *is* clear, however, that incredible numbers of children are being neglected, beaten physically, molested sexually and abused psychologically. While many cases of child abuse go unreported, others lead to hospitalization and so many deaths that child abuse has been called "the major killer of children in the United States . . . one of the primary destroyers of their emotional and physical well-being."[20]

There is no typical child abuser—the problem is too large and diverse for that—but studies have shown a cluster of characteristics often seen in the abusive parents, in the abusing circumstances and in the abused child.[21] *Abusive parents* frequently were themselves abused or neglected in childhood. Often there are unrealistic expectations for children, a dislike of or disappointment in the child who is abused, a strong parental belief in corporal punishment, and a frustration with the child, often accompanied by a feeling that one can't cope. Also seen at times are unhappy marriages, excessive use of drugs or alcohol, and isolation from family members or others who can help parents with the children. There is no evidence that child abuse is limited to specific socioeconomic or racial groups.

Child abuse almost always comes as the result of events or frustrations which we might term *abusing circumstances*. Excessive demands from children, perpetual crying, continuing sickness, or even the routine of dirty diapers and messy eating habits can put a strain on any parent. If the family is also characterized by financial pressure, cramped living quarters, job insecurity, isolation from relatives, marital tension, or similar stresses, the pressure of a demanding child can be overwhelming. In an attempt to "shut up the kid" or get a little privacy parents can increase the child's tension and this, in turn, accentuates the crying or other stressful behavior. Eventually it is easy to lose control. Probably all of us have overreacted to children, at times, and it may be true that given enough stress, any one of us could abuse a child.

As parents and circumstances vary, so do their *abused children*. Some have argued that abused children usually are unwanted, physically deformed, unattractive, or handicapped. While some abused children fit these categories, many do not. In time, however, abused children develop their own uniquenesses. While some are hyperactive and aggressive, a larger number are compliant, tense and withdrawn, almost all are distrustful, looking for love, and delayed in social, intellectual and sometimes physical development.

Counselors might look through their list of counselees or congregation members to spot families which could be under special stress.[22] Table 30–1 lists some other warning signs that could be considered. A thoughtful (not patronizing or accusing) offer to give practical assistance especially in handling the children can often relieve some of the stress and help prevent child abuse. Lay assistance and listening are especially helpful, but it should be realized that prevention is rarely that simple. Parents may need long-term counseling, encouragement, education concerning child-rearing, and support from a community of Christian believers. It should never be assumed that child abuse is limited to nonbelievers or a taboo subject for Christians.

When child abuse is detected, medical treatment for the child is of prime importance, sometimes followed by foster care. The counselor must recognize that legal implications sometimes determine who will help the child psychologically and where. Traditional forms of child treatment including

Table 30-1

Checklist of Conditions Leading to Child Abuse *

1. As a child was the parent repeatedly beaten or deprived?
2. Does the parent have a record of mental illness or criminal activities?
3. Is the parent suspected of physical abuse in the past?
4. Is the parent suffering lost self-esteem, social isolation, or depression?
5. Has the parent experienced multiple stresses, such as marital discord, divorce, debt, frequent moves, significant losses?
6. Does the parent have violent outbursts of temper?
7. Does the parent have rigid, unrealistic expectations of the child's behavior?
8. Does the parent punish the child harshly?
9. Does the parent see the child as difficult and provocative (whether or not the child is)?
10. Does the parent reject the child or have difficulty forming a bond with the child?
11. Are there currently excessive stresses in the family or parent's life?

*From Ruth S. Kempe and C. Henry Kempe, *Child Abuse* (Cambridge, MA: Harvard University Press, 1978), p. 67.

play therapy may be used. Almost always the children will need love, firm guidance, and a sense of security.

Parents can be helped in two ways: by giving them immediate help and by providing them with long-range counseling. Immediate help may include caring for the child temporarily and helping the parent cope with immediate crises. This can relieve the immediate pressure. Long-range help may be resisted (especially when it is ordered by the courts), but the goal is to help parents overcome the effects of their own depressing or abusive past histories, develop self-control, learn about normal child behavior, and acquire coping techniques so that they can love and care for the children, accept themselves as God accepts them, and learn how to deal with stresses in themselves and in their children. Like the children, these parents often have a great need for love, acceptance and approval. They need concrete, attainable goals and a counselor's guidance in dealing with specifics in their past and present lives.

Space does not permit more than brief mention of another abuse problem which may be increasing: the abuse of mates. It is well known that many murders occur in the home, and wives especially are victims of beatings, rejection, sexual abuse and emotional trauma.

For several reasons, wives often do not report, resist, or flee from such aggressive encounters in the home. Some have negative self-concepts and unconsciously may feel that they somehow deserve the abuse. Others are convinced that their husbands (or aggressive children) will reform, that they could not survive economically if they left, that divorce is wrong, or that they could not get along in a hostile world. Some sincere Christian women have been led to believe that beatings are to be endured as the duty of submissive wives.[23]

Many counselors can offer practical help, guidance and acceptance for such victims. Within recent years, some communities and churches have been working to provide safe and quiet places (including private homes) where "battered wives" and their children can go in times of crisis for safety, rest and counsel concerning their options. Ideally the mate-abuser, like the childabuser, should also be counseled. Such counseling may be resisted, although pastors and other Christian leaders, unlike professional counselors, sometimes are able to enter homes and engage in helping conversations which can lead to more in-depth counseling.

Counseling and the Handicapped

The term *disability* refers to a mental, physical or emotional condition (defect or impairment) which often hinders the person's ability to function normally. People whose disabilities interfere with optimal life adjustment are usually described as handicapped persons. These people may have handicaps ranging from minor issues which are almost unnoticed to disabilities which are severely inhibiting. The handicaps may be physical, mental or both. They may result from a congenital impairment or birth defect, from injury in childhood, or from loss of some capacity in later life.

It is rare to find completely handicapped people. While there are things which the handicapped person *cannot* do, there also are many things that he or she *can* do. Medical treatment is designed to assist the disabled person as much as possible in the physical area, and the rehabilitation task is to help the individual live with the disability and reach maximum effectiveness.

This rehabilitative task is not easy. Physical therapy, special education and occupational therapy may all be involved. The counselor may be helpful in assisting handicapped persons to face the handicap realistically, to overcome the social rejection which is common, and to deal with issues such as guilt, frustration, anger, insecurity, anxiety and a low self-concept.

> The optimal therapeutic objective may be to help such a person to appraise his disability realistically so that he will not exaggerate its negative consequences and see rejection where none exists, deny its existence and attempt tasks only achievable by a whole man, or engage in any other defense which is inappropriate and ineffective. Somehow the patient must be induced to accept his disability, to live with it, but of course not in the sense of using it to give up the struggle to live as fully and normally as possible.[24]

Counseling with the physically and mentally handicapped involves more than the traditional one-to-one interaction. It involves cooperative work with physical therapists, educators, physicians and other specialists. It involves cooperation with friends and family members. Sometimes it also involves family counseling.

It is extremely traumatic for parents to discover that their child is disabled or impaired. Parental guilt, rejection of the handicapped person, overprotection, and a number of other family reactions may appear and complicate the handicapped person's adjustment.

Jesus was much concerned about handicapped people—the lame, blind, deaf, epileptic and deformed. He accepted them completely and met their needs. The Christian counselor must do likewise. Counseling the handicapped may require creative approaches, forsaking some favorite techniques, and contact with a network of helpers. This can be very rewarding work, however, especially if one sees the disabled person growing in skills, psychological stability and spiritual maturity, insofar as the person's mental or physical capacities permit.

Counseling and the Question of "Why?"

When stress and problems arise, at some time people are likely to ask "Why?" "Why did this happen to me?" "Why did it happen now?" "Why did it not happen as I had expected?"

Christian laymen and theologians have struggled with these questions for centuries and the answers are, at best, incomplete.[25] We suffer, first, because we are part of a fallen human race. Pain comes when we are careless, exposed to disease, or lacking exercise and a proper diet. Secondly, suffering comes to help us grow and mature. For Christians, problems refine our faith, make us more Christlike, teach us about God, and produce perseverance and character.[26] Third, suffering enables us to understand and care more effectively for others.[27]

Does suffering also result from sin? All suffering ultimately results from mankind's fall into sin, and it is probable that some of our present problems come because of the sufferer's specific sin. It must be emphasized, however, that the Bible explicitly refutes the idea that specific sin automatically brings suffering.[28] People in need frequently conclude that "God must be punishing me," but such a conclusion is, at best, built on shaky theological evidence.

Apparently we cannot know for certain why people suffer. What we do know, however, is that God is compassionate, all-wise, all-knowing, and ever present. It is not wrong to struggle with the "why" questions of life; Christian counselors will be involved often in helping counselees with this struggle. But the ultimate answer is not likely to be found in intellectual debate. It comes from a willingness of counselee and counselor alike to acknowledge the certain truth that the sovereign, compassionate

God is aware of our problems and in control. He knows "why," and that is all that really matters.

Suggestions for Further Reading

Bassett, William T. *Counseling the Childless Couple.* Philadelphia: Fortress, 1965.

Kalmar, Roberta, ed. *Abortion: The Emotional Implications.* Dubuque, IA. Kendall/Hunt, 1977.

———— *Child Abuse: Perspectives on Diagnosis, Treatment and Prevention.* Dubuque, IA: Kendall/Hunt, 1977.

Kempe, Ruth S. and Kempe, C. Henry. *Child Abuse.* Cambridge, MA: Harvard University Press, 1978.

Koop, C. Everett. *The Right to Live; The Right to Die.* Wheaton, IL: Tyndale, 1976.

Nass, Deanna R. *The Rape Victim.* Dubuque, IA: Kendall/Hunt, 1977.

* Schaeffer, Edith. *Affliction.* Old Tappan, NJ: Revell, 1978.

Terkelsen, Helen E. *Counseling the Unwed Mother.* Philadelphia: Fortress, 1964.

* Yancey, Philip. *Where Is God When It Hurts?* Grand Rapids: Zondervan, 1977.

Footnotes

1. 1 Sam. 1:1–18.

2. Merrill Rogers Skrocki, "Infertility: The Loneliest Problem," *McCall's* 105 (August, 1978): 68–69

3. Ibid.

4. For information on infertility and referral information, contact RESOLVE, P.O. Box 474, Belmont, MA 02178, or The Fertility Institute, 42 E. 65th Street, New York, NY 10021. The family physician should be the first person consulted.

5. William T. Bassett, *Counseling the Childless Couple* (Philadelphia: Fortress, 1963), pp. 118, 119.

6. Helen E. Terkelsen, *Counseling the Unwed Mother* (Philadelphia: Fortress, 1967).

7. Roe et al. v. Wade, 93S Ct.705 (1973), p. 730. Quoted in Bill Horlacher, "Abortion: What Does the Bible Say?" *Worldwide Challenge* 5 (July 1978): 5–9.

8. Gen. 9:2–6; Pss. 51:5; 139:13–16; Jer. 1:4, 5; Luke 1:39–44.

9. See Cornelia Morrison Friedman, "Counseling for Abortion," and John D. Asher, "Abortion Counseling," both in *Abortion: The Emotional Implications,* ed. Roberta Kalmar (Dubuque, IA: Kendall/Hunt, 1977).

10. In a pamphlet written by Harold O. J. Brown, titled *Abortion on Demand?* and published by Christian Action Council (788 National Press Building, Washington, DC 20045), the abortion procedures are described as follows:

> Abortions fall into early, mid and late-term abortions. Early abortions, during the first three months of pregnancy, are performed by entering the uterus through the cervix, or mouth of the womb, with a sharp instrument or vacuum tube and scraping or sucking the developing fetus out. The fetus in such abortions is very small, but sufficiently well-developed so that the abortionist or his nurse must identify and count the individual members—head, arms, legs, torso—to make sure that nothing is left in the womb to cause complications.
>
> Mid-term (three to six months) abortions are usually performed by "salting out," i.e. removing some of the amniotic fluid surrounding the fetus and replacing it with salt water or another lethal solution. The fetus inhales and absorbs the poisonous fluid, dies, and is expelled as in an accidental miscarriage

Some fetuses have survived such abortions and emerged alive, but this is very rare.

Late abortions are performed by hysterotomy, which involves opening the womb surgically and removing the fetus, as in a Caesarean delivery, with the difference that instead of being cared for, the delivered fetus is either killed or allowed to die.

11. Marjory Mecklenberg and Judith Fink, "Developing Alternatives to Abortion," in *Facing the Future: The Church and Family Together,* ed. Gary R. Collins (Waco, TX: Word, 1976), pp. 123–36.

12. Norman R. Bernstein and Caroline B. Tinkham, "Group Therapy Following Abortion," in Kalmar, *Abortion,* pp. 108–23.

13. This definition and many of the concepts in this chapter are adapted from an unpublished paper by Mary Harvey, "Counseling the Rape Victim" (Trinity Evangelical Divinity School, 1978).

14. A. W. Burgess and L. L. Holmstrom, "Rape Trauma Syndrome," *American Journal of Psychiatry* 131 (September, 1974): 981–86. The paper is reprinted in *The Rape Victim,* ed. Deanna R. Nass (Dubuque, IA: Kendall/Hunt, 1977).

15. Daniel C. Silverman, "Sharing the Crisis of Rape: Counseling the Mates and Families of Victims," *American Journal of Orthopsychiatry* 48 (January, 1978): 166–73.

16. Burgess and Holmstrom, "Rape Trauma."

17. See for example, N. Connell and C. Wilson, eds., *Rape: The First Sourcebook for Women* (New York: Plume, 1974); and Susan Brownmiller, *Against Our Will* (New York: Simon & Schuster, 1975).

18. Brownmiller, *Against Our Will,* p. 209.

19. James Selkin, "Rape," *Psychology Today* 8 (January, 1975): 71–76.

20. Roberta Kalmar, ed., *Child Abuse: Perspectives on Diagnosis, Treatment and Prevention* (Dubuque, IA: Kendall/Hunt, 1977), p. iii.

21. These paragraphs are adapted from Kalmar, *Child Abuse;* and Ruth S. Kempe and C. Henry Kempe, *Child Abuse* (Cambridge, MA: Harvard University Press, 1978).

22. Carolyn Nystrom, "When Child Abuse Hits Home," *Moody Monthly* 73 (November, 1978): 54–60.

23. Joseph N. Bell, "Rescuing the Battered Wife," *Human Behavior* 6 (July, 1977): 16–23.

24. Walter S. Neff and Samuel A. Weiss, "Psychological Aspects of Disability," in *Handbook of Clinical Psychology,* ed. Benjamin B. Wolberg (New York: McGraw-Hill, 1965), p. 790.

25. The discussion in this section is adapted from Gary R. Collins, *The Joy of Caring* (in press).

26. 2 Cor. 12:7–10; 1 Pet. 1:5–7; Rom. 8:28; Heb. 12:11; Ps. 119:71; Rom. 5:3–5.

27. 2 Cor. 1:3–7.

28. John 9:1–41; Luke 13:1–5.

31

Families, Communities and Counseling

WITHIN RECENT YEARS, ONE OF THE MOST EXCITING AND POTEN-
tially revolutionary developments in the counseling field has been the
rediscovery of nonprofessionals. Of course, relatives, friends, classmates,
neighbors, fellow workers and church members have been offering their
own brand of counseling for centuries. With the rise of psychiatry, psychology, social work and related professional disciplines, however, the un-
trained lay person felt or was made to feel that he or she had nothing to
offer people in need. After a shaky start, pastoral counseling began to develop as a discipline and school counselors were not far behind in joining
the counselor ranks, but the lay person still felt unqualified to counsel.

Then, in 1960, the government-sponsored Joint Commission on Mental Illness and Health made what was then a startling observation and
proposal.

> A host of persons untrained or partially trained in mental health principles
> and practices—clergymen, family physicians, teachers, probation offi-
> cers, public health nurses, sheriffs, judges, public welfare workers, scout-
> masters, county farm agents, and others—are already trying to help and
> to treat the mentally ill in the absence of professional resources. With a
> moderate amount of training through short courses and consultation on
> the job, such persons can be fully equipped with an additional skill as
> mental health counselors.[1]

This proposal to train mental health counselors was not met with great
enthusiasm by professionals. Concerned about quackery, psychological
naïveté, harmful or blundering attempts at counseling or simplistic approaches to complex psychological problems, professionals hurried to
"protect the public" (and their professions) by pushing for legislation
which would limit counseling to those who were professionally trained and
legally licensed. Nevertheless, at the same time, many of these professionals began to teach counseling skills and to encourage lay helping in
accordance with the Joint Commission Report.

461

In the future, it is probable that professional counseling, including Christian counseling, will continue to grow as a field, and the requirements for licensing and certification will grow more stringent. As the world becomes more sophisticated psychologically and people become more open about their problems, however, the needs and demands for counseling will continue to be greater than the availability of professionals, especially Christian professionals. Friends, relatives and church members will continue to counsel one another—often with the blessing of overburdened professionals. After all, friends are more available, understanding, not bound by appointment hours, less threatening—and their services are free. In addition, it appears that for many problems, especially crises and the more transient problems of life, lay helpers are as good, if not better, than the professionals.[2]

Lay helpers can also do some things that professionals cannot do. Friends can give guidance, practical assistance, assurance of prayer and continued support to people with problems and to their families. People who are in counseling with professionals often find that friends and relatives give important encouragement between counseling sessions. And if the person in need refuses to get help, the trained counselor can often teach the family and friends how they, in turn, can help a friend.

In this chapter, we want to focus on these families, neighbors, and other support groups who can supplement Christian counseling and thus engage in the long-existing but recently revived art of nonprofessional people-helping.

Support Groups and Counseling

At several places in the preceding pages, we have mentioned the value of friends, family, church members and others who can give emotional support and practical help including guidance, more objective observations, friendship, sympathy, challenge, "feedback," and tangible assistance (such as money or food) to help one another in times of need. Professionals refer to this network of friends as a *support system*.[3] Most of us get help from the system of people who back us up, and most of us are part of several systems which support others. These support systems show us that others care, and there is evidence that people who have well-developed support systems have less mental or physical illness and are better able to cope with stress.[4]

Support systems can include individuals who give one-to-one help to a friend, natural groups such as families or classmates, religious groups such as participants in a Bible study or the members of a local church, and "mutual self-help groups,"[5] such as the people in Alcoholics Anonymous, encounter groups, Weight Watchers, Recovery, Inc., and others. In addition to giving care and guidance, these groups provide acceptance, training in social and coping skills, encouragement during behavior change, help with will power or self-control, and (for many people) a feeling of significance. If the members of a support system organize formally, they can have great political influence in a community. Sometimes they challenge or criticize professionals, but more often they supplement the counselor's work.

Active participation in a support group can even help those with problems. This has been called the "helper-therapy principle," [6] which, in its simplest form, states that those who help are helped the most. This has led some counselors to encourage their counselees to get involved in helping others. It is well known that "the best way to learn is to teach." It appears that one of the best ways to get help is to help others.

In helping others, many people "do what comes naturally"—giving the best advice and guidance that they can give. Regretfully, this type of amateur help can be ineffective, unhelpful and sometimes harmful. With a minimum of training, however, lay people can learn basic helping skills which can increase their effectiveness significantly. Of course, this training does not turn nonprofessionals into professional counselors, but the training can greatly enhance the ability of support group members to help one another. "Doing what comes naturally" is replaced by the ability to be a capable people-helper.

As the counseling profession develops and changes, a new role for counselors is emerging: the training of nonprofessional lay helpers. Lay persons in the church are prime candidates for this training, and to this end several programs have been developed.[7] A discussion of these training programs is beyond the scope of this book, but an awareness of their existence and potential is important for any Christian counselor. When people are trained to help their friends, problems can be prevented, solutions can be found sooner, and the counselor's work can be more effective because the counselee is "backed up" by an effective support system which includes lay helpers.

The Family and Counseling

There are two major ways by which the family can be involved in counseling. The family can be a support system in which the members *give* help and guidance to one another, and the family as a unit can *receive* counseling help and treatment.

1. *The Family As a Support System.* Although many families are scattered geographically or split by disagreements and tension, the "extended" family (which includes the grandparents, aunts, uncles and cousins) nevertheless provides help in a variety of ways. According to Caplan,[8] the family

—collects and disseminates information about the world;

—provides a place where individuals can get feedback about their behavior;

—gives guidance in solving problems;
—provides information about the sources of outside help;
—mediates disputes;
—gives practical assistance when needs arise;
—provides a haven for rest and recuperation;
—controls behavior which gets "out of line";
—gives people an identity;
—helps individuals master emotions such as anxiety, depression, guilt or feelings of hopelessness; and
—gives support during crises and through the much longer periods involved in adjusting to loss and deprivation.

The family is also the major source of the beliefs, values and ethical standards that individuals develop. In this respect, families and churches work together as a support system. Caplan's description of this is technical in language but significant for Christian counselors:

> The family group is a major source of the belief systems, value systems, and codes of behavior that determine an individual's understanding of the nature and meaning of the universe. . . . These systems of belief and values provide the individual with a map of his universe, and with a set of goals and missions, as well as a compass in finding his way. . . .
>
> [There is] a reciprocal reinforcement of family units and religious denominations. Most denominations recruit their members from family units. Religious rituals focus on developmental incidents and transitions of family life. . . . Religious denominations deal with the entire family as a unit throughout its developmental history. Conversely, families inculcate and foster among their members the value and belief systems and code of ethics of their religious denominations and strive to recruit the marital partners of their children to the same beliefs, as well as to ensure that grandchildren follow a similar path. . . .
>
> Years of crisis research have given me many illustrations of the advantage of individuals who conform to family and religious traditions over the nonconformists, the rebels, and the irreligious. . . .[9]

The family and church together can help people meet crises and cope with the realities of life. Christian counselors who work with individuals should not overlook the helping, supportive roles of families and their churches. As support systems and adjuncts to Christian counseling, the family and the church are without parallel in the society.

2. *The Family As a Therapy System.* There are many times, however, when the family is part (sometimes a major part) of the counselee's problem. Even when family members sincerely want to help the counselee, they sometimes interfere with the counseling and create continuing stress for the counselee. For this reason many counselors work with whole families as well as with the counselee.

Several years ago a number of counselors began to conclude that an individual's problems *never* exist in isolation. As we have seen, the family does much to shape human behavior, provide values and beliefs, and teach people how to deal with crises. If an individual family member is having problems, this may indicate as much or more about the counselee's family attitudes and communication as it does about the counselee. The person who comes for counseling, then, may be a "symptom-bearer" whose highly visible problems really signal that something is amiss in the family. Treating the counselee will not help much if he or she continues to live in an unhealthy family. Indeed, if the counselee starts to change behavior and improve, this could create confusion and even chaos with a family's values and ways of operating. This family confusion in turn can create more problems for the counselee.

Consider, for example, a three-person family with an alcoholic father. As long as the father is drinking, the mother and child may have a clear purpose—to protect themselves and to work at changing the alcoholic's drinking behavior. Now let us assume that the alcoholic goes for treatment, stops drinking, and determines to assume his role as head of the family. Suddenly the child, but especially the mother, may have no purpose for living. As a result she may get depressed, so the father and child team up to care for the mother. In one actual family (and probably many others) a seesaw arrangement has continued for years. If the husband is drinking, the wife is complaining but otherwise fine. If he stops drinking, she gets depressed and so hard to live with that he starts drinking again. When this happens, she gets better—and so the cycle continues.

Clearly this entire family needs help and that is the goal of the *systems approach* to counseling. While the original counselee may be seen alone, the family members also come together for counseling as a unit. The counselor watches the family interact, mediates their disputes, and teaches them more effective ways to communicate and relate to one another. The family members learn how to listen, to express themselves—including the expression of their feelings—to be flexible, to understand one another, to deal more effectively with conflict, and to develop a greater sense of mutual awareness and support.[10]

Family therapy is a growing and progressively complex field. It is a specialty which Christian counselors are only beginning to enter and influence, but it holds great potential for Christian counseling in the future.

The Community and Counseling

Although everyone is a member of some family, almost all of us also belong to a community. We are involved in neighborhoods, recreational groups, schools, places of employment, and churches. Neighbors, friends, local merchants, government leaders, schoolteachers, law enforcement officers, church leaders and a host of other people interact with us to both create tension and give support.

Within recent years a new approach has appeared known as *community counseling*. Just as family counselors believe that it is ineffective to help a counselee apart from the family, so community counselors assume that one cannot really help people without dealing with the community at the same time. The community counselor and counselee participate in a mutual exploration which asks:

1. To what extent is the individual capable of resolving the issue through personal change?
2. What resources in the environment are available to help the individual grow?
3. To what extent does the solution really rest in the environment instead of the individual?
4. How can the counselor and/or the counselee act to bring about the necessary changes in the environment? [11]

In addition to personal counseling, community counselors are involved in activities such as providing educational programs; giving training in self-help skills; assisting governments and social service agencies in planning social programs; identifying community support groups; working to establish telephone hot lines, rehabilitation centers and other community resources, and at times partcipating in political movements in an effort to improve the community.

Community counselors recognize that they are not alone in trying to improve the community. For this reason they work with a variety of professional, political and other resource people to bring about change. By improving the community it is assumed that community residents will be enabled to better cope with life and its problems.

It takes only a casual look at the literature to discover that the field of community counseling says very little about the church. If we consider the helping ministry of Jesus, however, we might conclude that he was a community counselor. He tenderly and sensitively helped individuals with their doubts and struggles, but he also spoke out against hypocrisy and poverty. He drove the moneychangers out of the temple, criticized the government, and spoke of a day when his kingdom would come and eliminate injustice.

In view of the recent trends in community counseling, it is exciting to ponder how Christian counseling might change in the future. Christians live in communities too, and believers—including counselors—must have an active concern about hunger, poverty, injustice, crime and the other social ills which give rise to many of the issues discussed in previous chapters. The church, as a community within a community, must ask how it can have an impact both on the unchurched and on church members. Following his oft-quoted instruction that we should "bear one another's burdens," Paul wrote:

> Let us not lose heart in doing good, for in due time we shall reap if we do not grow weary. So then, while we have opportunity, let us do good to all men, and especially to those who are of the household of the faith.[12]

Christian community counseling is a virgin territory, clearly consistent with the teachings of the Bible.

The Environment and Counseling

Several times in this book we have mentioned the effect of environment on counselees and their counselors. Four of these environmental influences are of special importance.

1. *Weather.* A large amount of research has attempted to study the influence of weather on human behavior.[13] Everyone knows that people feel sluggish and tired when the heat and humidity are high. It has also been shown that weather can influence suicide and accident rates, crime, academic performance, productivity, degree of participation in social activities, mood, subjective feelings, and attitudes. When weather conditions are extreme—as in heat waves, intense blizzards or storms—an additional stress is applied to everyone. People who are under stress already may see these weather pressures as "the last straw" which then produces dramatic change in behavior. Following a recent snowstorm in Chicago, for example, travel was restricted, people were forced to stay home, frustration and domestic quarrels increased, and the number of family murders rose sharply.

2. *Noise.* In urban areas especially, people constantly are bombarded by noise from traffic, aircraft, radios, typewriters, construction, barking dogs, people talking, telephones, and other sources of "noise pollution." While some sounds (such as desired music) can be soothing and relaxing, other noises can increase tension and irritability, prevent sleep, interfere with job performance and even lead to a reduction in sex drive or a loss of appetite.[14] People who live in noisy environments often find the perpetual sound to be annoying, and this can be stress-producing.

3. *Crowding.* Most people enjoy having a little, but not too much distance between themselves and other human beings. We like a little stimulation from others but too much or too little can be harmful to our well-being. We like to be near people, but we don't like to be crowded. At times we each need a quiet place, where we can withdraw for a time of solitude. When such withdrawal is impossible (as often is the case in crowded cities, campus dormitories, ships at sea or some mission compound situations) tensions build, tempers often flare, and people can feel trapped.[15]

4. *Architecture.* Architects and interior decorators have long recognized that room shape, colors, type and arrangement of furniture, decorations (such as pictures or books), temperature and lighting can all affect

people psychologically. These architectural and design effects have a subtle bearing on work productivity, interpersonal relations, attitudes, emotions and the extent to which people feel comfortable and relaxed.

These environmental factors influence counseling in two important ways. First, they can create stress and complicate counseling. In the midst of his busy life, Jesus moved away from the noise, crowds, and other environmental pressures to get alone with his Father. Counselees and counselors at times need to do the same.[16] The sensitive counselor keeps alert to environmental stresses which may intensify both the counselor's and the counselee's pressures and thus hinder counseling effectiveness.

This brings us to a second influence of the environment on counseling. The place where we do our counseling can be important. It is not necessary or always desirable to counsel in a formal office. When one does use an office, however, recognize that comfortable chairs, pleasant surroundings, neatness, warm colors (like yellow, brown, red or even blue—never white), soft floor coverings, comfortable temperatures, soothing music (or silence) can all reduce tension—providing the counselee feels comfortable in this kind of environment.[17] If you are counseling in a restaurant or public place, be alert to the potentially adverse influences of background music, commotion, architectural design and other environmental influences.

Groups and Counseling

The major emphasis of this book has concerned the counseling of individuals on a one-to-one basis. It is well known, however, that much counseling also occurs in groups. Led by a trained counselor, the group participants come together to share their problems and help one another. Within the group there is acceptance, freedom to share, and a sense of solidarity. Group members feel a closeness with others, especially when there is no nearby family or other support system.

The early church probably consisted of small groups of believers, meeting together for the teaching, fellowship, breaking of bread and prayer mentioned in Acts 2:42. Undoubtedly there was mutual support, encouragement, sharing and burden-bearing. It could be argued, therefore, that small group counseling is at least as old as the early church.

Today, in more modern times, there is a revival of interest in the formation of both groups in the church and small counseling groups. Literally thousands of techniques have been developed to facilitate group discussion and interaction. A consideration of these techniques is beyond the scope of this book, but Christian counselors should be aware of the unique benefits of small group counseling, of the technical expertise required for effective group leadership, and of the current upsurge of interest in group counseling as a way to help people in need. Christian counselors who want to start group counseling should seek further information about group techniques,[18] and attempt to get training in the process of group therapy.

The Church and Counseling

A Christian psychologist named Lawrence Crabb has suggested that psychological problems arise from inaccurate thoughts or ideas about life, ineffective patterns of behavior and a lack of involvement with other people. Effective biblical counseling involves enlightenment (to help people think right), exhortation (to help people "do right"), and encouragement from a caring community (to help people "live right").[19]

Crabb believes that the local church should provide all three of these elements. *Encouragement* should be the responsibility of every church member. People with training in basic helping skills can, in addition, counsel with *exhortation* (helping people "solve all conflicts in a manner consistent with scripture"). Then, especially sensitive, gifted Christian people should be given intensive training which enables them to do "*enlightenment* counseling." These people would "need to understand psychological functioning in some depth; how childhood experiences channel our thinking in wrong directions, where feelings come from, what controls behavior, how to unravel the tightly woven knots of foolish thinking, how to figure out the real causes behind surface problems, and so on."[20]

Crabb's creative ideas have stimulated the thinking of many Christian leaders. While some have called them simplistic, and others have argued that they too quickly sweep aside the special expertise and positive influence of professional counselors, the encouragement-exhortation-enlightenment model deserves further study and testing nevertheless. This view points Christian counseling away from the exclusive domain and secluded office of the professional, and back where it belongs—in the context of the church.

This was where we began this book, discussing the church and counseling. There continues to be a need for professionally trained Christian counselors, but we also need effective Christian lay people who know the joy of caring. Psychological theories and techniques will continue to be used to help people in need, but the Scriptures alone must be absolutely authoritative and the ultimate standard against which all counseling methods are tested. Bearing burdens and individually counseling people who have problems will surely continue to be an important task for many Christians, but especially in our public meetings we must also emphasize the prevention of problems and the elimination of environmental circumstances which create human misery.

The first sentence of chapter 1 described a pastor who argued that counseling is a waste of time. For some, this always will be true. But for those who seek to be led by the Holy Spirit, enlightened by the Word of God and acquainted with the insights of modern psychology, Christian counseling can be one of the most fulfilling tasks to which any believer may be called.

Suggestions for Further Reading

* Collins, Gary R. *How to Be a People Helper.* Santa Ana: Vision House, 1976.
Drakeford, John W. *People-to-People Therapy.* New York: Harper & Row, 1978.
Ferber, Andrew; Mendelsohn, Marilyn; and Napier, Augustus. *The Book of Family Therapy.* New York: Aronson, 1972.
Gartner, Alan, and Riessman, Frank. *Self-Help in the Human Services.* San Francisco: Jossey-Bass, 1977.
Haley, Jay, ed. *Changing Families: A Family Therapy Reader.* New York: Grune & Stratton, 1971.
Lewis, Judith A., and Lewis, Michael D. *Community Counseling: A Human Services Approach.* New York: Wiley, 1977.
Reid, Clyde. *Groups Alive—Church Alive.* New York: Harper & Row, 1969.
* Welter, Paul. *Family Problems and Predicaments: How to Respond.* Wheaton, IL: Tyndale, 1977.
* ————. *How to Help a Friend.* Wheaton, IL: Tyndale, 1978.

Footnotes

1. Joint Commission on Mental Illness and Health, *Action for Mental Health* (New York: Science Editions, 1961), p. xii.

2. See for example, Robert R. Carkhuff and Charles B. Traux, "Lay mental health counseling: the effects of lay group counseling," *Journal of Consulting Psychology* 29 (1965): 426–31; and R. R. Carkhuff, "Differential Functioning of Lay and Professional Helpers," *Journal of Counseling Psychology* 15 (1968): 117–28.

3. For more information on support systems see Gerald Caplan, *Support Systems and Community Mental Health* (New York: Behavioral Publications, 1974); and Gerald Caplan and Marie Killilea, *Support Systems and Mutual Help: Multidisciplinary Explorations* (New York: Grune & Stratton, 1976). Used by permission.

4. J. C. Cassel, "Psychiatric Epidemiology," in *American Handbook of Psychiatry,* ed. Gerald Caplan (New York: Basic Books, 1974). 2:401–11.

5. For an evaluation of self-help groups see Caplan, *Support Systems and Community Mental Health;* John W. Drakeford, *People-to-People Therapy* (Waco, TX: Word, 1978); Alan Gartner and Frank Riessman, *Self-Help in the Human Sciences* (San Francisco: Jossey-Bass, 1977); and A. H. Katz and E. I. Bender, eds., *The Strength in Us: Self-Help Groups in the Modern World* (New York: New Viewpoints, 1976).

6. Frank Riessman, "The 'Helper-Therapy' Principle," *Social Work* 10 (1965): 27–32.

7. To stimulate interest in helping it is suggested that lay persons read *The Joy of Caring,* by Gary R. Collins. For a book on lay helping see Paul Welter, *How to Help a Friend* (Wheaton, IL: Tyndale, 1978). Among the many training programs for Christian lay counselors is Gary R. Collins, *How to Be a People Helper* (with the accompanying *People Helper Growthbook* and training tapes) (Santa Ana: Vision House, 1976). See also H. Norman Wright, *Training Christians to Counsel. A Resource and Training Manual* (Denver: Christian Marriage Enrichment [8000 E. Girard], 1977).

8. Caplan and Killilea, *Support Systems and Mutual Help.* Used by permission.

9. Ibid., pp. 23, 24.

10. For an elaboration of this approach see Virginia Sater, *Conjoint Family Therapy* (Palo Alto, CA: Science and Behavior Books, 1964).

11. Judith A. Lewis and Michael D. Lewis, *Community Counseling: A Human Services Approach* (New York: Wiley, 1977).

12. Gal. 6:9, 10.

13. Rudolph H. Moos, *The Human Context: Environmental Determinants of Behavior* (New York: Wiley, 1976).

14. Ibid.

15. Ray Mulry, *Tension Management and Relaxation* (Glendale, CA: Mulry, 1976).

16. Mark 1:32–35.

17. Greg Hullinger, "How to Decorate a Pastor's Office," *Christianity Today*, 16 February 1979, pp. 32, 33.

18. Among the many available books, see part two of Wayne W. Dyer and John Vriend, *Counseling Techniques That Work* (Washington: APGA Press [1607 New Hampshire Ave., N.W.], 1975); Robert C. Leslie, *Sharing Groups in the Church* (Nashville: Abingdon, 1970); Harold D. Minor, ed., *Techniques and Resources for Guiding Adult Groups* (Nashville: Abingdon, 1972); and Clyde Reid, *Groups Alive—Church Alive* (New York: Harper & Row, 1969).

19. Lawrence J. Crabb, Jr., "Moving the Couch into the Church," *Christianity Today* 22 September 1978, p. 18.

20. Ibid., p. 19.

Index

abilities 236, 239, 240, 242, 258, 267, 349, 350
abortion 44, 291, 432, 449, 450–452, 459–460
—counseling and 450–452
acceptance 29, 75, 81, 82, 124, 135, 184, 222, 231, 259, 262, 308, 322, 324, 325, 352, 403, 438, 449, 453, 456, 462
accident(s) 100, 207, 214, 416, 467
"accident proneness" 90, 107, 123, 192
action 52–53, 68, 69
activities 275
Adams, Jay 18, 30, 102, 285
addiction 376–395
—Bible and 377–379
—causes of 379–384
—counseling and 385–391
—effects of 384–385
—preventing 391–392
Adler, Alfred 347
adolescence 220–234, 235, 250, 252, 253, 254, 286, 287, 381, 383, 416, 454
—Bible and 223
—causes of problems in 223–226
—counseling and 228–231
—effects of problems in 226–228
—preventing problems of 231–233
adoption 448, 449, 452
adultery 124, 126, 188, 189, 282, 283, 286, 287, 289, 292, 301, 433
advice 27, 28, 70
aggression 100, 107, 209, 348
alcohol, alcoholism 66, 77, 90, 100, 191, 222, 227, 304, 323, 376–395, 455, 465
Alcoholics Anonymous 54, 97, 382, 389, 462
alienation 78
Allport, Gordon 25
American Personnel and Guidance Association 43
American Psychological Association 22, 25, 43, 55, 65, 223
anger 28, 31, 40, 48, 49, 70, 76, 88, 89, 91, 92, 96, 100–115, 123, 136, 137, 150, 170, 187, 190, 192, 195, 196, 206, 208, 228, 247, 255, 257, 258, 287, 289, 290, 291, 295, 300, 305, 306, 308, 316, 322, 333, 334, 337, 361, 396, 400, 403, 405, 406, 407, 409, 414, 418, 420, 423, 434, 436, 437, 447, 448, 449, 451, 453, 457

—Bible and 100–104
—causes of 104–105
—counseling and 108–111
—effects of 105–108
—preventing 111–113
anxiety 37, 40, 43, 48, 50, 51, 59–71, 72, 74, 84, 91, 106, 117, 122, 163, 170, 192, 195, 206, 207, 209, 215, 216, 221, 222, 223, 224, 226, 228, 229, 247, 260, 267, 281, 288, 289, 290, 292, 296, 304, 305, 308, 326, 336, 361, 367, 380, 381, 382, 388, 400, 401, 403, 404, 408, 409, 411, 436, 449, 451, 453, 454, 457, 464
—Bible and 60–61
—causes of 61–65
—counseling and 66–69
—effects of 65–66
—preventing 69–70
—types of
—acute 59
—chronic 59
—free-floating 59, 64
—high 60
—moderate 60
—moral 61
—neurotic 60, 61
—normal 59
—realistic 61
apathy 84, 268
appointments 38
apprehension 70
aptitudes 239, 240, 243
architecture 467–468
atonement 125
attending 26
attitude 29, 42, 78, 93, 162, 163, 172, 176, 190, 193, 258, 269, 273, 274, 275, 290, 291, 307, 323, 334, 335, 338, 347, 361, 403, 408, 413, 423, 433, 452, 465, 467
Augsburger, David 339
Augustine 77
autism 210, 214
avoidance 181

Barrett, Roger 89
Barth, Karl 282
"battered wives" 457, also see mate beating
bed-wetting 209, 214
Beck, Aaron 87
behavior therapy 388
beliefs 65, 162, 176, 220, 226, 251, 306, 399, 414, 415, 464
bereavement, see grief
"bibliotherapy" 33
birth control 232, 286

bitterness 66, 100, 102, 103, 107, 112, 126, 134, 136, 137, 170, 192, 205, 257, 333, 337, 344, 396, 406, 423, 433, 434, 441
Boice, James Montgomery 101
boredom 174, 191, 250, 254, 257, 260, 303, 381, 405, 437
brain damage 210
Browning, Robert 264
burden-bearing 18, 24

Caplan, G. 463, 464
caring 15, 24, 34, 37, 97, 156, 160, 197, 199, 228, 356, 397, 404, 425, 441, 452, 453, 456, 469
cassette(s) 31, 32, 55, 56, 166, 310
catharsis 27, 111
child abuse 75, 191, 206, 454–457
child molesting 281
child rearing 139, 203–219
—Bible and 204–206
—causes of problems in 206–208
—counseling and problems in 210–215
—effects of problems in 208–210
—preventing problems in 215–217
childhood 223, 253
childlessness 446–448
children 74, 196, 203, 219, 255, 257, 260, 274, 319, 327, 339, 380, 418, 421, 422, 424, 454, 455
Christian Education 23, 357, 368, 438
Clinebell, Howard 380, 392
cohabitation 281, 286
communication 23–24, 43, 46, 60, 75, 79, 81, 139, 149, 162, 164, 170, 171, 176, 177, 180, 181, 184, 212, 213, 216, 222, 284, 287, 296, 308, 311, 312, 332, 335, 336, 338, 340, 342, 343, 344, 357, 406, 408, 423, 425, 465
community 351, 356, 461–471
companionship 81, 145
compassion 323, 328, 397, 403, 430, 442
conditioning 61
confession 28, 103, 109, 123, 124, 125, 338, 418, 440, 442
confidentiality 44
conflict 61, 63, 64, 70, 158, 159, 170, 173, 174, 180, 184, 211, 306, 311, 327, 333, 335, 338,

473